EARLY MODERN EUROPE:
A Book of Source Readings

EDITED BY
Herbert H. Rowen
Rutgers University
Carl J. Ekberg
Illinois State University

Early Modern Europe

A BOOK OF SOURCE READINGS

F. E. PEACOCK PUBLISHERS, INC.
ITASCA, ILLINOIS

Library of Congress
Catalog Card No. 72–79877

PREFACE 

The editors' conception of the function and method of this book of source readings may aid the reader in assimilating its content. We see three main functions. The first is to illustrate the general exposition to be found in any historical account of the early modern era as a whole. No matter what the skill of a modern historian in narration, analysis, and interpretation, he must cover his material broadly. In these pages the reader will find pages devoted to what may be allotted only a sentence or a phrase in a general history. The inevitable price of such detail is selectivity, but this does not dismay us, for all historical work rests upon selection. We will present here in all candor the principles of our choice, but our readers will quite properly bring their own principles of understanding and judgment to this book.

Second, these selections will, we hope, provide the reader with a sense of immediacy. However skillful, history as writing about the past is by its nature a re-creation of an aspect of the past. Most historical knowledge must come from works of this kind, which cannot give the direct feel of the past that is associated with the sources themselves. While sources require critical analysis for understanding, they convey the quality of a time and a place in a way that the modern study cannot possibly match. Nowhere, paradoxically, does the historical past come more alive than in the dusty archives.

But the sources do not speak for themselves, they answer only when questioned. The student who reads these selections and actively seeks to grasp what they can, and cannot, reveal to him will have begun to understand by his own experience the task of the historical scholar. He will see how "facts"—the building blocks of our knowledge—are drawn from the sources, varying according to what one seeks from them and yet retaining an inner hardness that remains independent. Study of this book will not by itself make a reader a historian, to be sure, but it will provide a better grasp of how the historian works and therefore a better understanding of what the contribution of historical method is to knowledge in general. This is our third function.

In determining our methods with these functions in mind, we have first of all limited ourselves to the presentation of sources. A scattering of excerpts from the writings of modern historians could not present an adequate picture of their work, and we believe that it is better to leave that task to other books, general histories or historiographical samplers. We prefer to do one thing, and hope to do it well.

Second, our sources are varied but not all-inclusive. We have sought out materials that can be understood to a significant extent by themselves. The reader should be aware, however, that there are many important kinds of sources that provide bits of information whose meaning can be seen only when fitted into the larger structure of the historian's study. For example, a parish register, with its lists of births, marriages, and deaths, provides invaluable information for social and demographic history, or for a biographer, but a page from such a document could by itself only illustrate a kind of source.

Third, we have kept the introductions to the individual chapters quite short. These cannot effectively replace a general history, and we do not imagine that this book would be likely to be used by itself. All that can be done in these introductions is to set the themes for the selections that follow.

Fourth, the introductions to the selections are relatively ample. We have tried to indicate the significance of the selections, providing both context (as it were, the questions the source can answer) and the necessary data about author and work. The reader should not need to refer to an encyclopedia or biographical dictionary for an adequate comprehension of the material.

Finally, the annotation is strictly limited to material required for an understanding of the significance of the selection. Terms are not defined nor names identified unless the reader is not likely to know them but needs to do so in order to grasp the meaning of the source.

If the reader can find in this work some of the joys—especially those of difficulties overcome—which the editors have known in their historical work, they will be satisfied that they have not failed in what they set out to do.

H. H. R.
C. J. E.

CHAPTER I

THE RENAISSANCE

THE CULTURAL LIFE of early modern Europe was dominated by a vast movement in arts, letters, and thought called the Renaissance. It consisted of scholarship and literature as applied in the work of the humanists, who revived classical Latin and turned to the study of classical Greek and who took the classical authors as models in literature and philosophy. This movement was paralleled in the arts, where the imitation and assimilation of antiquity were also undertaken, particularly in architecture and sculpture. This was the Renaissance in the specific sense, as its contemporaries knew it.

After the work of the Renaissance had been completed and the period lost its innovative force, historians who looked back to these centuries came to regard the Renaissance as something wider and deeper than a movement of writers and artists. They saw it as a unified epoch in which the revival of antiquity was only the outward sign of a tremendous transformation of society in general. The heart of that great change they took to be the rise of modern individualism as a replacement for the collective universalism of medieval man.

This view of the Renaissance, which was given its classic expression by the Swiss historian Jacob Burckhardt in the 19th century, has come to be challenged in the 20th. Medievalists have greatly modified our understanding of the Middle Ages and other scholars have found a persistence of medieval themes and attitudes in the Renaissance that had previously gone unobserved. The reduction of modernity to the phenomenon of individualism has also been disputed, and the relationship of the Renaissance and the Reformation (see Chapter II) has been seen to be more complex than had been assumed. There has also been a questioning of the affirmation of the essential unity of the Renaissance by scholars who call the existence of such a "spirit of the times" into question.

The debate over the Renaissance is likely to be one of the perennial conflicts among historians. The events of the period are rich enough to bear, indeed require, varied interpretations to bring out all their many aspects. Such debates as these, if they are not terminated by dogmatism, reflect the continuing vitality of historical study.

1. THE CULT OF ANTIQUITY

The Renaissance began as a deliberate turning to classical antiquity—the culture of ancient Greece and Rome—for models in the arts and literature. While the literary works of the ancients had not been forgotten in the Middle Ages, they had been copied and used with a certain naïveté, as if classical and medieval civilizations were the same. Medieval Latin, the international language of scholarship, was a rough-and-ready instrument usually very well adapted to the needs to which it was applied, but quite different in vocabulary and style from the Latin used by writers from Cicero to Augustine. Its primary functions were practical, not literary.

Outstanding works of literature were composed in the medieval vernacular languages, however, and one of the greatest of the late medieval masters of vernacular poetry was the Italian Petrarch (in Italian, Francesco Petrarca [1304-1374]), whose sonnets and odes rank him with Dante. But Petrarch, by education a lawyer and by occupation a churchman and diplomat, began to look at the classical authors in a new way; he set himself to write as they did, with their vocabulary and in their style. A favorite exercise of Petrarch's was to compose "letters" to ancient authors, which were designed to display to his contemporaries the qualities he admired in classical literature. When his friend Giovanni Boccaccio sent him in 1354 a volume containing some of the writings of Marcus Terentius Varro, a Roman poet of the first century B.C., he wrote one of these letters to Varro. It is typical of the genre and illustrates what he admired in the ancients.

Francesco Petrarch

Letter to Marcus Varro

Thy rare integrity, thine activity, and the great splendor of thy name urge me to love and in fact revere thee. There are some, indeed, whom we love even after their death, owing to the good and righteous deeds that live after them; men who mold our character by their teaching and comfort us by their example when the rest of mankind offends both our eyes and our nostrils; men who, though they have gone hence to the common abode of all (as Plautus says in the Casina), nevertheless continue to be of service to the living. Thou, however, art of no profit to us, or, at best, of only small profit. But the fault is not thine—it is due to Time, which destroys all things. All thy works are lost to us of today. And why not? 'Tis only of gold that the present age is desirous; and when, pray, is anyone a careful guardian of things despised?

Thou didst dedicate thyself to the pursuit of knowledge with incredible zeal and incomparable industry, and yet thou didst not for that reason abandon a life of action. Thou didst distinguish thyself in both directions, and deservedly didst become dear to those supremely eminent men, Pompey the Great and Julius Caesar. Thou didst serve as a soldier under the one; to the other thou didst address works worthy of admiration and full of the most varied learning—a most remarkable fact when we consider that they were composed 'mid the widely conflicting duties of war and of peace. Thou art deserving of great praise not only for thy genius and for thy resolve to keep both mind and body in unremitting activity, but also for having had the power and the wish to be of service both to thy age and to all succeeding ages. But alas, thy works, conceived and elaborated with such great care, have not been deemed worthy of passing down to posterity through our hands. Our shameless indifference has undone all thine ardor. Never has there been a father ever so thrifty but that an extravagant son has been able to squander within a short time the accumulated savings of years.

But why should I now enumerate thy lost works? Each title is a stigma upon our name. It is better, therefore, to pass them over in silence; for probing only opens the wound afresh, and a sorrow once allayed is renewed by the memory of the loss incurred. But how incredible is the

---

SOURCE: *Petrarch's Letters to Classical Authors*, translated by Mario E. Cosenza (Chicago: University of Chicago Press, 1910), pp. 69–75.

power of fame! The name lives on, even though the works be buried in oblivion. We have practically nothing of Varro, yet scholars unanimously agree that Varro was most learned. Thy friend Marcus Cicero does not fear to make this unqualified assertion in those very books in which he maintains that nothing is to be asserted as positive. It is as if the splendor of thy name had dazzled him; as if, in speaking of thee, he had lost sight of the principles of his school. Some there are who would accept this testimony of Cicero only within the narrow bounds of Latin literature, with whom therefore thou, O Varro, passest as the most learned of the Romans. But there are some who include Greek literature as well, particularly Lactantius, a Roman most famous both for his eloquence and his piety, who does not hesitate to declare that no man has ever been more learned than Varro, not even among the Greeks.

Among thy countless admirers, however, two stand out pre-eminently: one is he whom I have already mentioned, thy contemporary, thy fellow-citizen, and thy fellow-disciple, Cicero, with whom thou didst exchange numerous literary productions, thus devoting thy leisure moments to a useful occupation, in obedience to the precepts of Cato. And if Cicero's works were more long-lived than thine, it must be accounted for by the charm of his style. The second of thy pre-eminent admirers is a most holy man, and one endowed with a divine intellect, St. Augustine, African by birth, in speech Roman. Would that thou hadst been able to consult him when writing thy books on divine matters! Thou wouldst surely have become a very great theologian, seeing that thou hadst so accurately and so carefully laid down the principles of that theology with which thou wert acquainted. It has been written of thee that thou wert such an omnivorous reader as to cause wonder that thou couldst find any time for writing, and that thou wert so prolific a writer as to make it scarcely credible to us that anyone could even have read all that thou didst write. And yet, that I may withhold nothing concerning the present condition of thy works, I shall say that there is not one extant, or at best they are only in a very fragmentary state. But I remember having seen some a long time ago, and I am tortured by the memory of a sweetness tasted only with the tip of the tongue, as the saying goes. I am of the opinion that those very books on human and divine matters, which greatly increased the reputation of thy name, are still perchance in hiding somewhere, in search of which I have worn myself out these many years. For there is nothing in life more distressing and consuming than a constant and anxious hope ever unfulfilled.

But enough of this. Be of good cheer. Treasure the moral comfort deriving from thy uncommon labors, and grieve not that mortal things have perished. Even while writing thou must have known that thy work was destined to perish; for nothing immortal can be written by mortal man. Forsooth, what matters it whether our work perish immediately or after the lapse of a hundred thousand years, seeing that at some time it must necessarily die? There is, O Varro, a long line of illustrious men whose works were the result of an application equal to thine own, and who have not been a whit more fortunate than thou. And although not one of them was thy peer, yet thou shouldst follow their example and bear thy lot with greater equanimity. Let me enumerate some of this glorious company, for the mere utterance of illustrious names gives me pleasure. The following occur to me: Marcus Cato the censor, Publius Nigidius, Antonius Gnipho, Julius Hyginus, Ateius Capito, Gaius Bassus, Veratius Pontificalis, Octavianus Herennius, Cornelius Balbus, Masurius Sabinus, Servius Sulpitius, Cloacius Verus, Gaius Flaccus, Pompeius Festus, Cassius Hemina, Fabius Pictor, Statius Tullianus, and many others whom it would be tedious to enumerate, men once illustrious and now mere ashes blown hither and thither by every gust of wind. With the exception of the first two, their very names are scarcely known today. Pray greet them in my name, but alas, with thy lips. I do not send greetings to the Caesars Julius and Augustus and several others of that rank, even though they were devoted to letters and very learned, and though I know that thou wert very intimate with some of them. It will be better, I am sure, to leave the sending of such greetings to the emperors of our own age, provided they are not ashamed of their predecessors, whose care and courage built up an empire which they have overturned. Farewell forever, O illustrious one.

Written in the land of the living, in the capital of the world, Rome, which was thy fatherland and became mine, on the Kalends of November, in the year from the birth of Him whom I would thou hadst known, the thirteen hundred and fiftieth.

2. A HUMANIST AND THE CHRISTIAN ETHIC

Petrarch's friend Giovanni Boccaccio (1313-1375) illustrates the complex character of the emerging Renaissance humanism. Besides adapting the medieval lays and fabliaux popular in France to the form of an Italian prose tale in the famed *Decameron*, he wrote many other works in verse and prose which contributed to the creation of the Italian literary language. The *Decameron* combined the earthy realism and sardonic anticlericalism that formed the underside of medieval religious life with a literary refinement that reflected Boccaccio's admiration for the ancient masters. A pastoral poem like the *The Nymph of Fiesole*, the first part of which is reprinted below,

(A), was an attempt to reproduce the works of antiquity in their purity, although in the vernacular.

Like Petrarch, Boccaccio also composed works in classical Latin and considered them his major achievement. As he entered middle age, he began to turn to religious themes, reaffirming the verities of Christianity as they had been taught for a thousand years. The lighthearted laughter of the *Decameron* and the artificialities of *The Nymph of Fiesole* were replaced by sober thoughts of mortality and eternal life. This change is illustrated in one of the short chapters of his *The Fates of Illustrious Men* (1356-64), on "The Dark Blindness of Mankind" (B).

A. Giovanni Boccaccio

The Nymph of Fiesole

Here begins the book called the NINFALE, and first of all the author shows that Love is the cause of his writing it

Love makes me speak which long has lodged within my heart making his dwelling there, holding it captive with those fettering beams against which armor was no defense when they passed inward with the favor of my lady's eyes. She is the cause of all my many woes, my sighs by day, my tears by night.

Love guides me and directs me in the work I now begin. Love prompts me and endows me with the wit and strength to do it. Love is my pilot and my light and makes me worthy to discourse of him. Love presses me to tell a very ancient tale of love.

Therefore I wish the honor to be his alone, since it is he who guides my pen. He is sent by my lady whose worth is such that every other one seems base to me. As she is gentler and fairer than the rest, so in all virtues she exceeds all others. Nor would a single thing be lacking to her if she were but a whit more merciful.

Now I pray that every faithful lover will be my shield and my defense in this against the slanderers, the envious, and those devoid of love. And you, dear damsels, who are not cruel and flinty hearted, I beg you to pray my haughty lady not to be harsh to me, her humble servant.

Before Fiesole had been furnished with palings, wall, or fortress, it was inhabited by but few people; and those few had taken to the heights of the surrounding hills. The plain lay entirely abandoned because of the wild torrents and the extensive marsh which fed into a wide river at the foot of the hills.

SOURCE: Giovanni Boccaccio, *The Nymph of Fiesole: Il Ninfale Fiesolano,* translated by Daniel J. Donno (New York: Columbia University Press, 1960), pp. 3–7.

In those times there existed the false creed of the wicked, corrupt, and lying gods; and so much had their evil seed increased that all the people believed them as gracious in heaven as they seemed on earth. They sacrificed to them with solemn feasts and honors, here as elsewhere glorifying Jove above all others.

There also reigned at that time a goddess named Diana, and many ladies held her in devotion. But chiefly those who hated lust and wished to remain virgins chose to dedicate themselves to her. She welcomed them with great rejoicing, and kept them in the woods and in the forests.

Many maidens besides were offered to her by fathers and by mothers who had promised them, some for favors and some for gifts received. Diana accepted them all with open arms so long as they were willing to observe chastity, to renounce men and vanities, and to do her service.

Thus was this goddess adored through all the world. But to return now to the hills of Fiesole where she was honored and glorified more than elsewhere, I must tell you of her lovely band of virgins, called nymphs in those days, who always went about armed with bows and arrows.

Diana had assembled among those hills a large number of these virgins from the surrounding countryside, though rarely living with them openly, for she had many such throughout the world to guard from the assaults of men. However, when she came to Fiesole, she appeared before them in this form and manner:

She was tall and of a slenderness suited to her height. Her eyes and countenance shone brighter than a star. Truly it seemed she had been fashioned in paradise, for she irradiated light so like a flame one could not fix his gaze on her. Her hair was curled and blond, yet not like gold but of a shade that suited it far better.

Often she wore it parted over her slender neck. And her apparel, cut in the manner of a robe, was made of sendal so fine that it scarcely concealed the flesh. It was entirely white, with neither strip nor inset, and girdled at the waist. At times she wore a handsome crimson mantle.

In years she seemed a youthful twenty-five. She carried a bow in her left hand, while from her right side hung a quiver full of arrows which she discharged at savage beasts or, at times, even at men who might molest her or her nymphs. And thus she slew them.

In such fashion Diana came to Fiesole to visit with her nymphs. With reverent and pleasing manner she would often have them gather around cool fountains or in the leafy shade, as is the custom when the sun kindles the summer air. In winter they gathered in the sunlight.

Here she would warn them to keep close guard over their chastity. But sometimes she would talk with them about the hunts on which they had gone into the nearby hills, following the tracks of the wild beasts, catching and slaying many; and she would order them to slay still more. Such was their conversation, as I have said. And when Diana prepared to leave them, she would quickly summon forth a nymph to be her deputy for the entire troop, and she would make the others vow their obedience to her if they did not wish to die as victims of her bow.

The nymph selected was obeyed by everyone as though she were Diana herself. Each of the band, appareled in a cloak of thinly woven linen, made many a beast the target of her arrows, and every one who bore the whetted dart was swifter than the swiftest leopard.

B. Giovanni Boccaccio

The Fates of Illustrious Men

The Dark Blindness of Mankind

Why are we always duped by outward appearances, and why do we always search after trifles?

What misery is this? What blindness? What crime? If the earth is shaken a little, we immediately leave the cities and flee into the country. If a wild animal breaks out of his cage, immediately we bar our doors. If a river overflows, we climb its banks to higher ground. We call a doctor so we may save the oppressive life of the body a little longer. But we run after a bauble that is certain to ruin us and will frequently destroy our body and soul. Alas, I have said to myself, how foolish we are to run after it. Even when this desire is not at hand we seek it ardently through heat and cold, through mountains, plains, and the sea; through a thousand mortal hazards, through crimes and violence, with nervous exertion and insuperable labor. When our lives are devoid of such experiences, we proclaim we are truly miserable.

We do not care for the sky, remarkable for its clear serenity, the brilliant sun, the silvery moon, the glittering stars, and the other permanent beauties of the heavens circling around us in continual motion. God, calling us to the true glory with paternal affection, promising us His eternal kingdom, His unfailing truth following His judgment, all this we despise as a lie. I do not know by what madness it is that with deadly seriousness we fix our eyes on the ground, stop up our ears, harden our

---

SOURCE: Giovanni Boccaccio, *The Fates of Illustrious Men*, translated and abridged by Louis Brewer Hall (New York: Frederick Ungar Publishing Co., 1965), pp. 86–88.

heart, and while we do not see what cares worldly glitter may hide, what poisons it may bear, and what chances it may be subject to, we think only of all the delights that have fallen to us and forget what God has taught us. Worse, we see that glitter droops, falls, is reduced to nothing; but still, to our misfortune, we imagine it to be fixed and everlasting.

Oh, miserable creatures that we are, let us put aside this insatiable desire by which the eyes of our soul are blinded. Let our belief give way to reason. Although we are weary of regarding the Heavens and listening to God, at least every day we should be intent upon those things that are come right in front of our eyes. And so that heaps of treasure, numerous acquaintances, or the splendor of honors may not deceive us, among the many who emerged from that recent group, let us study Xerxes. That king, who left Persia with the greatest pomp and fully armed, who had the greatest hope in himself and his plans, returned to his country unarmed, obscure instead of triumphant, and received the mourning of his people. He who commanded the downfall of the gods (whatever was trivial, he regarded highly) was slaughtered in his own palace by Artabanus.

Why should we say more? What more can we ask in order to see what riches, power, and a temporal kingdom can do? What do we strive after, search for, hope for, or even know? I ignore the hidden cares by which all outward show is infected, and invoke the outward appearance only. Would it not have been better for Xerxes to be deprived of those outward things? And is it not one of the greatest misfortunes that he was happy? Why do we not drive this cloud of ignorance away from our eyes? But we, miserable creatures, turn aside. God may have many a Themistocles and Leonidas, but we have even a larger army than Xerxes. Yet finally deprived of our temporal abundance, in flight and powerless, we in vain beg the inexorable boatmen, not at the Hellespont, but on Acheron's shore; and naked, alone, and mournful, we cry exhausted, having lost the hope of a better life.

3. A HUMANIST VISION OF THE CREATION OF MAN

The humanists, in their endeavor to recapture the style of classical antiquity, often found themselves captured also by the substance of what they studied. While they were enraptured by pagan thought, they did not therefore abandon the Christian world view. Instead they decked Christian ideas in pagan garb, calling God Jove, or they worked pagan thoughts into Christian conceptions, changing them without rejecting them. This may be seen with particular clarity in the works of an Italian philosopher-scholar of the late 15th century, the gifted Count Giovanni Pico della Mirandola (1463-1494). He studied Aramaic and Hebrew as well as Greek and Latin, and his bold attempt to defend all sorts of ideas gleaned from his reading led him to the brink of accusations of heresy. Not long before his death, he was won back to a strict Catholicism by the reforming monk Savonarola. His most influential work was a tract on *The Dignity of Man,* from which the following selection was taken. Its very title clashed with the traditional Christian doctrine of man's unworthiness and need to evidence proper humility.

Pico della Mirandola

On the Dignity of Man

. . . But, when the work was finished, the Craftsman kept wishing that there were someone to ponder the plan of so great a work, to love its beauty, and to wonder at its vastness. Therefore, when everything was done (as Moses and Timaeus bear witness), He finally took thought concerning the creation of man. But there was not among His archetypes that from which He could fashion a new offspring, nor was there in His treasurehouses anything which He might bestow on His new son as an inheritance, nor was there in the seats of all the world a place where the latter might sit to contemplate the universe. All was now complete; all things had been assigned to the highest, the middle, and the lowest orders. But in its final creation it was not the part of the Father's power to fail as though exhausted. It was not the part of His wisdom to waver in a needful matter through poverty of counsel. It was not the part of His kindly love that he who was to praise God's divine generosity in regard to others should be compelled to condemn it in regard to himself.

At last the best of artisans ordained that that creature to whom He had been able to give nothing proper to himself should have joint possession of whatever had been peculiar to each of the different kinds of being. He therefore took man as a creature of indeterminate nature and, assigning him a place in the middle of the world, addressed him thus: "Neither a fixed abode nor a form that is thine alone nor any function peculiar to thyself have we given thee, Adam, to the end that according to thy longing and according to thy judgment thou mayest have and possess what abode, what form, and what functions thou thyself shalt desire. The

---

SOURCE: Ernst Cassirer *et al.* (eds.), *Petrarca, Valla, Ficino, Pico, Pomponazzi, Vives: The Renaissance Philosophy of Man,* passage translated by Elizabeth L. Forbes (Chicago: University of Chicago Press, 1948), pp. 224–27.

nature of all other beings is limited and constrained within the bounds of laws prescribed by Us. Thou, constrained by no limits, in accordance with thine own free will, in whose hand We have placed thee, shalt ordain for thyself the limits of thy nature. We have set thee at the world's center that thou mayest from thence more easily observe whatever is in the world. We have made thee neither of heaven nor of earth, neither mortal nor immortal, so that with freedom of choice and with honor, as though the maker and molder of thyself, thou mayest fashion thyself in whatever shape thou shalt prefer. Thou shalt have the power to degenerate into the lower forms of life, which are brutish. Thou shalt have the power, out of thy soul's judgment, to be reborn into the higher forms, which are divine."

O supreme generosity of God the Father, O highest and most marvelous felicity of man! To him it is granted to have whatever he chooses, to be whatever he wills. Beasts as soon as they are born (so says Lucilius) bring with them from their mother's womb all they will ever possess. Spiritual beings, either from the beginning or soon thereafter, become what they are to be for ever and ever. On man when he came into life the Father conferred the seeds of all kinds and the germs of every way of life. Whatever seeds each man cultivates will grow to maturity and bear in him their own fruit. If they be vegetative, he will be like a plant. If sensitive, he will become brutish. If rational, he will grow into a heavenly being. If intellectual, he will be an angel and the son of God. And if, happy in the lot of no created thing, he withdraws into the center of his own unity, his spirit, made one with God, in the solitary darkness of God, who is set above all things, shall surpass them all. Who would not admire this our chameleon? Or who could more greatly admire aught else whatever? . . .

. . . The Pythagoreans degrade impious men into brutes and, if one is to believe Empedocles, even into plants. Mohammed, in imitation, often had this saying on his tongue: "They who have deviated from divine law become beasts," and surely he spoke justly. For it is not the bark that makes the plant but its senseless and insentient nature; neither is it the hide that makes the beast of burden but its irrational, sensitive soul; neither is it the orbed form that makes the heavens but its undeviating order; nor is it the sundering from body but his spiritual intelligence that makes the angel. For if you see one abandoned to his appetites crawling on the ground, it is a plant and not a man you see; if you see one blinded by the vain illusions of imagery, as it were of Calypso, and, softened by their gnawing allurement, delivered over to his senses, it is a beast and not a man you see. If you see a philosopher determining all things by means of right reason, him you shall reverence: he is a heavenly being and not of this earth. If you see a pure contemplator, one unaware of the body and confined to the inner reaches of the mind, he is neither an earthly nor a heavenly being; he is a more reverend divinity vested with human flesh.

Are there any who would not admire man, who is, in the sacred writings of Moses and the Christians, not without reason described sometimes by the name of "all flesh," sometimes by that of "every creature," inasmuch as he himself molds, fashions, and changes himself into the form of all flesh and into the character of every creature? For this reason the Persian Euanthes, in describing the Chaldaean theology, writes that man has no semblance that is inborn and his very own but many that are external and foreign to him; whence this saying of the Chaldaeans: "Hanorish tharah sharinas," that is, "Man is a being of varied, manifold, and inconstant nature." But why do we emphasize this? To the end that after we have been born to this condition—that we can become what we will—we should understand that we ought to have especial care to this, that it should never be said against us that, although born to a privileged position, we failed to recognize it and became like unto wild animals and senseless beasts of burden but that rather the saying of Asaph the prophet should apply: "Ye are all angels and sons of the Most High," and that we may not, by abusing the most indulgent generosity of the Father, make for ourselves that freedom of choice He has given into something harmful instead of salutary. Let a certain holy ambition invade our souls, so that, not content with the mediocre, we shall pant after the highest and (since we may if we wish) toil with all our strength to obtain it.

4. THE PRINCE OF SCURRILITY

The Renaissance stylistic forms were used for a broad variety of subject matter, from the most elevated to the basest. No humanist writer combined the most scurrilous and ribald of material with a deft style more effectively than the Italian Pietro Aretino (1492-1556). Although he studied painting as well as literature, it was as a writer that he made his fame. His satirical assaults upon his contemporaries, marked by venomous castigation of their vices, earned him both the nickname of "Scourge of Princes" and the payments of those who wished to be spared depiction by this blackmailer of genius. His *Ragionamenti* are pornographic dialogues, written at Venice, where he took refuge in 1527, after having served popes and soldiers with his witty pen. His most lasting work is his *Letters,* a kind of early journalism. Two of these, the first describing a house on the Grand Canal in Venice (A) and the second addressed to Angela Zaffeta (B), whom he called "an honest whore," are reprinted here.

A. Pietro Aretino

A House on the Grand Canal

Aretino to M. Domenico Bolani

It seems to me, honored sir, that I would commit the sin of ingratitude, if I did not repay with praises some part of the debt which I owe to the heavenly site on which your house stands. I now dwell in that house with more happiness that I have ever had in my life.

For it is so placed that neither above it nor below it, neither if it were here nor there, could you find the slightest improvement. As a result, I am almost as afraid to begin upon its merits as I would be to begin upon those of the Emperor.

Certainly its builder chose for it the high honor of the finest place upon the Grand Canal, and since that canal is the patriarch of all others, and since Venice is the Lady Pope of all cities, I can truthfully say that I enjoy both the finest highway and the most jocund view in all the world.

I never look out of my windows at the hour when the merchants foregather that I do not see a thousand persons and as many gondolas. On my right hand, are the meat markets and the fish markets. On my left hand are the Bridge and the warehouses of the German Merchants. In the middle, is the Rialto, that gathering place of busy men.

There are grapes in the barges, game and game birds in the shops, and vegetables laid out upon the pavement. Nor do I have to long for streams rippling through the meadows when every morning I can gaze upon waters that are covered with every sort of different thing, each one in its own season.

What a ball I have when I watch those who bring great quantities of fruit and vegetables passing them ashore to those who carry them to the booths set up for them! All is animated confusion, except perhaps aboard the twenty to twenty-five sailboats laden with melons. Moored side by side, they make a sort of island, and then the crowd surges aboard them sniffing and weighing to find out whether the cargo was of high quality or not.

Of the good wives, seated proudly in their gondolas and gleaming in silk and gold and jewels, I will not speak. I do not wish to advertise their pomp and circumstance. But I will say that I cracked my jaws laughing

---

SOURCE: *The Letters of Pietro Aretino*, translated by Thomas C. Chubb (Hamden, Conn.: Archon Books [The Shoe String Press, Inc.], 1967), pp. 84–87.

at the hoots, whistles, and catcalls which the gondoliers hurled at those who had themselves rowed about by servants without scarlet breeches.

And who would not have guffawed until he wet himself if he had seen a boatload of Germans who had just reeled out of a tavern capsize into the cold waters of the canal? That is what Giulio Camillo and I did. Giulio is the good fellow who pleasantly remarked that the land entry to my house is like the terrible name that I have earned for myself by spewing forth the truth. That is because it is dark, badly designed, and has a broken-down stairway. But he then added that anyone who came to know me, would find that my disinterested, straightforward and innate friendship gave you the same tranquil contentment that you found in passing through its portico and coming out upon the balcony above.

Nothing is lacking which might delight my eyes. For, look you, on one side I am able to gaze on the orange trees that gild the base of the Palázzo de Camerlinghi, and on the other on the little canal and on the bridge of San Giovanni Crisostomo, nor does the winter sun ever deign to rise and shine without first sending word to my bedroom, to my study, to my chambers and my great hall.

Yet more even than by that, am I pleased by the distinction of my neighbors. For just across the piazza dwells His Eloquent and Honorable Magnificence, Maffeo Lioni. It was his genius that instilled learning, science and good manners into the fine intellects of Girolamo, Piero and Luigi, his most admirable sons. There too dwells Angela Sirena, life and inspiration of my studies, and the magnifico Francesco Mocinigo who is always giving splendid feasts to knights and gentlemen. Next door is the worthy Messer Giambattista Spinelli whose paternal dwelling place sheltered my friends, the Cavorlini—may God pardon Fortune for the wrongs done to them by Fate! Nor do I consider the least of my blessings the dear and pleasant propinquity of Monna Jacopa.

In short, if I could nourish my touch and other senses as I can my sight, the room which I praise would be paradise, since in it I can satisfy myself with all the pleasures which these loved objects give it.

And I must not forget either the great foreign and Venetian lords who are continually passing me as I stand at my door, nor the pride which lifts me up to heaven when I see the *Bucentaur* plying hither and thither, nor the regattas, nor the festivals which are always being celebrated in the canal which I look down on like a lord. And what too of the lights? After dusk they seem like stars which have been scattered upon those very places where they sell what we need for our feastings and our banquets. And what of the music? What of the harmonies that soothe my ears all night long?

I could far more easily express the profound judgement which you have in things literary and in the affairs of state than I could come to the end of the delights I see before me. And I assure you that if any genius breathes in the trifles which I have written, it comes not from the light and not from the shade, not from the violet nor from the verdant, but from the inspiration which is given me by them from the airy happiness of this your mansion.

May God grant that I live out in it in health and vigor those years which a man of good deeds ought to have!

VENICE, October 27, 1537

B. Pietro Aretino

An Honest Whore

Aretino to Angela Zaffetta

Even though Rumor, pretending that she really knows something, has gone about Italy spreading the report that in your person and by your doings, Love has done me wrong, the truth is that I have always held your favor to be a fine thing since there is no fraud in anything which you do.

Indeed, I give you the palm among all those of your kind there ever were. More than anyone else you know how to put the mask of decency upon the face of lust, gaining by your wisdom and discretion both riches and praise.

You do not use your wiles—which are the essence of a harlot's trade —to betray men, but rather with such skill that he who spends his money on you, swears he is the gainer. It would not be possible to describe the charms with which you win new friends, nor the means you employ to draw to your house those who are doubtful and hesitate between a *yes* and a *no*. It would be difficult even to imagine the effort you make to keep the affection of those who have become your servants.

You distribute so well your kisses, your caresses, your laughter and your bed sharings that no one ever hears anyone quarrel nor curse at you nor complain. Modest in your demands, you take what is given you without trying to appropriate what is not. Your anger only comes at the right time, yet you are not anxious to become known as "the mistress of flatteries," nor, either, to keep people dancing on a string. You hold in contempt all those who study the devices of Nanna and of Pippa.

You are not suspicious when there is no need to be suspicious, thus

---

SOURCE: *The Letters of Pietro Aretino*, translated by Thomas C. Chubb (Hamden, Conn.: Archon Books [The Shoe String Press, Inc.], 1967), pp. 120–22.

making people jealous who never even thought of it. You do not pull woes and consolations from your pocket, nor, pretending that you are in love, do you die and come to life again whenever you wish.

You do not rowel the flanks of gullible suitors with the spurs of your serving maids whom you have taught to swear that you do not eat, drink, sleep or find any peace on their account, and whom you make assert that you had come near to hanging yourself because your lover visited another lady. By God no, you are not one of those who are always ready with tears, and who, when they do weep, mingle their weeping with certain little sighs and sobs which come all too easily from the heart, the while they scratch their heads and bite their fingers with an "Alas! So be it!" in a hoarse and scarce-heard voice. Nor do you busy yourself with keeping those who want to go, while sending off the ones who long to stay. There is no place in your soul for such niggling deceits.

Your womanly wisdom moves, rather, in a royal manner, nor is feminine gossip to your taste, nor do you gather around you frivolous ladies and conceited men. Those who deal honorably rejoice in your gentle beauty which makes you shine in a most rare fashion. Your hopes remain unshaken that you will attain a position in which you can triumph over the things which you must do.

Lying, envy, and slander—once again the innate characteristics of a harlot—do not keep your mind and your tongue in a constant turmoil. You caress virtue and adore the virtuous. This is something which is usually a stranger to the habits and the nature of those who, for a price, yield to the desires of others.

And so I give myself to your ladyship, feeling that your ladyship is worthy.

VENICE, December 15, 1537

5. REBIRTH IN THE ARTS

The same impulse that fostered humanism in literature—the desire to follow the ancients as models of perfection—was active in the visual arts. But in this field it was only possible to study and attempt to recreate styles and forms of examples that remained from antiquity, and these were overwhelmingly limited to architecture and sculpture. Paintings and mosaics from Roman times were to be discovered only later in the remains of Pompey, Herculaneum, and other buried towns. Thus it was that Renaissance artists, in rejecting inherited Gothic styles (Romanesque and Gothic in architecture and Byzantine in painting), could directly follow the ancients in architecture, but in pictorial art they had to imagine what the classical forms would be. They retained far more of the methodology of the immediately preceding centuries than they realized, because it was so familiar. Their vaunted realism draws on both a faithfulness to what was seen that was in fact characteristic of medieval art and a deliberate creation of mathematical rules of composition that was truly novel and made possible the solution of the difficult problem of perspective.

The decline of ancient art with the fall of the Roman Empire in the West and the eventual rebirth of the arts (whence the name "Renaissance" for the cultural changes of the movement and the age itself) are described below by a 16th-century Italian artist. Giorgio Vasari (1511-1574) was an architect and painter of something less than the first order, but his gift of words enabled him to set forth, in his *Lives of the Most Eminent Painters, Sculptors and Architects,* what the Renaissance artists were conceived to have accomplished as their age came to an end.

Giorgio Vasari

Lives of the Painters

. . . .

But as fortune, when she has raised either persons or things to the summit of her wheel, very frequently casts them to the lowest point, whether in repentance or for her sport, so it chanced that, after these things, the barbarous nations of the world arose, in divers places, in rebellion against the Romans; whence there ensued, in no long time, not only the decline of that great empire, but the utter ruin of the whole, and more especially of Rome herself, when all the best artists, sculptors, painters, and architects, were in like manner totally ruined, being submerged and buried, together with the arts themselves, beneath the miserable slaughters and ruins of that much renowned city. Painting and sculpture were the first to suffer, as arts ministering rather to pleasure than utility; while architecture, being requisite to the comfort and safety of life, was still maintained, although not in its earlier excellence. Indeed, had it not been that sculpture and painting still placed before the eyes of the existing generation, the representations of those whom they were accustomed to honour, and to whom they gave an immortality, the very memory, both of one and the other, would have been soon extinguished. . . .

But infinitely more ruinous than all other enemies to the arts above named, was the fervent zeal of the new Christian religion, which, after long and sanguinary combats, had finally overcome and annihilated the

---

SOURCE: Giorgio Vasari, *Lives of the Most Eminent Painters, Sculptors and Architects,* translated by Mrs. Jonathan Foster, 5 vols. (London: G. Bell & Sons, 1910), Vol. I, pp. 20–22, 27, 32–33.

ancient creeds of the pagan world, by the frequency of miracles exhibited, and by the earnest sincerity of the means adopted; and ardently devoted, with all diligence, to the extirpation of error, nay, to the removal of even the slightest temptation to heresy, it not only destroyed all the wondrous statues, paintings, sculptures, mosaics, and other ornaments of the false pagan deities, but at the same time extinguished the very memory, in casting down the honours, of numberless excellent ancients, to whom statues and other monuments had been erected, in public places, for their virtues, by the most virtuous times of antiquity. Nay, more than this, to build the churches of the Christian faith, this zeal not only destroyed the most renowned temples of the heathens, but, for the richer ornament of St. Peter's, and in addition to the many spoils previously bestowed on that building, the tomb of Adrian, now called the castle of St. Angelo, was deprived of its marble columns, to employ them for this church, many other buildings being in like manner despoiled, and which we now see wholly devastated. And although the Christian religion did not effect this from hatred to these works of art, but solely for the purpose of abasing and bringing into contempt the gods of the Gentiles, yet the result of this too ardent zeal did not fail to bring such total ruin over the noble arts, that their very form and existence was lost. . . .

. . . . .

In the year 1013, we nevertheless perceive, that the art had regained somewhat of her ancient vigour; and this we infer, from the rebuilding of that most beautiful church San Miniato sul Monte, constructed in the time of Messer Alibrando, citizen and bishop of Florence; for to say nothing of the marble ornaments by which it is embellished, both within and without, the façade gives us clear proof that the Tuscan architects here made efforts to imitate the fine proportions and pure taste of the antique in columns, arches, cornices, doors, and windows, correcting and improving their perceptions by the study of that most ancient temple, the church of San Giovanni, in their own city. At the same period, painting, which had been little less than totally extinguished, was seen to be slowly regaining life, as may be proved by the mosaic executed in the principal chapel of this church of San Miniato.

From this commencement, then, the arts of design began to make progress in Tuscany by slow degrees, advancing gradually towards a better state of things as we see from the first steps taken by the Pisans towards the construction of their cathedral, in 1016.

. . . . .

Thus much I have thought it advisable to say respecting the first commencement of sculpture and painting, and may perhaps have spoken at greater length than was here needful; but this I have done, not so much because I was carried on by my love of art, as because I desire to be useful and serviceable to the whole body of artists, for they, having here seen the manner in which art proceeded from small beginnings, until she attained the highest summit, and next how she was precipitated from that exalted position into the deepest debasement; and considering that it is the nature of art, as of human existence, to receive birth, to progress, to become old, and to die, may thus more perfectly comprehend and follow the progress of her second birth to the high perfection which she has once more attained in these our days. I have further thought, that if even it should chance at any time, which may God forbid, that by the neglect of men, the malice of time, or the will of heaven, which but rarely suffers human things to remain long without change, the arts should once again fall into their former decay, these my labours, both what has been said and what yet remains to be said, should they be found worthy of a more happy fortune, may avail to keep those arts in life, or may at least serve as an incentive to exalted minds to provide them with more efficient aids and support, so that, by my own good intentions, and the help of such friends, the arts may abound in those facilities, of which, if it be permitted to speak the truth freely, they have ever been destitute even to this day.

6. A RENAISSANCE IMAGE OF AN IDEAL WOMAN

Renaissance culture was to a large extent centered in princely courts which gave their patronage to humanist scholars and poets and to artists. It reflected therefore the idealistic self-image of princes and courtiers as men of wide-ranging abilities who could do many things well—make music and talk, dance and hunt, and, in a word, live graciously—as well as do a few things with professional perfection—govern states and fight as soldiers. Such a "universal man" was depicted by Baldesar (or Baldassare) Castiglione (1478-1529), who served as diplomat and courtier to the dukes of Milan and Urbino, as well as papal nuncio to Spain. His *Book of the Courtier*, published in 1528, is a dialogue set at the Urbino court of Guidobaldo da Montefeltro. In the course of the work, Castiglione takes up the qualities of the "perfect Court Lady," which, though somewhat different from those of the male courtier, made her "perhaps worthy" of being considered his equal and perfect in her own way.

Baldassare Castiglione

The Book of the Courtier

. . . . .

Then the Magnifico, turning to the Duchess, said: "Since it is your pleasure, Madam, I will say what I have to say, but with great fear that I shall give no satisfaction. Certainly, it would cause me far less toil to imagine a lady worthy of being the queen of the world than to imagine a perfect Court Lady, because I do not know w[h]ere to find my model for the latter; whereas, for the Queen, I should not need to go very far, since it would be enough for me to set forth the divine accomplishments of a lady whom I know and, in contemplating those accomplishments, set all my thoughts to expressing clearly in words what many see with their eyes; and if I could do no more, I should have performed my task by merely uttering her name."

Then said the Duchess: "Do not exceed bounds, signor Magnifico, but hold to the order given, and describe the Court Lady so that such a noble lady may have someone capable of serving her worthily."

The Magnifico continued: "Then, Madam, in order to show that your commands can induce me to attempt what I do not even know how to do, I will speak of this excellent Lady as I would wish her to be; and when I have fashioned her to my taste, and since then I may not have another, like Pygmalion I will take her for my own. And, though signor Gasparo has said that the same rules which serve for the Courtier serve also for the Lady, I am of a different opinion; for although some qualities are common to both and are as necessary for a man as for a woman, there are yet others that befit a woman more than a man, and others that befit a man and to which a woman ought to be a complete stranger. I say this of bodily exercises; but above all I think that in her ways, manners, words, gestures, and bearing, a woman ought to be very unlike a man; for just as he must show a certain solid and sturdy manliness, so it is seemly for a woman to have a soft and delicate tenderness, with an air of womanly sweetness in her every movement, which, in her going and staying, and in whatever she says, shall always make her appear the woman without any resemblance to a man.

"Now, if this precept be added to the rules which these gentlemen have taught the Courtier, then I think she ought to be able to follow many such and adorn herself with the best accomplishments, as signor Gasparo says. For I hold that many virtues of the mind are as necessary to a woman as to a man; also, gentle birth; to avoid affectation, to be naturally graceful in all her actions, to be mannerly, clever, prudent, not arrogant, not envious, not slanderous, not vain, not contentious, not inept, to know how to gain and hold the favor of her mistress and of all others, to perform well and gracefully the exercises that are suitable for women. And I do think that beauty is more necessary to her than to the Courtier, for truly that woman lacks much who lacks beauty. Also she must be more circumspect, and more careful not to give occasion for evil being said of her, and conduct herself so that she may not only escape being sullied by guilt but even by the suspicion of it, for a woman has not so many ways of defending herself against false calumnies as a man has. But since Count Ludovico has set forth in great detail the chief profession of the Courtier, and has insisted that this be arms, I think it is also fitting to state what I judge that of the Court Lady to be, and when I have done this I shall think to have discharged the greater part of my assignment.

"Leaving aside, then, those virtues of the mind which she is to have in common with the Courtier (such as prudence, magnanimity, continence, and many others), as well as those qualities that befit all (such as kindness, discretion, ability to manage her husband's property and house and children, if she is married, and all qualities that are requisite in a good mother), I say that, in my opinion, in a Lady who lives at court a certain pleasing affability is becoming above all else, whereby she will be able to entertain graciously every kind of man with agreeable and comely conversation suited to the time and place and to the station of the person with whom she speaks, joining to serene and modest manners, and to that comeliness that ought to inform all her actions, a quick vivacity of spirit whereby she will show herself a stranger to all boorishness; but with such a kind manner as to cause her to be thought no less chaste, prudent, and gentle than she is agreeable, witty, and discreet: thus, she must observe a certain mean (difficult to achieve and, as it were, composed of contraries) and must strictly observe certain limits and not exceed them.

"Now, in her wish to be thought good and pure, this Lady must not be so coy, or appear so to abhor gay company or any talk that is a little loose, as to withdraw as soon as she finds herself involved, for it might easily be thought that she was pretending to be so austere in order to hide something about herself which she feared others might discover; for manners so unbending are always odious. Yet, on the other hand, for the sake of appearing free and amiable she must not utter unseemly words or enter into any immodest and unbridled familiarity or into ways such as might cause others to believe about her what is perhaps not true; but when she finds herself present at such talk, she ought to listen with a light blush of shame.

"Likewise, she must avoid an error into which I have seen many women fall, which is to gossip and eagerly listen to evil spoken of other women. For those women who, when they hear of the unchaste ways of other women, bristle and pretend that the thing is incredible and that a woman so immodest is a monster, in making so much of the fault give cause to think that they might be guilty of it themselves. And those others who continually go about prying into other women's love affairs, relating them in such detail and with such glee, appear envious and desirous that everyone should know of this case in order that the same thing may not through error be imputed to them; and thus they emit certain laughs and assume certain attitudes, making it evident that they relish it all. And the result of this is that men, although they appear to listen to them willingly, usually conceive a bad opinion of such women and have little respect for them, and take these ways of theirs to be an invitation to go further; and they often do go so far with them that it quite justly brings shame upon them, and in the end they esteem them so little as to care nothing for their company, and even come to despise them. On the other hand, there is no man so profligate and so forward as not to have reverence for those women who are esteemed to be good and virtuous, because a certain gravity, tempered with wisdom and goodness, is like a shield against the insolence and brutishness of presumptuous men; wherefore we see that a word, a laugh, or an act of kindness, however small, coming from a virtuous woman is more esteemed by everyone than all the blandishments and caresses of those who so openly show their want of shame —and if they are not unchaste, by their wanton laughter, loquacity, insolence, and scurrilous behavior of this sort, they appear to be so.

"And since words that have no subject matter of importance are vain and puerile, the Court Lady must have not only the good judgment to recognize the kind of person with whom she is speaking, but must have knowledge of many things, in order to entertain that person graciously; and let her know how in her talk to choose those things that are suited to the kind of person with whom she is speaking, and be careful lest, unintentionally, she might sometimes utter words that could offend him. Let her take care not to disgust him by indiscreet praise of herself or by being too prolix. Let her not proceed to mingle serious matters with playful or humorous discourse, or mix jests and jokes with serious talk. Let her not show ineptitude in pretending to know what she does not know, but let her seek modestly to do herself credit in what she does know—in all things avoiding affectation, as has been said. In this way she will be adorned with good manners; she will perform with surpassing grace the bodily exercises that are proper to women; her discourse will be fluent and most prudent, virtuous, and pleasant; thus, she will be not only loved but revered by everyone, and perhaps worthy of being considered the equal of this great Courtier, both in qualities of mind and of body."

. . . .

Then signor Gasparo said: "I would not have us get into such subtleties, for these ladies would not understand us; and, even if I should answer you with the best of arguments, they would believe (or at least pretend to believe) that I am wrong, and would proceed to pronounce judgment according to their own liking. Yet since we have already begun, I will say only that in the opinion of very wise men, as you know, man is as the form and woman as the matter; and therefore, just as the form is more perfect than the matter—nay, gives it its being—so man is far more perfect than woman. And I recall once having heard that a great philosopher says in his *Problems:* 'Why is it that a woman always naturally loves the man to whom she first gave herself? And why, on the contrary, does a man hate the woman he first enjoyed?' And, in giving the reason, he affirms that this is because in such an act the woman takes on perfection from the man, and the man imperfection from the woman; and that everyone naturally loves that which makes him perfect, and hates that which makes him imperfect. And, besides this, it greatly argues the perfection of man and the imperfection of woman that all women without exception desire to be men, by a certain natural instinct that teaches them to desire their own perfection."

The Magnifico Guiliano replied immediately: "The poor creatures do not desire to be men in order to become more perfect, but in order to gain freedom and to escape that rule over them which man has arrogated to himself by his own authority. And the analogy you give of matter and form does not apply in every respect; for woman is not made perfect by man as matter by form, because matter receives its being from form, and cannot exist without it; nay, in the degree that forms have matter, they have imperfection, and are most perfect when separated from matter. But woman does not receive her being from man; on the contrary, even as she is perfected by him, she also perfects him. . . .

7. A WORLD WITHOUT WALLS

Where the highest ideal of the medieval world had been the monastic life, with its embodiment of Christian ascetism (the rejection of the pleasures of this world and the chastisement and subjugation of the senses), there developed within the world of Renaissance humanism a contrary vision that accepted life but ennobled and purified it. This attitude was expressed nowhere more vividly than in the work of a French monk and physician, François Rabelais (c. 1494-1553). Yet the contradictions of the Renaissance movement, with its classicist revivalism often superimposed on powerful medieval habits and attitudes, are evidenced in Rabelais's great romance *Gargantua and Pantagruel* (1533-64). On the one hand, this series of novels consists of rambling accounts of the adventures of the giants Gargantua and his son Pantagruel, full of bawdy humor and satire and quite in the tradition of medieval folk tales. On the other hand, integral to the stories is a vision of a life of vigor and enjoyment lived to the full, in a world marked by aristocratic virtues. Thus the Abbey of Thélème, depicted in the selections below, is inhabited by monks who are neither ascetics of the Christian tradition nor self-indulgent rascals such as Boccaccio depicted. Rather they are indeed courtiers, men and women of the highest nobility of blood and habit, such as Castiglione described.

François Rabelais

The Abbey of Thélème

There was left only the monk to provide for, whom Gargantua would have made Abbot of Sevillé, but he refused it. He would have given him the Abbey of Bourgueil, or of Sanct Florent, which was better, or both, if it pleased him; but the monk gave him a very peremptory answer, that he would never take upon him the charge nor government of monks. For how shall I be able, said he, to rule over others, that have not full power and command of myself? If you think I have done you, or may hereafter do any acceptable service, give me leave to found an abbey after my own mind and fancy. The motion pleased Gargantua very well, who thereupon offered him all the country of Thélème by the river of Loire till within two leagues of the great forest of Port-Huault. The monk then requested Gargantua to institute his religious order contrary to all others. First, then, said Gargantua, you must not build a wall about your convent, for all other abbeys are strongly walled and mured about. See, said the monk, and not without cause (seeing wall and mur signify but one and the same thing); where there is mur before and mur behind, there is store of murmur, envy, and mutual conspiracy. . . .

Item, Because in the convents of women men come not but underhand,

---

Source: François Rabelais, *Five Books of the Lives, Heroic Deeds and Sayings of Gargantua and his Son Pantagruel*, translated by Sir Thomas Urquhart and Peter Antony Motteux (Philadelphia: George Barrie, n.d.), Vol. I, pp. 123–24, 131–34.

privily, and by stealth, it was therefore enacted that in this house there shall be no women in case there be not men, nor men in case there be not women.

Item, Because both men and women that are received into religious orders after the expiring of their novitiate or probation year were constrained and forced perpetually to stay there all the days of their life, it was therefore ordered that all whatever, men or women, admitted within this abbey, should have full leave to depart with peace and contentment whensoever it should seem good to them so to do.

. . . . .

The ladies at the foundation of this order were apparalled after their own pleasure and liking; but, since that of their own accord and free-will they have reformed themselves, their accoutrement is in manner as followeth. They wore stockings of scarlet crimson, or ingrained purple dye, which reached just three inches above the knee, having a list beautified with exquisite embroideries and rare incisions of the cutter's art. Their garters were of the color of their bracelets, and circled the knee a little both over and under. Their shoes, pumps, and slippers were either of red, violet, or crimson-velvet, pinked and jagged like lobster waddles. . . .

The men were apparalled after their fashion. Their stockings were of tamine or of cloth serge, of white, black, scarlet, or some other ingrained color. Their breeches were of velvet, of the same color with their stockings, or very near, embroidered and cut according to their fancy. Their doublet was of cloth of gold, of cloth of silver, of velvet, satin, damask, taffeties, etc., of the same colors, cut, embroidered, and suitably trimmed up in perfection. The points were of silk of the same colors; the tags were of gold well enamelled. Their coats and jerkins were of cloth of gold, cloth of silver, gold, tissue or velvet embroidered, as they thought fit. Their gowns were every whit as costly as those of the ladies. Their girdles were of silk, of the color of their doublets. Every one had a gallant sword by his side, the hilt and handle whereof were gilt, and the scabbard of velvet, of the color of his breeches, with a chape of gold, and pure goldsmith's work. The dagger was of the same. . . .

All their life was spent not in laws, statutes, or rules, but according to their own free-will and pleasure. They rose out of their beds when they thought good; they did eat, drink, labor, sleep, when they had a mind to it and were disposed for it. None did awake them, none did offer to constrain them to eat, drink, nor to do any other thing; for so had Gargantua established it. In all their rule and strictest tie of their order there was but this one clause to be observed:

DO WHAT THOU WILT;

because men that are free, well-born, well-bred, and conversant in honest companies, have naturally an instinct and spur that prompteth them unto virtuous actions, and withdraws them from vice, which is called honor. Those same men, when by base subjection and constraint they are brought under and kept down, turn aside from that noble disposition by which they formerly were inclined to virtue, to shake off and break that bond of servitude wherein they are so tyrannously enslaved; for it is agreeable with the nature of man to long after things forbidden and to desire what is denied us.

8. LEARNING REGENERATED

The rise of Renaissance humanism did not by any means bring an end to the Scholastic learning of medieval universities. The sources and methods employed by the Schoolmen continued to be practiced at most universities and were considered by most theologians to be the necessary foundation of their science. Scholasticism and humanism often coexisted in the same institutions, and sometimes in the same individual. Yet criticism of the narrowly analytic methodology of Scholasticism increased, leading early in the 17th century to a survey of the state of knowledge and proposals for its reform by the English philosopher Sir Francis Bacon (1561-1626).

Bacon's *The Advancement of Learning* (1605) was intended to be the introduction to a general encyclopedia of knowledge which he never completed. Bacon rose to the highest legal office in England, the lord chancellor's post, and was named to the peerage in 1618, although it is not customary to call him by his noble titles of Baron Verulam and Viscount St. Albans. He was a philosopher who conceived of the new physical sciences as an instrument for the domination of nature, an essayist who employed both English and Latin with great power, and a would-be educational reformer. His political career collapsed in 1621 when he was charged with corruption and confessed, but his works, such as the *Advancement of Learning*, from which the following extracts are taken, assure him a very high place in the annals of modern thought.

Francis Bacon

The Advancement of Learning

. . . Surely, like as many substances in nature which are solid do putrify and corrupt into worms; so it is the property of good and sound

SOURCE: Francis Bacon, *The Advancement of Learning*, edited by William Aldis Wright, 5th ed. (Oxford, England: Clarendon Press, 1926), pp. 31–34, 78–79. By permission of the Clarendon Press, Oxford.

knowledge to putrify and dissolve into a number of subtle, idle, unwholesome, and (as I may term them) vermiculate questions, which have indeed a kind of quickness and life of spirit, but no soundness of matter or goodness of quality. This kind of degenerate learning did chiefly reign amongst the schoolmen: who having sharp and strong wits, and abundance of leisure, and small variety of reading, but their wits being shut up in the cells of a few authors (chiefly Aristotle their dictator) as their persons were shut up in the cells of monasteries and colleges, and knowing little history, either of nature or time, did out of no great quantity of matter and infinite agitation of wit spin out unto us those laborious webs of learning which are extant in their books. For the wit and mind of man, if it work upon matter, which is the contemplation of the creatures of God, worketh according to the stuff and is limited thereby; but if it work upon itself, as the spider worketh his web, then it is endless, and brings forth indeed cobwebs of learning, admirable for the fineness of thread and work, but of no substance or profit. . . .

Notwithstanding, certain it is that if those schoolmen to their great thirst of truth and unwearied travail of wit had joined variety and universality of reading and contemplation, they had proved excellent lights, to the great advancement of all learning and knowledge; but as they are, they are great undertakers indeed, and fierce with dark keeping. But as in the inquiry of the divine truth, their pride inclined to leave the oracle of God's word, and to vanish in the mixture of their own inventions; so in the inquisition of nature, they ever left the oracle of God's works, and adored the deceiving and deformed images which the unequal mirror of their own minds, or a few received authors or principles, did represent unto them. And thus much for the second disease of learning.

. . . . .

First therefore, amongst so many great foundations of colleges in Europe, I find strange that they are all dedicated to professions, and none left free to arts and sciences at large. For if men judge that learning should be referred to action, they judge well; but in this they fall into the error described in the ancient fable, in which the other parts of the body did suppose the stomach had been idle, because it neither performed the office of motion, as the limbs do, nor of sense, as the head doth: but yet notwithstanding it is the stomach that digesteth and distributeth to all the rest. So if any man think philosophy and universality to be idle studies, he doth not consider that all professions are from thence served and supplied. And this I take to be a great cause that hath hindered the progression of learning, because these fundamental knowledges have been studied but in passage. For if you will have a tree bear more fruit than it hath used to do, it is not anything you can do to the boughs, but it is the stirring of the earth and putting new mould about the roots that must work it. Neither is it to be forgotten, that this dedicating of foundations and dotations to professory learning hath not only had a malign aspect and influence upon the growth of sciences, but hath also been prejudicial to states and governments. For hence it proceedeth that princes find a solitude in regard of able men to serve them in causes of estate, because there is no education collegiate which is free; where such as were so disposed mought give themselves to histories, modern languages, books of policy and civil discourse, and other the like enablements unto service of estate.

9. RENAISSANCE ARCHITECTURE REDUCED TO RULE

Like their contemporaries in literature, Renaissance architects in Italy could turn to models that were easily available in response to interest in neoclassical styles and forms. Ancient Roman and some Greek buildings could be seen in many parts of Italy, and available for reference were the writings of such classicists as Vitruvius, a first-century Roman architect and engineer. During the 16th century, the principles of design in these monuments and writings were elaborated by a practicing architect who had been born Andrea di Petro and given the name of Palladio (1508-1580), supposedly by his patron. After studying in Rome he went to Venice and its possessions, including his home town of Vicenza, to work at his profession. His treatise *The Four Books of Architecture*, which he conceived of as presenting the pure rules of restored classical architecture, was published in 1570. In fact, however, he added his personal touch to the work, and the style he taught is called *Palladian* after him. The following extracts from his preface are taken from a translation made in England by G. Leoni and first published in 1715.

Andrea Palladio

The Four Books of Architecture

My natural inclination leading me, from my very Infancy, to the Study of *Architecture*, I resolv'd to apply myself to it: And because I ever was of opinion, that the ancient *Romans* did far exceed all that have come after them, as in many other things so particularly in Building, I proposed to myself *Vitruvius* both as my Master and Guide, he being the only ancient Author that remains extant on this Subject. Then, I betook myself to the

---

SOURCE: From *A Documentary History of Art*, Vol. II, pp. 47–49, by Elizabeth Holt. Copyright 1947, 1958 by Princeton University Press. Reprinted by permission of Doubleday & Company, Inc.

Search and Examination of such Ruins of ancient Structures as, in spight of Time and the rude Hands of *Barbarians*, are still remaining; and finding that they deserved a much more diligent Observation than I thought at first Sight, I began with the utmost Accuracy to measure even the minutest part by itself: And indeed, I became so scrupulous an Examiner of them (not discovering that any thing, of this kind, was perform'd, without the justest Reason and the finest Proportion) that I afterwards, not once only, but very often, took Journies to several parts of *Italy*, and even out of it, that I might be able, from such Fragments, to comprehend what the whole must needs have been, and to make Draughts accordingly. Whereupon, considering how widely different the Building, commonly in use, is from the Observations I made on the said Edifices, and from what I read in *Vitruvius*, in *Leo Baptista Alberti*, and other excellent Writers since *Vitruvius's* Time, as well as from Buildings of my own Performance, which raised my Reputation, and gave no small satisfaction to those who were pleased to employ me; I thought it an Undertaking worthy of a Man who considers that he was not born for himself only, but likewise for the good of others, to publish to the World the Designs (or Draughts) of those Edifices, which with equal Expence of Time and Danger to my Person, I have collected; and briefly to set down what seem'd to me most worthy to be consider'd in them; and further, to give those Rules which I have hitherto follow'd in Building, and which I still follow, to the end that they who shall read my Books, may be able to practise whatever they find useful in them, and to supply what is wanting, as many such things there may be. Thus Men, by degrees, will learn to lay aside the strange Abuses, the barbarous Inventions, the superfluous Expences and (what imports them more than all the rest) to avoid the various and continual Ruins which have happened in several Buildings. I have moreover apply'd myself to this Undertaking with the greater Alacrity, because at this time I see abundance of others become studious of this Profession, many of whom are worthily and honourably mentioned in the Books of that rare Painter and Architect, *George Vasari Aretino;* which makes me hope that the way of Building will be reduced to general Utility, and very soon arrive to that Pitch of Perfection, which, in all Arts, is so much desired. We appear to come very near it, in this part of *Italy*, seeing that not only Venice (where all the polite Arts do flourish, and which City alone affords an Example of the Grandeur and Magnificence of the *Romans*) there begin to appear Fabricks of good taste, since that most celebrated Carver and Architect, *Giacomo Sansovino*, first introduced the true manner, as may be seen, not to mention his fine Performances in the new Palace of *Procuracy*, which is perhaps the most sumptuous and the most beautiful Edifice that has been erected since the time of the Ancients; but also in several other Places of less renown, and particularly in the City of *Vicenza*, which tho' of no great Extent, yet is full of very refined Genius's and sufficiently abounds in Riches. There I had first occasion to put that in practice, which I now publish for the common Good.

10. ART AS NATURE'S TEACHER

Renaissance ideas about beauty and the relation of art to nature continued to develop during the 17th century, evolving into modern academic classicism. This school of thought holds that art does not imitate nature as it is, with all its flaws, but embodies instead the idealized "idea" of a thing which in reality can be only an imperfect example. The Italian writer and painter Giovanni Pietro Bellori (1615-1696) was an influential spokesman of this concept. His antiquarian interests earned him both the post of librarian in Rome for the self-exiled Queen Christina of Sweden and the title of "Antiquarian of Rome" from Pope Clement X. Bellori dedicated his *Lives of Modern Painters, Sculptors and Architects* (1672) to the French Minister of State J. B. Colbert, who was the founder of France's Academy of Fine Arts. The selection below, "The Idea of the Painter, The Sculptor, and the Architect Chosen from the Higher Natural Beauties of Nature," which is the introduction to the *Lives*, was given as a lecture in 1664 to the Academy of St. Luke in Rome. Bellori's ideas about art paralleled the neoclassical purism of such contemporary literary critics as Boileau.

Giovanni Bellori

Lives of Modern Painters

The Idea of the Painter, the Sculptor, and the Architect Chosen from the Higher Natural Beauties of Nature

When that high and eternal intellect, the creator of nature, made his marvelous works by reflecting deeply within himself, he established the first forms called *Ideas*. Each species was derived from that first *Idea* and so was formed the admirable web of created things. The celestial bodies above the moon, not being subject to change, remained forever beautiful

---

Source: From *A Documentary History of Art*, Vol. II, pp. 94–98, by Elizabeth Holt. Copyright 1947, 1958 by Princeton University Press. Reprinted by permission of Doubleday & Company, Inc. This selection translated by Kenneth Donahue; translated quotations from Cicero and Raphael inserted in the body of the text in place of the original Latin and Italian by the editors.

and in harmony; and because of their measured spheres and because of the splendor of their appearance we recognize them to be in all eternity of the highest perfection and beauty. On the other hand, sublunar bodies are subject to change and to ugliness and, although nature always means to produce excellence in its workings, nevertheless forms are altered through the inequality of matter, and human beauty in particular is muddled, as we see from the countless deformities and disproportions that are in us.

For this reason the noble painters and sculptors imitate that first creator, and form in their minds also an example of superior beauty and, reflecting on it, improve upon nature until it is without fault of color or of line.

This *Idea*, or we might say goddess of painting and sculpture, after opening the sacred curtains of the exalted genius of men like Daedalus and Apelles, unveils herself to us, and descends upon the marbles and canvases. Originating from nature, she rises above her origin and becomes herself the original of art; gauged by the compass of the intellect, she becomes the measure of the hand; and animated by imagination, she gives life to the image. Certainly according to the opinions of the greatest philosophers there exist in the souls of artists the Exemplary Causes which without uncertainty and for eternity remain most beautiful and most perfect.

The *Idea* of the painter and sculptor is that perfect and excellent exemplar in the mind, with imagined form, which by imitation, the things that appear to human sight resemble; such is the definition of Cicero in the Book of the Orator for Brutus: "Accordingly, as there is something perfect and surpassing in the case of sculpture and painting—an intellectual ideal by reference to which the artist represents those objects which themselves appear to the eye—so with our minds we conceive the ideal of perfect eloquence, but with our ears we catch only the copy." [Cicero, *Orator*, III, 9.] Thus the *Idea* constitutes the perfection of natural beauty, and unites the true to the semblance of things present to the eye; she always aspires to the best and the wonderful, whereby she not only emulates but surpasses nature and manifests to us as elegant and accomplished the creations which nature is not wont to show perfect in every part.

Proclus confirms this high opinion in the Timaeus, saying that if you take a man made by nature, and one made by the art of sculpture, the natural one will be less excellent, because art works more accurately. Zeuxis, who selected five virgins to form the famous image of Helen that is proffered as an example by Cicero in the *Orator*, teaches the painter and the sculptor alike to keep in mind the *Idea* of the best natural forms and to make a selection from different bodies, choosing what is most elegant in each. For Zeuxis did not believe that he could find in one body only all the perfections that he sought for the beauty of Helen, because nature does not make any particular thing perfect in all its parts.

. . . Also Maximus Tyrius holds that when the painters create an image by choosing from diverse bodies, a beauty is brought forth that is not to be found in any single natural body, close as this might come to beautiful statues. Parrhasius admitted the same to Socrates, namely, that the painter desiring natural beauty in each form ought to take from diverse bodies all that which in each single one is most perfect, and ought to join it together since it is difficult to find a single one that is perfect.

More than that, nature for this reason is so much inferior to art that the copying artists, that is, those who scrupulously imitate bodies without discrimination and regard to the *Idea,* were reproved. Demetrius was remarked upon for relying too much on nature; Dionysius was blamed for having painted men like unto us, and was commonly called anthropographos,[1] that is, painter of men. Pauson and Peiraeikos were condemned, mainly for having depicted the worst and vilest, as Michelangelo da Caravaggio in our times was too naturalistic; he painted men just as they are; and Bamboccio worse than they are.

Lysippus, likewise, used to reprove the mass of sculptors that they made men as they are found in nature, and prided himself on forming them as they ought to be, following the basic precept given by Aristotle to poets as well as to painters. Phidias, on the other hand, was not accused of this failing, who evoked wonder in spectators by the forms of the heroes and gods, in which he imitated the *Idea* rather than nature. And Cicero, speaking of him, affirms that Phidias, when he carved Jupiter and Minerva, did not contemplate any object from which to take the likeness, but considered in his mind a form full of beauty on which he concentrated, and to the likeness of which he directed his mind and hand. . . . Wherefore to Seneca, although a Stoic, and a rigorous judge of our arts, it appeared a fine thing, and he was amazed, that this sculptor, without ever seeing either Jupiter or Minerva, nevertheless was able to conceive in his mind their divine forms. . . . Apollonius of Tyana teaches us the same, that imagination renders the painter wiser than does imitation, because the latter makes only the things that it sees, while the former makes even the things that it does not see, relating them to those that it sees.

Now, to join to the precepts of the ancient philosophers the best maxims of our modern ones, Leon Battista Alberti teaches that in all things one should love not only the appearance, but principally the beauty, and that one ought to select the most praised parts from the most beautiful

---

[1] In Greek type in the original text.

bodies. Thus Leonardo da Vinci instructs the painter to form this *Idea*, and to think about what he sees and question himself about it, so as to select the most excellent part of each thing. Raphael of Urbino, the great master of those who know, thus writes to Castiglione of his Galatea: In order to paint a beautiful woman, it would be necessary for me to see many beautiful women, but since there is a scarcity of them, I make use of a certain Idea which comes to my mind.

CHAPTER II

THE REFORMATION

DURING THE LATE MEDIEVAL PERIOD, Roman Catholicism was the universal Christian church of all western and central Europe. Yet it was a church which even its own leaders admitted was deeply in need of reform. Until the second decade of the 16th century, the needed reforms were seen as mainly administrative and moral. Their chief aims were to weaken the hold of the civilian world upon the wealth and power of the Church and to return it to the task of ministering to the faithful. In 1517, a new force was loosed in Germany with the religious rebellion of Martin Luther. Although he sought at first only a more precise definition of admittedly important theological issues, a different kind of church eventually evolved. However, Protestantism failed to achieve the unity of Catholicism, and it became a movement of sects and denominations.

Catholicism reacted to the rise of Protestantism by its own reform and a counteroffensive, the Counter-Reformation or Catholic Reformation. Some abuses were removed, but other practices that had been denounced by Protestants were defended and reaffirmed. The question of the church's independence from worldly states was not resolved, and the crisis of the Protestant revolt only intensified the need of the Church for the sword of princes.

11. A WISE FOOLISHNESS

One of the sources of the Protestant Reformation was the critical attitude fostered by the Renaissance, especially in the work of the Dutch scholar Desiderius Erasmus (c. 1465-1536). The most eminent humanist of the early 16th century, Erasmus was from the beginning a *Christian* humanist who put the new learning at the service of his faith and clarified his principles with the understanding that came from knowledge. His feelings about his society and its people were embodied in a work of his middle years, called with characteristic irony *The Praise of Folly* (1510). The "I" of the book is Folly, but what she says indicates that it is the customary worldly wisdom that is truly foolish. The ambiguity of such irony did not cloud, but rather intensified the clarity of the fundamental message, as can be seen in the following selections. The first is directed against the monastic life, which Erasmus had himself rejected. The second turns its fire upon the use of the offices and revenues of the Church for the material advantage of the princes of the Church instead of for service to the community of believers. But Erasmus did not turn against the Catholic Church or its fundamental doctrines; he was a critic from within, not an enemy from outside.

Desiderius Erasmus

The Praise of Folly

. . . . .

Coming nearest to these in felicity are the men who generally call themselves "the religious" and "monks"—utterly false names both, since most of them keep as far away as they can from religion and no people are more in evidence in every sort of place. But I do not see how anything could be more dismal than these monks if I did not succor them in many ways. For though people as a whole so detest this race of men that meeting one by accident is supposed to be bad luck, yet they flatter themselves to the queen's taste. For one thing, they reckon it the highest degree of piety to have no contact with literature, and hence they see to it that they do not know how to read. For another, when with asinine voices they bray out in church those psalms they have learned, by rote rather than by heart, they are convinced that they are anointing God's ears with the blandest of oil. Some of them make a good profit from their

---

SOURCE: From Desiderius Erasmus, *The Praise of Folly,* translated by Hoyt Hopewell Hudson (copyright 1941 © 1969 by Princeton University Press; Princeton Paperback, 1970), pp. 85–87, 97–99. Reprinted by permission of Princeton University Press.

dirtiness and mendicancy, collecting their food from door to door with importunate bellowing; nay, there is not an inn, public conveyance, or ship where they do not intrude, to the great disadvantage of the other common beggars. Yet according to their account, by their very dirtiness, ignorance, want of manners, and insolence, these delightful fellows are representing to us the lives of the apostles.

What is funnier than to find that they do everything by rule, employing, as it were, the methods of mathematics; and to slip up is a great crime. There must be just so many knots for each shoe and the shoe-string must be of a certain color; the habit must be decked with just so much trimming; the girdle must be of a certain material and the width of so many straws; the cowl of a certain shape and a certain number of bushels in capacity; the hair so many fingers long; and one must sleep just so many hours. Who does not see that all this equality is really very unequal, in view of the great diversity of bodies and temperaments? Yet on the basis of such details they hold other people as mere nutshells. What is more, the members of one order, amid all their professions of apostolic charity, will turn and condemn the members of some other, making an admirable hubbub over the way their habit is belted or the slightly darker color of it. Among the monks you will see some so rigorously pious that they will wear no outer garment unless it be of Cilician goat's hair, while their inner garment is of Milesian wool; some others, on the contrary, are linen on the outside, but still wool underneath. Members of certain orders start back from the mere touch of a piece of money as if it were aconite. They do not, however, withdraw from the touch of a glass of wine, or of a woman. In short, all orders take remarkable care that nothing in their way of life shall be consistent; nor is it so much their concern to be like Christ as to be unlike each other. Thus a great part of their felicity derives from their various names. Those of one order delight to call themselves Cordeliers, but among them some are Coletes, some Minors, some Minims, some Crutched. Again, there are the Benedictines and the Bernardines; the Bridgetines and the Augustinians; the Williamists and the Jacobines; as if it were not enough to be called Christians.

. . . . .

Our popes, cardinals, and bishops for some time now have earnestly copied the state and practice of princes, and come near to beating them at their own game. Let a bishop but consider what his alb, the white emblem of sincerity, should teach him, namely, a life in every way blameless; and what is signified on his part by the two-horned miter, the two peaks bound by the same knot—I suppose it is a perfect knowledge of the Old and New Testaments; what is meant by covering his hands with gloves, a clean administration of the sacrament and one unsullied by any taint of human concerns; what the crozier symbolizes, most watchful care of the flock put under his charge; what is indicated by the cross that is carried before him, to wit, a victory over all carnal affections. If he would contemplate these and other lessons of the sort, I say, would he not lead a sad and troubled life? But as it is, they do well enough by way of feeding themselves; as for the other, the care of the sheep, they delegate that to Christ himself, or else refer it to their suffragans, as they call them, or other deputies. Nor do they keep in mind the name they bear, or what the word "bishop" means—labor, vigilance, solicitude. Yet in raking in moneys they truly play the bishop, overseeing everything—and overlooking nothing.

In a similar way the cardinals, if they considered the fact that they have succeeded to the places of the apostles, would see that the same works are required of them as were performed by their predecessors; that they are not lords, but stewards, of spiritual things, and that shortly they are to render an exact account of what they hold in trust. Yes, let them too philosophize a bit concerning their vestments, and question themselves in this fashion: "What does the whiteness of this upper garment mean? Is it not a notable and singular purity of heart? What the crimson lower garment? Is it not a burning love of God? What, again, that outer robe flowing down in broad folds and spreading over the mule of his Exalted Reverence, though it would suffice to cover a camel? Is it not charity ample enough to embrace all men in its helpfulness, by way of teaching, exhorting, chastising, admonishing, ending wars, resisting wicked princes, and freely spending blood—not money alone—for the flock of Christ? And wherefore all this money, anyway, for those who hold the places of the needy apostles?" If they would weigh these things, I repeat, they would not be so ambitious for the post, and would willingly give it up, or at least they would lead a toilsome and watchful life of the sort lived by those ancient apostles.

As to these Supreme Pontiffs who take the place of Christ, if they tried to emulate His life, I mean His poverty, labors, teaching, cross, and contempt for safety, if even they thought upon the title of Pope—that is, Father—or the addition "Most Holy," who on earth would be more afflicted? Who would purchase that seat at the price of every resource and effort? Or who defend it, when purchased, by the sword, by poison, or by anything else? Were wisdom to descend upon them, how it would inconvenience them! Wisdom, did I say? Nay, even a grain of salt would do it—a grain of that salt which is spoken of by Christ. It would lose them all that wealth and honor, all those possessions, triumphal progresses, offices, dispensations, tributes, and indulgences; it would lose them so many horses, mules, and retainers; so many pleasures. (See how I have comprehended in a few words many marketsful, a great harvest, a wide ocean, of goods!) In place of these it would bring vigils, fasts, tears, prayers, sermons, studies, sighs, and a thousand troublesome tasks of the sort. Nor should we pass over the circumstance that all those copyists and notaries would be in want, as would all those advocates, promoters, secretaries, muleteers, grooms, bankers, and pimps—I was about to add something more tender, though rougher, I am afraid, on the ears. In short, that great host of men which burdens—I beg your pardon, I mean adorns—the Roman See would beg for their bread. This would be inhuman and downright abominable, and, what is more accursed, those very princes of the church and true lights of the world would themselves be reduced to a staff and a wallet.

As it is now, what labor turns up to be done they hand over to Peter and Paul, who have leisure for it. But the splendor and the pleasure they take care of personally. And so it comes about—by my doing, remember—that scarcely any kind of men live more softly or less oppressed with care; believing that they are amply acceptable to Christ if with a mystical and almost theatrical finery, with ceremonies, and with those titles of Beatitude and Reverence and Holiness, along with blessing and cursing, they perform the office of bishops. To work miracles is primitive and old-fashioned, hardly suited to our times; to instruct the people is irksome; to interpret the Holy Scriptures is pedantry; to pray is otiose; to shed tears is distressing and womanish; to live in poverty is sordid; to be beaten in war is dishonorable and less than worthy of one who will hardly admit kings, however great, to kiss his sacred foot; and finally, to die is unpleasant, to die on the cross a disgrace.

12. INDULGENCES IN RELIGION

Late medieval Catholicism was in trouble because of its very success in adapting to the institutions of secular society. Although it was in doctrine a mystical body that guided the faithful away from the temptations of this world toward the eternal rewards of the life hereafter, in practice it had become largely a livelihood (Englishmen even called a benefice or ecclesiastical office a "living"), a source of wealth and a means of power. For ordinary believers it was all too frequently a means of evading the penalties of sin, an attitude exemplified by the indulgence. In principle this was an exemption from the pains of mortal sins granted by the Papacy to penitents upon the basis of the treasury of merits stored up by Christ and the saints in Heaven. But what the indulgence had become in practice was a means for getting the faithful to pay hard cash beyond the usual church taxes, and the requirement of penitence was quickly slipped over in the preachings of such men as Johann Tetzel (c. 1465-1519), a Dominican prior appointed by Archbishop Albert of Mainz in 1517 to sell indulgences, the proceeds of which were to be shared between the treasuries of the archbishop and Pope Leo X. Tetzel, an excerpt from whose sermon to parish clergy on indulgences is reproduced here, sparked the outbreak of the Protestant Reformation when he sold the indulgences in ducal Saxony, across the border from the university town of Wittenberg, where the professor of Bible and court preacher was Dr. Martin Luther.

Johann Tetzel

Sermon on Indulgences

Venerable Sir, I pray you that in your utterances you may be pleased to make use of such words as shall serve to open the eyes of the mind and cause your hearers to consider how great a grace and gift they have had and now have at their very doors. Blessed eyes indeed, which see what they see, because already they possess letters of safe conduct by which they are able to lead their souls through that valley of tears, through that sea of the mad world, where storms and tempests and dangers lie in wait, to the blessed land of Paradise. Know that the life of man upon earth is a constant struggle. We have to fight against the flesh, the world and the devil, who are always seeking to destroy the soul. In sin we are conceived,—alas! what bonds of sin encompass us, and how difficult and almost impossible it is to attain to the gate of salvation without divine aid; since He causes us to be saved, not by virtue of the good works which we accomplish, but through His divine mercy; it is necessary then to put on the armor of God.

You may obtain letters of safe conduct from the vicar of our Lord Jesus Christ, by means of which you are able to liberate your soul from the hands of the enemy, and convey it by means of contrition and confession, safe and secure from all pains of Purgatory, into the happy kingdom. For know that in these letters are stamped and engraven all the merits of Christ's passion there laid bare. Consider, that for each and every mortal sin it is necessary to undergo seven years of penitence after confession and contrition, either in this life or in Purgatory.

Source: Department of History, University of Pennsylvania, *Translations and Reprints from the Original Sources of European History* (Philadelphia: University of Pennsylvania Press, n.d.), Vol. II, pp. 9–10. Reprinted by permission of the University of Pennsylvania Press.

How many mortal sins are committed in a day, how many in a week, how many in a month, how many in a year, how many in the whole course of life! They are well-nigh numberless, and those that commit them must needs suffer endless punishment in the burning pains of Purgatory.

But with these confessional letters you will be able at any time in life to obtain full indulgence for all penalties imposed upon you, in all cases except the four reserved to the Apostolic See. Therefore throughout your whole life, whenever you wish to make confession, you may receive the same remission, except in cases reserved to the Pope, and afterwards, at the hour of death, a full indulgence as to all penalties and sins, and your share of all spiritual blessings that exist in the church militant and all its members.

Do you not know that when it is necessary for anyone to go to Rome, or undertake any other dangerous journey, he takes his money to a broker and gives a certain per cent—five or six or ten—in order that at Rome or elsewhere he may receive again his funds intact, by means of the letter of this same broker? Are you not willing, then, for the fourth part of a florin, to obtain these letters, by virtue of which you may bring, not your money, but your divine and immortal soul safe and sound into the land of Paradise?

Wherefore I counsel, order, and by virtue of my authority as shepherd, I command that they shall receive together with me and other priests, this precious treasure, especially those who were not confessed at the time of the holy Jubilee, that they may be able to obtain the same forever. For the time may come when you may desire, but yet be unable to obtain the least portion of the grace.

Also on the part of SS. D. N. the Pope and of the most holy apostolic See and of the most reverend sir, my legate, to each and every one who shall have profited by the sacred Jubilee and made confession, and to all who may profit by this present brief opportunity, and who shall have lent a helping hand to the construction of the aforesaid house of the Prince of the Apostles, they shall all be participants and sharers in all prayers, suffrages, alms, fasts, supplications, masses, canonical hours, disciplines, pilgrimages, papal stations, benedictions, and all other spiritual goods which now exist or may exist forever in the church militant, and in all of these, not only they themselves, but their relatives, kindred, and benefactors who have passed away; and as they were moved by charity, so God, and SS. Peter and Paul, and all the saints whose bodies rest in Rome, shall guard them in peace in this vale, and conduct them through it to the heavenly kingdom. Give everlasting thanks in the aforesaid names and in mine to the reverend secular priests and prelates, etc.

13. WORKS, FAITH, AND SALVATION

The indulgence issue brought to a head Martin Luther's inner conflict over the true means of salvation. Was it the acts of men—"works," particularly the sacraments—or the faith given by God to man? Though Catholic theology regarded them as interdependent, the indulgence practice demonstrated to Luther (1438-1546) both the appeal and the dangers of the approach to salvation through works. In 1517, he distributed his famous 95 theses challenging the principle of indulgences (the hoary tradition that he nailed them to the church door of Wittenberg on October 31 seems to have been disproved). Luther was an Augustinian friar who joined the faculty of the new Wittenberg University in 1508 and became professor of Bible three years later. He had gone through a deep personal religious crisis because his sense of sin had failed to be removed by the stern practice of the church's ascetic discipline, and he found release in the idea that man is saved by faith, of which good works are only an outward sign and result. During the controversy over his theses, Luther found he was being driven to break completely with the Catholic Church, and his reform of doctrine developed into a religious revolution, the Protestant Reformation of the 16th century. Among the most influential of his early writings was *The Babylonian Captivity of the Church,* one of his three great tracts published in 1520. The following selections are directed to the central problem of works and faith.

Martin Luther

The Babylonian Captivity of the Church

. . . . .

It is already easy to see what is the inevitable result of this extinguishing of the faith, namely, the most godless superstition of works. For where faith dies and the word of faith is silent, there works and the prescribing of works immediately crowd into their place. By them we have been carried away out of our own land, as into a Babylonian captivity, and despoiled of all our precious possessions. This has been the fate of the mass; it has been converted by the teaching of godless men into a good work. They themselves call it an *opus operatum,* and by it they presume themselves to be all-powerful with God. Next they proceed to the very height of madness, and after inventing the lie that the mass is effective simply by virtue of the act having been performed, they add another one to the effect that the mass is none the less profitable to others

---

SOURCE: Abdel Ross Wentz (ed.), *Luther's Works,* Vol. XXXVI (Philadelphia: Fortress Press, 1959), pp. 47, 66–67. Reprinted by permission of Fortress Press.

even if it is harmful to some wicked priest who may be celebrating it. On such a foundation of sand they base their applications, participations, brotherhoods, anniversaries, and numberless other lucrative and profitable schemes of that kind.

These fraudulent disguises are so powerful, so numerous, and so firmly entrenched that you can scarcely prevail against them unless you exercise unremitting care and bear well in mind what the mass is and what has been said above. You have seen that the mass is nothing else than the divine promise or testament of Christ, sealed with the sacrament of his body and blood. If that is true, you will understand that it cannot possibly be in any way a work; nobody can possibly do any thing in it, neither can it be dealt with in any other way than by faith alone. However, faith is not a work, but the lord and life of all work.

. . . . .

Thus it is not baptism that justifies or benefits anyone, but it is faith in that word of promise to which baptism is added. This faith justifies, and fulfils that which baptism signifies. For faith is the submersion of the old man and the emerging of the new [Eph. 4:22–24; Col. 3:9–10]. . . .

It cannot be true, therefore, that there is contained in the sacraments a power efficacious for justification, or that they are "effective signs" of grace. All such things are said to the detriment of faith, and out of ignorance of the divine promise. Unless you should call them "effective" in the sense that they certainly and effectively impart grace where faith is unmistakably present. But it is not in this sense that efficacy is now ascribed to them; as witness the fact that they are said to benefit all men, even the wicked and unbelieving, provided they do not set an obstacle in the way—as if such unbelief were not in itself the most obstinate and hostile of all obstacles to grace. To such an extent they have exerted themselves to turn the sacrament into a command and faith into a work. For if the sacrament confers grace on me because I receive it, then indeed I receive grace by virtue of my work, and not by faith; and I gain not the promise in the sacrament but only the sign instituted and commanded by God. Thus you see clearly how completely the sacraments have been misunderstood by the theologians of the *Sentences*. In their discussions of the sacraments they have taken no account either of faith or of promise. They cling only to the sign and the use of the sign, and draw us away from faith to the work, away from the word to the sign. Thus, as I have said, they have not only taken the sacraments captive, but have completely destroyed them, as far as they were able.

Therefore let us open our eyes and learn to pay heed more to the word than to the sign, more to faith than to the work or use of the sign. We know that wherever there is a divine promise, there faith is required, and that these two are so necessary to each other that neither can be effective apart from the other. For it is not possible to believe unless there is a promise, and the promise is not established unless it is believed. But where these two meet, they give a real and most certain efficacy to the sacraments. Hence, to seek the efficacy of the sacrament apart from the promise and apart from the faith is to labor in vain and to find condemnation. Thus Christ says: "He who believes and is baptized will be saved; but he who does not believe will be condemned" [Mark 16:16]. He shows us in this word that faith is such a necessary part of the sacrament that it can save even without the sacrament, and for this reason he did not add: "He who does not believe, and is not baptized."

14. FAITH AS BONDAGE TO GOD

Erasmus, in his elaboration of Christian humanism, could not escape the complications of theological debate, much as he disliked them. In stressing the ethical over the mystical side of Christianity, he took the commonsense approach of practical men, for whom morality concerns the choices made by men. Such an affirmation of free will went counter to the religious vision of Luther, who saw man as powerless on his own (except to sin) and salvation as the work of a God who saved some souls out of his mercy alone. Luther realized that Erasmus, however sharply he criticized the abuses of the Catholic church, was on opposite sides when it came to fundamentals of faith and lashed out at the great scholar in a lengthy work of 1520, *The Bondage of the Will*, a specific reply to Erasmus's *Freedom of the Will*. The Wittenberger's point of view was central to the two most powerful new churches that emerged from the Protestant Reformation, his own Lutheranism and the Calvinism that came soon after.

Martin Luther

On the Bondage of the Will

. . . . .

It is then, fundamentally necessary and wholesome for Christians to know that God foreknows nothing contingently, but that He foresees, purposes, and does all things according to His own immutable, eternal and infallible will. This bombshell knocks "free-will" flat, and utterly

---

SOURCE: Martin Luther, *On the Bondage of the Will*, translated by J. I. Packer and O. R. Johnston (London, England: James Clarke & Co., Ltd., 1957), pp. 80–81, 234–35, 313–14. Reprinted by permission of James Clarke & Co.

shatters it; so that those who want to assert it must ether deny my bombshell, or pretend not to notice it, or find some other way of dodging it. Before I establish this point by my own arguments and Scriptural authority, I shall first state it with the aid of *your* words.

Surely it was you, my good Erasmus, who a moment ago asserted that *God is by nature just, and kindness itself*? If this is true, does it not follow that He is *immutably* just and kind? that, as His nature remains unchanged to all eternity, so do His justice and kindness? And what is said of His justice and kindness must be said also of His knowledge, His wisdom, His goodness, His will, and the other Divine attributes. But if it is religious, godly and wholesome, to affirm these things of God, as you do, what has come over you, that now you should contradict yourself by affirming that it is irreligious, idle and vain to say that God foreknows by necessity? You insist that we should learn the immutability of God's will, while forbidding us to know the immutability of His foreknowledge! Do you suppose that He does not will what He foreknows, or that He does not foreknow what He wills? If He wills what He foreknows, His will is eternal and changeless, because His nature is so. From which it follows, by resistless logic, that all we do, however it may appear to us to be done mutably and contingently, is in reality done necessarily and immutably in respect of God's will. For the will of God is effective and cannot be impeded, since power belongs to God's nature; and His wisdom is such that He cannot be deceived. Since, then His will is not impeded, what is done cannot but be done where, when, how, as far as, and by whom, He foresees and wills.

. . . . .

Behold, therefore, the wickedness of the human heart! When God saves the undeserving without merit, yes, and justifies the ungodly, with all their great demerit, yes, and justifies the ungodly, with all their great demerit, man's heart does not accuse God of iniquity, nor demand to know why He wills to do so, although by its own reckoning such action is most unprincipled; but because what God does is in its own interest, and welcome, it considers it just and good. But when He damns the undeserving, because this is against its interest, it finds the action iniquitious and intolerable; and here man's heart protests, and grumbles, blasphemes. So you see that the Diatribe and its friends do not judge in this matter according to equity, but according to their passionate regard for their own interest. If the Diatribe regarded equity, it would expostulate as much with God for His crowning of the unworthy as it does with Him for the damnation of the undeserving; and, conversely, it would praise and extol God in the same measure for damning and undeserving as it does when He saves the unworthy. The impropriety is the same in each case, if you regard our own judgment. Would it not have been equally improper to praise Cain for his murder and make him a king, while innocent Abel was cast into prison or executed?

Now, since Reason praises God when He saves the unworthy but finds fault with Him when He damns the undeserving, it stands convicted of not praising God as God, but as One who serves its own convenience—that is, what it looks for and praises in God is self, and the things of self, and not God and the things of God. But if a God who crowns the undeserving pleases you, you ought not be displeased when He damns the undeserving! If He is just in the one case, He cannot but be just in the other. In the one case, He pours out grace and mercy upon the unworthy; in the other, He pours out wrath and severity upon the undeserving; in both He transgresses the bounds of equity in man's sight, yet is just and true in His own sight. *How* it is just for Him to crown the unworthy is incomprehensible now; but we shall see it when we reach the place where He will be no more an object of faith, but we shall with open face behold Him. So, too, it is at present incomprehensible how it is just for Him to damn the undeserving; yet faith will continue to believe that it is so, till the Son of Man shall be revealed.

. . . .

I frankly confess that, for myself, even if it could be, I should not want "free-will" to be given me, nor anything to be left in my own hands to enable me to endeavour after salvation; not merely because in face of so many dangers, and adversities, and assaults of devils, I could not stand my ground and hold fast my "free-will" (for one devil is stronger than all men, and on these terms no man could be saved); but because, even were there no dangers, adversities, or devils, I should still be forced to labour with no guarantee of success, and to beat my fists at the air. If I lived and worked to all eternity, my conscience would never reach comfortable certainty as to how much it must do to satisfy God. Whatever work I had done, there would still be a nagging doubt as to whether it pleased God, or whether He required something more. The experience of all who seek righteousness by works proves that; and I learned it well enough myself over a period of many years, to my own great hurt. But now that God has taken my salvation out of the control of my own will, and put it under the control of His, and promised to save me, not according to my working or running, but according to His own grace and mercy, I have the comfortable certainty that He is faithful and will not lie to me, and that He is also great and powerful, so that no devils or opposition can break Him or pluck me from Him. "No one," He says, "shall pluck them out of my hand, because my Father which gave them me is greater than all" (John 10:28–29). Thus it is that, if not all, yet some, indeed many, are saved; whereas, by the power of "free-will" none at all could be saved, but every one of us would perish.

Furthermore, I have the comfortable certainty that I please God, not by reason of the merit of my works, but by reason of His merciful favour promised to me; so that, if I work too little, or badly, He does not impute it to me, but with fatherly compassion pardons me and makes me better. This is the glorying of all the saints in their God.

15. WHAT THE CHRISTIAN OWES TO THE STATE

The revolution wrought by Luther was not easily limited to the arena of religion, although his intentions did not extend any further. Some of those who heard his bristling words of emancipation from the established authority of the Catholic Church carried them over to their political and social experience, and heresy became civil war. Germany was shaken by a Peasants' War in 1524–25, in which peasants rebelled against princes and manorial lords under slogans they believed were derived from Luther's teaching (see Section 43). Luther, however, had given a judgment in 1523 on the duties of a Christian towards his government which taught the necessity of obedience to rulers. His tract *Temporal Authority,* from which the following extracts were taken, set forth his teaching that while the princes did not have power over men's souls, Christians as good subjects had only the right of passive resistance to tyrants and the duty to accept the punishments inflicted upon them. In view of these doctrines, it ought not be surprising that Luther denounced the peasant rebels as miscreants to be destroyed, even though he had warned the rulers against their misconduct.

Martin Luther

Temporal Authority

. . . . .

First, we must provide a sound basis for the civil law and sword so no one will doubt that it is in the world by God's will and ordinance. The passages which do this are the following: Romans 12, "Let every soul [*seele*] be subject to the governing authority, for there is no authority except from God; the authority which everywhere [*allenthalben*] exists has been ordained by God. He then who resists the governing authority resists the ordinance of God, and he who resists God's ordinance will incur judgment." Again, in I Peter 2 [:13–14], "Be subject to every kind

---

SOURCE: Walther I. Brandt (ed.), *Luther's Works,* Vol. XLV (Philadelphia: Fortress Press, 1962), pp. 85–86, 99, 104–5, 111–12, 124–26. Reprinted by permission of Fortress Press.

of human ordinance, whether it be to the king as supreme, or to governors, as those who have been sent by him to punish the wicked and to praise the righteous."

. . . . .

Moreover, we have the clear and compelling text of St. Paul in Romans 13 [:1], where he says, "The governing authority has been ordained by God"; and further, "The governing authority does not bear the sword in vain. It is God's servant for your good, an avenger upon him who does evil" [Rom. 13:4]. Be not so wicked, my friend, as to say, "A Christian may not do that which is God's own peculiar work, ordinance, and creation." Else you must also say, "A Christian must not eat, drink, or be married," for these are also God's work and ordinance. If it is God's work and creation, then it is good, so good that everyone can use it in a Christian and salutary way, as Paul says in II Timothy 4 [I Tim. 4:4, 3], "Everything created by God is good, and nothing is to be rejected by those who believe and know the truth." Under "everything created by God" you must include not simply food and drink, clothing and shoes, but also authority and subjection, protection and punishment.

. . . . .

We come now to the main part of this treatise. Having learned that there must be temporal authority on earth, and how it is to be exercised in a Christian and salutary manner, we must now learn how far its arm extends and how widely its hand stretches, lest it extend too far and encroach upon God's kingdom and government. It is essential for us to know this, for where it is given too wide a scope, intolerable and terrible injury follows; on the other hand, injury is also inevitable where it is restricted too narrowly. In the former case, the temporal authority punishes too much; in the latter case, it punishes too little. To err in this direction, however, and punish too little is more tolerable, for it is always better to let a scoundrel live than to put a godly man to death. The world has plenty of scoundrels anyway and must continue to have them, but godly men are scarce.

It is to be noted first that the two classes of Adam's children—the one in God's kingdom under Christ and the other in the kingdom of the world under the governing authority, as was said above—have two kinds of law. For every kingdom must have its own laws and statutes; without law no kingdom or government can survive, as everyday experience amply shows. The temporal government has laws which extend no further than to life and property and external affairs on earth, for God cannot and will not permit anyone but himself to rule over the soul. Therefore, where the temporal authority presumes to prescribe laws for the soul, it encroaches upon God's government and only misleads souls and destroys them. We want to make this so clear that everyone will grasp it, and that our fine gentlemen, the princes and bishops, will see what fools they are when they seek to coerce the people with their laws and commandments into believing this or that.

. . . . .

If your prince or temporal ruler commands you to side with the pope, to believe thus and so, or to get rid of certain books, you should say, "It is not fitting that Lucifer should sit at the side of God. Gracious sir, I owe you obedience in body and property; command me within the limits of your authority on earth, and I will obey. But if you command me to believe or to get rid of certain books, I will not obey; for then you are a tyrant and overreach yourself, commanding where you have neither the right nor the authority," etc. Should he seize your property on account of this and punish such disobedience, then blessed are you; thank God that you are worthy to suffer for the sake of the divine word. Let him rage, fool that he is; he will meet his judge. For I tell you, if you fail to withstand him, if you give in to him and let him take away your faith and your books, you have truly denied God.

. . . . .

Here you will ask: "Is a prince then not to go to war, and are his subjects not to follow him into battle?" Answer: This is a far-reaching question, but let me answer it very briefly. To act here as a Christian, I say, a prince should not go to war against his overlord—king, emperor, or other liege lord—but let him who takes, take. For the governing authority must not be resisted by force, but only by confession of the truth. If it is influenced by this, well and good; if not, you are excused, you suffer wrong for God's sake. If, however, the antagonist is your equal, your inferior, or of a foreign government, you should first offer him justice and peace, as Moses taught the children of Israel. If he refuses, then—mindful of what is best for you—defend yourself against force by force, as Moses so well describes it in Deuteronomy 20 [:10–12]. But in doing this you must not consider your personal interests and how you may remain lord, but those of your subjects to whom you owe help and protection, that such action may proceed in love. Since your entire land is in peril you must make the venture, so that with God's help all may not be lost. If you cannot prevent some from becoming widows and orphans as a consequence, you must at least see that not everything goes to ruin until there is nothing left except widows and orphans.

In this matter subjects are in duty bound to follow, and to devote their life and property, for in such a case one must risk his goods and himself for the sake of others. In a war of this sort it is both Christian and an act of love to kill the enemy without hesitation, to plunder and burn and injure him by every method of warfare until he is conquered (except that one must beware of sin, and not violate wives and virgins). And when victory has been achieved, one should offer mercy and peace to those who surrender and humble themselves. In such a case let the proverb apply, "God helps the strongest." This is what Abraham did when he smote the four kings, Genesis 14; he certainly slaughtered many, and showed little mercy until he conquered them. Such a case must be regarded as sent by God as a means to cleanse the land for once and drive out the rascals.

What if a prince is in the wrong? Are his people bound to follow him then too? Answer: No, for it is no one's duty to do wrong; we must obey God (who desires the right) rather than men [Acts 5:29]. What if the subjects do not know whether their prince is in the right or not? Answer: So long as they do not know, and cannot with all possible diligence find out, they may obey him without peril to their souls.

16. ERASMUS AND THE REFORMATION

Although Erasmus's foes within the Catholic Church accused him of having fathered the Protestant Reformation by his criticism of the church's abuses and even its fundamental institutions, such as monasticism, he continued to feel an essential tie to the ancient church. What he sought was reform, not overthrow, he said; he could not be blamed for what other men did. He set forth these ideas in a letter to Cardinal Thomas Wolsey, the Primate of England, early in 1519. The key passages are given here.

Desiderius Erasmus

Letter to Cardinal Wolsey

ANTWERP, May 18, 1519

. . . . .

For myself, rejoicing, as I do, in the general felicity, I am not sorry that my own name is cast into the shade by more recent lights, when I see those around me, compared with whom I appear no wiser than a child. Enough for me to claim this praise, if indeed I can fairly do so,—to be described as one of those, who have done their best to drive out of this part of the world that barbarous ignorance of languages, with which

SOURCE: *The Epistles of Erasmus*, translated by Francis Morgan Nichols (London, England, and New York: Longmans, Green & Co., 1901–8), Vol. III, pp. 380–82, 384. (Nichols misdates this letter May 18, 1517; the correct date is given in P. S. Allen [ed.], *Opus Epistolarum Des. Erasmi Roterodami*, Tom. III, p. 587.)

Italy was wont to reproach us. How far I have been successful in this, I know not; that I have striven to do so I know, and striven not without some of that jealousy, which accompanies and pursues exceptional efforts, as the shadow follows the light. But the majority is now more kind; only a few still hold out, too old to hope, too stupid to learn, or too arrogant to wish to know better!

These people see only too plainly, that their own authority will fall to the ground, if we have the Sacred Books accessible in an amended form, and seek their meaning at the fountain-head. And so high a value do they set upon their own importance, that they had rather have many things unknown, many things mis-read and cited amiss from the Divine Books, than appear to be ignorant themselves of any point. But inasmuch as they are conscious of their own inferiority in argument, and aware that, if they deal with books, they do nothing but betray their own ignorance and folly, making themselves a laughing-stock to the learned, they have given up open fighting, and have recourse to stratagems, loading with their slanders literature and its defenders, and me above all, whom they judge to have had some influence in the revival of these studies. Whatever writing of an invidious nature may be published, they fasten it upon Erasmus; and here you will detect the very Genius of Calumny at work, when the cause of Good Letters is mixed up with the affairs of Reuchlin or of Luther, whereas they have no proper connection with each other.

For my own part, I never had any fancy for the Cabala or the Thalmud; and as for Reuchlin himself, I have only once met him at Frankfort, when nothing passed between us, except such friendly civilities as are usual between scholars. Not that I am ashamed to have joined in friendly correspondence with him; he has a letter of mine, in which, before I knew him by sight, I advised him to abstain from those plain terms of abuse of his opponents in which after the German fashion he indulges in his Apology; so far is it from the truth, that I have ever encouraged writings affecting any one's good name!

Luther is no more known to me than to any stranger he might meet; and as for the man's books, I have not had time to turn over more than one or two pages. And yet it is pretended,—so I am told,—that he has had my help in his work! If he has written aright, no credit is due to me; and if the reverse, I deserve no blame, seeing that in all his lucubrations not a tittle is mine. Any one who cares to investigate the matter, will find this to be quite true. The man's life is by a wide and general consent approved; and it is no small presumption in his favour, that his moral character is such, that even his foes can find no fault with it. If I had had ample leisure to read his works, I do not claim so much authority, as to pass judgment upon the writings of so important a person; although in these days you find boys everywhere pronouncing with the greatest temerity, that this proposition is erroneous and that heretical. And indeed we were at one time all the more inclined to find fault with Luther, for fear of a prejudice that might arise against Literature, upon which I did not wish a further burden to be laid. For I saw plainly enough, how invidious an act it is to disturb the stability of things from which a rich harvest is reaped by Priests or Monks.

The first of these writings which came out were several propositions concerning Papal pardons. These were followed by one or two pamphlets about Confession and Penance; and when I became aware that some persons were intent upon their publication, I did my best to discourage it, that they might not strengthen the prejudice against Good Letters. This circumstance will be shown by the evidence even of those who are Luther's well-wishers. At last a whole swarm of pamphlets came out; no one saw me reading them; no one heard me give any opinion either for or against them. I am not so rash as to approve that which I have not read, nor such a sycophant as to condemn that which I do not know; although in these days this is commonly done by those who have least excuse for doing so.

. . . . .

I have advised by letter all those young German writers to control their excessive freedom of language, and certainly to abstain from any attack upon persons of authority in the Church,—lest they should prejudice against literature those by whose patronage they might be able to stand up against their foes. What more am I to do? I can advise, but have no power to compel; I may temper my own style, but to control the pen of another is not in my power. The absurdest thing of all is, that the work which was lately written by the Bishop of Rochester against Lefèvre was suspected to be mine, when there is so great a difference of style,—and indeed I have no pretentions to the erudition of that divine Prelate. There were also persons to be found, who ascribed More's *Utopia* to my authorship, every thing new, whether I like it or not, being attributed to me!

17. PREDESTINATION AND THE COVENANT OF LIFE

The principles of Lutheran's form of Christianity were adopted widely in Germany and throughout Scandinavia, eventually becoming the established religion there. The impetus of the Protestant revolt continued, however, and the French theologian John Calvin (1509-1564) was its principal exponent. A lawyer by training, Calvin had to flee for his life from France in 1533 after he had adopted the Reformed doctrines, and he became an exile in Switzerland and the Rhineland. When Geneva took him as its spiritual leader in 1541, after a period of disputed authority, he organized the city as an independent theocratic state. His *Institutes of the Christian Religion*, first published in Basel in 1536, presents his conception of Christian theology, marked by emphasis upon the principle of predestination. This doctrine reinforced Luther's rejection of works as the means of salvation by attributing faith to the election of God from the beginning of time. Thus God granted salvation to some and denied it to others. The following selections from the *Institutes* examine the searing problem of predestination.

John Calvin

Institutes of the Christian Religion

. . . . .

THE covenant of life is not preached equally to all, and among those to whom it is preached, does not always meet with the same reception. This diversity displays the unsearchable depth of the divine judgment, and is without doubt subordinate to God's purpose of eternal election. But if it is plainly owing to the mere pleasure of God that salvation is spontaneously offered to some, while others have no access to it, great and difficult questions immediately arise, questions which are inexplicable, when just views are not entertained concerning election and predestination. To many this seems a perplexing subject, because they deem it most incongruous that of the great body of mankind some should be predestinated to salvation, and others to destruction. How causelessly they entangle themselves will appear as we proceed. We may add, that in the very obscurity which deters them, we may see not only the utility of this doctrine, but also its most pleasant fruits. We shall never feel persuaded as we ought that our salvation flows from the free mercy of God as its fountain, until we are made acquainted with his eternal election, the grace of God being illustrated by the contrast, viz., that he does not adopt all promiscuously to the hope of salvation, but gives to some what he denies to others. It is plain how greatly ignorance of this principle detracts from the glory of God, and impairs true humility. But though thus necessary to be known, Paul declares that it cannot be known unless God, throwing works entirely out of view, elects those whom he has predestined. His words are, "Even so then at this present time also, there is a remnant according to the election of grace. And if by grace, then it is no more of works: otherwise grace is no more grace. But if it be of

---

SOURCE: John Calvin, *Institutes of the Christian Religion*, translated by Henry Beveridge (Edinburgh; Scotland: Calvin Translation Society, 1845), vol. II, pp. 529, 534, 540.

works, then it is no more grace: otherwise work is no more work," (Rom. xi. 6.) If to make it appear that our salvation flows entirely from the good mercy of God, we must be carried back to the origin of election, then those who would extinguish it, wickedly do as much as in them lies to obscure what they ought most loudly to extol, and pluck up humility by the very roots.

. . . . .

The predestination by which God adopts some to the hope of life, and adjudges others to eternal death, no man who would be thought pious ventures simply to deny; but it is greatly cavilled at, especially by those who make prescience its cause. We, indeed, ascribe both prescience and predestination to God; but we say, that it is absurd to make the latter subordinate to the former . . . When we attribute prescience to God, we mean that all things always were, and ever continue, under his eye; that to his knowledge there is no past or future, but all things are present, and indeed so present, that it is not merely the idea of them that is before him, (as those objects are which we retain in our memory,) but that he truly sees and contemplates them as actually under his immediate inspection. This prescience extends to the whole circuit of the world, and to all creatures. By predestination we mean the eternal decree of God, by which he determined with himself whatever he wished to happen with regard to every man. All are not created on equal terms, but some are preordained to eternal life, others to eternal damnation; and, accordingly, as each has been created for one or other of these ends, we say that he has been predestinated to life or to death.

. . . . .

. . . We say, then, that Scripture clearly proves this much, that God by his eternal and immutable counsel determined once for all those whom it was his pleasure one day to admit to salvation, and those whom, on the other hand, it was his pleasure to doom to destruction. We maintain that this counsel, as regards the elect, is founded on his free mercy, without any respect to human worth, while those whom he dooms to destruction are excluded from access to life by a just and blameless, but at the same time incomprehensible judgment. In regard to the elect, we regard calling as the evidence of election, and justification as another symbol of its manifestation, until it is fully accomplished by the attainment of glory. But as the Lord seals his elect by calling and justification, so by excluding the reprobate either from the knowledge of his name or the sanctification of his Spirit, he by these marks in a manner discloses the judgment which awaits them. I will here omit many of the fictions which foolish men have devised to overthrow predestination. There is no need of refuting objections which the moment they are produced abundantly betray their hollowness. I will dwell only on those points which either form the subject of dispute among the learned, or may occasion any difficulty to the simple, or may be employed by impiety as specious pretexts for assailing the justice of God.

18. THE COMMUNITY OF THE ELECT

Luther and Calvin became the founders of great churches which won the adherence of millions and domination over powerful states. But the same impulse to seek a new way in religion also led to the formation of a swarm of sects, with followers numbered at most in the thousands. The followers of these sects were considered heretics by Lutherans and Calvinists as well as by Catholics and were relentlessly persecuted almost everywhere in Europe, primarily because they called into question aspects of Christianity the major reformers had left untouched.

Most important of these changes was the rejection of infant baptism, which brought the newborn child into the community of Christians. Proclaiming that only understanding adults could profess the faith, these sects practiced "rebaptism" (anabaptism). The concept of a community of goods (property) embraced by many of the early Anabaptist groups intensified the fury of the ruling groups against them. They formed small, often secret communities both to avoid persecution and because they saw themselves as "saints" living apart from the world of sinners.

One of the earliest ordinances for the life of an Anabaptist community in the Tirol was written in 1527, probably by its leader, Hans Schlaffer, who was martyred the following year. The text below was translated from a manuscript copy by Elizabeth Horsch Bender and edited by Robert Friedmann, who has added in brackets material in another version, the Hutterite Chronicle (*Geschicht-Buch*) published in 1923.

Rules for an Anabaptist Community, 1527

Discipline of the Believers: How a Christian Is to Live

Introduction (missing in the Geschicht-Buch)

Since the almighty God and heavenly Father is permitting His eternal and all-powerful Word to be proclaimed to all creatures in these most perilous times (Col. 1) and has called us at this time out of pure grace into His marvelous light (I Pet. 3) to one body, one spirit, and one faith,

---

Source: Robert Friedmann, "The Oldest Church Discipline of the Anabaptists," *The Mennonite Quarterly Review,* Vol. XXIX (1955), pp. 164-66. Reprinted by permission of *The Mennonite Quarterly Review.*

united in the bonds of love (Eph. 4; I Cor. 1), to which we have all agreed, in order that our calling be found worthy, not only with the word of the mouth but in the truth and power (II Thess. 1; I Thess. 1; I Cor. 4; James 1), we have all in one another's presence openly agreed to regulate everything in the best possible way. For the improvement of our brotherhood [*Gemein,* so translated throughout], for the praise and honor of the Lord, and for the service of all the needy, we have unanimously agreed that this *Ordnung* shall be kept among us by all the brethren and sisters. When, however, a brother or sister is able to produce a better *Ordnung* it shall be accepted from him at any time (I Cor. 14).

First Article

And beginning: when the brethren are together they shall sincerely ask God for grace that He might reveal His divine will and help us to note it (Psalm 86, 118) and when the brethren part they shall thank God and pray for all the brethren and sisters of the entire brotherhood (I Thess. 1 and 5; II Thess. 1 and 2; II Cor. 1; Col. 1, 3, 4).

Second Article

In the second place: we shall sincerely and in a Christian spirit admonish one another in the Lord to remain constant (Heb. 10:1; Acts 14, 15, 18: Col. 2). To meet often, at least four or five times, and if possible . . . even at midweek [prayer meetings?] (I Cor. 11, 14; Acts 1, 2, 9, 11, 20; Heb. 10; II Cor. 6; Matt. 18).

Third Article

In the third place: when a brother or sister leads a disorderly life it shall be punished: if he does so publicly [he] shall be kindly admonished before all the brethren (Gal. 2, 6; I Cor. 5; II Thess. 3): if it is secret it shall be punished in secret, according to the command of Christ (Matt. 18).

Fourth Article

In the fourth place: every brother or sister shall yield himself in God to the brotherhood completely with body and life, and hold in common all gifts received of God (Acts 2 and 4; I Cor. 11, 12; II Cor. 8 and 9), [and] contribute to the common need so that brethren and sisters will always be helped (Rom 12); needy members shall receive from the brotherhood as among the Christians at the time of the apostles (Acts 2, 4, 5; I Cor. 11, 12; Eph. 4; Prov. 5; Matt. 8, 15, 16, 17, 19; Luke 3, 6, 8, 9, 10, 12, 14, 18; I John 1, 2, 3, 4; Mark 3, 10, 12; Gal. 6; Heb. 13; Dan. 4, 8; Luke 6, 8; I Tim. 1; I Cor. 14, 16; Rom. 6, 18; James 1; Phil. 2).

Fifth Article

The elders [*Vorsteher*] and preachers chosen for the brotherhood shall with zeal look after the needs of the poor, and with zeal in the Lord according to the command of the Lord extend what is needed for the sake of and instead of the brotherhood (Gal. 2; II Cor. 8, 9; Rom. 15; Acts 6).

Sixth Article

In the sixth place: a decent conduct *(ehrbarer Wandel)*, shall be kept among them (Rom. 12, 13; Phil. 1, 2; I Pet. 2, 3; I Cor. 1, 3; Gal. 5; Eph. 5) before everyone (Titus 3; Matt. 5; I Pet. 3) and no one shall carelessly conduct himself before the brotherhood both with words or deeds (Rom. 1, 6; II Tim. 2), nor before those who are "outside" (I Thess. 5; I Pet. 3).

Seventh Article

In the seventh place: in the meeting one is to speak and the others listen and judge what is spoken, and not two or three stand together (I Cor. 14). No one shall curse or swear (Matt. 5; Rom. 3; James 5) nor shall idle gossip be carried on, so that the weak may be spared (I Cor. 15; Eph. 5; Col. 3; II Tim. 2; Psalm 118). [*Geschicht-Buch* here cites only Ecclesiasticus 23.]

Eighth Article

In the eighth place: when the brethren assemble they shall not fill up with eating and drinking, but avoid expenses [reduce expenditures] to the least, [eat] a soup and vegetable or whatever God gives (I Cor. 11; I Pet. 4; Gal. 5; Rom. 13; Eph. 5; Eccles. 37; Luke 21), and when they have eaten, all the food and drink shall again be removed [*Geschicht-Buch:* "from the table"] (John 6; Matt. 4; Luke 9; Mark 6), for one should use with thanksgiving and moderation the creatures which God has created, pure and good, for our subsistence.

Ninth Article

In the ninth place; what is officially done among the brethren and sisters in the brotherhood [*Geschicht-Buch:* "or is judged"] shall not be made public before the world. The good-hearted [an interested but not yet converted or committed] person, before he comes to the brethren in the brotherhood shall be taught [*Geschicht-Buch:* "the Gospel"] (Mark 16; Rom. 1; Col. 1). When he has learned [*Geschicht-Buch:* "understood"] and bears a sincere desire for it, and if he agrees to the content of the Gospel, he shall be received by the Christian brotherhood as a brother or a sister, that is, as a fellow member of Christ (Matt. 7; Prov. 19, 29; Col. 4; Rom.

14; II Cor. 6; I Cor. 10; I Tim. 6; Matt. 10). But this shall not be made public before the world to spare the conscience and for the sake of the spouse (I Cor. 9, 10; Matt. 15).

Tenth Article

In the tenth place: all the brethren and sisters after they have committed themselves, shall accept and bear with patience all that He sends us [*Geschicht-Buch*: "accept with gratitude and bear with patience"] (Rom. 6; John 13; Matt. 16; Luke 9; I Pet. 4; II Cor. 12), and [shall] not let themselves be easily frightened by every wind and cry.[1]

Eleventh Article

When brethren and sisters are together, being one body and one bread in the Lord and of one mind, then they shall keep the Lord's Supper as a memorial of the Lord's death (Matt. 26; Mark 14; Luke 22; I Cor. 11), whereby each one shall be admonished to become conformed to the Lord in the obedience of the Father (Phil. 2, 3; I Pet. 2, 4; Rom. 8; I John 2.—Obedience: Rom. 2; Phil. 2; II Cor. 2, 10; II Thess. 1; I Pet. 1).

Twelfth Article

In the twelfth place: as we have taught and admonished the brethren and sisters we shall always watch and wait for the Lord that we may be worthy to enter [the kingdom] with Him when He comes, and to escape or flee from the evil that will come to the world. Amen. (Matt. 25; Luke 21; I Thess. 5; I Pet. 5; II Pet. 3; Rom. 2)

God be merciful to me. I commend my spirit and your spirit with our brother in Christ into the hand of the eternal Father. Amen.

19. CATHOLIC REFORMATION

The Catholic Church responded to the challenge of Protestantism in two ways. The first, generally known as the Counter-Reformation, was an assault upon Protestant heresies and Protestant states waged with the weapons of debate, teaching, and political suppression. The sword was the work of self-reform undertaken by the church which built upon older traditions of internal criticism; this is often called the Catholic Reformation, to set it parallel to Protestant reform movements.

Definition of the purpose and method of the Catholic Reformation was achieved with the Council of Trent, held intermittently between 1545 and

[1]The *Geschicht-Buch* adds as a marginal note: "to be ready for cross and suffering."

1563 in that Alpine city. The decrees and canons that evolved first of all reaffirmed the theological traditions of the Roman Church, although much of the breadth of medieval theological debate was lost. Other decrees ordained removal of the most notorious and admitted abuses within the Roman Church, such as impropriety in the lives of clerics, inadequate facilities for education of priests, concubinage, and the holding of multiple benefices by clergymen. The decisions of the Council of Trent as to these points are given in the selection below.

Canons and Decrees of the Council of Trent

ON THE SACRAMENTS IN GENERAL

CANON I. If any one saith, that the sacraments of the New Law were not all instituted by Jesus Christ, our Lord; or, that they are more, or less, than seven, to wit, Baptism, Confirmation, the Eucharist, Penance, Extreme Unction, Order, and Matrimony; or even that any one of these seven is not truly and properly a sacrament; let him be anathema.

CANON II. If any one saith, that these said sacraments of the New Law do not differ from the sacraments of the Old Law, save that the ceremonies are different, and different the outward rites; let him be anathema.

CANON III. If any one saith, that these seven sacraments are in such wise equal to each other, as that one is not in any way more worthy than another; let him be anathema.

CANON IV. If any one saith, that the sacraments of the New Law are not necessary unto salvation, but superfluous; and that, without them, or without the desire thereof, men obtain of God, through faith alone, the grace of justification;—though all (the sacraments) are not indeed necessary for every individual; let him be anathema.

CANON V. If any one saith, that these sacraments were instituted for the sake of nourishing faith alone; let him be anathema.

CANON VI. If any one saith, that the sacraments of the New Law do not contain the grace which they signify; or, that they do not confer that grace on those who do not place an obstacle thereunto; as though they were merely outward signs of grace or justice received through faith, and certain marks of the Christian profession, whereby believers are distinguished amongst men from unbelievers; let him be anathema.

CANON VII. If any one saith, that grace, as far as God's part is concerned, is not given through the said sacraments, always, and to all men,

---

SOURCE: *Canons and Decrees of the Council of Trent*, translated by J. Waterworth (London: C. Dolman, 1848), pp. 54-55, 162-163, 187, 270, 224.

even though they receive them rightly, but (only) sometimes, and to some persons; let him be anathema.

CANON VIII. If any one saith, that by the said sacraments of the New Law grace is not conferred through the act performed [*ex opere operato*], but that faith alone in the divine promise suffices for the obtaining of grace; let him be anathema.

CANON IX. If any one saith, that, in the three sacraments, Baptism, to wit, Confirmation, and Order, there is not imprinted in the soul a character, that is, a certain spiritual and indelible sign, on account of which they cannot be repeated; let him be anathema.

CANON X. If any one saith, that all Christians have power to administer the word, and all the sacraments; let him be anathema.

CANON XI. If any one saith, that, in ministers, when they effect, and confer the sacraments, there is not required the intention at least of doing what the Church does; let him be anathema.

CANON XII. If any one saith, that a minister, being in mortal sin,—if so be that he observe all the essentials which belong to the effecting, or conferring of, the sacrament,—neither effects, nor confers the sacrament; let him be anathema.

. . . . .

The Canons relative to the life, and propriety of conduct of Clerics are renewed

There is nothing that continually *instructs others unto piety,* and the service of God, more than the life and example of those who have dedicated themselves to the divine ministry. For as they are seen to be raised to a higher position, above the things of this world, others fix their eyes upon them as upon a mirror, and derive from them what they are to imitate. Wherefore clerics called to have the Lord for their portion, ought by all means so to regulate their whole life and conversation, as that in their dress, comportment, gait, discourse, and all things else, nothing appear but what is grave, regulated, and replete with religiousness; avoiding even slight faults, which in them would be most grievous; that so their actions may impress all with veneration. Whereas, therefore, the more useful and decorous these things are for the Church of God, the more carefully also are they to be attended to; the holy Synod ordains, that those things which have been heretofore copiously and wholesomely enacted by sovereign pontiffs and sacred councils,—relative to the life, propriety of conduct, dress, and learning of clerics, and also touching the luxuriousness, feastings, dances, gambling, sports, and all sorts of crime whatever, as also the secular employments, to be by them shunned,—the same shall be henceforth observed, under the same penalties, or greater, to be imposed at the discretion of the Ordinary; nor shall any appeal suspend the execution hereof, as relating to the correction of manners.

. . . . .

Method of establishing Seminaries for Clerics, and of educating the same therein

Whereas the age of youth, unless it be rightly trained, is prone to follow after the pleasures of the world; and unless it be formed, from its tender years, unto piety and religion, before habits of vice have taken possession of the whole man, it never will perfectly, and without the greatest, and well-nigh special, help of Almighty God, persevere in ecclesiastical discipline; the holy Synod ordains, that all cathedral, metropolitan, and other churches greater than these, shall be bound, each according to its means and the extent of the diocese, to maintain, to educate religiously, and to train in ecclesiastical discipline, a certain number of youths of their city and diocese, or, if that number cannot be met with there, of that province, in a college to be chosen by the bishop for this purpose near the said churches, or in some other suitable place.

. . . . .

The manner of proceeding against Clerics who keep concubines is prescribed

How shameful a thing, and how unworthy it is of the name of clerics who have devoted themselves to the service of God, to live in the filth of impurity, and unclean bondage, the thing itself doth testify, in the common scandal of all the faithful, and the extreme disgrace entailed on the clerical order. To the end, therefore, that the ministers of the Church may be recalled to that continency and integrity of life which becomes them; and that the people may hence learn to reverence them the more, that they know them to be more pure of life: the holy Synod forbids all clerics whatsoever to dare to keep concubines, or any other woman of whom any suspicion can exist, either in their own houses, or elsewhere, or to presume to have any intercourse with them: otherwise they shall be punished with the penalties imposed by the sacred canons, or by the statutes of the (several) churches. . . .

. . . . .

In what case it is lawful to confer more than one benefice upon one individual; and for him to retain the same

Whereas ecclesiastical order is perverted when one cleric fills the offices of several, the sacred canons have holily provided that no one ought to be enrolled in two churches. But, seeing that many, through the passion of ungodly covetousness deceiving themselves, not God, are not ashamed to elude, by various artifices, what has been so excellently ordained, and to hold several benefices at the same time; the holy Synod, desiring to restore the discipline required for the government of the church, doth by this present decree,—which It orders to be observed in regard of all persons whatsoever, by whatsoever title distinguished, even though it be by the dignity of the Cardinalate, –ordain, that, for the future, one ecclesiastical benefice only shall be conferred on one and the same person. If indeed that benefice be not sufficient to afford a decent livelihood to the person on whom it is conferred, it shall then be lawful to bestow on him some other simple benefice that may be sufficient; provided that both do not require personal residence. . . .

20. THE OBSESSION OF WITCHCRAFT

Medieval Christianity not only stressed with great force of imagination and belief the battle of good and evil but embodied that combat in good and evil spirits. Wizards and witches—the male and female spirits who did the devil's work—seemed to be everywhere present, the cause of the pain that was so much a part of life. The belief in witchcraft not only survived the rise of humanism, with its strong component of rationality; it was, if anything, intensified by the religious hatreds that accompanied the storm of the Protestant Reformation. Protestants were as easily persuaded of the malign works of witches as Catholics were, and they were no less ready to try them for their crimes and punish them with horrible deaths. Perhaps the most fearful denunciation of witches was a book printed in 1486, the *Hammer of Witches*, by two German theologians, Jacobus Sprenger and Heinrich Krämer. The following sections from this work "explain" why witches were even more prevalent than wizards and why they had to suffer the extreme penalty.

Jacobus Sprenger and Heinrich Krämer

The Hammer of Witchcraft

Question I [poses] Whether the Belief that there are such Beings as Witches is so Essential a Part of the Catholic Faith that Obstinacy to maintain the Opposite Opinion manifestly savours of Heresy. [It is answered that such belief is indeed heresy, both in ecclesiastical and civil

SOURCE: Jacobus Sprenger and Heinrich Krämer, *Malleus Maleficarum: The Hammer of Witchcraft*, edited by Pennethorne Hughes and translated by Montague Summers (London: Folio Society, 1968), pp. 25, 28–29, 31–32. From the Benjamin Blom Inc. 1970 edition.

law, and ends:] This then is our proposition: devils by their art do bring about evil effects through witchcraft, yet it is true that without the assistance of some agent they cannot make any form, either substantial or accidental, and we do not maintain that they can inflict damage without the assistance of some agent, but with such an agent diseases, and any other human passions or ailments, can be brought about, and these are real and true. How these agents or how the employment of such means can be rendered effective in co-operation with devils will be made clear in the following chapters.

. . . . .

[Question VI:] As for the question, why a greater number of witches is found in the fragile feminine sex than among men; it is indeed a fact that it were idle to contradict, since it is accredited by actual experience, apart from the verbal testimony of credible witnesses. And without in any way detracting from a sex in which God has always taken great glory that His might should be spread abroad, let us say that various men have assigned various reasons for this fact, which nevertheless agree in principle. Wherefore it is good, for the admonition of women, to speak of this matter; and it has often been proved by experience that they are eager to hear of it, so long as it is set forth with discretion.

For some learned men propound this reason; that there are three things in nature, the Tongue, an Ecclesiastic, and a Woman, which know no moderation in goodness or vice; and when they exceed the bounds of their condition they reach the greatest heights and the lowest depths of goodness and vice. When they are governed by a good spirit, they are most excellent in virtue; but when they are governed by an evil spirit, they indulge the worst possible vices.

[It quotes various authorities, proceeding in these terms:] Now the wickedness of women is spoken of in Ecclesiasticus XXV: There is no head above the head of a serpent: and there is no wrath above the wrath of a woman. I had rather dwell with a lion and a dragon than to keep house with a wicked woman. And among much which in that place precedes and follows about a wicked woman, he concludes: All wickedness is but little to the wickedness of a woman. Wherefore St. John Chrysostom says on the text, It is not good to marry (St. Matthew XIX): What else is woman but a foe to friendship, an unescapable punishment, a necessary evil, a natural temptation, a desirable calamity, a domestic danger, a delectable detriment, an evil of nature, painted with fair colours! Therefore if it be a sin to divorce her when she ought to be kept, it is indeed a necessary torture; for either we commit adultery by divorcing her, or we must endure daily strife. Cicero in his second book of "The Rhetorics" says: The many lusts of men lead them into one sin, but the one lust of women leads them into all sins; for the root of all woman's vices is avarice. And Seneca says in his "Tragedies": A woman either loves or hates; there is no third grade. And the tears of a woman are a deception, for they may spring from true grief, or they may be a snare. When a woman thinks alone, she thinks evil.

[This later continues:] All witchcraft comes from carnal lust, which is in women insatiable. See Proverbs XXX: There are three things that are never satisfied, yea, a fourth thing which says not, It is enough; that is, the mouth of the womb. Wherefore for the sake of fulfilling their lusts they consort even with devils. More such reasons could be brought forward, but to the understanding it is sufficiently clear that it is no matter for wonder that there are more women than men found infected with the heresy of witchcraft. And in consequence of this, it is better called the heresy of witches than of wizards, since the name is taken from the more powerful party. And blessed by the Highest Who has so far preserved the male sex from so great a crime: for since He was willing to be born and to suffer for us, therefore He has granted to men this privilege.

[After this partial exemption the diatribe continues:] And touching this we may say what is known by experience; that these women satisfy their filthy lusts not only in themselves, but even in the mighty ones of the age, of whatever state and condition; causing by all sorts of witchcraft the death of their souls through the excessive infatuation of carnal love, in such a way that for no shame or persuasion can they desist from such acts. And through such men, since the witches will not permit any harm to come to them either from themselves or from others once they have them in their power, there arises the great danger of the time, namely, the extermination of the Faith. And in this way do witches every day increase.

. . . . .

[Question XIV expatiates on the enormity of witchcraft, and explains:] The crimes of witches, then, exceed the sins of all others; and we now declare what punishment they deserve, whether as Heretics or as Apostates. Now Heretics, according to St. Raymund, are punished in various ways, as by excommunication, deposition, confiscation of their goods, and death. The reader can be fully informed concerning all these by consulting the law relating to the sentence of excommunication. Indeed even their followers, protectors, patrons, and defenders incur the heaviest penalties. For, besides the punishment of excommunication inflicted on them, Heretics, together with their patrons, protectors, and defenders, and with their children to the second generation on the father's side, and to the first degree on the mother's side, are admitted to no benefit or office of the Church. And if a Heretic have Catholic children, for the heinousness of his crime they are deprived of their paternal inheritance. And if a man be convicted, and refuse to be converted and abjure his heresy, he must at once be burned, if he is a layman. For if they who counterfeit money are summarily put to death, how much more must they who counterfeit the Faith? But if he is a cleric, after solemn degradation he is handed over to the secular Court to be put to death. But if they return to the Faith, they are to be imprisoned for life. But in practice they are treated more leniently after recantation than they should be according to the judgement of the Bishops and the Inquisition, as will be shown in the Third Part, where the various methods of sentencing such are treated of; that is to say, those who are arrested and convicted and have recanted their error.

But to punish witches in these ways does not seem sufficient, since they are not simple Heretics, but Apostates. More than this, in their very apostasy they do not deny the Faith for any fear of men or for any delight of the flesh, as has been said before; but, apart from their abnegation, even give homage to the very devils by offering them their bodies and souls. It is clear enough from this that, however much they are penitent and return to the Faith, they must not be punished like other Heretics with lifelong imprisonment, but must suffer the extreme penalty.

21. THE PERSECUTION OF WITCHES

The obsession with witchcraft in the early modern era became if anything more intense than it had been during the medieval period. Although the rise of scientific attitudes roused some to dismiss or diminish the notion of "spirits" at loose in the world, some good but mainly evil, most continued to believe that evil-minded people could command these spirits to do harm against men, beasts, or even crops. Virtually all religious creeds took witches and wizards for granted, although it was the female of the species that received most attention. They were hunted down and tried on accusations that eventually became suspect. The arguments for the existence of witches and the duty to destroy them was put in flaming words by an eloquent preacher of colonial New England, Cotton Mather (1663–1728). His sermon "A Discourse on Witchcraft" was preached in Boston in 1689 and printed the same year in his *Memorable Providences relating to Witchcraft and Possessions.* Much of the notorious Salem persecution of witches in 1692 is attributed to its influence, although Mather himself eventually came to think the trials a miscarriage of justice. His father, Increase Mather, helped end the use of death sentences in witchcraft cases.

Cotton Mather

Memorable Providences relating to Witchcraft and Possessions

THE NATURE AND REALITY OF WITCHCRAFT

Such an Hellish thing there is as *Witchcraft* in the World. There are Two things which will be desired for the advantage of this Assertion. It should *first* be show'd,

WHAT *Witchcraft* is;

My Hearers will not expect from me an accurate *Definition* of the *vile Thing;* since the Grace of God has given me the Happiness to speak without *Experience* of it. But from Accounts both by *Reading* and *Hearing* I have learn'd to describe it so.

WITCHCRAFT is the Doing of *Strange* (and for the most part *Ill*) Things by the help of *evil Spirits, Covenanting* with (and usually *Representing* of) the woful children of men.

This is the *Diabolical Art* that *Witches* are notorious for.

First. *Witches* are the Doers of *Strange* Things. They cannot indeed perform any proper *Miracles*; those are things to be done only by the *Favourites* and *Embassadours* of the LORD. But *Wonders* are often produced by them, though chiefly such Wonders as the Apostle calls in *2. Thes.* 2. 9. *Lying wonders.* There are *wonderful Storms* in the *great* World, and *wonderful Wounds* in the *little* World,[1] often effected by these *evil Causes.* They do things which transcend the ordinary *Course* of Nature, and which puzzle the ordinary *Sense* of Mankind. Some *strange* things are done by them in a way of *Real Production.* They do really *Torment,* they do really *Afflict* those that their Spite shall extend unto. Other *Strange* Things are done by them in a way of *Crafty Illusion.* They do craftily make of the *Air,* the *Figures* and *Colours* of things that never can be truly created by them. All men might *see,* but, I believe, no man could *feel,* some of the Things which the *Magicians* of *Egypt* exhibited of old.

Secondly. They are not only *strange* Things, but *Ill* Things, that *Witches* are the Doers of. In this regard also they are not the Authors of *Miracles:* those are things *commonly* done for the *Good* of Man, *alwaies* done for the *Praise* of *God.* But of these *Hell-hounds* it may in a special manner be said,

---

SOURCE: Department of History, University of Pennsylvania, *Translations and Reprints from the Original Sources of European History* (Philadelphia: University of Pennsylvania Press, n. d.), Vol. III, pp. 2–5. Reprinted by permission of the University of Pennsylvania Press.

[1] I. e., in Man—the microcosm. The "great world" is the universe [orig. ed.].

as in *Psal.* 52, 3. *Thou lovest evil more than good.* For the most part they labour to robb *Man* of his *Ease* or his *Wealth;* they labour to wrong *God of* His *Glory.* There is Mention of Creatures that they call *White Witches,* which do only *Good-Turns* for their Neighbours. I suspect that there are none of that sort; but rather think, *There is none that doeth good, no, not one.* If they *do good,* it is only that they *may do hurt.*

Thirdly. It is by virtue of *evil Spirits* that *Witches* do what they do. We read in *Ephes.* 2, 2. about the *Prince of the power of the air.* There is confined unto the *Atmosphere* of our *Air* a vast *Power,* or *Army* of *Evil Spirits,* under the Government of a Prince who employes them in a continual Opposition to the Designs of GOD: The Name of that *Leviathan,* who is the *Grand-Seigniour of Hell,* we find in the Scripture to be *Belzebub.* Under the Command of that mighty Tyrant, there are vast *Legions & Myriads* of Devils, whose *Businesses & Accomplishments* are not all the same. Every one has his *Post,* and his *Work;* and they are all glad of an opportunity to be *mischievous* in the World. These are they by whom *Witches* do exert their Devillish and malignant Rage upon their *Neighbours*: And especially Two Acts concur hereunto. The *First* is, Their *Covenanting* with the Witches. There is a most hellish *League* made between them, with various *Rites* and *Ceremonies.* The *Witches* promise to serve the *Devils,* and the *Devils* promise to *help* the witches; *How?* It is not convenient[2] to be related. The *Second* is, their *Representing* of the Witches. And hereby indeed these are drawn into *Snares* and *Cords* of Death. The Devils, when they go upon the Errands of the *Witches,* do bear their *Names;* and hence do *Harmes* too come to be carried from the *Devils* to the *Witches.* We need not suppose such a wild thing as the *Transforming* of those Wretches into *Bruits* or *Birds,* as we too often do.

It should next be proved *THAT* Witchcraft *is.*

The *Being* of such a thing is denied by many that place *a great part* of their *small wit* in derideing the Stories that are told of it. Their chief Argument is, That they never *saw* any Witches, therefore there are *none.* Just as if you or I should say, We never met with any *Robbers* on the Road, therefore there never was any *Padding* there.

Indeed the *Devils* are loath to have true Notions of *Witches* entertained with us. I have beheld them to put out the eyes of an enchaunted Child, when a Book that proves, *There is Witchcraft,* was laid before her. But there are especially Two Demonstrations that evince the Being of that Infernal mysterious thing.

First. We have the Testimony of *Scripture* for it. We find *Witchcrafts* often mentioned, sometimes by way of *Assertion,* sometimes by way of

---

[2] I. e., not seemly: perhaps because the details are too vile, perhaps because the preacher will not tempt his hearers [orig. ed.].

Allusion, in the Oracles of God. Besides that, We have there the History of diverse *Witches* in these infallible and inspired Writings. Particularly, the Instance of the *Witch* at *Endor*, in I *Sam.* 28. 7, is so plain and full that *Witchcraft* it self is not a more amazing thing, than any *Dispute* about the Being of it, after this. The Advocates of *Witches* must use more *Tricks* to make Nonsense of the *Bible*, than ever the *Witch of Endor* used in her Magical Incantations, if they would evade the Force of that famous History. They that will believe no *Witches*, do imagine that *Jugglers* only are meant by them whom the Sacred Writ calleth so. But what do they think of that law in *Exod.* 22. 18. *Thou shalt not suffer a Witch to live!* Methinks 'tis a little too hard to punish every silly *Juggler* with so great Severity.

Secondly. We have the *Testimony* of *Experience* for it. What will those *Incredulous*, who must be the only *Ingenious* men, say to This? Many *Witches* have like those in *Act.* 19. 18. *Confessed and shewed their Deeds.* We see those things done, that it is impossible any *Disease* or any *Deceit* should procure. We see some hideous *Wretches* in hideous *Horrours* confessing, *That they did the Mischiefs.* This *Confession* is often made by them that are owners of as much Reason as the people that laugh at all *Conceit* of *Witchcraft:* the exactest Scrutiny of skilful Physicians cannot find any Distraction in their minds. This *Confession* is often made by them that are apart One from another, and yet they *agree* in all the Circumstances of it. This *Confession* is often made by them that at the same time will produce the *Engines* and *Ensignes* of their *Hellish Trade*, and give the standers-by an *Ocular Conviction* of *what* they do, and *how.* There can be no Judgment left of any *Humane Affairs*, if such *Confessions* must be Ridiculed: all the *Murders*, yea, and all the *Bargains* in the World must be meer *Imaginations* if such *Confessions* are of no Account.

CHAPTER III

ECONOMIC LIFE: THE OLDEN WAY

IF THE ESSENTIAL CHARACTERISTIC of modern economics is seen as industrialization, the process of modernization moved very slowly during the early modern period. Agriculture, still bound by a system of limited fertility, required the labors of most men and enabled only a fairly small number to engage in what economists call the secondary and tertiary sectors, the production of goods and services. The principal force for economic change and the expansion of wealth in the early modern period was commerce, which expanded greatly during the 16th and 17th centuries with the exploitation of the newly discovered Americas and the discovery of direct oceanic routes to the East. Industry remained overwhelmingly artisan in character, with productivity limited to the possibilities of handicraft tools. Banking was already a vital economic force, although it was not to become separated from mercantile business for centuries.

The first impact of the new discoveries was not so much the introduction of new goods into the European market as a new supply of immense quantities of precious metals, particularly silver. The expansion of the quantity of money that resulted contributed to a rapid rise of prices in Europe during the 16th century, the so-called "Price Revolution." Overall, the European population expanded during the 16th century, which was a sure sign of general prosperity, but in the following century, which was marked by lengthy general wars, economic expansion halted and the growth of population ceased.

Economic policy was largely directed to the amassing of wealth in the form of money. Mercantilism, the system of achieving this aim by a favorable balance of trade, was the dominant economic theory of this age. It was disputed, however, by the Dutch, who gained a near monopoly of shipping and trade during the 17th century. They found their advantage in the principle of free trade, at least in Europe.

22. PARTNERS IN THE NAME OF GOD AND PROFIT

The rise of modern business has a long and complicated history. Operations inaugurated by individual craftsmen and merchants have become the world-spanning activities of immense corporations organized as stock companies. In the earlier phases of this process, the combination of skills and resources necessary for the expansion of business was found usually in one or another form of partnership, by which members pooled responsibilities as well as capital. Some of the most famous of these partnerships were those formed by the Medici family in Florence in the 15th century. The Medici engaged in many lines of business and, as merchant-bankers, rose to become grand dukes of Tuscany and to give two daughters as wives to kings of France. The taproot of their wealth and prosperity was the woolen trade; they operated their own shop in Florence and engaged in large-scale transactions in the trade. Medici business organizations were partnerships, to which members of the family contributed money and service for a given period of time. When a partnership was dissolved after the contractual term or because a member died, it had to be reorganized. The terms of operation of one of these partnerships, formed in 1434, is described in the following selection. The *Arte di Lana* mentioned was the associated clothmakers' guilds of Florence.

Article of Association of the Medici

ARTICLE OF ASSOCIATION INVOLVING GIOVENCO DI GIULIANO DE' MEDICI, GIOVENCO D'ANTONIO DE' MEDICI, AND BERNARDO D'ANTONIO DE' MEDICI, ALL OF FLORENCE, June 1, 1434

SOURCE: Gertrude Randolph Bramlette Richards (ed.), *Florentine Merchants in the Age of the Medici: Letters and Documents from the Selfridge Collection of Medici Manuscripts* (Cambridge, Mass.: Harvard University Press, 1932), pp. 237–40. Reprinted by permission of Harvard University Press.

In the name of God, Amen, the first day of June, 1434

Be it known to whomsoever shall see or read the present contract made the year and month mentioned above, that it is declared in the name of God and of profit, that Bernardo d'Antonio de' Medici on the one part, and Giovenco d'Antonio de' Medici on another part, and Giovenco di Giuliano [de' Medici] on the other part, all three Florentine citizens and merchants, have made this present new Company under the *Arte di Lana*, in the *Convento* of San Martino, with this pact and condition and agreement that thus they make a partnership. That is:

In the first place, they are agreed that the capital of the said Company shall be, and must be, 4000 gold florins, and that this shall be contributed in cash within twelve months from now in this wise: the said Bernardo d'Antonio [shall put therein] 2200 florins; the said Giovenco d'Antonio [shall put therein] 1500 florins; and the above-said Giovenco di Giuliano shall put therein 300 for the said term of one year, as stated above, so that in all the sum [shall be] 4000 gold florins. Each one shall put in the above-said amount for the time mentioned, and whosoever shall fail to put in the stated sum within one year for the use of the said Company shall be obliged to make good to the said Company [with interest at] ten per cent of his account at the beginning of the year, according to what he has lacked.

And the said Giovenco di Giuliano promises his person and assistance and service and usefulness to the said Company and traffic under the *Arte di Lana*, and [he promises] to go to the looms and to other places generally at other times, always in whatever place is necessary, without other provision or salary. And the said Bernardo and Giovenco d'Antonio are not held to any such service in the said shop more than they give voluntarily during the said time. And if it pleases Giovenco d'Antonio to withdraw himself [from the firm] for any reason during the said time, that such absence is possible, providing that it appears to Bernardo d'Antonio and to Giovenco di Giuliano that it is possible; and that such salary [as he may receive] shall be paid into the said shop and Company.

And they are agreed that the said shop and traffic under the *Arte di Lana* shall be conducted in the *Convento* of San Martino in Florence and that the name of this Company shall be Bernardo d'Antonio de' Medici and Company with this sign that appears here on the side. This Company is agreed that they commence and are bound to commence on the 1st day of June, 1434, and are to continue for the next three years and that this contract terminates the 1st day of June, 1437, and at that time the said sign shall remain with the said Bernardo d'Antonio.

And they are agreed that the profit which our Lord God concedes through His mercy and grace will be divided in this manner: that is, that Bernardo d'Antonio shall draw on the basis of 1800 florins and Giovenco d'Antonio shall draw on the basis of 1300 florins, and Giovenco di Giuliano shall draw on the basis of 900 florins; and similarly during this time if any damage occurs, which God forbid, [each shall contribute on this basis]; and also each may draw out [his share] of their [joint] profits at any time, and at each withdrawal there shall be a balancing of accounts.

And they are agreed that Giovenco di Giuliano de' Medici may draw for his needs 4 florins the month, and similarly Bernardo d'Antonio may draw, and similarly Giovenco d'Antonio may draw, as their necessities demand, such money without paying any costs; and that whoever draws more, must restore the lack at 10 per cent the florin at the beginning of the year.

And they are agreed that the said Giovenco di Giuliano may not carry on or have carried on any other business or service to another traffic outside of this firm under any [condition] on the pain of paying 200 florins in gold, and if he does so engage, he must pay the said sum to the said Bernardo d'Antonio and Giovenco d'Antonio who may force him if he breaks this agreement. And furthermore, if he engages in any outside enterprise, whether he pays this fine or not, the said Bernardo d'Antonio and Giovenco d'Antonio may claim whatever profits or salary he has made, and he shall be responsible for whatever damages [may be incurred in this other business].

And they are agreed that the said Bernardo and Giovenco d'Antonio may manufacture or engage in other traffic of any sort in Florence or out of Florence.

And they are agreed that if any of the said Company shall hold in that Company any amount of money above the original capital, they may receive for it 8 florins the hundred as interest, but that this money may not be put into the Company without consent of all members thereof. And it [the interest] is to be paid from the time when it is deposited as if on interest with a third person, and such money may be withdrawn whenever its owner wishes, providing the others agree.

And they are agreed that the said Giovenco di Giuliano shall not engage any credits [run up debts] outside the business without the express permission of the said Bernardo and Giovenco d'Antonio or at least one or the other of them; and that in case he so does, the fact shall be entered against his account for the day; and the said Giovenco shall not be permitted to extend credit or make any guarantees for the said Company for a sum exceeding 20 florins without permission of both of the senior partners, and that any violation of the above shall incur a fine of 100 florins for each offense.

And they are agreed that when the termination of this Company shall draw near, and if any one of the partners does not wish to continue or reconfirm the traffic, in such case the one or the other must speak; and if he gives six months' notice, the firm shall be discontinued. The said Giovenco di Giuliano shall be obligated to stay in the shop until all the *panni* and samples have been restored to the stock of the said shop. And within two months Bernardo and Giovenco must have cancelled all debts so that within such time they shall be free of all obligations; and the stock shall be divided among them in this proportion: To Bernardo, 1800 florins in gold; to Giovenco d'Antonio, 1300 florins in gold; to Giovenco di Giuliano, 900 florins in gold. And the merchandise shall be divided among them, each receiving according to his share. And whosoever of the partners has taken goods on good security, must pay in money for what is outstanding.

And similarly, if through the given time it should please our Lord God to call to Himself any one of the said Company (which may God in His mercy forbid), the said Company shall be terminated and the division of the property shall follow the above-mentioned terms.

And they are agreed that all of the aforesaid terms, acts, and capitulations, as set forth in this article, shall be fully observed in all ways and by all and on their good faith as merchants without any other expression of faith; and the said Bernardo and Giovenco d'Antonio and Giovenco di Giuliano subscribe with their hands to observe all these terms now and in the future, grateful for all benefits which have come to them, and submitting to every ordinance set forth by the city of Florence, and especially those governing the *Mercanzia*.

And they are agreed that the said Bernardo d'Antonio shall be willing and desirous of placing at the service of the association, and of the accounts of the firm, that is of the ledger, Giovanni di Bernardo Bencini; and to him he shall give a salary which seems appropriate for that service which he shall make for the community of the said Company; and this salary shall be paid during the existence of the said Company while the said youth performs his service; and if the said youth is lacking [in his service] (which God forbid), then in that case Bernardo may put in his place whomsoever he wishes, paying him on the above terms.

I, the above-said Bernardo d'Antonio de' Medici, am satisfied and obligate myself to what is written in this above article, and do pledge that I will observe the terms faithfully. With my own hand, I set forth this subscription.

I, the above-said Giovenco di Giuliano de' Medici, am content, and obligate myself to obey the above stated article, and as pledge that I will observe its terms faithfully, I subscribe with my own hand this year, month, and day mentioned above.

23. A BANKER SERVES AN EMPEROR

The political role the great merchant-bankers could play because of their wealth was never more evident than in the contested election in 1519 for the throne of the Holy Roman Empire, in which Charles of Habsburg, King of Spain and Duke of Burgundy, and Francis I, King of France, were rival candidates. Francis offered huge cash bribes to the electoral princes of Germany, but the Habsburg agents were able to counter with promises of even greater sums to be given after Charles was elected. They could safely make such promises because Jacob Fugger, the merchant-banker of Augsburg, had opened his purse strings to the House of Austria (Habsburg). When Charles was elected, the Fuggers were rewarded with lucrative concessions in Europe and the new Spanish colonies in America. The self-assurance of the Fuggers in this relationship is displayed in a letter written in 1523 by Jacob Fugger, the head of the firm, to the Emperor himself to remind him of his obligations.

Jacob Fugger

Letter to Charles V

Your Imperial Majesty doubtless knows how I and my kinsmen have ever hitherto been disposed to serve the House of Austria in all loyalty to the furtherance of its well-being and prosperity; wherefore, in order to be pleasing to Your Majesty's Grandsire, the late Emperor Maximilian, and to gain for Your Majesty the Roman Crown, we have held ourselves bounden to engage ourselves towards divers princes who placed their Trust and Reliance upon myself and perchance on No Man besides. We have, moreover, advanced to Your Majesty's Agents for the same end a Great Sum of Money, of which we ourselves have had to raise a large part from our Friends. It is well known that Your Imperial Majesty could not have gained the Roman Crown save with mine aid, and I can prove the same by the writings of Your Majesty's Agents given by their own hands. In this matter I have not studied mine own Profit. For had I left the House of Austria and had been minded to further France, I had obtained much money and property, such as was then offered to me. How

---

Source: Richard Ehrenberg, *Capital and Finance in the Age of the Renaissance: A Study of the Fuggers and their Connections*, translated by H. M. Lucas (New York: Augustus M. Kelley Publishers, 1963), p. 80.

grave a Disadvantage had in this case accrued to Your Majesty and the House of Austria, Your Majesty's Royal Mind well knoweth.

24. THE GOLD OF THE INDIES AND SPANISH REVENUES

Although the precious metals mined in Spanish America struck the imagination of Europeans in an age when gold and silver were in short supply, the fundamental revenues of the Spanish monarchy continued to come from the taxes paid by Spain itself and by its European possessions in Italy and the Low Countries. This remained true even after the middle of the 16th century, when shipments of silver increased sharply. The fiscal position of Philip II, who came to the throne in 1556 on the abdication of his father, Charles V, was described to the Venetian government by its returning ambassador, Michele Soriano, in 1559. The "Relation" from which this selection is taken was one of the great series of ambassadorial reports by Venetian diplomats which kept the government of Venice one of the best informed in Europe even after its power declined.

Michele Soriano

Relation from Spain

From New Spain are obtained gold and silver, cochineal (little insects like flies), from which crimson dye is made, leather, cotton, sugar and other things; but from Peru nothing is obtained except minerals. The fifth part of all that is produced goes to the king, but since the gold and silver is brought to Spain and he has a tenth part of that which goes to the mint and is refined and coined, he eventually gets one-fourth of the whole sum, which fourth does not exceed in all four or five hundred thousand ducats, although it is reckoned not alone at millions, but at millions of pounds. Nor is it likely that it will long remain at this figure, because great quantities of gold and silver are no longer found upon the surface of the earth, as they have been in past years; and to penetrate into the bowels of the earth requires greater effort, skill and outlay, and the Spaniards are not willing to do the work themselves, and the natives cannot be forced to do so, because the Emperor has freed them from all obligation of service as soon as they accept the Christian religion. Where-

---

SOURCE: Department of History, University of Pennsylvania, *Translations and Reprints from the Original Sources of European History* (Philadelphia: University of Pennsylvania Press, n.d.), Vol. III, pp. 5–7. Reprinted by permission of the University of Pennsylvania Press.

fore it is necessary to acquire negro slaves, who are brought from the coasts of Africa, both within and without the Straits, and these are selling dearer every day, because on account of their natural lack of strength and the change of climate, added to the lack of discretion upon the part of their masters in making them work too hard and giving them too little to eat, they fall sick and the greater part of them die. . . .

From these his realms his majesty receives every year an income of five millions of gold in times of peace: one and one-half millions from Spain; a half million from the Indies; one from Naples and Sicily, and another from Flanders and the Low Countries. But his expenses are six millions, and this excess is covered by extraordinary taxes according to his pleasure, whence it appears that he could control only a small amount of money for special undertakings, since he consumes for his ordinary needs everything that he derives from his realms. But looked at from another point of view, the Emperor, his father, although he had the same burdens, was nevertheless able to carry on extensive wars and enterprises in Italy and outside of Italy, both by land and sea, and the same king was able in these later years to maintain great armies in Flanders, in Piedmont, in Lombardy and in the kingdom, and many soldiers in Africa against the Turk. So that we may calculate that he spent more than ten millions of gold; wherefore it may be put down as a fact that although expenses may exceed income, yet a way is not wanting to great princes, whereby they may find large sums of money in times of great need, particularly in the case of the king of Spain, not so much on account of the mines which are found in Spain and the Indies, of which the Spanish nation, according to its custom, makes no great account, as from the fact that he has so many states and so many subjects and nearly all are rich, and from them he has had so much aid, not through force or violence, but for the most part with common consent of the people, persuaded that public and private interest demanded such a policy.

It would appear that the great results which the Spaniards have accomplished are not to be ascribed to the financial strength derived from the mines, because you see on one side France and the Turk, extremely rich without mines, and on the other the Emperor, with more mines in his realms than all the rest of Europe possesses, always in need.

25. A REVOLUTION IN PRICES

The 16th century saw a tripling or quadrupling of prices which was deeply disturbing to all, particularly those whose incomes were based upon fixed sums of money. The quickest but flimsiest explanation was that evil merchants were indulging their greed and taking advantage of customers, but this overrated the traders' ability to set prices and overlooked the relation between supply and demand in the marketplace. A more ingenious and penetrating explanation was given by a Frenchman, Malestroit by name, who suggested that the true price of goods was not the nominal price but the equivalent value in gold or silver, which he believed had not actually changed. Nevertheless, the value of precious metals had in fact gone down, or (what is the same thing) the prices of goods had gone up.

A more realistic explanation was offered by the French thinker Jean Bodin (1530–1596), best known for his work in political theory (see below, section 48). He believed the rise in prices was due to the fact that the supply of gold and silver had risen at a greater rate than that of the goods they bought and explained how this had come about in his *Reply to the Paradox of Monsieur de Malestroit* (1568). Although modern economic historians would consider also such factors as the rate of circulation of money and the use of credit instruments (which serve as a kind of paper money), Bodin's *Reply* continues to be one of the early classics of careful, systematic economic thought.

Jean Bodin

Reply to the Paradox of Monsieur de Malestroit

To Monsieur Prevost, Seigneur de Morsan, presiding for the King in his Court of Parlement.

You know, Monsieur, the usual complaints made about the dearness of all things: the assemblies called in all quarters of this city to consider it: the trouble that has been taken to find whence this dearness came. . . . Finally, Monsieur de Malestroit, a man deserving of a reply from a more important person than I, employed in this matter by command of the King, published a little booklet of paradoxes, in which he maintained against everyone's opinion that nothing has become dearer for three hundred years. He made some believe this, and by this means appeased the complaints of many men. But, having read his treatise these last days, I bethought myself to answer him briefly, to clarify and make understood this matter which is of great consequence to all in general and to each in particular: on the condition, if it please you, that you shall be the judge, being confident that Monsieur de Malestroit will agree. . . .

Before proceeding, I shall state briefly the arguments of Monsieur de

---

Source: Contemporary Civilization Staff of Columbia College, Columbia University, *Introduction to Contemporary Civilization in the West: A Source Book*, 2d ed. (New York: Columbia University Press, 1954), Vol. I, pp. 447, 449–52. Reprinted by permission of Columbia University Press.

Malestroit. One cannot complain, he says, that a thing is dearer now than it was three hundred years ago: unless, in order to buy it, one has to pay more gold or silver now than one paid then. Now, in buying all things, one does not pay more gold or silver than one paid then. Hence nothing has grown dearer in France since that time. There is his conclusion, which is necessary if one grants his minor premise, and, in proof of the latter, in the time of King Philip de Valois, he says, an ell of velvet cost only four *écus*, as good as or of even better weight and value than our *écus soleils*, and each *écu* was worth only twenty *sous* silver coin: while now, when the *écu* is worth fifty *sous*, it costs ten *livres*, which are worth no more than the four *écus*, an ell. Therefore the said ell of velvet is no dearer now than it was then. He proceeds in the same manner with regard to all Latin goods [luxury products], even to our wines and grains, but nevertheless he has no proof.

. . . . .

I find that the dearness we observe comes from four or five causes. The principal and almost the only one (to which no one has heretofore referred) is the abundance of gold and silver, which is much greater in this kingdom today than it was four hundred years ago. I do not go further back since the extracts of the registers of the court and of the chamber which I have do not go beyond four hundred years. The rest has to be drawn from old histories with little certainty. The second cause of dearness comes in part from monopolies. The third is scarcity, which is caused as much by exports as by waste. The fourth is the pleasure of kings and great nobles, who raise the prices of the things they like. The fifth is the price of money, debased from its old valuation. I shall treat briefly all these points.

The principal cause which raises the price of everything wherever it be is the abundance of that which gives valuation and price to things. Plutarch and Pliny testify that after the conquest of the Kingdom of Macedonia under King Perseus, Captain Paulus Aemilius brought so much gold and silver to Rome that the people were freed from paying taxes, and the price of lands in the Romagna at once rose two thirds. Now it was not a scarcity of lands, which cannot increase or diminish, nor monopoly, which cannot exist in such a case, but the abundance of gold and silver which caused their depreciation, and the dearness of things priced [in terms of them]. . . .

It is therefore necessary to show that there was not so much gold and silver three hundred years ago as there is now, which one perceives at a glance. For if there is money in a country it cannot be so well hidden that princes do not find it when they are in need. Now King Jean [II, reigned 1350–64] was totally unable to get sixty thousand *francs* (let us speak in terms of *écus*) on credit in his extreme need, and during the eight years after the battle of Poitiers when he was a prisoner of the English, neither his children, nor his friends, nor his people, nor he himself who came in person, could raise his ransom, and he was forced to return to England and wait until money was obtained for him. Saint Louis [Louis IX, reigned 1226–70] was in the same trouble while a prisoner in Egypt. It is unlikely that the French people, who naturally love their king, and then more than now, and especially such a king, who had not then and perhaps will have even less hereafter his equal, should wish to suffer to see him a slave of the Mohammedans, whom they then detested. . . . Further, we read in our old histories that for lack of silver they made money of leather with a silver nail. I confide myself to the judgement of facts. And, if we come to our own age, we shall find that in six months the King raised in Paris, without going further, more than three million four hundred thousand *livres.* . . . Let Monsieur de Malestroit leaf through the registers of the Chamber and he will agree with me that more gold and silver have been obtained for the needs of the king and the state between the years 1515 and 1568 than they had been able to raise in two hundred years before. . . .

But, someone will say, from where has so much gold and silver come since that time? I hold that the merchant and artisan, who cause gold and silver to come, were idle then. For the Frenchman, having one of the most fertile countries in the world, devoted himself to tilling the soil and raising cattle, which is the greatest industry in France, so that the Levant trade was not followed, for fear of the Barbary pirates who held the African coast, and of the Arabs, whom our fathers called Saracens, who controlled the entire Mediterranean sea, treating the Christians they captured like galley slaves. And as for the western trade, it was entirely unknown before the Spaniard set sail in the Indian sea. In addition, the English, who held the ports of Guyenne and Normandy, had closed the routes to Spain and the islands. Further, the quarrels of the houses of Anjou and Aragon cut us off from the ports of Italy. But one hundred twenty years ago we drove out the English, and the Portuguese, sailing the high seas by compass, made himself master of the Persian Gulf, and partly of the Red Sea, and by this means filled his ships with the riches of the Indies and fruitful Arabia, circumventing the Venetians and Genoese, who took goods from Egypt and Syria, where it had been brought by the caravans of the Arabs and the Persians to sell it to us at retail and at its weight in gold. At the same time, the Castilian, having brought under his power the new lands full of gold and silver, filled Spain with them, and showed our pilots the ways to voyage around Africa with wonderful profit. . . .

Now the Spaniard, who subsists only because of France, being inevitably compelled to get here grains, cloths, dry goods, woad, *rodon,* paper, books, even cabinet work and all handicraft products, goes to the end of the world to seek gold and silver and spices for us. On the other hand the English, Scotch and all the people of Norway, Sweden, Denmark and the Baltic coast, who have an infinity of mineral deposits, dig the metals from the center of the earth to buy our wines, our saffron, our prunes, our woad, and above all our salt, which is a manna that God gives us of special grace, with little labor. . . . This causes the English, Flemings and Scotch, who carry on a large trade in salt fish, often to load their ships with sand, for lack of other goods, to come to buy our salt with hard cash.

The other cause of the great wealth that has come to us in the last hundred and twenty or forty years is the tremendous population that has grown up in this kingdom since the civil wars between the houses of Orléans and Burgundy came to an end: which has made us feel the sweetness of peace and enjoy its fruits for a long time, until the religious troubles, for the foreign war we have had since then was merely a purgation of bad humors necessary to the entire body politic. Previously the level country had been deserted, and the cities nearly so, because of the ravages of the civil wars, during which the English had sacked cities, burned villages, murdered, pillaged, killed a good part of the French people, and gnawed the rest to the bones: which was sufficient to bring agriculture, trade and the mechanical arts to a halt. But during the past hundred years we have cleared a vast expanse of forests and wastelands, built many villages, peopled the cities. . . .

There is yet another cause for the wealth of France, that is the Levant trade, opened to us by the friendship of the House of France with the House of the Ottomans in the time of King Francis I. So that since that time French merchants have kept shop in Alexandria, Cairo, Beirut, Tripoli as well as the Venetians, and have no less credit at Fez and Morocco than the Spaniard. Which was revealed to us when the Jews, driven from Spain by Ferdinand, withdrew to the lowlands of Languedoc and accustomed us to trading in Barbary.

Another cause of the abundance of gold and silver has been the Bank of Lyon, which was opened, to tell the truth, by King Francis I, who began by borrowing money at eight, and his successor at ten, then at sixteen and up to twenty per cent in his necessity. Suddenly the Florentines, Luccans, Genoese, Swiss, Germans, lured by the great profits, brought a tremendous amount of gold and silver into France, and some settled here, both because of the mildness of the climate, the natural goodness of the people and the fertility of the country. By the same means, the fixed charges of the City of Paris, which amount to three million three hundred fifty thousand *livres* each year, enticed the foreigner, who brought his cash here to make a profit, and finally settled here: which greatly enriched this city. It is true that the mechanical arts and commerce would make greater progress, in my opinion, without being diminished by the money trade that is carried on: and the city would be much richer if they did as they do in Genoa, where the house of Saint George takes the money of all who wish to bring it at five per cent, and lends it to merchants to trade with at eight and one third or six and two thirds per cent [*denier douze ou quinze*], which is a measure that has caused the greatness and wealth of that city, and which seems to me very advisable for the public and the individual. . . .

There, Monsieur, are the means which have brought us gold and silver in abundance during the last two hundred years. There is much more in Spain and Italy than in France, because in Italy even the nobility engage in trade, and the people of Spain have no other occupation. Hence everything is dearer in Spain and Italy than in France, and more so in Spain than in Italy, and even domestic service and handcrafts, which attracts our Auvergnats and Limousins to Spain, as I know from them themselves, because they earn three times as much as they do in France: for the rich, haughty and indolent Spaniard sells his effort very dearly, as witness Cleynaerts, who writes in his letters, in the the chapter on expenses, in a single entry, for being shaved in Portugal, fifteen *ducats* a year. It is therefore an abundance of gold and silver which in part causes the dearness of things.

26. THE NOWHERE LAND OF PERFECTION

One of the most subtle and yet effective forms of social criticism is the depiction of a "perfect" society, the perfection of which consists of the absence of those attributes of the existing order that are seen to be faulty. There is no reason to believe that Sir Thomas More (1478-1535) envisioned his *Utopia* as an ideal society (1516), based on what were to become Communist economic principles, which men should actually seek to bring into existence. More was a practical statesman who rose to be lord chancellor of England, but he refused to acknowledge his king, Henry VIII, as sovereign over the church and was beheaded for treason. The principle for which he deliberately accepted death was not the ideal of a new and perfect society on earth, but the old faith and order of Roman Catholicisim. It has been brilliantly argued by a modern scholar (J. H. Hexter) that More was illustrating in a novel way the Catholic condemnation of the traditional vices—greed, envy, hatred, and ambition. Generations of men who dream of building perfect societies have overlooked More's purpose and failed to recognize that he was no utopian in this sense. Like his great predecessor, Plato (the author of the *Republic*), More has become a teacher of social reformers and revolutionaries. Raphael, a wise and observant world traveler, upon whose speculations the *Utopia* is largely based, begins the dialogue in the following extract.

Sir Thomas More

Utopia

. . . . .

" 'However the case may be, it seems to me by no means profitable to the common weal to keep for the emergency of a war a vast multitude of such people as trouble and disturb the peace. You never have war unless you choose it, and you ought to take far more account of peace than of war. Yet this is not the only situation that makes thieving necessary. There is another which, as I believe, is more special to you Englishmen.'

" 'What is that?' asked the Cardinal.

" 'Your sheep,' I answered, 'which are usually so tame and so cheaply fed, begin now, according to report, to be so greedy and wild that they devour human beings themselves and devastate and depopulate fields, houses, and towns. In all those parts of the realm where the finest and therefore costliest wool is produced, there are noblemen, gentlemen, and even some abbots, though otherwise holy men, who are not satisfied with the annual revenues and profits which their predecessors used to derive from their estates. They are not content, by leading an idle and sumptuous life, to do no good to their country; they must also do it positive harm. They leave no ground to be tilled; they enclose every bit of land for pasture; they pull down houses and destroy towns, leaving only the church to pen the sheep in. And, as if enough English land were not wasted on ranges and preserves of game, those good fellows turn all human habitations and all cultivated land into a wilderness.

" 'Consequently in order that one insatiable glutton and accursed plague of his native land may join field to field and surround many thousand acres with one fence, tenants are evicted. Some of them, either circumvented by fraud or overwhelmed by violence, are stripped even of their own property, or else, wearied by unjust acts, are driven to sell. By hook or by crook the poor wretches are compelled to leave their homes—men and women, husbands and wives, orphans and widows, parents with little children and a household not rich but numerous, since

---

SOURCE: St. Thomas More, *Utopia*, edited by Edward Surtz, S.J. (New Haven, Conn.: Yale University Press, 1964), pp. 24–25, 52–54, 60–61, 68–71, 82–83, 146–48. Reprinted by permission of Yale University Press.

farm work requires many hands. Away they must go, I say, from the only homes familiar and known to them, and they find no shelter to go to. All their household goods which would not fetch a great price if they could wait for a purchaser, since they must be thrust out, they sell for a trifle.

" 'After they have soon spent that trifle in wandering from place to place, what remains for them but to steal and be hanged—justly, you may say!—or to wander and beg. And yet even in the latter case they are cast into prison as vagrants for going about idle when, though they most eagerly offer their labor, there is no one to hire them. For there is no farm work, to which they have been trained, to be had, when there is no land for plowing left. A single shepherd or herdsman is sufficient for grazing livestock on that land for whose cultivation many hands were once required to make it raise crops. . . .' "

. . . . .

"Yet surely, my dear More, to tell you candidly my heart's sentiments, it appears to me that wherever you have private property and all men measure all things by cash values, there it is scarcely possible for a commonwealth to have justice or prosperity—unless you think justice exists where all the best things flow into the hands of the worst citizens or prosperity prevails where all is divided among very few—and even they are not altogether well off, while the rest are downright wretched.

"As a result, when in my heart I ponder on the extremely wise and holy institutions of the Utopians, among whom, with very few laws, affairs are ordered so aptly that virtue has its reward, and yet, with equality of distribution, all men have abundance of all things, and then when I contrast with their policies the many nations elsewhere ever making ordinances and yet never one of them achieving good order—nations where whatever a man has acquired he calls his own private property, but where all these laws daily framed are not enough for a man to secure or to defend or even to distinguish from someone else's the goods which each in turn calls his own, a predicament readily attested by the numberless and ever new and interminable lawsuits—when I consider, I repeat, all these facts, I become more partial to Plato and less surprised at his refusal to make laws for those who rejected that legislation which gave to all an equal share in all goods.

"This wise sage, to be sure, easily foresaw that the one and only road to the general welfare lies in the maintenance of equality in all respects. I have my doubts that the latter could ever be preserved where the individual's possessions are his private property. When every man aims at absolute ownership of all the property he can get, be there never so great abundance of goods, it is all shared by a handful who leave the rest in poverty. It generally happens that the one class preeminently deserves the lot of the other, for the rich are greedy, unscrupulous, and useless, while the poor are well-behaved, simple, and by their daily industry more beneficial to the commonwealth than to themselves. I am fully persuaded that no just and even distribution of goods can be made and that no happiness can be found in human affairs unless private property is utterly abolished. While it lasts, there will always remain a heavy and inescapable burden of poverty and misfortunes for by far the greatest and by far the best part of mankind. . . ."

. . . . .

As the report goes and as the appearance of the ground shows, the island once was not surrounded by sea. But Utopus, who as conqueror gave the island its name (up to then it had been called Abraxa) and who brought the rude and rustic people to such a perfection of culture and humanity as makes them now superior to almost all other mortals, gained a victory at his very first landing. He then ordered the excavation of fifteen miles on the side where the land was connected with the continent and caused the sea to flow around the land. He set to the task not only the natives but, to prevent them from thinking the labor a disgrace, his own soldiers also. With the work divided among so many hands, the enterprise was finished with incredible speed and struck the neighboring peoples, who at first had derided the project as vain, with wonder and terror at its success.

The island contains fifty-four city-states, all spacious and magnificent, identical in language, traditions, customs, and laws. They are similar also in layout and everywhere, as far as the nature of the ground permits, similar even in appearance. None of them is separated by less than twenty-four miles from the nearest, but none is so isolated that a person cannot go from it to another in a day's journey on foot. From each city three old and experienced citizens meet to discuss the affairs of common interest to the island once a year at Amaurotum, for this city, being in the very center of the country, is situated most conveniently for the representatives of all sections. It is considered the chief as well as the capital city.

The lands are so well assigned to the cities that each has at least twelve miles of country on every side, and on some sides even much more, to wit, the side on which the cities are farther apart. No city has any desire to extend its territory, for they consider themselves the tenants rather than the masters of what they hold.

Everywhere in the rural districts they have, at suitable distances from one another, farmhouses well equipped with agricultural implements. They are inhabited by citizens who come in succession to live there. No rural household numbers less than forty men and women, besides two serfs attached to the soil. Over them are set a master and a mistress, serious in mind and ripe in years. . . .

. . . . .

Agriculture is the one pursuit which is common to all, both men and women, without exception. They are all instructed in it from childhood, partly by principles taught in school, partly by field trips to the farms closer to the city as if for recreation. Here they do not merely look on, but, as opportunity arises for bodily exercise, they do the actual work.

Besides agriculture (which is, as I said, common to all), each is taught one particular craft as his own. This is generally either wool-working or linen-making or masonry or metal-working or carpentry. There is no other pursuit which occupies any number worth mentioning. As for clothes, these are of one and the same pattern throughout the island and down the centuries, though there is a distinction between the sexes and between the single and married. The garments are comely to the eye, convenient for bodily movement, and fit for wear in heat and cold. Each family, I say, does its own tailoring.

Of the other crafts, one is learned by each person, and not the men only, but the women too. The latter as the weaker sex have the lighter occupations and generally work wool and flax. To the men are committed the remaining more laborious crafts. For the most part, each is brought up in his father's craft, for which most have a natural inclination. But if anyone is attracted to another occupation, he is transferred by adoption to a family pursuing that craft for which he has a liking. Care is taken not only by his father but by the authorities, too, that he will be assigned to a grave and honorable householder. Moreover, if anyone after being thoroughly taught one craft desires another also, the same permission is given. Having acquired both, he practices his choice unless the city has more need of the one than of the other.

The chief and almost the only function of the syphogrants is to manage and provide that no one sit idle, but that each apply himself industriously to his trade, and yet that he be not wearied like a beast of burden with constant toil from early morning till late at night. Such wretchedness is worse than the lot of slaves, and yet it is almost everywhere the life of workingmen—except for the Utopians. The latter divide the day and night into twenty-four equal hours and assign only six to work. There are three before noon, after which they go to dinner. After dinner, when they have rested for two hours in the afternoon, they again give three to work and finish up with supper. Counting one o'clock as beginning at midday, they go to bed about eight o'clock, and sleep claims eight hours.

The intervals between the hours of work, sleep, and food are left to every man's discretion, not to waste in revelry or idleness, but to devote the time free from work to some other occupation according to taste. These periods are commonly devoted to intellectual pursuits. For it is their custom that public lectures are daily delivered in the hours before daybreak. Attendance is compulsory only for those who have been specially chosen to devote themselves to learning. A great number of all classes, however, both males and females, flock to hear the lectures, some to one and some to another, according to their natural inclination. But if anyone should prefer to devote this time to his trade, as is the case with many minds which do not reach the level for any of the higher intellectual disciplines, he is not hindered; in fact, he is even praised as useful to the commonwealth.

After supper they spend one hour in recreation, in summer in the gardens, in winter in the common halls in which they have their meals. There they either play music or entertain themselves with conversation. Dice and that kind of foolish and ruinous game they are not acquainted with. They do play two games not unlike chess. The first is a battle of numbers in which one number plunders another. The second is a game in which the vices fight a pitched battle with the virtues. In the latter is exhibited very cleverly, to begin with, both the strife of the vices with one another and their concerted opposition to the virtues; then, what vices are opposed to what virtues, by what forces they assail them openly, by what stratagems they attack them indirectly, by what safeguards the virtues check the power of the vices, by what arts they frustrate their designs; and, finally, by what means the one side gains the victory.

. . . . .

Now you can see how nowhere is there any license to waste time, nowhere any pretext to evade work—no wine shop, no alehouse, no brothel anywhere, no opportunity for corruption, no lurking hole, no secret meeting place. On the contrary, being under the eyes of all, people are bound either to be performing the usual labor or to be enjoying their leisure in a fashion not without decency. This universal behavior must of necessity lead to an abundance of all commodities. Since the latter are distributed evenly among all, it follows, of course, that no one can be reduced to poverty or beggary.

In the senate at Amaurotum (to which, as I said before, three are sent annually from every city), they first determine what commodity is in plenty in each particular place and again where on the island the crops have been meager. They at once fill up the scarcity of one place by the surplus of another. This service they perform without payment, receiving nothing in return from those to whom they give. Those who have given out of their stock to any particular city without requiring any return from it receive what they lack from another to which they have given nothing. Thus, the whole island is like a single family.

. . . . .

Now I have described to you, as exactly as I could, the structure of that commonwealth which I judge not merely the best but the only one which can rightly claim the name of a commonwealth. Outside Utopia, to be sure, men talk freely of the public welfare—but look after their private interests only. In Utopia where nothing is private, they seriously concern themselves with public affairs. Assuredly in both cases they act reasonably. For, outside Utopia, how many are there who do not realize that, unless they make some separate provision for themselves, however flourishing the commonwealth, they will themselves starve? For this reason, necessity compels them to hold that they must take account of themselves rather than of the people, that is, of others.

On the other hand, in Utopia, where everything belongs to everybody, no one doubts, provided only that the public granaries are well filled, that the individual will lack nothing for his private use. The reason is that the distribution of goods is not niggardly. In Utopia there is no poor man and no beggar. Though no man has anything, yet all are rich.

For what can be greater riches for a man than to live with a joyful and peaceful mind, free of all worries not troubled about his food or harassed by the querulous demands of his wife or fearing poverty for his son or worrying about his daughter's dowry, but feeling secure about the livelihood and happiness of himself and his family: wife, sons, grandsons, great-grandsons, great-great-grandsons, and all the long line of their descendants that gentlefolk anticipate? Then take into account the fact that there is no less provision for those who are now helpless but once worked than for those who are still working.

At this point I should like anyone to be so bold as to compare this fairness with the so-called justice prevalent in other nations, among which, upon my soul, I cannot discover the slightest trace of justice and fairness. What brand of justice is it that any nobleman whatsoever or goldsmith-banker or moneylender or, in fact, anyone else from among those who either do no work at all or whose work is of a kind not very essential to the commonwealth, should attain a life of luxury and grandeur on the basis of his idleness or his nonessential work? In the meantime, the common laborer, the carter, the carpenter, and the farmer perform work so hard and continuous that beasts of burden could scarcely endure it and work so essential that no commonwealth could last even one year without it. Yet they earn such scanty fare and lead such a miserable life that the condition of beasts of burden might seem far preferable. The latter do not have to work so incessantly nor is their food much worse (in fact, sweeter to their taste) nor do they entertain any fear for the future. The workmen, on the other hand, not only have to toil and suffer without return or profit in the present but agonize over the thought of an indigent old age. Their daily wage is too scanty to suffice even for the day: much less is there an excess and surplus that daily can be laid by for their needs in old age.

27. FOR THE RELIEF OF THE POOR

The wrenching economic changes of the 16th century in England led to the adoption of An Act for the Relief of the Poor in 1598, which was confirmed in 1601. It laid down principles that guided the system of assistance to those who could not earn their own livelihoods, even a barely sufficient one. Such relief was no longer the province of the church, as it had been in the Middle Ages, but had been accepted by the state. It was the duty of the local government in each parish to provide grants and labor in workshops for the poor at the expense of their neighbors, through a local tax for this purpose. The principal provisions of the 1598 act are given below.

Poor Relief Act of 1598

Be it enacted by the authority of this present Parliament, That the Churchwardens of every parish, and four substantial householders there . . . who shall be nominated yearly in Easter week, under the hand and seal of two or more Justices of the Peace in the same county, whereof one to be of the Quorum, dwelling in or near the same parish, shall be called Overseers of the Poor of the same parish; and they or the greater part of them shall take order from time to time by and with the consent of two or more such Justices of Peace for setting to work of the children of all such whose parents shall not by the said persons be thought able to keep and maintain their children, And also all such persons married or unmarried as having no means to maintain them use no ordinary and daily trade of life to get their living by; and also to raise weekly or otherwise (by taxation of every inhabitant and every occupier of lands in the said parish in such competent sum and sums of money as they shall think fit) a convenient stock of flax, hemp, wool, thread, iron, and other necessary ware and stuff to set the poor on work, and also competent sums of money for and towards the necessary relief of the lame, impotent, old, blind, and such other among them being poor and not able to work, and also for the putting out of such children to be apprentices, to be gathered out of the same parish according to the ability of the said parish; and to do and execute all other things, as well for disposing of the said stock as otherwise concerning the premises, as to them shall seem convenient: Which said Churchwardens, and Overseers so to be nominated, or

---

SOURCE: J. R. Tanner (ed.), *Tudor Constitutional Documents, A. D. 1485–1603* (Cambridge, England: Cambridge University Press, 1951), pp. 488–90.

such of them as shall not be let by sickness or other just excuse to be allowed by such two Justices of Peace or more, shall meet together at the least once every month in the church of the said parish, upon the Sunday in the afternoon after divine service, there to consider of some good course to be taken and of some meet orders to be set down in the premises; and shall within four days after the end of their year, and after other overseers nominated as aforesaid, make and yield up to such two Justices of Peace a true and perfect account of all sums of money by them received, or rated and cessed and not received, and also of such stock as shall be in their hands or in the hands of any of the poor to work, and of all other things concerning their said office, and such sum or sums of money as shall be in their hands shall pay and deliver over to the said Churchwardens and Overseers newly nominated and appointed as aforesaid: upon pain that every one of them absenting themselves without lawful cause as aforesaid from such monthly meeting for the purpose aforesaid, or being negligent in their office or in the execution of the orders aforesaid being made by and with the assent of the said Justices of Peace, to forfeit for every such default twenty shillings.

II. And be it also enacted, That if the said Justices of Peace do perceive that the inhabitants of any parish are not able to levy among themselves sufficient sums of money for the purposes aforesaid, That then the said Justices shall and may tax, rate, and assess as aforesaid any other of other parishes, or out of any parish within the hundred where the said parish is, to pay such sum and sums of money to the Churchwardens and Overseers of the said poor parish for the said purposes as the said Justices shall think fit, according to the intent of this law; And if the said hundred shall not be thought to the said Justices able and fit to relieve the said several parishes not able to provide for themselves as aforesaid, then the Justices of Peace at their general Quarter Sessions, or the greater number of them, shall rate and assess as aforesaid, . . . other parishes . . . as in their discretion shall seem fit.

III. And that it shall be lawful for the said Churchwardens and Overseers or any of them, by warrant from any such two Justices of Peace, to levy as well the said sums of money of every one that shall refuse to contribute according as they shall be assessed, by distress and sale of the offender's goods, as the sums of money or stock which shall be behind upon any account to be made as aforesaid, rendering to the party the overplus; and in defect of such distress, it shall be lawful for any such two Justices of the Peace to commit him to prison, there to remain without bail or mainprize till payment of the said sum or stock; And the said Justices of Peace or any one of them to send to the House of Correction such as shall not employ themselves to work being appointed thereunto as aforesaid; And also any two such Justices of Peace to commit to prison every one of the said Churchwardens and Overseers which shall refuse to account, there to remain without bail or mainprize till he have made a true account and satisfied and paid so much as upon the said account shall be remaining in his hands.

IV. And be it further enacted, That it shall be lawful for the said Churchwardens and Overseers or the greater part of them, by the assent of any two Justices of the Peace, to bind any such children as aforesaid to be apprentices where they shall see convenient, till such man-child shall come to the age of four and twenty years, and such woman-child to the age of one and twenty years; the same to be as effectual to all purposes as if such child were of full age and by indenture of covenant bound him or herself.

28. THE DUTCH REACH THE EAST INDIES

The Spanish and Portuguese monopoly of the new transoceanic trade routes and overseas colonies of the 16th century was not successfully breached until the very end of the century. It was the naval and commercial prowess of the Dutch, who had broken loose from the sovereignty of Philip II two decades before, that made this achievement possible. The immediate spur to Dutch voyages directly to the East Indies was the decision of Philip II to bar Dutch ships from his harbors in Spain and Portugal; this action ended the anomalous situation in which the Dutch rebels supplied Spain with grain and other supplies from the North in exchange for coin that enabled the Dutch to continue their resistance to Spanish power in the Low Countries. Independent Dutch voyages were undertaken in defiance of the Spanish monopoly after an itinerary of the route was published in 1596 by Jan Huygens van Linschoten, a Dutch bookkeeper who had served for six years in Goa and then returned to Holland. The return of the richly laden ships in 1599 created great excitement, as did similarly successful trips by Dutch and English ships the following year from both the East and West Indies. The news was sent to the Fuggers, the merchant-bankers of Augsburg, by their correspondents in Amsterdam and Antwerp. Two of their reports are given below.

FUGGER NEWS-LETTERS

From AMSTERDAM, the 24th day of July 1599

Out of the eight Dutch ships which left fourteen and a half months ago for India to obtain spices, four arrived here this week. They are richly

SOURCE: Victor von Klarwill (ed.), *The Fugger News-Letters*, translated by Pauline de Chary (New York: G. P. Putnam's Sons, 1925), pp. 222, 229.

laden. Their most important consignment is nearly three hundred loads of pepper, which should come to over four thousand packets. The remaining cargo consists of other kinds of spices, such as cloves, nutmeg, cinnamon, etc. The ships have a capacity of two hundred and twenty-five, two hundred and fifteen, seventy and forty loads respectively. The other four ships with soldiery have been left at Banca. These have set sail for the Moluccas and are to follow in a few months. This is considered here as great tidings, and much wonder is expressed that they should have taken such a short time over the journey. It took them seven months to make the East Indies and they lay two months in Banca. There they procured all their cargo, and have returned in five and a half months. Never have the Portuguese accomplished such a journey.

The Indians of Banca traded with them in most friendly spirit, and the Dutch paid the inhabitants of Banca for all the damage they had caused them three years before. In the meantime, the Portuguese attacked the town of Banca, but with the help of the Dutch, the Indians have killed eight hundred of these and captured the rest with the ships. Whereas the Dutch have succeeded so greatly in this sea journey they will undertake others, and if the King of Spain does not beware and put a stop to them, in time great harm will befall the kingdom of Portugal and the Venetians.

These ships are valued at three hundred thousand Flemish pounds. They will make yearly a great trade in spices and cause many others to alter their course. The Dutch States wish to go out again to India with these ships and to send an envoy to the King of Banca. They will never relinquish this desire unless the King of Spain prevent them by force.

. . . . .

From ANTWERP, the 2nd day of July 1600

From Holland and Zeeland we get written tidings that four ships from the East Indies and others from the West Indies have again sailed into Plymouth in England heavily laden with spices. Altogether they have brought ninety loads of pepper, which are estimated at about 324,000 lb.; also cloves and mace. Besides these there are nine other ships expected in Zeeland, Amsterdam and Rotterdam. The consignment of the two ships which have recently come from the Moluccas amounts to 620,000 lb. of nutmeg, 65,000 lb. of mace, 35,000 lb. of cloves and 700 lb. of pepper, which altogether is estimated at 230,000 Flemish pounds. In exchange these two ships have carried away with them 300,000 Flemish pounds in cash. It is said that six more ships are due to sail for the East Indies, namely four of the old and two of the new Company. This route becomes therefore of universal use, which is very harmful to the Spaniards, because it has been decided in Holland and Zeeland that this journey should be made through Portuguese and Spanish waters. It is announced from Emden that a ship has come here from Pernambuco in Brazil, the sailors of which report that the fleet of the United Provinces with seven ships have captured two forts in Brazil, and that afterwards they attacked the town and carried off between seven and eight thousand cases of sugar.

29. A FAVORABLE BALANCE OF TRADE

The rivalry between England and the Dutch Republic was fiercest in the East Indies, where the two countries' East India companies competed for control of the lucrative spice trade. It was a director of the English company, Thomas Mun (1571-1641), who gave the clearest statement of the principles of mercantilism in his arguments to Parliament for measures against the Dutch. Mun noted that only a state that sold more abroad than it bought would have a monetary advantage in the end. Such "treasure" he considered to be true wealth, both for governments and for people. His arguments were developed most fully in his *England's Treasure by Forraign Trade*, which was published posthumously "for the common good" in 1664, when England was on the verge of a second war with the Dutch (the first, 1652–54, had been fought and won by Cromwell). Two key chapters of this work are reprinted below.

Thomas Mun

England's Treasure by Forraign Trade

The means to enrich this Kingdom, and to encrease our Treasure

Although a Kingdom may be enriched by gifts received, or by purchase taken from some other Nations, yet these are things uncertain and of small consideration when they happen. The ordinary means therefore to encrease our wealth and treasure is by *Forraign Trade*, wherein wee must ever observe this rule; to sell more to strangers yearly than wee consume of theirs in value. For suppose that when this Kingdom is plentifully served with the Cloth, Lead, Tinn, Iron, Fish and other native commodities, we doe yearly export the overplus to forraign Countries to the value of twenty two hundred thousand pounds; by which means we are enabled beyond the Seas to buy and bring in forraign wares for

---

Source: Thomas Mun, *England's Treasure by Forraign Trade* (Oxford, England: Basil Blackwell, 1949), pp. 5–6, 87–88. Reprinted by permission of Basil Blackwell Publisher.

our use and Consumptions, to the value of twenty hundred thousand pounds; By this order duly kept in our trading, we may rest assured that the Kingdom shall be enriched yearly two hundred thousand pounds, which must be brought to us in so much Treasure; because that part of our stock which is not returned to us in wares must necessarily be brought home in treasure.

For in this case it cometh to pass in the stock of a Kingdom, as in the estate of a private man; who is supposed to have one thousand pounds yearly revenue and two thousand pounds of ready money in his Chest: If such a man through excess shall spend one thousand five hundred pounds *per annum*, all his ready mony will be gone in four years; and in the like time his said money will be doubled if he take a Frugal course to spend but five hundred pounds *per annum;* which rule never faileth likewise in the Commonwealth, but in some cases (of no great moment) which I will hereafter declare, when I shall shew by whom and in what manner this ballance of the Kingdoms account ought to be drawn up yearly, or so often as it shall please the State to discover how much we gain or lose by trade with forraign Nations. But first I will say something concerning those ways and means which will encrease our exportations and diminish our importations of wares; which being done, I will then set down some other arguments both affirmative and negative to strengthen that which is here declared, and thereby to shew that all the other means which are commonly supposed to enrich the Kingdom with Treasure are altogether insufficient and meer fallacies.

. . . . .

The conclusion upon all that hath been said concerning the Exportation or Importation of Treasure

The sum of all that hath been spoken, concerning the enriching of the Kingdom, and th' encrease of our treasure by commerce with strangers, is briefly thus. That it is a certain rule in our forraign trade, in those places where our commodities exported are overballanced in value by forraign wares brought into this Realm, there our mony is undervalued in exchange; and where the contrary of this is performed, there our mony is overvalued. But let the Merchants exchange be at a high rate, or at a low rate, or at the *Par pro pari*, or put down altogether; Let Forraign Princes enhance their Coins, or debase their Standards, and let His Majesty do the like, or keep them constant as they now stand; Let forraign Coins pass current here in all payments at higher rates than they are worth at the Mint; Let the Statute for employments by Strangers stand in force or be repealed; Let the meer Exchanger do his worst; Let Princes oppress, Lawyers extort, Usurers bite, Prodigals wast, and lastly let Merchants carry out what mony they shall have occasion to use in traffique. Yet all these actions can work no other effects in the course of trade than is declared in this discourse. For so much Treasure only will be brought in or carried out of a Commonwealth, as the Forraign Trade doth over or under ballance in value. And this must come to pass by a Necessity beyond all resistance. So that all other courses (which tend not to this end) howsoever they may seem to force mony into a Kingdom for a time, yet are they (in the end) not only fruitless but also hurtful: they are like to violent flouds which bear down their banks, and suddenly remain dry again for want of waters.

Behold then the true form and worth of forraign Trade, which is, *The great Revenue of the King, The honour of the Kingdom, The Noble profession of the Merchant, The School of our Arts, The supply of our wants, The employment of our poor, The improvement of our Lands, The Nurcery of our Mariners, The walls of the Kingdoms, The means of our Treasure, The Sinnews of our wars, The terror of our Enemies.* For all which great and weighty reasons, do so many well governed States highly countenance the profession, and carefully cherish the action, not only with Policy to encrease it, but also with power to protect it from all forraign injuries: because they know it is a Principal in Reason of State to maintain and defend that which doth Support them and their estates.

30. THE ADVANTAGE OF PRODUCTIVE AGRICULTURE

Although mercantilism is often looked upon as a single system of economic doctrine and practice, it is actually a blanket term for a variety of policies. Where Mun, a merchant, thought in terms of the profits to be made in trade, the French statesman Maximilien de Béthune, Baron de Rosny and Duc de Sully (1560–1641) saw his country's strength in its agriculture, and he opposed expensive efforts under Henry IV to establish new manufactures, as favored by his rival, Barthélemy de Laffemas. Sully recognized how important the products of French agriculture were in bringing in revenues from exports and favored reducing expenditures on imported luxuries by sumptuary laws that limited or forbade the wearing of certain apparel or the making of other expenditures. Sully, a Huguenot who, after fighting alongside Henry of Navarre in his early years, became a state minister after Henry came to the throne in 1589, recorded his presentation of these views to the king in the section of his *Memoirs* (1638) presented below. Finance and agriculture were his principal responsibilities.

Maximilien de Béthune, Duc de Sully

Memoirs

. . . . .

The king, wishing to establish in his kingdom the raising of mulberry trees, the art of silk, and all sorts of foreign manufactures which were not made in this country; for that purpose, caused to be brought in, at great expense, workers in all these crafts, and to be constructed large buildings to house them. You [i.e., Sully] did everything you could to prevent all that, but he desired it passionately. He came to you about it at the Arsenal one day and said, "I don't know what fancy has taken hold of you, so that you wish, as I am told, to oppose yourself to what I want to establish for my own satisfaction, the embellishment and enrichment of my realm, and the removal of idleness from among my people."

"Sire," you replied to him, "as regards your satisfaction, I would deeply regret to oppose myself to it formally, whatever it might cost; because having endured so many labors, difficulties, troubles, and dangers from your birth to the present, it is quite reasonable, now that your state is quiet and that things are going better in all sections, that you should also have some pleasure and recreation . . . if the expense were not excessive; . . . but to say that to your pleasure is joined the convenience, the embellishment, and the enrichment of your kingdom and of your peoples, that is what I cannot understand. If it please Your Majesty to listen patiently to my reasons, I am sure, knowing as I do the quickness of your wit and the soundness of your judgment, that you will agree with me."

"Go ahead, indeed I wish it," said the king. "I'm glad to hear your reasons, but also I want you to listen to mine afterwards, because I am sure they are better than yours. . . ."

"As for my reasons, since it pleases Your Majesty to take the trouble to listen to them, I will mingle them with arguments, which, though you may scorn them now, you will perhaps regret in the future not having considered more carefully. Because in the first place, Sire, Your Majesty must realize that as there are different climates, regions, and countries, so does it seem likewise that God wished to have them supplied variously with possessions, commodities, goods, materials, special and exclusive

---

SOURCE: Charles Woolsey Cole, *Colbert and a Century of French Mercantilism* (New York: Columbia University Press, 1939), Vol. I, pp. 42–44. Reprinted by permission of Columbia University Press.

arts and crafts, which are not common to all, or at least not as good in other places, so that by trade and commerce in these things (of which some have abundance and others a lack), intercourse, communication, and human association might be maintained between nations, however far they might be from one another, as the long voyages to the East and West prove.

"In the second place, it is essential to examine whether this kingdom has not a climate, a situation, an elevation of the sun, a temperate atmosphere, a quality of the land, and a natural inclination of the peoples which are contrary to the designs of Your Majesty.

"In the third place, there is the question whether the season of the spring here is not too cold, humid, and late both for the hatching and raising of silkworms and for supplying mulberry leaves to feed them, of which it would be impossible to obtain a sufficient quantity in five or six years, no matter what diligence was exhibited in sowing and planting.

"And in the fourth place, there is the question whether the employment of your subjects in this sort of life, which seems meditative, idle, and sedentary rather than active, will not render them unused to that toilsome, difficult, and laborious life in which they have need to be trained to make good soldiers; as I have heard Your Majesty say many times that it is among such people of toil and labor that one finds the best fighters; that having in a productive state so much good land, with which France is better provided than any other kingdom in the world (except that of Egypt), of which the great products consist of grains, vegetables, wines, dyes, oils, ciders, salts, flax, hemp, wool, linens, woolens, sheep, hogs, and mules, is the cause of all the gold and silver that enters into France, and that consequently these occupations are worth more than all the silk and silk goods which are produced in Sicily, Spain, or Italy. And also the establishment of these scarce and rich stuffs, far from aiding your peoples and enriching your state would lead them into the luxury, the pleasure, the idleness, and the excessive expenditure which have always been the chief causes of the ruin of kingdoms and commonwealths, denuding them of loyal, valiant, and hardy soldiers of whom Your Majesty has more need than of all these little good-for-nothing coxcombs of the court and cities, clothed in gold and purple. Because, as for the export of gold and silver out of your kingdom, already so often alleged by those who propose the establishment of the rich and expensive foreign stuffs, there is nothing so easy as to avoid it without harm to any one at all, [by] forbidding all display and luxury and reducing all persons of all stations, men, women, and children alike, in regard to their personal clothing, their furniture, buildings, dwellings, plants, gardens, jewels, silver vessels, horses, carriages, equipages, servants, gildings, paintings, stucco or marble work, marriages, purchases of offices, banquets, feasts, perfumes, and other superfluities to what was practiced in the times of Kings Louis XI, Charles VIII, and Louis XII; especially as regards those people connected with justice, administration, and finance, and secretaries, and bourgeois who are the ones who today indulge in the most luxury. During those reigns it is well known that chancellors, first presidents, government secretaries, and the most important financiers had only the most modest lodgings without slates, bricks, stucco or marble work, gildings or paintings; did not wear silk materials richer than taffetas; and the wives of most of them wore plain cloth hoods; they had neither costly tapestries nor silken beds, nor vessels of silver, nor even plates; they gave only small weddings for their children; they had relatives and friends in to meals only if each one of them brought his share to the table; and by excess of these things there is now consumed ten times more gold and silver than all that causes so much worry because it is exported from here for manufactures of foreign countries."

"Are these," the king then said to you, "the good reasons that you were to explain to me. Ha! Mine are better, being in short that I wish to experiment with the propositions that are made to me, and I would fight the king of Spain in three pitched battles rather than all those people of justice and finance, secretaries, and city folk, and especially all their wives and daughters, whom you would throw on my hands by so many odd rules, which I think I shall put off till another year."

"Then since such is your absolute wish, Sire," you said, "I won't talk about it any more, and time and experience will teach you that France is not fit for such playthings."

31. FRENCH MERCANTILISM

Like England, France also took up the challenge of Dutch maritime preponderance. The leader in this campaign was Jean Baptiste Colbert (1619-1683), the great finance minister under Louis XIV. Unlike Sully, Colbert believed strongly in building up the domestic manufactures of France and vigorously sought to encourage the development of independent French shipping and merchant enterprises that could take from the Dutch the lucrative trade in French products. One such measure was the establishment in 1664 of a French East India Company. It is interesting to observe the rationale in the declaration of Louis XIV announcing its formation (A), for the reasons combine both the narrowly mercantilist aims of Colbert and the broad view of the king as a "god on earth" that was central to French royalist theory.

Colbert's deep anxieties about the Dutch as "mortal enemies" of his plans are revealed in a letter to his cousin, Colbert de Terron (B), who was the intendant at the port of Rochefort. The Northern Company was designed to bring into French hands the important trade between France and the Baltic countries. He became more confident when French plans to undertake a direct military assault upon the United Provinces were confirmed in the summer of 1670 by an offensive military alliance with Charles II of England. When the Dutch responded to France's virtual exclusion of Dutch ships from their ports by taking measures of retaliation, in particular barring the import of French brandy, Colbert planned on "repaying them in kind." However, his further remarks to the French ambassador at The Hague (C) indicate that he counted on the forthcoming war to defeat the Dutch as much as on strictly commerical measures.

A. Louis XIV

Declaration Establishing the French East India Company

DECLARATION OF THE KING CONSISTING IN THE ESTABLISHMENT OF A COMPANY FOR THE EAST INDIES TRADE AND ON BEHALF OF OFFICERS OF HIS COUNCIL AND SOVEREIGN COURTS HOLDING AN INTEREST IN THE SAID COMPANY AND IN THE WEST INDIA COMPANY.

VINCENNES, August 1664

LOUIS, [etc.]

All the attention and diligence we have given until now to reform the abuses which crept into every order of our state during the long war the late king, our most honored lord and father of glorious memory, and we ourselves, were compelled to sustain, seem to us to have clearly won God's approval by the success which His divine goodness has deigned to give to our plans, equal and greater than we could hope for; and we are greatly persuaded that we cannot worthily reply to the favors we receive from His all-powerful hands except by giving to the people who owe us allegiance the same marks of paternal goodness we receive from Him each day in our own person and in those of our royal family; so that we are therefore called upon all the more to redouble our assiduous and unrelenting labors to obtain for the people the peace and alleviation which they have so greatly merited from us by their assistance to us during such a long war.

And since we know clearly that the happiness of the people consists not only in the considerable reduction of the taxes which we granted to them during the last two or three years, but even more in the restoration

---

SOURCE: Pierre Clément (ed.), *Lettres, instructions et mémoires de Colbert* Vol. II, Part 2 (Paris: Imprimerie Impériale, 1863), p. 50. Translated by Herbert H. Rowen.

of trade in our kingdom, by which means alone prosperity can be attracted to it and serve not the luxuries and lavishness of a few, as occurred before because of the dissipation of our finances, but in spreading to the people as a whole by means of the manufacture and consumption of goods and employment of a multitude of persons of every age and sex produced by trade; which reconciles most happily the abundance of temporal and spiritual goods, since the people when they work steadily are kept from all kinds of occasions to act badly which are inseparable from idleness.

And having reflected several times upon a matter of such great scope, we have principally fixed among all the means we have frequently examined for attaining this good purpose upon the trade which results from long voyages; for it is certain both by ordinary and natural reason and by the experience of our neighbors that the profit from reaching such distant countries immensely exceeds the pains and labor required. This is, furthermore, entirely in conformity with the character and glory of this nation and with the advantage it possesses above all others of succeeding easily in whatever it undertakes.

These things have obliged us to employ all our efforts for the organization of a powerful company to trade with the East Indies; and as we see a host of our subjects of every status impatient to join this company and to form it, for which purpose they await a declaration of our will to establish it and to guide it to a successful conclusion, we can no longer delay informing them of all things we are disposed to undertake on this occasion for their profit.

For these reasons, ...

B. Jean Baptiste Colbert

Letter to a Royal Intendant

Colbert to Colbert de Terron

Paris, 12 August 1669

I am convinced that the Northern Company is in good hands and that it will succeed because of the great assistance the King is giving to the directors and the favors he has granted to them. I will be very pleased to hear monthly what they have done, so that I will see if anything else can be added to make the company even stronger. Above all, you must inform the directors that in the moderate and wise policy they propose

---

Source: Pierre Clément (ed.), *Lettres, instructions et mémoires de Colbert* Vol. II, Part 2 (Paris: Imprimerie Impériale, 1863), p. 581. Translated by Herbert H. Rowen.

to follow, which I strongly approve, they should be wary especially of the Dutch and consider them as mortal enemies who will employ every means possible to bring about their ruin. I must admit to you that I was disturbed when I read in your letter that they wish to send ten vessels with cargoes of salt to Holland, to be sold there so that they can pay for all the things they want to buy there. They must expect the Dutch to destroy their ships and their cargoes if they can find the opportunity to do so; and it seems to me that it would be much better and just as easy to offer them for sale at Hamburg and Lübeck.

These are matters for their judgment; but it is certain that they must do without the Dutch if possible.

C. Jean Baptiste Colbert

Letter to a French Ambassador

Colbert to Arnauld de Pomponne

SAINT-GERMAIN, 21 November 1670

. . . I have seen in the hands of merchants reports from Holland and Rotterdam to the effect that the States have put a ban on our brandy and have decided to place such high duties on our other manufactures and products that they also will be excluded. I look for confirmation of these reports in your letters, so that if they are true I can consider means of repaying them in kind. I hope that we will not find much difficulty in doing so, especially since by banning our brandy they are directly infringing treaties. But they have gotten the habit of paying little attention to the obligations of their treaties in more important matters; what will hurt them is that I do not see that the King is willing to tolerate and accept it as in the past, and I hope that you will shortly see that they will have every reason to repent having begun this skirmish.

32. ENGLISH MERCANTILISM

During the half century that followed the breaking of the Iberian colonial monopoly by the Dutch and the English, the Dutch rapidly outpaced their

---

SOURCE: Pierre Clément (ed.), *Lettres, instructions et mémoires de Colbert* Vol. II, Part 2 (Paris: Imprimerie Impériale, 1863), p. 583. Translated by Herbert H. Rowen.

rivals across the North Sea and established an extraordinary supremacy in overseas trade, both in European waters and overseas. English merchants were infuriated, especially when the Dutch, who had proclaimed a doctrine of freedom of the seas, created their own monopoly in the East Indies. But they were also resentful, if less outraged, by the success of the Dutch in dominating European interregional shipping. Under the ineffectual reigns in Britain of James I and Charles I, little could be done except to write tracts and to complain to the States General at The Hague; but when Cromwell came to power, he created a powerful new navy that successfully contested Dutch maritime dominance. A Navigation Act adopted in 1651 barred the Dutch from most trade with England and her American colonies; it was renewed in 1660 when Charles II was restored to the throne. Its results in overcoming the Dutch advantage were gradual but became virtually irresistible when the Dutch had to become allies of the English, and lesser partners to boot, during the wars against Louis XIV. The principal provisions of the 1660 act are given below.

The English Navigation Act of 1660

For the increase of shipping and encouragement of the navigation of this nation, wherein under the good providence and protection of God the wealth, safety and strength of this kingdom is so much concerned, be it enacted . . . that from and after the first day of December one thousand six hundred and sixty . . . no goods or commodities whatsoever shall be imported into or exported out of any lands, islands, plantations or territories to his Majesty belonging or in his possession, or which may hereafter belong unto or be in the possession of his Majesty, his heirs and successors, in Asia, Africa or America, in any other ship or ships, vessel or vessels whatsoever, but in such ships or vessels as do truly and without fraud belong only to the people of England or Ireland, dominion of Wales or town of Berwick-upon-Tweed, or are of the built of and belonging to any of the said lands, islands, plantations or territories as the proprietors and right owners thereof, and whereof the master and three fourths of the mariners at least are English, under the penalty of the forfeiture and loss of all the goods and commodities which shall be imported into, or exported out of, any the aforesaid places in any other ship or vessel, as also of the ship or vessel with all its guns, furniture, tackle, ammunition and apparel, one third part thereof to his Majesty, his heirs and successors, one third part to the governor of such land, plantation, island or territory where such default shall be committed, in case the said ship or goods be there seized, or otherwise that third part also to his Majesty,

---

SOURCE: From *English Historical Documents, Volume 8, 1660-1714*, pp. 533–34, edited by Andrew Browning.

his heirs and successors, and the other third part to him or them who shall seize, inform or sue for the same. . . . And all admirals and other commanders at sea of any the ships of war or other ship having commission from his Majesty, or from his heirs or successors, are hereby authorized and strictly required to seize and bring in as prize all such ships or vessels as shall have offended contrary hereunto, and deliver them to the Court of Admiralty, there to be proceeded against; and in case of condemnation one moiety of such forfeitures shall be to the use of such admirals or commanders and their companies, to be divided and proportioned amongst them according to the rules and orders of the sea in cases of ships taken prize, and the other moiety to the use of his Majesty, his heirs and successors.

II. And be it enacted, that no alien or person not born within the allegiance of our sovereign lord the king, his heirs and successors, or naturalized or made a free denizen, shall from and after the first day of February which shall be in the year of our Lord one thousand six hundred sixty-one exercise the trade or occupation of a merchant or factor in any the said places, upon pain of the forfeiture and loss of all his goods and chattels, or which are in his possession, one third to his Majesty, his heirs and successors, one third to the governor of the plantation where such person shall so offend, and the other third to him or them that shall inform or sue for the same in any of his Majesty's courts in the plantation where such offence shall be committed. . . .

III. And it is further enacted . . . that no goods or commodities whatsoever of the growth, production or manufacture of Africa, Asia or America, or of any part thereof, . . . be imported into England, Ireland or Wales, islands of Guernsey or Jersey or town of Berwick-upon-Tweed, in any other ship or ships . . . under the penalty of the forfeiture of all such goods and commodities, and of the ship or vessel in which they were imported. . . .

IV. And it is further enacted . . . that no goods or commodities that are of foreign growth, production or manufacture, and which are to be brought into England, Ireland, Wales, the islands of Guernsey and Jersey or town of Berwick-upon-Tweed in English-built shipping, or other shipping belonging to some of the aforesaid places, and navigated by English mariners as abovesaid, shall be shipped or brought from any other place or places, country or countries, but only from those of their said growth, production or manufacture, or from those ports where the said goods and commodities can only or are or usually have been first shipped for transportation, . . . under the penalty of the forfeiture of all such of the aforesaid goods as shall be imported from any other place or country contrary to the true intent and meaning hereof, as also of the ship in which they were imported. . . .

CHAPTER IV

EUROPEAN DISCOVERY AND COLONIZATION

NOTHING SETS medieval and modern Europe so clearly apart as the great wave of exploration that began in the 15th century. Although Italian navigators and geographers contributed their skills, it was largely an achievement of the nations facing the Atlantic, which had developed ships suitable for long oceanic voyages. Within less than a century after the first Portuguese probings down the western coast of Africa, the unknown continent across the Atlantic had been discovered, the East Indies had been reached round the Cape of Good Hope, and the globe had been circumnavigated. Although much discovery and exploration remained to be done, the essential tasks had been accomplished.

Portugal and Spain, which had been the principal actors in the great drama, were also the first beneficiaries from the newly established trade routes and the new colonies formed in America and the East. The characteristic problem of colonization, the relations between and mutual transformation of the "mother country" and the colonized lands, soon arose to challenge men's minds and consciences. But those countries that had not yet established colonies, like France, England, and Holland, were concerned only with catching up to the achievement of their Iberian rivals.

33. EXPLORATION AND THE REASONS WHY

European exploration of the oceans in modern times began with the expeditions organized by Prince Henry of Portugal (1394-1460), who was known as Henry the Navigator although he did not himself undertake any voyages of discovery. After taking part in the Portuguese conquest of Ceuta in 1415, he established an observatory and naval school at the southwestern tip of Portugal, from which he sent out sea captains to explore southward along the coast of Africa. These difficult voyages round the jutting coastline to Guinea, which were the basis for later Portuguese explorations all the way to the East Indies, were chronicled by Gomes Eannes de Azurara at the request of King Alfonso V in 1452–53. Azurara's presentation of the reasons that moved Prince Henry (the "Lord Infant") to undertake sponsorship of the voyages of discovery may be set against the "causes" historians of later centuries, with their different patterns of explanation, have attributed to the venture.

Gomes Eannes de Azurara

The Chronicle of the Discovery and Conquest of Guinea

. . . . .

We imagine that we know a matter when we are acquainted with the doer of it and the end for which he did it. And since in former chapters we have set forth the Lord Infant [Prince Henry] as the chief actor in these things, giving as clear an understanding of him as we could, it is meet that in this present chapter we should know his purpose in doing them. And you should note well that the noble spirit of this Prince, by a sort of natural constraint, was ever urging him both to begin and to carry out very great deeds. For which reason, after the taking of Ceuta he always kept ships well armed against the Infidel, both for war, and because he had also a wish to know the land that lay beyond the isles of Canary and that Cape called Bojador, for that up to his time, neither by writings, nor by the memory of man, was known with any certainty the nature of the land beyond that Cape. Some said indeed that Saint Brandan had passed that way; and there was another tale of two galleys rounding the Cape, which never returned. But this doth not appear at all likely to be true, for it is not to be presumed that if the said galleys went there, some other ships would not have endeavoured to learn what

---

SOURCE: Gomes Eannes de Azurara, *The Chronicle of the Discovery and Conquest of Guinea*, translated by Charles Raymond Beazley and Edgar Prestage (London, England: Hakluyt Society, 1896), Vol. I, pp. 27–30.

voyage they had made. And because the said Lord Infant wished to know the truth of this,—since it seemed to him that if he or some other lord did not endeavour to gain that knowledge, no mariners or merchants would ever dare to attempt it—(for it is clear that none of them ever trouble themselves to sail to a place where there is not a sure and certain hope of profit)—and seeing also that no other prince took any pains in this matter, he sent out his own ships against those parts, to have manifest certainty of them all. And to this he was stirred up by his zeal for the service of God and of the King Edward his Lord and brother, who then reigned. And this was the first reason of his action.

The second reason was that if there chanced to be in those lands some population of Christians, or some havens, into which it would be possible to sail without peril, many kinds of merchandise might be brought to this realm, which would find a ready market, and reasonably so, because no other people of these parts traded with them, nor yet people of any other that were known; and also the products of this realm might be taken there, which traffic would bring great profit to our countrymen.

The third reason was that, as it was said that the power of the Moors in that land of Africa was very much greater than was commonly supposed, and that there were no Christians among them, nor any other race of men; and because every wise man is obliged by natural prudence to wish for a knowledge of the power of his enemy; therefore the said Lord Infant exerted himself to cause this to be fully discovered, and to make it known determinately how far the power of those infidels extended.

The fourth reason was because during the one and thirty years that he had warred against the Moors, he had never found a Christian king, nor a lord outside this land, who for the love of our Lord Jesus Christ would aid him in the said war. Therefore he sought to know if there were in those parts any Christian princes, in whom the charity and the love of Christ was so ingrained that they would aid him against those enemies of the faith.

The fifth reason was his great desire to make increase in the faith of our Lord Jesus Christ and to bring to him all the souls that should be saved,—understanding that all the mystery of the Incarnation, Death, and Passion of our Lord Jesus Christ was for this sole end—namely the salvation of lost souls—whom the said Lord Infant by his travail and spending would fain bring into the true path. For he perceived that no better offering could be made unto the Lord than this; for if God promised to return one hundred goods for one, we may justly believe that for such great benefits, that is to say for so many souls as were saved by the efforts of this Lord, he will have so many hundreds of guerdons in the kingdom of God, by which his spirit may be glorified after this life in the celestial realm. For I that wrote this history saw so many men and women of those parts turned to the holy faith, that even if the Infant had been a heathen, their prayers would have been enough to have obtained his salvation. And not only did I see the first captives, but their children and grandchildren as true Christians as if the Divine grace breathed in them and imparted to them a clear knowledge of itself.

But over and above these five reasons I have a sixth that would seem to be the root from which all the others proceeded: and this is the inclination of the heavenly wheels. For, as I wrote not many days ago in a letter I sent to the Lord King, that although it be written that the wise man shall be Lord of the stars, and that the courses of the planets (according to the true estimate of the holy doctors) cannot cause the good man to stumble; yet it is manifest that they are bodies ordained in the secret counsels of our Lord God and run by a fixed measure, appointed to different ends, which are revealed to men by his grace, through whose influence bodies of the lower order are inclined to certain passions. And if it be a fact, speaking as a Catholic, that the contrary predestinations of the wheels of heaven can be avoided by natural judgment with the aid of a certain divine grace, much more does it stand to reason that those who are predestined to good fortune, by the help of this same grace, will not only follow their course but even add a far greater increase to themselves. But here I wish to tell you how by the constraint of the influence of nature this glorious Prince was inclined to those actions of his. And that was because his ascendent was Aries, which is the house of Mars and exaltation of the sun, and his lord in the XIth house, in company of the sun. And because the said Mars was in Aquarius, which is the house of Saturn, and in the mansion of hope, it signified that this Lord should toil at high and mighty conquests, especially in seeking out things that were hidden from other men and secret, according to the nature of Saturn, in whose house he is. And the fact of his being accompanied by the sun, as I said, and the sun being in the house of Jupiter, signified that all his traffick and his conquests would be loyally carried out, according to the good pleasure of his king and lord.

34. THE DISCOVERY OF AMERICA

Thanks to the Spanish historian Bartolomé de Las Casas (1474-1566), who is best known as the champion of the Indians, we possess something of the logbook Columbus kept of his first epic voyage in 1492. Although the original manuscript has vanished, Las Casas abstracted it in detail for his *History of the Indies,* reproducing many passages verbatim. Las Casas's working version was printed in 1825 in Spanish and appeared in English translation two years later. In the text Columbus is referred to as the Admiral.

Bartolomé de Las Casas

Columbus's Logbook

Sunday, Oct. 7th. Continued their course W. and sailed twelve miles an hour, for two hours, then eight miles an hour. Sailed till an hour after sunrise, twenty-three leagues; reckoned to the crew eighteen. At sunrise the caravel Niña, who kept ahead on account of her swiftness in sailing, while all the vessels were striving to out-sail one another, and gain the reward promised by the King and Queen by first discovering land—hoisted a flag at her mast head, and fired a *lombarda*,[1] as a signal that she had discovered land, for the Admiral had given orders to that effect. He had also ordered that the ships should keep in close company at sunrise and sunset, as the air was clearer and more favourable at those times for seeing at a distance. In the afternoon, seeing nothing of the land which the Niña had made signals for, and observing large flocks of birds coming from the N. and making for the S.W. whereby it was rendered probable that they were either going to land to pass the night, or abandoning the countries of the North, on account of the approaching winter, he determined to alter his course, knowing also that the Portuguese had discovered most of the islands they possessed by attending to the flight of birds. The Admiral accordingly shifted his course from W. to W.S.W. with a resolution to continue two days in that direction. This was done about an hour after sunset. Sailed in the night nearly five leagues, and twenty-three in the day: in all twenty-eight.

Monday, Oct. 8th. Steered W.S.W. and sailed day and night eleven or twelve leagues; it seems that at times during the night they made fifteen miles an hour (if the handwriting is not deceptive). Found the sea like the river at Seville, "thanks to God," says the Admiral. The air soft as that of Seville in April, and so fragrant that it was delicious to breathe it. The weeds appeared very fresh. Many land birds, one of which they took, flying towards the S.W. also *grajaos*, ducks, and a gannet were seen.

Tuesday, Oct. 9th. Sailed S.W. five leagues, when the wind changed, and they stood W. by N. four leagues. Sailed, with eleven leagues by day

---

SOURCE: A. W. Lawrence and Jean Young, *Narratives of the Discovery of America* (New York: Jonathan Cape and Harrison Smith, 1931, pp. 93–98. Reprinted by permission of Jonathan Cape and Harrison Smith Publishers.

[1] A sort of cannon, first brought from Lombardy.

and the night, twenty leagues and a half; reckoned to the crew seventeen. All night heard birds passing.

Wednesday, Oct. 10th. Steered W.S.W. and sailed at times ten miles an hour, at others twelve, and at others, seven; day and night made fifty-nine leagues progress; reckoned to the crew but forty-four. Here the men lost all patience, and complained of the length of the voyage, but the Admiral encouraged them in the best manner he could, representing the profits they were about to acquire, and adding that it was to no purpose to complain, since he had come to the Indies, and that so he must continue on till, with the help of our Lord, he found them.

Thursday, Oct. 11th. Steered W.S.W.; and encountered a heavier sea than they had met with before in the whole voyage. Saw sandpipers and a green rush near the vessel. The crew of the caravel Pinta saw a cane and a log; they also picked up a stick which appeared to have been carved with an iron tool, a piece of cane, another plant which grows on land, and a board. The crew of the Niña saw other signs of land, and a stalk loaded with rose-hips. These signs made them all grow cheerful again. Sailed this day till sunset, twenty-seven leagues.

After sunset steered their original course W. and sailed twelve miles an hour till two hours after midnight, going ninety miles, which are twenty-two leagues and a half; and as the Pinta was the swiftest sailer, and kept ahead of the Admiral, she discovered land and made the signals which had been ordered. The land was first seen by a sailor called Rodrigo de Triana, although the Admiral at ten o'clock that evening standing on the quarter-deck saw a light, but so small a body that he could not affirm it to be land; calling to Pero Gutierrez, groom of the King's wardrobe, he told him he saw a light, and bid him look that way, which he did and saw it; he did the same to Rodrigo Sanchez of Segovia, whom the King and Queen had sent with the squadron as comptroller, but he was unable to see it from his situation. The Admiral again perceived it once or twice, appearing like the light of a wax candle moving up and down, which some few thought an indication of land. But the Admiral held it for certain that land was near; for which reason, after they had said the *Salve* which the seamen are accustomed to repeat and chant after their fashion, the Admiral asked and admonished them to keep a strict watch upon the forecastle and look out diligently for land, and to him who should first discover it he promised a silken jacket, besides the reward which the King and Queen had offered, which was an annuity of ten thousand *maravedis.* At two o'clock in the morning, the land was discovered, at two leagues distance; they took in sail and remained under the square-sail without peaks, lying to till day, which was Friday, when they found themselves near a small island, one of the Lucayos, called in the Indian language Guanahani. Presently they descried people, naked, and the Admiral landed in the boat, which was armed, along with Martin Alonso Pinzon, and Vincent Yañez his brother, captain of the Niña. The Admiral bore the royal standard, and the two captains each a banner of the Green Cross, which all the ships had carried for an ensign; this contained an F and a Y,[2] one letter on each side of the cross, and a crown over each. Arrived on shore, they saw trees very green, many streams of water, and diverse sorts of fruits. The Admiral called upon the two Captains, and the rest of those who jumped ashore, as also to Rodrigo de Escovedo, notary of the fleet, and Rodrigo Sanchez, of Segovia, to bear faithful witness that he before all others took possession (as in fact he did) of that island for the King and Queen his sovereigns, making the requisite declarations, which are more at large set down there in writing. Numbers of the people of the island straightway collected together. . . . [In] the precise words of the Admiral, in his book of his first navigation and discovery of the Indies. . . .

"Weapons they have none, nor are acquainted with them, for I showed them swords which they grasped by the blades, and cut themselves through ignorance. They have no iron, their javelins being without it, and nothing more than sticks, though some have fish-bones or other things at the ends. They are all of a good size and stature, and handsomely formed. I saw some with scars of wounds upon their bodies, and demanded by signs the cause of them; they answered me in the same way, that there came people from the other islands in the neighbourhood who endeavoured to make prisoners of them, and they defended themselves. I thought then, and still believe, that these came here from the continent to take captives. It appears to me, that the people are ingenious, and would be good servants, for I saw that they very quickly grasped all that was said to them; and I am of opinion that they would very readily become Christians, as they appear to have no religion. If it please our Lord, I intend at my return to carry home six of them to your Highnesses, that they may learn our language. I saw no beasts of any kind in the island, except parrots." These are the very words of the Admiral.

35. NAMING A NEW CONTINENT

The new continent discovered by Columbus received not his name but that of a fellow Italian, Amerigo Vespucci (1451-1512). A Florentine navigator, Vespucci began a series of voyages to the new land in 1497 or 1499—the date

[2] The initials of King Ferdinand and Queen Isabella.

is uncertain because the first journey is reported only in a letter attributed to him and first published in 1504. If the letter is authentic, Vespucci reached the mainland of South America a year before Columbus, but some historians have held it to be forged. The letter was reprinted by the German geographer and cartographer Martin Waldseemüller in 1507 as an appendix to his *Introduction to Cosmography*. Waldseemüller, who points out that the names of the continents of the Old World could be traced to mythology and ancient history, realized that the new land was not the Indies sought by Columbus but a hitherto unknown "island" and proposed to give it the name of Amerige or America, after Vespucci's given name. The latter form of the name quickly took hold, even though Waldseemüller took it off his map of 1516 after he had learned more about Columbus's voyages.

Martin Waldseemüller

Introduction to Cosmography

Of Certain Elements of Cosmography

It is clear from astronomical demonstrations that the whole earth is a point in comparison with the entire extent of the heavens; so that if the earth's circumference be compared to the size of the celestial globe, it may be considered to have absolutely no extent. There is about a fourth part of this small region in the world which was known to Ptolemy and is inhabited by living beings like ourselves. Hitherto it has been divided into three parts, Europe, Africa, and Asia.

Europe is bounded on the west by the Atlantic Ocean, on the north by the British Ocean, on the east by the river Tanais (modern Don), Lake Maeotis (modern Sea of Azov), and the Black Sea, and on the south by the Mediterranean Sea. It includes Spain, Gaul, Germany, Raetia, Italy, Greece, and Sarmatia. Europe is so called after Europa, the daughter of King Agenor. While with a girl's enthusiasm she was playing on the sea-shore accompanied by her Tyrian maidens and was gathering flowers in baskets, she is believed to have been carried off by Jupiter, who assumed the form of a snow-white bull, and after being brought over the seas to Crete seated upon his back to have given her name to the land lying opposite.

Africa is bounded on the west by the Atlantic Ocean, on the south by the Ethiopian Ocean, on the north by the Mediterranean Sea, and on the east by the river Nile. It embraces the Mauritanias, viz., Tingitana (mod-

---

Source: Martin Waldseemüller, *Cosmographiae Introductio*, translated by Joseph Fischer and Franz von Wieser (Ann Arbor, Mich.: University Microfilms, 1966), pp. 68–70. Reprinted by permission of University Microfilms, Inc.

ern Tangiers) and Caesarea, inland Libya, Numidia (also called Mapalia), lesser Africa (in which is Carthage, formerly the constant rival of the Roman empire), Cyrenaica, Marmarica (modern Barca), Libya (by which name also the whole of Africa is called, from Libs, a king of Mauritania), inland Ethiopia, Egypt, etc. It is called Africa because it is free from the severity of the cold.

Asia, which far surpasses the other divisions in size and in resources, is separated from Europe by the river Tanais (Don) and from Africa by the Isthmus, which stretching southward divides the Arabian and the Egyptian seas. The principal countries of Asia are Bithynia, Galatia, Cappadocia, Pamphylia, Lydia, Cilicia, greater and lesser Armenia, Colchis, Hyrcania, Iberia, and Albania; besides many other countries which it would only delay us to enumerate one by one. Asia is so called after a queen of that name.

Now, these parts of the earth have been more extensively explored and a fourth part has been discovered by Amerigo Vespucci (as will be set forth in what follows). Inasmuch as both Europe and Asia received their names from women, I see no reason why any one should justly object to calling this part Amerige, i.e., the land of Amerigo, or America, after Amerigo, its discoverer, a man of great ability. Its position and the customs of its inhabitants may be clearly understood from the four voyages of Amerigo, which are subjoined.

Thus the earth is now known to be divided into four parts. The first three parts are continents, while the fourth is an island, inasmuch as it is found to be surrounded on all sides by the ocean. Although there is only one ocean, just as there is only one earth, yet, being marked by many seas and filled with numberless islands, it takes various names. . . .

36. CONQUEROR ON THE VERGE OF CONQUEST

The conquests of Spain on the mainland of America, notably of Mexico and Peru, were stupendous achievements by small military parties. Their success was due less to a technical superiority of arms than to luck in intruding into lands on the brink of civil war, with rulers who faced internal enemies and were willing to accept the assistance of strangers. Also essential was something of their own, a desperate willingness to dare the worst in the hope of bettering themselves. We can see the beginnings of the conquest of Mexico by Hernando Cortés in 1519–21 through the eyes of a extraordinary common soldier in his ranks, Bernal Díaz del Castillo (c.1492-c.1581). Díaz managed to retain his human (and humane) sensitivity in a world of cruelties and could see places, events, and men with plain honesty. He put these qualities into the strong, quickly moving prose of *The Discovery and Conquest of Mexico*, which he began to write when he was well past 60. The following passages from his work, which was first published in 1632, relate the preparations for Cortés's expedition and the approach to the capital city of Mexico.

Bernal Díaz del Castillo

The Discovery and Conquest of Mexico

. . . . .

As soon as Hernando Cortés had been appointed General he began to search for all sorts of arms, guns, powder and crossbows, and every kind of warlike stores which he could get together, and all sorts of articles to be used for barter, and other things necessary for the expedition.

Moreover he began to adorn himself and be more careful of his appearance than before, and he wore a plume of feathers with a medal, and a gold chain, and a velvet cloak trimmed with knots of gold, in fact he looked like a gallant and courageous Captain. However, he had no money to defray the expenses I have spoken about, for at that time he was very poor and much in debt, although he had a good *encomienda* of Indians who were getting him a return from his gold mines, but he spent all of it on his person and on finery for his wife, whom he had recently married, and on entertaining some guests who had come to visit him. For he was affable in his manner and a good talker, and he had twice been chosen *Alcalde* [Mayor] of the town of Santiago Baracoa where he had settled, and in that country it is esteemed a great honour to be chosen as *Alcalde.*

When some merchant friends of his saw that he had obtained this command as Captain General, they lent him four thousand gold dollars in coin and gave him merchandise worth another four thousand dollars secured on his Indians and estates. Then he ordered two standards and banners to be made, worked in gold with the royal arms and a cross on each side with a legend which said, "Comrades, let us follow the sign of the holy Cross with true faith, and through it we shall conquer." And he ordered a proclamation to be made with the sound of drums and trumpets in the name of His Majesty and by Diego Velásquez in the King's name, and in his own as Captain General, to the effect that whatsoever person might wish to go in his company to the newly discovered lands to conquer them and to settle there, should receive his share of the gold, silver and riches which might be gained, and an *encomienda* of

---

SOURCE: Reprinted with the permission of Farrar, Straus & Giroux, Inc. from *The Discovery and Conquest of Mexico* by Bernal Díaz del Castillo, pp. 32–33, 189–92. Copyright 1956 by Farrar, Straus & Cudahy. Translated by A. P. Maudslay.

Indians after the country had been pacified, and that to do these things Diego Velásquez held authority from His Majesty.

. . . . .

As soon as the messengers had been despatched, we set out for Mexico, and as the people of Huexotzingo and Chalco had told us that Montezuma had held consultations with his Idols and priests, who had said he was to allow us to enter and that then he could kill us, and as we are but human and feared death, we never ceased thinking about it. As that country is very thickly peopled we made short marches, and commended ourselves to God and to Our Lady his blessed Mother, and talked about how and by what means we could enter the City, and it put courage into our hearts to think that as our Lord Jesus Christ had vouchsafed us protection through past dangers, he would likewise guard us from the power of the Mexicans.

We went to sleep at a town called Iztapalatengo where half the houses are in the water and the other half on dry land, and there they gave us a good supper.

The Great Montezuma, when he heard the reply which Cortés had sent to him, at once determined to send his nephew named Cacamatzin, the Lord of Texcoco, with great pomp to bid welcome to Cortés and to all of us, and one of our scouts came in to tell us that a large crowd of friendly Mexicans was coming along the road clad in rich mantles. It was very early in the morning when this happened, and we were ready to start, and Cortés ordered us to wait in our quarters until he could see what the matter was.

At that moment four chieftains arrived, who made deep obeisance to Cortés and said that close by there was approaching Cacamatzin, the great Lord of Texcoco, a nephew of the Great Montezuma, and he begged us to have the goodness to wait until he arrived.

He did not tarry long, for he soon arrived with greater pomp and splendour than we had ever beheld in a Mexican Prince, for he came in a litter richly worked in green feathers, with many silver borderings, and rich stones set in bosses made out of the finest gold. Eight Chieftains, who, it was said were all Lords of Towns, bore the litter on their shoulders. When they came near to the house where Cortés was quartered, the Chieftains assisted Cacamatzin to descend from the litter, and they swept the ground, and removed the straws where he had to pass, and when they came before our Captain they made him a deep reverence, and Cacamatzin said:

"Malinche, here we have come, I and these Chieftains to place ourselves at your service, and to give you all that you may need for yourself and your companions and to place you in your home, which is our city, for so the Great Montezuma our Prince has ordered us to do, and he asks your pardon that he did not come with us himself, but it is on account of ill-health that he did not do so, and not from want of every good will which he bears towards you."

When our Captain and all of us beheld such pomp and majesty in those chiefs, especially in the nephew of Montezuma, we considered it a matter of the greatest importance, and said among ourselves, if this Cacique bears himself with such dignity, what will the Great Montezuma do?

When Cacamatzin had delivered his speech, Cortés embraced him, and gave many caresses to him and all the other Chieftains, and gave him three stones which are called Margaritas, which have within them many markings of different colours, and to the other Chieftains he gave blue glass beads, and he told them that he thanked them and when he was able he would repay the Lord Montezuma for all the favours which every day he was granting us.

As soon as the speech-making was over, we at once set out, and as the Caciques whom I have spoken about brought many followers with them, and as many people came out to see us from the neighbouring towns, all the roads were full of them.

During the morning, we arrived at a broad Causeway and continued our march towards Iztapalapa, and when we saw so many cities and villages built in the water and other great towns on dry land and that straight and level Causeway going towards Mexico, we were amazed and said that it was like the enchantments they tell of in the legend of Amadis, on account of the great towers and cues and buildings rising from the water, and all built of masonry. And some of our soldiers even asked whether the things that we saw were not a dream. It is not to be wondered at that I here write it down in this manner, for there is so much to think over that I do not know how to describe it, seeing things as we did that had never been heard of or seen before, not even dreamed about.

Thus, we arrived near Iztapalapa, to behold the splendour of the other Caciques who came out to meet us, who were the Lord of the town named Cuitlahuac, and the Lord of Culuacan, both of them near relations of Montezuma. And then when we entered the city of Iztapalapa, the appearance of the palaces in which they lodged us! How spacious and well built they were, of beautiful stone work and cedar wood, and the wood of other sweet scented trees, with great rooms and courts, wonderful to behold, covered with awnings of cotton cloth.

When we had looked well at all of this, we went to the orchard and garden, which was such a wonderful thing to see and walk in, that I was never tired of looking at the diversity of the trees, and noting the scent which each one had, and the paths full of roses and flowers, and the many fruit trees and native roses, and the pond of fresh water. There was another thing to observe, that great canoes were able to pass into the garden from the lake through an opening that had been made so that there was no need for their occupants to land. And all was cemented and very splendid with many kinds of stone [monuments] with pictures on them, which gave much to think about. Then the birds of many kinds and breeds which came into the pond. I say again that I stood looking at it and thought that never in the world would there be discovered other lands such as these, for at that time there was no Peru, nor any thought of it. Of all these wonders that I then beheld to-day all is overthrown and lost, nothing left standing.

Let us go on, and I will relate that the Caciques of that town and of Coyoacan brought us a present of gold, worth more than two thousand pesos.

Early next day we left Iztapalapa with a large escort of those great Caciques whom I have already mentioned. We proceeded along the Causeway which is here eight paces in width and runs so straight to the City of Mexico that it does not seem to me to turn either much or little, but, broad as it is, it was so crowded with people that there was hardly room for them all, some of them going to and others returning from Mexico, besides those who had come out to see us, so that we were hardly able to pass by the crowds of them that came; and the towers and cues were full of people as well as the canoes from all parts of the lake. It was not to be wondered at, for they had never before seen horses or men such as we are.

Gazing on such wonderful sights, we did not know what to say, or whether what appeared before us was real, for on one side, on the land, there were great cities, and in the lake ever so many more, and the lake itself was crowded with canoes, and in the Causeway were many bridges at intervals, and in front of us stood the great City of Mexico, and we—we did not even number four hundred soldiers! and we well remembered the words and warnings given us by the people of Huexotzingo and Tlaxcala, and the many other warnings that had been given that we should beware of entering Mexico, where they would kill us, as soon as they had us inside.

37. OUTRAGEOUS AND SENSELESS ACTIONS

Although until recent decades the "black legend" of Spanish cruelties in the conquest and rule of their American colonies dominated the history of these lands as seen by historians in England and the United States, the legend itself rests upon the testimony of Spanish officials and churchmen. That fact, although it does not contradict the legend, lends it ambiguity and irony, for not only was it Spaniards who did "outrageous and senseless" things, it was also Spaniards who denounced these deeds. The pleas of Bishop Las Casas for the Indians were repeated by Alonso de Zorita in his description of Mexican life during the years of his service as a royal judge (*oidor*) in New Spain. Zorita (1512–80) wrote *Life and Labor in Ancient Mexico: The Brief and Summary Relation of the Lords of New Spain* after his return to Spain in 1566. Although he wrote with compassion and honesty about what he observed, he idealized the Aztec empire the Spaniards had overthrown, as an obvious reaction to a distasteful present.

Alonso de Zorita

Life and Labor in Ancient Mexico

How this relation came to be written, and why it was not written until now

In December 1553, there was issued at Valladolid a royal cedula that commanded the Audiencias of the Indies to make inquiry into certain matters about which His Majesty wished to be informed. They were to inquire who were the lords of the land, what tribute the natives paid them in the time of their heathendom, and what tribute they have been paying since they came under the Royal Crown of Castile. When the Audiencias had gathered this information, they were to send it together with their opinions to His Majesty.

At the time this royal cedula was received by the Audiencia de los Confines, in which I served as oidor, I left for Mexico City, whither His Majesty sent me to serve as oidor in the Audiencia of that capital. When I arrived in Mexico City, the Audiencia there had already completed its inquiry and had dispatched its report and opinion. The Audiencia de los Confines, on the other hand, made its inquiry after I had left. Since I was in His Majesty's service when his royal cedula was issued and when the inquiries were made and the reports sent, and since it does not excuse me that I was absent from both Audiencias when the matter was under discussion, I feel an obligation to say what I think about it.

I wish to relate what I learned in the nineteen years I served His Majesty in those parts. The first two I passed as oidor in the town of Santo Domingo, and the next three in the New Kingdom of Granada, in Santa Marta, Cartegena, and Cabo de la Vela, where by His Majesty's order I went to hold a *residencia* of the governor of those provinces. On my return to Santo Domingo to resume my office, I received His Majesty's

---

SOURCE: *Life & Labor in Ancient Mexico: The Brief and Summary Relation of the Lords of New Spain*, by Alonso de Zorita, translated and with an introduction by Benjamin Keen, pp. 84–85, 200–02, 216–17. Rutgers University Press, New Brunswick, New Jersey, 1971.

instructions ordering me to go to serve him as oidor in the Audiencia de los Confines. There I passed three years during which I visited almost every part of the province of Guatemala. The rest of the time I resided in Mexico City. Because of the press of work, I found it impossible to write this relation, as I greatly wished. Now that I am unoccupied, having returned to Spain with His Majesty's permission because the state of my health prevented me from serving him with my wonted diligence and care, I have determined to put in finished form the material I kept for many years in my notebooks and papers. I have done this by putting in the form of a reply to each article of the royal cedula the material relating to that article.

. . . . .

Article 10

You will inform yourselves if the Christian Spaniards, when they conquered that land, imposed new tributes on the Indians in addition to those they paid in the time of their paganry, and how they used the Indians. You will also inform yourselves whether the Spaniards were careful not to require other tribute or service of the Indians than what they used to give their universal ruler, and whether the requirement that the Indian towns give food to their Spanish encomenderos was a new imposition and how this was done.

The actions of the Spaniards at first were so outrageous and senseless (and still are in some places) that if I had to tell all that pertains to this article it would make a very long story. To make it as short as possible I shall comment with all brevity, considering that I could write endlessly about the matters with which this article deals. For a better understanding of these matters I shall have to refer to events and conditions both past and present.

This article contains two questions: First, were new tributes imposed on the Indians when the land was conquered. Second, how did the Spaniards use the Indians.

In reply to the first question, I say that as soon as the land was won, Captain Hernando Cortés summoned the lords and caciques to Coyoacán, which is an important Indian town, two leagues from Mexico City, that Cortés took for himself along with some other important towns of this region. Those who could went to Coyoacán; and when they were assembled, Cortés told them that they were no longer to take their tribute to the ruler of Mexico or to the rulers of Texcoco or Tlacopan, as they used to do, but that they were to give it to the Emperor, delivering it in his name to Cortés himself and the other Spaniards who were there. The Indians were not to cultivate the tribute land as they used to do; and each town of any consequence was to be independent of every other. The lords and caciques who were present, having fresh in their minds the treatment they and their people had received from the Spaniards, accepted what Cortés told them. One can imagine how freely they gave their consent!

Cortes distributed the land among his Spaniards and to himself without stipulating how, or when, or how much was to be paid in tribute, so that each Spaniard arranged with the lord and principales of the town commended to him what they must give him every eighty days. Some, but very few, went to the Captain for confirmation of their agreement. Since their appetite and greed were their only measure and rule, they demanded all they could in tribute, personal services, and slaves, never caring whether the Indians were able to comply. One can judge from this whether care was taken that the Indians pay no greater tribute than they had been accustomed to pay their lords. The Spaniards compelled them to give whatever they asked, and inflicted unheard-of cruelties and tortures upon them. Because of this, and because of the plagues that have afflicted them, of which more later, so many people have died that there is not one third the number there used to be.

. . . . .

Who shall tell the sum of the miseries and hardships these poor unfortunate people suffer, without help or succor from any quarter! Who does not turn his face against them, who does not persecute and vex them, who does not rob them and live by their sweat! Since I cannot tell all, but have told enough to make clear the need for a remedy, let me be silent concerning the innumerable crimes that I have personally seen and verified or that I have heard of from trustworthy persons.

The ancient kings and lords never ruled in this way, never took the Indians from their towns, never disrupted their way of life and labor. I cannot believe that Your Majesty or the members of Your Majesty's Council know or have been informed about what is taking place. If they knew of it, they would surely take steps to preserve Your Majesty's miserable vassals and would not allow the Indians to be entirely destroyed in order to gratify the wishes of the Spaniards. If the Indians should die out (and they are dying with terrible rapidity), those realms will very quickly become depopulated, as has already happened in the Antilles, the great province of Venezuela, and the whole coast of northern South America and other very extensive lands that have become depopulated in our time. The wishes of Your Majesty and his Royal Council are well known and are made very plain in the laws that are issued every day in favor of the poor Indians and for their increase and preservation. But these laws are obeyed and not enforced, wherefore there is no end to the destruction of the Indians, nor does anyone care what Your Majesty decrees. How many decrees, cedulas, and letters were sent by our lord, the Emperor, who is in glory, and how many necessary orders are sent by Your Majesty! How little good have all these orders done! Indeed, the more laws and decrees are sent, the worse is the condition of the Indians by reason of the false and sophistical interpretation that the Spanish officials give these laws, twisting their meaning to suit their own purposes. It seems to me that the saying of a certain philosopher well applies to this case: Where there is a plenty of doctors and medicines, there is a plenty of ill health. Just so, where there are many laws and judges, there is much injustice.

We have a multitude of laws, judges, viceroys, governors, *presidentes*, oidores, corregidores, alcaldes mayores, a million lieutenants, and yet another million alguaciles. But this multitude is not what the Indians need, nor will it relieve their misery. Indeed, the more such men there are, the more enemies do the Indians have. For the more zeal these men display against the Indians, the more influence do they wield; the Spaniards call such men Fathers of their Country, saviors of the state, and proclaim them to be very just and upright. The more ill will such men show against the Indians and friars, the more titles and lying encomiums are heaped upon them. But let an official favor the Indians and the religious (who are bound together, one depending upon the other), and this alone suffices to make him odious and abhorrent to all. For the Spaniards care for one thing alone, and that is their advantage; and they give not a rap whether these poor and miserable Indians live or die, though the whole being and welfare of the country depend upon them.

38. HOW BARBAROUS THE BARBARIANS?

Almost from the beginning of the explorations, European thinkers were faced with the problem of grasping the intellectual and moral implications of their confrontations with new civilizations. The initial response (and for long the only significant one) was that these were heathen peoples whom the Europeans had the opportunity, and the duty, to Christianize. However, those thinkers who were to a significant degree out of tune with their own cultures saw it differently. Already by the later 16th century, during the turmoil of the French wars of religion, the French essayist Michel de Montaigne (1533-1592) was developing the attitude now called "cultural relativism," which was in line with his compassionate skepticism, in response to accounts of heathen societies in the New World. The essay "On Cannibalism" is an attempt to understand the practices of barbarians, rather than condemning them offhand.

Michel de Montaigne

On Cannibalism

. . . . .

Now, to return to my subject, I think there is nothing barbarous and savage in that nation, from what I have been told, except that each man calls barbarism whatever is not his own practice; for indeed it seems we have no other test of truth and reason than the example and pattern of the opinions and customs of the country we live in. *There* is always the perfect religion, the perfect government, the perfect and accomplished manners in all things. Those people are wild, just as we call wild the fruits that Nature has produced by herself and in her normal course; whereas really it is those that we have changed artificially and led astray from the common order, that we should rather call wild. The former retain alive and vigorous their genuine, their most useful and natural, virtues and properties, which we have debased in the latter in adapting them to gratify our corrupted taste. And yet for all that, the savor and delicacy of some uncultivated fruits of those countries is quite as excellent, even to our taste, as that of our own. It is not reasonable that art should win the place of honor over our great and powerful mother Nature. We have so overloaded the beauty and richness of her works by our inventions that we have quite smothered her. Yet wherever her purity shines forth, she wonderfully puts to shame our vain and frivolous attempts:

> Ivy comes readier without our care;
> In lonely caves the arbutus grows more fair;
> No art with artless bird song can compare.
>
> PROPERTIUS

All our efforts cannot even succeed in reproducing the nest of the tiniest little bird, its contexture, its beauty and convenience; or even the web of the puny spider. All things, says Plato, are produced by nature, by fortune, or by art; the greatest and most beautiful by one or the other of the first two, the least and most imperfect by the last.

These nations, then, seem to me barbarous in this sense, that they have been fashioned very little by the human mind, and are still very close to their original naturalness. The laws of nature still rule them, very little

---

SOURCE: Reprinted from *The Complete Essays of Montaigne*, translated by Donald M. Frame, with the permission of the publishers, Stanford University Press, pp. 152–59.

corrupted by ours; and they are in such a state of purity that I am sometimes vexed that they were unknown earlier, in the days when there were men able to judge them better than we. I am sorry that Lycurgus and Plato did not know of them; for it seems to me that what we actually see in these nations surpasses not only all the pictures in which poets have idealized the golden age and all their inventions in imagining a happy state of man, but also the conceptions and the very desire of philosophy. They could not imagine a naturalness so pure and simple as we see by experience; nor could they believe that our society could be maintained with so little artifice and human solder. This is a nation, I should say to Plato, in which there is no sort of traffic, no knowledge of letters, no science of numbers, no name for a magistrate or for political superiority, no custom of servitude, no riches or poverty, no contracts, no successions, no partitions, no occupations but leisure ones, no care for any but common kinship, no clothes, no agriculture, no metal, no use of wine or wheat. The very words that signify lying, treachery, dissimulation, avarice, envy, belittling, pardon—unheard of. How far from this perfection would he find the republic that he imagined:

Men fresh sprung from the gods [Seneca].

These manners nature first ordained.

VIRGIL

For the rest, they live in a country with a very pleasant and temperate climate, so that according to my witnesses it is rare to see a sick man there; and they have assured me that they never saw one palsied, bleary-eyed, toothless, or bent with age. They are settled along the sea and shut in on the land side by great high mountains, with a stretch about a hundred leagues wide in between. They have a great abundance of fish and flesh which bear no resemblance to ours, and they eat them with no other artifice than cooking. The first man who rode a horse there, though he had had dealings with them on several other trips, so horrified them in this posture that they shot him dead with arrows before they could recognize him.

Their buildings are very long, with a capacity of two or three hundred souls; they are covered with the bark of great trees, the strips reaching to the ground at one end and supporting and leaning on one another at the top, in the manner of some of our barns, whose covering hangs down to the ground and acts as a side. They have wood so hard that they cut with it and make of it their swords and grills to cook their food. Their beds are of a cotton weave, hung from the roof like those in our ships, each man having his own; for the wives sleep apart from their husbands.

They get up with the sun, and eat immediately upon rising, to last them through the day; for they take no other meal than that one. Like some other Eastern peoples, of whom Suidas tells us, who drank apart from meals, they do not drink then; but they drink several times a day, and to capacity. Their drink is made of some root, and is of the color of our claret wines. They drink it only lukewarm. This beverage keeps only two or three days; it has a slightly sharp taste, is not at all heady, is good for the stomach, and has a laxative effect upon those who are not used to it; it is a very pleasant drink for anyone who is accustomed to it. In place of bread they use a certain white substance like preserved coriander. I have tried it; it tastes sweet and a little flat.

The whole day is spent in dancing. The younger men go to hunt animals with bows. Some of the women busy themselves meanwhile with warming their drink, which is their chief duty. Some one of the old men, in the morning before they begin to eat, preaches to the whole barnful in common, walking from one end to the other, and repeating one single sentence several times until he has completed the circuit (for the buildings are fully a hundred paces long). He recommends to them only two things: valor against the enemy and love for their wives. And they never fail to point out this obligation, as their refrain, that it is their wives who keep their drink warm and seasoned.

There may be seen in several places, including my own house, specimens of their beds, of their ropes, of their wooden swords and the bracelets with which they cover their wrists in combats, and of the big canes, open at one end, by whose sound they keep time in their dances. They are close shaven all over, and shave themselves much more cleanly than we, with nothing but a wooden or stone razor. They believe that souls are immortal, and that those who have deserved well of the gods are lodged in that part of heaven where the sun rises, and the damned in the west.

They have some sort of priests and prophets, but they rarely appear before the people, having their home in the mountains. On their arrival there is a great feast and solemn assembly of several villages—each barn, as I have described it, makes up a village, and they are about one French league from each other. The prophet speaks to them in public, exhorting them to virtue and their duty; but their whole ethical science contains only these two articles: resoluteness in war and affection for their wives. He prophesies to them things to come and the results they are to expect from their undertakings, and urges them to war or holds them back from it; but this is on the condition that when he fails to prophesy correctly, and if things turn out otherwise than he has predicted, he is cut into a thousand pieces if they catch him, and condemned as a false prophet. For this reason, the prophet who has once been mistaken is never seen again.

Divination is a gift of God; that is why its abuse should be punished as imposture. Among the Scythians, when the soothsayers failed to hit the mark, they were laid, chained hand and foot, on carts full of heather and drawn by oxen, on which they were burned. Those who handle matters subject to the control of human capacity are excusable if they do the best they can. But these others, who come and trick us with assurances of an extraordinary faculty that is beyond our ken, should they not be punished for not making good their promise, and for the temerity of their imposture?

They have their wars with the nations beyond the mountains, further inland, to which they go quite naked, with no other arms than bows or wooden swords ending in a sharp point, in the manner of the tongues of our boar spears. It is astonishing what firmness they show in their combats, which never end but in slaughter and bloodshed; for as to routs and terror, they know nothing of either.

Each man brings back as his trophy the head of the enemy he has killed, and sets it up at the entrance to his dwelling. After they have treated their prisoners well for a long time with all the hospitality they can think of, each man who has a prisoner calls a great assembly of his acquaintances. He ties a rope to one of the prisoner's arms, by the end of which he holds him, a few steps away, for fear of being hurt, and gives his dearest friend the other arm to hold in the same way; and these two, in the presence of the whole assembly, kill him with their swords. This done, they roast him and eat him in common and send some pieces to their absent friends. This is not, as people think, for nourishment, as of old the Scythians used to do; it is to betoken an extreme revenge. And the proof of this came when they saw the Portuguese, who had joined forces with their adversaries, inflict a different kind of death on them when they took them prisoner, which was to bury them up to the waist, shoot the rest of their body full of arrows, and afterward hang them. They thought that these people from the other world, being men who had sown the knowledge of many vices among their neighbors and were much greater masters than themselves in every sort of wickedness, did not adopt this sort of vengeance without some reason, and that it must be more painful than their own; so they began to give up their old method and to follow this one.

I am not sorry that we notice the barbarous horror of such acts, but I am heartily sorry that, judging their faults rightly, we should be so blind to our own. I think there is more barbarity in eating a man alive than in eating him dead; and in tearing by tortures and the rack a body still full of feeling, in roasting a man bit by bit, in having him bitten and mangled by dogs and swine (as we have not only read but seen within fresh memory, not among ancient enemies, but among neighbors and fellow citizens, and what is worse, on the pretext of piety and religion), than in roasting and eating him after he is dead.

Indeed, Chrysippus and Zeno, heads of the Stoic sect, thought there was nothing wrong in using our carcasses for any purpose in case of need, and getting nourishment from them; just as our ancestors, when besieged by Caesar in the city of Alesia, resolved to relieve their famine by eating old men, women, and other people useless for fighting.

> The Gascons once, 'tis said, their life renewed
> By eating of such food.
>
> JUVENAL

And physicians do not fear to use human flesh in all sorts of ways for our health, applying it either inwardly or outwardly. But there never was any opinion so disordered as to excuse treachery, disloyalty, tyranny, and cruelty, which are our ordinary vices.

So we may well call these people barbarians, in respect to the rules of reason, but not in respect to ourselves, who surpass them in every kind of barbarity.

Their warfare is wholly noble and generous, and as excusable and beautiful as this human disease can be; its only basis among them is their rivalry in valor. They are not fighting for the conquest of new lands, for they still enjoy that natural abundance that provides them without toil and trouble with all necessary things in such profusion that they have no wish to enlarge their boundaries. They are still in that happy state of desiring only as much as their natural needs demand; anything beyond that is superfluous to them.

They generally call those of the same age, brothers; those who are younger, children; and the old men are fathers to all the others. These leave to their heirs in common the full possession of their property, without division or any other title at all than just the one that Nature gives to her creatures in bringing them into the world.

If their neighbors cross the mountains to attack them and win a victory, the gain of the victor is glory, and the advantage of having proved the master in valor and virtue; for apart from this they have no use for the goods of the vanquished, and they return to their own country, where they lack neither anything necessary nor that great thing, the knowledge of how to enjoy their condition happily and be content with it. These men of ours do the same in their turn. They demand of their prisoners no other ransom than that they confess and acknowledge their defeat. But there is not one in a whole century who does not choose to die rather than to relax a single bit, by word or look, from the grandeur of an invincible courage; not one who would not rather be killed and eaten than so much as ask not to be. They treat them very freely, so that life may be all the dearer to them, and usually entertain them with threats of their coming death, of the torments they will have to suffer, the preparations that are being made for that purpose, the cutting up of their limbs, and the feast that will be made at their expense. All this is done for the sole purpose of extorting from their lips some weak or base word, or making them want to flee, so as to gain the advantage of having terrified them and broken down their firmness. For indeed, if you take it the right way, it is in this point alone that true victory lies:

> It is no victory
> Unless the vanquished foe admits your mastery.
>
> CLAUDIAN

. . . . .

To return to our story. These prisoners are so far from giving in, in spite of all that is done to them, that on the contrary, during the two or three months that they are kept, they wear a gay expression; they urge their captors to hurry and put them to the test; they defy them, insult them, reproach with their cowardice and the number of battles they have lost to the prisoners' own people.

I have a song composed by a prisoner which contains this challenge, that they should all come boldly and gather to dine off him, for they will be eating at the same time their own fathers and grandfathers, who have served to feed and nourish his body. "These muscles," he says, "this flesh and these veins are your own, poor fools that you are. You do not recognize that the substance of your ancestors' limbs is still contained in them. Savor them well; you will find in them the taste of your own flesh." An idea that certainly does not smack of barbarity. Those that paint these people dying, and who show their execution, portray the prisoner spitting in the face of his slayers and scowling at them. Indeed, to the last gasp they never stop braving and defying their enemies by word and look. Truly here are real savages by our standards; for either they must be thoroughly so, or we must be; there is an amazing distance between their character and ours.

The men there have several wives, and the higher their reputation for valor the more wives they have. It is a remarkably beautiful thing about their marriages that the same jealousy our wives have to keep us from the affection and kindness of other women, theirs have to win this for them. Being more concerned for their husbands' honor than for anything else, they strive and scheme to have as many companions as they can, since that is a sign of their husbands' valor.

Our wives will cry "Miracle!" but it is no miracle. It is a properly matrimonial virtue, but one of the highest order. In the Bible, Leah, Rachel, Sarah, and Jacob's wives gave their beautiful handmaids to their husbands; and Livia seconded the appetites of Augustus, to her own disadvantage; and Stratonice, the wife of King Deiotarus, not only lent her husband for his use a very beautiful young chambermaid in her service, but carefully brought up her children, and backed them up to succeed to their father's estates.

And lest it be thought that all this is done through a simple and servile bondage to usage and through the pressure of the authority of their ancient customs, without reasoning or judgment, and because their minds are so stupid that they cannot take any other course, I must cite some examples of their capacity. Besides the warlike song I have just quoted, I have another, a love song, which begins in this vein: "Adder, stay; stay, adder, that from the pattern of your coloring my sister may draw the fashion and the workmanship of a rich girdle that I may give to my love; so may your beauty and your pattern be forever preferred to all other serpents." This first couplet is the refrain of the song. Now I am familiar enough with poetry to be a judge of this: not only is there nothing barbarous in this fancy, but it is altogether Anacreontic. Their language, moreover, is a soft language, with an agreeable sound, somewhat like Greek in its endings.

Three of these men, ignorant of the price they will pay some day, in loss of repose and happiness, for gaining knowledge of the corruptions of this side of the ocean; ignorant also of the fact that of this intercourse will come their ruin (which I suppose is already well advanced: poor wretches, to let themselves be tricked by the desire for new things, and to have left the serenity of their own sky to come and see ours!)—three of these men were at Rouen, at the time the late King Charles IX was there. The king talked to them for a long time; they were shown our ways, our splendor, the aspect of a fine city. After that, someone asked their opinion, and wanted to know what they had found most amazing. They mentioned three things, of which I have forgotten the third, and I am very sorry for it; but I still remember two of them. They said that in the first place they thought it very strange that so many grown men, bearded, strong, and armed, who were around the king (it is likely that they were talking about the Swiss of his guard) should submit to obey a child, and that one of them was not chosen to command instead. Second (they have a way in their language of speaking of men as halves of one another), they had noticed that there were among us men full and gorged with all sorts of good things, and that their other halves were beggars at their doors, emaciated with hunger and poverty; and they thought it strange that these needy halves could endure such an injustice, and did not take the others by the throat, or set fire to their houses.

I had a very long talk with one of them; but I had an interpreter who followed my meaning so badly, and who was so hindered by his stupidity in taking in my ideas, that I could get hardly any satisfaction from the man. When I asked him what profit he gained from his superior position among his people (for he was a captain, and our sailors called him king), he told me that it was to march foremost in war. How many men followed him? He pointed to a piece of ground, to signify as many as such a space could hold; it might have been four or five thousand men. Did all his authority expire with the war? He said that this much remained, that when he visited the villages dependent on him, they made paths for him through the underbrush by which he might pass quite comfortably.

All this is not too bad—but what's the use? They don't wear breeches.

39. THE FRENCH DISCOVERY OF CANADA

During the 16th century, while the Spaniards were extending their conquests and turning them to profit, the French and English engaged in a series of explorations, sometimes spiced with piratical raids upon Spanish settlements. Canada—that is, the valley of the St. Lawrence River—was discovered by a Breton sailor, Jacques Cartier (1491-1557) during three voyages. In 1534 he explored the Gulf of Saint Lawrence, sailed up the river of the same name to the present site of Montreal two years later, and returned in 1541–42 to make an unsuccessful effort to colonize the country. Effective settlement by France was to come only in the next century. Cartier's voyage of 1535 was described in a *Short and Brief Narration of the Navigations to the Islands of Canada*, published in 1545.

Jacques Cartier

Narration of the Navigations to the Islands of Canada

In the yeere of our Lord 1535, upon Whitsunday, being the 16. of May, by the commandement of our Captaine James Cartier, and with a common accord, in the Cathedrall Church of S. Malo we devoutly each one confessed our selves, and received the Sacrament: and all entring into the Quier of the sayd Church, wee presented our selves before the Reverend Father in Christ, the Lord Bishop of S. Malo, who blessed us all, being in his Bishops roabes. The Wednesday following, being the 19. of May, there arose a good gale of wind, and therefore we hoysed sayle with three ships . . .

. . . . .

SOURCE: Henry S. Burrage (ed.), *Early English and French Voyages Chiefly from Hakluyt, 1534–1608* (New York: Charles Scribner's Sons, 1906), pp. 37, 40–42, 58–59.

. . . All this coast is full of shoulds and very dangerous, albeit in sight many good havens seeme to be there, yet is there nought else but shelves and sands. We staied and rested our selves in the sayd haven, until the seventh of August being Sonday: on which day we hoysed sayle, and came toward land on the South side toward Cape Rabast,[1] distant from the sayd haven about twentie leagues Northnortheast, and Southsouthwest: but the next day there rose a stormie and a contrary winde, and because we could find no haven there toward the South, thence we went coasting along toward the North, beyond the abovesayd haven about ten leagues, where we found a goodly great gulfe, full of Islands, passages, and entrances toward what wind soever you please to bend: for the knowledge of this gulfe there is a great Island that is like to a Cape of lande, stretching somewhat further foorth than the others, and about two leagues within the land, there is an hill fashioned as it were an heape of corne.[2] We named the sayd gulfe Saint Laurence his bay.[3] The twelfth of the sayd moneth wee went from the sayd Saint Laurence his Bay, or gulfe, sayling Westward, and discovered a Cape[4] of land toward the South, that runneth West and by South, distant from the sayd Saint Laurence his Bay, about five and twenty leagues. And of the two wilde men which wee tooke in our former voyage, it was tolde us, that this was part of the Southerne coaste, and that there was an Island, on the Southerly parte of which is the way to goe from Honguedo[5] (where the yeere before we had taken them) to Canada, and that two dayes journey from the sayd Cape and Island began the Kingdome of Saguenay, on the North shore extending toward Canada, and about three leagues athwart the sayd Cape, there is above a hundreth fadome water. Moreover I beleeve that there were never so many Whales seen as wee saw that day about the sayd Cape. The next day after being our Ladie day of August the fifteenth of the moneth,[6] having passed the Straight, we had notice of certaine lands that wee left toward the South, which landes are full of very great and high hills, and this Cape wee named The Island of the Assumption,[7] and one Cape of the said high countreys lyeth Eastnortheast, and Westsouthwest, the distance betweene which is about five and twenty leagues. The Countreys lying North may plainely be perceived to be higher then the Southerly, more then thirty leagues in length. We trended the sayd landes about toward the South: from the sayd day untill Tewesday noone following, the winde came West, and therefore wee bended toward the

[1] Cow Point on the island of Anticosti.
[2] Mount St. Genevieve.
[3] Pillage Bay.
[4] North Cape on Anticosti Island.
[5] Gaspe.
[6] The feast of the Assumption of the Virgin Mary.
[7] Anticosti.

North, purposing to goe and see the land that we before had spied. Being arrived there, we found the sayd landes, as it were joyned together, and low toward the Sea. And the Northerly mountains that are upon the sayd low lands stretch East, and West, and a quarter of the South.[8] Our wild men told us that there was the beginning of Saguenay,[9] and that it was land inhabited, and that thence commeth the red Copper, of them named Caignetdaze. There is betweene the Southerly lands and the Northerly about thirty leagues distance, and more than two hundreth fadome depth. The sayd men did moreover certifie unto us, that there was the way and beginning of the great river of Hochelaga[10] and ready way to Canada, which river the further it went the narrower it came, even unto Canada, and that then there was fresh water, which went so farre upwards, that they had never heard of any man who had gone to the head of it, and that there is no other passage but with small boates. Our Captaine hearing their talke, and how they did affirme no other passage to be there, would not at that time proceede any further, till he had seene and noted the other lands, and coast toward the North, which he had omitted to see from S. Laurence his gulfe, because he would know, if between the lands toward the North any passage might be discovered.

. . . . .

Our Captaine the next day very earely in the morning, having very gorgeously attired himselfe, caused all his company to be set in order to go to see the towne and habitation of those people, and a certaine mountaine[11] that is somewhat neere the citie: with whom went also five Gentlemen and twentie Mariners, leaving the rest to keepe and looke to our boates: we tooke with us three men of Hochelaga to bring us to the place. All along as we went we found the way as well beaten and frequented as can be, the fairest and best countrey that possibly can be seene, full of as goodly great Okes as are in any wood in France, under which the ground was all covered over with faire Akornes. After we had gone about foure or five miles, we met by the way one of the chiefest Lords of the citie, accompanied with many moe, who so soone as he sawe us beckned and made signes upon us, that we must rest us in that place where they had made a great fire, and so we did. After that we had rested our selves there a while, the said Lord began to make a long discourse, even as we have saide above, they are accustomed to doe in signe of mirth and friendship, shewing our Captaine and all his company a joyfull countenance, and good will, who gave him two hatchets, a paire of knives and

---

[8] High lands on the north side of the river near Cape des Monts.

[9] The country westward from the river of that name.

[10] St. Lawrence.

[11] Mont Royal as below, whence the name Montreal. Hochelaga stood near the present site of Montreal.

a crosse which he made him to kisse, and then put it about his necke, for which he gave our Captaine heartie thankes. This done, we went along, and about a mile and a halfe farther, we began to finde goodly and large fieldes, full of such corne as the countrie yeeldieth. It is even as the Millet of Bresil, as great and somewhat bigger than small peason, wherewith they live even as we doe with ours. In the midst of those fields is the citie of Hochelaga, placed neere, and as it were joyned to a great mountaine that is tilled round about, very fertill, on the top of which you may see very farre, we named it Mount Roiall.

40. COLONIES, THE GIFT OF GOD

The enterprises of exploration and colonialization were spurred by a variety of motives, but one almost invariable reason cited in an age as passionately religious as the 16th century was the service of God. To bring Christianity and salvation to heathens seemed to Europeans a worthy cause, one which it was only fitting should be rewarded by commerical advantages. Rivalries among nations also played a role, and each nation that ventured across the oceans was sure that it was doing God's work by enhancing its own power.

With such notions, how could success be seen as anything but God's grace, a gift to the nation of His choice? This is the tone of the introductory paragraphs of the *Voyage of Sir Humphrey Gilbert, Knight, 1583,* by Edward Haies. Sir Humphrey Gilbert (c. 1539-1583) served as a military commander in Ireland and the Netherlands before attempting two voyages to the Americas in quest of the Northwest Passage to the Far East. An unsuccessful voyage in 1578–79 was followed by another in 1583, during which an English colony was founded at what is now Saint John's, Newfoundland. Gilbert was lost on the return journey; Haies, aboard one of the other ships, returned safely.

Edward Haies

Sir Humphrey Gilbert's Voyage to America

VOYAGE OF SIR HUMFREY GILBERT KNIGHT, 1583

A report of the voyage and successe thereof, attempted in the yeere of our Lord 1583 by sir Humfrey Gilbert knight, with other gentlemen assisting him in that action,

---

SOURCE: Henry S. Burrage (ed.), *Early English and French Voyages, Chiefly from Hakluyt, 1534–1608* (New York: Charles Scribner's Sons, 1906), pp. 179–82.

intended to discover and to plant Christian inhabitants in place convenient, upon those large and ample countreys extended Northward from the cape of Florida, lying under very temperate Climes, esteemed fertile and rich in Minerals, yet not in the actuall possession of any Christian prince, written by M. Edward Haies gentleman, and principall actour in the same voyage, who alone continued unto the end, and by Gods speciall assistance returned home with his retinue safe and entire.

Many voyages have bene pretended, yet hitherto never any thorowly accomplished by our nation of exact discovery into the bowels of those maine, ample and vast countreys, extended infinitely into the North from 30 degrees, or rather from 25 degrees of Septentrionall [Northern] latitude, neither hath a right way bene taken of planting a Christian habitation and regiment [government] upon the same, as well may appeare both by the little we yet do actually possesse therein, and by our ignorance of the riches and secrets within those lands, which unto this day we know chiefly by the travell and report of other nations, and most of the French, who albeit they can not challenge such right and interest unto the sayd countreys as we, neither these many yeeres have had opportunity nor meanes so great to discover and to plant (being vexed with the calamnities of intestine warres) as we have had by the inestimable benefit of our long and happy peace: yet have they both waies performed more, and had long since attained a sure possession and setled government of many provinces in those Northerly parts of America, if their many attempts into those forren and remote lands had not bene impeached by their garboils at home.

The first discovery of these coasts (never heard of before) was well begun by John Cabot the father, and Sebastian his sonne, an Englishman borne, who were the first finders out of all that great tract of land stretching from the cape of Florida unto those Islands which we now call the Newfoundland: all which they brought and annexed unto the crowne of England. Since when, if with like diligence the search of inland countreys had bene followed, as the discovery upon the coast, and out-parts therof was performed by those two men: no doubt her Majesties territories and revenue had bene mightily inlarged and advanced by this day. And which is more: the seed of Christian religion had bene sowed amongst those pagans, which by this time might have brought foorth a most plentifull harvest and copious congregation of Christians; which must be the chiefe intent of such as shall make any attempt that way: or els whatsoever is builded upon other foundation shall never obtaine happy successe nor continuance.

And although we can not precisely judge (which onely belongeth to God) what have bene the humours of men stirred up to great attempts of discovering and planting in those remote countreys, yet the events do shew that either Gods cause hath not bene chiefly preferred by them, or els God hath not permitted so abundant grace as the light of his word and knowledge of him to be yet revealed unto those infidels before the appointed time.

But most assuredly, the only cause of religion hitherto hath kept backe, and will also bring forward at the time assigned by God, an effectuall and compleat discovery and possession by Christians both of those ample countreys and the riches within them hitherto concealed: whereof notwithstanding God in his wisdome hath permitted to be revealed from time to time a certaine obscure and misty knowledge, by little and little to allure the mindes of men that way (which els will be dull enough in the zeale of his cause) and thereby to prepare us unto a readinesse for the execution of his will against the due time ordeined, of calling those pagans unto Christianity.

In the meane while, it behooveth every man of great calling, in whom is any instinct of inclination unto this attempt, to examine his owne motions: which if the same proceed of ambition or avarice, he may assure himselfe it commeth not of God, and therefore can not have confidence of Gods protection and assistance against the violence (els irresistable) both of sea, and infinite perils upon the land; whom God yet may use an instrument to further his cause and glory some way, but not to build upon so bad a foundation.

Otherwise, if his motives be derived from a vertuous and heroycall minde, preferring chiefly the honour of God, compassion of poore infidels captived by the devill, tyrannizing in most woonderfull and dreadfull maner over their bodies and soules; advancement of his honest and well disposed countreymen, willing to accompany him in such honourable actions: reliefe of sundry people within this realme distressed: all these be honourable purposes, imitating the nature of the munificent God, wherwith he is well pleased, who will assist such an actour beyond expectation of man. And the same, who feeleth this inclination in himselfe, by all likelihood may hope, or rather confidently repose in the preordinance of God, that in this last age of the world (or likely never) the time is compleat of receiving also these Gentiles into his mercy, and that God will raise him an instrument to effect the same: it seeming probable by event of precedent attempts made by the Spanyards and French sundry times, that the countreys lying North of Florida, God hath reserved the same to be reduced unto Christian civility by the English nation. For not long after that Christopher Columbus had discovered the Islands and continent of the West Indies for Spaine, John and Sebastian Cabot made discovery also of the rest from Florida Northwards to the behoofe of England.

And whensoever afterwards the Spanyards (very prosperous in all their Southerne discoveries) did attempt any thing into Florida and those regions inclining towards the North they proved most unhappy, and were at length discouraged utterly by the hard and lamentable successe of many both religious and valiant in armes, endevouring to bring those Northerly regions also under the Spanish jurisdiction; as if God had prescribed limits unto the Spanish nation which they might not exceed; as by their owne gests recorded may be aptly gathered.

41. AUTHORITY TO COLONIZE

Gilbert's half-brother, Sir Walter Raleigh (c.1552-1618), who had accompanied him on his first quasi-piratical voyage of 1578–79, took up the challenge of colonization after Gilbert's death. He was granted "letters patent" by Queen Elizabeth I on March 25, 1584, authorizing him to organize expeditions to seize and settle "heathen and barbarous" lands not yet claimed or inhabited by other European peoples. Seven voyages of exploration with an eye to colonization were organized under this authority between 1584 and 1590. To the territory north of the Spanish possessions of Mexico Raleigh gave the name "Virginia," in honor of the queen. Attempted settlements on Roanoke Island failed, with one body of colonizers returning to England and the other disappearing. The powers and limitations imposed upon such efforts at private colonization under public authority are illustrated by the letters patent, to Raleigh, dated March 25, 1584, as reprinted below.

Letters Patent to Walter Raleigh

Elizabeth by the grace of God &c To all people to whome thes p*re*sent*es* shall come greting Know yee that of our especiall grace c*er*teyne science and meere mocyon [motion] We haue gyuen [given] and graunted and by thes p*re*sent*es* for vs our heyres and successors doe geve and graunte to our trusty and welbeloved servaunte Walter Raleighe Esquier and to his heyres and assignes for ever free lib*er*ty and license from tyme to tyme and at all tymes for ever hereafter to discover search fynde out and viewe such remote heathen and barbarous landes Contries and territories not actually possessed of any Christian Prynce and inhabited by Christian people as to him his heyres and assignes and to every or any of them shall seme good and the same to haue holde occupy and enioye [enjoy] to him his heyres and assignes for ever with all p*re*rogataves comodities iurisdic-

SOURCE: David Beers Quinn (ed.), *The Roanoke Voyages, 1584–1590* (London, England: The Hakluyt Society, 1955), Vol. I, pp. 82–84.

cions and royalties priviledges Fraunchises and p*re*eminenc*es* there or thereabout*es* bothe by sea and lande what so ever we by our l*ett*res patent*es* may grante and as we or any of our noble Progenitors haue heretofore graunted to any p*er*son or p*er*sons bodies politique or corporate And the said Walter Raleigh his heyres and assignes and all such as from tyme to tyme by license of vs our heyres and successors shall goe or travell thither to inhabite or remayne there to buylde and fortifye at the discresyon of the said Walter Raleighe his heyres and assignes the statutes or actes of Parliamente made againste fugityues [fugitives] or against such as shall departe remayne or contynue out of our Realme of England without lycense or any other Acte statute lawe or ordinaunce whatsoever to the contrary in any wise notwithstanding And we doe likewise by thes p*re*sent*es* of our grace especiall meere moc*i*on and c*er*teyne knowledge for vs our heyres and successors, gyve and graunte full authority lib*er*ty and power to the said Walter Raleighe his heyres and assignes and every of them That he and they and every or any of them shall and maye at all and every tyme and tymes hereafter haue take and leade in the sayde voyages to travell thitherward or to inhabite there with him or them and every or any of them such and so many of our subiect*es* as shall willingly accompany him and them and them [*sic*] and every or any of them to whome also by these p*re*sent*es* we doe gyue full lib*er*ty Power and aucthority in that behalf and also to haue take employ and vse sufficient shippyng and furniture for theire transportac*i*ons and Nauigac*i*ons in that behalf so that none of the same p*er*sons nor any of them be such as hereafter shalbe restreyned by vs our heyres or successors And further that he the said Walter Raleighe his heyres and assignes and every of them shall haue holde occupy and enioye to him his heyres and assignes and every of them for ever all the soyle of all such landes Countryes and t*er*ritories so to be discovered or possessed as aforesaid and of all Cittyes Castles townes villages and places in the same with the right*es* royalities francheses and Iurisdicc*i*ons as well maryne as other within the sayd landes or Countryes or the seas therevnto adioyning to be had or vsed with full power to dispose therof and of every p*ar*te in fee simple or otherwise according to the order of the lawes of England as nere as the same conveniently may be at his and theire will and plesure to any p*er*son then beyng or that shall remayne within the allegiance of vs our heires and successors Reseruing alwayes to vs our heyres and successors for all s*er*uices dueties and demaundes the fifte parte of all the owre of Gold and silver that from tyme to tyme and at all tymes after such discovery subduyng and possessing shal be there gotten or obteyned All which landes Countreys and territories shall for ever be holden by the said Walter Raleigh his heyres and assignes of vs our heyres and successors by homage and by the said paymente of the said fifte parte before reserued onely for all s*er*uices . . . .

CHAPTER V

THE POLITICS OF EUROPE: THE SIXTEENTH CENTURY

DURING THE 16TH CENTURY a process that had been begun at the height of the Middle Ages—the creation of sovereign territorial states to replace the feudal order—was continued in the political system of Europe. But the emergence of a clear concept of sovereignty and the development of sole dominion over a given country by no means solved another central problem of politics. This problem was the relation of the ruler and the ruled. Much as it was taken for granted in political theory that governments existed for the benefit of those they ruled, the rulers saw to their own welfare just as the people sought advantage in the activity of the state.

These were the issues fought over and debated during the century of the Reformation, in the setting of religious struggles that whipped up passions and made savagery seem a godly deed. In the course of these conflicts, however, political life moved along the path of modernization. Institutions were developed and created that would be of service centuries later, and ideas were put forward and examined that would feed future political debates. All in all, the result of this ferment was more an inner transformation of the medieval political order in the triumph of some elements over others than a new creation.

42. A KING FALLS, A KING RISES

The reality of political life in the 16th century was as truly mirrored in the Biblical dictum that those who lived by the sword would die by it as in Machiavelli's teachings of victory by any means. "Revolution" at that time meant the turning of the wheel of fortune. One of the most dramatic of such "revolutions" was the Battle of Bosworth Field in England in 1485, in which King Richard III was defeated by Henry, Earl of Richmond, who as Henry VII founded the Tudor dynasty that reigned in England for a little more than a century. The battle, characteristic of late medieval warfare before combat was dominated by firearms, was described by Polydore Vergil (c.1470-c.1555) in his *Anglica Historia* ("English History") of 1534. Vergil, an Italian-born ecclesiastic, came to England in 1502 as a papal official; his abilities as a Renaissance humanist and historian led the Tudor kings to invite him to remain in their service. This selection from the *English History* is a modernized version of an English translation made about 1540.

Polydore Vergil

The Battle of Bosworth, 1485

In the mean time King Richard, hearing that the enemy drew near, came first to the place of fight, a little beyond Leicester (the name of that village is Bosworth), and there, pitching his tents, refreshed his soldiers that night from their travails, and with many words exhorted them to the fight to come. It is reported that King Richard had that night a terrible dream; for he thought in his sleep that he saw horrible images as it were of evil spirits hovering clearly about him, as it were before his eyes, and that they would not let him rest . . . his heart told him upon this that the result of the following battle would be grievous, and he did not buckle himself to the conflict with such liveliness of courage and countenance as before. . . . But I believe it was no dream but a conscience guilty of heinous offences. . . . The next day afterwards King Richard, furnished thoroughly with all manner of things, drew his whole host out of their tents, and arrayed his vanguard, stretching it forth of a wondrous length . . . and in the front were placed his archers . . . of these archers he made John Duke of Norfolk the leader. After this long vanguard followed the king himself with a choice force of soldiers. In the mean

---

SOURCE: From *English Historical Documents, Volume 4, 1327-1485*, edited by A. R. Myers, pp. 345–47. © 1969 Eyre & Spottiswoode. Reprinted by permission of Oxford University Press, Inc.

time Henry, having returned from the conference with his friends, began to take better heart, and without any delay encamped himself near his enemies, where he rested all night, and early in the morning commanded the soldiers to arm themselves, sending as well to Thomas Stanley, who had now approached the place of fight, as in the mid-way between the two battles, that he would come with his forces. . . . He made a slender vanguard for the small number of his people; before the same he placed archers, of whom he made captain John, Earl of Oxford; in the right wing of the vanguard he placed Gilbert Talbot to defend the same; on the left truly he set John Savage; and himself, trusting to the aid of Thomas Stanley, did follow with one troop of horsemen, and a few footmen; for the number of all his soldiers, altogether, was scarcely 5,000, besides the Stanleyans, of whom about 3,000 were at the battle, under the conduct of William. The king's forces were twice as many and more. . . . There was a marsh between both hosts, which Henry purposely left on the right hand, that it might serve his men instead of a fortress; by doing this he left the sun upon his back; but when the king saw the enemies past the marsh, he commended his soldiers to charge against them. They made suddenly great shouts and assaulted the enemy first with arrows; their foes were not at all loath to fight and began also to shoot fiercely; but when they came to hand strokes the matter then was dealt with by blades. . . . While the battle continued thus hot on both sides between the vanguards, King Richard understood . . . when Earl Henry was afar off with a small force of soldiers about him; then after drawing nearer he knew it perfectly by evident signs and tokens that it was Henry. Wherefore, all inflamed with ire, he struck his horse with the spurs, and ran against him out of his own army ahead of the vanguard. . . . King Richard at the first brunt killed some men, overthrew Henry's standard, together with William Brandon the standard bearer. Then he matched himself against John Cheney, a man of much strength, far exceeding the common sort, who strove with him as he came; but the king with great force drove him to the ground, making way with his weapon on every side. But yet Henry abode the brunt longer than even his own soldiers would have thought, who were now almost out of hope of victory, when suddenly William Stanley with 3,000 men came to the rescue. Then truly in a moment the remainder all fled, and King Richard was killed fighting manfully in the thickest press of his enemies. In the mean time also the Earl of Oxford after a little skirmishing put to flight those who fought in the van, whereof a great company were killed in the chase. But many more forbore to fight, who came to the field with King Richard for awe, and for no goodwill, and departed without any danger, as men who desired not the safety but destruction of that prince whom they hated. There were about 1,000 men killed, and amongst them of warrior noblemen were John, Duke of Norfolk, "Gwalter L. Ferryse" (Walter, Lord Ferrers of Chartley), Robert Brackenbury, Richard Radcliffe, and many more. . . . And of those who took to their feet Francis Lovell, Humphrey Stafford, with Thomas his brother and much more company, fled into the sanctuary of St. John, which is at Colchester. . . . As for the number of captives it was very great . . . amongst them the chief were Henry, Earl of Northumberland, and Thomas, Earl of Surrey. The latter was committed to prison, where he long remained; the former as a friend at heart was received unto favour. Henry lost in that battle scarcely a hundred soldiers, amongst whom there was one principal man, William Brandon, who bore Earl Henry's standard. . . .

The report is that King Richard might have sought to save himself by flight; but he . . . is said to have answered that that very day he would make an end either of war or of life, such great fierceness and such huge force of mind he had; wherefore, knowing certainly that that day would either yield him a peaceable and quiet reign thenceforth or else perpetually bereave him of the same, he came to the field with a crown upon his head, that thereby he might either make a beginning or end of his reign.

After the victory was obtained, Henry gave forthwith thanks unto Almighty God for the same; then afterwards . . . the soldiers cried "God save King Henry, God save King Henry" and with heart and hand uttered all the show of joy that might be; which, when Thomas Stanley did see, he at once set King Richard's crown, which was found among the spoil in the field, upon his head. . . . After that . . . Henry with his victorious army proceeded in the evening to Leicester where, for refreshing of his soldiers from their travail and pains, and to prepare for going to London he tarried two days.

In the mean time the body of King Richard, naked of all clothing, and laid upon a horse's back, with the arms and legs hanging down on both sides, was brought to the abbey of Franciscan monks [*sic*] at Leicester, a miserable spectacle in good truth, but not unworthy for the man's life, and was buried there two days afterwards without any pomp or solemn funeral. He reigned two years and so many months and one day over. He was little of stature, deformed of body, the one shoulder being higher than the other, with a curt and sour countenance, which seemed to savour of mischief, and manifested clearly craft and deceit. While he was thinking of any matter, he did continually bite his nether lip, as though that cruel nature of his did so rage against itself in that little carcase. Also he was wont to be ever with his right hand pulling out of the sheath to the middle, and putting in again, the dagger which he did always wear. Truly he had a sharp wit, cautious and subtle, apt both to counterfeit and dissemble; his courage also high and fierce, which failed him not in the very death. When his men forsook him, he preferred rather to take death with the sword, than by foul flight to prolong his life, uncertain what death perchance soon afterwards to suffer by sickness or other violence.

43. THE PEASANTS' REVOLT IN GERMANY

In addition to wars among states and between ruling groups in each country, another ever-present threat, as it had been for centuries, was rebellion of the lower classes. The most important of such risings in the 16th century was the great revolt of the peasantry that began in southwestern Germany in 1524–25 and eventually shook the entire country to its foundations. Much as it was inspired by Lutheran preachings, it was only to a limited extent a religious movement. Its principal targets were the abuses of the manorial system and the continuation of the institution of serfdom, as can be seen from the key clauses (reprinted below) of the Twelve Articles into which the peasants put their demands. The revolt was put down with fierce violence by the rulers.

Demands of The Peasants, 1524

The First Article. First, it is our humble petition and desire, as also our will and resolution, that in the future we should have power and authority so that each community should choose and appoint a pastor, and that we should have the right to depose him should he conduct himself improperly. The pastor thus chosen should teach us the Gospel pure and simple, without any addition, doctrine or ordinance of man. For to teach us continually the true faith will lead us to pray God that through his grace this faith may increase within us and become a part of us. For if his grace work not within us we remain flesh and blood, which availeth nothing; since the Scripture clearly teaches that only through true faith can we come to God. Only through his mercy can we become holy. Hence such a guide and pastor is necessary, and in this fashion grounded upon the Scriptures.

The Second Article. According as the just tithe is established by the Old Testament and fulfilled in the New, we are ready and willing to pay the fair tithe of grain. The word of God plainly provides that in giving according to right to God and distributing to his people the services of

---

SOURCE: Department of History, University of Pennsylvania, *Translations and Reprints from the Original Sources of European History* (Philadelphia: University of Pennsylvania Press, n.d.), Vol. II, pp. 26–29. Reprinted by permission of University of Pennsylvania Press.

a pastor are required. We will that for the future our church provost, whomsoever the community may appoint, shall gather and receive this tithe. From this he shall give to the pastor, elected by the whole community, a decent and sufficient maintenance for him and his (*im und den seynen*), as shall seem right to the whole community [*or*, with the knowledge of the community]. What remains over shall be given to the poor of the place, as the circumstances and the general opinion demand. Should anything farther remain, let it be kept, lest anyone should have to leave the country from poverty. Provision should also be made from this surplus to avoid laying any land tax on the poor. In case one or more villages have themselves sold their tithes on account of want, and the village has taken action as a whole, the buyer should not suffer loss, but we will that some proper agreement be reached with him for the repayment of the sum by the village with due interest. But those who have tithes which they have not purchased from a village, but which were appropriated by their ancestors, should not, and ought not, to be paid anything farther by the village, which shall apply its tithes to the support of the pastors elected as above indicated, or to solace the poor, as is taught by the Scriptures. The small tithes, whether ecclesiastical or lay, we will not pay at all, for the Lord God created cattle for the free use of man. We will not, therefore, pay farther an unseemly tithe which is of man's invention.

The Third Article. It has been the custom hitherto for men to hold us as their own property, which is pitiable enough, considering that Christ has delivered and redeemed us all, without exception, by the shedding of his precious blood, the lowly as well as the great. Accordingly, it is consistent with Scripture that we should be free and wish to be so. Not that we would wish to be absolutely free and under no authority. God does not teach us that we should lead a disorderly life in the lusts of the flesh, but that we should love the Lord our God and our neighbor. We would gladly observe all this as God has commanded us in the celebration of the communion. He has not commanded us not to obey the authorities, but rather that we should be humble, not only towards those in authority, but towards everyone. We are thus ready to yield obedience according to God's law to our elected and regular authorities in all proper things becoming to a Christian. We, therefore, take it for granted that you will release us from serfdom, as true Christians, unless it should be shown us from the Gospel that we are serfs.

The Fourth Article. In the fourth place it has been the custom heretofore, that no poor man should be allowed to touch venison or wild fowl, or fish in flowing water, which seems to us quite unseemly and unbrotherly, as well as selfish and not agreeable to the word of God. In some places the authorities preserve the game to our great annoyance and loss, recklessly permitting the unreasoning animals to destroy to no purpose our crops, which God suffers to grow for the use of man, and yet we must remain quiet. This is neither godly nor neighborly. For when God created man he gave him dominion over all the animals, over the birds of the air and over the fish in the water. Accordingly it is our desire if a man holds possession of waters that he should prove from satisfactory documents that his right has been unwittingly acquired by purchase. We do not wish to take it from him by force, but his rights should be exercised in a Christian and brotherly fashion. But whosoever cannot produce such evidence should surrender his claim with good grace.

The Fifth Article. In the fifth place we are aggrieved in the matter of wood-cutting, for the noble folk have appropriated all the woods to themselves alone. If a poor man requires wood he must pay double for it, [*or perhaps,* two pieces of money]. It is our opinion in regard to a wood which has fallen into the hands of a lord, whether spiritual or temporal, that unless it was duly purchased it should revert again to the community. It should, moreover, be free to every member of the community to help himself to such firewood as he needs in his own home. Also, if a man requires wood for carpenter's purposes he should have it free, but with the knowledge of a person appointed by the community for that purpose. Should, however, no such forest be at the disposal of the community, let that which has been duly bought be administered in a brotherly and Christian manner. If the forest, although unfairly appropriated in the first instance, was later duly sold, let the matter be adjusted in a friendly spirit and according to the Scriptures.

The Sixth Article. Our sixth complaint is in regard to the excessive services demanded of us, which are increased from day to day. We ask that this matter be properly looked into so that we shall not continue to be oppressed in this way, and that some gracious consideration be given us, since our forefathers were required only to serve according to the word of God.

The Seventh Article. Seventh, we will not hereafter allow ourselves to be farther oppressed by our lords, but will let them demand only what is just and proper according to the word of the agreement between the lord and the peasant. The lord should no longer try to force more services or other dues from the peasant without payment, but permit the peasant to enjoy his holding in peace and quiet. The peasant should, however, help the lord when it is necessary, and at proper times, when it will not be disadvantageous to the peasant, and for a suitable payment.

The Eighth Article. In the eighth place, we are greatly burdened by holdings which cannot support the rent exacted from them. The peasants suffer loss in this way and are ruined; and we ask that the lords may appoint persons of honor to inspect these holdings, and fix a rent in accordance with justice, so that the peasant shall not work for nothing, since the laborer is worthy of his hire.

The Ninth Article. In the ninth place, we are burdened with a great evil in the constant making of new laws. We are not judged according to the offence, but sometimes with great ill will, and sometimes much too leniently. In our opinion we should be judged according to the old written law, so that the case shall be decided according to its merits, and not with partiality.

The Tenth Article. In the tenth place, we are aggrieved by the appropriation by individuals of meadows and fields which at one time belonged to a community. These we will take again into our own hands. It may, however, happen that the land was rightfully purchased, but when the land has unfortunately been purchased in this way, some brotherly arrangement should be made according to circumstances.

The Eleventh Article. In the eleventh place we will entirely abolish the due called *Todfall* [*i.e.*, heriot], and will no longer endure it, nor allow widows and orphans to be thus shamefully robbed against God's will, and in violation of justice and right, as has been done in many places, and by those who should shield and protect them. These have disgraced and despoiled us, and although they had little authority they assumed it. God will suffer this no more, but it shall be wholly done away with, and for the future no man shall be bound to give little or much.

44. ABSOLUTE VERSUS LIMITED MONARCHY AT THE END OF THE MIDDLE AGES

The Middle Ages had been a time of frequent violence and disputes over power, but the distribution of political authority among a multitude of ruling persons and bodies which characterized feudalism had largely thwarted the concentration of effective force or acknowledgement of the right to rule in any single person—emperor, king, or other "prince." The notion of sovereignty (the right to rule without being ruled) was slowly taking shape, usually in the form of rejection of papal overlordship in secular principalities. But the notion that one prince could legitimately hold all political power in his hand as an absolute ruler, that is, with undivided and undistributed sovereignty, was still strange to a world where feudalism was far from dead. Even monarchical rule was usually shared with assemblies of "estates," or economic-social orders, within the realm. The English Parliament was one of the most celebrated of these.

A distinguished English jurist, Sir John Fortescue (c. 1394–c. 1476), contrasted the government of France, where the king claimed all power and many lawyers defended his claim, with the government of England. He called the first "royal dominion," which a later age would designate as absolute monarchy, and the second "political and royal dominion," or limited monarchy. ("Dominion" here means simply "rule.") The following selection is taken from Fortescue's *The Governance of England,* which was first printed in 1714.

Sir John Fortescue

The Governance of England

. . . . .

There are two kinds of kingdoms, one of which is a lordship called in Latin *dominium regale*[1] and the other is called *dominium politicum et regale.*[2] And they differ in that the first king may rule his people by such laws as he makes himself, and therefore he may set upon them tallies and other impositions, such as he wills himself, without their assent. The second king may not rule his people by other laws than such as they assent unto, and therefore he may set upon them no impositions without their own assent. . . .

And why is it that the French king reigns upon his people *dominio regali,*[3] yet Saint Louis,[4] sometimes king there, and his progenitors never set tallies or other imposition upon the people of that land without the assent of the three estates, which when they are assembled are like the court of the parliament in England. And many of his successors kept this order into recent times, when the English waged such war in France that the three estates dare not come together. Then, for that reason and because of the great necessity which the French king had of means for the defense of that land, he took upon him to set tallies and other impositions upon the commons without the assent of the three estates, but he would not and did not set any such charge upon the nobles for fear of rebellion. And because the commons there, though they have complained, have not rebelled and are not so bold as to rebel, the French kings have yearly set such charges upon them and so augmented the same charges that the same commons are so impoverished and destroyed that they cannot live. They drink water, they eat apples, with bread right brown made of rye; they eat no flesh except quite seldom a little pork

---

SOURCE: Sir John Fortescue, *The Governance of England,* edited by Charles Plummer 1885 (Oxford, England: Oxford University Press, 1926), pp. 109, 113–15. The text has been modernized. Reprinted by permission of The Clarendon Press, Oxford.

[1] Royal dominion.

[2] Political and royal dominion.

[3] By means of royal dominion.

[4] Louis IX of France.

or the entrails and heads of beasts slain for the nobles and merchants of the land. They wear no woollen except a poor coat under their outermost garments made of heavy canvas and called a frock. Their hose are of the same canvas and do not pass their knees, for which reason they wear garters and their thighs are bare. Their wives and children go barefoot; they cannot live in any other way. For some of them, who were wont to pay a rent to the lord of a crown a year, now pay to the king over that five crowns. As a result they are compelled by necessity to watch, labor, and grub in the ground for their sustenance, their nature is wasted, and their families brought to nought. They go crooked and are feeble, not able to fight or to defend the realm; nor do they have weapons or the money to buy weapons. But in truth they live in the most extreme poverty and misery and yet they dwell in the most fertile realm of the world. As a consequence the French king does not have men of his own able to defend it except his nobles, who do not carry such impositions, and therefore they are quite able-bodied. This is the reason why the king of France is compelled to recruit his armies and retinues for defense of his country from foreigners, such as the Scots, Aragonese, Germans and men of other nations; for otherwise all his enemies might overrun him, as he has no defense of his own except his castles and fortresses. As we see, this is the fruit of his *Jus regale*.[5]

If the realm of England, which is an isle and therefore cannot easily obtain assistance from other countries, were ruled by a prince of this kind, it would become a prey to all other nations that would conquer, rob and devour it. This was well proved in the time of the Britons, when the Scots and the Picts so beat and oppressed this land, that the people thereof sought help of the Romans to whom they had been tributary. And when they could not be defended by them, they sought help of the Duke of Brittany (or little Britain) and accepted his brother Constantine as their king. And he was therefore made king here and reigned many years, and his children after him, of which Arthur the Great was one of their issue. But blessed by God, this land is ruled under a better law, and therefore its people are not in such penury nor damaged in their persons as a result, but they are prosperous and have all things necessary to the sustenance of nature. As a result they are powerful and able to resist the adversaries of this realm, and to defeat other realms that do or would do them wrong. As we see, this is the fruit of *Jus politicum et regale*[6] under which we live.

---

[5] Royal law.
[6] Political and royal law.

45. THE FRENCH MONARCHY PRAISED

French jurists saw the royal power in their country with a somewhat different eye than their English counterparts did. They had battled in earlier centuries with all the skill of their pens against papal suzerainty over France, and they proclaimed that the king was truly "emperor"—independent and sovereign—in his own realm. Yet they did not see his power as "totally absolute," a form of rule they found embodied only in Eastern despotisms. Not only did the king of France reign by a law of fixed succession, but curbs existed to prevent arbitrary and evil government. These curbs were France's religion, a passionate Roman Catholicism; her judicial system; and her "political order," the fundamental laws that even the kings obeyed.

Claude de Seyssel (c.1450-1520), a Savoyard-born jurist, diplomat, and historian, spent almost all of his career in the service of Charles VIII and Louis XII of France and was rewarded with the bishopric of Marseille. After the accession of Francis I in 1515, he returned to Turin as archbishop (1517). His *Great Monarchy of France*, written during his final years in France and published in 1519, was the outstanding treatise on French government in the early 16th century. Unlike Fortescue, he did not see the Estates General or the provincial Estates, which continued to exist in France, as the principal force working against royal tyranny. The French assemblies, particularly the national body, did not meet regularly and had not acquired the central role in taxation and legislation that had been won by the English Parliament. The "Parlements" referred to in this selection were law courts, not representative assemblies.

Claude de Seyssel

The Great Monarchy of France

. . . . .

But the Monarchy of France would have nothing distinctive to set it above the other kingdoms and monarchical states which are governed in the same way if it did not have some special characteristics; and nonetheless I wish to show that the Monarchy of France is governed in a better way than any other of which we have knowledge to date or of which we may have memory through ancient history, so that it is able not only to endure for a long time and to preserve and maintain itself but also to prosper and to achieve greater power and domination, and even to cor-

---

SOURCE: Claude de Seyssel, *La monarchie de France et deux autres fragments politiques*, edited by Jacques Poujol (Paris: Librairie d'Argences, 1961), pp. 112–19. Translated by Herbert H. Rowen. Reprinted by permission of the publisher.

rect those imperfections which it has—of which I shall speak later—as a thing easy to do when the Prince and Monarch will wish to.

Why it is good that the Kingdom should pass by masculine succession

The first characteristic which I find good in it is that this kingdom passes by masculine succession and cannot fall into the hands of a woman, according to what the French call the "Salic" law, which is a very good thing. For, if it were to pass by feminine succession, it can come into the hands and power of a man of foreign nation, which is a pernicious and dangerous thing; but he who comes from a foreign nation has been differently nourished and brought up, has different manners, language and way of life from those of the country to which he comes to rule. And he usually wishes to promote those of his own nation and grant them the greatest and principal authority in the management of affairs, and to give them greater preference in honors and profits, for he always bears them more love and confidence and follows their manners and condition more than those of the country to which he has newly come. From this there always results envy and dissension between the people of the country and the foreigners, and indignation against the princes, as we have often seen in our experience and still see every day. Therefore, when the succession is from male to male, the heir is always certain and remains of the same blood as those who ruled before. By this the subjects all have such love and reverence for them as they do not have for the others, which does not falter nor feel any scruple, so that they address themselves to the new king as soon as the former has died, even when he is a distant relation and there are daughters by the former king, without any change or difficulty arising, as we saw at the death of the late kings Charles VIII and Louis XII. And although there were in former times great debates and quarrels on such occasions (from which followed great wars, persecutions and desolation of the kingdom), it was nonetheless more by other causes (under cover of such quarrels, although they were known to be frivolous and unfounded) than for good reasons. And matters finally came out right and were so established that there can never be any more a quarrel or difficulty on this account. And I have included, in describing this Monarchy, the state of France as it is at present, joining the ancient laws, customs and observances with the new and most recent.

How the authority and power of the King is controlled and curbed in France by three bridles

There is another thing which I consider to be most important for the preservation and increase of this Monarchy, which is that the House and all its members are controlled by such good order that it can fall into dissension only with difficulty, at least until—by the will of God and the common course of Nature which can neither create nor produce any everlasting thing which is not subject to corruption and change—it has reached the time of its fall and dissolution: which is necessary sooner or later as we have said of all others. But just as mortal men live longer and in better health when they have a better complexion and live a better way, so Lordships and States which are better established and governed maintain themselves longer and better. And to explain more clearly what I mean by this Governance of France, I assume that the greatest danger for monarchical states of falling into rottenness and confusion is caused by the change of princes, even when it occurs by natural succession of the nearest of kin, as in this realm. For it often happens that a good and valiant king is succeeded by one who is an imbecile or suffers from various vices or is merely a young child; from which result various disorders and arbitrary deeds caused by the bad government of such a vicious king or those who have the administration of the king when he is a child or wholly incompetent, which can be the occasion of great desolation and destruction in the whole state, as has been seen several times even in this kingdom. . . . For, to speak of the disorder which can result from the imperfection of the Heads and Monarchs, there are several remedies for curbing their absolute authority if they are depraved and wilful; and even more of those who may have the management of the kingdom, if the kings are incompetent by reason of age or otherwise. And nonetheless the dignity and royal authority remains complete, neither totally absolute nor too restrained either but controlled and curbed by good laws, ordinances and customs, which are so established that they are difficult to break and destroy (although here and there, and at certain times, some infraction and violence may result). And, speaking of the curbs by which the absolute power of the kings of France is controlled, I find three principal ones, the first of which is Religion, the second Justice, and the third, Political Order (*la Police*).

Of Religion, which is the first curb upon kings

As to the first, it is certain that the people of France has been and still is a pious and religious nation among all the other peoples and nations. . . . And the Princes and People of France have always been more ardent and prompt than any other in driving out heretics and unbelievers and in defending the Roman Catholic church. And even now all the nations of Christendom come to the University of Paris to learn theology at its true source, from which perfect doctrine flows: for which reasons this kingdom is called the Most Christian, and the kings, the Most Christian.

For which reason it is very necessary that whoever is King demonstrate to the people by his actual and visible example that he is zealous in the observance of the Christian Faith and Religion and wishes to maintain and augment its power. For if the people thought otherwise, they would hate him and perchance obey him faultily, so that all the troubles which would occur in the kingdom would be imputed by the people to the King's lack of faith and imperfect religion. . . .

But when the King lives according to the Christian Law and Religion, he cannot do tyrannical things. And if he should do such, it is permissible for any prelate or other man of religion who lives well and has the good esteem of the people to remonstrate with him and accuse him, and for a simple preacher to take him up and argue with him publicly and to his face. And yet the King would not dare to mistrust him or hurt him for this (even if he so wished) in order not to provoke the ill will and indignation of the people: which is not true in any other realm, at least so far as I know. . . .

Of Justice, which is the second curb

The second is Justice, which without dispute has more authority in France than in any other country of the world that I know of, just because of the Parlements which were instituted principally for this cause and purpose of curbing the absolute power which the Kings might wish to use. And from the beginning there were established grand personages in such number and with such power that the Kings have always been subject to them for distributive justice: in such wise that in civil cases there is reasons and justice with regard to them as well as to subjects; and among private persons, their authority cannot prejudice anyone else's rights, but their letters and rescripts are subject to the judgment of these Parlements in such cases. . . .

And as for criminal cases, their pardons and remissions are so much debated, and those who obtain them subject to such discussion, that there are few persons who dare to do evil and execrable things in the hope or confidence of pardon. . . . And this Justice is the more authoritative because the Officials assigned to try cases are perpetual and the King does not have the power to depose them, except by forfeiture. . . .

Of the Political Order, which is the third curb

The third curb is the Political Order, that is, the various ordinances which were made by the Kings themselves and tend to the general and individual preservation of the king by repeated confirmation and approval. And because they have been followed for so long, the Princes make no effort to derogate from them; and if they wished to do so, their orders would not be obeyed, even with regard to their domain and royal patrimony which they cannot alienate without necessity. . . .

46. THE ETHICS OF POLITICAL AMORALISM

The new states that emerged in Europe during the early modern era were not only sovereign territories but secular states as well. The ultimate purpose of power was considered to be success in this world rather than service to the Christian church and its otherworldly mission. The result of this shift was to weaken the inhibitions put on political action by the Christian moral code. There had been fierceness and villainy a-plenty in the struggles for power during the Middle Ages, but the obligation to obey the ethical imperatives taught by the church had not been denied; those who murdered and betrayed their way to the top were beset by remorse and penitence. At the height of the Renaissance in Italy there was a plainer recognition of the fact that the price of political success, at least for the creators of new states, was disregard of the traditional code and affirmation that the needs of the people for peace and order required a strong state, however established.

The greatest of 16th-century political thinkers, the Florentine Niccolò Machiavelli (1469-1527), virtually enshrined political victory as a kind of moral achievement on the principle that the moral end justifies otherwise evil means. The most famous and influential statement of this doctrine is Machiavelli's *The Prince,* first published in 1513. Extracts from Chapters 13–18 are given below. Yet, as even Machiavelli recognized in the strong republicanism of his *Discourses* (1512–19), other purposes and other moral imperatives continued to work in political life. Subsequent history was to show that religious and ideological movements could also adopt the principle that the end justifies the means and triumph at the cost of their own principles.

Niccolò Machiavelli

The Prince

. . . . .

An army is auxiliary (this is the other kind of profitless army) when you summon a powerful man to bring his forces to aid and defend you. So in recent times Pope Julius did, for seeing in his expedition against Ferrara the poor showing of his mercenary soldiers, he turned to auxiliary ones and made an agreement with Ferdinand, King of Spain, who was to aid him with military forces. Such troops can be useful and good in themselves, but for him who invites them are almost always harmful;

SOURCE: From Allan Gilbert, trans., *Chief Works of Machiavelli,* Vol. 1., pp. 51–54, 57–59, 64–67. Reprinted by permission of the Publisher.

losing, you are done for; winning, you are their prisoner. Even though ancient histories are full of such instances, none the less I am not going to abandon this fresh instance of Pope Julius II, whose decision could not have been more ill-advised; in order to get Ferrara, he threw himself entirely into the hands of a foreigner. But his good fortune made a third thing come about, so that he did not gather the fruit of his bad choice: when his auxiliaries were defeated at Ravenna, the Swiss rose up and chased off the winners—against all expectation, both his own and that of others. Hence he was not left as the prisoner of his enemies, who had run away, nor of his auxiliaries, since he had conquered with other weapons than theirs. . . .

. . . Wise princes, therefore, always reject these armies and turn to their own; they choose rather to lose with their own soldiers than to win with the others, judging that not a true victory which they gain with foreign armies. . . .

. . . In short, the armor of another man either falls off your back or weighs you down or binds you.

After Charles VII, King Louis XI's father, had with his fortune and his ability delivered France from the English, he recognized such a need for arming himself with his own weapons, and set up in his realm the ordinance about men-at-arms and infantry. Then King Louis, his son, abolished that of the infantry and took to hiring Swiss. Practical experience now shows that this mistake, followed by others, is one cause of that kingdom's perils: by giving prestige to the Swiss, the King discredited all his own soldiers, because his own infantry he wholly abolished and his men-at-arms he made dependent on the soldiers of another country; being accustomed to fight in company with the Swiss, the French cavalry believe they cannot conquer without them. The result is that French against Swiss are not adequate, and without Swiss they do not risk themselves against others. Thus the French king's army is mixed, partly mercenary and partly his own. Such a force is on the whole much better than one purely auxiliary or purely mercenary, though much inferior to an army entirely his own. The instance just given is enough, because the French kingdom would be unconquerable if Charles's method had been developed or retained.

But men in their imprudence often enter upon some policy which at the moment pleases them without envisaging the poison underneath it, as I said above of the hectic fever. So a prince who does not recognize the ills in his state when they spring up is not truly wise; but this power is given to very few. On considering the chief cause for the fall of the Roman Empire, we find it was solely that she took to hiring Gothic mercenaries. After that beginning, the Empire's forces steadily failed, for she stripped away all her own vigor to give it to the Goths.

I conclude, then, that without her own armies no princedom is secure; on the contrary, she is entirely dependent on Fortune, not having strength that in adversity loyally defends her. Wise men have always said and believed that "nothing is so weak or shaky as the reputation of a power that does not rely on its own strength." Armies of your own are those made up of your subjects or of citizens of your state or of dependents; all the others are either mercenary or auxiliary. . . .

. . . . .

Now it remains to examine the wise prince's methods and conduct in dealing with subjects or with allies. And because I know that many have written about this, I fear that, when I too write about it, I shall be thought conceited, since in discussing this material I depart very far from the methods of the others. But since my purpose is to write something useful to him who comprehends it, I have decided that I must concern myself with the truth of the matter as facts show it rather than with any fanciful notion. Yet many have fancied for themselves republics and principalities that have never been seen or known to exist in reality. For there is such a difference between how men live and how they ought to live that he who abandons what is done for what ought to be done learns his destruction rather than his preservation, because any man who under all conditions insists on making it his business to be good will surely be destroyed among so many who are not good. Hence a prince, in order to hold his position, must acquire the power to be not good, and understand when to use it and when not to use it, in accord with necessity.

Omitting, then, those things about a prince that are fancied, and discussing those that are true, I say that all men, when people speak of them, and especially princes, who are placed so high, are labeled with some of the following qualities that bring them either blame or praise. To wit, one is considered liberal, one stingy (I use a Tuscan word, for the *avaricious* man in our dialect is still one who tries to get property through violence; *stingy* we call him who holds back too much from using his own goods); one is considered a giver, one grasping; one cruel, one merciful; one a promise-breaker, the other truthful; one effeminate and cowardly, the other bold and spirited; one kindly, the other proud; one lascivious, the other chaste; one reliable, the other tricky; one hard, the other tolerant; one serious, the other light-minded; one religous, the other unbelieving; and the like.

I am aware that everyone will admit that it would be most praiseworthy for a prince to exhibit such of the above-mentioned qualities as are considered good. But because no ruler can possess or fully practice them, on account of human conditions that do not permit it, he needs to be so prudent that he escapes ill repute for such vices as might take his position away from him, and that he protects himself from such as will not take it away if he can; if he cannot, with little concern he passes over the latter vices. He does not even worry about incurring reproach for those vices without which he can hardly maintain his position, because when we carefully examine the whole matter, we find some qualities that look like virtues, yet—if the prince practices them—they will be his destruction, and other qualities that look like vices, yet—if he practices them—they will bring him safety and well-being.

. . . . .

How praiseworthy a prince is who keeps his promises and lives with sincerity and not with trickery, everybody realizes. Nevertheless, experience in our time shows that those princes have done great things who have valued their promises little, and who have understood how to addle the brains of men with trickery; and in the end they have vanquished those who have stood upon their honesty.

You need to know, then, that there are two ways of fighting: one according to the laws, the other with force. The first is suited to man, the second to the animals; but because the first is often not sufficient, a prince must resort to the second. Therefore he needs to know well how to put to use the traits of animal and of man. This conduct is taught to princes in allegory by ancient authors, who write that Achilles and many other well-known ancient princes were given for upbringing to Chiron the Centaur, who was to guard and educate them. This does not mean anything else (this having as teacher one who is half animal and half man) than that a prince needs to know how to adopt the nature of either animal or man, for one without the other does not secure him permanence.

Since, then, a prince is necessitated to play the animal well, he chooses among the beasts the fox and the lion, because the lion does not protect himself from traps; the fox does not protect himself from the wolves. The prince must be a fox, therefore, to recognize the traps and a lion to frighten the wolves. Those who rely on the lion alone are not perceptive. By no means can a prudent ruler keep his word—and he does not—when to keep it works against himself and when the reasons that made him promise are annulled. If all men were good, this maxim would not be good, but because they are bad and do not keep their promises to you, you likewise do not have to keep yours to them. Never has a shrewd prince lacked justifying reasons to make his promise-breaking appear honorable. Of this I can give countless modern examples, showing how many treaties of peace and how many promises have been made null and empty through the dishonesty of princes. The one who knows best how to play the fox comes out best, but he must understand well how to disguise the animal's nature and must be a great simulator and dissimulator. So simple-minded are men and so controlled by immediate necessities that a prince who deceives always finds men who let themselves be deceived.

I am not willing, among fresh instances, to keep silent about one of them. Alexander VI never did anything else and never dreamed of anything else than deceiving men, yet he always found a subject to work on. Never was there a man more effective in swearing and who with stronger oaths confirmed a promise, but yet honored it less. Nonetheless, his deceptions always prospered as he hoped, because he understood well this aspect of the world.

For a prince, then, it is not necessary actually to have all the above-mentioned qualities, but it is very necessary to appear to have them. Further, I shall be so bold as to say this: that if he has them and always practices them, they are harmful; and if he appears to have them, they are useful; for example, to appear merciful, trustworthy, humane, blameless, religious—and to be so—yet to be in such measure prepared in mind that if you need to be not so, you can and do change to the contrary. And it is essential to realize this: that a prince, and above all a prince who is new, cannot practice all those things for which men are considered good, being often forced, in order to keep his position, to act contrary to truth, contrary to charity, contrary to humanity, contrary to religion. Therefore he must have a mind ready to turn in any direction as Fortune's winds and the variability of affairs require, yet, as I said above, he holds to what is right when he can but knows how to do wrong when he must.

A wise prince, then, is very careful never to let out of his mouth a single word not weighty with the above-mentioned five qualities; he appears to those who see him and hear him talk, all mercy, all faith, all integrity, all humanity, all religion. No quality does a prince more need to possess —in appearance—than this last one, because in general men judge more with their eyes than with their hands, since everybody can see but few can perceive. Everybody sees what you appear to be; few perceive what you are, and those few dare not contradict the belief of the many, who have the majesty of the government to support them. As to the actions of all men and especially those of princes, against whom charges cannot be brought in court, everybody looks at their result. So if a prince succeeds in conquering and holding his state, his means are always judged honorable and everywhere praised, because the mob is always fascinated by appearances and by the outcome of an affair; and in the world the mob is everything; the few find no room there when the many crowd together. A certain prince of the present time, whom I refrain from naming, never preaches anything except peace and truth, and to both of them he is utterly opposed. Either one, if he had practiced it, would many times have taken from him either his reputation or his power.

47. ON THE BITTERNESS OF WAR

The return of the Renaissance writers to the works of antiquity served not only to capture the savor of classical authors in diction and form; it also provided them a wealth of new ideas or new ways of expressing long-held values. Erasmus used his command of pure classical Latin to present his distinctive view of man. Tolerant, governed by a deep personal morality, and skeptical of big words and bold doctrines, he defended the worth of unheroic man. This view is presented in his "Adages," a collection of essays on quotations from classical authors. The adage presented in the selection below, that "war is sweet to those who have not tried it," is drawn from the Greek poet Pindar and the Roman military writer Vegetius, but the commentary is distinctively Erasmus's.

Desiderius Erasmus

War Is Sweet to Those Who Have Not Tried It

'DULCE BELLUM INEXPERTIS'

Among the choicest proverbs, and widely used in literature, is the adage: *Glykus speiro polemos,*[1] that is, war is sweet to those who have not tried it. Vegetius uses it thus, in his book on the Art of War, III, chapter xiv, "Do not be too confident, if a new recruit hankers after war, for it is to the inexperienced that fighting is sweet." There is a quotation from Pindar: "War is sweet to those who have not tried it, but anyone who knows what it is is horrified beyond measure if he should meet it."

There are some things in the affairs of men, fraught with dangers and evils of which one can have no idea until one has put them to the test.

> How sweet, untried, the favour of the great!
> But he who knows it, fears it.[2]

It seems a fine and splendid thing to walk among the nobles at court, to be occupied with the business of kings, but old men who know all about the matter from experience are glad enough to deny themselves this pleasure. It seems delightful to be in love with girls, but only to those

---

SOURCE: Margaret Mann Phillips, *The "Adages" of Erasmus: A Study with Translations* (Cambridge, England: Cambridge University Press, 1964), pp. 308–9, 314–15, 339–40, 349. Reprinted by permission of Cambridge University Press.

[1] In Greek type in the original text.

[2] Horace, *Epistles,* I, 18, 86–87.

who have not yet felt what bitter there is in the sweet. In the same way this idea can be applied to any enterprise carrying with it great risks and many evils, such as no one would undertake unless he were young and without experience. Indeed Aristotle in his *Rhetoric* says this is the reason why youth tends to be bold and age to be diffident, because the former is given confidence by inexperience, and the latter acquires diffidence and hesitancy from familiar knowledge of many ills. If there is anything in mortal affairs which should be approached with hesitancy, or rather which ought to be avoided in every possible way, guarded against and shunned, that thing is war; there is nothing more wicked, more disastrous, more widely destructive, more deeply tenacious, more loathsome, in a word more unworthy of man, not to say of a Christian. . . .

. . . . .

. . . But to me it seems more than savage, more than brutish, to resort to armed conflict. In the first place, most of the wild animals live in peace and good understanding with their own kind, they go in herds, and support each other with mutual help. Not all wild creatures are given to fighting (for there are some quite harmless ones, like hares and fallow deer) but only the really savage ones like lions, wolves, and tigers. And even these do not make war on each other as we do; dog does not eat dog, fierce lions do not fight each other, there is peace between snake and snake, venomous creatures agree together. But there is no wild beast more harmful to man than man. And then when they do fight, they fight with their own weapons, but we use instruments invented against nature by the art of demons, to arm men for the destruction of men. If the animals turn fierce, it is not for any casual reason, but because hunger drives them to madness, or they know they are being hunted, or they are afraid for their young. But we men, O God in heaven, what tragic conflicts we stir up for what frivolous reasons! For the emptiest of claims "on property," out of mere childish spite, because of "the interception of" a woman, or for reasons much sillier than these. And then among wild animals it is single combat, and very short, and however bloody the battle, as soon as one or other is wounded they break it up. Who ever heard of a hundred thousand animals rushing together to butcher each other, which men do everywhere? . . .

"But," they say, "it is permissible to sentence a criminal to punishment; therefore it is permissible to take vengeance on a state by war." What is there to say in answer to this? So much, that one can hardly begin. I will only point out the difference between the two cases; that the felon has been convicted in the courts before he is punished by the law, but in war each side is prosecuting the other; in the first case the suffering falls only on the person who did wrong, and the example is before everyone, but in the second case the greatest part of the suffering falls on those who have least deserved it, namely on the peasants, old people, wives, orphans, young girls. Moreover, if there is any advantage to be gained from this worst of all experiences, it is entirely drawn off by a few thieving scoundrels—it goes to pay the mercenaries, the out-and-out profiteers, perhaps a few leaders by whose instigation the war was stirred up (for this very reason) and who are never so well off as when the state is on the rocks. In the case of the felon, the reason for not sparing one is that all should be the safer; but in war, it is for the sake of taking vengeance on a few, or perhaps even one person, that we inflict such cruel suffering on so many thousands of innocent people. It would be better for the fault of a few to go unpunished than to demand an uncertain retribution from one or another, and meanwhile throw both our own people and those whom we call our enemies—our neighbours, who have done us no harm—into certain danger. Better leave the wound alone, if no surgery can be done without grave harm to the whole body. If anyone cries that it is unjust that the sinner should go unpunished, I answer that it is much more unjust to bring desperate calamity on so many thousands of innocent people who have not deserved it.

. . . . .

There are those who go to war for no other reason than because it is a way of confirming their tyranny over their own subjects. For in times of peace the authority of the council, the dignity of the magistrates, and the force of the laws stand in the way, to a certain extent, of the prince's doing just what he likes. But once war has been declared, then all the affairs of the State are at the mercy of the appetites of a few. Up go the ones who are in the prince's favour, down go the ones with whom he is angry. Any amount of money is exacted. Why say more? It is only then that they feel they are really kings. Meanwhile the generals act in collusion to pick the unfortunate population to the bone. When people are in this frame of mind, do you think they will be slow to seize any opportunity which presents itself of making war?

Then we cloak our disease with respectable titles. I am really hankering after the riches of the Turks, and I cover it up with the defence of religion; I am obeying my private hatred, and I use as an excuse the rights of the Church. I am the slave of ambition, I am moved by anger, I am carried away by my fierce and undisciplined character, and I allege as my reasons for action a broken treaty, a violated alliance, some omission in betrothal arrangements, or something else of the kind. It is amazing how rulers fail to achieve the very thing they are striving after, and while they are stupidly seeking to avoid this or that misfortune, fall into another, or even much deeper into the original one. For truly, if they are led by the hope of glory, it is more splendid by far to preserve than to destroy, much finer to build a city than demolish it. . . .

48. THE EXTENT OF SOVEREIGN POWER

As the Middle Ages passed into the early modern period, political power tended to be consolidated into sovereign territorial states, smaller than the universal empire dreamed of by medieval thinkers and larger than fiefdoms. Such states sought not only to establish their rule within fixed boundaries but to exclude all rival rulers, whether external powers, including (for Catholic states) the Papacy, or domestic elements claiming by right a share in government. While legal and political thinkers affirmed the desirability and legitimacy of such unshared power, which they called "sovereignty," and the experience of civil wars reinforced their arguments, they still had to define the proper limits of sovereignty. One of the most insightful and influential of these thinkers, the Frenchman Jean Bodin (1530-1596), in his *Six Books of the Commonwealth* (1576) described sovereignty as absolute, perpetual, and indivisible. As in the selections below, however, he also affirmed the subjection of rulers to divine and human laws and accepted the legitimacy of a sovereign people as an alternate (if inferior) form of rule to monarchy.

Jean Bodin

Six Books of the Commonwealth

CONCERNING SOVEREIGNTY

Sovereignty is that absolute and perpetual power vested in a commonwealth which in Latin is termed *majestas* . . . . The term needs careful definition, because although it is the distinguishing mark of a commonwealth, and an understanding of its nature fundamental to any treatment of politics, no jurist or political philosopher has in fact attempted to define it. . . . .

I have described it as *perpetual* because one can give absolute power to a person or group of persons for a period of time, but that time expired they become subjects once more. Therefore even while they enjoy power, they cannot properly be regarded as sovereign rulers, but only as the lieutenants and agents of the sovereign ruler, till the moment comes when it pleases the prince or the people to revoke the gift. The true

---

SOURCE: Jean Bodin, *Six Books of the Commonwealth*, abridged and translated by M. J. Tooley (Oxford, England: Basil Blackwell, 1953), pp. 25, 27–29, 51–53. Reprinted by permission of Basil Blackwell Publisher.

sovereign remains always seized of his power. Just as a feudal lord who grants lands to another retains his eminent domain over them, so the ruler who delegates authority to judge and command, whether it be for a short period, or during pleasure, remains seized of those rights of jurisdiction actually exercised by another in the form of a revocable grant, or precarious tenancy. For this reason the law requires the governor of a province, or the prince's lieutenant, to make a formal surrender of the authority committed to him, at the expiration of his term of office. In this respect there is no difference between the highest officer of state and his humblest subordinate. If it were otherwise, and the absolute authority delegated by the prince to a lieutenant was regarded as itself sovereign power, the latter could use it against his prince who would thereby forfeit his eminence, and the subject could command his lord, the servant his master. This is a manifest absurdity, considering that the sovereign is always excepted personally, as a matter of right, in all delegations of authority, however extensive. However much he gives there always remains a reserve of right in his own person, whereby he may command, or intervene by way of prevention, confirmation, evocation, or any other way he thinks fit, in all matters delegated to a subject, whether in virtue of an office or a commission. Any authority exercised in virtue of an office or a commission can be revoked, or made tenable for as long or short a period as the sovereign wills.

. . . . .

Let us now turn to the other term of our definition and consider the force of the word *absolute*. The people or the magnates of a commonwealth can bestow simply and unconditionally upon someone of their choice a sovereign and perpetual power to dispose of their property and persons, to govern the state as he thinks fit, and to order the succession, in the same way that any proprietor, out of his liberality, can freely and unconditionally make a gift of his property to another. Such a form of gift, not being qualified in any way, is the only true gift, being at once unconditional and irrevocable. Gifts burdened with obligations and hedged with conditions are not true gifts. Similarly sovereign power given to a prince charged with conditions is neither properly sovereign, nor absolute, unless the conditions of appointment are only such as are inherent in the laws of God and of nature. . . .

On the other hand it is the distinguishing mark of the sovereign that he cannot in any way be subject to the commands of another, for it is he who makes law for the subject, abrogates law already made, and amends obsolete law. No one who is subject either to the law or to some other person can do this. That is why it is laid down in the civil law that the prince is above the law, for the word *law* in Latin implies the command of him who is invested with sovereign power. Therefore we find in all statutes the phrase "notwithstanding all edicts and ordinances to the contrary that we have infringed, or do infringe by these present." This clause applies both to former acts of the prince himself, and to those of his predecessors. For all laws, ordinances, letters patent, privileges, and grants whatsoever issued by the prince, have force only during his own lifetime, and must be expressly, or at least tacitly, confirmed by the reigning prince who has cognizance of them. . . . In proof of which, it is the custom of this realm for all corporations and corporate bodies to ask for the confirmation of their privileges, rights, and jurisdictions, on the accession of a new king. Even Parlements and high courts do this, as well as individual officers of the crown.

If the prince is not bound by the laws of his predecessors, still less can he be bound by his own laws. One may be subject to laws made by another, but it is impossible to bind oneself in any matter which is the subject of one's own free exercise of will. As the law says, "there can be no obligation in any matter which proceeds from the free will of the undertaker." It follows of necessity that the king cannot be subject to his own laws. Just as, according to the canonists, the Pope can never tie his own hands, so the sovereign prince cannot bind himself, even if he wishes. For this reason edicts and ordinances conclude with the formula "for such is our good pleasure," thus intimating that the laws of a sovereign prince, even when founded on truth and right reason, proceed simply from his own free will.

It is far otherwise with divine and natural laws. All the princes of the earth are subject to them, and cannot contravene them without treason and rebellion against God. His yoke is upon them, and they must bow their heads in fear and reverence before His divine majesty. The absolute power of princes and sovereign lords does not extend to the laws of God and of nature. He who best understood the meaning of absolute power, and made kings and emperors submit to his will, defined his sovereignty as a power to override positive law; he did not claim power to set aside divine and natural law.

. . . . .

Of the Different Kinds of Commonwealth

Now that we have determined what sovereignty is, and have described its rights and attributes, we must consider in whom it is vested in every kind of commonwealth, in order to determine what are the various possible types of state. If sovereignty is vested in a single prince we call the state a monarchy. If all the people share in it, it is a popular state. If only a minority, it is an aristocracy. . . .

If sovereignty is, of its very nature, indivisible, as we have shown, how can a prince, a ruling class, and the people, all have a part in it at the same time? The first attribute of sovereignty is the power to make law binding on the subject. But in such a case who will be the subjects that obey, if they also have a share in the law-making power? And who will be the law-giver if he is also himself forced to receive it from those upon whom he has imposed it? One is forced to the conclusion that if no one in particular has the power to make law, but it belongs to all indifferently, then the commonwealth is a popular state. If power is given to the people to make law, and appoint to office, but all other powers are denied them, it must nevertheless be recognized that these other powers, vested in officials, really belong to the people, and are only entrusted by them to the magistrates. The people, having instituted the latter, can also deprive them, and the state therefore remains a popular one. . . .

49. THE KING'S PREROGATIVE: WITH OR WITHOUT PARLIAMENT?

The issue of royal absolutism was posed not in the abstract, like a theorem in geometry, but as a question of the extent of the king's powers in his own right, what in English law was called his prerogative. Did the monarch exercise these rights of sovereignty—particularly legislation, taxation, and punishment—alone, although customarily with the participation of Parliament and courts? Or was his rule shared with those through whom he governed? The first position is taken in the following selection by William Stanford, writing in 1548 during the reign of Edward VI (A). John Aylmer, writing in 1559 (B), a year after the ascension of Elizabeth I, on the contrary upheld the notion of a "mixed" monarchy, with elements of both aristocracy and democracy. Aylmer (1521-1594), whose Protestant views compelled him to flee to the Continent during the reign of the Catholic Mary I (1553–58), was consecrated Bishop of London in 1577.

A. William Stanford

The King's Prerogative

Prerogativa is as much to say as a privilege or preeminence that any person hath before another, which, as it is tolerable in some, so it is most

Source: G. R. Elton (ed.), *The Tudor Constitution: Documents and Commentary* (Cambridge, England: Cambridge University Press, 1960), pp. 18–19. Reprinted by permission of Cambridge University Press.

to be permitted and allowed in a prince or sovereign governor of a realm. For besides that that he is the most excellentest and worthiest part or member of the common body of the wealth, so is he also (through his good governance) the preserver, nourisher and defender of all the people, being the rest of the same body. . . . For which cause the laws do attribute unto him all honour, dignity, prerogative and preeminence, which prerogative doth not only extend to his own person but also to all other his possessions, goods and chattels. As that his person shall be subject to no man's suit, his possessions cannot be taken from him by any violence or wrongful disseisin, his goods and chattels are under no tribute, toll nor custom, nor otherwise distrainable: with an infinite number of prerogatives more, which were tedious here to recite. Howbeit, forasmuch as in every realm the king's prerogatives are no small part of the profits and commodities of the Crown of the same, and namely within this realm of England it hath been thought good heretofore to declare and set forth in writing certain of the most highest and weightiest matters and articles touching the said prerogatives. And hereupon was there as declaration made in writing by the authority of Parliament holden in the 17th year of the reign of King Edward the 2nd. . . . Howbeit, this Parliament maketh no part of the king's prerogative, but long time before it had his being by the order of the common law, as plainly may appear by them that have written before the making of the said statute of prerogative. . . .

B. John Aylmer

On Kingship

The regiment of England is not a mere monarchy, as some for lack of consideration think, nor a mere oligarchy, nor democracy, but a rule mixed of all these . . . the image whereof, and not the image but the thing indeed, is to be seen in the Parliament House, wherein you shall find these three estates: the king or queen, which representeth the monarch; the noblemen which be the aristocracy; and the burgesses and knights the democracy. . . . . If the Parliament use their privileges, the King can ordain nothing without them. If he do, it is his fault in usurping it and their folly in permitting it; wherefore in my judgment those that in King Henry VIII's days would not grant him that his proclamations should

---

SOURCE: G. R. Elton (ed.), *The Tudor Constitution: Documents and Commentary* (Cambridge, England: Cambridge University Press, 1960), p. 16. Reprinted by permission of Cambridge University Press.

have the force of a statute were good fathers of the country and worthy commendation in defending their liberty. . . . To declare that it is not in England so dangerous a matter to have a woman ruler as men take it to be. For first it is not she that ruleth but the laws, the executors whereof be her judges, appointed by her, her justices of the peace and such other officers. . . . She maketh no statutes or laws but the honourable court of Parliament. . . . What may she do alone wherein is peril? She may grant pardon to an offender, that is her prerogative wherein if she err it is a tolerable and pitiful error to save life. She may misspend the revenues of the crown wantonly; so can kings do too, and commonly do, and yet they be kings. If on the other part the regiment were such as all hanged upon the king's or queen's will and not upon the laws written; if she might decree and make laws alone, without her senate; if she judged offences according to her wisdom and not by limitation of statutes and laws; if she might dispose alone of war and peace; if, to be short, she were a mere monarch and not a mixed ruler, you might peradventure make me to fear the matter the more. . . .

50. RESISTANCE TO TYRANNY

The civil wars of the later 16th century prompted some thinkers (like Bodin) to argue in support of the absolute power of monarchs as the only way to achieve peace for the people. But those who spoke war against the kings saw them not as preservers of the welfare of the community but as tyrants who abused their powers for their own gain and that of the nefarious interests that backed them. Such attitudes were intensified when, as frequently happened, the civil wars were also wars of religion, setting Catholic against Protestant or one Protestant group against another. The ancient problem of resistance to tyrants came to the fore again and with it the recurrent question of what legitimizes rulers. The principle of tyrannicide—that it is right and proper to slay iniquitous princes who oppress their peoples—had been enunciated long before and was held by Catholics and Protestants alike. It was set forth with particular clarity and force by the Huguenot leader Philippe du Plessis-Mornay (1549-1623) in a work, the *Vindiciae Contra Tyrannos* ("The Defense of Liberty against Tyrants"), published anonymously in 1574–75, in the aftermath of the massacre of Huguenots in Paris on St. Bartholomew's Eve in August 1572.

Philippe du Plessis-Mornay

The Defense of Liberty against Tyrants

MAY A PRINCE WHO OPPRESSES OR DEVASTATES A COMMONWEALTH BE RESISTED; AND TO WHAT EXTENT, BY WHOM, IN WHAT FASHION, AND BY WHAT PRINCIPLE OF LAW?

[What follows will be approved by proper kings and give offense to tyrants only.]

Kings Are Created by the People

. . . We have already shown that it is God who makes kings, gives kingdoms, and selects rulers. And now we say that it is the people that establishes kings, gives them kingdoms. and approves their selection by its vote. For God willed that every bit of authority held by kings should come from the people, after Him, so that kings would concentrate all their care, energy, and thought upon the people's interests. And kings are not to think that they are of a higher nature than the rest of men and rule as men rule over cattle. Born the same as all the rest of men, they are always to remember that they were raised up from below to their estates, upon all others' shoulders, as it were, so that thereafter the burdens of the commonwealth should fall, for the most part, upon theirs.

. . . . .

And since no one is born a king, and no one is a king by nature; and since a king cannot rule without a people, while a people can rule itself without a king, it is clear, beyond all doubt, that the people is prior to the king and that kings were originally established by the people. By adhering to the virtues of their forebears, the sons and relatives of kings sometimes seem to have rendered a kingdom hereditary, and in certain regions the right of free elections almost seems no longer to exist. And yet in all properly constituted kingdoms, the practice still remains inviolate. Children do not properly succeed to the fathers' thrones until they are established, as if *de novo,* by the people. They are not kings by birth, or by inheritance, but become kings only when they have received the office, together with the sceptre and the crown, from those who represent the people's majesty.

SOURCE: From *Constitutionalism and Resistance in the Sixteenth Century: Three Treatises by Hotman, Beza and Mornay,* edited and translated by Julian H. Franklin, pp. 158, 160-62, 165–67.

In Christian kingdoms now reputed to descend by succession, these traces of election are quite evident. The kings of France, Spain, England, and other countries are normally inaugurated by the estates of the realm—that is, by the peers, patricians, and magnates, who represent the people as a whole and who put the king into possession of the kingdom, as it were. In Germany, the emperors are chosen by the electors, and the king of Poland by the Wojewodowie, or palatines, since in both of these countries the right of election is preserved intact. Furthermore, the cities of a kingdom do not accord an incumbent regal honors until he has been properly inaugurated. And in ancient times the beginning of a reign was dated from the day of coronation, a practice followed very strictly in France. But so that we are not misled by recurrent series of direct successions in these kingdoms, it should be noted that the Estates have often preferred the uncle to the son, the younger brother to the elder—as in France Louis was preferred over his brother, Robert, Count of Evreux; and Henry, the king's brother, over Robert Capet, the surviving son of Henry's older brother. And in France the crown was also transferred from family to family by the authority of the people—from the Merovingians to the Carolingians and from these to the Capetians.

[Additional evidence of election in early French history is given.]

Thus, at the beginning all kings were elected. And even those who seem today to come to the throne by succession must first be inaugurated by the people. Furthermore, even if a people has customarily chosen its kings from a particular family because of its outstanding merits, that decision is not so unconditional that if the established line degenerates, the people may not select another. Indeed, even the nearest kin of the selected family are not born kings but are made such. At their birth they are considered not kings but rather candidates for kingship.

The People Is Greater than the King

Since kings, then, are created by the people, it seems to follow that the people as a whole is greater than the king. This is an implication of the term itself, since one who is created by another is considered his inferior. Potiphar set Joseph over his family, Nebuchadnezzar set Daniel over his provinces of Babylon; Darius created 180 governors to superintend his kingdom. Masters set up slaves; kings, ministers. And the people sets up a king as a kind of minister to the commonwealth. . . .

[Kings are made for the people, not the people for the king. The people are compared to the owner, the king to the pilot of a ship. The conquests of a king belong not to him but to the people. There can be no king without a people, but a people can exist without a king. A king is powerless if the people do not support him.]

The People as a Whole Is Represented by the Officers of the Kingdom Ordinarily and by the Assembly of the Estates Either Extraordinarily or Annually

Moreover, what we have said of the whole people also applies, as was shown in our second question, to those who lawfully represent the whole people of the kingdom or of a single region, and who are commonly called officers, not of the king, but of the kingdom. Officers of the king are created and removed at his discretion. When the king dies, their tenure ends, and they too are deemed to be in some sense dead. Officers of the kingdom, on the other hand, receive, or at least used to receive, their authority from the people in public council and cannot be removed unless that body consents. Hence, the former depend upon the king, the latter, on the kingdom; the former, on the supreme officer of the kingdom, that is, upon the king, the latter, upon the supreme dominion of the people on whom the king himself depends as well. The duty of the first is to look after the well-being of the king; the duty of the second is to look after the safety of the commonwealth. The charge of the first is that they should attend and wait upon the king like domestics on a master; of the second, that they should protect the people's rights and privileges and make sure that the king himself commits no crime against the people nor neglects his duty toward them. The former, finally, are ministers, servants, and domestics of the king established only to obey him; the latter, on the other hand, are like assistants (*assessores*) of the king in reaching legal judgment and are associates in the royal power, so that all of them are bound, just like the king, to look after the welfare of the commonwealth. The king is like a president among them who possesses only primacy of place. For as the entire people is above the king, so these officers, although below the king as individuals, are above him when taken as a body. . . .

. . . . .

Hence, even today, the Parlement of Paris, which is called the "court of peers" or "of patricians," is judge between the king and the people, and especially between the king and particular individuals, for it is supposed to give justice to the individual if the king should seek to act against him in contravention of the law. Furthermore, if the king passes any edict or decision in his private council, or if a war is to be declared or peace is to be made, as under Charles V not long ago, the authorization of the Senate must be asked. In fact, everything relating to the commonwealth has to be entered in the record of its acts, since nothing is considered ratified until approval has been given by the Senate. And to protect the Senators from intimidation by the king, there was a time when no one could be coopted to its ranks unless he had been nominated by the Senate, and no one could be deprived of office without its authorization and for a cause prescribed by law.

Finally, unless letters of the king are also signed by a secretary of the kingdom and unless his decrees are countersigned by the chancellor (who has the power to annul them [*cancel-landi*]), they are invalid. And there are dukes, marquises, counts, viscounts, barons, and chatelains; and also, in the towns, elders, vicars, consuls, syndics, *échevins*, and so on, who are established to protect the people within their jurisdiction. And although some of these offices are now hereditary, they were all conferred by the several towns and districts.

So much, then, for ordinary checks. Beyond these, there is the Assembly of the Three Estates, which was at one time summoned every year, and although it has met less regularly since, it is always convened in dire times at least. All the districts and towns of any importance sent deputies to this assembly; and commoners (*plebeii*), nobles, and ecclesiastics there met together publicly and decided all matters of importance to the commonwealth. The authority of this assembly, moreover, was unquestioned. Whether it concluded peace, made war, named a regent, or imposed a tax, anything it decreed was considered binding and inviolable. By its authority, kings were sent off to monasteries for extravagance, neglect, or tyranny; and an entire line might be deprived of succession to the throne by the same authority that called it to the kingship in the first place. Thus kings who had been created by consent were, by its withdrawal, driven out. And children who enjoyed an almost hereditary claim through imitation of their fathers' virtue were disinherited as unworthy or unsuitable if their character had degenerated or was disagreeable. It is, therefore, clear enough that [hereditary] succession was tolerated only insofar as it was a convenient remedy for rebellions, secessions, interregna, and other dangers of election. But where succession threatened even greater dangers, where the kingdom was in jeopardy of tyranny or a tyrant had usurped the throne, a lawful assembly of the people had unquestioned authority to expel a tyrannical or incompetent king, and to install a good king in his place, albeit very often from the old king's male relations on his father's side. The French took this practice over from the Gauls, as is clearly indicated in Caesar Bk. 5, where Ambiorix, king of the Eburones, avows that the powers of the kings of Gaul were such that the people lawfully assembled had no less authority over the king than the king over the people. And this is also documented by the example of Vercingetorix, who justified his plans to the assembled people.

In the kingdoms of Spain, and especially in Aragon, Valencia, and Catalonia, it is very much the same. In Aragon, the *Justicia*, as he is called, is the highest authority in the kingdom. The magnates, who represent the people, proudly address the king, at his coronation and every third year thereafter, in the following terms: "We are as strong as you; and above us both there is someone (the *Justicia* of Aragon is understood) who has more authority than you." Furthermore, there is no country in the world where a tax can be imposed without the authorization of some assembly like this. In England and Scotland, sovereignty (*summa rerum*) resides in the Parliament, which is normally convoked each year. By Parliament they mean the assembly of the estates of the realm in which bishops, counts, barons, and deputies from the towns and districts deliberate on the condition of the commonwealth and make decisions by their joint consent. And so inviolable is its authority that a king who abrogates what it has once decided is considered guilty of a crime. Moreover, all officers of the kingdom, including those who sit in the council of the king or queen, normally receive their insignia from this assembly.

Finally, it is clear, from written history or living memory, that the other Christian kingdoms—Hungary, Bohemia, Denmark, Sweden, and the rest—also have officials of the kingdom who are associates in the royal power and who have, on various occasions, even made use of that authority even to depose the king himself. . . . .

51. REGICIDE AND ILLEGITIMACY

The doctrine of tyrannicide could be debated at the lofty level of political theory, but it ran squarely against a general feeling that it was "a deed of slander," a violation of the political and moral order that brought retribution upon usurpers and devastating civil war upon the peoples. The problem of tyrannicide and usurpation runs like a scarlet thread through the histories and tragedies of Shakespeare. He painted with great imaginative insight the characteristic crises of monarchical power, even though his plays are not based on any effort to reconstruct the past "as it actually was," in the famous phrase of a modern historian. Noteworthy in the following passages is the poet's memorable expression of the concept that regicide is a crime.

In the first selection from *Richard II,* Act III, Scene 2 (A), King Richard responds to the news that his cousin, Henry Bolingbroke, has just risen in rebellion against him. In the second selection from the same play, Act V, Scene 6 (B), the king is Henry Bolingbroke, who has just become Henry IV by the assassination of Richard II (Richard of Bordeaux), and Sir Pierce of Exton is the murderer. The third selection, from *Henry IV,* Part II, Act IV, Scene 5 (C), depicts Henry IV on his deathbed telling his son, who will succeed him as Henry V, how difficult and long is the way towards the legitimacy—the uncontested acknowledgement by the whole people—of a crown won by "crooked ways."

A. William Shakespeare

On the Divine Right of Kings

King Richard Discomfortable cousin! know'st thou not
That when the searching eye of heaven is hid,
Behind the globe, that lights the lower world,
Then thieves and robbers range abroad unseen
In murders and in outrage, boldly here;
But when from under this terrestrial ball
He fires the proud tops of the eastern pines
And darts his light through every guilty hole,
Then murders, treasons and detested sins,
The cloak of night being pluck'd from off their backs,
Stand bare and naked, trembling at themselves?
So when this thief, this traitor, Bolingbroke,
Who all this while hath revell'd in the night,
Whilst we were wandering with the antipodes,
Shall see us rising in our throne, the east,
His treasons will sit blushing in his face,
Not able to endure the sight of day,
But self-affrighted tremble at his sin.
Not all the water in the rough rude sea
Can wash the balm off from an anointed king;
The breath of worldly men cannot depose
The deputy elected by the Lord:
For every man that Bolingbroke hath press'd
To lift shrewd steel against our golden crown,
God for his Richard hath in heavenly pay
A glorious angel: then, if angels fight,
Weak men must fall, for heaven still guards the right.

B. William Shakespeare

On Regicide

Exton. Great king, within this coffin I present
Thy buried fear: herein all breathless lies

SOURCE: *The Works of William Shakespeare,* edited by William Aldis Wright (London: Macmillan, 1891), Vol. IV, pp. 192–93.

SOURCE: *The Works of William Shakespeare,* edited by William Aldis Wright (London: Macmillan, 1891), Vol. IV, pp. 258–59.

The mightiest of thy greatest enemies,
Richard of Bordeaux, by me hither brought.
Boling. Exton, I thank thee not; for thou hast wrought
A deed of slander, with thy fatal hand,
Upon my head and all this famous land.
Exton. From your own mouth, my lord, did I this deed.
Boling. They love not poison that do poison need,
Nor do I thee: though I did wish him dead,
I hate the murderer, love him murdered.
The guilt of conscience take thou for thy labour,
But neither my good word nor princely favour:
With Cain go wander through shades of night,
And never show thy head by day nor light.
Lords, I protest, my soul is full of woe,
That blood should sprinkle me to make me grow:
Come, mourn with me for that I do lament,
And put on sullen black incontinent:
I'll make a voyage to the Holy Land,
To wash this blood off from my guilty hand:
March sadly after; grace my mournings here;
In weeping after this untimely bier.

C. William Shakespeare

On Royal Succession

King. Come hither, Harry, sit thou by my bed;
And hear, I think, the very latest counsel
That ever I shall breathe. God knows, my son,
By what by-paths and indirect crook'd ways
I met this crown; and I myself know well
How troublesome it sat upon my head.
To thee it shall descend with better quiet,
Better opinion, better confirmation;
For all the soil of the achievement goes
With me into the earth. It seem'd in me
But as an honour snatch'd with boisterous hand,
And I had many living to upbraid

SOURCE: *The Works of William Shakespeare*, edited by William Aldis Wright (London: Macmillan, 1891), Vol. IV, pp. 535–36.

My gain of it by their assistances;
Which daily grew to quarrel and to bloodshed,
Wounding supposed peace: all these bold fears
Thou see'st with peril I have answered;
For all my reign hath been but as a scene
Acting that argument: and now my death
Changes the mode; for what in me was purchased,
Falls upon thee in a more fairer sort;
So thou the garland wear'st successively.
Yet, though thou stand'st more sure than I could do,
Thou art not firm enough, since griefs are green;
And all my friends, which thou must make thy friends,
Have but their stings and teeth newly ta'en out;
By whose fell working I was first advanced
And by whose power I well might lodge a fear
To be again displaced: which to avoid,
I cut them off; and had a purpose now
To lead out many to the Holy Land,
Lest rest and lying still might make them look
Too near unto my state. Therefore, my Harry,
Be it thy course to busy giddy minds
With foreign quarrels; that action, hence borne out,
May waste the memory of the former days.
More would I, but my lungs are wasted so
That strength of speech is utterly denied me.
How I came by the crown, O God forgive;
And grant it may with thee in true peace live!

CHAPTER VI

THE POLITICS OF EUROPE: THE SEVENTEENTH CENTURY

THE STATES OF EUROPE found themselves moving in one of two ways during the 17th century—toward absolutism or toward the participation of the ruled in government. The classical example of absolute monarchy was provided in France, where it was created by the cardinal-ministers Richelieu and Mazarin and practiced by King Louis XIV. English history, on the contrary, was centered upon the conflict between the Stuart kings, who sought to extend the monarch's prerogative as far as possible, and the political forces that advocated rule by king with Parliament, or even by Parliament alone. These alternative paths were reflected in contemporary political theory. King James I of England was a clear advocate of absolutism, and John Locke of a form of sovereignty of the nation. The program of the Levellers in England was a democratic form of the parliamentary system.

The 17th century was also marked by unusually long and fierce wars. These strained the resources of states to the utmost, set the soldiery in conflict with the inhabitants of the lands they occupied no less than with enemy forces, and threatened the vitality of European civilization. War remained the "ultimate argument" of political conflict, almost unquestioned when it was fought between states, even though the ideal goal of political life within countries was civil peace.

52. A KING ON KINGSHIP

The attitude of a real monarch, not a fictional one like Shakespeare's Henry IV, can be seen in the writings of the scholar-king James I of England. An effective ruler in an unruly Scotland, where he had been king since 1567, James never quite mastered the intricacies of practical politics in England, where he came to the throne in 1603 at the age of 46. His reputation has suffered from his habit of combining bold statements of principle with extreme caution in action. He responded to a first-class education with vigorous interest in theology and political theory and fancied himself a major thinker. His writings in political theory, at least, are important because few actual rulers have been able to state their ideas with his clear command of scholarship. His concept of monarchy—not just in England but everywhere—was set forth in a speech to Parliament on March 21, 1610, from which the following passages are taken. It will be observed that he conceived of kingly power as limited not by subjects or representative assemblies but by the duty of justice imposed by God.

James I

Speech to Parliament, March 21, 1610

The state of monarchy is the supremest thing upon earth; for kings are not only God's lieutenants upon earth, and sit upon God's throne, but even by God himself they are called gods. There be three principal similitudes that illustrate the state of monarchy: one taken out of the word of God, and the two other out of the grounds of policy and philosophy. In the Scriptures kings are called gods, and so their powers after a certain relation compared to the divine power. Kings are also compared to fathers of families, for the king is truly *parens patriae*, the politic father of his people. And lastly, kings are compared to the head of this microcosm of the body of man.

Kings are justly called gods for that they exercise a manner or resemblance of divine power upon earth, for if you will consider the attributes to God you shall see how they agree in the person of a king. God hath power to create or destroy, make or unmake, at his pleasure, to give life or send death, to judge all and to be judged not accountable to none; to raise low things and to make high things low at his pleasure; and to God

---

SOURCE: J. P. Kenyon (ed.), *The Stuart Constitution, 1603–1688: Documents and Commentary* (Cambridge, England: Cambridge University Press, 1966), pp. 12–14. Reprinted by permission of Cambridge University Press.

are both soul and body due. And the like power have kings: they make and unmake their subjects; they have power of raising, and casting down; of life, and of death, judges over all their subjects, and in all causes, and yet accountable to none but God only. They have power to exalt low things, and abase high things, and make of their subjects like men at the chess—a pawn to take a bishop or a knight—and cry up or down any of their subjects, as they do their money. And to the king is due both the affection of the soul and the service of the body of his subjects. . . .

But yet is all this power ordained by God, *ad aedificationem, non ad destructionem.* For although God hath power as well of destruction, as of creation or maintenance, yet will it not agree with the wisdom of God to exercise his power in the destruction of nature, and overturning the whole frame of things, since his creatures were made, that his glory might thereby be the better expressed. So were he a foolish father that would disinherit or destroy his children without a cause, or leave off the careful education of them; and it were an idle head that would in place of physic so poison or phlebotomise the body as might breed a dangerous distemper or destruction thereof.

But now in these our times we are to distinguish between the state of kings in their first original, and between the state of settled kings and monarchies that do at this time govern in civil kingdoms; for even as God, during the time of the Old Testament, spake by oracles and wrought by miracles, yet how soon it pleased him to settle a Church, which was bought and redeemed by the blood of his only son Christ, then was there a cessation of both, he even after governing his people and Church within the limits of his revealed will; so in the first original of kings, whereof some had their beginning by conquest, and some by election of the people, their wills at that time served for law, yet how soon kingdoms began to be settled in civility and policy, then did kings set down their minds by laws, which are properly made by the king only, but at the rogation of the people, the king's grant being obtained thereunto. And so the king became to be *lex loquens* after a sort, binding himself by a double oath to the observation of the fundamental laws of the kingdom: tacitly, as by being a king, and so bound to protect as well the people as the laws of his kingdom; and expressly, by his oath at his coronation. So, as every just king in a settled kingdom is bound to observe that paction made to his people by his laws, in framing his government agreeable thereto, according to that paction which God made with Noah after the deluge, "Hereafter seed time and harvest, cold and heat, summer and winter, and day and night shall not cease, so long as the earth remains"; and therefore a king governing in a settled kingdom leaves to be a king, and degenerates into a tyrant, as soon as he leaves off to rule according to his laws. . . . As for my part, I thank God I have ever given good proof that I never had intention to the contrary, and I am sure to go to my grave with that reputation and comfort, that never king was in all his time more careful to have his laws duly observed, and himself to govern thereafter, than I.

I conclude then this point touching the power of kings with this axiom of Divinity, that as to dispute what God may do is blasphemy, but *quid vult Deus,* that divines may lawfully and do ordinarily dispute and discuss, for to dispute *a posse ad esse* is both against logic and divinity; so is it sedition in subjects to dispute what a king may do in the height of his power, but just kings will ever be willing to declare what they will do, if they will not incur the curse of God. I will not be content that my power be disputed upon, but I shall ever be willing to make the reason appear of all my doings, and rule my actions according to my laws.

53. THE ABOLITION OF KINGSHIP

After James I's son took the throne as Charles I in 1625, the English monarchy experienced some 15 years of increasing royal power, with Parliament first overridden and then left in abeyance, neither abolished nor convened. Not until the king attempted to enforce the royal prerogative over the established church of Scotland, which was Calvinist in doctrine and Presbyterian in form, did he meet with firm resistance. This developed into a decade of civil war that swept over England and only ended when the king was captured by a rebel army representing the authority of Parliament. Charles was tried for high treason by a special parliamentary court and executed in January 1649. Parliament soon drew the logical conclusion from its action and abolished the monarchy on March 17, creating a Commonwealth or republic for which it claimed all the obedience due sovereigns by their subjects. Unlike the Dutch republic, which only emerged because attempts to find a prince to rule over it on its own terms were unsuccessful, the English Commonwealth was deliberately created.

An Act for the Abolishing the Kingly Office in England and Ireland, March 17, 1649

Whereas Charles Stuart, late King of England . . . [etc.], hath by authority derived from Parliament been, and is hereby declared to be justly condemned, adjudged to die, and put to death, for many treasons, mur-

---

SOURCE: J. P. Kenyon (ed.), *The Stuart Constitution, 1603–1688: Documents and Commentary* (Cambridge, England: Cambridge University Press, 1966), pp. 339–41. Reprinted by permission of Cambridge University Press.

ders and other heinous offences committed by him, by which judgement he stood, and is hereby declared to be attainted of high treason, whereby his issue and posterity, and all other pretending title under him, are become incapable of the said crowns, or of being king or queen of the said kingdom or dominions, or either or any of them; be it therefore enacted and ordained . . . by this present parliament and by the authority thereof, that all the people of England and Ireland . . . , of what degree or condition soever, are discharged of all fealty, homage and allegiance which is or shall be pretended to be due unto any of the issue and posterity of the said late King, or any claiming under him; and that Charles Stuart, eldest son, and James called Duke of York, second son, and all other the issue and posterity of him the said late King, and all and every person and persons pretending title from, by or under him, are and be disabled to hold or enjoy the said Crown of England and Ireland. . . .

And whereas it is and hath been found by experience that the office of a king in this nation and Ireland, and to have the power thereof in any single person, is unnecessary, burdensome and dangerous to the liberty, safety and public interest of the people, and that for the most part use hath been made of the regal power and prerogative to oppress and impoverish and enslave the subject, and that usually and naturally any one person in such power makes it his interest to encroach upon the just freedom and liberty of the people, and to promote the setting up of their own will and power above the laws, that so they might enslave these kingdoms to their own lust, be it therefore enacted and ordained by this present Parliament . . . that the office of a king in this nation shall not henceforth reside in or be exercised by any one single person, and that no one person whatsoever shall or may have or hold the office, style, dignity, power or authority of king of the said kingdoms and dominions, or any of them, or of the Prince of Wales, any law . . . notwithstanding.

And whereas by the abolition of the kingly office provided for in this Act a most happy way is made for this nation (if God see it good) to return to its just and ancient right of being governed by its own Representatives[1] or National Meetings in Council, from time to time chosen and entrusted for that purpose by the people; it is therefore resolved and declared by the Commons assembled in Parliament, that they will put a period to the sitting of this present Parliament, and dissolve the same, so soon as may possibly stand with the safety of the people that hath betrusted them, and with what is absolutely necessary for the preserving and upholding the government now settled in the way of a Commonwealth, and that they will carefully provide for the certain choosing, meeting and sitting of the next and future Representatives with such other circumstances of free-

[1] That is, "representative assemblies" [J. P. Kenyon's note].

dom in choice and equality in distribution of Members to be elected thereunto as shall most conduce to the lasting freedom and good of this Commonwealth.

And it is hereby further enacted and declared, notwithstanding anything contained in this Act, [that] no person or persons of what condition and quality soever, within the Commonwealth of England and Ireland, Dominion of Wales, the Islands of Guernsey and Jersey, and [the] town of Berwick upon Tweed, shall be discharged from the obedience and subjection which he and they owe to the government of this nation, as it is now declared, but all and every of them shall in all things render and perform the same, as of right is due unto the Supreme Authority hereby declared to reside in this and the successive Representatives of the people of this nation, and in them only.

54. DEMOCRATIC RADICALISM

During the long struggle between king and Parliament, a new force, the Levellers, appeared upon the political scene. In religion they were extreme Puritans and in politics advocates of democratic government and social justice, although they did not go as far as the smaller, less influential movement of the Diggers, which attacked the very institution of private property. The Levellers were led by a former parliamentary officer, John Lilburne (c. 1614-1657), who continued to steadfastly resist the Commonwealth government of Oliver Cromwell, as he had the royal government of Charles I. Lilburne had a democratic concept of government, in which a House of Commons freed of restraints by king or lords would be subjected to frequent elections and restrained from interfering with the liberties of subjects. This opposition to a new parliamentary tyranny was set down in a "Humble Petition" submitted to Parliament on September 11, 1648, which was probably drafted by Lilburne himself and became the fundamental programmatic statement of the Levellers.

John Lilburne

The Humble Petition

To the Right Honorable, the Commons of England in Parliament Assembled. The humble Petition of divers wel affected Persons in-

Source: William Haller and Godfrey Davies (eds.), *The Leveller Tracts, 1647–1653* (Gloucester, Mass.: Peter Smith, 1964), pp. 148, 151–52, 154. Reprinted by permission of Peter Smith Publishers.

HABITING THE CITY OF LONDON, WESTMINSTER, THE BOROUGH OF SOUTHWORK, HAMBLETS, AND PLACES ADJACENT. WHEREUNTO IS ANNEXED, THE HUMBLE DESIRES OF THE SAID PETITIONERS FOR THE HOUSES RESOLUTION THEREON, BEFORE THEY PROCEED WITH THE PERSONAL TREATY

Sheweth,

That although we are as earnestly desirous of a safe and wel-grounded Peace, and that a finall end were put to all the troubles and miseries of the Common-wealth, as any sort of men whatsoever: Yet considering upon what grounds we engaged on your part in the late and present Wars, and how far (by our so doing) we apprehend our selves concerned, Give us leave (before you conclude as by the Treaty in hand) to acquaint you first with the ground and reason which induced us to aid you against the King and his Adherents. Secondly, What our Apprehensions are of this Treaty. Thirdly, What we expected from you, and do still most earnestly desire.

Be pleased therefore to understand, that we had not engaged on your part, but that we judged this honourable House to be the supream Authority of England, as chosen by, and representing the people; and entrusted with absolute power for redresse of Grievances, and provision for Safety: and that the King was but at the most the chief publike Officer of this Kingdom, and accomptable to this House (the Representative of the People, from whom all just Authority is, or ought to be derived) for discharge of his Office: And if we had not bin confident hereof, we had bin desperately mad to have taken up Armes or to have bin aiding and assisting in maintaining a War against Him; The Laws of the Land making it expresly a crime no lesse than Treason for any to raise War against the King.

. . . . .

And if you consider what new wars, risings, revolting invasions, and plottings have been since this last cry for a Personall Treaty, you will not blame us if we wonder at your hasty proceedings thereunto: especially considering the wonderfull victories which God hath blessed the Army withall.

We professe we cannot chuse but stand amazed to consider the inevitable danger we shall be in, though all things in the Propositions were agreed unto, the Resolutions of the King and his party have been perpetually violently and implacably prosecuted & manifested against us, and that with such scorn and indignation, that it must be more than such ordinary bonds that must hold them.

And it is no lesse a wonder to us, that you can place your own security therein, or that you can ever imagine to see a free Parliament any more in England.

The truth is (and we see we must either now speak it [or] for ever be silent,) We have long expected things of another nature from you, and such as we are confident would have given satisfaction to all serious people of all Parties.

1. That you would have made good the supreme [authority] of the people, in this Honourable House, from all pretences of Negative Voices, either in King or Lords.

2. That you would have made lawes for election of representatives yearly and of course without writ or summons.

3. That you would have set expresse times for their meeting Continuance and Dissolution: as not to exceed 40 or 50 daies at the most, and to have fixed an expressed time for the ending of this present Parl[iament].

4. That you would have exempted matters of Religion and God, from the compulsive or restrictive power of any Authoritie upon earth, and reserved to the supreme authoritie an uncompulsive power only of appointing a way for the publick [worship], whereby abundance of misery, persecution, and hart-burning would for ever be avoyded.

5. That you would have disclaimed in your selvs and all future Representatives, a power of Pressing and forcing any sort of men to serve in warrs, there being nothing more opposite to freedom, nor more unreasonable in an authoritie impowered for raising monies in all occasions, for which, and a just cause, assistants need not be doubted: the other way serving rather to maintain injustice and corrupt parties.

6. That you would have made both Kings, Queens, Princes, Dukes, Earls, Lords, and all Persons, alike liable to every Law of the Land, made or to be made; that so all persons even the Highest might fear & stand in aw and neither violate the publick peace, nor private right of person or estate, (as hath been frequent) without being lyable to accompt as other men.

7. That you would have freed all Commoners from the jurisdiction of the Lords in all cases: and to have taken care that all tryalls should be only of twelve sworn men, and no conviction but upon two or more sufficient known witnesses.

8. That you would have freed all men from being examined against themselves, and from being questioned or punished for doing of that against which no Law hath bin provided.

9. That you would have abbreviated the proceedings in Law, mitigated and made certain the charge thereof in all particulars.

10. That you would have freed all Trade and Marchandising from all Monopolizing and Engrossing, by Companies or otherwise.

11. That you would have abolished Excise, and all kinds of taxes, except subsidies, the old and onely just way of England.

12. That you would have laid open all late Inclosures of Fens, and

other Commons, or have enclosed them onely or chiefly to the benefit of the poor.

13. That you would have considered the many thousands that are ruined by perpetual imprisonment for debt, and provided to their enlargement.

14. That you would have ordered some effectual course to keep people from begging and beggery, in so fruitful a Nation as through Gods blessing this is.

15. That you would have proportioned Punishments more equal to offences; that so mens Lives and Estates might not be forfeited upon trivial and slight occasions.

. . . . .

27. That you would have laid to heart all the abundance of innocent bloud that hath bin spilt, and the infinite spoil and havock that hath been made of peaceable harmlesse people, by express Commissions from the King; and seriously to have considered whether the justice of God be likely to be satisfyed, or his yet continuing wrath appeased, by an Act of Oblivion.

55. THE CONTRACT OF SOVEREIGNTY

The turmoil of the English civil war led one English thinker, the philosopher Thomas Hobbes, to reconsider the basis of political authority. Hobbes (1588-1679) had fled to France in 1641 to escape possible parliamentary harassment for his royalist opinions, but his philosophical boldness led him to fear persecution in France and he returned to England in 1652, reconciling himself to Cromwell's government. It was an act which infuriated Cavalier (royalist) friends, although Charles II, whom he had tutored in mathematics as a youth, was later to protect him and give him a pension.

Hobbes's great exposition of political theory was the *Leviathan, or the Matter, Form, and Power of a Commonwealth, Ecclesiastical and Civil* (1651), in which the state is portrayed in the image of the Leviathan, a Biblical monster. It is a complex work which attempts to derive the true principles of politics from a materialist (but, despite hostile allegations, not atheist) philosophy. Its central political concept is that of the political covenant, by which men set a sovereign (either a monarch or an assembly, such as Parliament or the States of the Dutch) over them, to bring order and peace in the place of the civil war that is inevitable without such a higher authority or power. Although Hobbes's hard, passionate rhetoric, so reminiscent of Machiavelli's, led many to describe him as a defender of absolutist tyranny, he attempted to distinguish interest, obligation, and justice and to set limits to the effective reach of sovereign power. He even envisioned a legitimate revolt when the ruler could not enforce his power and protect his subjects. The following selections give only some high points of an intricate, subtle, and suggestive book.

Thomas Hobbes

Leviathan

Of the Natural Condition of Mankind as Concerning Their Felicity, and Misery

. . . . .

Againe, men have no pleasure, (but on the contrary a great deale of griefe) in keeping company, where there is no power able to over-awe them all. For every man looketh that his companion should value him, at the same rate he sets upon himselfe: And upon all signes of contempt, or undervaluing, naturally endeavours, as far as he dares (which amongst them that have no common power to keep them in quiet, is far enough to make them destroy each other,) to extort a greater value from his contemners, by dommage; and from others, by the example.

So that in the nature of man, we find three principall causes of quarrell. First, Competition; Secondly, Diffidence; Thirdly, Glory.

The first, maketh men invade for Gain; the second, for Safety; and the third, for Reputation. The first use Violence, to make themselves Masters of other mens persons, wives, children, and cattell; the second, to defend them; the third, for trifles, as a word, a smile, a different opinion, and any other signe of undervalue, either direct in their Persons, or by reflexion in their Kindred, their Friends, their Nation, their Profession, or their Name.

Hereby it is manifest, that during the time men live without a common Power to keep them all in awe, they are in that condition which is called Warre; and such a warre, as is of every man, against every man. For Warre, consisteth not in Battell onely, or the act of fighting; but in a tract of time, wherein the Will to contend by Battell is sufficiently known: and therefore the notion of *Time*, is to be considered in the nature of Warre; as it is in the nature of Weather. For as the nature of Foule weather, lyeth

---

Source: Thomas Hobbes, *Leviathan*, edited by A. R. Waller (Cambridge, England: Cambridge University Press, 1935), pp. 83–84, 118–19, 121–23, 129, 152–54, 156. Reprinted by permission of Cambridge University Press.

not in a showre or two of rain; but in an inclination thereto of many dayes together: So the nature of War, consisteth not in actual fighting; but in the known disposition thereto, during all the time there is no assurance to the contrary. All other time is PEACE.

. . . . .

OF THE CAUSES, GENERATION, AND DEFINITION OF A COMMON-WEALTH

The only way to erect such a Common Power, as may be able to defend them from the invasion of Forraigners, and the injuries of one another, and thereby to secure them in such sort, as that by their owne industrie, and by the fruites of the Earth, they may nourish themselves and live contentedly; is, to conferre all their power and strength upon one Man, or upon one Assembly of men, that may reduce all their Wills, by plurality of voices, unto one Will: which is as much as to say, to appoint one Man, or Assembly of men, to beare their Person; and every one to owne, and acknowledge himselfe to be Author of whatsoever he that so beareth their Person, shall Act, or cause to be Acted, in those things which concerne the Common Peace and Safetie; and therein to submit their Wills, every one to his Will, and their Judgements, to his Judgment. This is more than Consent, or Concord; it is a reall Unitie of them all, in one and the same Person, made by Covenant of every man with every man, in such manner, as if every man should say to every man, *I Authorise and give up my Right of Governing my selfe, to this Man, or to this Assembly of men, on this condition, that thou give up thy Right to him, and Authorise all his Actions in like manner.* This done, the Multitude so united in one Person, is called a COMMON-WEALTH, in latine CIVITAS. This is the Generation of that great LEVIATHAN, or rather (to speake more reverently) of that *Mortall God,* to which wee owe under the *Immortall God,* our peace and defence. For by this Authoritie, given him by every particular man in the Common-Wealth, he hath the use of so much Power and Strength conferred on him, that by terror thereof, he is inabled to forme the wills of them all, to Peace at home, and mutuall ayd against their enemies abroad. And in him consisteth the Essence of the Common-wealth; which (to define it,) is *One Person, of whose Acts a great Multitude, by mutuall Covenants one with another, have made themselves every one the Author, to the end he may use the strength and means of them all, as he shall think expedient, for their Peace and Common Defence.*

And he that carryeth this Person, is called SOVERAIGNE, and said to have *Soveraigne Power;* and every one besides, his SUBJECT.

. . . . .

Of the Rights of Soveraignes by Institution

Secondly, Because the Right of bearing the Person of them all, is given to him they make Soveraigne, by Covenant onely of one to another, and not of him to any of them; there can happen no breach of Covenant on the part of the Soveraigne; and consequently none of his Subjects, by any pretence of forfeiture, can be freed from his Subjection. . . .

Fourthly, because every Subject is by this Institution Author of all the Actions, and Judgments of the Soveraigne Instituted; it followes, that whatsoever he doth, it can be no injury to any of his Subjects; nor ought he to be by any of them accused of Injustice. For he that doth any thing by authority from another, doth therein no injury to him by whose authority he acteth: But by this Institution of a Common-wealth, every particular man is Author of all the Soveraigne doth; and consequently he that complaineth of injury from his Soveraigne, complaineth of that whereof he himselfe is Author; and therefore ought not to accuse any man but himselfe; no nor himselfe of injury; because to do injury to ones selfe, is impossible. It is true that they that have Soveraigne power, may commit Iniquity; but not Injustice, or Injury in the proper signification.

Fifthly, and consequently to that which was sayd last, no man that hath Soveraigne power can justly be put to death, or otherwise in any manner by his Subjects punished. For seeing every Subject is Author of the actions of his Soveraigne; he punisheth another, for the actions committed by himselfe.

. . . . .

Of the Severall Kinds of Common-wealth by Institution, and of Succession to the Soveraigne Power.

The difference of Common-wealths, consisteth in the difference of the Soveraign, or the Person representative of all and every one of the Multitude. And because the Soveraignty is either in one Man, or in an Assembly of more than one; and into that Assembly either Every man hath right to enter, or not every one, but Certain men distinguished from the rest; it is manifest, there can be but Three kinds of Common-wealth. For the Representative must needs be One man, or More: and if more, then it is the Assembly of All, or but of a Part. When the Representative is One man, then, is the Common-wealth a MONARCHY: when an Assembly of All that will come together, then it is a DEMOCRACY, or Popular Common-wealth: when an Assembly of a Part onely, then it is called an ARISTOCRACY. Other kind of Common-wealth there can be none: for either One, or More, or All, must have the Soveraign Power (which I have shewn to be indivisible) entire.

. . . . .

Of the Liberty of Subjects

To come now to the particulars of the true Liberty of a Subject; that is to say, what are the things, which though commanded by the Soveraign, he may neverthelesse, without Injustice, refuse to do; we are to consider, what Rights we passe away, when we make a Common-wealth; or (which is all one,) what Liberty we deny our selves, by owning all the Actions (without exception) of the Man, or Assembly we make our Soveraign. For in the act of our *Submission,* consisteth both our *Obligation,* and our *Liberty;* which must therefore be inferred by arguments taken from thence; there being no Obligation on any man, which ariseth not from some Act of his own; for all men equally, are by Nature Free. And because such arguments, must either be drawn from the expresse words, *I Authorise all his Actions,* or from the Intention of him that submitteth himselfe to his Power, (which Intention is to be understood by the End for which he so submitteth;) The Obligation, and Liberty of the Subject, is to be derived, either from those Words, (or others equivalent;) or else from the End of the Institution of Soveraignty; namely, the Peace of the Subjects within themselves, and their Defence against a common Enemy.

First therefore, seeing Soveraignty by Institution, is by Covenant of every one to every one; and Soveraignty by Acquisition, by Covenants of the Vanquished to the Victor, or Child to the Parent; It is manifest, that every Subject has Liberty in all those things, the right whereof cannot by Covenant be transferred. I have shewn before in the 14. Chapter, that Covenants, not to defend a mans own body, are voyd. Therefore,

If the Soveraign command a man (though justly condemned,) to kill, wound, or mayme himselfe; or not to resist those that assault him; or to abstain from the use of food, ayre, medicine, or any other thing, without which he cannot live; yet hath that man the Liberty to disobey.

If a man be interrogated by the Soveraign, or his Authority, concerning a crime done by himselfe, he is not bound (without assurance of Pardon) to confesse it; because no man (as I have shewn in the same Chapter) can be obliged by Covenant to accuse himselfe.

Again, the Consent of a Subject to Soveraign Power, is contained in these words, *I Authorise, or take upon me, all his actions;* in which there is no restriction at all, of his own former naturall Liberty: For by allowing him to *kill me,* I am not bound to kill my selfe when he commands me.

'Tis one thing to say, *Kill me, or my fellow, if you please;* another thing to say, *I will kill my selfe, or my fellow.* It followeth therefore, that

No man is bound by the words themselves, either to kill himselfe, or any other man; And consequently, that the Obligation a man may sometimes have, upon the Command of the Soveraign to execute any dangerous, or dishonourable Office, dependeth not on the Words of our Submission; but on the Intention; which is to be understood by the End thereof. When therefore our refusall to obey, frustrates the End for which the Soveraignty was ordained; then there is no Liberty to refuse: otherwise there is.

Upon this ground, a man that is commanded as a Souldier to fight against the enemy, though his Soveraign have Right enough to punish his refusall with death, may neverthelesse in many cases refuse, without Injustice; as when he substituteth a sufficient Souldier in his place: for in this case he deserteth not the service of the Common-wealth. And there is allowance to be made for naturall timorousnesse, not onely to women, (of whom no such dangerous duty is expected,) but also to men of feminine courage. When Armies fight, there is on one side, or both, a running way; yet when they do it not out of trechery, but fear, they are not esteemed to do it unjustly, but dishonourably. For the same reason, to avoyd battell, is not Injustice, but Cowardise. But he that inrowleth himselfe a Souldier, or taketh imprest mony, taketh away the excuse of a timorous nature; and is obliged, not onely to go to the battell, but also not to run from it, without his Captaines leave. And when the Defence of the Common-wealth, requireth at once the help of all that are able to bear Arms, every one is obliged; because otherwise the Institution of the Common-wealth, which they have not the purpose, or courage to preserve, was in vain.

. . . . .

The Obligation of Subjects to the Soveraign, is understood to last as long, and no longer, than the power lasteth, by which he is able to protect them. For the right men have by Nature to protect themselves, when none else can protect them, can by no Covenant be relinquished. The Soveraignty is the Soule of the Common-wealth; which once departed from the Body, the members doe no more receive their motion from it. The end of Obedience is Protection; which, wheresoever a man seeth it, either in his own, or in anothers sword, Nature applyeth his obedience to it, and his endeavour to maintaine it. And though Soveraignty, in the intention of them that make it, be immortall; yet is it in its own nature, not only subject to violent death, by forreign war; but also through the ignorance, and passions of men, it hath in it, from the very institution, many seeds of a naturall mortality, by Intestine Discord.

56. THE TRIBUNAL OF NATURAL LAW

In disputes among men and groups of men the alternatives seemed to be an appeal to force, and hence ultimately to war, or to a higher authority. Hobbes and other proponents of the theory of the political covenant relied on the force of a sovereign to overcome endemic violence. There emerged no higher authority to decide disputes among states, however, and war or the threat of war remained ever present. During the early 16th century one such dispute spanned the world, pitting the Spanish monarchy (which had included the Portuguese Crown since 1580) against all those who, like the Dutch, refused to accept the Iberian monopoly over trade to the Indies, East and West.

A great Dutch jurist, Hugo Grotius (1583–1645), seeking to escape the necessity of an appeal to force by his countrymen, urged the rightness of their cause in *The Freedom of the Seas*, published in 1625 when he was in exile. Grotius argued that the laws of justice and equity were not the enactments of those who happened to possess power but arose from the nature of man as created by God; there was therefore a law of nations to which all states were subject. But where such laws of nature were written, who judged disputes under them, and who enforced decisions, not as an interested party but as an impartial policeman, were questions that Grotius could answer only in part, as long as the states remained independent and sovereign.

It was significant that the Spaniards and Portuguese lost their monopoly over trade to the Indies not because they were persuaded by Grotius' arguments but because Dutch ships and cannon broke their resistance. Nor were the Spaniards (and, indeed, the English) slow in pointing out that the Dutch destroyed the Portuguese monopoly of trade in the East only to replace it by their own, which they maintained by force.

Hugo Grotius

The Freedom of the Seas

TO THE RULERS AND TO THE FREE AND INDEPENDENT NATIONS OF CHRISTENDOM

The delusion is as old as it is detestable with which many men, especially those who by their wealth and power exercise the greatest influence, persuade themselves, or as I rather believe, try to persuade them-

SOURCE: Hugo Grotius, *The Freedom of the Seas*, translated by Ralph Van Deman Magoffin and edited by James Brown Scott (New York: Oxford University Press, 1916), pp. 1–5.

selves, that justice and injustice are distinguished the one from the other not by their own nature, but in some fashion merely by the opinion and the custom of mankind. Those men therefore think that both the laws and the semblance of equity were devised for the sole purpose of repressing the dissensions and rebellions of those persons born in a subordinate position, affirming meanwhile that they themselves, being placed in a high position, ought to dispense all justice in accordance with their own good pleasure, and that their pleasure ought to be bounded only by their own view of what is expedient. This opinion, absurd and unnatural as it clearly is, has gained considerable currency; but this should by no means occasion surprise, inasmuch as there has to be taken into consideration not only the common frailty of the human race by which we pursue not only vices and their purveyors, but also the arts of flatterers, to whom power is always exposed.

But on the other hand, there have stood forth in every age independent and wise and devout men able to root out this false doctrine from the minds of the simple, and to convict its advocates of shamelessness. For they showed that God was the founder and ruler of the universe, and especially that being the Father of all mankind, He had not separated human beings, as He had the rest of living things, into different species and various divisions, but had willed them to be of one race and to be known by one name; that furthermore He had given them the same origin, the same structural organism, the ability to look each other in the face, language too, and other means of communication, in order that they all might recognize their natural social bond and kinship. They showed too that He is the supreme Lord and Father of this family; and that for the household or the state which He had thus founded, He had drawn up certain laws not graven on tablets of bronze or stone but written in the minds and on the hearts of every individual, where even the unwilling and the refractory must read them. That these laws were binding on great and small alike; that kings have no more power against them than have the common people against the decrees of the magistrates, than have the magistrates against the edicts of the governors, than have the governors against the ordinances of the kings themselves; nay more, that those very laws themselves of each and every nation and city flow from that Divine source, and from that source receive their sanctity and their majesty. . . .

If it be thought that the small society which we call a state cannot exist without the application of these principles (and certainly it cannot), why will not those same principles be necessary to uphold the social structure of the whole human race and to maintain the harmony thereof? If any one rebels against these principles of law and order you are justly indignant, and you even decree punishments in proportion to the magnitude of the offence, for no other reason than that a government cannot be tranquil where trespasses of that sort are allowed. If king act unjustly and violently against king, and nation against nation, such action involves a disturbance of the peace of that universal state, and constitutes a trespass against the supreme Ruler, does it not? There is however this difference: just as the lesser magistrates judge the common people, and as you judge the magistrates, so the King of the universe has laid upon you the command to take cognizance of the trespasses of all other men, and to punish them; but He has reserved for Himself the punishment of your own trespasses. But although He reserves to himself the final punishment, slow and unseen but none the less inevitable, yet He appoints to intervene in human affairs two judges whom the luckiest of sinners does not escape, namely, Conscience, or the innate estimation of oneself, and Public Opinion, or the estimation of others. These two tribunals are open to those who are debarred from all others; to these the powerless appeal; in them are defeated those who are wont to win by might, those who put no bounds to their presumption, those who consider cheap anything bought at the price of human blood, those who defend injustice by injustice, men whose wickedness is so manifest that they must needs be condemned by the unanimous judgment of the good, and cannot be cleared before the bar of their own souls.

To this double tribunal we bring a new case. It is in very truth no petty case such as private citizens are wont to bring against their neighbors about dripping eaves or party walls; nor is it a case such as nations frequently bring against one another about boundary lines or the possession of a river or an island. No! It is a case which concerns practically the entire expanse of the high seas, the right of navigation, the freedom of trade!! Between us and the Spaniards the following points are in dispute: Can the vast, the boundless sea be the appanage of one kingdom alone, and it not the greatest? Can any one nation have the right to prevent other nations which so desire, from selling to one another, from bartering with one another, actually from communicating with one another? Can any nation give away what it never owned, or discover what already belonged to some one else? Does a manifest injustice of long standing create a specific right?

In this controversy we appeal to those jurists among the Spanish themselves who are especially skilled both in divine and human law; we actually invoke the very laws of Spain itself. If that is of no avail, and those whom reason clearly convicts of wrong are induced by greed to maintain that stand, we invoke your majesty, ye Princes, your good faith, ye Peoples, whoever and wherever ye may be. . . .

The law by which our case must be decided is not difficult to find, seeing that it is the same among all nations; and it is easy to understand, seeing that it is innate in every individual and implanted in his mind. Moreover the law to which we appeal is one such as no king ought to deny to his subjects, and one no Christian ought to refuse to a non-Christian. For it is a law derived from nature, the common mother of us all, whose bounty falls on all, and whose sway extends over those who rule nations, and which is held most sacred by those who are most scrupulously just.

57. A CONTRACT AGAINST ABSOLUTISM

The theory of a political covenant or "social contract" that Hobbes used to justify absolute sovereign government was turned around by the English philosopher John Locke (1632-1704) to make all legitimate government dependent upon the people. Locke was the principal theorist of the Whig Party, which arose in England after the restoration of Charles II. He put his political ideas into *Two Treatises of Government,* published in 1689 after he returned from exile in Holland to join the government of King William III. The treatises began as a refutation of the Tory arguments of Sir Robert Filmer, who considered government as the patrimony of the ruler by reason of his descent from Adam. Although drafted a decade before, they remained in manuscript until the revolution of 1688, when a few changes were made to refer to recent events. The following selections are taken from Peter Laslett's modern edition, which is based on Locke's manuscripts and his corrections of the first editions.

John Locke

Second Treatise of Government

. . . . .

Of the State of Nature

To understand Political Power right, and derive it from its Original, we must consider what State all Men are naturally in, and that is, a *State of perfect Freedom* to order their Actions, and dispose of their Possessions, and Persons as they think fit, within the bounds of the Law of Nature,

---

Source: John Locke, *Two Treatises of Government,* edited by Peter Laslett (Cambridge, England: Cambridge University Press, 1960), pp. 287–90, 293–94, 298, 341–43, 382–86, 424–25, 430–31, 445–46. Reprinted by permission of Cambridge University Press.

without asking leave, or depending upon the Will of any other Man.

A *State* also *of Equality,* wherein all the Power and Jurisdiction is reciprocal, no one having more than another: there being nothing more evident, than that Creatures of the same species and rank promiscuously born to all the same advantages of Nature, and the use of the same faculties, should also be equal one amongst another without Subordination or Subjection, unless the Lord and Master of them all, should by any manifest Declaration of his Will set one above another, and confer on him by an evident and clear appointment an undoubted Right to Dominion and Sovereignty. . .

But though this be a *State of Liberty,* yet it is *not a State of Licence,* though man in that State have an uncontroleable Liberty, to dispose of his Person or Possessions, yet he has not Liberty to destroy himself, or so much as any Creature in his Possession, but where some nobler use, than its bare Preservation calls for it. The *State of Nature* has a Law of Nature to govern it, which obliges every one: And Reason, which is that Law, teaches all Mankind, who will but consult it, that being all equal and independent, no one ought to harm another in his Life, Health, Liberty, or Possessions. For Men being all the Workmanship of one Omnipotent, and infinitely wise Maker; All the Servants of one Sovereign Master, sent into the World by his order and about his business, they are his Property, whose Workmanship they are, made to last during his, not one anothers Pleasure. And being furnished with like Faculties, sharing all in one Community of Nature, there cannot be supposed any such *Subordination* among us, that may Authorize us to destroy one another, as if we were made for one anothers uses, as the inferior ranks of Creatures are for ours. Every one as he is *bound to preserve himself,* and not to quit his Station wilfully; so by the like reason when his own Preservation comes not in competition, ought he, as much as he can, *to preserve the rest of Mankind,* and may not unless it be to do Justice on an Offender, take away, or impair the life, or what tends to the Preservation of the Life, the Liberty, Health, Limb or Goods of another.

And that all Men may be restrained from invading others Rights, and from doing hurt to one another, and the Law of Nature be observed, which willeth the Peace and *Preservation of all Mankind,* the *Execution* of the Law of Nature is in that State, put into every Mans hands, whereby every one has a right to punish the transgressors of that Law to such a Degree, as may hinder its Violation. For the *Law of Nature* would, as all other Laws that concern Men in this World, be in vain, if there were no body that in the State of Nature, had a *Power to Execute* that Law, and thereby preserve the innocent and restrain offenders, and if any one in the State of Nature may punish another, for any evil he has done, every one may do so. For in that *State of perfect Equality,* where naturally there is no superiority or jurisdiction of one, over another, what any may do in Prosecution of that Law, every one must needs have a Right to do.

. . . . .

To this strange Doctrine, *viz.* That *in the State of Nature, every one has the Executive Power* of the Law of Nature, I doubt not but it will be objected, That it is unreasonable for Men to be Judges in their own Cases, that Self-love will make Men partial to themselves and their Friends. And on the other side, that Ill Nature, Passion and Revenge will carry them too far in punishing others. And hence nothing but Confusion and Disorder will follow, and that therefore God hath certainly appointed Government to restrain the partiality and violence of Men. I easily grant, that *Civil Government* is the proper Remedy for the Inconveniences of the State of Nature, which must certainly be Great, where Men may be Judges in their own Case, since 'tis easily to be imagined, that he who was so unjust as to do his Brother an Injury, will scarce be so just as to condemn himself for it: But I shall desire those who make this Objection, to remember that *Absolute Monarchs* are but Men, and if Government is to be the Remedy of those Evils, which necessarily follow from Mens being Judges in their own Cases, and the State of Nature is therefore not to be endured, I desire to know what kind of Government that is, and how much better it is than the State of Nature, where one Man commanding a multitude, has the Liberty to be Judge in his own Case, and may do to all his Subjects whatever he pleases, without the least liberty to any one to question or controle those who Execute his Pleasure? And in whatsoever he doth, whether led by Reason, Mistake or Passion, must be submitted to? Much better it is in the State of Nature wherein Men are not bound to submit to the unjust will of another: And if he that judges, judges amiss in his own, or any other Case, he is answerable for it to the rest of Mankind.

. . . . .

Of the State of War

And here we have the plain *difference between the State of Nature, and the State of War*, which however some Men have confounded, are as far distant, as a State of Peace, Good Will, Mutual Assistance, and Preservation, and a State of Enmity, Malice, Violence, and Mutual Destruction are one from another. Men living together according to reason, without a common Superior on Earth, with Authority to judge between them, is *properly the State of Nature*. But force, or a declared design of force upon the Person of another, where there is no common Superior on Earth to appeal to for relief, *is the State of War*.

. . . . .

Of Political or Civil Society

Man being born, as has been proved, with a Title to perfect Freedom, and an uncontrouled enjoyment of all the Rights and Priviledges of the Law of Nature, equally with any other Man, or Number of Men in the World, hath by Nature a Power, not only to preserve his Property, that is, his Life, Liberty and Estate, against the Injuries and Attempts of other Men; but to judge of, and punish the breaches of that Law in others, as he is perswaded the Offence deserves, even with Death it self, in Crimes where the heinousness of the Fact, in his Opinion, requires it. But because no *Political Society* can be, nor subsist without having in it self the Power to preserve the Property, and in order thereunto punish the Offences of all those of that Society; there, and there only is *Political Society,* where every one of the Members hath quitted this natural Power, resign'd it up into the hands of the Community in all cases that exclude him not from appealing for Protection to the Law established by it. And thus all private judgement of every particular Member being excluded, the Community comes to be Umpire, by settled standing Rules, indifferent, and the same to all Parties; and by Men having Authority from the Community, for the execution of those Rules, decides all the differences that may happen between any Members of that Society, concerning any matter of right; and punishes those Offences, which any Member hath committed against the Society, with such Penalties as the Law has established: Whereby it is easie to discern who are, and who are not, in *Political Society* together. Those who are united into one Body, and have a common establish'd Law and Judicature to appeal to, with Authority to decide Controversies between them, and punish Offenders, *are in Civil Society* one with another: but those who have no such common Appeal, I mean on Earth, are still in the state of Nature, each being, where there is no other, Judge for himself, and Executioner; which is, as I have before shew'd it, the perfect *state of Nature.* . . .

Where-ever therefore any number of Men are so united into one Society, as to quit every one his Executive Power of the Law of Nature, and to resign it to the publick, there and there only is a *Political, or Civil Society.* And this is done where-ever any number of Men, in the state of Nature, enter into Sociey to make one People, one Body Politick under one Supreme Government, or else when any one joyns himself to, and incorporates with any Government already made. For hereby he authorizes the Society, or which is all one, the Legislative thereof to make Laws for him as the publick good of the Society shall require; to the Execution whereof, his own assistance (as to his own Decrees) is due. And this *puts*

Men out of a State of Nature *into* that of a *Commonwealth*, by setting up a Judge on Earth, with Authority to determine all the Controversies, and redress the Injuries, that may happen to any Member of the Commonwealth; which Judge is the Legislative, or Magistrates appointed by it. And where-ever there are any number of Men, however associated, that have no such decisive power to appeal to, there they are still *in the state of Nature*. . . .

. . . . .

Of the Legislative, Executive, and Federative Power of the Commonwealth

The *Legislative* Power is that which has a right *to direct* how *the Force of the Commonwealth* shall be imploy'd for preserving the Community and the Members of it. But because those Laws which are constantly to be Executed, and whose force is always to continue, may be made in a little time; therefore there is no need, that the *Legislative* should be always in being, not having always business to do. And because it may be too great a temptation to humane frailty apt to grasp at Power, for the same Persons who have the Power of making Laws, to have also in their hands the power to execute them, whereby they may exempt themselves from Obedience to the Laws they make, and suit the Law, both in its making and execution, to their own private advantage, and thereby come to have a distinct interest from the rest of the Community, contrary to the end of Society and Government: Therefore in well order'd Commonwealths, where the good of the whole is so considered, as it ought, the *Legislative* Power is put into the hands of divers Persons who duly Assembled, have by themselves, or jointly with others, a Power to make Laws, which when they have done, being separated again, they are themselves subject to the Laws, they have made; which is a new and near tie upon them, to take care, that they make them for the publick good.

But because the Laws, that are at once, and in a short time made, have a constant and lasting force, and need a *perpetual Execution*, or an attendance thereunto: Therefore 'tis necessary there should be a *Power always in being*, which should see to the *Execution* of the Laws that are made, and remain in force. And thus the *Legislative* and *Executive Power* come often to be separated. .

Of the Subordination of the Powers of the Commonwealth

Though in a Constituted Commonwealth, standing upon its own Basis, and acting according to its own Nature, that is, acting for the preservation of the Community, there can be but *one Supream Power,* which is *the Legislative,* to which all the rest are and must be subordinate, yet the Legislative being only a Fiduciary Power to act for certain ends, there remains still *in the People a Supream Power* to remove or *alter the Legislative,* when they find the *Legislative* act contrary to the trust reposed in them. For all *Power given with trust* for the attaining an *end,* being limited by that end, whenever that *end* is manifestly neglected, or opposed, the *trust* must necessarily be *forfeited,* and the Power devolve into the hands of those that gave it, who may place it anew where they shall think best for their safety and security. And thus the *Community* perpetually *retains a Supream Power* of saving themselves from the attempts and designs of any Body, even of their Legislators, whenever they shall be so foolish, or so wicked, as to lay and carry on designs against the Liberties and Properties of the Subject. For no Man, or Society of Men, having a Power to deliver up their *Preservation,* or consequently the means of it, to the Absolute Will and arbitrary Dominion of another; whenever any one shall go about to bring them into such a Slavish Condition, they will always have a right to preserve what they have not a Power to part with; and to rid themselves of those who invade this Fundamental, Sacred, and unalterable law of *Self-Preservation,* for which they enter'd into Society. And thus the *Community* may be said in this respect to be *always the Supream Power,* but not as considered under any Form of Government, because this Power of the People can never take place till the Government be dissolved.

In all Cases, whilst the Government subsists, the *Legislative is the Supream Power.* For what can give Laws to another, must needs be superiour to him: and since the Legislative is no otherwise Legislative of the Society, but by the right it has to make Laws for all the parts and for every Member of the Society, prescribing Rules to their actions, and giving power of Execution, where they are transgressed, the *Legislative* must needs be the *Supream,* and all other Powers in any Members or parts of the Society, derived from and subordinate to it.

. . . . .

Of the Dissolution of Government

He that will with any clearness speak of the *Dissolution of Government,* ought, in the first place to distinguish between the *Dissolution of the Society,* and the *Dissolution of the Government.* That which makes the Community, and brings Men out of the loose State of Nature, into *one Politick Society,* is the Agreement which every one has with the rest to incorporate, and act as one Body, and so be one distinct Commonwealth. The usual, and almost only way whereby *this Union is dissolved*, is the Inroad of Foreign Force making a Conquest upon them. For in that Case, (not being able to maintain and support themselves, as *one intire* and *independent Body*) the Union belonging to that Body which consisted therein, must necessarily cease, and so every one return to the state he was in before, with a liberty to shift for himself, and provide for his own Safety as he thinks fit in some other Society. Whenever the *Society is dissolved*, 'tis certain the Government of that Society cannot remain. Thus Conquerours Swords often cut up Governments by the Roots, and mangle Societies to pieces, separating the subdued or scattered Multitude from the Protection of, and Dependence on that Society which ought to have preserved them from violence. The World is too well instructed in, and too forward to allow of this way of dissolving of Governments to need any more to be said of it: and there wants not much Argument to prove, that where the *Society is dissolved*, the Government cannot remain; that being as impossible, as for the Frame of an House to subsist when the Materials of it are scattered, and dissipated by a Whirl-wind, or jumbled into a confused heap by an Earthquake.

Besides this over-turning from without, *Governments are dissolved from within*,

First, When the *Legislative* is *altered*. Civil Society being a State of Peace, amongst those who are of it, from whom the State of War is excluded by the Umpirage, which they have provided in their Legislative, for the ending all Differences, that may arise amongst any of them, 'tis in their *Legislative*, that the Members of a Commonwealth are united, and combined together into one coherent living Body. This *is the Soul that gives Form, Life, and Unity* to the Commonwealth: From hence the several Members have their mutual Influence, Sympathy, and Connexion: And therefore when the *Legislative* is broken, or *dissolved*, Dissolution and Death follows. For the *Essence and Union of the Society* consisting in having one Will, the Legislative, when once established by the Majority, has the declaring, and as it were keeping of that Will.

. . . . .

There is therefore, secondly, another way whereby *Governments are dissolved*, and that is; when the Legislative, or the Prince, either of them act contrary to their Trust.

First, The *Legislative acts against the Trust* reposed in them, when they endeavour to invade the Property of the Subject, and to make themselves, or any part of the Community, Masters, or Arbitrary Disposers of the Lives, Liberties, or Fortunes of the People.

The Reason why Men enter into Society, is the preservation of their Property; and the end why they chuse and authorize a Legislative, is, that there may be Laws made, and Rules set as Guards and Fences to the Properties of all the Members of the Society, to limit the Power, and moderate the Dominion of every Part and Member of the Society. For since it can never be supposed to be the Will of the Society, that the Legislative should have a Power to destroy that, which every one designs to secure, by entering into Society, and for which the People submitted themselves to the Legislators of their own making; whenever the *Legislators endeavour to take away, and destroy the Property of the People,* or to reduce them to Slavery under Arbitrary Power, they put themselves into a state of War with the People, who are thereupon absolved from any farther Obedience, and are left to the common Refuge, which God hath provided for all Men, against Force and Violence. Whensoever therefore the *Legislative* shall transgress this fundamental Rule of Society; and either by Ambition, Fear, Folly or Corruption, *endeavour to grasp* themselves, *or put into the hands of any other an Absolute Power* over the Lives, Liberties, and Estates of the People; By this breach of Trust they *forfeit the Power,* the People had put into their hands, for quite contrary ends, and it devolves to the People, who have a Right to resume their original Liberty, and, by the Establishment of a new Legislative (such as they shall think fit) provide for their own Safety and Security, which is the end for which they are in Society. What I have said here, concerning the Legislative, in general, holds true also concerning the *supreame Executor,* who having a double trust put in him, both to have a part in the Legislative, and the supreme Execution of the Law, Acts against both, when he goes about to set up his own Arbitrary Will, as the Law of the Society.

. . . . .

To conclude, The *Power that every individual gave the Society,* when he entered into it, can never revert to the Individuals again, as long as the Society lasts, but will always remain in the Community; because without this, there can be no Community, no Common-wealth, which is contrary to the original Agreement: So also when the Society hath placed the Legislative in any Assembly of Men, to continue in them and their Successors, with Direction and Authority for providing such Successors, *the Legislative can never revert to the People* whilst that Government lasts: Because having provided a Legislative with Power to continue for ever, they have given up their Political Power to the Legislative, and cannot resume it. But if they have set Limits to the Duration of their Legislative, and made this Supreme Power in any Person, or Assembly, only temporary: Or else when by the Miscarriages of those in Authority, it is forfeited; upon the Forfeiture of their Rulers, or at the Determination of the Time set, *it reverts to the Society,* and the People have a Right to act as Supreme, and continue the Legislative in themselves, or erect a new Form, or under the old form place it in new hands, as they think good.

58. RULES FOR RULING WELL

Some of the most penetrating analysis of the problems of politics in 17th-century Europe came from one of its most able political leaders, Cardinal Richelieu, who became the prime minister of France in 1624. Armand Jean du Plessis, Duke de Richelieu (1585-1642), one of the greatest statesmen of his age, led the government of France for Louis XIII during the Thirty Years' War, from 1624 to 1642. He put down rebellions of Huguenots and noblemen, strengthened the central government on principles of royalist absolutism, and brought France into the war against the Spanish and Austrian Habsburgs and prepared their defeat, which he did not live to see acknowledged in the treaties of Westphalia (1648) and the Pyrenees (1659). Although he was well read in theology and political thought, his approach to the problem of government was highly concrete.

But it was not enough to state that only the king rightly possessed sovereignty; it was also necessary to guide the king to rule effectively and to good purpose. These ideas Richelieu set forth in his *Political Testament*, compiled about 1646 from various memoranda and commentaries he prepared during his years as the king's chief minister and first published in Amsterdam in 1688. The portions reprinted below were translated from the modern edition, which is based on the original manuscripts, edited by Louis André.

Armand Jean du Plessis, Cardinal Richelieu

Political Testament

General Statement of the Royal Program

When Your Majesty resolved to admit me both to your council and to an important place in your confidence for the direction of your affairs, I may say that the Huguenots shared the state with you; that the nobles conducted themselves as if they were not your subjects, and the most powerful governors of the provinces as if they were sovereign in their offices.

Source: From Henry Bertram Hill, editor and translator, *The Political Testament of Cardinal Richelieu* (Madison: University of Wisconsin Press; © 1961 by the Regents of the University of Wisconsin), pp. 9–11, 37, 39–40, 76, 118. Reprinted by permission of the University of Wisconsin Press.

I may say that the bad example of all of these was so prejudicial to the welfare of this realm that even the best courts were affected by it, and endeavored, in certain cases, to diminish your legitimate authority as far as it was possible in order to carry their own powers beyond the limits of reason.

I may say that everyone measured his own merit by his audacity; that in place of esteeming the benefits which they received from Your Majesty at their proper worth, they all valued them only as they satisfied the demands of their imaginations; that the most scheming were held to be the wisest, and often found themselves the most prosperous.

I may further say that foreign alliances were scorned, private interests being preferred to those of the public, and in a word, the dignity of the royal majesty was so disparaged, and so different from what it should be, because of the misdeeds of those who conducted your affairs, that it was almost impossible to recognize it. It was impossible, without losing all, to tolerate longer the conduct of those to whom Your Majesty had intrusted the helm of state; and yet everything could not be changed at once without violating the laws of prudence, which do not permit the passing from one extreme to another without preparation.

The bad state of your affairs seemed to force you to precipitate decisions, without a choice of time or of means. And yet it was imperative to make a choice of both in order to profit by the change which necessity demanded of your prudence.

The best minds did not think that it would be possible to pass without shipwreck all the rocks in such uncertain times. The court was full of people who censured the temerity of those who wished to undertake a reform, and all well knew that princes find it easy to impute to those who are near them the bad outcome of the undertakings upon which they have been well advised. So few people, consequently, expected good results from the change which it was announced I wished to make, that many held my fall assured even before Your Majesty had elevated me.

Notwithstanding these difficulties which I explained to Your Majesty, knowing how much kings may do when they make good use of their power, I dared to promise you, with assurance, that you would soon find remedies for the disorders in your state, and that your prudence, your courage, and the benediction of God would give a new aspect to this realm. I promised Your Majesty to employ all my industry and all the authority which it should please you to give to me to ruin the Huguenot party, to abase the pride of the nobles, to bring all your subjects back to their duty, and to restore your reputation among foreign nations to the station it ought to occupy.

. . . . .

The Role of the King

. . . I cannot help repeating again a plea I have made many times before to Your Majesty, begging you to apply yourself to the matters of greatest importance to your country, disdaining the little ones as beneath your thought and interest. It would be useful and inspiring for you to dwell often upon the vast prospects of the trend of events. If you preoccupy yourself with the small matters, you will not only fail to gain benefit therefrom, you will even bring misfortune upon yourself. Not only does such a preoccupation divert you from a better one. Just as little thorns are more capable of pricking than larger ones, which are more easily seen, so it would be impossible for you to protect yourself from many unpleasant happenings inconsequential for public business and bad for your own health.

. . . . .

Although it is common enough with many men to act only when driven by some emotion, so that one may conceive of them as being like incense which smells sweet only when it is being burned, I cannot help reminding Your Majesty that such a character trait is dangerous in any kind of person, and it is particularly so in kings, who more than all others should be motivated by reason. If emotion once in a while does in fact bring good results, it is only a matter of luck, since by its very nature it misleads men so much that it blinds those who are possessed by it. If a man so deprived of sight occasionally does find the proper course, it is a marvel if he does not stray and get lost completely. And if he does not fall down he will certainly need the best of good fortune not to falter many times. Often indeed have evils befallen princes and their countries when they have been more inclined to follow their emotions than their minds, especially when guided by their whims rather than by considerations of the public interest. Because of this it is impossible for me not to beg Your Majesty to reflect frequently on this matter in order to confirm more and more in yourself your natural tendency to do the right thing.

. . . . .

Public Interest the First Objective

The public interest ought to be the sole objective of the prince and his councillors, or, at the least, both are obliged to have it foremost in mind, and preferred to all private gain. It is impossible to overestimate the good which a prince and those serving him in government can do if they religiously follow this principle, and one can hardly imagine the evils which befall a state if private interest is preferred to the public good and actually gains the ascendency. True philosophy, as well as the precepts of both Christianity and sound politics, teach this truth so clearly that a prince's councillors can hardly too often remind him of so necessary a principle, nor the prince punish too severely those members of his council despicable enough not to practice it.

. . . . .

THE POWER OF THE PRINCE

Power being one of the things most necessary to the grandeur of kings and the success of their governments, those who have the principal management of states are particularly obliged to omit nothing which could contribute to making their masters fully and universally respected. As goodness is the object of love, so power is the cause of fear. It is certain that of all the forces capable of producing results in public affairs, fear, if based on both esteem and reverence, is the most effective, since it can drive everyone to do his duty. If this principle is of great efficacy with regard to internal affairs, it is of no less value externally, since both foreigners and subjects take the same view of redoubtable power and both refrain from offending a prince whom they recognize as being able to hurt them if he so wishes. I have said already that this power of which I speak should be based on esteem and respect.

59. THE LAWS OF POLITICAL PRUDENCE

The doctrine that political necessity makes its own laws, which had been enunciated with chilly rhetoric by Machiavelli, came to be known as the principle of "reason of state." It was applied with great skill not only by Richelieu but also by his successor, Cardinal Mazarin, who became prime minister on the accession of Louis XIV in 1643. Jules Mazarin (1602-1661), an Italian-born diplomat, who had been brought into the French government by Richelieu, continued his task of defeating the Habsburgs. Although the Austrian Habsburgs accepted defeat with the Treaty of Westphalia in 1648, their Spanish cousins stubbornly continued the war against France. The rise of the English Commonwealth seemed to afford Spain an opportunity to salvage victory, or at least avert overwhelming defeat. The execution of Charles I was quite naturally execrated by all monarchs, but especially by the king of France, for Charles's widow was Louis XIV's aunt. Mazarin, in a letter to the queen mother, Anne of Austria (Louis was only 12 years of age), explained why, despite the laws of honor and justice, France had to seek the friendship of Cromwell, regicide though he was, to thwart the purposes of Spain.

Jules Mazarin

Letter to Anne of Austria

. . . It seems at first sight . . . that if we are guided by the laws of honor or justice, we ought not to recognize this Commonwealth; as the King could do nothing more prejudicial to his reputation than to consent to a recognition by which he would abandon the interest of the legitimate king, his near relative, neighbor, and ally; and nothing more unjust than to recognize usurpers who have imbrued their hands in the blood of their sovereign. . . . But as the laws of honor or justice should never lead us to do anything contrary to the dictates of prudence, it must be considered that all the demonstrations which we might now make in favor of the King of England, would not lead to his restoration; that a longer refusal to recognize the Commonwealth will serve in no way to augment or confirm the rights of the King; . . . that whatever the necessities of the time and of our affairs may compel us to do in favor of the Commonwealth, will not prevent us from afterwards being able to take advantage of any favorable conjunctures that may present themselves, when we shall be in a better condition to attempt some great enterprise; . . . that, moreover, there is reason to fear that, if the Spaniards once become more intimately allied with the English, as they are ardently laboring to be, they will prevent them from consenting to any accommodation with us, and will persuade them, if not to make open war upon us, at least to give them powerful assistance against us. There accordingly remains no room for doubt that we should without delay enter into negotiations with the Commonwealth of England, and give it the title which it desires. One condition is, nevertheless, absolutely necessary; and without it, it would be useless to pledge ourselves to grant this recognition; and that is, to be assured beforehand that we shall derive from it some utility, capable of counterbalancing the prejudice which may accrue by it to our reputation; . . . it would be doubly prejudicial to condescend to an act of meanness, if, after we had done it, the English should continue in a state of indifference and coolness towards us; and if our advances only served

---

SOURCE: F. P. G. Guizot, *History of Oliver Cromwell and the English Commonwealth*, translated by Andrew R. Scobie (Philadelphia: Blanchard and Lea, 1854), Vol. I, pp. 222–24.

to make them more haughty and unyielding, in the conditions of the treaty which must be made with them for the accommodation of the differences which exist between us.

60. THE GRAND MONARCH ON THE MANNER OF RULING

A different kind of wisdom about monarchical rule was evidenced by Mazarin's pupil, King Louis XIV of France. The "Grand Monarch," who became the very model of European kingship, was deeply dedicated to the task of governing his state well, that is, both effectively and justly. Possessing a shrewd intelligence in political calculations and in human relations, he had little interest in or understanding of the subtler distinctions and perplexing problems of political theory. During the two decades after he took over the personal administration of the royal government on Mazarin's death in 1661, he wrote (or more usually, dictated) his comments on his actions and his conclusions about the nature of royal rule for the eventual instruction of his elder son, the Dauphin (as the heir to the French throne was called). The first part of the selection below from these *Mémoires* discusses the "mild and courteous association" a strong ruler of France could and should have with his subjects. The second part, which deals with memories of the civil war of the Fronde (1648–1653) during his minority, expresses his sharp hatred for any popular share in the royal power.

Louis XIV

Mémoires for the Instruction of the Dauphin

. . . There are some nations where the majesty of kings consists mostly of not letting themselves be seen, and this may have its reasons among spirits accustomed to servitude who can only be governed by fear and by terror; but this is not the character of our French, and as far back as we can go in our history, if there is any unique characteristic about this monarchy, it is the free and easy access of the subjects to the prince. It is a community of justice between them that holds them, so to speak, in a mild and courteous association, notwithstanding their almost infinite difference in birth, rank, and power. That this system is good and useful for us, experience has already shown, since there is no memory in all past times of any empire having lasted as long as this one, and yet it does not seem about to end.

SOURCE: Reprinted with permission of The Macmillan Company from *Louis XIV: Mémoires for the Instruction of the Dauphin*, translated by Paul Sonnino, pp. 101–2, 130–31.

And it is a notable thing, my son, that the most unscrupulous political thinkers, the least affected by principles of equity, of goodness, and of honor seem to have predicted immortality for this state, insofar as it is humanly possible, for they maintain that these other empires where terror rules and where the caprice of the prince is the only law are perhaps more difficult to pierce, but that their first wound is mortal, there being hardly any subject who does not wish for a change and who does not favor it as soon as there is any hope for it; whereas in France, they say, if it is easy to depart from natural conditions, it is even easier to return to them, there being no other empire where private individuals, and especially the principal ones, once they have had a taste of it, find so many things to their interest and advantage as in this one.

It may seem to you, perhaps, my son, that I am carrying this reflection a little too far, but it does not fail to come right to the point. I confess, my son—and everything that I have already told you makes it sufficiently clear to you—that this liberty, this mildness, and, so to speak, this laxity of the monarchy had gotten out of hand during my minority and the troubles of my state, and that it had turned into license, confusion, and disorder. But the more necessary it was to find some acceptable remedies to this excess, the more I was obliged to preserve and cultivate carefully whatever, without diminishing my authority and the respect that was due me, bound my people, and especially persons of quality, to me by affection, so as to show them thereby that it was neither aversion for them, nor affected severity, nor rudeness of manners, but simply reason and duty that rendered me more reserved and more strict toward them in other things. This community of pleasures that produces a courteous familiarity between our courtiers and ourselves strikes them and charms them beyond words. The people, on the other hand, enjoy a spectacle which, basically, is always aimed at pleasing them, and all our subjects, in general, are delighted to see that we share their tastes for what they do best. We sometimes hold their minds and their hearts more effectively by this, perhaps, than by rewards and by favors; and in regard to foreigners, when they see that a state is otherwise flourishing and orderly, what might be considered as superfluous expenses make a very favorable impression of magnificence, power, wealth, and greatness upon them, aside from the fact that physical dexterity, which can only be maintained and confirmed by this, is always becoming in a prince and produces a favorable estimate of his hidden qualities.

. . . . .

What makes for the greatness and the majesty of kings is not so much the scepter that they bear as the manner in which they bear it. It is perverting the order of things to attribute decisions to the subjects and deference to the sovereign, and if I have described to you elsewhere the miserable condition of princes who commit their people and their dignity to the conduct of a prime minister, I have good cause to portray to you here the misery of those who are abandoned to the indiscretion of a popular assembly; for indeed, the prime minister is a man whom you choose as you see fit, whom you associate to your power only insofar as you please, and who has the greatest influence in your affairs only because he has the first place in your heart. In appropriating your possessions and your authority, he at least retains some gratitude and some respect for your person, and however great we may make him, he cannot avoid his ruin if we have but the strength to will it. At the most, you have only a single partner on the throne. If he despoils you of part of your glory, he unburdens you at the same time of your thorniest cares. The interest of his own greatness engages him to sustain yours. He wishes to preserve your rights as a possession that he enjoys in your name, and if he shares your diadem with you, he at least works to leave it intact to your descendants.

But this is not the case with the power of a popular assembly. The more you grant it, the more it demands; the more you caress it, the more it scorns you; and what it once has in its possession is retained by so many hands that it cannot be torn away without extreme violence. Out of so many persons who compose these great bodies, it is always the least sensible who assume the greatest license. Once you defer to them, they claim the right forever to control your plans according to their fancy, and the continual necessity of defending yourself against their assaults alone produces many more cares for you than all the other interests of your crown, so that a prince who wants to bequeath lasting tranquillity to his people and his dignity completely intact to his successors cannot be too careful to suppress this tumultuous temerity.

But I am dwelling too long on a reflection that seems useless for you, or that can at most serve you only to recognize the misery of our neighbors, since it is patent that you will reign in a state where you will find no authority that is not honored to derive its origin and its status from you, no body that dares to depart from expressions of respect, no corporation that does not see its principal greatness in the good of your service and its sole security in its humble submission.

61. A TALE OF WARFARE AWAY FROM BATTLE

From the agonies of the Thirty Years' War emerged one of the masterpieces of literature, *The Adventurous German Simplicissimus*, which was published in 1669, just 21 years after the holocaust ended. The subtitle describes it as the life story of "a queer strolling scholar named Melchior Sternfels von Fuchshaim," but its hero is always called Simplicissimus, "The Most Simple One." Simplicius Simplicissimus passes through a succession of careers—soldier and clown, townsman and pilgrim, slave and hermit—and in each he undergoes or observes the horrors of warfare. The author of Simplicissimus was Johann Jakob Christoffel von Grimmelshausen (c. 1620-1676), a writer and churchman who served as a soldier during the war. The following excerpts emphasize not the dramatic clashes of huge masses of troops upon the battlefield but the small and bitter conflicts between the soldiery and the population upon whom they preyed. The work combines vivid realism and bold imagination and is written in an earthy style worthy of its subject.

Johann Jakob von Grimmelshausen

The Adventurous German Simplicissimus

Simplicius lets himself drift, like a piece of reed on a pond

A few days after my dear and worthy hermit's demise, I made my way to the parson mentioned above, reported my master's death to him, and asked his advice on how to act in this situation. Although he tried very hard to dissuade me from staying longer in the woods, and pointed out the obvious danger of doing so, I followed in my predecessor's footsteps bravely, and all summer long did as a pious anchorite should. But as time changes everything, the grief I felt for my hermit gradually lessened, and the severe cold of winter outside extinguished the ardor of my intentions inside. The more I began to waver, the lazier I became about my prayers, and instead of contemplating divine and heavenly things, I was overcome by a desire to look at the world. And since I wasn't much good anymore in the forest, I resolved to see the parson again and to find out if he would still advise me to leave the woods. To this end, I walked toward the village, and when I got there I saw it in flames; a troop of cavalry had just plundered and set it on fire, killed some of the peasants, run off many and captured a few, among them the parson. Oh, my God! How full of trials and tribulations is a man's life?! One misfortune hardly stops before another overtakes us.

The cavalrymen were about to leave, and the parson was led by a rope like a poor sinner and slave. Some were screaming, "Shoot the bastard!" Others wanted money from him. He raised his hands and begged them, for the sake of their souls, to spare him and treat him with Christian mercy—in vain, for one of them rode roughshod over him and hit him

---

Source: From Johann Jakob Christoffel von Grimmelshausen: *Simplicius Simplicissimus*, translated by George Schulz-Gehrend, pp. 26–32, copyright © 1965, by The Bobbs-Merrill Company, Inc., reprinted by permission of the publisher.

such a wallop over the head that blood trickled down; he fell, commended his soul to God, and lay there like a dead dog. The captured peasants didn't fare much better.

When it looked as if these horsemen had lost their minds in their tyrannical cruelty, an armed gang of peasants like an angry swarm of yellow jackets came charging out of the woods. They raised such a ghastly war whoop, attacked so furiously, and fired so savagely that my hair stood on end, for I had never attended this kind of free-for-all. Nobody's likely to make monkeys of our peasants from the Spessart—nor of the ones from Hesse, Sauerland, Vogelsberg, or the Black Forest! The horsemen made tracks, not only leaving the stolen cattle behind, but also throwing away the loot as they ran, giving up their prey lest they fall prey to the peasants. A few who were captured were given rough treatment.

This introductory entertainment almost spoiled my desire to see the world; I thought if this is the way things are, the wilderness is far more attractive. Still, I wanted to hear the parson's explanations, but he was rather faint from his injuries and the beating he had received. He admonished me that he couldn't help or advise me because in his present condition he would soon have to make a living as a beggar, and even if I wanted to stay in the woods, he wouldn't be able to give me any help, because, as I could see, his church and parsonage were at that very moment going up in smoke.

With these words I trotted sadly back toward the woods and my home. Since I had experienced little comfort on my journey (rather, I had become much more devout again), I decided never to leave the wilderness, but meant to conclude my life like a hermit, in contemplation of divine things. I was already figuring out how to get along without salt (which the parson had previously given me) and thus do without anybody's help.

A strange story of five peasants

So that I might follow my decision at once and be a genuine hermit, I dressed in the late hermit's hair shirt and put on his chain—not because I needed to mortify my rebellious flesh, but to resemble my predecessor in appearance as well as in manner of living and also to protect myself better against the cold of winter.

The day after the village had been plundered and burned, I was just sitting in my hut, frying yellow turnips and praying at the same time, when some forty or fifty musketeers surrounded me. Although they hardly believed their eyes when they saw me, those boys turned my place upside down looking for something that absolutely wasn't there, for I had only a couple of books, and they threw them helter-skelter because they were no good to them. After a while, when they had taken a second look at me and seen by the feathers what kind of bird they had caught, they decided there was no hope of booty. Then they wondered about my hard way of living and took pity on my tender youth, particularly the officer in charge. He did me the honor of requesting me to show them the way out of the woods, in which they had been lost for some time. I did not refuse for a moment. To get rid of these unfriendly guests as soon as possible, I led them by the nearest road to the village where the parson had been manhandled. Truth to tell, that was the only road I knew.

But before we got out of the woods we saw about ten peasants, some armed with guns, the others busy burying something. The soldiers approached them and shouted, "Halt!" The peasants answered with their guns. And when they saw how many soldiers there were, they rushed off this way and that so that the musketeers (who were tired) couldn't catch any of them. Then the soldiers wanted to uncover what the peasants had covered up—an easy job because the spades and picks were still there. They had hardly started when a voice came up from below and said, "You bloody rascals! You dirty crooks! You damn bastards! Do you think heaven will let you go unpunished for your unchristian cruelty? There are plenty of stout fellows who will retaliate for your bestiality, so that nobody will come to lick your ass!" The soldiers looked at each other and didn't know what to do next. Some thought they were hearing a ghost, but I thought I was dreaming. Their officer told them to go on digging. Soon they struck a barrel, opened it, and found inside a man whose nose and ears had been cut off. But he was still alive. As soon as this fellow had recovered enough to recognize some of the group, he told how the peasants had captured six soldiers who had been reconnoitering for feed. Only an hour ago, they had shot five of these, standing them one behind the other; since the bullet, having had to go through five bodies before him, had not killed him, the sixth in the line, they had cut off his ears and nose. But first they had forced him (I beg the reader's pardon) to lick their asses. When he saw himself so degraded by these dishonorable and dastardly knaves, he called them the vilest names he could think of, hoping to trick them into killing him, though they had vouchsafed his life, but in vain. After he had embittered them, they stuck him in this barrel and buried him alive, saying that since he tried so hard for death, for reasons of spite they did not want to humor him.

While this man was telling of his misery, another group of soldiers, infantry, came up out of the woods. They had captured five of the fugitive peasants and shot the others. Among the captives were four peasants to whom the mistreated cavalryman had been forced to do as he was told. Now, when both groups of soldiers discovered they were from the same army, the horseman had to tell once more what had happened to him and his comrades in arms.

You should have seen what happened to the peasants there! Some of the soldiers in their first fury wanted to fill them full of lead, but others said that these gay birds ought to be tortured a little; they ought to get a taste of what they did to our buddy. In the meantime, their ribs were being tickled with musket stocks. Finally a soldier stepped forward and said, "Gentlemen, since it is a crying shame to all soldiers that five peasants abused this rascal (he pointed to the cavalryman), it is no more than fair for us to erase this blot and let these bastards kiss our friend a hundred times." Another said, "This rat is not worthy of the honor. If he hadn't been such a numbskull he would have died a thousand times rather than act in a manner unbecoming to a soldier."

Finally they resolved that each of the peasants was to reciprocate on ten soldiers. Then they wanted to decide what else to do to the peasants. But the peasants were so obstinate that they could in no way be coerced. One soldier took the fifth peasant aside and promised to let him go where he pleased, if he denied God and all his saints. The peasant answered that he had never given a damn for the saints and his personal acquaintance with God had been slight. He swore he did not know God and wanted no part of his kingdom. The soldier fired a bullet at his head, but it ricocheted as if it had hit a steel wall. Then he pulled out his sword bayonet and shouted, "Is that the kind you are? I promised to let you go where you wanted, but since you don't want to go to heaven, I am now sending you to hell!" And he split his head apart down to the teeth. "This is the way to get revenge," said the soldier. "Send these villains to hell and keep 'em there!"

Meanwhile the soldiers tied the other four peasants (the same whose asses the soldier had had to lick) over a fallen tree in such a way that their rumps stuck up. After removing their trousers, they took yards and yards of fuse cord, made knots in it, and neatly ran the knotted cord through the cleft of their behinds until they drew blood. "This is the way to dress their backsides," they said. The peasants screamed like pigs, but a lot of good it did them! The soldiers didn't stop until they struck the bone. I was sent back to my hut because the second troop knew the way, so I didn't find out what else they did to the peasants.

Simplicius is raided, and has a wondrous dream about peasants and how it goes in time of war

When I got back home, I found that all my firewood, my household goods, and all the frugal food I had saved and harvested in the garden all summer for the coming winter were completely gone. "What now?"

I thought. At that moment, need taught me to pray. I called on all my modest wit to decide what would be best for me. But since my experience was limited and indifferent, I could not reach a good decision. The best I could do was to commend myself to God and to put my trust in him; otherwise I would surely have despaired and perished. Moreover, the predicaments of the injured parson and the five miserably wounded peasants which I had witnessed that day were before me all the time, and I thought not so much about food and survival as about the hatred that existed between soldiers and peasants. But in my simplicity I could not help thinking that since Adam's creation there must surely be not one but two kinds of people on earth—wild ones and tame ones—who cruelly chase each other like unreasoning animals. I was cold and troubled, and with such thoughts I fell asleep, on an empty stomach.

Then, as in a dream, I saw how all the trees standing around the place where I lived were suddenly changing and taking on an utterly different appearance. On top of each tree sat a cavalier; and instead of bearing leaves the branches were decorated with all sorts of men. Some of these fellows had long pikes, others muskets, pistols, halberds, small flags, and drums and fifes. The sight was a pleasure to look at, for everything was neatly divided by rank. The root was made up of lowly people like day-laborers, craftsmen, peasants, and such, who nevertheless gave the tree its strength and imparted vigor anew when it had been lost. In fact, to their own great disadvantage and even peril they made up for the deficiency caused by the fallen leaves. They were complaining about those sitting in the tree; and they had good cause, for the whole load rested on them and pressed them so hard that all their money was being squeezed out of their pockets and even out of the strongboxes which they had secured with seven locks. But if money was not forthcoming, certain commissioners curried them with combs (a process called military execution), and because of this there issued sighs from their hearts, tears from their eyes, blood from their nails, and marrow from their bones. Yet among them there were some jokers called funny birds who were little troubled by it all. They took everything easy, and in their misery they came up with all sorts of raillery so that they needed no consolation.

62. GERMAN DISUNITY SEALED

When the Thirty Years' War ended in 1648 with the Peace of Westphalia (so called because it was negotiated at the Westphalian towns of Münster and Osnabrück), it marked the end both of the effort of the Austrian Habsburgs to transform the Holy Roman Empire into an effective sovereign territorial state and of the period of religious wars that had begun with the Lutheran revolt more than a century before. Both Calvinism and Lutheranism were now accepted as legal religions, along with Catholicism. Some of the key clauses of the principal treaty, between the emperor and his allies on the one side and France, Sweden, and the electoral princes on the other, are given below. "His most Christian Majesty" was the king of France, Louis XIV. The Confession of Augsburg refers to the Lutheran religion. The Peace of Westphalia set the basic pattern of European international relations until the French Revolution by splitting the House of Habsburg and establishing the ascendancy of France as the preponderant power in Europe.

The Peace of Westphalia, 1648

Article I

That there shall be a Christian and Universal Peace, and a perpetual, true, and sincere Amity, between his Sacred Imperial Majesty, and his most Christian Majesty; as also, between all and each of the Allies, and Adherents of his said Imperial Majesty, the House of *Austria*, and its Heirs, and Successors; but chiefly between the Electors, Princes, and States of the Empire on the one side; and all and each of the Allies of his said Christian Majesty, and all their Heirs and Successors, chiefly between the most Serene Queen and Kingdom of *Swedeland*, the Electors respectively, the Princes and States of the Empire, on the other part. That this Peace and Amity be observ'd and cultivated with such a Sincerity and Zeal, that each Party shall endeavour to procure the Benefit, Honour and Advantage of the other; that thus on all sides they may see this Peace and Friendship in the *Roman* Empire, and the Kingdom of *France* flourish, by entertaining a good and faithful Neighbourhood.

. . . . .

Article XXVIII

That those of the Confession of *Augsburg*, and particularly the Inhabitants of *Oppenheim*, shall be put in possession again of their Churches, and Ecclesiastical Estates, as they were in the Year 1624, as also that all others of the said Confession of *Augsburg*, who shall demand it, shall have the free Exercise of their Religion, as well in publick Churches at the appointed Hours, as in private in their own Houses, or in others chosen

---

Source: Fred L. Israel (ed.), *Major Peace Treaties of Modern History, 1648-1967* (New York: Chelsea House Publishers, 1967), Vol. I, pp. 9, 16, 27–28.

for this purpose by their Ministers, or by those of their Neighbours, preaching the Word of God.

. . . . .

Article LXIV

And to prevent for the future any Differences arising in the Politick State, all and every one of the Electors, Princes and States of the *Roman* Empire, are so establish'd and confirm'd in their antient Rights, Prerogatives, Libertys, Privileges, free exercise of Territorial Right, as well Ecclesiastick, as Politick Lordships, Regales, by virtue of this present Transaction: that they never can or ought to be molested therein by any whomsoever upon any manner of pretence.

Article LXV

They shall enjoy without contradiction, the Right of Suffrage in all Deliberations touching the Affairs of the Empire; but above all, when the Business in hand shall be the making or interpreting of Laws, the declaring of Wars, imposing of Taxes, levying or quartering of Soldiers, erecting new Fortifications in the Territorys of the States, or reinforcing the old Garisons; as also when a Peace of Alliance is to be concluded, and treated about, or the like, none of these, or the like things shall be acted for the future, without the Suffrage and Consent of the Free Assembly of all the States of the Empire: Above all, it shall be free perpetually to each of the States of the Empire, to make Alliances with Strangers for their Preservation and Safety; provided, nevertheless, such Alliances be not against the Emperor, and the Empire, nor against the Publick Peace, and this Treaty, and without prejudice to the Oath by which every one is bound to the Emperor and the Empire.

CHAPTER VII

THE SCIENTIFIC REVOLUTION

NOWHERE WERE THE INNOVATIONS of the early modern era more striking than in the field of science. A revolution of ideas and practice of almost unlimited scope took place, with far-reaching consequences for man's power over nature and abiding influence on man's ideas about the universe and his place in it. The new science, the greatest triumph of which was the Newtonian world system, did not suddenly emerge as a fully developed discipline. It was the creation of men who struggled with established ideas as they battled their way to new concepts, and some of the greatest minds of the age could not accept all the assumptions and conclusions of the new science.

The scientific revolution was in the first place a new conception of the physical universe that linked astronomy and terrestrial mechanics in a single theory. It was successful not only in simultaneously encompassing two bodies of knowledge, itself an extraordinary feat, but also in leading to new investigations and new understanding reached on the basis of what came to be recognized as a new method. The same methods that led to Newton's triumph were also applied to the study of living things. Biological knowledge, which called for vastly more complex processes than physics, progressed more slowly and hesitantly, and its greatest successes were to lie centuries ahead. The groundwork, however, was laid during the early modern period.

63. A NEW MODEL OF THE UNIVERSE

The scientific revolution began by almost literally tearing the earth from its moorings. The established theory of the cosmos set the earth at its fixed center and put all the celestial bodies in spheres at various distances from it. The astronomer Nicolaus Copernicus (1473-1543), by profession a physician and churchman, became dissatisfied with the mathematical difficulties in current theories about the relative movements of sun, moon, planets, and stars and spent several decades working out a new model of the universe. In it the sun became the center of the universe, and the earth, one of the planets. Because Biblical text, common sense, and the mythological and philosophical conceptions then associated with Christian doctrine all supported the so-called Ptolemaic theory, Copernicus did not publish his work, *On the Revolutions of the Heavenly Spheres,* when it was virtually completed early in the 1530s. Fearing the storm it would arouse, he held off having it printed, and the book which represented his life's work did not appear until 1543, the year of his death. He dedicated it to Pope Paul III in a preface which attempted to explain its general intent and defended his way of describing the world "built for us by the Best and Most Orderly Workman of all."

Nicolaus Copernicus

•

On the Revolutions of the Heavenly Spheres

Preface and Dedication to Pope Paul III

I can reckon easily enough, Most Holy Father, that as soon as certain people learn that in these books of mine which I have written about the revolutions of the spheres of the world I attribute certain motions to the terrestrial globe, they will immediately shout to have me and my opinion hooted off the stage. For my own works do not please me so much that I do not weigh what judgments others will pronounce concerning them. And although I realize that the conceptions of a philosopher are placed beyond the judgment of the crowd, because it is his loving duty to seek the truth in all things, in so far as God has granted that to human reason;

Source: Nicolaus Copernicus, *On the Revolutions of the Heavenly Spheres,* in *Great Books of the Western World,* Vol. 16 (Chicago: Encyclopaedia Britannica, Inc., 1952), pp. 506–9. Reprinted by permission of Encyclopaedia Britannica.

nevertheless I think we should avoid opinions utterly foreign to rightness. And when I considered how absurd this "lecture" would be held by those who know that the opinion that the Earth rests immovable in the middle of the heavens as if their centre had been confirmed by the judgments of many ages—if I were to assert to the contrary that the Earth moves; for a long time I was in great difficulty as to whether I should bring to light my commentaries written to demonstrate the Earth's movement, or whether it would not be better to follow the example of the Pythagoreans and certain others who used to hand down the mysteries of their philosophy not in writing but by word of mouth and only to their relatives and friends—witness the letter of Lysis to Hipparchus. They however seem to me to have done that not, as some judge, out of a jealous unwillingness to communicate their doctrines but in order that things of very great beauty which have been investigated by the loving care of great men should not be scorned by those who find it a bother to expend any great energy on letters—except on the money-making variety—or who are provoked by the exhortations and examples of others to the liberal study of philosophy but on account of their natural stupidity hold the position among philosophers that drones hold among bees. Therefore, when I weighed these things in my mind, the scorn which I had to fear on account of the newness and absurdity of my opinon almost drove me to abandon a work already undertaken. . . .

But perhaps Your Holiness will not be so much surprised at my giving the results of my nocturnal study to the light—after having taken such care in working them out that I did not hesitate to put in writing my conceptions as to the movement of the Earth—as you will be eager to hear from me what came into my mind that in opposition to the general opinion of mathematicians and almost in opposition to common sense I should dare to imagine some movement of the Earth. And so I am unwilling to hide from Your Holiness that nothing except my knowledge that mathematicians have not agreed with one another in their researches moved me to think out a different scheme of drawing up the movements of the spheres of the world. For in the first place mathematicians are so uncertain about the movements of the sun and moon that they can neither demonstrate nor observe the unchanging magnitude of the revolving year. Then in setting up the solar and lunar movements and those of the other five wandering stars, they do not employ the same principles, assumptions, or demonstrations for the revolutions and apparent movements. For some make use of homocentric circles only, others of eccentric circles and epicycles, by means of which however they do not fully attain what they seek. For although those who have put their trust in homocentric circles have shown that various different movements can be composed of such circles, nevertheless they have not been able to establish anything for certain that would fully correspond to the phenomena. But even if those who have thought up eccentric circles seem to have been able for the most part to compute the apparent movements numerically by those means, they have in the meanwhile admitted a great deal which seems to contradict the first principles of regularity of movement. Moreover, they have not been able to discover or to infer the chief point of all, *i.e.*, the form of the world and the certain commensurability of its parts. But they are in exactly the same fix as someone taking from different places hands, feet, head, and the other limbs—shaped very beautifully but not with reference to one body and without correspondence to one another—so that such parts made up a monster rather than a man. And so, in the process of demonstration which they call "method," they are found either to have omitted something necessary or to have admitted something foreign which by no means pertains to the matter; and they would by no means have been in this fix, if they had followed sure principles. For if the hypotheses they assumed were not false, everything which followed from the hypotheses would have been verified without fail; and though what I am saying may be obscure right now, nevertheless it will become clearer in the proper place.

Accordingly, when I had meditated upon this lack of certitude in the traditional mathematics concerning the composition of movements of the spheres of the world, I began to be annoyed that the philosophers, who in other respects had made a very careful scrutiny of the least details of the world, had discovered no sure scheme for the movements of the machinery of the world, which has been built for us by the Best and Most Orderly Workman of all. Wherefore I took the trouble to reread all the books by philosophers which I could get hold of, to see if any of them even supposed that the movements of the spheres of the world were different from those laid down by those who taught mathematics in the schools. And as a matter of fact, I found first in Cicero that Nicetas thought that the Earth moved. And afterwards I found in Plutarch that there were some others of the same opinion: I shall copy out his words here, so that they may be known to all:

> Some think that the Earth is at rest; but Philolaus the Pythagorean says that it moves around the fire with an obliquely circular motion, like the sun and moon. Herakleides of Pontus and Ekphantus the Pythagorean do not give the Earth any movement of locomotion, but rather a limited movement of rising and setting around its centre, like a wheel.

Therefore I also, having found occasion, began to meditate upon the mobility of the Earth. And although the opinion seemed absurd, nevertheless because I knew that others before me had been granted the liberty of constructing whatever circles they pleased in order to demonstrate astral phenomena, I thought that I too would be readily permitted to test whether or not, by the laying down that the Earth had some movement, demonstrations less shaky than those of my predecessors could be found for the revolutions of the celestial spheres.

And so, having laid down the movements which I attribute to the Earth farther on in the work, I finally discovered by the help of long and numerous observations that if the movements of the other wandering stars are correlated with the circular movement of the Earth, and if the movements are computed in accordance with the revolution of each planet, not only do all their phenomena follow from that but also this correlation binds together so closely the order and magnitudes of all the planets and of their spheres or orbital circles and the heavens themselves that nothing can be shifted around in any part of them without disrupting the remaining parts and the universe as a whole.

Accordingly, in composing my work I adopted the following order: in the first book I describe all the locations of the spheres or orbital circles together with the movements which I attribute to the earth, so that this book contains as it were the general set-up of the universe. But afterwards in the remaining books I correlate all the movements of the other planets and their spheres or orbital circles with the mobility of the Earth, so that it can be gathered from that how far the apparent movements of the remaining planets and their orbital circles can be saved by being correlated with the movements of the Earth. And I have no doubt that talented and learned mathematicians will agree with me, if—as philosophy demands in the first place—they are willing to give not superficial but profound thought and effort to what I bring forward in this work in demonstrating these things. And in order that the unlearned as well as the learned might see that I was not seeking to flee from the judgment of any man, I preferred to dedicate these results of my nocturnal study to Your Holiness rather than to anyone else; because, even in this remote corner of the earth where I live, you are held to be most eminent both in the dignity of your order and in your love of letters and even of mathematics; hence, by the authority of your judgment you can easily provide a guard against the bites of slanderers, despite the proverb that there is no medicine for the bite of a sycophant.

But if perchance there are certain "idle talkers" who take it upon themselves to pronounce judgment, although wholly ignorant of mathematics, and if by shamelessly distorting the sense of some passage in Holy Writ to suit their purpose, they dare to reprehend and to attack my work; they worry me so little that I shall even scorn their judgments as foolhardy. For it is not unknown that Lactantius, otherwise a distinguished writer but hardly a mathematician, speaks in an utterly childish fashion concerning the shape of the Earth, when he laughs at those who have affirmed that the Earth has the form of a globe. And so the studious need not be surprised if people like that laugh at us. Mathematics is written for mathematicians; and among them, if I am not mistaken, my labours will be seen to contribute something to the ecclesiastical commonwealth, the principate of which Your Holiness now holds. For not many years ago under Leo X when the Lateran Council was considering the question of reforming the Ecclesiastical Calendar, no decision was reached, for the sole reason that the magnitude of the year and the months and the movements of the sun and moon had not yet been measured with sufficient accuracy. From that time on I gave attention to making more exact observations of these things and I was encouraged to do so by that most distinguished man, Paul, Bishop of Fossombrone, who had been present at those deliberations. But what have I accomplished in this matter I leave to the judgment of Your Holiness in particular and to that of all other learned mathematicians. And so as not to appear to Your Holiness to make more promises concerning the utility of this book than I can fulfill, I now pass on to the body of the work.

64. THE CELESTIAL HARMONIES

Copernicus's system came to be accepted by most astronomers by the end of the 16th century. Yet, although it explained the motions of the planets on the basis of simpler principles, it was not marked by significantly greater precision, and certain anomalies could not be removed. Not until Johannes Kepler (1571-1630), applied the accumulated data of Tycho Brahe, a master observer who accepted Copernicus's ideas only in part, did the pieces of the puzzle fall into place. Kepler conceived the planetary orbits to be elliptical, not circular, as Copernicus had. His discovery, formulated in his famous three laws, did not draw its impulse from purely astronomical interests. He was also a mystic in the Neoplatonic tradition, with its belief in celestial harmonies, and he adored the sun, as may be seen in the following passages from his *The Harmonies of the World* (1619).

Johannes Kepler

The Harmonies of the World

A Summary of Astronomical Doctrine Necessary for Speculation into the Celestial Harmonies

First of all, my readers should know that the ancient astronomical hypotheses of Ptolemy, in the fashion in which they have been unfolded

---

SOURCE: Johannes Kepler, *The Harmonies of the World: V*, in *Great Books of the Western World*, Vol. 16 (Chicago: Encyclopaedia Britannica, Inc., 1952), pp. 1014–16, 1080–81. Reprinted by permission of Encyclopaedia Britannica.

in the *Theoricae* of Peurbach and by the other writers of epitomes, are to be completely removed from this discussion and cast out of the mind. For they do not convey the true lay out of the bodies of the world and the polity of the movements.

Although I cannot do otherwise than to put solely Copernicus' opinion concerning the world in the place of those hypotheses and, if that were possible, to persuade everyone of it; but because the thing is still new among the mass of the intelligentsia [*apud vulgus studiosorum*], and the doctrine that the Earth is one of the planets and moves among the stars around a motionless sun sounds very absurd to the ears of most of them: therefore those who are shocked by the unfamiliarity of this opinion should know that these harmonical speculations are possible even with the hypotheses of Tycho Brahe—because that author holds, in common with Copernicus, everything else which pertains to the lay out of the bodies and the tempering of the movements, and transfers solely the Copernican annual movement of the Earth to the whole system of planetary spheres and to the sun, which occupies the centre of that system, in the opinion of both authors. For after this transference of movement it is nevertheless true that in Brahe the Earth occupies at any time the same place that Copernicus gives it, if not in the very vast and measureless region of the fixed stars, at least in the system of the planetary world. And accordingly, just as he who draws a circle on paper makes the writing-foot of the compass revolve, while he who fastens the paper or tablet to a turning lathe draws the same circle on the revolving tablet with the foot of the compass or stylus motionless; so too, in the case of Copernicus the Earth, by the real movement of its body, measures out a circle revolving midway between the circle of Mars on the outside and that of Venus on the inside; but in the case of Tycho Brahe the whole planetary system (wherein among the rest the circles of Mars and Venus are found) revolves like a tablet on a lathe and applies to the motionless Earth, or to the stylus on the lathe, the midspace between the circles of Mars and Venus; and it comes about from this movement of the system that the Earth within it, although remaining motionless, marks out the same circle around the sun and midway between Mars and Venus, which in Copernicus it marks out by the real movement of its body while the system is at rest. Therefore, since harmonic speculation considers the eccentric movements of the planets, as if seen from the sun, you may easily understand that if any observer were stationed on a sun as much in motion as you please, nevertheless for him the Earth, although at rest (as a concession to Brahe), would seem to describe the annual circle midway between the planets and in an intermediate length of time. Wherefore, if there is any man of such feeble wit that he cannot grasp the movement of the earth among the stars, nevertheless he can take pleasure in the most excellent spectacle of this most divine construction, if he applies to their image in the sun whatever he hears concerning the daily movements of the Earth in its eccentric—such an image as Tycho Brahe exhibits, with the Earth at rest.

And nevertheless the followers of the true Samian philosophy have no just cause to be jealous of sharing this delightful speculation with such persons, because their joy will be in many ways more perfect, as due to the consummate perfection of speculation, if they have accepted the immobility of the sun and the movement of the earth.

Firstly [I], therefore, let my readers grasp that today it is absolutely certain among all astronomers that all the planets revolve around the sun, with the exception of the moon, which alone has the Earth as its centre: the magnitude of the moon's sphere or orbit is not great enough for it to be delineated in this diagram in a just ratio to the rest. Therefore, to the other five planets, a sixth, the Earth, is added, which traces a sixth circle around the sun, whether by its own proper movement with the sun at rest, or motionless itself and with the whole planetary system revolving.

Secondly [II]: It is also certain that all the planets are eccentric, *i.e.*, they change their distances from the sun, in such fashion that in one part of their circle they become farthest away from the sun, and in the opposite part they come nearest to the sun.

. . . . .

Epilogue Concerning the Sun, by way of Conjecture

From the celestial music to the hearer, from the Muses to Apollo the leader of the Dance, from the six planets revolving and making consonances to the Sun at the centre of all the circuits, immovable in place but rotating into itself. For although the harmony is most absolute between the extreme planetary movements, not with respect to the true speeds through the ether but with respect to the angles which are formed by joining with the centre of the sun the termini of the diurnal arcs of the planetary orbits; while the harmony does not adorn the termini, *i.e.*, the single movements, in so far as they are considered in themselves but only in so far as by being taken together and compared with one another, they become the object of some mind; and although no object is ordained in vain, without the existence of some thing which may be moved by it, while those angles seem to presuppose some action similar to our eyesight or at least to that sense-perception whereby . . . the sublunary nature perceived the angles of rays formed by the planets on the Earth: still it is not easy for dwellers on the Earth to conjecture what sort of sight is present in the sun, what eyes there are, or what other instinct there is for perceiving those angles even without eyes and for evaluating the harmonies of the movements entering into the antechamber of the mind by whatever doorway, and finally what mind there is in the sun. None the less, however those things may be, this composition of the six primary spheres around the sun, cherishing it with their perpetual revolutions and as it were adoring it (just as, separately, four moons accompany the globe of Jupiter, two Saturn, but a single moon by its circuit encompasses, cherishes, fosters the Earth and us its inhabitants, and ministers to us) and this special business of the harmonies, which is a most clear footprint of the highest providence over solar affairs, now being added to that consideration, wrings from me the following confession: not only does light go out from the sun into the whole world, as from the focus or eye of the world, as life and heat from the heart, as every movement from the King and mover, but conversely also by royal law these returns, so to speak, of every lovely harmony are collected in the sun from every province in the world, nay, the forms of movements by twos flow together and are bound into one harmony by the work of some mind, and are as it were coined money from silver and gold bullion; finally, the curia, palace, and praetorium or throne-room of the whole realm of nature are in the sun, whatsoever chancellors, palatines, prefects the Creator has given to nature: for them, whether created immediately from the beginning or to be transported hither at some time, has He made ready those seats. For even this terrestrial adornment, with respect to its principal part, for quite a long while lacked the contemplators and enjoyers, for whom however it had been appointed; and those seats were empty. Accordingly the reflection struck my mind, what did the ancient Pythagoreans in Aristotle mean, who used to call the centre of the world (which they referred to as the "fire" but understood by that the sun) "the watchtower of Jupiter," . . . what, likewise, was the ancient interpreter pondering in his mind when he rendered the verse of the Psalm as: "He has placed His tabernacle in the sun."

65. THE NEW ASTRONOMY AND THE OLD PHILOSOPHY

The Aristotelian philosophy of nature, which had become imbedded in the structure of Christian theology during the Middle Ages, found itself threatened by the implications of the Copernican revolution. The Aristotelian system conceived of the heavens as being perfect and permanent, while the earth was the seat of change and imperfection. Copernicus had taken the earth out of the center of the universe, and man's position as the purpose of God's creation was called into question.

The Italian astronomer Galileo Galilei (1564-1642), who had built one of the first telescopes and had observed the sunspots, the moons of Jupiter, and the rings of Saturn, also questioned celestial perfection. The debate that ensued between the defenders of Aristotelianism's preference for the Ptolemaic cosmology on the one hand and the Copernican system on the other was brilliantly summarized by Galileo in his *Dialogue concerning the Two Chief World Systems* (1632). Politically it was too brilliant, for it brought down upon Galileo the wrath of the Papal Inquisition for violating the ban on defense of Copernicanism that had been placed on him for an earlier book, and he was sentenced to live in exile on his estate near Florence. In the dialogue, Salviati stands for Galileo himself, Simplicio for a learned but stubborn Aristotelian, and Sagredo for an intelligent layman.

Galileo Galilei

Dialogue concerning the Two Chief World Systems

SALVIATI. Yesterday we resolved to meet today and discuss as clearly and in as much detail as possible the character and the efficacy of those laws of nature which up to the present have been put forth by the partisans of the Aristotelian and Ptolemaic position on the one hand, and by the followers of the Copernican system on the other. Since Copernicus places the earth among the movable heavenly bodies, making it a globe like a planet, we may well begin our discussion by examining the Peripatetic steps in arguing the impossibility of that hypothesis; what they are, and how great is their force and effect. For this it is necessary to introduce into nature two substances which differ essentially. These are the celestial and the elemental, the former being invariant and eternal; the latter, temporary and destructible. This argument Aristotle treats in his book *De Caelo,* introducing it with some discourses dependent upon certain general assumptions, and afterwards confirming it by experiments and specific demonstrations. Following the same method, I shall first propound, and then freely speak my opinion, submitting myself to your criticisms—particularly those of Simplicio, that stout champion and defender of Aristotelian doctrines. . . .

. . . Therefore leaving the general contemplation of the whole, let us get to the consideration of the parts. Aristotle in his first division separates the whole into two differing and, in a way, contrary parts; namely, the celestial and the elemental, the former being ingenerable, incorrupti-

---

SOURCE: Galileo Galilei, *Dialogue concerning the Two Chief World Systems—Ptolemaic and Copernican,* translated by Stillman Drake (Berkeley and Los Angeles: University of California Press, 1953), pp. 13–14, 51–57. Originally published by the University of California Press; reprinted by permission of The Regents of the University of California.

ble, inalterable, impenetrable, etc.; the latter being exposed to continual alteration, mutation, etc. He takes this difference from the diversity of local motions as his original principle. With this step he proceeds.

. . . . .

Now, getting back to the subject, I say that things which are being and have been discovered in the heavens in our own time are such that they can give entire satisfaction to all philosophers, because just such events as we have been calling generations and corruptions have been seen and are being seen in particular bodies and in the whole expanse of heaven. Excellent astronomers have observed many comets generated and dissipated in places above the lunar orbit, besides the two new stars of 1572 and 1604, which were indisputably beyond all the planets. And on the face of the sun itself, with the aid of the telescope, they have seen produced and dissolved dense and dark matter, appearing much like the clouds upon the earth; and many of these are so vast as to exceed not only the Mediterranean Sea, but all of Africa, with Asia thrown in. Now, if Aristotle had seen these things, what do you think he would have said and done, Simplicio?

SIMP[LICIO]. I do not know what would have been done or said by Aristotle, who was the master of all science, but I know to some extent what his followers do and say, and what they ought to do and say in order not to remain without a guide, a leader, and a chief in philosophy.

As to the comets, have not these modern astronomers who wanted to make them celestial been vanquished by the *Anti-Tycho?* Vanquished, moreover, by their own weapons; that is, by means of parallaxes and of calculations turned about every which way, and finally concluding in favor of Aristotle that they are all elemental. A thing so fundamental to the innovators having been destroyed, what more remains to keep them on their feet?

SALV. Calm yourself, Simplicio. What does this modern author of yours say about the new stars of 1572 and 1604, and of the solar spots? As far as the comets are concerned I, for my part, care little whether they are generated below or above the moon, nor have I ever set much store by Tycho's verbosity. Neither do I feel any reluctance to believe that their matter is elemental, and that they may rise as they please without encountering any obstacle from the impenetrability of the Peripatetic heavens, which I hold to be far more tenuous, yielding, and subtle than our air. And as to the calculation of parallaxes, in the first place I doubt whether comets are subject to parallax; besides, the inconstancy of the observations upon which they have been computed renders me equally suspicious of both his opinions and his adversary's—the more so because it seems to me that the *Anti-Tycho* sometimes trims to its author's taste those observations which do not suit his purposes, or else declares them to be erroneous.

SIMP. With regard to the new stars, the *Anti-Tycho* thoroughly disposes of them in a few words, saying that such recent new stars are not positively known to be heavenly bodies, and that if its adversaries wish to prove any alterations and generations in the latter, they must show us mutations made in stars which have already been described for a long time and which are celestial objects beyond doubt. And this can never possibly be done.

As to that material which some say is generated and dissolved on the face of the sun, no mention is made of it at all, from which I should gather that the author takes it for a fable, or for an illusion of the telescope, or at best for some phenomenon produced by the air; in a word, for anything but celestial matter.

SALV. But you, Simplicio, what have you thought of to reply to the opposition of these importunate spots which have come to disturb the heavens, and worse still, the Peripatetic philosophy? It must be that you, as its intrepid defender, have found a reply and a solution which you should not deprive us of.

SIMP. I have heard different opinions on this matter. Some say, "They are stars which, like Venus and Mercury, go about the sun in their proper orbits, and in passing under it present themselves to us as dark; and because there are many of them, they frequently happen to collect together, and then again to separate." Others believe them to be figments of the air; still others, illusions of the lenses; and still others, other things. But I am most inclined to believe—yes, I think it certain—that they are a collection of various different opaque objects, coming together almost accidentally; and therefore we often see that in one spot there can be counted ten or more such tiny bodies of irregular shape that look like snowflakes, or tufts of wool, or flying moths. They change places with each other, now separating and now congregating, but mostly right under the sun, about which, as their center, they move. But it is not therefore necessary to say that they are generated or decay. Rather, they are sometimes hidden behind the body of the sun; at other times, though far from it, they cannot be seen because of their proximity to its immeasurable light. For in the sun's eccentric sphere there is established a sort of onion composed of various folds, one within another, each being studded with certain little spots, and moving; and although their movements seem at first to be inconstant and irregular, nonetheless it is said to be ultimately observed that after a certain time the same spots are sure to return. This seems to me to be the most appropriate expedient that has so far been found to account for such phenomena, and at the same time to maintain the incorruptibility and ingenerability of the heavens. And if this is not enough, there are more brilliant intellects who will find better answers.

SALV. If what we are discussing were a point of law or of the humanities, in which neither true nor false exists, one might trust in subtlety of mind and readiness of tongue and in the greater experience of the writers, and expect him who excelled in those things to make his reasoning most plausible, and one might judge it to be the best. But in the natural sciences, whose conclusions are true and necessary and have nothing to do with human will, one must take care not to place oneself in the defense of error; for here a thousand Demostheneses and a thousand Aristotles would be left in the lurch by every mediocre wit who happened to hit upon the truth for himself. Therefore, Simplicio, give up this idea and this hope of yours that there may be men so much more learned, erudite, and well-read than the rest of us as to be able to make that which is false become true in defiance of nature. And since among all opinions that have thus far been produced regarding the essence of sunspots, this one you have just explained appears to you to be the correct one, it follows that all the rest are false. Now to free you also from that one—which is an utterly delusive chimera—I shall, disregarding the many improbabilities in it, convey to you but two observed facts against it.

One is that many of these spots are seen to originate in the middle of the solar disc, and likewise many dissolve and vanish far from the edge of the sun, a necessary argument that they must be generated and dissolved. For without generation and corruption, they could appear there only by way of local motion, and they all ought to enter and leave by the very edge.

The other observation, for those not in the rankest ignorance of perspective, is that from the changes of shape observed in the spots, and from their apparent changes in velocity, one must infer that the spots are in contact with the sun's body, and that, touching its surface, they are moved either with it or upon it, and in no sense revolve in circles distant from it. Their motion proves this by appearing to be very slow around the edge of the solar disc, and quite fast toward its center; the shapes of the spots prove the same by appearing very narrow around the sun's edge in comparison with how they look in the vicinity of the center. For around the center they are seen in their majesty and as they really are; but around the edge, because of the curvature of the spherical surface, they show themselves foreshortened. . . .

SIMP. To tell the truth, I have not made such long and careful observations that I can qualify as an authority on the facts of this matter; but certainly I wish to do so, and then to see whether I can once more succeed in reconciling what experience presents to us with what Aristotle teaches. For obviously two truths cannot contradict one another.

SALV. Whenever you wish to reconcile what your senses show you with the soundest teachings of Aristotle, you will have no trouble at all. Does not Aristotle say that because of the great distance, celestial matters cannot be treated very definitely?

SIMP. He does say so, quite clearly.

SALV. Does he not also declare that what sensible experience shows ought to be preferred over any argument, even one that seems to be extremely well founded? And does he not say this positively and without a bit of hesitation?

SIMP. He does.

SALV. Then of the two propositions, both of them Aristotelian doctrines, the second—which says it is necessary to prefer the senses over arguments—is a more solid and definite doctrine than the other, which holds the heavens to be inalterable. Therefore it is better Aristotelian philosophy to say, "Heaven is alterable because my senses tell me so," than to say, "Heaven is inalterable because Aristotle was so persuaded by reasoning." Add to this that we possess a better basis for reasoning about celestial things than Aristotle did. He admitted such perceptions to be very difficult for him by reason of the distance from his senses, and conceded that one whose senses could better represent them would be able to philosophize about them with more certainty. Now we, thanks to the telescope, have brought the heavens thirty or forty times closer to us than they were to Aristotle, so that we can discern many things in them that he could not see; among other things these sunspots, which were absolutely invisible to him. Therefore we can treat of the heavens and the sun more confidently than Aristotle could.

SAGR[EDO]. I can put myself in Simplicio's place and see that he is deeply moved by the overwhelming force of these conclusive arguments. But seeing on the other hand the great authority that Aristotle has gained universally; considering the number of famous interpreters who have toiled to explain his meanings; and observing that the other sciences, so useful and necessary to mankind, base a large part of their value and reputation upon Aristotle's credit; Simplicio is confused and perplexed, and I seem to hear him say, "Who would there be to settle our controversies if Aristotle were to be deposed? What other author should we follow in the schools, the academies, the universities? What philosopher has written the whole of natural philosophy, so well arranged, without omitting a single conclusion? Ought we to desert that structure under which so many travelers have recuperated? Should we destroy that haven, that Prytaneum where so many scholars have taken refuge so comfortably; where, without exposing themselves to the inclemencies of the air, they can acquire a complete knowledge of the universe by merely turning over a few pages? Should that fort be leveled where one may abide in safety against all enemy assaults?"

I pity him no less than I should some fine gentleman who, having built a magnificent palace at great trouble and expense, employing hundreds and hundreds of artisans, and then beholding it threatened with ruin because of poor foundations, should attempt, in order to avoid the grief of seeing the walls destroyed, adorned as they are with so many lovely murals; or the columns fall, which sustain the superb galleries, or the gilded beams; or the doors spoiled, or the pediments and the marble cornices, brought in at so much cost—should attempt, I say, to prevent the collapse with chains, props, iron bars, buttresses, and shores.

SALV. Well, Simplicio need not yet fear any such collapse; I undertake to insure him against damage at a much smaller cost. There is no danger that such a multitude of great, subtle, and wise philosophers will allow themselves to be overcome by one or two who bluster a bit. Rather, without even directing their pens against them, by means of silence alone, they place them in universal scorn and derision. It is vanity to imagine that one can introduce a new philosophy by refuting this or that author. It is necessary first to teach the reform of the human mind and to render it capable of distinguishing truth from falsehood, which only God can do. . . .

66. WHIRLINGS IN THE SKY

In the interval between Galileo's death and the work of the English physicist Newton, a bold explanation of the planetary system was put forward by the French philosopher René Descartes (1596-1650). With a mathematical mind of immense power and inventiveness as well as great philosophical subtlety, Descartes turned to the problem of explaining the astronomical system that had been created by Copernicus in a way that seemed to him physically and philosophically sound. Like Aristotle, Descartes believed the explanation would have to correspond to observations and to common sense immensely refined. Because he was unable to conceive of action at a distance or through a void, he decided that space was full of an extraordinarily thin liquid that caused bodies (such as the planets) floating in it to move by means of whirlpools.

This vortex theory of astronomy, which fitted the observed mathematical data and was drawn from study of the phenomenon of eddies on earth, was published in Descartes's *Philosophical Principles,* first in Latin in 1644 and then in French in 1647. It competed for almost a century with Newton's somewhat later gravitational theory for the support of European scientists and was abandoned when they no longer began to feel Descartes's revulsion for the notion of field forces, which was a restatement of the Scholastic doctrine that nature abhors a vacuum.

René Descartes

On Vortices

. . . . .

Finally, it is not difficult to infer from all of this that the earth and the sky are made of the same matter; and that even if there existed an infinity of worlds they would be made only of this matter; from which it follows that there cannot be several kinds, because we conceive as manifest that matter, whose nature consists only in its being what is extended, now occupies all imaginable space where these other worlds might exist, and because we are not able to discover in ourselves the idea of any other matter.

There is, then, only one matter in the whole universe, and we know it only because of its extension; because all the properties which we *distinctly* perceive in it are related to the fact that it can be divided and moved in its parts, and because it can enter into all the various arrangements which we observe can happen by the movement of its parts. For, although we can simulate in thought causing divisions in this matter, nonetheless it is obvious that *our thought does not have the power* to make any changes in it, and that the entire diversity of forms which we meet in it depend upon local movement. This has no doubt been noticed by the Philosophers, all the more because *in many places* they have said that nature is the origin (*principe*) of movement and rest and that they understood by nature that which caused bodies to arrange themselves as we see them in experience.

Now, movement (that is, the movement which occurs from one place to another, for it is the only one I conceive and also do not think that there can be a necessity to presuppose another in nature) is therefore, if we take it as we ordinarily do, nothing else than THE ACTION BY WHICH A BODY PASSES FROM ONE PLACE TO ANOTHER. And just as we remarked above that the same thing at the same time changes place and does not do so, so we can say that at the same time it moves and it does not move. For someone who is seated at the poop of a ship driven by the wind, for example, believes he is moving when he pays attention only to the shore he has left and considers he is motionless when he pays attention only to the ship where he is, because he does not change his position with

---

SOURCE: Charles Adam and Paul Tannery (eds.), *Œuvres de Descartes,* Vol. IX, Part 2 (Paris: Librairie Philosophique J. Vrin, 1964), pp. 75–76, 112–16. Translated by Herbert H. Rowen. Reprinted by permission of Librairie Philosophique J. Vrin.

regard to its parts. In any case, because we are accustomed to thinking that there is no movement without action, we will say that he who is seated in that position is at rest, because he feels no action in himself, and *that this is customary.*

But if, instead of stopping at that which has no other foundation than ordinary usage, we wish to know what movement is in truth, we will say, in order to attribute to it a determinate nature, that it is THE TRANSPORT OF THE PART OF MATTER, OR OF A BODY, FROM THE PROXIMITY OF THOSE WHICH TOUCH IT DIRECTLY AND WHICH WE CONSIDER TO BE AT REST, TO THE PROXIMITY OF SEVERAL OTHERS. By a BODY, or indeed by A PART OF MATTER, I mean all that is transported together, even though it may perhaps be composed of several parts which *nonetheless employ their agitation to cause* other movements. And I say that it is the TRANSPORT and not the force or action which transports, in order to show that the movement is always in that which is moved and not in what moves it; for it seems to me that we are not accustomed to distinguish these two things with enough care. Furthermore, I understand that it is a *property* of that which is moved and not a substance; just as the drawing is a *property* of the thing which is drawn and not of the thing which is at rest.

. . . .

But it seems to me that several are in error when, desiring to attribute to the sky the property of being liquid, they imagine it to be an entirely empty space, which not only offers no resistance to the movement of other bodies, but also which has no force to move them and carry them along with itself; for, besides the fact that there cannot be such a void in nature, it has this in common with all liquids that the reason why it does not resist the movement of other bodies *is not that they possess less matter than the latter, but that they have as much or more* agitation, and that their *small parts* can easily be caused to move on every side and when it happens that these are all caused to move *together* to the same side, this necessarily causes them to carry along with them all the bodies which they embrace and surround on every side, and which are not prevented from following them by any external cause, although these bodies are wholly at rest, and hard and solid, as follows evidently from what has been said above *about the nature of liquid bodies.*

In the fourth place, since we see that the Earth is not supported by columns nor suspended in the air by cables but is surrounded on every side by a very liquid Sky, let us think that it is at rest and possesses no propensity for movement, since we remark none in it; but also let us not believe that this can prevent its being carried along by the course of the Sky and following its movement without itself moving: just as a ship which is not propelled by either the wind or oars and is not held by anchors either, remains at rest in the middle of the sea, although perhaps the *ebb or flow* of this great mass of water imperceptibly carries it along with it.

And just as all the other Planets resemble the Earth in being opaque and reflecting the rays of the Sun, we have reason to believe that they resemble it also in remaining *like it* at rest in the part of the Sky where each one is located, and that all the change which we observe in their location arises only from their obeying the movement of the matter of the Sky which contains them.

We will recall also at this place what has been said above regarding the nature of movement, to wit, that properly speaking it is only the transport of a body from the proximity of those which touch it directly and which we consider to be at rest to the proximity of several others; but that, in common usage, we often give the name of movement to any action which causes a body to pass from one place to another; and that in this sense we may say that the same object is moved and not moved at the same time, depending on the diverse ways in which we determine its place. Now, we cannot find in the Earth or the other Planets any movement in the proper sense of this word, because they are not transported from the proximity of the parts of the Sky which touch them, insofar as we consider these parts to be at rest; for in order to be transported in this way, they would have to move off at the same time from all parts of this Sky taken together, which does not happen. But since the matter of the Sky is liquid *and the parts which compose it are highly agitated*, sometimes some of these parts move away from the Planet which they touch, and sometimes others, by a movement which belongs to them and which must be attributed to them rather than to the Planet *which they are leaving:* just as we attribute the individual transports of air or water which occur on the surface of the Earth to the air or water and not to the Earth. . . .

After having removed by these arguments all the scruples which we may have regarding the movement of the Earth, let us think that the matter of the Sky in which the Planets are located turns constantly around, like a whirlpool which would have the Sun at its center and whose parts close to the Sun move faster than those which are further away, *up to a certain distance*, and that all the Planets (among which we shall hereafter include the Earth) remain always suspended among the same parts of this matter of the Sky. For by this alone, and without employing other devices, we will easily understand all the things which we observe in them. This is all the more so because if a few straws *or other very light bodies* float on the water in the bends of a river, where the water curls back on itself and turns in circles, we can see that it carries them along and makes them go around together with it; and we can even observe that there are often some of these straws which also turn around their own centers, and those which are closer to the center of the whirlpool which contains them complete their turn sooner than those which are further away; and finally, that although these whirlpools of water always seem to be turning around, they almost never describe wholly perfect circles but sometimes become longer and sometimes broader, *so that all the parts of the circumference which they describe are not equally distant from the center.* Thus, we can easily imagine that the same things happen to the Planets; and nothing but this is needed to explain all their phenomena.

67. GRAVITY: THE FORCE THAT ATTRACTS

The solution of the problem posed by Galileo of bringing the celestial and terrestrial systems into a unified theory was solved by the Englishman Sir Isaac Newton (1642-1727). Even more than his invention of the calculus or his fundamental work on the theory of light, this achievement marked him as one of the supreme scientific minds of all time. In his *Mathematical Principles of Natural Philosophy* (1687), known more usually by its Latin title, *Principia,* Newton set down a series of natural laws which applied equally in the heavens and on earth and which explained precisely the Keplerian model of the solar system. One of Newton's key conceptions was the law of universal gravitation, which explained the movement of bodies toward each other. Another of the laws he formulated—that of inertial momentum—defined the natural motion of bodies as in a straight line at a steady velocity. The key passage of the *Principia* that explained the law of gravitation is given below.

Sir Isaac Newton

Principia

On Gravity

Proposition LXXVI

If spheres be however dissimilar (as to density of matter and attractive force) in the same ratio onward from the center to the circumference, but everywhere similar at every given distance from the center, on all sides round about; and the attractive force of every point decreases as the square of the distance of the body attracted:

Source: H. S. Thayer (ed.), *Newton's Philosophy of Nature* (New York: Hafner Publishing Co., 1953), pp. 105–12.

I say that the whole force with which one of these spheres attracts the other will be inversely proportional to the square of the distance of the centers.

Corollary III

The motive attractions, or the weights of the spheres toward one another, will be at equal distances of the centers conjointly as the attracting and attracted spheres; that is, as the products arising from multiplying the spheres into each other.

Corollary IV

And at unequal distances directly as those products and inversely as the squares of the distances between the centers.

The intensities of the forces and the resulting motions in individual cases.

Therefore the absolute force of every globe is as the quantity of matter which the globe contains; but the motive force by which every globe is attracted toward another and which, in terrestrial bodies, we commonly call their weight, is as the content under the quantities of matter in both globes divided by the square of the distance between their centers (by Corollary IV, Proposition LXXVI), to which force the quantity of motion by which each globe in a given time will be carried toward the other is proportional. And the accelerative force by which every globe according to its quantity of matter is attracted toward another is as the quantity of matter in that other globe divided by the square of the distance between the centers of the two . . . to which force the velocity by which the attracted globe will, in a given time, be carried toward the other is proportional. And from these principles well understood, it will now be easy to determine the motions of the celestial bodies among themselves.

Proposition IV

That the moon gravitates toward the earth, and by the force of gravity is continually drawn off from a rectilinear motion and retained in its orbit.

Scholium

The demonstration of this Proposition may be more diffusely explained after the following manner. Suppose several moons to revolve about the earth, as in the system of Jupiter or Saturn; the periodic times of these moons (by the argument of induction) would observe the same law which Kepler found to obtain among the planets, and therefore their centripetal forces would be inversely as the squares of the distances from the center of the earth. . . . Now if the lowest of these were very small and were so near the earth as almost to touch the tops of the highest mountains, the centripetal force thereof, retaining in its orbit, would be nearly equal to the weights of any terrestrial bodies that should be found upon the tops of those mountains, as may be known by the foregoing computation. Therefore, if the same little moon should be deserted by its centrifugal force that carries it through its orbit, and be disabled from going onward therein, it would descend to the earth; and that with the same velocity with which heavy bodies actually fall upon the tops of those very mountains, because of the equality of the forces that oblige them both to descend. And if the force by which the lowest moon would descend were different from gravity, and if the moon were to gravitate toward the earth, as we find terrestrial bodies do upon the tops of mountains, it would then descend with twice the velocity, as being impelled by both these forces conspiring together. Therefore, since both these forces, that is, the gravity of heavy bodies and the centripetal force of the moons, are directed to the center of the earth and are similar and equal between themselves, they will (by Rules I and II) have one and the same cause. And therefore the force which retains the moon in its orbit is that very force which we commonly call "gravity," because otherwise this little moon at the top of a mountain must either be without gravity or fall twice as swiftly as heavy bodies are wont to do.

Scholium

The force which retains the celestial bodies in their orbits has been hitherto called "centripetal force," but it being now made plain that it can be no other than a gravitating force we shall hereafter call it "gravity." For the cause of that centripetal force which retains the moon in its orbit will extend itself to all the planets, by Rules I, II, and IV.

Proposition VI

That all bodies gravitate toward every planet; and that the weights of bodies toward any one planet, at equal distances from the center of the planet, are proportional to the quantities of matter which they severally contain.

It has been now for a long time observed by others that all sorts of heavy bodies (allowance being made for the inequality of retardation which they suffer from a small power of resistance in the air) descend to the earth *from equal heights* in equal times, and that equality of times we may distinguish to a great accuracy by the help of pendulums. I tried experiments with gold, silver, lead, glass, sand, common salt, wood, water, and wheat. I provided two wooden boxes, round and equal; I filled the one with wood and suspended an equal weight of gold (as exactly as I could) in the center of oscillation of the other. The boxes, hanging by equal threads of 11 feet, made a couple of pendulums perfectly equal in weight and figure and equally receiving the resistance of the air. And, placing the one by the other, I observed them to play together forward and backward for a long time with equal vibrations. And therefore the quantity of matter in the gold . . . was to the quantity of matter in the wood as the action of the motive force (or *vis motrix*) upon all the gold to the action of the same upon all the wood, that is, as the weight of the one to the weight of the other; and the like happened in the other bodies. By these experiments, in bodies of the same weight, I could manifestly have discovered a difference of matter less than the thousandth part of the whole, had any such been. But, without all doubt, the nature of gravity toward the planets is the same as toward the earth. For, should we imagine our terrestrial bodies taken to the orbit of the moon and there, together with the moon, deprived of all motion, to be let go so as to fall together toward the earth, it is certain, from what we have demonstrated before, that in equal times they would describe equal spaces with the moon, and of consequence are to the moon, in quantity of matter, as their weights to its weight. Moreover, since the satellites of Jupiter perform their revolutions in times which observe the 3/2th power of the proportion of their distances from Jupiter's center, their accelerative gravities toward Jupiter will be inversely as the squares of their distances from Jupiter's center, that is, equal at equal distances. And therefore these satellites, if supposed to fall *toward Jupiter* from equal heights, would describe equal spaces in equal times, in like manner as heavy bodies do on our earth. And, by the same argument, if the circumsolar planets were supposed to be let fall at equal distances from the sun, they would, in their descent toward the sun, describe equal spaces in equal times. But forces which equally accelerate unequal bodies must be as those bodies; that is to say, the weights of the planets *toward the sun* must be as their quantities of matter. Further, that the weights of Jupiter and of his satellites toward the sun are proportional to the several quantities of their matter appears from the exceedingly regular motions of the satellites. . . . For if some of those bodies were more strongly attracted to the sun in proportion to their quantity of matter than others, the motions of the satellites would be disturbed by that inequality of attraction. . . . If at equal distances from the sun any satellite, in proportion to the quantity of its matter, did gravitate toward the sun with a force greater than Jupiter in proportion to his, according to any given proportion, suppose of *d* to *e*, then the distance between the centers of the sun and of the satellite's orbit would be always greater than the distance between the centers of the sun and of Jupiter, nearly as the square root of that proportion, as by some computations I have found. And if the satellite did gravitate toward the sun with a force less in the proportion of *e* to *d*, the distance of the center of the satellite's orbit from the sun would be less than the distance of the center of Jupiter from the sun as the square root of the same proportion. Therefore if, at equal distances from the sun, the accelerative gravity of any satellite toward the sun were greater or less than the accelerative gravity of Jupiter toward the sun but by one 1/1,000 part of the whole gravity, the distance of the center of the satellite's orbit from the sun would be greater or less than the distance of Jupiter from the sun by one 1/2,000 part of the whole distance; that is, by a fifth part of the distance of the utmost satellite from the center of Jupiter, an eccentricity of the orbit which would be very sensible. But the orbits of the satellites are concentric to Jupiter, and therefore the accelerative gravities of Jupiter and of all its satellites toward the sun are equal among themselves. And by the same argument the weights of Saturn and of his satellites toward the sun, at equal distances from the sun, are as their several quantities of matter; and the weights of the moon and of the earth toward the sun are either none or accurately proportional to the masses of matter which they contain. But some weight they have, by Corollaries I and III, Proposition V.

But further, the weights of all the parts of every planet toward any other planet are one to another as the matter in the several parts; for if some parts did gravitate more, others less, than for the quantity of their matter, then the whole planet, according to the sort of parts with which it most abounds, would gravitate more or less than in proportion to the quantity of matter in the whole. Nor is it of any moment whether these parts are external or internal; for if, for example, we should imagine the terrestrial bodies with us to be raised to the orbit of the moon, to be there compared with its body, if the weights of such bodies were to the weights of the external parts of the moon as the quantities of matter in the one and in the other respectively, but to the weights of the internal parts in a greater or less proportion, then likewise the weights of those bodies would be to the weight of the whole moon in a greater or less proportion, against what we have shown above.

Corollary I

Hence the weights of bodies do not depend upon their forms and textures; for if the weights could be altered with the forms, they would be greater or less, according to the variety of forms, in equal matter, altogether against experience.

Corollary II

Universally, all bodies about the earth gravitate toward the earth; and the weights of all, at equal distances from the earth's center, are as the quantities of matter which they severally contain. This is the quality of all bodies within the reach of our experiments, and therefore (by Rule III) to be affirmed of all bodies whatsoever. If the ether, or any other body, were either altogether void of gravity or were to gravitate less in proportion to its quantity of matter, then, because (according to Aristotle, Descartes, and others) there is no difference between that and other bodies but in mere form of matter, by a successive change from form to form, it might be changed at last into a body of the same condition with those which gravitate most in proportion to their quantity of matter; and, on the other hand, the heaviest bodies, acquiring the first form of that body, might by degrees quite lose their gravity. And therefore the weights would depend upon the forms of bodies and, with those forms, might be changed, contrary to what was proved in the preceding Corollary.

Corollary III

All spaces are not equally full; for if all spaces were equally full, then the specific gravity of the fluid which fills the region of the air, on account of the extreme density of the matter, would fall nothing short of the specific gravity of quicksilver or gold or any other the most dense body, and therefore neither gold nor any other body could descend in air, for bodies do not descend in fluids unless they are specifically heavier than the fluids. And if the quantity of matter in a given space can, by any rarefaction, be diminished, what should hinder a diminution to infinity?

Corollary IV

If all the solid particles of all bodies are of the same density and cannot be rarefied without pores, then a void, space, or vacuum must be granted. By "bodies of the same density" I mean those whose inertias are in the proportion of their bulks.

Corollary V

The power of gravity is of a different nature from the power of magnetism, for the magnetic attraction is not as the matter attracted. Some bodies are attracted more by the magnet, others less; most bodies not at all. The power of magnetism in one and the same body may be increased and diminished, and is sometimes far stronger, for the quantity of matter, than the power of gravity; and in receding from the magnet decreases, not as the square, but almost as the cube of the distance, as nearly as I could judge from some rude observations.

68. ANATOMY BY OBSERVATION

Part of the scientific revolution was the development of a new way of looking at natural events that combined precise observation and measurement with theories of explanation tied to data rather than to traditional doctrines. The great work that initiated this approach in the biological field was published, by coincidence, in 1543, the same year in which Copernicus's book appeared. This work was *On the Fabric of the Human Body*, by Andreas Vesalius (1514-1564), who was named professor of anatomy and surgery at Padua in 1537, the day after he passed his doctoral examination. He did not follow the practice of traditional anatomists, who lectured on Galen's description of the human body from the podium while a barber-surgeon dissected a corpse and a servant pointed out the parts of the cadaver. Instead, he did the dissection in person and described what he saw, not, as was customary, what was to be found in Galen even when it differed from visual observation. The *Fabric of the Human Body* profoundly influenced anatomical knowledge not only by its text but also by a remarkable series of woodcuts. After 1544, when Vesalius became personal physician to Emperor Charles V and then to his son Philip II, his scientific work declined, and he may have been in trouble with the Inquisition in Spain.

Andreas Vesalius

Fabric of the Human Body

THE EPITOME OF HIS BOOKS ON THE FABRIC OF THE HUMAN BODY BY ANDREAS VESALIUS OF BRUSSELS

TO THE MOST SERENE PRINCE PHILIP, SON AND HEIR OF THE DIVINE EMPEROR CHARLES THE FIFTH, MIGHTIEST AND MOST INVINCIBLE, ANDREAS VESALIUS SENDS GREETINGS:

Within the slender compass of these pages, greatest prince Philip, adorned with the splendor of your immortal name and under its good auspices, there is sent forth unto the common use of learning the descrip-

---

SOURCE: *The Epitome of Vesalius*, transalted by L. R. Lind (Cambridge, Mass.: The M.I.T. Press, 1969, pp. xxxiii–xxxv. Reprinted by permission of L. R. Lind.

tion of the human body, which I have so divided in the manner of an enumeration, and singly related, that the principal branch of natural philosophy, treating the finished product of a creation most perfected and nigh the most worthy of all, may in the manner of an image be set before the eyes of those studious of the works of Nature. This has been done with as much conciseness as possible, and with less labor it describes those matters which I have embraced more amply in my seven books upon the subject. To those books this *Epitome* is, as it were, a footpath, or, as it will also be rightly considered, an appendix, gathering into summary form the chapters which are set forth with detail in those books; it lays out everything in such a fashion I may prophesy that you, with the amazing liberality of culture in which you eagerly welcome whatsoever slightest offering of the writer's craft, will not utterly cast it from your sight. Moreover, as you are now entering upon a period in your life distinguished by such various virtues, you are held fast by a wondrous and most generous love of all art and learning. And when your spacious spirit shall one day rule the whole world, you may perhaps at times consider it pleasant to be acquainted with my work and to regard it as a situation wretched and unworthy of the greatest Emperors, Kings, and Consuls, that in the pursuit of studies so varied, the harmony of the human body which we shall publish to the world should lie constantly concealed; that man be completely unknown to himself; and that the structure of instruments so divinely created by the Great Artificer of all things should remain unexamined: since it is by the function of these instruments that those things we look upon as most, and almost solely, important are brought to pass.

Truly, although for this reason my undertaking will perhaps be not wholly displeasing to your admirable judgment, if I should nevertheless refuse to give forth this companion to physicians because, while I strive to be useful to them yet at the same time I am anxious to snatch opportunity from the hands of certain rascally printers who may later seize in possession upon the labors of another to reduce them ineptly into small space and publish them under their own names (creatures born for the destruction of letters!), I might in either case prove a grievous hindrance. For no one is ignorant how much is lost in all sciences by the use of compendiums. Though indeed they seem to provide a certain way and systematic approach to the perfect and complete knowledge of things and seem to contain in short and in sum that which is set down elsewhere with more space and prolixity and are for this reason considered in the light of an index or the very abode of memory, in which matters written down at length are fitly reduced to their proper place, nevertheless, compendiums do signal injury and wreak a great havoc upon literature; for, given to the use of compendiums alone, we read scarcely anything else through to the end these days. This is true even for those who have delivered themselves completely to learning, to this degree aspiring only to the shadow and superstructure of science, digging little or not at all beneath the surface.

However, although this evil wanders widely amid almost all studies, it is a charge to be laid most gravely at the door of the mob of physicians that they perform their duty so carelessly in distinguishing the parts of the human body that not even enumeration is made use of in learning them. For when, beyond the function and use of each part, its location, form, size, color, the nature of its substance, the principle of its connection with the other parts, and many things of this sort in the medical examination of the parts may never be sufficiently perceived, how many can be found who know even the number of the bones, cartilages, ligaments, muscles, and veins, arteries, and nerves running in a numerous succession throughout the entire body and of the viscera which are found in the cavities of the body? I pass over in silence those pestilent doctors who encompass the destruction of the common life of mankind, who never even stood by at a dissection: whereas in the knowledge of the body no one could produce anything of value who did not perform dissections with his own hands as the kings of Egypt were wont to do and in like manner busied himself frequently and sedulously with dissections and with simple medicines. Whence also those most prudent members of the household of Asclepius will never be sufficiently praised, who, as children in the home learn reading and writing, so they exercised the dissection of cadavers and, learned in this wise, under the happy auspices of the Muses, they bent to their studies. Furthermore, whatever our sloth in the thorough mastery of Anatomy as the basis and foundation of the medical art, I have assumed that no demonstration is required of how necessary the knowledge of human parts is for us who have enlisted under the banner of medicine, since the conscience of each and all will bear full testimony to the fact that in the cure of illness the knowledge of those parts lays rightful claim to first, second, and third place; and this knowledge is to be sought primarily from the affected portion, without, of course, neglecting the due application of subsidiary remedies. Indeed, those who are now dedicated to the ancient study of medicine, almost restored to its pristine splendor in many schools, are beginning to learn to their satisfaction how little and how feebly men have labored in the field of Anatomy to this day from the times of Galen, who, although easily chief of the masters, nevertheless did not dissect the human body; and the fact is now evident that he described (not to say imposed upon us) the fabric of the ape's body, although the latter differs from the former in many respects.

69. AN UNPLANNED EXPERIMENT

Another aspect of the method of investigation that evolved in the scientific revolution was the experiment, or the organization of experience (which in Latin and the Romance languages has the same root as the word "experiment") in such a way that causes could be detected for effects. Normally such experiments would be deliberate arrangements of materials and events, but accidental events thoughtfully observed might yield the same results. This method can be seen in the description by the famed French army surgeon Ambroise Paré (1510-1590) of the way he found a better treatment for gunshot wounds, which is reprinted from his *Works* below. He also solved an essential problem in surgery, control of hemorrhaging.

Ambroise Paré

Treatment for Gunshot Wounds

Fowling pieces which men usually carry upon their shoulders, are of the middle ranke of these engines, as also Muskets and Caleevers, which you cannot well discharge unlesse lying upon a Rest, which therefore may be called Breast-guns for that they are not laid to the cheeke, but against the Breast by reason of their weight and shortness; All which have beene invented for the commodity of footemen, and light horsemen. This middle sort of engine we call in Latine by a generall name Sclopus, in imitation of the sound, and the Italians who terme it Sclopetere; the French call it Harquebuse, a word likewise borrowed from the Italians, by reason of the touch-hole by which you give fire to the peice, for the Italians call a hole Buzio.

In the year of our Lord 1536, Francis the French King, for his acts in warre and peace stiled the Great, sent a puissant Army beyond the Alpes, under the Government and leading of Annas of Mommorancie high Constable of France, both that he might releeve Turin with victualls, souldiers, and all things needefull, as also to recover the Citties of that Province taken by the Marquis du Guast, Generall of the Emperours forces. I was in the Kings Army the Chirurgion of Monsieur of Montejan, Generall of the foote. The Imperialists had taken the straits of Suze, the Castle of Villane, and all the other passages, so that the Kings army was

---

SOURCE: From Logan Clendening (ed.), *Source Book of Medical History* (New York: Dover Publications, Inc., 1942), pp. 192–93. Reprinted through permission of the publisher.

not able to drive them from their fortifications but by fight. In this conflict there were many wounded on both sides with all sorts of weapons but cheefely with bullets. I will tell the truth, I was not very expert at that time in matters of Chirurgery; neither was I used to dresse wounds made by gunshot. Now I had read in Iohn de Vigo that wounds made by Gunshot were venerate or poisoned, and that by reason of the Gunpouder; Wherefore for their cure, it was expedient to burne or cauterize them with oyle of Elders scalding hot, with a little Treacle mixed therewith.

But for that I gave no great credite neither to the author, nor remedy, because I knew that caustickes could not be powred into wounds, without excessive paine; I, before I would runne a hazard, determined to see whether the Chirurgions, who went with me in the army, used any other manner of dressing to these wounds. I observed and saw that all of them used that Method of dressing which Vigo prescribes; and that they filled as full as they could, the wounds made by Gunshot with Tents and pledgets dipped in the scalding Oyle, at the first dressings; which encouraged me to doe the like to those, who came to be dressed of me.

It chanced on a time, that by reason of the multitude that were hurt, I wanted this Oyle. Now because there were some few left to be dressed, I was forced, that I might seeme to want nothing, and that I might not leave them undrest, to apply a digestive made of the yolke of an egg, oyle of Roses, and Turpentine. I could not sleep all that night, for I was troubled in minde, and the dressing of the precedent day, (which I judged unfit) troubled my thoughts; and I feared that the next day I should finde them dead, or at the point of death by the poyson of the wound, whom I had not dressed with the scalding oyle. Therefore I rose early in the morning. I visited my patients and beyond expectation, I found such as I had dressed with a digestive onely, free from vehemencie of paine to have had good rest, and that their wounds were not inflamed, nor tumifyed; but on the contrary the others that were burnt with the scalding oyle were feaverish, tormented with much paine, and the parts about their wounds were swolne. When I had many times tryed this in divers others I thought this much, that neither I nor any other should ever cauterize any wounded with Gun-shot.

70. THE HEART AS BLOOD PUMP

A different kind of experiment was conducted by the English physician William Harvey (1578-1657) to solve one of the most central problems in physiology, the role of the heart and the blood vessels. Until Harvey, the blood was conceived of as a means of conveying nutrition to the body and the lungs as a way of lightening the blood; the heart itself was believed to mix heavy and light blood through the walls of its cavities. The movement of blood in the arteries and veins, whose function could not be clearly differentiated, was seen as a kind of ebb and flow. Harvey, building on the speculative work of predecessors, demonstrated the circulation of the blood by vivisection, dissection, and coherent analysis of all the parts of the system, including the capillaries that linked arteries to veins. His analysis treated the heart as a pumping machine and the flow of blood as a problem in volumes and rates of flow. A key section of his book *Anatomical Exercises on the Motion of the Heart and Blood in Animals* (1628) is given below.

William Harvey

On the Motion of the Heart and Blood

Thus far I have spoken of the passage of the blood from the veins into the arteries, and of the manner in which it is transmitted and distributed by the action of the heart; points to which some, moved either by the authority of Galen or Columbus, or the reasonings of others, will give in their adhesion. But what remains to be said upon the quantity and source of the blood which thus passes, is of so novel and unheard-of character, that I not only fear injury to myself from the envy of a few, but I tremble lest I have mankind at large for my enemies, so much doth wont and custom, that become as another nature, and doctrine once sown and that hath struck deep root, and respect for antiquity influence all men: Still the die is cast, and my trust is in my love of truth, and the candour that inheres in cultivated minds. And sooth to say, when I surveyed my mass of evidence, whether derived from vivisections, and my various reflections on them, or from the ventricles of the heart and the vessels that enter into and issue from them, the symmetry and size of these conduits,—for nature doing nothing in vain, would never have given them so large a relative size without a purpose,—or from the arrangement and intimate structure of the valves in particular, and of the other parts of the heart in general, with many things besides, I frequently and seriously bethought me, and long revolved in my mind, what might be the quantity of blood which was transmitted, in how short a time its passage might be effected, and the like; and not finding it possible that this could be supplied by the juices of the ingested aliment without the veins on the one hand becoming drained, and the arteries on the other getting ruptured through the excessive charge of blood,

---

Source: Logan Clendening (ed.), *Source Book of Medical History* (New York: Dover Publications, 1942), pp. 163–64. Reprinted through permission of the publisher.

unless the blood should somehow find its way from the arteries into the veins, and so return to the right side of the heart; I began to think whether there might not be A MOTION AS IT WERE, IN A CIRCLE. Now this I afterwards found to be true; and I finally saw that the blood, forced by the action of the left ventricle into the arteries, was distributed to the body at large, and its several parts, in the same manner as it is sent through the lungs, impelled by the right ventricle into the pulmonary artery, and that it then passed through the veins and along the vena cava, and so round to the left ventricle in the manner already indicated. Which motion we may be allowed to call circular, in the same way as Aristotle says that the air and the rain emulate the circular motion of the superior bodies; for the moist earth, warmed by the sun, evaporates; the vapours drawn upwards are condensed, and descending in the form of rain, moisten the earth again; and by this arrangement are generations of living things produced; and in like manner too are tempests and meteors engendered by the circular motion, and by the approach and recession of the sun.

71. A WAY TO TAME SMALLPOX

In the field of medicine, remedies often were discovered and applied long before the reasons for their operation were understood. Insofar as a connection of cause and effect was perceived and put to use, however, such innovations lay within the realm of the development of science, as distinct from "old wives' cures," which were not put to any rigorous test. The first great example of such a new remedy was new only in Europe, because it was already in use in Turkey; this was the inoculation for smallpox. It was reported by Lady Mary Wortley Montagu, the wife of the British ambassador in Turkey, in 1717. The passage of her letter of April 1, 1717, to a friend from Adrianople that relates to inoculation for smallpox is given here. When she returned to England the next year, she campaigned vigorously for the adoption of the practice, as she had planned.

Lady Mary Wortley Montagu

Letter on Inoculation

A propos of Distempers, I am going to tell you a thing that I am sure will make you wish your selfe here. The Small Pox so fatal and so general

SOURCE: Robert Halsband (ed.), *The Complete Letters of Lady Mary Wortley Montagu* (Oxford, England: Clarendon Press, 1965), Vol. I, pp. 338–39. Reprinted by permission of the Clarendon Press, Oxford.

amongst us is here entirely harmless by the invention of engrafting (which is the term they give it). There is a set of old Women who make it their business to perform the Operation. Every Autumn in the month of September, when the great Heat is abated, people send to one another to know if any of their family has a mind to have the small pox. They make partys for this purpose, and when they are met (commonly 15 or 16 together) the old Woman comes with a nutshell full of the matter of the best sort of small-pox and asks what veins you please to have open'd. She immediately rips open that you offer to her with a large needle (which gives you no more pain than a common scratch) and puts into the vein as much venom as can lye upon the head of her needle, and after binds up the little wound with a hollow bit of shell, and in this manner opens 4 or 5 veins. The Grecians have commonly the superstition of opening one in the Middle of the forehead, in each arm and on the breast to mark the sign of the cross, but this has a very ill Effect, all these wounds leaving little Scars, and is not done by those that are not superstitious, who chuse to have them in the legs or that part of the arm that is conceal'd. The children or young patients play together all the rest of the day and are in perfect health till the 8th. Then the fever begins to seize 'em and they keep their beds 2 days, very seldom 3. They have very rarely above 20 or 30 in their faces, which never mark, and in 8 days time they are as well as before their illness. Where they are wounded there remains running sores during the Distemper, which I don't doubt is a great releife to it. Every year thousands undergo this Operation, and the French Ambassador says pleasantly that they take the Small pox here by way of diversion as they take the Waters in other Countrys. There is no example of any one that has dy'd in it, and you may beleive I am very well satisfy'd of the safety of the Experiment since I intend to try it on my dear little Son. I am Patriot enough to take pains to bring this usefull invention into fashion in England, and I should not fail to write to some of our Doctors very particularly about it if I knew any one of 'em that I thought had Virtue enough to destroy such a considerable branch of their Revenue for the good of Mankind, but that Distemper is too beneficial to them not to expose to all their Resentment the hardy wight that should undertake to put an end to it. Perhaps if I live to return I may, however, have courrage to war with 'em.

72. THE MICROSCOPE AND THE LITTLE BEASTIES

The development of scientific biology also depended upon the ability to examine living things and their parts that were smaller than the eye could see. The application of the microscope to the investigation of "very little animalcules" was the work of the 17th-century Dutch naturalist Antony van Leeuwenhoek (1632-1723). With simple one-lens microscopes of incredible accuracy which he ground himself, he investigated the abounding life invisible to the naked eye that inhabited the waters of a lake not far from his home in Delft. What he found was described in a letter reprinted below to Henry Oldenburg, secretary of the English Royal Society, on September 7, 1674. Leeuwenhoek, although without formal training, was an honored member of the society and regularly reported his findings to it.

Antony van Leeuwenhoek

Observations of Very Little Animalcules

About two hours distant from this Town there lies an inland lake, called the Berkelse Mere, whose bottom in many places is very marshy, or boggy. Its water is in winter very clear, but at the beginning or in the middle of summer it becomes whitish, and there are then little green clouds floating through it; which, according to the saying of the country folk dwelling thereabout, is caused by the dew, which happens to fall at that time, and which they call honey-dew. This water is abounding in fish, which is very good and savoury. Passing just lately over this lake, at a time when the wind blew pretty hard, and seeing the water as above described, I took up a little of it in a glass phial; and examining this water next day, I found floating therein divers earthy particles, and some green streaks, spirally wound serpent-wise, and orderly arranged, after the manner of the copper or tin worms, which distillers use to cool their liquors as they distil over. The whole circumference of each of these streaks was about the thickness of a hair of one's head. Other particles had but the beginning of the foresaid streak; but all consisted of very small green globules joined together: and there were very many small green globules as well. Among these there were, besides, very many little animalcules, whereof some were roundish, while others, a bit bigger, consisted of an oval. On these last I saw two little legs near the head, and two little fins at the hindmost end of the body. Others were somewhat longer than an oval, and these were very slow a-moving, and few in number. These animalcules had divers colours, some being whitish and transparent; others with green and very glittering little scales; others again were green in the middle, and before and behind white; others yet were ashen grey. And the motion of most of these animalcules in the

SOURCE: Clifford Dobell, Ed. and Transl. *Antony Van Leeuwenhoek and His "Little Animals,"* [1932] New York: Russell & Russell, 1958, pp. 109–11.

water was so swift, and so various, upwards, downwards, and round about, that 'twas wonderful to see: and I judge that some of these little creatures were above a thousand times smaller than the smallest ones I have ever yet seen, upon the rind of cheese, in wheaten flour, mould, and the like.

73. A SCIENTIFIC WAY OF GIVING NAMES

One of the most subtle of the important problems in the foundation of a science is an effective way of naming the things studied. Without such a system, precision is impossible; yet it cannot be established until such a level of understanding of what is being studied has been achieved that nomenclature will not be arbitrary or irrelevant but will arise out of essential elements. The first major figure in modern science to make nomenclature his central concern was the Swedish botanist Carolus Linnaeus (1707-1778). After taking a medical degree at a Dutch university, he remained in Holland for several years, writing a number of works, including the *Critica Botanica* (1737), from which the following selection is taken. Linnaeus urged a scientifically adequate system of nomenclature that would use dual (or even triple) names, specifying the genus and then the species (and variety) upon the basis of plant physiology. He later applied this principle in a series of works that established modern botanic nomenclature.

Carolus Linnaeus

Critica Botanica

Generic Names

210. The classification being made, let Nomenclature, the other of the two foundations of Botany, forthwith bestow names.

We have laid down the twofold foundation of Botany, the Classification and the Nomenclature of plants, in undertaking either of which the botanist must use judgment.

If anyone should distinguish precisely all the plants in the world ac-

---

Source: *The "Critica Botanica" of Linnaeus*, translated by Sir Arthur Hort and revised by Miss M. L. Green. (London: The Ray Society, 1938), pp. 1–3. Reprinted by permission of The Ray Society.

cording to the characters stamped on them, and yet bestow no names on the plants themselves, he would be keeping his learning entirely to himself. Even a rustic knows plants, and so maybe does a brute beast, but neither can make anyone else the wiser: hence in the words of Isidorus, "If you know not the names, the knowledge of things too is wasted."

Wherefore the Botanist is distinguished from the layman by the fact that the former is able to give a name which fits one particular plant and not another, and which can be understood by anyone all the world over.

The names bestowed on plants by the ancient Greeks and Romans I commend, but I shudder at the sight of most of those given by modern authorities: for these are for the most part a mere chaos of confusion, whose mother was barbarity, whose father dogmatism, and whose nurse prejudice. Now is there anything surprising in this? For what novice was ever well versed in nomenclature? Who has ever given for the naming of plants principles, conclusive arguments or examples? Those who in recent times have made the attempt have forthwith experienced shipwreck: they have avoided sundry rocks, but have often fallen victims to Scylla in their desire to escape Charybdis.

Tournefort has been the chief chooser of names, Ruppius has chosen a certain number, Dillenius has proceeded with greater caution than the rest. But both these botanists and others would have rejected far more names, had not men advanced in years been too scrupulous about parting with names which had become familiar to them, and which they defended as they would their own hearths and homes. Yet a beginning must some time be made, even though one risks one's reputation over the attempt: for the assent of one wise man counts for more with me than the idle reproaches of a hundred laymen.

There is no spell to bind me before the publication of Sherard's Pinax: after its appearance Threlkeld has threatened with anathema anyone who should change the names of plants. To that anathema I indeed would subscribe, if only he would in the meanwhile provide suitable names. But, as so far this has not been done, I need feel no scruple in putting forward suggestions of my own and submitting them to the criticism of others.

Only when plants have been classified under genera, and not before, should names be assigned to them. Hence no names that have been assigned to plants must be adopted if they do not fit the genera—neither those assigned by the ancients, nor the official names, nor any other accepted names which include different genera under a single designation: *Where a single genus is concerned, there shall be but one name!*

211. It is only real botanists who have the power of assigning true names to plants.

By a botanist I mean one who understands how to observe the genera of Nature. I judge unworthy of the name of botanist the meddlesome person who is indifferent to genera.

Again the foundation of all classification of plants depends on Genera and Species: let those things which agree in genus, or species come under the same generic or specific name: and let the converse of this rule hold. Therefore it follows that no one can assign true names to plants unless he be a botanist and understands the genera and the known species.

Further it is required of the botanist that he should use judgment in assigning names, and not merely assign the first that occur to his mind. We see from the examples cited how absurd, foolish and ridiculous are the names assigned by the Commentators when these studies had lately been revived and the science had not yet been developed: and so we ought to learn wisdom from the example of others.

We reject all the names assigned to plants by anyone, unless they have been either invented by the Systematists or confirmed by them. For none of those given by the ancients are of this kind: if any of their names are good, it is only by accident.

Nor is there any need for one to be afraid about assigning a new name to a plant which has been already named by some collector: for the name which he gave is bound to be untrue in so far as he did not understand genera—unless by pure accident he hit on a suitable name, or some more learned person taught him about the plant.

We exclude all new names given in memory of botanists by anyone who was not himself a real botanist: for in truth he who desires a name given by himself to be permanent must observe the plant's character.

We do reverence to the omnipotence of the Creator, and to His sublime mysteries as discerned in plants: but we do not admit those names which have a religious significance. . . .

CHAPTER VIII

THE RESPONSE TO SCIENCE

THE RESPONSE to the new science was varied and contradictory. For some it was a weapon of understanding in the struggle to master nature and put it to man's uses. They were concerned with working out its principles and creating institutions in which it could function more efficiently. They saw no conflict with religion, for the laws of nature were God's laws. Science, indeed, was almost a new religion, to be brought to the people by all the skills of the literary art, a way of thinking that need not be reserved for the physical world alone.

For others, however, the challenge was not just to man's rational powers but to the very place that man held in the universe, both the visible universe of the cosmos and the invisible one of divine purpose and will. While the new science might be true, it was no less troubling, for they could find no meaning in an infinite universe in which man was the least of specks. When science seemed to shatter the traditional bonds of man to God, they responded by reaffirming those bonds by faith.

74. A NEW LOGIC FOR THE NEW SCIENCE

The experimental method of the new science rested upon a new conception of the investigation of nature in which observation was the primary method and conclusions were based upon experimentation. The English philosopher Sir Francis Bacon (1561-1626) took note of the shift from deductive to inductive logic in his work on the general principles of the new science called "The Great Instauration," published as part of *The New Organon* in 1620. Bacon was more effective in his assault against the old syllogistic methods of abstract proof practiced by the Scholastics than he was in personal practice of the new science. He saw science too simply, as a massive accumulation of data from which, upon inspection, general conclusions could be drawn. He therefore failed to grasp the creative quality of scientific thought and the direction given to experimental research by the problems posed in scientific theory. Nor did Bacon appreciate the major scientific innovations of his own time, which transcended his essentially common-sense vision. Nevertheless, his dictum that science meant control over nature, not just an understanding of it, became one of the motivating ideas of the scientific enterprise.

Francis Bacon

The Great Instauration

. . . . .

Having thus coasted past the ancient arts, the next point is to equip the intellect for passing beyond. To the second part, therefore, belongs the doctrine concerning the better and more perfect use of human reason in the inquisition of things, and the true helps of the understanding, that thereby (as far as the condition of mortality and humanity allows) the intellect may be raised and exalted, and made capable of overcoming the difficulties and obscurities of nature. The art which I introduce with this view (which I call "Interpretation of Nature") is a kind of logic, though the difference between it and the ordinary logic is great, indeed, immense. For the ordinary logic professes to contrive and prepare helps and guards for the understanding, as mine does; and in this one point they agree. But mine differs from it in three points especially—viz., in the end aimed at, in the order of demonstration, and in the starting point of the inquiry.

For the end which this science of mine proposes is the invention not of arguments but of arts; not of things in accordance with principles, but of principles themselves; not of probable reasons, but of designations and directions for works. And as the intention is different, so, accordingly, is the effect; the effect of the one being to overcome an opponent in argument, of the other to command nature in action.

In accordance with this end is also the nature and order of the demonstrations. For in the ordinary logic almost all the work is spent about the syllogism. Of induction, the logicians seem hardly to have taken any serious thought, but they pass it by with a slight notice and hasten on to the formulae of disputation. I, on the contrary, reject demonstration by syllogism as acting too confusedly and letting nature slip out of its hands. For although no one can doubt that things which agree in a middle term agree with one another (which is a proposition of mathematical certainty), yet it leaves an opening for deception, which is this: the syllogism consists of propositions—propositions of words; and words are the tokens and signs of notions. Now if the very notions of the mind (which are as the soul of words and the basis of the whole structure) be improperly and overhastily abstracted from facts, vague, not sufficiently definite, faulty—in short, in many ways, the whole edifice tumbles. I therefore reject the syllogism, and that not only as regards principles (for to principles the logicians themselves do not apply it) but also as regards middle propositions, which, though obtainable no doubt by the syllogism, are, when so obtained, barren of works, remote from practice, and altogether unavailable for the active department of the sciences. Although, therefore, I leave to the syllogism and these famous and boasted modes of demonstration their jurisdiction over popular arts and such as are matter of opinion (in which department I leave all as it is), yet in dealing with the nature of things I use induction throughout, and that in the minor propositions as well as the major. For I consider induction to be that form of demonstration which upholds the sense, and closes with nature, and comes to the very brink of operation, if it does not actually deal with it.

Hence it follows that the order of demonstration is likewise inverted. For hitherto the proceeding has been to fly at once from the sense and particulars up to the most general propositions, as certain fixed poles for the argument to turn upon, and from these to derive the rest by middle terms—a short way, no doubt, but precipitate and one which will never lead to nature, though it offers an easy and ready way to disputation. Now my plan is to proceed regularly and gradually from one axiom to another, so that the most general are not reached till the last; but then, when you do come to them, you find them to be not empty notions but well defined, and such as nature would really recognize as her first principles, and such as lie at the heart and marrow of things.

But the greatest change I introduce is in the form itself of induction and the judgment made thereby. For the induction of which the logicians speak, which proceeds by simple enumeration, is a puerile thing, concludes at hazard, is always liable to be upset by a contradictory instance, takes into account only what is known and ordinary, and leads to no result.

Now what the sciences stand in need of is a form of induction which shall analyze experience and take it to pieces, and by a due process of exclusion and rejection lead to an inevitable conclusion. And if that ordinary mode of judgment practiced by the logicians was so laborious, and found exercise for such great wits, how much more labor must we be prepared to bestow upon this other, which is extracted not merely out of the depths of the mind, but out of the very bowels of nature.

Nor is this all. For I also sink the foundations of the sciences deeper and firmer; and I begin the inquiry nearer the source than men have done heretofore, submitting to examination those things which the common logic takes on trust. For first, the logicians borrow the principles of each science from the science itself; secondly, they hold in reverence the first notions of the mind; and lastly, they receive as conclusive the immediate informations of the sense, when well disposed. Now upon the first point, I hold that true logic ought to enter the several provinces of science armed with a higher authority than belongs to the principles of those sciences themselves, and ought to call those putative principles to account until they are fully established. Then with regard to the first notions of the intellect, there is not one of the impressions taken by the intellect when left to go its own way, but I hold it as suspect and no way established until it has submitted to a new trial and a fresh judgment has been thereupon pronounced. And lastly, the information of the sense itself I sift and examine in many ways. For certain it is that the senses deceive; but then at the same time they supply the means of discovering their own errors; only the errors are here, the means of discovery are to seek.

The sense fails in two ways. Sometimes it gives no information, sometimes it gives false information. For first, there are very many things which escape the sense, even when best disposed and no way obstructed, by reason either of the subtlety of the whole body or the minuteness of the parts, or distance of place, or slowness or else swiftness of motion, or familiarity of the object, or other causes. And again when the sense does apprehend a thing its apprehension is not much to be relied upon. For the testimony and information of the sense has reference always to man, not to the universe; and it is a great error to assert that the sense is the measure of things.

To meet these difficulties, I have sought on all sides diligently and faithfully to provide helps for the sense—substitutes to supply its failures, rectifications to correct its errors; and this I endeavor to accomplish not so much by instruments as by experiments. For the subtlety of experiments is far greater than that of the sense itself, even when assisted by exquisite instruments—such experiments, I mean, as are skillfully and artificially devised for the express purpose of determining the point in question. To the immediate and proper perception of the sense, therefore, I do not give much weight; but I contrive that the office of the sense shall be only to judge of the experiment, and that the experiment itself shall judge of the thing. And thus I conceive that I perform the office of a true priest of the sense (from which all knowledge in nature must be sought, unless men mean to go mad) and a not unskillful interpreter of its oracles; and that while others only profess to uphold and cultivate the sense, I do so in fact. Such then are the provisions I make for finding the genuine light of nature and kindling and bringing it to bear. And they would be sufficient of themselves if the human intellect were even and like a fair sheet of paper with no writing on it. But since the minds of men are strangely possessed and beset so that there is no true and even surface left to reflect the genuine rays of things, it is necessary to seek a remedy for this also.

Now the idols, or phantoms, by which the mind is occupied are either adventitious or innate. The adventitious come into the mind from without—namely, either from the doctrines and sects of philosophers or from perverse rulers of demonstration. But the innate are inherent in the very nature of the intellect, which is far more prone to error than the sense is. For let men please themselves as they will in admiring and almost adoring the human mind, this is certain: that as an uneven mirror distorts the rays of objects according to its own figure and section, so the mind, when it receives impressions of objects through the sense, cannot be trusted to report them truly, but in forming its notions mixes up its own nature with the nature of things.

And as the first two kinds of idols are hard to eradicate, so idols of this last kind cannot be eradicated at all. All that can be done is to point them out, so that this insidious action of the mind may be marked and reproved (else as fast as old errors are destroyed new ones will spring up out of the ill complexion of the mind itself, and so we shall have but a change of errors, and not a clearance); and to lay it down once for all as a fixed and established maxim that the intellect is not qualified to judge except by means of induction, and induction in its legitimate form. This doctrine, then, of the expurgation of the intellect to qualify it for dealing with truth is comprised in three refutations: the refutation of the philosophies; the refutation of the demonstrations; and the refutation of the natural human reason. The explanation of which things, and of the true relation between the nature of things and the nature of the mind, is as the strewing and decoration of the bridal chamber of the mind and the universe, the divine goodness assisting, out of which marriage let us hope (and be this the prayer of the bridal song) there may spring helps to man, and a line and race of inventions that may in some degree subdue and overcome the necessities and miseries of humanity. This is the second part of the work.

But I design not only to indicate and mark out the ways, but also to enter them. And therefore the third part of the work embraces the "phenomena of the universe"; that is to say, experience of every kind, and such a natural history as may serve for a foundation to build philosophy upon. For a good method of demonstration or form of interpreting nature may keep the mind from going astray or stumbling, but it is not any excellence of method that can supply it with the material of knowledge. Those, however, who aspire not to guess and divine, but to discover and know, who propose not to devise mimic and fabulous worlds of their own, but to examine and dissect the nature of this very world itself, must go to facts themselves for everything. . . .

. . . .

The sixth part of my work (to which the rest is subservient and ministrant) discloses and sets forth that philosophy which by the legitimate, chaste, and severe course of inquiry which I have explained and provided is at length developed and established. The completion, however, of this last part is a thing both above my strength and beyond my hopes. I have made a beginning of the work—a beginning, as I hope, not unimportant: the fortune of the human race will give the issue, such an issue, it may be, as in the present condition of things and men's minds cannot easily be conceived or imagined. For the matter in hand is no mere felicity of speculation, but the real business and fortunes of the human race, and all power of operation. For man is but the servant and interpreter of nature: what he does and what he knows is only what he has observed of nature's order in fact or in thought; beyond this he knows nothing and can do nothing. For the chain of causes cannot by any force be loosed or broken, nor can nature be commanded except by being obeyed. And so those twin objects, human knowledge and human power, do really meet in one; and it is from ignorance of causes that operation fails.

And all depends on keeping the eye steadily fixed upon the facts of nature and so receiving their images simply as they are. For God forbid that we should give out a dream of our own imagination for a pattern of the world; rather may he graciously grant to us to write an apocalypse or true vision of the footsteps of the Creator imprinted on his creatures.

Therefore do thou, O Father, who gavest the visible light as the first fruits of creation, and didst breathe into the face of man the intellectual light as the crown and consummation thereof, guard and protect this work, which coming from thy goodness returneth to thy glory. Thou when thou turnedst to look upon the works which thy hands had made, sawest that all was very good, and didst rest from thy labors. But man, when he turned to look upon the work which his hands had made, saw that all was vanity and vexation of spirit, and could find no rest therein. Wherefore if we labor in thy works with the sweat of our brows, thou wilt make us partakers of thy vision and thy sabbath. Humbly we pray that this mind may be steadfast in us, and that through these our hands, and the hands of others to whom thou shalt give the same spirit, thou wilt vouchsafe to endow the human family with new mercies.

75. A NEW WAY TO CERTAIN TRUTH

The problem of how to know truth that had occupied the minds of philosophers since antiquity continued in the early modern period to beset those who rose above the level of naïveté. What was involved was not primarily the detection of lies but rather the provision of adequate grounds for certitude. The corrosive questions of the skeptics—How can we know that our senses do not deceive us? What force can personal conviction have when honest men disagree? How can we assert the proofs of mathematics and logic, when we cannot prove the axioms on which they rest?—were deeply troubling.

The new science ultimately required positive answers to these questions, and René Descartes sought to provide them in a magnificently ingenious paradox. In his *Discourse on Method* (1637), he applied the process of skeptical thought to obtain a first truth—the existence of the skeptic himself. From this truth he could proceed to the necessary certitudes. In one respect, the *Discourse,* with its elaborate proofs, is one of the last masterpieces of philosophy in the Scholastic manner. In another, its refusal to accept any authority whatever other than experience marks it as one of the first studies in the modern manner. The passages from the *Discourse* in which Descartes defines his problem and arrives at his first solution are given here.

René Descartes

Discourse on Method

. . . .

Thus I came to think that the sciences found in books, at least those whose reasonings are made up merely of plausible arguments and yield no demonstrations, built up, as they are, little by little, from the opinions of many different contributors, do not get so near to the truth as the simple reasonings which a man of good sense, making use of his natural

---

SOURCE: René Descartes, *Philosophical Writings,* edited and translated by Norman Kemp Smith (New York: The Modern Library, 1958), pp. 102–7, 118–20. Reprinted by permission of St. Martin's Press, Inc., Macmillan & Co., Ltd.; and Macmillan London and Basingstoke. (One correction, noted in a footnote, has been made in the translation.)

powers, can carry out respecting what happens to come before him. Then further, since we have all passed through the state of infancy before being men, and have therefore of necessity been long governed by our sensuous impulses and by our teachers (teachers who were often at variance with one another, and none of whom, perhaps, counseled us always for the best), I also came to think that it is well-nigh impossible our judgments can be so correct and so reliable as they would have been, had we from the moment of our birth been in entire possession of our reason and been all along guided by it alone.

To be sure, we do not proceed to pull down all the houses of a town, simply for the purpose of rebuilding them differently, to make the streets more beautiful. Often, however, it does happen that this or that house is pulled down with a view to rebuilding; and sometimes this is due to their being in danger of themselves falling, their foundations being insecure. In analogy with this, I persuaded myself that it is not indeed reasonable for a private individual to think of reforming a State by changing everything in it, overturning it in order to re-establish it; and that it is not likely that the whole body of the sciences, or the manner of teaching them, as established in the Schools, can be remodeled. In respect, however, of the opinions which I have hitherto been entertaining, I thought that I could not do better than decide on emptying my mind of them one and all, with a view to the replacing of them by others more tenable, or, it may be, to the re-admitting of them, on their being shown to be in conformity with reason. I was firmly of the belief that by this means I should succeed much better in the conduct of my life than if, building on the old foundations, I relied on principles of which in my youth I had allowed myself to be persuaded, and into the truth of which I had never inquired. Of the many difficulties involved I was very well aware. These are not, however, without remedy, nor are they comparable to those which face us in reforming, even in quite minor ways, what is of direct public concern. Great public institutions, if once overthrown, are excessively difficult to re-establish, or even to maintain erect if once seriously shaken; and their fall cannot but be very violent. As to their imperfections, if they have any—and their very diversity is sufficient to assure us that they do—usage has doubtless greatly mitigated them, eliminating, or at least insensibly correcting, many evils which could never have been so effectively countered in a deliberately reflective manner. Almost always the imperfections are more tolerable than the changes required for their removal. Do not highways that wind about among the mountains, by being much frequented, become gradually so smooth and convenient, that the following of them is vastly preferable to attempting the straighter route, scaling high rocks and clambering down precipices?

This is why I cannot at all approve of those reckless quarrelsome spirits who, though not called by birth or fortune to take part in the management of public affairs, yet never fail to be always on the hunt for some new reform. If I thought that in this essay there were the least ground for supposing me to be guilty of any such folly, I should never willingly consent to its publication. My design has all along been limited to the reform of my own thoughts, and to the basing of them on a foundation entirely my own. Although these labors have given me considerable satisfaction—this is what has led me to give you an account of them—I have no desire to counsel all others to engage in them. Those whom God has more amply endowed will perhaps entertain more exalted designs; but I fear that even what I am here proposing will for many be too hazardous. The resolve to strip oneself of all opinions hitherto believed is not one that everyone is called upon to take. There are among men two types of mind, to neither of which is it at all suited: first, those who, owing to undue confidence in their powers, are precipitate in their judgments and have not the patience required for the orderly arranging of their thoughts. Should men of this type assume themselves free to doubt received opinions and to deviate from the common highway, they will never be able to find, and to hold to, the one straight path that leads aright. Instead they will, throughout all the rest of their lives, find themselves hopelessly astray. Secondly, there are those who have reason or modesty enough to realize that they are less capable of distinguishing between the true and the false than others from whom they can gain instruction. They ought to be well content to follow the opinions of those others, and not to attempt to improve on them by efforts of their own.

As for myself, I should no doubt have belonged to the latter class, had I never had more than one instructor and had I never known how from time immemorial even the most learned of men have continued in disagreement one with another. Already in my college days I had been brought to recognize that there is no opinion, however strange, and however difficult of belief, which has not been upheld by one or other of the philosophers. Afterwards, too, in the course of my travels, I observed that those whose sentiments are very contrary to ours are not on this account barbarous and savage, and that many of them make as good or, it may be, better use of reason than we do ourselves. Bearing also in mind how the selfsame man, with the mental equipment proper to him, if nurtured from infancy among the French or the Germans, would come to be different from what he would have been had he lived always among the Chinese or the cannibals; and how, in respect of fashions in dress, what pleased us ten years ago, and which will again please ten years hence, appears to us at the present moment extravagant and ridiculous. Thus I came to see that custom and example have a much more persuasive power than any certitude obtained by way of inquiry. In respect of truths which are not readily discoverable, plurality of supporting votes is of no value as proof; it is much more likely that the discovery will be made by one man than by all and sundry. I was, however, unable to decide on any one person whose opinion seemed worthy of preference, and so had no option save to look to myself for guidance.

But like those who walk alone and after nightfall, I resolved to proceed so slowly, and with such meticulous circumspection, that if my advance was but small, I should at least guard myself from falling. I had no intention of forthwith discarding any of the opinions which had established themselves in my mind unintroduced by reason. Like the dwellers in an outworn house, who do not start to pull it down until they have planned another in its place, I had first to allow myself time to think out the project on which I was entering, and to seek out and decide on the true method, a method that I could rely upon as guiding me to a knowledge of all the things my mind is capable of knowing.

Along with other philosophical disciplines I had, in my early youth, made some little study of logic, and, in the mathematical field, of geometrical analysis and of algebra—three arts or sciences, which, it seemed to me, ought to be in some way helpful toward what I had in view. But on looking into them I found that in the case of logic, its syllogisms and the greater part of its other precepts are serviceable more for the explaining to others the things we know (or even, as in the art of Lully,[1] for speaking without judgment of the things of which we are ignorant) than for the discovery of them; and that while it does indeed yield us many precepts which are very good and true, there are so many others, either harmful or superfluous, mingled with them, that to separate out what is good and true is almost as difficult as to extract a Diana or a Minerva from a rough unshaped marble block. As to the analysis of the ancients and the algebra of the moderns, besides extending only to what is highly abstract and seemingly of no real use, the former is so confined to the treatment of shapes that it cannot exercise the understanding without greatly fatiguing the imagination, and the latter is in such subjection to certain rules and other requirements that out of it they have made an obscure and difficult art, which encumbers the mind, not a science helpful in improving it. I was thus led to think that I must search for some other method which will comprise all that is advantageous in these three disciplines, while yet remaining exempt from their defects. A multiplicity of laws often furnishes the vicious with excuses for their evil-doing, and a community is much the better governed if, with only a very few laws, it insists on a quite strict observance of them. So, in like manner, in place

[1] Raymond Lully's *Ars brevis*, composed in 1308, was printed for the first time in 1481, and repeatedly thereafter [N. K. Smith's note].

of the numerous precepts which have gone to constitute logic, I came to believe that the four following rules would be found sufficient, always provided I took the firm and unswerving resolve never in a single instance to fail in observing them.

The first was to accept nothing as true which I did not evidently know to be such, that is to say, scrupulously to avoid precipitance and prejudice, and in the judgments I passed to include nothing additional to what had presented itself to my mind so clearly and so distinctly that I could have no occasion for doubting it.

The second, to divide each of the difficulties I examined into as many parts as may be required for its adequate solution.

The third, to arrange my thoughts in order, beginning with things the simplest and easiest to know, so that I may then ascend little by little, as it were step by step, to the knowledge of the more complex, and, in doing so, to assign an order of thought even to those objects which are not of themselves in any such order of precedence.

And the last, in all cases to make enumerations so complete, and reviews so general, that I should be assured of omitting nothing.

Those long chains of reasonings, each step simple and easy, which geometers are wont to employ in arriving even at the most difficult of their demonstrations, have led me to surmise that all the things we human beings are competent to know are interconnected in the same manner, and that none are so remote as to be beyond our reach or so hidden that we cannot discover them—that is, provided we abstain from accepting as true what is not thus related, i.e., keep always to the order required for their deduction one from another. And I had no great difficulty in determining what the objects are with which I should begin, for that I already knew, viz., that it was with the simplest and easiest. Bearing in mind, too, that of all those who in time past have sought for truth in the sciences, the mathematicians alone have been able to find any demonstrations, that is to say, any reasons which are certain and evident, I had no doubt that it must have been by a procedure of this kind that they had obtained them. In thus starting from what is simplest and easiest I did not as yet anticipate any other advantage than that of accustoming my mind to pasture itself on truths, and to cease from contenting itself with reasons that are false.

. . . . .

I hesitate to tell you of the first meditations there [Holland] made by me; they are so metaphysical and so unusual as not, perhaps, to be generally acceptable. None the less, since they are necessary in judging whether the foundations I have laid are sufficiently secure, I have no option save to speak of them. In practical life, as I had long observed, it is sometimes necessary to follow opinions which we know to be highly uncertain; and, as above said, to hold steadfastly to them, as if they were indeed indubitable. But as I was then minded to give myself entirely to the search for truth, I thought that what was required of me was the directly opposite course, and that I ought to reject as downright false all opinions which I could imagine to be in the least degree open to doubt—my purpose being to discover whether, after so doing, there might not remain, as still calling for belief, something entirely indubitable. Thus, on the ground that our senses sometimes deceive us, I was prepared to suppose that no existing thing is such as the senses make us image it to be; and because in respect even of the very simplest geometrical questions some men err in reasoning and commit paralogisms, I therefore rejected as false (recognizing myself to be no less fallible than others) all the reasonings I had previously accepted as demonstrations; and, finally, when I considered that all the thoughts we have when awake can come to us in sleep (none of the latter being then true), I resolved to feign that all the things which had entered my mind were no more true than the illusions of my dreams. But I immediately became aware that while I was thus disposed to think that all was false, it was absolutely necessary that I who thus thought should be something [2]; and noting that this truth *I think, therefore I am,* was so steadfast and so assured that the suppositions of the skeptics, to whatever extreme they might all be carried, could not avail to shake it, I concluded that I might without scruple accept it as being the first principle of the philosophy I was seeking.

Next, on attentively examining what I was, while recognizing that I could feign that I had no body, that there was no world, nor any place in which I might be, I likewise noted that, notwithstanding this, I could not on that account feign that I was not. Quite the contrary: from this very circumstance that I thought to doubt the truth of those other things, it very evidently and very certainly followed that I was, whereas I had only to cease to think for an instant of time and I should then (even although all the other things I had imaged still remained true [i.e., real existents]) have no ground for believing that I can have existed in that instant. From this I knew that I was a substance whose whole essence or nature consists entirely in thinking, and which, for its existence, has no need of place, and is not dependent on any material thing; so that this I, that is to say, the soul by which I am what I am, is entirely distinct from the body, and is indeed more easy to know than the body, and would not itself cease to be all that it is, even should the body cease to exist.

I then proceeded to consider, in a general manner, what is requisite to the truth and certainty of a proposition. Having found one—*I think, therefore I am*—which I knew to be true and certain, I thought that I ought

---

[2] Corrected from "somewhat": French "quelque chose" [editors' note].

also to know in what this certainty consists; and having noted that in this proposition nothing assures me of its truth save only that I see very clearly that in order to think it is necessary to be, I judged that I could take as being a general rule, that the things we apprehend very clearly and distinctly are true—bearing in mind, however, that there is some difficulty in rightly determining which are those we apprehend distinctly.

76. A SHATTERED UNIVERSE

The implications of the Scientific Revolution for the philosophy of life held by thoughtful men were either vastly exhilarating or devastating. Those who were exhilarated saw science as the instrument of man's power over nature, the fulfillment of the promise in Genesis that the earth was given to man for his use. Those who felt that the cosmos must continue to be conceived of as it was in the great Scholastic synthesis found no comfort in science's power for tiny man on tiny earth.

These believers could conceive of no relation between human life, with its passions and dreams, its pains and pleasures, and the endless emptiness of an infinite universe in which the earth was not the center, either physically or spiritually. This feeling was given masterly statement by the English poet John Donne (1572-1631) in his "An Anatomie of the World," parts of which are given below (A). The French philosopher Blaise Pascal (1623-1662), who had abandoned a career as a mathematical prodigy and a scientist of the first order to devote himself to religious contemplation and mystic ecstasies, said the same thing in a few lines in his *Thoughts* (*Pensées*) (B).

A. John Donne

An Anatomie of the World

. . . .

And new Philosophy calls all in doubt,
The Element of fire is quite put out;
The Sun is lost, and th'earth, and no mans wit
Can well direct him where to looke for it.
And freely men confesse that this world's spent,

Source: John Donne, *Complete Poetry and Selected Prose*, edited by John Hayward. (Bloomsbury, N.J.: Nonesuch Press, 1929), pp. 202–6.

When in the Planets, and the Firmament
They seeke so many new; then see that this
Is crumbled out againe to his Atomies.
'Tis all in peeces, all cohaerence gone;
All just supply, and all Relation:
Prince, Subject, Father, Sonne, are things forgot,
For every man alone thinkes he hath got
To be a Phoenix, and that then can bee
None of that kinde, of which he is, but hee.
This is the worlds condition now, and now
She that should all parts to reunion bow,
She that had all Magnetique force alone,
To draw, and fasten sundred parts in one;
She whom wise nature had invented then
When she observ'd that every sort of men
Did in their voyage in this worlds Sea stray,
And needed a new compasse for their way;
She that was best, and first originall
Of all faire copies, and the generall
Steward to Fate; she whose rich eyes, and breast
Guilt the West Indies, and perfum'd the East;
Whose having breath'd in this world, did bestow
Spice on those Iles, and bad them still smell so,
And that rich Indie which doth gold interre,
Is but as single money, coyn'd from her:
She to whom this world must it selfe refer,
As Suburbs, or the Microcosme of her,
Shee, shee is dead; shee's dead: when thou knowst this,
Thou knowst how lame a cripple this world is.
And learn'st thus much by our Anatomy,
That this worlds generall sickenesse doth not lie
In any humour, or one certaine part;
But as thou sawest it rotten at the heart,
Thou seest a Hectique feaver hath got hold
Of the whole substance, not to be contrould,
And that thou hast but one way, not t'admit
The worlds infection, to be none of it.
For the worlds subtilst immateriall parts
Feele this consuming wound, and ages darts.
For the worlds beauty is decai'd, or gone,
Beauty, that's colour, and proportion.
We thinke the heavens enjoy their Sphericall,
Their round proportion embracing all.
But yet their various and perplexed course,
Observ'd in divers ages, doth enforce
Men to finde out so many Eccentrique parts,
Such divers downe-right lines, such overthwarts,
As disproportion that pure forme: It teares
The Firmament in eight and forty sheires,
And in these Constellations then arise
New starres, and old doe vanish from our eyes:

As though heav'n suffered earthquakes, peace or war,
When new Towers rise, and old demolish't are.
They have impal'd within a Zodiake
The free-borne Sun, and keepe twelve Signes awake
To watch his steps; the Goat and Crab controule,
And fright him backe, who else to either Pole
(Did not these Tropiques fetter him) might runne:
For his course is not round; nor can the Sunne
Perfit a Circle, or maintaine his way
One inch direct; but where he rose to-day
He comes no more, but with a couzening line,
Steales by that point, and so is Serpentine:
And seeming weary with his reeling thus,
He meanes to sleepe, being now falne nearer us.
So, of the Starres which boast that they doe runne
In Circle still, none ends where he begun.
All their proportion's lame, it sinkes, it swels.
For of Meridians, and Parallels,
Man hath weav'd out a net, and this net throwne
Upon the Heavens, and now they are his owne.
Loth to goe up the hill, or labour thus
To goe to heaven, we make heaven come to us.
We spur, we reine the starres, and in their race
They're diversly content t'obey our pace.
But keepes the earth her round proportion still?
Doth not a Tenarif, or higher Hill
Rise so high like a Rocke, that one might thinke
The floating Moone would shipwrack there, and sinke?
Seas are so deepe, that Whales being strooke to day,
Perchance to morrow, scarse at middle way
Of their wish'd journies end, the bottome, die.
And men, to sound depths, so much line untie,
As one might justly thinke, that there would rise
At end thereof, one of th'Antipodies:
If under all, a Vault infernall bee,
(Which sure is spacious, except that we
Invent another torment, that there must
Millions into a straight hot roome be thrust)
Then solidnesse, and roundnesse have no place.
Are these but warts, and pock-holes in the face
Of th'earth? Thinke so: but yet confesse, in this
The worlds proportion disfigured is;
That those two legges whereon it doth rely,
Reward and punishment are bent awry.
And, Oh, it can no more be questioned,
That beauties best, proportion, is dead,
Since even griefe it selfe, which now alone
Is left us, is without proportion.
Shee by whose lines proportion should bee
Examin'd, measure of all Symmetree,

Whom had that Ancient seen, who thought soules made
Of Harmony, he would at next have said
That Harmony was shee, and thence infer,
That soules were but Resultances from her,
And did from her into our bodies goe,
As to our eyes, the formes from objects flow:
Shee, who if those great Doctors truly said
That the Arke to mans proportions was made,
Had been a type for that, as that might be
A type of her in this, that contrary
Both Elements, and Passions liv'd at peace
In her, who caus'd all Civill war to cease.
Shee, after whom, what forme soe'r we see,
Is discord, and rude incongruitie;
Shee, shee is dead, shee's dead; when thou knowst this,
Thou knowst how ugly a monster this world is:
And learn'st thus much by our Anatomie,
That here is nothing to enamour thee:
And that, not only faults in inward parts,
Corruptions in our braines, or in our hearts,
Poysoning the fountaines, whence our actions spring,
Endanger us: but that if every thing
Be not done fitly'and in proportion,
To satisfie wise, and good lookers on,
(Since most men be such as most thinke they bee)
They're lothsome too, by this Deformitee.

B. Blaise Pascal

Thoughts on Man's Place in the Universe

When I consider the brief span of my life absorbed into the eternity which comes before and after—*as the remembrance of a guest that tarrieth but a day*—the small space I occupy and which I see swallowed up in the infinite immensity of spaces of which I know nothing and which know nothing of me, I take fright and am amazed to see myself here rather than there: there is no reason for me to be here rather than there, now rather than then. Who put me here? By whose command and act were this time and place allotted to me? . . .

The eternal silence of these infinite spaces fills me with dread.

SOURCE: Blaise Pascal, *Pensées,* translated by A. J. Krailsheimer (Baltimore: Penguin Books, 1966), pp. 48, 95.

77. THE TASKS OF AN ACADEMY OF SCIENCE

One of the most famous of the academies devoted to the study of science which were founded in many parts of Europe in the 17th and 18th centuries was the Royal Society of London. It was set up by English scientists shortly after the restoration of Charles II in 1660, and the king granted it a formal charter in 1662. Unlike the French Academy of Sciences, which provided salaries and facilities for research to its members out of the royal treasury, the Royal Society was self-supporting and served primarily as a meeting place for discussion and publication of members' works. Bishop Thomas Sprat (1635-1713), whose history of the Royal Society was published in 1667, describes its purposes and discusses its relations with theology in the sections reprinted below.

Thomas Sprat

The History of the Royal Society

. . . . .

I will here, in the first place, contract into few Words, the whole *summe* of their *Resolutions;* which I shall often have occasion, to touch upon in *parcels.* Their purpose is, in short, to make faithful *Records,* of all the Works of *Nature,* or *Art,* which can come within their reach: that so the present Age, and posterity, may be able to put a mark on the Errors, which have been strengthned by long prescription: to restore the Truths, that have lain neglected: to push on those, which are already known, to more various uses: and to make the way more passable, to what remains unreveal'd. This is the compass of their Design. And to accomplish this, they have indeavor'd, to separate the knowledge of *Nature,* from the colours of *Rhetorick,* the devices of *Fancy,* or the delightful deceit of *Fables.* They have labor'd to inlarge it, from being confin'd to the custody of a few; or from servitude to private interests. They have striven to preserve it from being over-press'd by a confus'd heap of vain, and useless particulars; or from being straitnd and bounded too much by General Doctrines. They have try'd, to put it into a condition of perpetual increasing; by settling an inviolable correspondence between the hand, and the brain.

SOURCE: Thomas Sprat, *The History of the Institution, Design, and Progress, of the Royal Society of London. For the Advancement of Experimental Philosophy.* (London, 1667), pp. 61–62, 81–83.

They have studi'd, to make it, not onely an Enterprise of one season, or of some lucky opportunity; but a business of time; a steddy, a lasting, a popular, an uninterrupted Work. They have attempted, to free it from the Artifice, and Humors, and Passions of Sects; to render it an Instrument, whereby Mankind may obtain a Dominion over *Things,* and not onely over one anothers *Judgements.* And lastly, they have begun to establish these Reformations in Philosophy, not so much, by any solemnity of Laws, or ostentation of Ceremonies; as by solid Practice, and examples: not, by a glorious pomp of Words; but by the silent, effectual, and unanswerable Arguments of real Productions. . . .

Of the *extent* of the *matter,* about which they have been already conversant, and intend to be hereafter; there can be no better measure taken, than by giving a *general prospect* of all the objects of mens thoughts: which can be nothing else, but either *God,* or *Men,* or *Nature.*

As for the First, they meddle no otherwise with *Divine things,* than onely as the *Power,* and *Wisdom,* and *Goodness* of the *Creator,* is display'd in the admirable order, and workman-ship of the Creatures. It cannot be deny'd, but it lies in the *Natural Philosophers* hands, best to advance that part of *Divinity:* which, though it fills not the mind, with such *tender,* and *powerful contemplations,* as that which shews us Man's *Redemption* by a *Mediator;* yet it is by no means to be pass'd by unregarded: but is an excellent ground to establish the other. This is *a Religion,* which is confirm'd, by the unanimous agreement of all sorts of Worships: and may serve in respect to *Christianity,* as *Solomon's* Porch to the *Temple;* into the one the Heathens themselves did also enter; but into the other, onely God's *peculiar People.*

In men, may be consider'd the *Faculties,* and operations of their *Souls;* The *constitution of their Bodies,* and the *works of their Hands.* Of these, the *first* they omit: both because the knowledge and direction of them have been before undertaken, by some *Arts,* on which they have no mind to intrench, as the *Politicks, Morality,* and *Oratory:* and also because the *Reason,* the *Understanding,* the *Tempers,* the *Will,* the *Passions* of Men, are so hard to be reduc'd to any certain observation of the *senses;* and afford so much more room to the *observers* to falsifie or counterfeit: that if such discourses should be once entertain'd; they would be in danger of falling into *talking,* instead of *working,* which they carefully avoid. Such subjects therefore as these, they have hitherto kept out. But yet, when they shall have made more progress, in *material* things, they will be in a condition, of pronouncing more boldly on them too. For, though Man's *Soul,* and *Body* are not onely one *natural Engine* (as some have thought) of whose motions of all sorts, there may be as certain an accompt given, as of those of a Watch or Clock: yet by long studying of the *Spirits,* of the *Bloud,* of the *Nourishment,* of the parts, of the *Diseases,* of the *Advantages,* of the accidents which belong to *humane bodies* (all which will come within their Province) there, without question, be very neer ghesses made, even at the more *exalted*, and *immediate* Actions of the Soul; and that too, without destroying its *Spiritual* and *Immortal* Being.

These two Subjects, *God*, and the *Soul*, being onely forborn: In all the rest, they wander, at their pleasure: In the frame of *Mens bodies*, the ways for strong, healthful, and long life: In the *Arts of Mens Hands*, those that either *necessity*, *convenience*, or *delight* have produc'd: In the *works* of *Nature*, their helps, their varieties, redundancies, and defects: and in bringing all these to the *uses* of *humane Society*.

78. THE INVENTORS MOCKED

Jonathan Swift (1667–1745) judged the aspirations and activities of the Royal Society and similar associations of inventive minds with characteristic irony. In *Gulliver's Travels* (1726), he describes one such society, the Grand Academy of Lagado. It needs no introduction to be savored and enjoyed.

Jonathan Swift

The Grand Academy of Lagado

This Academy is not an entire single building, but a continuation of several houses on both sides of a street, which growing waste was purchased and applied to that use.

I was received very kindly by the Warden, and went for many days to the Academy. Every room hath in it one or more projectors, and I believe I could not be in fewer than five hundred rooms.

The first man I saw was of a meagre aspect, with sooty hands and face, his hair and beard long, ragged and singed in several places. His clothes, shirt, and skin were all of the same colour. He had been eight years upon a project for extracting sun-beams out of cucumbers which were to be put into vials hermetically sealed, and let out to warm the air in raw inclement summers. He told me he did not doubt in eight years more he should be able to supply the Governor's gardens with sunshine at a

---

SOURCE: Jonathan Swift, *Gulliver's Travels*, edited by William Alfred Eddy (New York: Oxford University Press, 1933), pp. 212–16. Reprinted by permission of Oxford University Press.

reasonable rate; but he complained that his stock was low, and entreated me to give him something as an encouragement to ingenuity, especially since this had been a very dear season for cucumbers. I made him a small present, for my lord had furnished me with money on purpose, because he knew their practice of begging from all who go to see them.

I went into another chamber, but was ready to hasten back, being almost overcome with a horrible stink. My conductor pressed me forward, conjuring me in a whisper to give no offence, which would be highly resented, and therefore I durst not so much as stop my nose. The projector of this cell was the most ancient student of the Academy; his face and beard were of a pale yellow; his hands and clothes daubed over with filth. When I was presented to him, he gave me a close embrace (a compliment I could well have excused). His employment from his first coming into the Academy, was an operation to reduce human excrement to its original food, by separating the several parts, removing the tincture which it receives from the gall, making the odour exhale, and scumming off the saliva. He had a weekly allowance from the society, of a vessel filled with human ordure, about the bigness of a Bristol barrel.

I saw another at work to calcine ice into gunpowder, who likewise showed me a treatise he had written concerning the malleability of fire, which he intended to publish.

There was a most ingenious architect who had contrived a new method for building houses, by beginning at the roof, and working downwards to the foundation, which he justified to me by the like practice of those two prudent insects, the bee and the spider.

There was a man born blind, who had several apprentices in his own condition: their employment was to mix colours for painters, which their master taught them to distinguish by feeling and smelling. It was indeed my misfortune to find them at that time not very perfect in their lessons, and the professor himself happened to be generally mistaken: this artist is much encouraged and esteemed by the whole fraternity.

In another apartment I was highly pleased with a projector, who had found a device of ploughing the ground with hogs, to save the charges of ploughs, cattle, and labour. The method is this: in an acre of ground you bury, at six inches distance and eight deep, a quantity of acorns, dates, chestnuts, and other mast or vegetables whereof these animals are fondest; then you drive six hundred or more of them into the field, where in a few days they will root up the whole ground in search of their food, and make it fit for sowing, at the same time manuring it with their dung. It is true, upon experiment they found the charge and trouble very great, and they had little or no crop. However, it is not doubted that this invention may be capable of great improvement.

I went into another room, where the walls and ceiling were all hung round with cobwebs, except a narrow passage for the artist to go in and out. At my entrance he called aloud to me not to disturb his webs. He lamented the fatal mistake the world had been so long in of using silk-worms, while we had such plenty of domestic insects, who infinitely excelled the former, because they understood how to weave as well as spin. And he proposed farther that by employing spiders the charge of dyeing silks should be wholly saved, whereof I was fully convinced when he showed me a vast number of flies most beautifully coloured, where-with he fed his spiders, assuring us that the webs would take a tincture from them; and as he had them of all hues, he hoped to fit everybody's fancy, as soon as he could find proper food for the flies, of certain gums, oils, and other glutinous matter to give a strength and consistence to the threads.

There was an astronomer who had undertaken to place a sun-dial upon the great weathercock on the town-house, by adjusting the annual and diurnal motions of the earth and sun, so as to answer and coincide with all accidental turnings by the wind.

I was complaining of a small fit of the colic, upon which my conductor led me into a room, where a great physician resided, who was famous for curing that disease by contrary operations from the same instrument. He had a large pair of bellows with a long slender muzzle of ivory. This he conveyed eight inches up the anus, and drawing in the wind, he affirmed he could make the guts as lank as a dried bladder. But when the disease was more stubborn and violent, he let in the muzzle while the bellows were full of wind, which he discharged into the body of the patient, then withdrew the instrument to replenish it, clapping his thumb strongly against the orifice of the fundament; and this being repeated three or four times, the adventitious wind would rush out, bringing the noxious along with it (like water put into a pump), and the patient recover. I saw him try both experiments upon a dog, but could not discern any effect from the former. After the latter, the animal was ready to burst, and made so violent a discharge, as was very offensive to me and my companions. The dog died on the spot, and we left the doctor endeavouring to recover him by the same operation.

I visited many other apartments, but shall not trouble my reader with all the curiosities I observed, being studious of brevity.

I had hitherto seen only one side of the Academy, the other being appropriated to the advancers of speculative learning, of whom I shall say something when I have mentioned one illustrious person more, who is called among them *the universal artist.* He told us he had been thirty years employing his thoughts for the improvement of human life. He had two large rooms full of wonderful curiosities, and fifty men at work. Some were condensing air into a dry tangible substance, by extracting the nitre, and letting the aqueous or fluid particles percolate; others softening marble for pillows and pin-cushions; others petrifying the hoofs of a living horse to preserve them from foundering. The artist himself was at that time busy upon two great designs; the first, to sow land with chaff, wherein he affirmed the true seminal virtue to be contained, as he demonstrated by several experiments which I was not skilful enough to comprehend. The other was, by a certain composition of gums, minerals, and vegetables outwardly applied, to prevent the growth of wool upon two young lambs; and he hoped in a reasonable time to propagate the breed of naked sheep all over the kingdom.

79. NEWTON FOR THE LAYMAN

The cause of Newton's gravitational theory as opposed to Descartes's vorticism was espoused in 18th-century France not only by scientists with a mastery of mathematics. It was also brilliantly popularized by François Marie Arouet (1694–1778), whose pen name was Voltaire. A 1734 letter of Voltaire's was a sketch for his later, more elaborate book on the subject, *Elements of Newton's Philosophy*. The letter, like the book, oversimplifies its subject, with transparent language and saucy wit. However, it could be read by intelligent and thoughtful men who could not grasp the difficult reasoning of Newton's own *Mathematical Principles of Natural Philosophy*.

Voltaire

Letter on Newton's Philosophy

I shall not enter here into a mathematical explanation of what is called attraction or gravity, but confine myself to the history of this new property of matter. Although it was guessed at long before Newton, it was demonstrated by him, so that what we provide here is in a way the history of a new creation.

Hardly had Copernicus, astronomy's Christopher Columbus, taught men what the order of the universe, so long distorted, truly was, and shown that the earth turns both upon itself and through a vast space, before the scholars all made about the same objections which their predecessors had put up against the antipodes. Saint Augustine had denied

---

SOURCE: Voltaire, *Œuvres complètes*, nouvelle éd., Vol. XXII (Paris: Garnier Frères, 1879), pp. 132–40. Translated by Herbert H. Rowen.

the existence of the antipodes, saying, "Indeed! They would have their heads at their feet and fall into the sky." The learned men told Copernicus, "If the earth turned upon itself, all its parts would come loose and fall into the sky." It is certain, replied Copernicus, that the earth does turn and that its parts do not fly off; there must therefore be a power which directs them all to the center of the earth. And he added that this property probably exists in all the globes of the sky, in the moon and the stars; it is an attribute given to matter by Divine Providence. This is the explanation which he gives in his first book *Of the Celestial Revolutions.* Perhaps he did not dare to go any further.

Kepler, who followed Copernicus and improved the admirable discovery of the true system of the world, came a little closer to the system of universal gravity. We see in his treatise on the star Mars the still malformed veins of the mine from which Newton took his gold. Kepler not only admits a universal tendency of all earthly bodies to go to the center but also one of the stars towards each other. He is bold enough to glimpse and say that if the earth and the moon were not held in their orbits, they would approach each other and join together. This astounding truth was obscured in his work by so many clouds and errors that it has been said that he guessed it by instinct.

Meanwhile the great Galileo, starting from a more mechanical principle, examined the fall of bodies on earth, how this fall is accelerated, and at what rate. And Lord Chancellor Bacon urged experiments to see if such falling occurred at greater depths and heights than had been reached.

It is quite odd that Descartes, who was the greatest mathematician of his time, should not have used this thread in the labyrinth which he built for himself. We find no trace of these truths in his work, and it is not surprising, therefore, that he went astray. He wished to create a universe, and he constructed a philosophy the way that you write a good novel: everything was plausible and nothing true. He imagined elements—the vortices—which seemed to provide a plausible cause for all the mysteries of nature; but in philosophy we must distrust what we believe we understand too easily as well as things which we do not understand at all. Descartes was more dangerous than Aristotle because he seemed to be more reasonable. Mr. Conduit, Sir Isaac Newton's nephew, assured me that his uncle had read Descartes when he was twenty years old; he scribbled in the margins of the first pages but made only one note, consisting in the word "error" which he repeated frequently, and then, tiring of writing "error" everywhere, tossed the book aside and never read it again.

After quitting the abyss of theology in which he had been educated for the truths of mathematics, Newton invented the infinitesimal calculus by the time he was twenty-three years of age, following the road opened for him by his teacher Wallis. He applied himself to the quest for the secret and universal principle of nature which Copernicus, Kepler and Bacon had already pointed to and which the celebrated Hooke had already grasped, that is, the cause of the weight and motion of all matter. After returning to his country home near Cambridge in 1666 because of the plague, he was walking one day in the garden and saw fruit dropping from a tree; he was drawn into a profound meditation upon weight, whose cause all philosophers had sought so long in vain (although the ordinary man does not even suspect that there exists a mystery). He said to himself, "No matter what the height from which these bodies fall in our hemisphere, their descent will certainly follow the progression discovered by Galileo, and the space they will travel will be in proportion to the square of the time. The power which causes heavy bodies to fall is the same without any perceptible decrease, however deep one goes below the ground or however high one goes up the mountain. Why should this power not extend to the moon? And if it is true that it reaches that far, isn't it very probable that this power holds it in its orbit and determines its movement? But if the moon obeys this principle, whatever it may be, isn't it also very reasonable to believe that the other planets are also subject to it?

"If this power exists, it must increase in the inverse ratio of the square of the distance (which, in fact, has been proved). We therefore have only to examine the path which a heavy body would follow in falling to the ground from a moderate height and the path which a body falling from the orbit of the moon would make in the same time. To learn this, we need only know the size of the earth and the distance from the moon to the earth."

This is how Mr. Newton reasoned. But at that time there existed in England only quite inaccurate measurements of our globe; they relied upon the uncertain estimation of pilots, who counted 60,000 English miles as one degree when the right figure is almost 70,000. This wrong calculation did not agree with the conclusions which Mr. Newton wished to draw from it and he abandoned it. A middling philosopher possessing only vanity would have made the measurement of the earth square as best he could with his system. Mr. Newton preferred to abandon his system at that time, but after M. Picard gave an exact measurement of the earth by drawing the meridian (so much to the honor of France), Mr. Newton returned to his first thoughts and succeeded by using M. Picard's calculations.

The other planets must be subject to this general law; and if this law exists, the planets must follow the rules discovered by Kepler. In fact, the planets do observe all these rules and ratios. The law of gravitation, which is their sole origin, solves all the apparent inequalities in the paths of the celestial globes. The variations of the moon become a necessary result of these laws. The ebb and flow of the tides is also a very simple effect of this attraction. The proximity of the full and the new moon and its distance when in its quarters, combined with the action of the sun, provide a perceptible cause for the rise and fall of the ocean.

Once he had explained the paths and the inequalities of the planets by this sublime theory, he subjected the comets to the bridle of the same law. He proved that they are solid bodies which move in the sun's sphere of action and describe an ellipse so eccentric and so close to a parabola that certain comets must take more than five hundred years in their revolution.

The learned Mr. Halley believes that the comet of 1680 was the same which appeared during the time of Julius Caesar. This serves more than anything else to show that the comets are hard, opaque bodies, for it descended so close to the sun that it was distant from it only the sixth part of its disc; in consequence it had to acquire a degree of heat 2,000 times greater than the hottest iron. It would have dissolved and been consumed in a short time if it had not been an opaque body. It then became the fashion to guess the path of the comets. The famous mathematician Jacques Bernouilli concluded under his own system that the famous comet of 1680 would reappear on May 17, 1719. There was not an astronomer in Europe who went to sleep that night of May 17, but the famous comet did not appear. If there is no greater assurance, it would be more adroit to give it 575 years to return. As for Mr. Wilston, the English geometer, he has seriously affirmed that during the time of the Flood, it was a comet which inundated our globe. In being surprised that men made fun of him, he committed an injustice. Antiquity had about the same ideas that Wilston; it believed that the comets were always heralds of some great misfortune upon earth. Newton, on the contrary, suspected that they were very beneficial and that the smoke which trailed after them served only to aid and vivify the planets which imbibe during their course all the particles which the sun has detached from the comets. This belief at least is more probable than the other.

This is not all. If this force of gravitation or attraction acts on all celestial globes, it no doubt acts upon every part of them. For, if the bodies attract each other in proportion to their masses, it can only be in accordance with the quantity of their parts; and if this power is lodged in the whole, so it is also beyond doubt in the half, the quarter, the eighth part, until the infinitely small. This, then, is the attraction which is the great mainspring making all nature move.

Newton had clearly foreseen that after he had demonstrated the existence of this principle there would be a revolt against its mere name. In more than one place of his book he warns his reader not to confuse it with the occult forces of the ancients and to be satisfied with knowing that there exists in all bodies a central force which acts from one end of the universe to the other upon the closest and the most distant bodies, according to the immutable laws of mechanics.

It is astounding, therefore, that after these solemn protestations of the great philosopher, M. Saurin and M. de Fontenelle, who also deserve that name, should reproach him specifically for accepting the chimeras of Peripatecism [Aristotelianism]. M. Saurin did this in the *Mémoires* of the Academy in 1709 and M. de Fontenelle in his funeral elegy for Mr. Newton, no less. Almost all Frenchmen, learned or not, have repeated this reproach. Everywhere we hear it said, "Why didn't Newton use the word 'impulsion,' which is understood so well here, rather than the word 'attraction,' which we do not understand?"

To these critics Newton could have replied:

"First, you do not understand the word 'impulsion' any better than that of 'attraction,' and if you do not conceive why a body tends to move toward the center of another body, you cannot grasp any better by what virtue a body can push another.

"Secondly, I cannot accept impulsion. To do so, I would have to know what celestial matter it is that in fact pushes the planets; but not only do I know nothing of such matter but I have proved that it does not exist.

"Thirdly, I use the word 'attraction' only to express an effect which I discovered in nature—a certain and indisputable effect of an unknown principle. It is a quality inherent in matter whose cause men more able than myself will find if they can."

"Then what have you taught us?" they continue to insist. "Why so many calculations to tell us something that you yourself do not understand?"

Newton could go on: "I have taught you that the mechanism of central forces alone causes the planets and comets to move in fixed ratios. I am (he would continue) in a different position from the ancients. For example, they saw water rise in a pump and said that the water rises because it has a horror of the void; but I am in the position of the man who first observed the rise of water in pumps and left to others the task of explaining the cause of this result. The anatomist who first said that the arm moves because the muscles contract taught men an incontestable truth. Is our obligation to him the less because he did not know why muscles contract? The cause of the spring of the air [air pressure] is unknown, but the man who discovered this spring rendered a great service to physics. The spring which I discovered is more hidden and more universal: therefore I have a right to greater gratitude. I have discovered a new property of matter which is one of the secrets of the Creator; I have calculated and demonstrated its effects. Are you going to quibble with me over the name I give it?"

It is the vortices which can be called an occult quality because their existence has never been proved. Attraction, on the contrary, is a real thing because its effects have been demonstrated and their proportions calculated. The cause of this cause is in the lap of God. *Procedes huc, et non ibis amplius.*[1]

---

[1] Go this far and no farther.

CHAPTER IX

THE ENLIGHTENMENT

THE CENTRAL INTELLECTUAL MOVEMENT of the 18th century was a tangled knot of ideas and feeling called the Enlightenment. It prided itself on being the philosophy of reason and rejected the rule of tradition and revealed faith. Nevertheless, it was in its turn a kind of faith in the possibilities of human betterment by the purposeful action of men of goodwill. While the Enlightenment viewed itself as the extension of science to morality and politics, its own practice was often based less on observation of what actually was than on affirmation of what ought to be. It was more social engineering than social science.

France was the homeland of the Enlightenment, and such figures as Voltaire, Diderot, and Rousseau were its most characteristic exponents. As the primary experience to which Enlightened thinkers addressed themselves, France was the object of the political and moral reform they sought. But the *philosophes*—the Enlightened philosophers of France—drew heavily upon English experience and thought, and they found sympathizers and imitators elsewhere in Europe who looked to them for inspiration. The Enlightenment thus became a European movement, which extended even to European colonies in America.

80. KNOWLEDGE THROUGH EXPERIENCE AND REFLECTION

At certain times in human history, expositions of abstract problems or philosophical analyses seem to possess significance not just for specialists but for broad groups of thoughtful men who find that new ideas fit circumstances that concern them. Such was the destiny of John Locke's *An Essay concerning Human Understanding,* which was published in England in 1690. The theories of philosophers about the nature of knowledge and existence during the Renaissance and Reformation had remained fundamentally those of their medieval predecessors, a more or less integrated system derived from Aristotle and Plato through a host of commentators. The scientific revolution of the 17th century implied a different world view, although it was seldom the scientists themselves who drew such conclusions. Locke provided a new way of handling the problem by arguing that all knowledge came from sensation, the experience of man's physical senses and his reflection upon it. This was to be the prevalent pattern for scientific explanation for some two centuries, and it became the accepted philosophical position of most Enlightenment thinkers.

John Locke

Essay concerning Human Understanding

NO INNATE PRINCIPLES IN THE MIND

The way shown how we come by any knowledge, sufficient to prove it not innate. It is an established opinion amongst some men, that there are in the understanding certain *innate principles;* some primary notions, *koinai ennoiai*[1] characters, as it were stamped upon the mind of man, which the soul receives in its very first being, and brings into the world with it. It would be sufficient to convince unprejudiced readers of the falseness of this supposition, if I should only show (as I hope I shall in the following parts of this discourse) how men, barely by the use of their natural faculties, may attain to all the knowledge they have, without the help of any innate impressions; and may arrive at certainty, without any such

---

SOURCE: John Locke, *Essay concerning Human Understanding,* edited by A. S. Pringle-Pattison (Oxford: Clarendon Press, 1964), pp. 16–19, 42–45. Reprinted by permission of The Clarendon Press, Oxford.

[1] Greek for "common ideas."

original notions or principles. For I imagine any one will easily grant, that it would be impertinent to suppose the ideas of colours innate in a creature to whom God hath given sight, and a power to receive them by the eyes from external objects: and no less unreasonable would it be to attribute several truths to the impressions of nature and innate characters, when we may observe in ourselves faculties fit to attain as easy and certain knowledge of them as if they were originally imprinted on the mind.

But because a man is not permitted without censure to follow his own thoughts in the search of truth, when they lead him ever so little out of the common road, I shall set down the reasons that made me doubt of the truth of that opinion, as an excuse for my mistake, if I be in one; which I leave to be considered by those who, with me, dispose themselves to embrace truth wherever they find it.

General assent the great argument. There is nothing more commonly taken for granted, than that there are certain principles, both *speculative* and *practical* (for they speak of both), universally agreed upon by all mankind; which therefore, they argue, must needs be the constant impressions which the souls of men receive in their first beings, and which they bring into the world with them, as necessarily and really as they do any of their inherent faculties.

Universal consent proves nothing innate. This argument, drawn from universal consent, has this misfortune in it, that if it were true in matter of fact, that there were certain truths wherein all mankind agreed, it would not prove them innate, if there can be any other way shown, how men may come to that universal agreement in the things they do consent in; which I presume may be done.

"What is, is," and "It is impossible for the same thing to be, and not to be," not universally assented to. But, which is worse, this argument of universal consent, which is made use of to prove innate principles, seems to me a demonstration that there are none such; because there are none to which all mankind give an universal assent. I shall begin with the speculative, and instance in these magnified principles of demonstration: "Whatsoever is, is," and "It is impossible for the same thing to be, and not to be," which, of all others, I think, have the most allowed title to innate. These have so settled a reputation of maxims universally received, that it will, no doubt, be thought strange if any one should seem to question it. But yet I take liberty to say, that these propositions are so far from having an universal assent, that there are a great part of mankind to whom they are not so much as known.

Not on the mind naturally imprinted, because not known to children, idiots, &c. For, first, it is evident, that all children and idiots have not the least apprehension or thought of them: and the want of that is enough to destroy that universal assent, which must needs be the necessary concomitant of all innate truths: it seeming to me near a contradiction to say, that there are truths imprinted on the soul which it perceives or understands not; imprinting, if it signify anything, being nothing else but the making certain truths to be perceived. No proposition can be said to be in the mind which it never yet knew, which it was never yet conscious of. For if any one may, then, by the same reason, all propositions that are true, and the mind is capable ever of assenting to, may be said to be in the mind, and to be imprinted; since if any one can be said to be in the mind, which it never yet knew, it must be only because it is capable of knowing it; and so the mind is of all truths it ever shall know. Nay, thus truths may be imprinted on the mind which it never did, nor ever shall know: for a man may live long, and die at last in ignorance of many truths which his mind was capable of knowing, and that with certainty. So that if the capacity of knowing be the natural impression contended for, all the truths a man ever comes to know will, by this account, be every one of them innate: and this great point will amount to no more, but only to a very improper way of speaking. But then, to what end such contest for certain innate maxims? If truths can be imprinted on the understanding without being perceived, I can see no difference there can be between any truths the mind is capable of knowing in respect of their original: they must all be innate, or all adventitious; in vain shall a man go about to distinguish them. He therefore that talks of innate notions in the understanding, cannot (if he intend thereby any distinct sort of truths) mean such truths to be in the understanding as it never perceived, and is yet wholly ignorant of. For if these words "to be in the understanding" have any propriety, they signify to be understood. If therefore these two propositions: "Whatsoever is, is," and, "It is impossible for the same thing to be, and not to be," are by nature imprinted, children cannot be ignorant of them; infants, and all that have souls, must necessarily have them in their understandings, know the truth of them, and assent to it.

. . . . .

Of Ideas in General and Their Original

Idea is the object of thinking. Every man being conscious to himself that he thinks, and that which his mind is applied about whilst thinking being the ideas that are there, it is past doubt that men have in their minds several ideas, such as are those expressed by the words, "whiteness, hardness, sweetness, thinking, motion, man, elephant, army, drunkenness," and others. It is in the first place then to be enquired, How he comes by them? I know it is a received doctrine, that men have native ideas and original characters stamped upon their minds in their very first being. This opinion I have at large examined already; and, I suppose, what I have said in the foregoing Book will be much more easily admitted, when I have shown whence the understanding may get all the ideas it has, and by what ways and degrees they may come into the mind; for which I shall appeal to every one's own observation and experience.

All ideas come from sensation or reflection. Let us then suppose the mind to be, as we say, white paper, void of all characters, without any ideas; how comes it to be furnished? Whence comes it by that vast store, which the busy and boundless fancy of man has painted on it with an almost endless variety? Whence has it all the materials of reason and knowledge? To this I answer, in one word, from EXPERIENCE; in that all our knowledge is founded, and from that it ultimately derives itself. Our observation, employed either about external sensible objects, or about the internal operations of our minds, perceived and reflected on by ourselves, is that which supplies our understandings with all the materials of thinking. These two are the fountains of knowledge, from whence all the ideas we have, or can naturally have, do spring.

The objects of sensation one source of ideas. First, our senses, conversant about particular sensible objects, do convey into the mind several distinct perceptions of things, according to those various ways wherein those objects do affect them; and thus we come by those *ideas* we have of yellow, white, heat, cold, soft, hard, bitter, sweet, and all those which we call sensible qualities; which when I say the senses convey into the mind, I mean, they from external objects convey into the mind what produces there those perceptions. This great source of most of the ideas we have, depending wholly upon our senses, and derived by them to the understanding, I call, SENSATION.

The operations of our minds the other source of them. Secondly, the other fountain, from which experience furnisheth the understanding with ideas, is the perception of the operations of our own minds within us, as it is employed about the ideas it has got; which operations, when the soul comes to reflect on and consider, do furnish the understanding with another set of ideas which could not be had from things without: and such are perception, thinking, doubting, believing, reasoning, knowing, willing, and all the different actings of our own minds; which we being conscious of, and observing in ourselves, do from these receive into our understanding as distinct ideas, as we do from bodies affecting our senses. This source of ideas every man has wholly in himself: and though it be not sense, as having nothing to do with external objects, yet it is very like it, and might properly enough be called internal sense. But as I call the other Sensation, so I call this REFLECTION, the ideas it affords being such only as the mind gets by reflecting on its own operations within itself. By Reflection, then, in the following part of this discourse, I would be understood to mean that notice which the mind takes of its own operations, and the manner of them, by reason whereof there come to be ideas of these operations in the understanding. These two, I say, viz., external material things as the objects of Sensation, and the operations of our own minds within as the objects of Reflection, are, to me, the only originals from whence all our ideas take their beginnings. The term *operations* here, I use in a large sense, as comprehending not barely the actions of the mind about its ideas, but some sort of passions arising sometimes from them, such as is the satisfaction or uneasiness arising from any thought.

All our ideas are of the one or the other of these. The understanding seems to me not to have the least glimmering of any ideas which it doth not receive from one of these two. *External objects* furnish the mind with the ideas of sensible qualities, which are all those different perceptions they produce in us; and *the mind* furnishes the understanding with ideas of its own operations. These, when we have taken a full survey of them, and their several modes, combinations, and relations, we shall find to contain all our whole stock of ideas; and that we have nothing in our minds which did not come in one of these two ways. Let any one examine his own thoughts, and thoroughly search into his understanding, and then let him tell me, whether all the original ideas he has there, are any other than of the objects of his senses, or of the operations of his mind considered as objects of his reflection; and how great a mass of knowledge soever he imagines to be lodged there, he will, upon taking a strict view, see that he has not any idea in his mind but what one of these two have imprinted, though perhaps with infinite variety compounded and enlarged by the understanding, as we shall see hereafter.

81. EDUCATION AND THE MALLEABILITY OF MAN

One of the significant implications of Locke's theory of knowledge concerned the nature and possibilities of education. At the same time that he was writing his *Essay concerning Human Understanding* during his exile in Holland, Locke was composing a shorter book, *Some Thoughts concerning Education*, which was published in 1693. For Locke, the notions of innate ideas and of innate capacity to learn had to be rejected. He believed men were principally what their education made them, and thus decisions in this area were of primary importance. This principle of the malleability of the human species became a central tenet of Enlightenment thought. Only a few more percipient thinkers realized the latent conflict with the tenet of natural moral judgments, a kind of "innate idea" under another name.

John Locke

Some Thoughts concerning Education

A Sound Mind in a sound Body, is a short, but full Description of a happy State in this World. He that has these two, has little more to wish for; and he that wants either of them, will be but little the better for any thing else. Men's Happiness or Misery is most part of their own making. He, whose Mind directs not wisely, will never take the right Way; and he, whose Body is crazy and feeble, will never be able to advance in it. I confess, there are some Men's Constitutions of Body and Mind so vigorous, and well fram'd by Nature, that they need not much Assistance from others; but by the strength of their natural Genius, they are from their Cradles carried towards what is excellent; and by the Privilege of their happy Constitutions, are able to do Wonders. But Examples of this Kind are but few; and I think I may say, that of all the Men we meet with, nine Parts of ten are what they are, good or evil, useful or not, by their Education. 'Tis that which makes the great Difference in Mankind. The little, or almost insensible Impressions on our tender Infancies, have very important and lasting Consequences: And there 'tis, as in the Fountains of some Rivers, where a gentle Application of the Hand turns the flexible Waters in Channels, that make them take quite contrary Courses; and by this Direction given them at first in the Source, they receive different Tendencies, and arrive at last at very remote and distant Places.

I imagine the Minds of Children as easily turn'd this or that Way, as Water it self: And though this be the principal Part, and our main Care should be about the Inside, yet the Clay-Cottage is not to be neglected. I shall therefore begin with the Case, and consider first the *Health* of the Body, as that which perhaps you may rather expect from that Study I have been thought more peculiarly to have apply'd my self to; and that also which will be soonest dispatch'd, as lying, if I guess not amiss, in a very little Compass.

. . . . .

Due Care being had to keep the Body in Strength and Vigour, so that it may be able to obey and execute the Orders of the *Mind;* the next and principal Business is, to set the *Mind* right, that on all Occasions it may

---

SOURCE: John Locke, *Some Thoughts concerning Education,* edited by R. H. Quick. (Cambridge, England: Cambridge University Press, 1913), pp. 1–2, 20–21.

be dispos'd to consent to nothing but what may be suitable to the Dignity and Excellency of a rational Creature.

If what I have said in the beginning of this Discourse be true, as I do not doubt but it is, *viz.* That the Difference to be found in the Manners and Abilities of Men is owing more to their *Education* than to any Thing else, we have reason to conclude, that great Care is to be had of the forming Children's *Minds*, and giving them that Seasoning early, which shall influence their Lives always after: For when they do well or ill, the Praise and Blame will be laid there; and when any Thing is done awkwardly, the common saying will pass upon them, that it's suitable to their *Breeding*.

82. EDUCATION AND THE DIFFERENCES AMONG MEN

Locke's ideas on education were taken up by the French materialist philosopher Claude Adrien Helvétius in his book *Man the Machine*, which treated them more dogmatically and pursued them further to logical extemes. A rebuttal of Helvétius's work came from an immensely subtler Enlightenment philosopher, Denis Diderot (1713-1784). Although in principle a materialist and an atheist, Diderot yearned for the solace of a personal God, and his "matter" was imbued with vitalist powers. He was a many-sided thinker, the principal editor of the great *French Encyclopedia*, and an author of plays, novels, essays, and criticism of drama and the arts. Deeply concerned with the problems of artistic imagination and expression, Diderot found Helvétius's ideas on the virtually total malleability of human ability and character impossible to accept.

Denis Diderot

Nature Plus Education

The author [Helvétius] uses the fifteen chapters composing this section to establish his favorite paradox, "that education by itself makes all the difference between individuals in a fairly good state of organization. . . ." This is a condition into which neither strength nor weakness, neither health nor illness, nor any of the physical and moral qualities which make temperaments and characters diverse enters.

Page 2. "I have considered the mind, genius and virtue as the product of education."

SOURCE: J. Assezat (ed.), *Œuvres complètes de Diderot* (Paris: Garnier Frères, 1875–77), Vol. II, pp. 276–79, 455–56. Translated by Herbert H. Rowen.

By itself?

"This idea has always seemed to me to be true."

It is false, for the reason that it can never be adequately proved.

"It has been conceded to me that education had more influence than has been believed upon genius and on the character of men and peoples."

And that is all that can be conceded to you.

Page 4. "If it is organization which makes us almost completely what we are, on what grounds can the teacher be reproached with the ignorance and stupidity of his pupils?"

I know no system which is more comforting for parents and encouraging for teachers. That is its advantage.

But I know none either which is more disheartening for the children whom we believe to be equally fit for anything, or which is more capable of fulfilling the conditions for a society of mediocre men and misguiding the genius who does only one thing well; nor one which is more dangerous because of the stubbornness which it must inspire in those in charge, who, having long and fruitlessly set a class of pupils to work on tasks for which they had no natural disposition, will expel them into a world in which they will no longer be good for anything. You cannot give a greyhound a sense of smell nor a setter the greyhound's speed; do what you will, the setter will keep his sense of smell and the greyhound his legs.

Page 5. "Man is born ignorant but he is not born a fool, and he does not become one without difficulty."

What we should say is almost exactly the contrary. Man is always born ignorant and very often a fool; and if he is not one, there is nothing easier than to make him one. Alas, there is nothing more in keeping with experience.

Stupidity and genius occupy the two extremes of the scale of the human mind. It is impossible to budge stupidity; it is easy to move genius.

Page 6. "There are two kinds of stupidity. One is natural and the other is acquired."

I would very much like to know how we can overcome natural stupidity. All men take a place somewhere between the greatest possible understanding and the most complete stupidity, between M. D'Alembert and M. D'Outrelot. Despite everything that education can do, everyone remains at about the same place on the rungs of the ladder. Let me try out a man and I will soon tell what he owes to diligence and what to nature. Anyone who cannot make such distinctions will often mistake the tool for the handiwork and the handiwork for the tool.

Between each rung of the ladder there is a small gap which it is impossible to cross. In order to alleviate natural inequality we must on the one hand apply stubborn effort and on the other almost equally continual neglect.

The man who is on the rung where nature has placed him can keep a steady foothold there without effort. He who leaps to a rung higher than his natural one totters there and is always unsure of himself; he meditates deeply upon the problem which the former solves even while he is being put in blinkers.

Our author has confused stupidity with ignorance.

Page 7. "Once the mind has accepted the burden of a learned ignorance, it will never again rise to the truth; it has lost the tendency which moved it thence. . . ."

And is this tendency, whether natural or acquired, the same in everyone?

"The man who knows nothing is able to learn; all that is involved is to kindle the desire in him."

And is everyone equally susceptible to this desire?

Page 8. "What makes a teacher? What is it he wishes to do? It is to release the wings of genius."

Then genius does exist before education.

"The ancients will maintain over the moderns a superiority in morality as well as in politics and legislation which they owe not to organization but to education."

And what does that prove?

"That one nation differs little from another."

Who told you that was not so?

"Frenchmen who would be educated like Romans would also have their Caesar, Scipio, Pompey and Cicero."

Why not? By this argument, in any nation whatsoever, good education will produce a great man, a Hannibal, an Alexander, an Achilles, a Thersites, anyone you name! Convince anyone else you please of that, but not me.

Why are these illustrious names so rare even among those nations whose citizens have all received the education you advocate? This is a small question, M. Helvétius. Take five hundred newborn infants who are abandoned to you to be raised at your discretion. Tell me, how many will you make into men of genius? Why not five hundred? Press hard on whatever answer you give, and you will find in the last analysis that it will resolve into the differences of organization. That is the original source of laziness, frivolity, stubbornness and the other vices and passions.

Page 12. "The true preceptors of our childhood are the objects which surround us."

That is true. But how do they teach us?

"By sensation."

Is it possible, then, that a sensation will remain the same when organization is different? The diversity of organization is such that if each individual could create a language analogous to what he is himself, there would be as many languages as individuals. One man would not say hello or good-bye like another.

"But is there, then, no truth or beauty or goodness?"

I do not think that there is none. The variety of such languages would not suffice to change these ideas.

. . . . .

Page 438. "The mind is only the assemblage of our ideas; ideas come through the senses; therefore mind is only something acquired."

Indeed, it is something which not everyone is able to acquire.

Ibid. "To attribute mind to organization and not be able to name its organ is to recall occult qualities."

Perhaps. But the organ has a name, the head.

Ibid. "Experience and history teach us that the mind is independent of the greater or lesser receptivity of the senses."

I do not know how far that is true.

Ibid. "Men of different constitutions are susceptible to the same passions."

That is false in every respect. We do not, each of us, give in to all passions. We are born with anger or lack of feeling, with brutality or tenderness. It is circumstances which arouse these passions in men. Even if all men had them in common, they would not have them to the same extent.

There is much that education can do but it does not and cannot do everything. Take ten children who are to be made discreet and cautious; they will certainly all be less indiscreet and less incautious than if no effort had been made to cultivate this virtue in them, but there may be one or two on whom education will do nothing or very little.

Page 439. "If the mind, character and passions of men depend on their organs, which are not equally perfect, and if each individual is a different machine, how could the justice of Heaven or even of the earth require the same results from dissimilar machines?"

The justice of the earth punishes equally machines which are dissimilar because it is incapable of either appreciating or taking into account these dissimilarities.

83. THE QUARREL OF THE ANCIENTS AND THE MODERNS

One sign that the Renaissance impulse was being quenched was the development of a debate among scholars over the relative merits of antiquity and the contemporary world. This "quarrel of the ancients and moderns" arose when the Renaissance innovations in literature and education had become everyday practice, and neoclassicism in France (and to a lesser extent in England) was productive and self-confident. In England the cause of the ancients (the Greek and Latin authors of classical antiquity) was pleaded by the diplomat and author Sir William Temple (1628-1699) in his *Essay of Ancient and Modern Learning,* first published in 1680 (A). It is one of the ironies of the history of culture that Temple's vigorous, clear prose had a distinctly modern style, thus making him one of the first of the English literary "moderns." On the other hand, the French writer Bernard le Bovier de Fontenelle (1657-1757), who defended the equality of the moderns in his *Digression upon the Ancients and Moderns* (1688) (B), was definitely a man of his own time, the very spirit of the growth of ideas from the age of Louis XIV to the Enlightenment.

A. Sir William Temple

Essay of Ancient and Modern Learning

. . . . .

The force of all that I have met with upon this subject, either in talk or writings is, first, as to knowledge, that we must have more than the ancients, because we have the advantage both of theirs and our own, which is commonly illustrated by the similitude of a dwarf's standing upon a giant's shoulders, and seeing more or farther than he. Next as to wit or genius, that nature being still the same, these must be much at a rate in all ages, at least in the same climates, as the growth and size of plants and animals commonly are; and if both these are allowed, they think the cause is gained. But I cannot tell why we should conclude that the ancient writers had not as much advantage from the knowledge of others that were ancient to them, as we have from those that are ancient to us. The invention of printing has not perhaps multiplied books, but only the copies of them; and if we believe there were six hundred thousand in the library of Ptolemy, we shall hardly pretend to equal it by any of ours, nor perhaps by all put together: I mean so many originals that have lived any time, and thereby given testimony of their having been thought worth preserving. For the scribblers are infinite, that like mushrooms or flies are born and die in small circles of time, whereas books, like proverbs, receive their chief value from the stamp and esteem of ages through which they have passed. Besides the account of this library at Alexandria, and others very voluminous in the Lesser Asia and Rome,

---

Source: Sir William Temple, *Five Miscellaneous Essays,* edited by Samuel Holt Monk (Ann Arbor: University of Michigan Press, 1963), pp. 38–39, 50–51, 62–65. Reprinted by permission of the University of Michigan Press.

we have frequent mention of ancient writers in many of those books which we now call ancient, both philosophers and historians. 'Tis true that besides what we have in Scripture concerning the original and progress of the Jewish nation, all that passed in the rest of our world before the Trojan war is either sunk in the depths of time, wrapped up in the mysteries of fables, or so maimed by the want of testimonies and loss of authors, that it appears to us in too obscure a shade to make any judgment upon it. For the fragments of Manethon about the antiquities of Egypt, the relations in Justin concerning the Scythian Empire, and many others in Herodotus and Diodorus Siculus, as well as the records of China, make such excursions beyond the periods of time given us by the Holy Scriptures that we are not allowed to reason upon them. And this disagreement itself, after so great a part of the world became Christian, may have contributed to the loss of many ancient authors. For Solomon tells us even in his time, of writing many books there was no end; and whoever considers the subject and the style of Job, which by many is thought more ancient than Moses, will hardly think it was written in an age or country that wanted either books or learning; and yet he speaks of the ancients then, and their wisdom, as we do now.

. . . . .

I have long thought that the different abilities of men, which we call wisdom or prudence for the conduct of public affairs or private life, grow directly out of that little grain of intellect or good sense which they bring with them into the world; and that the defect of it in men comes from some want in their conception or birth.

Dixitq; semel nascentibus auctor,
Quicquid scire licet.[1]

And though this may be improved or impaired in some degree by accidents of education, of study, and of conversation and business, yet it cannot go beyond the reach of its native force, no more than life can beyond the period to which it was destined by the strength or weakness of the seminal virtue.

If these speculations should be true, then I know not what advantages we can pretend to modern knowledge by any we receive from the ancients; nay 'tis possible, men may lose rather than gain by them; may lessen the force and growth of their own genius by constraining and forming it upon that of others; may have less knowledge of their own, for contenting themselves with that of those before them. So a man that

[1] "And the creator told only once all things they were permitted to know to those just born."

only translates shall never be a poet, nor a painter that only copies, nor a swimmer that swims always with bladders. So people that trust wholly to others' charity, and without industry of their own, will be always poor. Besides who can tell whether learning may not even weaken invention in a man that has great advantages from nature and birth; whether the weight and number of so many other men's thoughts and notions may not suppress his own, or hinder the motion and agitation of them, from which all invention arises, as heaping on wood, or too many sticks, or too close together, suppresses, and sometimes quite extinguishes, a little spark that would otherwise have grown up to a noble flame. The strength of mind, as well as of body, grows more from the warmth of exercise than of clothes; nay, too much of this foreign heat rather makes men faint, and their constitutions tender or weaker than they would be without them. Let it come about how it will, if we are dwarfs, we are still so though we stand upon a giant's shoulders; and even so placed, yet we see less than he, if we are naturally shorter sighted, or if we do not look as much about us, or if we are dazzled with the height, which often happens from weakness either of heart or brain.

. . . . .

. . . A boy at fifteen is wiser than his father at forty, the meanest subject than his prince or governors; and the modern scholars, because they have, for a hundred years past, learned their lesson pretty well, are much more knowing than the ancients their masters.

But let it be so, and proved by good reasons, is it so by experience too? Have the studies, the writings, the productions of Gresham College, or the late Academies of Paris, outshined or eclipsed the Lycaeum of Plato, the Academy of Aristotle, the Stoa of Zeno, the Garden of Epicurus? Has Harvey outdone Hippocrates; or Wilkins, Archimedes? Are d'Avila's and Strada's histories beyond those of Herodotus and Livy? Are Sleyden's commentaries beyond those of Caesar? The flights of Boileau above those of Virgil? If all this must be allowed, I will then yield *Gondibert* to have excelled Homer, as is pretended; and the modern French poetry, all that of the ancients. And yet, I think, it may be as reasonably said, that the plays in Moorfields are beyond the Olympic games; a Welsh or Irish harp excels those of Orpheus and Arison; the pyramid in London, those of Memphis; and the French conquests in Flanders are greater than those of Alexander and Caesar, as their operas and panegyrics would make us believe.

But the consideration of poetry ought to be a subject by itself. For the books we have in prose, do any of the modern we converse with appear of such a spirit and force, as if they would live longer than the ancient have done? If our wit and eloquence, our knowledge or inventions, would deserve it; yet our languages would not: there is no hope of their lasting long, nor of anything in them; they change every hundred years so as to be hardly known for the same, or anything of the former styles to be endured by the later; so as they can no more last like the ancients, than excellent carvings in wood, like those in marble or brass.

The three modern tongues most esteemed are Italian, Spanish, and French, all imperfect dialects of the noble Roman; first mingled and corrupted with the harsh words and terminations of those many different and barbarous nations, by whose invasions and excursions the Roman Empire was long infested, they were afterwards made up into these several languages by long and popular use, out of those ruins and corruptions of Latin, and the prevailing languages of those nations to which these several provinces came in time to be most and longest subjected (as the Goths and Moors in Spain, the Goths and Lombards in Italy, the Franks in Gaul) besides a mingle of those tongues which were original to Gaul and to Spain, before the Roman conquests and establishments there. Of these, there may be some remainders in Biscay or the Asturias; but I doubt, whether there be any of the old Gallic in France, the subjection there having been more universal, both to the Romans and Franks. But I do not find the mountainous parts on the north of Spain were ever wholly subdued, or formerly governed, either by the Romans, Goths, or Saracens, no more than Wales by Romans, Saxons, or Normans, after their conquests in our island, which has preserved the ancient Biscayan and British more entire, than any native tongue of other provinces where the Roman and Gothic or Norman conquests reached, and were for any time established. . . .

It may perhaps be further affirmed, in favour of the ancients, that the oldest books we have are still in their kind the best. The two most ancient that I know of in prose, among those we call profane authors, are Æsop's *Fables* and Phalaris's *Epistles*, both living near the same time, which was that of Cyrus and Pythagoras. As the first has been agreed by all ages since for the greatest master in his kind, and all others of that sort have been but imitations of his original, so I think the *Epistles* of Phalaris to have more race, more spirit, more force of wit and genius, than any others I have ever seen, either ancient or modern. I know several learned men (or that usually pass for such, under the name of critics) have not esteemed them genuine, and Politian, with some others, have attributed them to Lucian: but I think he must have little skill in painting, that cannot find out this to be an original; such diversity of passions, upon such variety of actions and passages of life and government, such freedom of thought, such boldness of expression, such bounty to his friends, such scorn of his enemies, such honour of learned men, such esteem of good, such knowledge of life, such contempt of death, with such fierceness of nature and cruelty of revenge, could never be represented but by him that possessed them; and I esteem Lucian to have been no more capable of writing than of acting what Phalaris did. In all one writ, you find the scholar or the sophist; and in all the other, the tyrant and the commander.

The next to these, in time, are Herodotus, Thucydides, Hippocrates, Plato, Xenophon, and Aristotle; of whom I shall say no more, than, what I think is allowed by all, that they are in their several kinds inimitable. So are Caesar, Sallust, and Cicero, in theirs, who are the ancientest of the Latin (I speak still of prose) unless it be some little of old Cato upon rustic affairs.

The height and purity of the Roman style, as it began towards the time of Lucretius, which was about that of the Jugurthin war, so it ended about that of Tiberius; and the last strain of it seems to have been Velleius Paterculus. The purity of the Greek lasted a great deal longer, and must be allowed till Trajan's time, when Plutarch wrote, whose Greek is much more estimable than the Latin of Tacitus his contemporary. After this last, I know none that deserves the name of Latin, in comparison of what went before them, especially in the Augustan age; if any, 'tis the little treatise of Minutius Felix. All Latin books that we have till the end of Trajan, and all Greek till the end of Marcus Antoninus, have a true and very esteemable value: all written since that time seem to me to have little more than what comes from the relation of events we are glad to know, or the controversy of opinions in religion or laws, wherein the busy world has been so much employed.

B. Bernard le Bovier de Fontenelle

Digression upon the Ancients and Moderns

. . . . .

The whole debate over the preeminence of the ancients or the moderns, once understood properly, is reduced to knowing whether the trees which used to grow in our countryside were larger than those which grow there now. If it be true that they used to be larger, then Homer, Plato and Demosthenes cannot be equalled at the present time; but if our trees are as large as those of earlier times, then we can equal Homer, Plato and Demosthenes.

Source: Bernard le Bovier de Fontenelle, *Digression sur les Anciens et les Modernes,* edited by Robert Shackleton (Oxford: Clarendon Press, 1955), pp. 161–63. Translated by Herbert H. Rowen. Reprinted by permission of The Clarendon Press, Oxford.

I should like to explain this paradox. If the ancients had better minds than we, it was because their brains were better arranged, constructed of stronger or finer fibers, and filled with more animal spirits: but what reason would there have been for brains to be better constructed then? Perhaps the trees were in fact larger and finer; for if nature was younger and more vigorous then, trees as well as men's brains should have responded to that vigor and youth.

Let those who admire the ancients consider this matter a little. When they tell us that the men of that time were the source of good taste and reason, and of the knowledge destined to enlighten all men after them, and that we are intelligent only when we admire them, that nature wore herself out in producing those great inventive geniuses, they are in fact making them out to be a different species from ourselves. Physics does not support all their fine phrases. Nature has in its hands a kind of dough which is always the same; it twists and retwists it endlessly in a thousand different ways and forms it into men, animals and plants; certainly it did not form Plato, Demosthenes or Homer of a finer or better prepared clay than our philosophers, orators and poets today. What concerns me in this respect in our minds, which are not material in nature, is only their connection with the brain, which is material and which by its different dispositions produces all the differences which exist among them.

But if the trees are all the same height in every century, this is not true of the trees in every country. There are differences of the same kind for minds. Different ideas are like plants or flowers which do not grow equally well in every sort of climate. It may be that our soil of France is not fit for the reasoning of Egyptians, any more than for their palm trees; and, without going any further, it may be that orange trees, which do not grow as well here as in Italy, indicate that a certain cast of mind exists in Italy which is not exactly like that of France. It remains a certainty, nonetheless, that the differences of climate which make themselves felt in plants must, because of the linkage and mutual dependence between all parts of the material world, extend all the way to the brain and have some effect upon it.

This effect, however, is smaller and less perceptible because art and culture have much more impact upon the brain than upon the earth, which is of a harder and more intractable substance. Thus the ideas of one country are more easily transported to another than are its plants, and we would have less difficulty in bringing the Italian genius into our product than in growing orange trees.

I am not at all sure that what I take to be the general opinion that there is more variety among minds than among faces is true. Looking at each other does not make faces much more alike, but that is what happens to minds in their meeting. Thus minds, which in nature differ as much as faces, come to have less difference.

The ease with which minds to a certain extent shape themselves upon each other has the result that the peoples do not preserve in its entirety the original cast which is produced by their climate. The reading of Greek books produces in us the same relative effect as if we took only Greek women for our wives. Beyond question such frequent alliances would lead to a change in the blood in Greece and France and the look of individual faces would change a little in both nations.

The small difference of climate which exists between two neighboring countries can easily be effaced with regard to minds by their mutual trade in books; the same would not be true of two very distant peoples. It is probable that the Negroes and the Lapps could read Greek books without absorbing much of the Greek spirit. As for me, I am inclined to believe that the torrid zone and the two frigid zones are not fitted for science. Until now it has not gone beyond Egypt and Mauretania on the one side and Sweden on the other; perhaps it is not an accident that it has remained confined to the region between the Atlas mountains and the Baltic Sea. I do not know whether these are boundaries which nature has placed upon science, and we must not hope ever to see great Lapp or Negro authors.

However that may be, it seems to me that this exhausts the great debate of the ancients and the moderns. The centuries create no natural differences between men, and the climates of Greece or Italy and France are too similar to establish any perceptible difference between the Greeks or Latins and ourselves; and if there were any, it would be very easy to remove it. We are therefore all perfectly equal, the ancients and the moderns, the Greeks, Latins and French. . . .

If the great men of this age felt charitably toward posterity, they would give it a warning not to admire them too much and always to aspire at least to equal them. Nothing is a greater barrier to progress, nothing so hampers the intellect, as excessive admiration of the ancients. Not only did philosophy fail to advance in any way because there was such devotion to the authority of Aristotle and truth was sought only in his enigmatic writings, never in nature; it also fell into an abyss of pretentious nonsense and unintelligible ideas from which it has been very difficult to extract it. Aristotle never produced a true philosopher but he stifled many who could have become philosophers if it had been permitted. And what is harmful is that once a fantasy of this kind is established among men, it lasts for a long time; it takes centuries to overcome it, even after it has been acknowledged to be ridiculous. If we were all to become intoxicated with Descartes and place him in Aristotle's place, just about the same harm would result.

84. CIVILIZATION AS FATAL ACCIDENT

The Renaissance had renewed interest in the pastoral romance, with its pretty pretense that the simple life of shepherds held more delight than the complexities faced by modern civilized man. But, as the quarrel of the ancients and moderns once more demonstrated, the acquisitions of high culture mattered greatly in the early modern period. Not until Jean Jacques Rousseau (1712-1778) began to publish his writings in the middle of the 18th century did a major thinker seriously argue that civilization represented a decline from the moral purity of the untutored savage. This idea was first expounded by Rousseau in his *Discourse on the Arts and Sciences* in 1750 and repeated in his *Discourse on Inequality* in 1754. The following selection is taken from the latter work.

The "myth of the noble savage" was accepted by many Enlightened thinkers, including Diderot. Voltaire, the most worldly and commonsensical of them all, found the idea silly. Although it contradicted the theory of progress which was so dominant in the Enlightenment, it was a convenient stick with which to beat the often jaded aristocratic courtly culture the Enlightenment both fed upon and fought.

Jean Jacques Rousseau

Discourse on Inequality

. . . . .

In proportion as ideas and sentiments succeed each other, and the head and the heart exercise themselves, men continue to shake off their original wildness, and their connections become more intimate and extensive. They now begin to assemble round a great tree: singing and dancing, the genuine offspring of love and leisure, become the amusement or rather the occupation of the men and women, free from care, thus gathered together. Every one begins to survey the rest, and wishes to be surveyed himself; and public esteem acquires a value. He who sings or dances best; the handsomest, the strongest, the most dexterous, the most eloquent, comes to be the most respected: this was the first step towards inequality,

---

SOURCE: Charles W. Eliot (ed.), *The Harvard Classics,* Vol. 34, "French and English Philosophers: Descartes, Rousseau, Voltaire, Hobbes" (New York: P. F. Collier & Son, 1961), pp. 203–6, 226–28. Reprinted by permission of Americana Interstate Corp., Mundelein, Ill.

and at the same time towards vice. From these first preferences there proceeded on one side vanity and contempt, on the other envy and shame; and the fermentation raised by these new leavens at length produced combinations fatal to happiness and innocence.

Men no sooner began to set a value upon each other, and know what esteem was, than each laid claim to it, and it was no longer safe for any man to refuse it to another. Hence the first duties of civility and politeness, even among savages; and hence every voluntary injury became an affront, as besides the mischief, which resulted from it as an injury, the party offended was sure to find in it a contempt for this person more intolerable than the mischief itself. It was thus that every man, punishing the contempt expressed for him by others in proportion to the value he set upon himself, the effects of revenge became terrible, and men learned to be sanguinary and cruel. Such precisely was the degree attained by most of the savage nations with whom we are acquainted. And it is for want of sufficiently distinguishing ideas, and observing at how great a distance these people were from the first state of nature, that so many authors have hastily concluded that man is naturally cruel, and requires a regular system of police [civil government] to be reclaimed; whereas nothing can be more gentle than he in his primitive state, when placed by nature at an equal distance from the stupidity of brutes, and the pernicious good sense of civilized man; and equally confined by instinct and reason to the care of providing against the mischief which threatens him, he is withheld by natural compassion from doing any injury to others, so far from being ever so little prone even to return that which he has received. For according to the axiom of the wise Locke, Where there is no property, there can be no injury.

But we must take notice, that the society now formed and the relations now established among men required in them qualities different from those, which they derived from their primitive constitution; that as a sense of morality began to insinuate itself into human actions, and every man, before the enacting of laws, was the only judge and avenger of the injuries he had received, that goodness of heart suitable to the pure state of nature by no means suited infant society; that it was necessary punishments should become severer in the same proportion that the opportunities of offending became more frequent, and the dread of vengeance add strength to the too weak curb of the law. Thus, though men were become less patient, and natural compassion had already suffered some alteration, this period of the development of the human faculties, holding a just mean between the indolence of the primitive state, and the petulant activity of self-love, must have been the happiest and most durable epoch. The more we reflect on this state, the more convinced we shall be, that it was the least subject of any to revolutions, the best for man, and that nothing could have drawn him out of it but some fatal accident, which, for the public good, should never have happened. The example of the savages, most of whom have been found in this condition, seems to confirm that mankind was formed ever to remain in it, that this condition is the real youth of the world, and that all ulterior improvements have been so many steps, in appearance towards the perfection of individuals, but in fact towards the decrepitness of the species.

As long as men remained satisfied with their rustic cabins; as long as they confined themselves to the use of clothes made of the skins of other animals, and the use of thorns and fish-bones, in putting these skins together; as long as they continued to consider feathers and shells as sufficient ornaments, and to paint their bodies of different colours, to improve or ornament their bows and arrows, to form and scoop out with sharp-edged stones some little fishing boats, or clumsy instruments of music; in a word, as long as they undertook such works only as a single person could finish, and stuck to such arts as did not require the joint endeavours of several hands, they lived free, healthy, honest and happy, as much as their nature would admit, and continued to enjoy with each other all the pleasures of an independent intercourse; but from the moment one man began to stand in need of another's assistance; from the moment it appeared an advantage for one man to possess the quantity of provisions requisite for two, all equality vanished; property started up; labour became necessary; and boundless forests became smiling fields, which it was found necessary to water with human sweat, and in which slavery and misery were soon seen to sprout out and grow with the fruits of the earth.

. . . . .

By thus discovering and following the lost and forgotten tracks, by which man from the natural must have arrived at the civil state; by restoring, with the intermediate positions which I have been just indicating, those which want of leisure obliges me to suppress, or which my imagination has not suggested, every attentive reader must unavoidably be struck at the immense space which separates these two states. 'Tis in this slow succession of things he may meet with the solution of an infinite number of problems in morality and politics, which philosophers are puzzled to solve. He will perceive that, the mankind of one age not being the mankind of another, the reason why Diogenes could not find a man was, that he sought among his contemporaries the man of an earlier period: Cato, he will then see, fell with Rome and with liberty, because he did not suit the age in which he lived; and the greatest of men served only to astonish that world, which would have cheerfully obeyed him, had he come into it five hundred years earlier. In a word, he will find himself in a condition to understand how the soul and the passions of men by insensible alterations change as it were their nature; how it comes to pass, that at the long run our wants and our pleasures change objects; that, original man vanishing by degrees, society no longer offers to our inspection but an assemblage of artificial men and factitious passions, which are the work of all these new relations, and have no foundation in nature. Reflection teaches us nothing on that head, but what experience perfectly confirms. Savage man and civilised man differ so much at bottom in point of inclinations and passions, that what constitutes the supreme happiness of the one would reduce the other to despair. The first sighs for nothing but repose and liberty; he desires only to live, and to be exempt from labour; nay, the ataraxy of the most confirmed Stoic falls short of his consummate indifference for every other object. On the contrary, the citizen always in motion, is perpetually sweating and toiling, and racking his brains to find out occupations still more laborious: He continues a drudge to his last minute; nay, he courts death to be able to live, or renounces life to acquire immortality. He cringes to men in power whom he hates, and to rich men whom he despises; he sticks at nothing to have the honour of serving them; he is not ashamed to value himself on his own weakness and the protection they afford him; and proud of his chains, he speaks with disdain of those who have not the honour of being the partner of his bondage. What a spectacle must the painful and envied labours of an European minister of state form in the eyes of a Caribbean! How many cruel deaths would not this indolent savage prefer to such a horrid life, which very often is not even sweetened by the pleasure of doing good? But to see the drift of so many cares, his mind should first have affixed some meaning to these words power and reputation; he should be apprised that there are men who consider as something the looks of the rest of mankind, who know how to be happy and satisfied with themselves on the testimony of others sooner than upon their own. In fact, the real source of all those differences, is that the savage lives within himself, whereas the citizen, constantly beside himself, knows only how to live in the opinion of others; insomuch that it is, if I may say so, merely from their judgment that he derives the consciousness of his own existence. It is foreign to my subject to show how this disposition engenders so much indifference for good and evil, notwithstanding so many and such fine discourses of morality; how everything, being reduced to appearances, becomes mere art and mummery; honour, friendship, virtue, and often vice itself, which we at last learn the secret to boast of; how, in short, ever inquiring of others what we are, and never daring to question ourselves on so delicate a point, in the midst of so much philosophy, humanity, and politeness, and so many sublime maxims, we have nothing to show for ourselves but a deceitful and frivolous exterior, honour without virtue, reason without wisdom, and pleasure without happiness. It is sufficient that I have proved that this is not the original condition of man, and that it is merely the spirit of society, and the inequality which society engenders, that thus change and transform all our natural inclinations.

I have endeavoured to exhibit the origin and progress of inequality, the institution and abuse of political societies, as far as these things are capable of being deduced from the nature of man by the mere light of reason, and independently of those sacred maxims which give to the sovereign authority the sanction of divine right. It follows from this picture, that as there is scarce any inequality among men in a state of nature, all that which we now behold owes its force and its growth to the development of our faculties and the improvement of our understanding, and at last becomes permanent and lawful by the establishment of property and of laws. It likewise follows that moral inequality, authorised by any right that is merely positive, clashes with natural right, as often as it does not combine in the same proportion with physical inequality: a distinction which sufficiently determines, what we are able to think in that respect of that kind of inequality which obtains in all civilised nations, since it is evidently against the law of nature that infancy should command old age, folly conduct wisdom, and a handful of men should be ready to choke with superfluities, while the famished multitude want the commonest necessaries of life.

85. THE VIRTUES OF CIVILIZATION

No one denounced more vigorously the romantic fantasies of Rousseau's primitivism and upheld the sanity and splendor of civilization with greater bluntness than the English lexicographer and author Samuel Johnson (1709-1784). He expressed these views repeatedly to his companion, James Boswell (1740-1795), who recorded them in his *Life of Johnson*, published in 1791. Boswell's work demonstrates how Johnson managed to combine personal kindliness and stubborn realism with vigorous and unrepentant Tory prejudices. The "Wilkes" of the first part of the selection below was the English radical John Wilkes.

James Boswell

Conversations with Dr. Johnson

Our next meeting at the Mitre was on Saturday the 15th of February [1766], when I presented to him my old and most intimate friend,

SOURCE: James Boswell, *The Life of Johnson* (New York: Oxford University Press, 1933), Book I, pp. 339, 494; Book II, 136–37, 193. Reprinted by permission of Oxford University Press.

the Reverend Mr. Temple, then of Cambridge. I having mentioned that I had passed some time with Rousseau in his wild retreat, and having quoted some remark made by Mr. Wilkes, with whom I had spent many pleasant hours in Italy, Johnson said (sarcastically,) "It seems, Sir, you have kept very good company abroad, Rousseau and Wilkes!" Thinking it enough to defend one at a time, I said nothing as to my gay friend, but answered with a smile, "My dear Sir, you don't call Rousseau bad company. Do you really think *him* a bad man?" JOHNSON. "Sir, if you are talking jestingly of this, I don't talk with you. If you mean to be serious, I think him one of the worst of men; a rascal who ought to be hunted out of society, as he has been. Three or four nations have expelled him; and it is a shame that he is protected in this country." BOSWELL. "I don't deny, Sir, but that his novel may, perhaps, do harm; but I cannot think his intention was bad." JOHNSON. "Sir, that will not do. We cannot prove any man's intention to be bad. You may shoot a man through the head, and say you intended to miss him; but the Judge will order you to be hanged. An alleged want of intention, when evil is committed, will not be allowed in a court of justice. Rousseau, Sir, is a very bad man. I would sooner sign a sentence for his transportation, than that of any felon who has gone from the Old Bailey these many years. Yes, I should like to have him work in the plantations." BOSWELL. "Sir, do you think him as bad a man as Voltaire?" JOHNSON. "Why, Sir, it is difficult to settle the proportion of iniquity between them."

. . . . .

The modes of living in different countries, and the various views with which men travel in quest of new scenes, having been talked of, a learned gentleman who holds a considerable office in the law, expatiated on the happiness of a savage life; and mentioned an instance of an officer who had actually lived for some time in the wilds of America, of whom, when in that state, he quoted this reflection with an air of admiration, as if it had been deeply philosophical: "Here am I, free and unrestrained, amidst the rude magnificence of Nature, with this Indian woman by my side, and this gun with which I can procure food when I want it: what more can be desired for human happiness?" It did not require much sagacity to foresee that such a sentiment would not be permitted to pass without due animadversion. JOHNSON. "Do not allow yourself, Sir, to be imposed upon by such gross absurdity. It is sad stuff; it is brutish. If a bull could speak, he might as well exclaim,—Here am I with this cow and this grass; what being can enjoy greater felicity?"

. . . . .

. . . I had long complained to him that I felt myself discontented in Scotland, as too narrow a sphere, and that I wished to make my chief residence in London, the great scene of ambition, instruction, and amusement: a scene, which was to me, comparatively speaking, a heaven upon earth. JOHNSON. "Why, Sir, I never knew any one who had such a *gust* for London as you have: and I cannot blame you for your wish to live there. . . ."

I suggested a doubt, that if I were to reside in London, the exquisite zest with which I relished it in occasional visits might go off, and I might grow tired of it. JOHNSON. "Why, Sir, you find no man, at all intellectual, who is willing to leave London. No, Sir, when a man is tired of London, he is tired of life; for there is in London all that life can afford." . . .

. . . . .

We talked of living in the country. JOHNSON. "No wise man will go to live in the country, unless he has something to do which can be better done in the country. For instance: if he is to shut himself up for a year to study a science, it is better to look out to the fields, than to an opposite wall. Then, if a man walks out in the country, there is nobody to keep him from walking in again: but if a man walks out in London, he is not sure when he shall walk in again. A great city is, to be sure, the school for studying life; and 'The proper study of mankind is man,' as Pope observes."

86. THE WORLDLY LIFE DEFENDED

What Johnson defended bluntly was argued subtly and with vivacious good humor by Voltaire in a poem of 1736, "The Worldling" (*Le Mondain*). This portrait of a man who enjoys life reflects Voltaire's rejection of the principle of asceticism; long before the appearance of Rousseau's discourses he had disavowed the primitivism they expressed. The poem's jests on the crudity of Adam and Eve led to court proceedings against Voltaire, and he took refuge in Holland for several months until the furor subsided. Voltaire became the central figure of the French Enlightenment. As dramatist and poet, essayist and pamphleteer, he presented a self-portrait of a man who luxuriated in the pleasures of life and made himself wealthy with his pen and yet could risk all to come to the defense of those persecuted by judicial injustice.

Voltaire

The Worldling

Others may with regret complain
That 'tis not fair Astrea's reign,

SOURCE: *The Works of Voltaire*, translated by William F. Fleming (New York: E. R. Du Mont, 1901), Vol. XXXVI, pp. 84–88.

That the famed golden age is o'er
That Saturn, Rhea rule no more:
Or, to speak in another style,
That Eden's groves no longer smile.
For my part, I thank Nature sage,
That she has placed me in this age:
Religionists may rail in vain;
I own, I like this age profane;
I love the pleasures of a court;
I love the arts of every sort;
Magnificence, fine buildings, strike me;
In this, each man of sense is like me.
I have, I own, a worldly mind,
That's pleased abundance here to find;
Abundance, mother of all arts,
Which with new wants new joys imparts
The treasures of the earth and main,
With all the creatures they contain:
These, luxury and pleasures raise;
This iron age brings happy days.
Needful superfluous things appear;
They have joined together either sphere.
See how that fleet, with canvas wings,
From Texel, Bordeaux, London brings,
By happy commerce to our shores,
All Indus, and all Ganges stores;
Whilst France, that pierced the Turkish lines,
Sultans make drunk with rich French wines.
Just at the time of Nature's birth,
Dark ignorance o'erspread the earth;
None then in wealth surpassed the rest,
For naught the human race possessed.
Of clothes, their bodies then were bare,
They nothing had, and could not share:
Then too they sober were and sage,
Martialo [1] lived not in that age.
Eve, first formed by the hand divine,
Never so much as tasted wine.
Do you our ancestors admire,
Because they wore no rich attire?
Ease was like wealth to them unknown,
Was't virtue? ignorance alone.
Would any fool, had he a bed,
On the bare ground have laid his head?
My fruit-eating first father, say,
In Eden how rolled time away?
Did you work for the human race,
And clasp dame Eve with close embrace!
Own that your nails you could not pare,

---

[1] The author of a treatise entitled "The French Cook."

And that you wore disordered hair,
That you were swarthy in complexion,
And that your amorous affection
Had very little better in't
Than downright animal instinct.
Both weary of the marriage yoke
You supped each night beneath an oak
On millet, water, and on mast,
And having finished your repast,
On the ground you were forced to lie,
Exposed to the inclement sky:
Such in the state of simple nature
Is man, a helpless, wretched creature.
Would you know in this cursed age,
Against which zealots so much rage,
To what men blessed with taste attend
In cities, how their time they spend?
The arts that charm the human mind
All at his house a welcome find;
In building it, the architect
No grace passed over with neglect.
To adorn the rooms, at once combine
Poussin, Correggio the divine,
Their works on every panel placed
Are in rich golden frames incased.
His statues show Bouchardon's skill,
Plate of Germain, his sideboards fill.
The Gobelin tapestry, whose dye
Can with the painter's pencil vie,
With gayest coloring appear
As ornaments on every pier.
From the superb salon are seen
Gardens with Cyprian myrtle green.
I see the sporting waters rise
By jets d'eau almost to the skies.
But see the master's self approach
And mount into his gilded coach,
A house in motion, to the eyes
It seems as through the streets it flies.
I see him through transparent glasses
Loll at his ease as on he passes.
Two pliant and elastic springs
Carry him like a pair of wings.
At Bath, his polished skin inhales
Perfumes, sweet as Arabian gales.
Camargot at the approach of night
Julia, Goffin by turns invite.
Love kind and bounteous on him pours
Of choicest favors plenteous showers.
To the opera house he must repair,
Dance, song and music charm him there.

The painter's art to strike the sight,
Does there with that blest art unite;
The yet more soft, persuasive skill,
Which can the soul with pleasure thrill.
He may to damn an opera go,
And yet perforce admire Rameau.
The cheerful supper next invites
To luxury's less refined delights.
How exquisite those sauces flavor!
Of those ragouts I like the savor.
The man who can in cookery shine,
May well be deemed a man divine.
Chloris and Aegle at each course
Serve me with wine, whose mighty force
Makes the cork from the bottle fly
Like lightning darting from the sky.
Bounce! to the ceiling it ascends,
And laughter the apartment rends.
In this froth, just observers see
The emblem of French vivacity.
The following day new joys inspires,
It brings new pleasures and desires.
Mentor, Telemachus descant
Upon frugality, and vaunt
Your Ithaca and your Salentum
To ancient Greeks, since they content them:
Since Greeks in abstinence could find
Ample supplies of every kind.
The work, though not replete with fire,
I for its elegance admire:
But I'll be whipped Salentum through
If thither I my bliss pursue.
Garden of Eden, much renowned,
Since there the devil and fruit were found,
Huetius, Calmet, learned and bold,
Inquired where Eden lay of old:
I am not so critically nice,
Paris to me's a paradise.

87. A RELIGION WITHOUT MIRACLES

During the late 17th and early 18th centuries, the traditional forms of Christianity based on the notion of a personal God working through both natural laws and miracles and speaking to man through revelation came under attack. The enemy was seldom atheism, with its total denial of the very existence of a deity, but rather deism, which accepted the idea of a personal God but limited his role to that of a master craftsman of the universe, working only through natural law and natural morality. This natural religion became predominant in the Enlightenment. One of its clearest statements was the book *Christianity as Old as the Creation*, by Matthew Tindal (c. 1653-1733). Tindal, who was educated as a lawyer and lived as a fellow of All Souls' College, Oxford, was for a period a Roman Catholic under James II but returned to his rationalist principles and became a stormy petrel in English religious circles. The book from which the selection below was taken was his last and was often called "the deist's Bible."

Matthew Tindal

Christianity as Old as the Creation

That the religion of nature consists in observing those things which our reason, by considering the nature of God and man, and the relation we stand in to him and one another, demonstrates to be our duty; and that those things are plain; and likewise what they are

By natural religion, I understand the belief of the existence of a God, and the sense and practice of those duties which result from the knowledge we, by our reason, have of him and his perfections; and of ourselves, and our own imperfections, and of the relation we stand in to him, and to our fellow-creatures; so that the religion of nature takes in everything that is founded on the reason and nature of things.

I suppose you will allow that it is evident by the light of nature that there is a God, or in other words, a being absolutely perfect, and infinitely happy in himself, who is the source of all other beings; and that what perfections soever the creatures have, they are wholly derived from him. It is equally demonstrable that the creatures can neither add to, or take away from, the happiness of that being; and that he could have no motive in framing his creatures, or in giving laws to such of them as he made capable of knowing his will, but their own good. It unavoidably follows, nothing can be a part of the divine law, but what tends to promote the common interest and mutual happiness of his rational creatures, and everything that does so must be a part of it.

As God can require nothing of us, but what makes for our happiness;

SOURCE: E. Graham Waring (ed.), *Deism and Natural Religion: A Source Book* (New York: Frederick Ungar Publishing Co., 1967), pp. 113–17. Reprinted by permission of Frederick Ungar Publishing Co.

so he, who can't envy us any happiness our nature is capable of, can forbid us those things only which tend to our hurt. From the consideration of these perfections, we cannot but have the highest veneration, nay, the greatest adoration and love for this supreme being, who, that we may not fail to be as happy as possible for such creatures to be, has made our acting for our present, to be the only means of obtaining our future happiness; and that we can't sin against him, but by acting against our reasonable natures.

Our reason, which gives us a demonstration of the divine perfections, affords us the same concerning the nature of those duties God requires, not only with relation to himself, but to ourselves, and one another.

With relation to ourselves, we can't but know how we are to act, if we consider that God has endowed man with such a nature as makes him necessarily desire his own good; and, therefore, he may be sure that God, who has bestowed this nature on him, could not require anything of him in prejudice of it; but on the contrary, that he should do everything which tends to promote the good of it. The health of the body and the vigor of the mind being highly conducing to our good, we must be sensible we offend our maker if we indulge our senses to the prejudice of these. We can't but know we ought to use great moderation with relation to our passions, or, in other words, govern all our actions by reason, that and our true interest being inseparable. And, in a word, whoever so regulates his natural appetites as will conduce most to the exercise of his reason, the health of his body, and the pleasure of his senses, taken and considered together (since herein his happiness consists), may be certain he can never offend his maker.

As to what God expects from man with relation to each other, everyone must know his duty who considers that the common parent of mankind has the whole species alike under his protection, and will equally punish him for injuring others, as he would others for injuring him; and consequently that it is his duty to deal with them, as he expects they should deal with him in the like circumstances. Considering the variety of circumstances men are under, and these continually changing, as well as being for the most part unforeseen, it is impossible to have rules laid down by any external revelation for every particular case. Therefore, there must be some standing rule, discoverable by the light of nature, to direct us in all such cases. And we can't be more certain that it is the will of God that those effects which flow from natural causes should so flow, than we are that it is the will of God that men should observe whatever the nature of things, and the relation they have to one another, make fit to be observed, should be so observed.

And I may add that the better to cause men to observe those rules which make for their mutual benefit, infinite goodness has sown in their hearts seeds of pity, humanity and tenderness, which, without much difficulty, cannot be eradicated; but nothing operates more strongly than that desire men have of being in esteem, credit, and reputation with their fellow creatures, not to be obtained without acting on the principles of natural justice, equity, benevolence, etc. In a word, as a most beneficent disposition in the supreme being is the source of all his actions in relation to his creatures, so he has implanted in man, whom he has made after his own image, a love for his species; the gratifying of which in doing acts of benevolence, compassion and good will, produces a pleasure that never satiates, as on the contrary actions of ill nature, envy, malice, etc., never fail to produce shame, confusion, and everlasting self-reproach.

From these premises, I think, we may boldly draw this conclusion, that if religion consists in the practice of those duties that result from the relation we stand in to God and man, our religion must always be the same. If God is unchangeable, our duty to him must be so too; if human nature continues the same, and men at all times stand in the same relation to one another, the duties which result from those relations must always be the same. And consequently, our duty to God and man must, from the beginning of the world to the end, always be the same, always alike plain and perspicuous, and can neither be changed in whole or part. Consequently, whoever acts what is best for himself, both in a public and private capacity, does all that either God or man can require. Hence I think we may define true religion to consist in a constant disposition of mind to do all the good we can, and thereby render ourselves acceptable to God in answering the end of his creation.

88. THE RELIGION OF FEELING

The reply of the established Anglican Church in England to the heresies of deism was partly persecution and partly counterargument. Nevertheless, Anglicanism during the 18th century moved strongly toward a latitudinarianism that adopted in practice much of deism's moral concerns while maintaining the traditional doctrines. A reply to deism that was more effective in reviving popular faith came from two brothers, John and Charles Wesley. After taking orders as priests of the Anglican church, they turned to active evangelism and preached widely, even in the newly founded American colony of Georgia and in the open fields of their homeland. They appealed to the feelings of their audiences not only with powerful sermons but with hundreds of hymns that aroused emotions in a way that was rare in a century characterized by spare, rationalist poetry. John broke away from the Anglican Church to ordain presbyters even though he did not hold the office of bishop, but Charles refused to make the same break. Two of the most famous of Charles Wesley's hymns are given here.

A. Charles Wesley

Jesus, Lover of My Soul

Jesus, Lover of my soul,
Let me to thy bosom fly;
While the nearer waters roll,
While the tempest still is high;
Hide me, O my Saviour, hide,
Till the storm of life is past;
Safe into the haven guide;
O receive my soul at last.

Other refuge have I none;
Hangs my helpless soul on thee;
Leave, ah, leave me not alone,
Still support and comfort me.
All my trust on thee is stayed,
All my help from thee I bring;
Cover my defenseless head
With the shadow of thy wing.

Thou, O Christ, art all I want,
More than all in thee I find;
Raise the fallen, cheer the faint,
Heal the sick, and lead the blind.
Just and holy is thy name,
I am all unrighteousness;
False, and full of sin I am,
Thou art full of truth and grace.

Plenteous grace with thee is found,
Grace to cover all my sin;
Let the healing streams abound;
Make and keep me pure within;
Thou of life the fountain art,
Freely let me take of thee;
Spring you up within my heart,
Rise to all eternity.

SOURCE: H. Augustine Smith, *Lyric Religion: The Romance of Immortal Hymns* (New York: D. Appleton-Century-Crofts, Educational Division, Meredith Corporation, 1931), pp. 195–98.

B. Charles Wesley

Regeneration and Witness of the Spirit

Author of faith, eternal Word,
  Whose Spirit breathes the active flame,
Faith, like its Finisher and Lord,
  Today as yesterday the same.

To thee our humble hearts aspire,
  And ask the gift unspeakable;
Increase in us the kindled fire,
  In us the work of faith fulfill.

By faith we know thee strong to save;
  Save us, a present Saviour thou:
Whate'er we hope, by faith we have;
  Future and past subsisting now.

To him that in thy name believes,
  Eternal life with thee is given;
Into himself he all receives,
  Pardon, and holiness, and heaven.

The things unknown to feeble sense,
  Unseen by reason's glimmering ray,
With strong, commanding evidence,
  Their heavenly origin display.

Faith lends its realizing light;
  The clouds disperse, the shadows fly;
The Invisible appears in sight,
  And God is seen by mortal eye.

89. FRANCE AS THE STRANGE LAND

Efforts to understand what was novel and different in the societies beyond the seas came, during the 18th century, to suggest a sly way of criticizing one's own society. Instead of depicting Europeans puzzling over barbarian manners and customs, however, the literary method showed men from another society attempting to understand a European one. The method was applied with brilliance by the French political thinker Montesquieu in his earliest important work, *The Persian Letters* (1721). In this book, Rica is a

---

Source: *The Methodist Hymnal* (New York: The Methodist Book Concern, 1905), Hymn 298.

Persian visiting France and describing and judging what he sees in letters to his friend Ibben, back home. One of these letters is given in the selection below. Charles de Secondat, baron de La Brède et de Montesquieu (1689-1755), was the presiding judge of the Parlement of Bordeaux before he retired to a career as a writer.

Charles de Secondat de Montesquieu

The Persian Letters

Letter XXIV

Rica to Ibben, at Smyrna

We arrived in Paris a month ago and have since been in constant motion. There is much to do before you can get settled, find the people to whom you are directed, and procure the things which are all needed at the same time.

Paris is as large as Ispahan, and the houses are so tall you would suppose them inhabited only by astrologers. You may well imagine that a city built in the air, with six or seven houses one on top of the other, is thickly populated, and that when everyone is in the streets there is great confusion.

You may not believe that in the month I have been here I have yet to see anyone walk. No people in the world make more use of their vehicles than the French. They run, they fly; the slow carriages of Asia, or the even pace of our camels, would throw them into a fit. However, I am not made for such speed, and as I often go walking without changing my gait, I sometimes get as angry as a Christian; for even if I did not object to being splashed with mud from head to foot, I cannot pardon the elbowing I regularly and periodically receive. One man, passing me from behind, shoves me half around; another, passing on the opposite side, pushes me back to my original position, and I am more weary after a hundred paces than if I had gone ten leagues.

You must know that at present I cannot speak knowingly to you of the manners and customs of the Europeans, for I myself have but the slightest idea of them and so far have had time only to be astonished.

The king of France [1] is the most powerful prince in Europe. He does not own gold mines, like his neighbor the king of Spain; but he is wealth-

---

[1] Louis XIV [translator's note].

ier, because his riches are extracted from the vanity of his subjects, which is more inexhaustible than any mine. He has undertaken and sustained great wars with marketable titles as his only source of revenue; and by so prodigious a display of human pride, his troops are paid, his towns fortified, and his fleets equipped.

Moreover, the king is a great magician, for he exercises dominion even over the minds of his subjects and makes them think as he wishes. If he has only a million *écus* in his treasury, and has need of two million, he has only to persuade them that one *écu* is worth two, and they believe it. If he has a hard war to sustain and no money at all, he has only to put in their heads the notion that a piece of paper is money, and they are instantly convinced. So great is his power over their minds that he has even made them believe that he cures all kinds of disease, simply by touching them.[2]

You ought not to be astonished by what I say of this prince, for there is an even stronger magician than he, who is master of the king's mind even as the king is sovereign over his subjects. This magician is called the pope. Sometimes he makes the prince believe that three is only one, or that the bread he eats is not bread, or that the wine drunk is not wine, and a thousand similar things.

And to keep the king always in condition and in the habit of belief, the pope sends him from time to time certain articles of faith to exercise upon. Two years ago he sent him a large document which he called the *Constitution*, and with threat of heavy punishment he insisted that the prince and his subjects believe everything contained in it.[3] He succeeded with the prince, who submitted immediately and gave the example to his subjects; some of them, however, revolted and said that they would not believe anything in the document. Women have been the prime movers in this rebellion, which divides the court, the entire kingdom, and every family, because this *Constitution* forbids their reading a book which all the Christians claim has come down from heaven; it is, in fact, their Koran. Indignant over this outrage to their sex, the women rose as a body against the *Constitution*, and have brought over to their side all the men, who are not anxious about their superiority in this affair. Indeed, one must admit that this mufti has not reasoned badly; and, by the great Hali,

---

[2] In the Middle Ages the "king's touch" was believed to be efficacious as a cure for scrofula; the practice was widely disbelieved and infrequently followed in the eighteenth century [translator's note].

[3] The papal bull *Unigenitus*, often simply called the *Constitution* in France, was promulgated by Clement XI in September, 1713; Montesquieu thus errs in referring to it in this letter dated 1712. The bull specifically condemned certain propositions in Quesnel's *Réflexions morales sur le Nouveau Testament* (1692); more generally and significantly, it was understood to condemn the Jansenist tradition in the French Catholic Church. . . . [translator's note].

it must be that he has been instructed in the principles of our sacred law: for since women are of a creation inferior to ours, and since our prophets tell us that they cannot enter paradise, why then should they trouble themselves to read a book intended only to teach the way to paradise?

I have heard some things ascribed to the king which seem incredible, and I have no doubt that you will hesitate to believe them.

It is said that while he was making war against all his neighbors who were leagued against him, he was surrounded in his own realm by an infinity of invisible enemies.[4] It is added that while he sought to uncover these enemies for over thirty years, and with the indefatigable aid of certain dervishes who hold his confidence,[5] he has not been able to find a single one. They live with him; they are at court, in the capital, in the army, in the law courts; nonetheless it is said that he will be unfortunate enough to die without having found them. One might say that they exist in general but not in particular, that they are a body without members. Doubtless, heaven means to punish this prince for not being moderate enough to his vanquished enemies by sending him invisible enemies whose genius and destiny are superior to his.

I will write again to tell you of things far removed from the Persian character and genius. The same earth carries us both, but the men of this courtry, and those where you are, are certainly different men.

PARIS, the 4th of the moon of Rebiab II, 1712

90. THE ABSOLUTISM OF POPULAR SOVEREIGNTY

The idea of the political compact underwent further evolution during the 18th century at the hands of the one of the boldest thinkers of the Enlightenment, Jean Jacques Rousseau. Drawing upon the experience of his native Geneva, Rousseau repeated the fundamental assertions of his predecessors regarding the transfer of individual rights to the sovereign. But for him the sovereign was not a person or body set over the people, even if it was ultimately accountable to them. Instead, the sovereign was the people themselves, as a body.

Where Hobbes and Locke had both emphasized the usefulness of the state to individuals in assuring them peace and civil order, Rousseau treated the question of a conflict of interests between the sovereign and the people as logical nonsense, since the sovereign people could not act against their own interests. He also made the grant of political power by the contracting

[4] The Jansenists [translator's note].

[5] The Jesuits. Montesquieu generally uses "dervish" as the equivalent of "monk" [translator's note].

people as complete and perpetual as Hobbes had done, but, bringing into political thought the concept of freedom that Luther had argued against Erasmus (see Section 14), he declared freedom was precisely being a member of a sovereign people.

A work as full of paradox and originality as Rousseau's *Social Contract* (1762), from which the selection below is taken, was bound to have many different meanings according to who read it. However, its proclamation of the principle of popular sovereignty worked in any case against the traditional claims of hereditary monarchy and established oligarchies.

Jean Jacques Rousseau

The Social Contract

My purpose is to consider if, in political society, there can be any legitimate and sure principle of government, taking men as they are and laws as they might be. In this inquiry I shall try always to bring together what right permits with what interest prescribes so that justice and utility are in no way divided.

I start without seeking to prove the importance of my subject. I may be asked whether I am a prince or a legislator that I should be writing about politics. I answer no: and indeed that that is my reason for doing so. If I were a prince or a legislator I should not waste my time saying what ought to be done; I should do it or keep silent.

Born as I was the citizen of a free state and a member of its sovereign body, the very right to vote imposes on me the duty to instruct myself in public affairs, however little influence my voice may have in them. And whenever I reflect upon governments, I am happy to find that my studies always give me fresh reasons for admiring that of my own country.

Man was born free, and he is everywhere in chains. Those who think themselves the masters of others are indeed greater slaves than they. How did this transformation come about? I do not know. How can it be made legitimate? That question I believe I can answer.

If I were to consider only force and the effects of force, I should say: "So long as a people is constrained to obey, and obeys, it does well; but as soon as it can shake off the yoke, and shakes it off, it does better; for

---

SOURCE: Jean Jacques Rousseau, *The Social Contract*, translated by Maurice Cranston (Baltimore, Md.: Penguin Books, 1968), pp. 49–50, 59–61, 63–64, 72–73. Reprinted by permission of A. D. Peters and Company.

since it regains its freedom by the same right as that which removed it, a people is either justified in taking back its freedom, or there is no justifying those who took it away." But the social order is a sacred right which serves as a basis for all other rights. And as it is not a natural right, it must be one founded on covenants. The problem is to determine what those covenants are.

. . . . .

I assume that men reach a point where the obstacles to their preservation in a state of nature prove greater than the strength that each man has to preserve himself in that state. Beyond this point, the primitive condition cannot endure, for then the human race will perish if it does not change its mode of existence.

Since men cannot create new forces, but merely combine and control those which already exist, the only way in which they can preserve themselves is by uniting their separate powers in a combination strong enough to overcome any resistance, uniting them so that their powers are directed by a single motive and act in concert.

Such a sum of forces can be produced only by the union of separate men, but as each man's own strength and liberty are the chief instruments of his preservation, how can he merge his with others' without putting himself in peril and neglecting the care he owes to himself? This difficulty, which brings me back to my present subject, may be expressed in these words:

"How to find a form of association which will defend the person and goods of each member with the collective force of all, and under which each individual, while uniting himself with the others, obeys no one but himself, and remains as free as before." This is the fundamental problem to which the social contract holds the solution.

The articles of this contract are so precisely determined by the nature of the act, that the slightest modification must render them null and void; they are such that, though perhaps never formally stated, they are everywhere the same, everywhere tacitly admitted and recognized; and if ever the social pact is violated, every man regains his original rights and, recovering his natural freedom, loses that social freedom for which he exchanged it.

These articles of association, rightly understood, are reducible to a single one, namely the total alienation by each associate of himself and all his rights to the whole community. Thus, in the first place, as every individual gives himself absolutely, the conditions are the same for all, and precisely because they are the same for all, it is in no one's interest to make the conditions onerous for others. . . .

Finally, since each man gives himself to all, he gives himself to no one; and since there is no associate over whom he does not gain the same rights as others gain over him, each man recovers the equivalent of everything he loses, and in the bargain he acquires more power to preserve what he has.

. . . . .

Now, as the sovereign is formed entirely of the individuals who compose it, it has not, nor could it have, any interest contrary to theirs; and so the sovereign has no need to give guarantees to the subjects, because it is impossible for a body to wish to hurt all of its members, and, as we shall see, it cannot hurt any particular member. The sovereign by the mere fact that it is, is always all that it ought to be. . . .

Hence, in order that the social pact shall not be an empty formula, it is tacitly implied in that commitment—which alone can give force to all others—that whoever refuses to obey the general will shall be constrained to do so by the whole body, which means nothing other than that he shall be forced to be free; for this is the condition which, by giving each citizen to the nation, secures him against all personal dependence, it is the condition which shapes both the design and the working of the political machine, and which alone bestows justice on civil contracts—without it, such contracts would be absurd, tyrannical and liable to the grossest abuse.

. . . . .

It follows from what I have argued that the general will is always rightful and always tends to the public good; but it does not follow that the decisions of the people are always equally right. We always want what is advantageous but we do not always discern it. The people is never corrupted, but it is often misled; and only then does it seem to will what is bad.

There is often a great difference between the will of all [what all individuals want] and the general will; the general will studies only the common interest while the will of all studies private interest, and is indeed no more than the sum of individual desires. But if we take away from these same wills, the pluses and minuses which cancel each other out, the sum of the difference is the general will.

91. A JUSTER JUSTICE

In Italy the Enlightenment had its strongest attraction for an élite of government officials, and the improvement of the laws was one of their central concerns. A Milanese nobleman, Cesare Bonesana, Marchese di Beccaria (c.1735-1794), who taught law and economics at the university of his native city, anticipated such major thinkers as Adam Smith, Thomas Malthus, and Jeremy Bentham. He is best known for his devastating critique of the highly diverse, vengeful, and often self-defeating punitive legal system of Europe under the old regime. In his great treatise, *On Crimes and Punishments* (1764), he advocated logically conceived laws that would match punishments to the magnitude of criminal acts, seek to reduce criminality rather than to revenge crimes, and make the laws "clear and simple" so that obedience to them would be easy for the citizen. Criminal jurisprudence in modern countries has its foundation in Beccaria's work.

Cesare Bonesana di Beccaria

On Crimes and Punishments

. . . . .

We have seen what the true measure of crimes is—namely, the *harm done to society*. This is one of those palpable truths which, though requiring neither quadrants nor telescopes for their discovery, and lying well within the capacity of any ordinary intellect, are, nevertheless, because of a marvelous combination of circumstances, known with clarity and precision only by some few thinking men in every nation and in every age. But notions of an Asiatic sort, and passions clothed with authority and power, usually with indiscernible but sometimes with violent impressions made on the timid credulity of men, have effaced the simple notions that perhaps formed the first philosophy of primitive societies—notions back to which the present enlightenment seems to be leading us, but with that greater degree of certitude obtainable through precise analysis, through a thousand unhappy experiences and from the very obstacles in its way.

They were in error who believed that the true measure of crimes is to be found in the intention of the person who commits them. Intention depends on the impression objects actually make and on the precedent disposition of the mind; these vary in all men and in each man, according to the swift succession of ideas, of passions, and of circumstances. It would be necessary, therefore, to form not only a particular code for each citizen, but a new law for every crime. Sometimes, with the best intentions, men do the greatest injury to society; at other times, intending the worst for it, they do the greatest good.

Others measure crimes rather by the dignity of the injured person than by the importance [of the offense] with respect to the public good. If this were the true measure of crimes, an irreverence toward the Being of beings ought to be more severely punished than the assassination of a monarch, the superiority of nature constituting infinite compensation for the difference in the injury.

Finally, some have thought that the gravity of sinfulness ought to enter into the measure of crimes. The fallacy of this opinion will at once appear to the eye of an impartial examiner of the true relations between men and men, and between men and God. The first are relations of equality. Necessity alone brought into being, out of the clash of passions and the opposition of interests, the idea of *common utility*, which is the foundation of human justice. The second are relations of dependence on a perfect Being and Creator, who has reserved to himself alone the right to be legislator and judge at the same time, because he alone can be such without inconvenience. If he has established eternal punishments for anyone who disobeys his omnipotence, what insect is it that shall dare to take the place of divine justice, that shall want to vindicate the Being who is sufficient unto himself, who cannot receive from things any impression of pleasure or pain, and who, alone among all beings, acts without suffering any reaction? The weight of sin depends on the inscrutable malice of the heart, which can be known by finite beings only if it is revealed. How then can a norm for punishing crimes be drawn from this? Men might in such a case punish where God forgives, and forgive where God punishes. If men can be in opposition with the Omnipotent in offending him, they may also be so in punishing.

. . . . .

It is better to prevent crimes than to punish them. This is the ultimate end of every good legislation, which, to use the general terms for assessing the good and evils of life, is the art of leading men to the greatest possible happiness or to the least possible unhappiness.

But heretofore, the means employed have been false and contrary to the end proposed. It is impossible to reduce the turbulent activity of mankind to a geometric order, without any irregularity and confusion. As the constant and very simple laws of nature do not impede the planets from disturbing one another in their movements, so in the infinite and very contrary attractions of pleasure and pain, disturbances and disorder cannot be impeded by human laws. And yet this is the chimera of narrow-minded men when they have power in their grasp. To prohibit a multitude of indifferent acts is not to prevent crimes that might arise from them, but is rather to create new ones; it is to define by whim the ideas of virtue and vice which are preached to us as eternal and immutable. To what should we be reduced if everything were forbidden us that might induce us to crime! It would be necessary to deprive man of the use of his senses. For one motive that drives men to commit a real crime there are a thousand that drive them to commit those indifferent acts which are called crimes by bad laws; and if the probability of crimes is proportionate to the number of motives, to enlarge the sphere of crimes is to increase the probability of their being committed. The majority of the laws are nothing but privileges, that is, a tribute paid by all to the convenience of some few.

Do you want to prevent crimes? See to it that the laws are clear and simple and that the entire force of a nation is united in their defense, and that no part of it is employed to destroy them. See to it that the laws favor not so much classes of men as men themselves. See to it that men fear the laws and fear nothing else. For fear of the laws is salutary, but fatal and fertile for crimes is one man's fear of another. Enslaved men are more voluptuous, more depraved, more cruel than free men. These study the sciences, give thought to the interests of their country, contemplate grand objects and imitate them, while enslaved men, content with the present moment, seek in the excitement of debauchery a distraction from the emptiness of the condition in which they find themselves. Accustomed to an uncertainty of outcome in all things, the outcome of their crimes remains for them problematical, to the advantage of the passions that determine them. If uncertainty regarding the laws befalls a nation which is indolent because of climate, its indolence and stupidity are confirmed and increased; if it befalls a voluptuous but energetic nation, the result is a wasteful diffusion of energy into an infinite number of little cabals and intrigues that sow distrust in every heart, make treachery and dissimulation the foundation of prudence; if it befalls a brave and powerful nation, the uncertainty is removed finally, but only after having caused many oscillations from liberty to slavery and from slavery back to liberty.

Do you want to prevent crimes? See to it that enlightenment accompanies liberty. Knowledge breeds evils in inverse ratio to its diffusion, and benefits in direct ratio. A daring impostor, who is never a common man, is received with adorations by an ignorant people, and with hisses by an enlightened one. Knowledge, by facilitating comparisons and by multiplying points of view, brings on a mutual modification of conflicting feelings, especially when it appears that others hold the same views and face the same difficulties. In the face of enlightenment widely diffused throughout the nation, the calumnies of ignorance are silenced and authority trembles if it be not armed with reason. The vigorous force of the laws, meanwhile, remains immovable, for no enlightened person can fail to approve of the clear and useful public compacts of mutual security when he compares the inconsiderable portion of useless liberty he himself has sacrificed with the sum total of liberties sacrificed by other men, which, except for the laws, might have been turned against him. Any person of sensibility, glancing over a code of well-made laws and observing that he has lost only a baneful liberty to injure others, will feel constrained to bless the throne and its occupant.

. . . . .

Finally, the surest but most difficult way to prevent crimes is by perfecting education—a subject much too vast and exceeding the limits I have prescribed for myself, a subject, I venture also to say, too intimately involved with the nature of government for it ever to be, even in the far-off happy ages of society, anything more than a barren field, only here and there cultivated by a few sages. A great man, who enlightens the world that persecutes him, [1] has indicated plainly and in detail what principal maxims of education are truly useful to men: they are, that it should consist less in a barren multiplicity of things than in a selection and precise definition of them; in substituting originals for the copies of the moral as well as physical phenomena which chance or willful activity may present to the fresh minds of youths; in leading them toward virtue by the easy way of feeling, and in directing them away from evil by the infallible one of necessity and inconvenience, instead of by the uncertain means of command which obtains only simulated and momentary obedience.

92. RELIGION WITHOUT PREJUDICE

Of all the varied doctrines held by Enlightenment thinkers, perhaps only one was shared by all—the principle that religious persecution was abhorrent. Where the Enlightenment in France (and to a lesser degree in England) adopted deism as its principal religious expression, in Germany the *Aufklärung* (which gave the name "enlightenment" to the movement) was pious in mood, although critical of the intolerance of established churches. The most eloquent expression of the belief that all religions were equally valid insofar as they shared essential truths of morality and divinity came from the dramatist Gotthold Ephraim Lessing (1729-1781). His poetic drama *Nathan the Wise* (1779) was startling not only because it took a Jew as its hero, but also because it argued for the equality of Judaism, Islam, and Christianity. The story of the three rings, which Lessing took from Boccaccio, is presented in the famous scene between Nathan and the sultan, Saladin, which is reprinted below.

---

[1] Reference is to Rousseau's *Émile* [translator's note].

Gotthold Ephraim Lessing

Nathan the Wise

. . . . .

SALADIN
I want your teaching as to something else;
Something far different—and since it seems
You are so wise, now tell me, I entreat,
What human faith, what theologic law,
Hath struck you as the truest and the best?

NATHAN
Sire, I'm a Jew.

SALADIN
And I a Mussulman;
And here we have the Christians to boot;
Of these three faiths one only can be true;
A man like you would never take his stand
Where chance or birth has cast him; or, if so,
'Tis from conviction, reasonable grounds,
And choice of that which is the best,—well, then,
Tell me of your view, and let me hear your grounds.

. . . . .

NATHAN
Well then:—In hoary antiquity there dwelt
In eastern lands a man who had received
From a loved hand a ring of priceless worth.
An opal was the stone it bore, which shot
A hundred fair and varied hues around,
And had the mystic power to render dear
Alike to God and man whoever wore
The ring with perfect faith. What wonder, then,
That eastern man would never lay it off,
And further made a fixed and firm resolve
That it should bide for ever with his race.
For this he left it to his dearest son,
Adding a stringent clause that he in turn
Should leave it to the son he loved the most,
And that in every age the dearest son,
Without respect to seniority,

SOURCE: *Lessing's Nathan the Wise*, translated by Major-General Patrick Maxwell (London: Walter Scott Ltd., n. d.), pp. 119, 123–28.

By virtue of the ring alone should be
The lord of all the race. Sultan, I ask
If you have marked me well.

SALADIN

Ay, ay,—proceed.

NATHAN

And thus the ring came down from sire to son,
Until it reached a father of three sons
Each equally obedient to his will,
And whom accordingly he was constrained
To love alike. And yet from time to time,
Whene'er the one or other chanced to be
Alone with him, and his o'erflowing heart
Was not divided by the other two,
The one who stood beside him still would seem
Most worthy of the ring; and thus it chanced
That he by kindly weakness had been led
To promise it in turn to each of them.
This state of matters lasted while it could,
But by-and-by he had to think of death,
And then this worthy sire was sore perplexed.
He could not brook the thought of breaking faith
With two dear sons to whom he'd pledged his word;
What now was to be done? He straightway sends
In secret for a skilled artificer,
And charges him to make two other rings
Precisely like the first, at any cost.
This the artificer contrives to do,
And when at last he brings him all three rings
Even the father can't say which is which.
With joyful heart he summons then his sons,
But singly and apart, bestows on each
His special blessing, and his ring—and dies.
You hear me, Sultan?

SALADIN *(looking aside in perplexity)*

Ay, I hear, I hear;
Come, make an end of it.

NATHAN

I'm at the end;
For what's to follow may be well conceived.
Scarce was the father dead, each several son
Comes with his ring and claims to be the lord
Of all his kindred. They investigate,
Recriminate, and wrangle—all in vain—
Which was the true original genuine ring
Was undemonstrable——
(After a pause, during which he closely marks the SULTAN.*)*
Almost as much
As now by us is undemonstrable
The one true faith.

SALADIN

Nathan, is this to pass
For answer to my question?

NATHAN

Sultan, no;
'Tis only meant to serve as my excuse
For better answer. How could I presume
E'er to pronounce distinction 'tween the rings
The father purposely designed to be
Quite indistinguishable?

SALADIN

Rings, forsooth!
Trifle not with me thus. I should have thought
The three religons which I named to you
Were easy to distinguish, if alone
By difference of dress and food and drink.

NATHAN

But not by fundamental difference.
Are they not founded all on history,
Traditional or written? History
Must still be taken upon trust alone;
And who are they who best may claim our trust?
Surely our people, of whose blood we are;
Who from our infancy have proved their love,
And never have deceived us, save, perchance,
When kindly guile was wholesomer for us
Than truth itself. Why should I less rely
Upon my ancestors than you on yours;
Or I ask of you to give the lie
To your forefathers, merely to agree
With mine?—and all that I have said applies
To Christians as well. Is this not so?

SALADIN *(aside)*

Now, by the living God, the man is right;
I must be silent.

NATHAN

Let us now return
Once more unto our rings. As I have said,
The sons now sued each other; each of them
Swore to the judge he had received his ring
Straight from his father's hand—as was the fact—
And that, too, after he had long enjoyed
His father's promise to bequeath the ring
To him alone—which also was the truth;
Each vowed the father never could have proved
So false to him; and rather than believe
A thing like this of such a loving sire,
He was constrained—however loath he was
To think unkindly of his brethren—
To charge them both with some nefarious trick,

And now he would unmask their treachery
And be avenged for such a cruel wrong.

SALADIN
Well, and the Judge? for I am fain to hear
What you will make *him* say,—tell on, tell on.

NATHAN
The Judge pronounced—Unless you bring your sire,
And place him here before the judgment-seat,
I must dismiss your suit. Think you I'm here
For solving riddles?—or perhaps you wait
Until the genuine ring declares itself.
Yet stay—you said the genuine ring contains
The magic power to make its wearer loved
More than all else, in sight of God and man;
This must decide the case—the spurious rings
Will not do this—say, which of you is he
The other two most love?—what, no reply?
Your rings would seem to work reflexively,
Not on external objects; since it seems
Each is enamoured of himself alone.
Oh, then, all three of you have been deceived,
And are deceivers too; and all three rings
Are spurious alike—the genuine ring
Was lost, most likely, and to hide his loss,
And to supply its place, your father caused
These three to be made up instead of it.

SALADIN
Bravo! bravo!

NATHAN
And then the Judge resumed—
Belike ye would not relish my advice
More than the judgment I have now pronounced;
In that case, go—but my advice is this:
Accept the case precisely as it stands;
If each of you in truth received his ring
Straight from his father's hand, let each believe
His own to be the true and genuine ring.
Perhaps your father wished to terminate
The tyranny of that especial ring
'Mid his posterity. Of this be sure,
He loved you all, and loved you all alike,
Since he was loath to injure two of you
That he might favour one alone; well, then,
Let each now rival his unbiassed love,
His love so free from every prejudice;
Vie with each other in the generous strife
To prove the virtues of the rings you wear;
And to this end let mild humility,
Hearty forbearance, true benevolence,
And resignation to the will of God,

Come to your aid,—and if, in distant times,
The virtues of the genuine gem be found
Amid your children's children, they shall then,
When many a thousand years have rolled away,
Be called once more before this judgment-seat,
Whereon a wiser man than I shall sit
And give his verdict—now, begone. Thus spake
That sapient Judge.

CHAPTER X

RULE AND REBELLION IN THE COLONIES

THE NEW COLONIAL POWERS during the 17th and 18th centuries were England, France, and Holland. As the Dutch displaced the Portuguese in the East Indies, they gradually built an empire. The efforts of the French and English in America were distinctive in that their colonies were formed by the settlement of Europeans rather than by imposing rule on native peoples (African slaves, however, were imported for labor in the Caribbean and southern mainland colonies). The new societies that emerged in America were therefore different from other colonies in character; they were simplified versions of the mother country rather than conquered lands.

The British colonies on the North American mainland were the most diverse in character and, from the beginning, the most independent in spirit. Distinctive colonial interests, combined with the institutions of self-government, provided the basis for a stubborn resistance to British rule after the Peace of Paris in 1763 deprived France of her colonies. With the American Revolution, the 13 colonies became the first to separate from their mother country by their own volition. The United States thus became an independent country rather than passing under the sovereignty of another colonial power.

93. THE PUNISHMENT OF BANISHMENT

The settlement of English colonists at Jamestown, Virginia, in 1607 proved permanent. Not all those who came to populate the new land were willing settlers; included were not only black slaves from Africa but also what a royal proclamation of December 23, 1617, called "notorious and wicked offenders." This proclamation named a commission to seek out troublemakers in the shires of Northumberland, Cumberland, and Westmoreland. No specific crime had to have been committed, no trials were to be held, and offenders who could be reformed only "by severity of punishment"—were to be sent either into military service or to Virginia. The paragraph of the proclamation concerning such punitive banishment is given below. The deportation of criminals to the "plantations" continued to be one of the methods of settlement in them in the late 18th and early 19th centuries, although not of first importance except in Australia.

Declaration for Deporting Notorious Offenders to Virginia, December 23, 1617

Item, for the more speedy suppressing, and freeing the said Countreis and places of notorious and wicked offenders that will not be reformed, but by severity of punishment; Wee have taken order for the making out a Commission to speciall Commissioners, to survey, search and finde out, and enforme Us of the most notorious and lewd persons, and of their faults, within the said Counties of Northumberland, Cumberland, and Westmerland, Riddesdale, and Bewcastle within the same: And We hereby signifie our pleasure to be upon Certificate of the said Commissioners, to send the most notorious ill livers, and misbehaved persons of them that shall so be certified, into Virginia, or to some other remote parts to serve in the Warres, or in Colonies, that they may no more infect the places where they abide within this our Realme.

94. COLONIAL SELF-GOVERNMENT

A colony of quite a different kind was set down at Plymouth, in what is now Massachusetts, in 1620. The Pilgrims obtained a grant of authority to settle from the Virginia Company, but before landing on Cape Cod they drew up the famous "Mayflower Compact" of November 11. While proclaiming their continued allegiance to King James I, they arranged for their own government. It was a "political covenant" or "social contract" before either Hobbes or Rousseau wrote their famous treatises. The full text, without the signatures, follows.

SOURCE: Clarence S. Brigham (ed.), *British Royal Proclamations relating to America, 1603–1783* (New York: Burt Franklin, 1964), p. 7.

The Mayflower Compact, November 11, 1620

In the Name of God, Amen. We, whose names are underwritten, the Loyal Subjects of our dread Sovereign Lord King *James*, by the Grace of God, of *Great Britian*, *France*, and *Ireland*, King, *Defender of the Faith*, &c. Having undertaken for the Glory of God, and Advancement of the Christian Faith, and the Honour of our King and Country, a Voyage to plant the first Colony in the northern Parts of Virginia; Do by these Presents, solemnly and mutually, in the Presence of God and one another, covenant and combine ourselves together into a civil Body Politick, for our better Ordering and Preservation, and Furtherance of the Ends aforesaid: And by Virtue hereof do enact, constitute, and frame, such just and equal Laws, Ordinances, Acts, Constitutions, and Officers, from time to time, as shall be thought most meet and convenient for the general Good of the Colony; unto which we promise all due Submission and Obedience. In Witness whereof we have hereunto subscribed our names at *Cape-Cod* the eleventh of *November*, in the Reign of our Sovereign Lord King *James*, of *England*, *France*, and *Ireland*, the eighteenth, and of *Scotland*, the fifty-fourth, *Anno Domini*, 1620.

95. A PROPRIETARY COLONY

The charter granted by Charles II to William Penn, the Quaker, in 1681 provided for rule of the province of Pennsylvania by Penn and his successors as proprietors. Although Penn was moved by motives of benefaction as well as self-interest, such government at its best would correspond to what would be called a century later "enlightened despotism." The use of the term "absolute" in the grant, reproduced here, indicates that the rule was unshared.

Royal Proclamation Granting Pennsylvania to William Penn, April 2, 1681

Charles R.

Whereas His Majesty, in consideration of the great Merit and Faithful Services of Sir William Penn deceased, and for divers other good Causes

Source: Ben Perley Poore (ed.), *The Federal and State Constitutions, Colonial Charters, and Other Organic Laws of the United States*, Part I (Washington, D.C.: Government Printing Office, 1877), p. 931.

Source: Clarence S. Brigham (ed.), *British Royal Proclamations relating to America, 1603–1783* (New York: Burt Franklin, 1964), pp. 133–34.

Him thereunto moving, hath been Graciously pleased by Letters Patents bearing Date the Fourth day of March last past, to Give and Grant unto William Penn Esquire, Son and Heir of the said Sir William Penn, all that Tract of Land in America, called by the Name of Pennsilvania, as the same is Bounded on the East by Delaware River, from Twelve Miles distance Northwards of Newcastle Town, unto the Three and fourtieth Degree of Northern Latitude, if the said River doth extend so far Northwards, and if the said River shall not extend so far Northward, then by the said River so far as it doth extend: And from the Head of the said River, the Eastern Bounds to be determined by a Meridian Line to be Drawn from the Head of the said River, unto the said Three and fourtieth Degree, the said Province to extend Westward Five Degrees in Longitude, to be Computed from the said Eastern Bounds, and to be Bounded on the North, by the Beginning of the Three and fourtieth Degree of Northern Latitude, and on the south by a Circle Drawn at Twelve Miles distance from Newcastle Northwards, and Westwards unto the Beginning of the Fourtieth Degree of Northern Latitude, and then by a straight line Westwards to the limit of Longitude above mentioned, together with all Powers, Prcheminencies and Jurisdictions necessary for the Government of the said Province, as by the said Letters Patents, Reference being thereunto had, doth more at large appear.

His Majesty doth therefore hereby Publish and Declare His Royal Will and Pleasure, That all Persons Settled or Inhabiting within the Limits of the said Province, do yield all Due Obedience to the said William Penn, His Heirs and Assigns, as absolute Proprietaries and Governours thereof, as also to the Deputy or Deputies, Agents or Lieutenants, Lawfully Commissionated by him or them, according to the Powers and Authorities Granted by the said Letters Patents; Wherewith His Majesty Expects and Requires a ready Complyance from all Persons whom it may concern, as they tender His Majesties Displeasure.

Given at the Court at Whitehall the Second day of April 1681. In the Three and thirtieth year of Our Reign.

To the Inhabitants and
Planters of the Province
of Pennsilvania.

By his Majesties Command,
CONWAY

96. ENGLAND'S WAR PRIZE: THE SLAVE TRADE CONTRACT

The labor needs of the Spanish American colonies were largely met by the importation of black slaves from the West Coast of Africa. Little attention was paid until late in the 18th century to the cruelties suffered by the slaves in the infamous "Middle Passage" across the Atlantic or in the plantations of America; what mattered was that it was an extremely profitable trade. With the decline of Spanish naval power in the 17th century, the contract (or *asiento)* for the supply of slaves was coveted by the great powers. Although it was given to France when the first Bourbon king of Spain, Philip V, came to the throne in 1700, one of the fruits of the English victory in the War of the Spanish Succession was the transfer of the *asiento* to the king of Great Britain. The relevant clause of the peace treaty between Spain and England, concluded at Utrecht on July 13, 1713, is given below.

Pacto de el Assiento de Negros, 1713

XII

The Catholick King doth furthermore hereby give and grant to her *Britannick* Majesty, and to the Company of her Subjects appointed for that purpose, as well the Subjects of *Spain* as all others being excluded, the Contract for introducing Negroes into several Parts of the Dominions of his Catholick Majesty in *America,* commonly called *el Pacto de el Assiento de Negros,* for the Space of 30 Years successively beginning from the 1st day of *May* 1713, with the same Conditions on which the *French* enjoy'd it, or any time might or ought to enjoy the same; together with a Tract or Tracts of Land to be allotted by the said Catholick King, and to be granted to the Company aforesaid, commonly called *la Compania de el Assiento,* in some convenient Place on the River of Plata, (no Dutys or Revenues being payable by the said Company on that account, during the Time of the abovementioned Contract, and no longer;) and this Settlement of the said Society, or those Tracts of Land, shall be proper and sufficient for planting and sowing, and for feeding Cattle for the Subsistence of those who are in the Service of the said Company, and of their Negroes; and that the said Negroes may be there kept in safety, till they

---

Source: Fred L. Israel (ed.), *Major Peace Treaties of Modern History, 1648–1967* (New York: Chelsea House Publishers, 1967), Vol. I, pp. 225–26. Reprinted with permission of Chelsea House Publishers, a division of Chelsea House Educational Communications, Inc. in association with McGraw-Hill Inc.

are sold; and moreover, that the Ships belonging to the said Company may come close to Land, and be secure from any Danger. But it shall always be lawful for the Catholick King to appoint an Officer in the said Place or Settlement to take care that nothing be done contrary to his Royal Interests. And all who manage the Affairs of the said Company there, or belong to it, shall be subject to the Inspection of the aforesaid Officer, as to all Matters relating to the Tracts of Land abovementioned. But if any Doubts, Difficultys, or Controversys should arise between the said Officer and the Managers for the said Company, they shall be referred to the Determination of the Governor of *Buenos Ayres.* The Catholick King has been likewise pleased to grant to the said Company several other extraordinary Advantages, which are more fully and amply explained in the Contract of the Assiento, made and concluded at *Madrid* the 26th of *March* of this present Year 1713. Which Contract, or *Assiento de Negros,* and all the Clauses, Conditions, Privileges and Immunitys contained therein, and which are not contrary to this Article, are and shall be deemed and taken to be Part of this Treaty, in the same manner as if they had been here inserted word for word.

97. PROTECTION OF COLONIAL PLANTATIONS

British relations with the colonies were guided by the principles of mercantilism, in which the interests of the merchants of the mother country were paramount. When such interests were not at stake, however, the advantages of colonial enterprisers were also attended to, especially for those who had powerful connections in the English business and political community, like the sugar growers of the British colonies in the Caribbean. It was to protect them against the competition of their rivals, particularly in the French sugar-growing colonies, that the Molasses Act was adopted by the British Parliament on May 17, 1733. As can be seen by its provisions given below, it applied high tariff duties on foreign rum and molasses imported into other British colonies. Since this in practice meant the British colonies on the North American mainland, this law protected one group of British colonists at the expense of another. It was resisted by agitation and massive smuggling.

The Molasses Act, May 17, 1733

Whereas the welfare and prosperity of your Majesty's sugar colonies in America are of the greatest consequence and importance to the trade,

---

navigation, and strength of this kingdom; and whereas the planters of the said sugar colonies have of late years fallen under such great discouragements that they are unable to improve or carry on the sugar trade upon an equal footing with the foreign sugar colonies without some advantage and relief be given to them from Great Britain; for remedy whereof, . . . be it enacted, . . . that from and after twenty-fifth day of December, one thousand seven hundred and thirty-three, there shall be raised, levied, collected and paid, unto and for the use of his Majesty, his heirs and successors, upon all rum or spirits of the produce or manufacture of any of the colonies or plantations in America, not in the possession or under the dominion of his Majesty, his heirs and successors, which at any time or times within or during the continuance of this act, shall be imported or brought into any of the colonies or plantations in America, which now are or hereafter may be in the possession or under the dominion of his Majesty, his heirs or successors, the sum of nine pence, money of Great Britain, to be paid according to the proportion and value of five shillings and six pence the ounce in silver, for every gallon thereof, and after that rate for any greater or lesser quantity; and upon all molasses or syrups of such foreign produce or manufacture as aforesaid, which shall be imported or brought into any of the said colonies or plantations of or belonging to his Majesty, the sum of six pence of like money for every gallon thereof, and after that rate for any greater or lesser quantity; and upon all sugars and paneles of such foreign growth, produce or manufacture as aforesaid, which shall be imported into any of the said colonies or plantations of or belonging to his Majesty, a duty after the rate of five shillings of like money, for every hundredweight avoirdupois, of the said sugar and paneles, and after that rate for a greater or lesser quantity.

98. A BATTLE AND THE DESTINY OF CANADA

William III's accession to the British throne in 1689 saw the beginning of a series of wars with France that was to last more than a century. For the British and French colonies in North America, this meant that they too were at war with one another. The British had the advantage of denser settlement; the French, of profitable trades with the Indians on routes reaching to the Great Lakes. A single battle, at Quebec on September 13, 1759, destroyed French power in Canada, and the Peace of Paris of 1763 confirmed the battle verdict which was not disturbed by the successful rebellion of the American colonists a decade later. The account given below of (A) of the battle by one of the English officers is taken from a collection of historic documents at Windsor Castle. It is followed by the clause of the Treaty of Paris that ceded Canada to England (B).

A. *An Account of the Action Which Happened Near Quebec, September 13, 1759*

An Account of the Action which happen'd on the 13th Sept[r] 1759 between the English commanded by General Wolfe, and the French commanded by the Marquis de Montcalm, on the 12th Sept[r] at 9 at night the light Infantry of the Army under the command of Colonel How, with Braggs, Kennedys, Lascelle's, and Anstruthers Regiments with part of the Highlanders and Moncton's Grenadiers amounting in the whole to 1800, embarqued near Cape Rouge from on board the men of War and Transports, and proceeded in the flat bottom'd boats down the River, the men of War, Transports, and Arm'd Sloops follow'd with the rest of the Troops, the two floating Batteries accompanied the first embarkation, about half an hour after four on the 13th in the morning the Boats arrived at Sellery Bay, being seven or eight miles from Capc Rouge, the Troops landed immediately at which time four pieces of Canon were instantly fired from a battery, to the left of the landing place, and a number of Musquetry from the top of the hill, but this did not hinder the light Infantry from advancing briskly up a small path which lead by several turnings to the Top, whilst two Regiments scrambled up an almost perpendicular Ascent on the right of the road, in short the Troops gained the summitt with little loss, the defence of which was committed to the care of a Captain with one hundred men, and might have been defended by a Serjeant and twelve men, as soon as this part of the army had got footing on the top of the hill, the boats returned to the men of War and Transports, who had by this time fallen down the river to the landing place, and brought on shore Amhersts Lawrences, Otways, another detachment from the Highlanders, and the Grenadiers from Louisbourgh, Webbs and Monckton's from the other side of the River, who had been drawn from Isle of Orleans, and Point Levi and were ready to come over before day break, the whole being landed amounted to 4,500, soon after our gaining the heights some light Infantry were sent to take possession of the four Gun Battery, which was effected with small loss, Lawrences battallion took post there, and in the two houses near it, as soon as it was

---

Source: Stanley Pargellis (ed.), *Military Affairs in North America, 1748–1765: Selected Documents from the Cumberland Papers in Windsor Castle* (New York: D. Appleton-Century Co., 1936), pp. 437–39.

broad day, we perceived the french in motion betwixt the Town and our little army, they appear'd to be very numerous, and we observ'd they had some Canon, the Genl. immediately disposed the Troops in order of battle, his right occupying the brow of the small eminence, and the left being cover'd by two small houses, into which we threw a Company of Grenadiers, a Battallion & some light Infantry, were extended from those two houses to another house surrounded with Pallisadoes, in the rear of our left from whence the light Infantry occupied the whole space to the battery which was on the rear of our Right, which disposition seemed doubly necessary as we had observed a large detachm[t] of the ennemy filing off from their main body towards our left Flank, and as we knew there was a body of Troops that had been sent up the River, & might be expected at our backs, upon the news of our landing the ennemy soon began to canonade us, and their Irregulars & Indians advancing among some bushes in our front annoy'd us much, as our light Infantry were otherwise disposed of, we were obliged from time to time to advance plattoons from the Battallions to keep these at a distance we had now got 2 short six pounders with which we play'd upon the enemy, who were formed in three Columns in our front, all their Irregulars being disposed of upon our left Flank and Rear, and along the face of the hill below our right, where the bushes afforded them all the advantages they could hope for, the two Armies remained sometime in this situation, our General having delay'd attacking the ennemy in hopes of his bringing up the rest of his field Artillery, but the French either willing to deprive us of this advantage, or fearing we might be reinforced; or perhaps from a contempt of our numbers, advanced upon us in three columns in front, & harrass'd our flanks at the same time with their Irregulars; when they were within 50 paces of our line, they began their fire, which our people received with great firmness for about two minutes, when they three [threw] in their whole fire upon them, which putting them into disorder our people immediately advanced upon them with their Bayonets, and in a few minutes put the whole to flight, which was very precipitate towards the Town and the River St. Charles, our Troops pursuing them with great slaughter, and making many Officers & men prisoners the Irregulars seeing the main body give way, soon follow'd them, and thus ended the Action, in which the French lost their General Montcalm, the 2[d] in command Mons[r] de Sansargues with about 30 officers, and 1500, men killed, wounded and taken, we lost Genl. Wolfe, Brigadier Monckton wounded with 30 Officers killed and wounded, the Ennemy left one field piece, and a great deal of Ammunition on the field in consequence of this victory, Quebec by capitulation surrender'd the 18th when our Troops took possession of it.

B. Treaty of Paris, February 10, 1763

IV

His most Christian Majesty renounces all pretensions, which he has heretofore formed, or might have formed, to Nova Scotia, or Acadia, in all its parts, and guaranties the whole of it, and with all its dependencies, to the King of Great Britain: Moreover, his most Christian Majesty cedes, and guaranties to his said Britannick Majesty, in full right, Canada, with all its dependencies, as well as the Island of Cape Breton, and all the other Islands and Coasts, in the gulph and river of St. Laurence, and in general, every thing that depends on the said Countries, Lands, Islands, and Coasts, with the sovereignty, property, possession, and all rights acquired by treaty, or otherwise, which the most Christian King, and the crown of France, have had, till now, over the said Countries, Islands, Lands, Places, Coasts, and their inhabitants, so that the most Christian King cedés and makes over the whole to the said King, and to the crown of Great-Britain, and that in the most ample manner and form, without restriction, and without any liberty to depart from the said cession and guaranty, under any pretence, or to disturb Great Britain in the possessions above-mentioned. His Brittannick Majesty, on his side, agrees to grant the liberty of the Catholick religion to the inhabitants of Canada: He will, in consequence, give the most precise and most effectual orders, that his new Roman Catholick subjects may profess the worship of their religion, according to the rites of the Romish Church, as far as the laws of Great Britain permit. His Britannick Majesty further agrees, that the French inhabitants, or others who had been subjects of the most Christian King in Canada, may retire, with all safety and freedom, wherever they shall think proper, and may sell their estates, provided it be to the subjects of his Britannick Majesty, and being away their effects, as well as their persons, without being restrained in their emigration, under any pretence whatsoever, except that of debts, or of criminal prosecutions: The term, limited for this emigration, shall be fixed to the space of eighteen months, to be computed from the day of the exchange of the ratification of the present treaty.

SOURCE: Fred L. Israel (ed.), *Major Peace Treaties of Modern History, 1648–1967* (New York: Chelsea House Publishers, 1967), Vol. I, pp. 308–9. Reprinted with permission of Chelsea House Publishers, a division of Chelsea House Educational Communications, Inc. in association with McGraw-Hill Inc.

99. THE COLONIES AND TAXATION

The mercantilist system of relations with colonies, in which chief consideration was given to the advantages of the mother country, began to feel the strain of opposing colonial interests after the Peace of Paris. The threat of a French-held Canada was removed and the government in London began to seek a fiscal contribution from the colonies beyond support of their own provincial governments. One of the principal measures to this end was the Stamp Act of 1765, and the debate over its legal and political basis was particularly vehement. The Pennsylvania Assembly sent the gifted journalist-scientist Benjamin Franklin (1706–1790) to England to argue for its repeal. He made the views of the colonists known not only to the House of Commons but also to the public, in an anonymous letter to the *Gazetteer* of January 23, 1766, replying to one by "A Friend to My Country" printed six days before.

Benjamin Franklin

Letter to the English Public, January 23, 1766

To the Printer.

The sketch in your last Friday's paper, of the *arguments on both sides*, relating to the American stamp act, (signed *A Friend to my Country*) is, I think, on the whole, a pretty fair one. There are, however, a few omissions in it, which I beg leave to supply.

On behalf of the colonies it is farther said, that, allowing the principle, which they do not, nor never did dispute, that they ought in justice to bear with other subjects their share of common burthens, yet the act was *unnecessary* whether we look backward or forward. As to what is *past*, they have in all wars exerted themselves fully equal to their abilities, and in the last, beyond them, which has been acknowledged by government here; and that they still are under a heavy load of debt incurred by that war, for which all their provincial land-taxes, taxes on personal property, excises, poll-taxes, taxes on the profits of business, &c. &c. during many years to come, are mortgaged. And as to the occasions of expence that may *hereafter*, arise, the ancient *established* method of calling on their

---

SOURCE: Verner W. Crane (ed.), *Benjamin Franklin's Letters to the Press, 1758-1775*. (Chapel Hill: University of North Carolina Press, 1950), pp., 53–54. Reprinted by permission of University of North Carolina Press.

assemblies by requisitory letters from the crown, is sufficient to answer all purposes; since they always should, as they always have done, think themselves obliged in duty, on such requisitions, to grant aids suitable to their circumstances. That besides this, they actually pay great taxes to this country, in the accumulated price (occasioned by its taxes) of all British manufactures they consume; and which, if it were not for the restraints on their trade, they might buy cheaper elsewhere. That the acts for regulating commerce and navigation, and the Post-office act, differ very materially from the stamp-act. The former lay duties on the importation of goods, which people may buy or let alone, and the other fixes a rate for the carriage of letters, that is merely a *quantum meruit* for service done, and which every man may do in another way, if he thinks it cheaper and safer, i.e. he may send his letter by a special messenger, or by his friend. But the stamp act *forces* the money from the country under *heavy penalties*, and denies *common justice* in the courts, unless they will submit to part with it, and this without the consent of the legislative body, in which only the country has representatives. And though it is true, that the distance between session and session gave time enough for "preparing proper arguments to oppose the stamp-act"; yet that time was rendered of no use, the petitions that were sent over from the colonies, containing their reasons against it, not being *admitted* or *so much as read*, because it was, it seems, contrary to an established rule, importing that petitions should not be received against a money bill. The parliament may have "asserted a right" to tax Ireland; but it is certain they have never practised it. And though it should be allowed right neither to tax Ireland or the colonies by act of a legislature in which they have no representative, it does not appear how "all the counties in England could found a like claim on that principle," since they are all represented; there not being a landed freehold estate above 40s. per ann. in any county, that does not give its owner a right to vote for a member of parliament.

A FRIEND TO BOTH COUNTRIES

100. LIBERTY AND TAXES

The taxation issue was also seen as central in the colonists' cause by the English statesman and political theorist Edmund Burke (1729–1797). When the American resistance turned to armed rebellion, Burke urged the House of Commons, of which he was a member, to conciliate the colonies by abandoning the innovations that had driven them to desperate measures. In his speech of March 22, 1775, part of which is given below, Burke reminded the assembly that the right to grant taxation by one's own representatives was one that Englishmen carried over to the colonies.

Edmund Burke

Speech on America, March 22, 1775

. . . . .

In this character of the Americans a love of freedom is the predominating feature which marks and distinguishes the whole: and as an ardent is always a jealous affection, your colonies become suspicious, restive, and untractable, whenever they see the least attempt to wrest from them by force, or shuffle from them by chicane, what they think the only advantage worth living for. This fierce spirit of liberty is stronger in the English colonies, probably, than in any other people of the earth, and this from a great variety of powerful causes; which, to understand the true temper of their minds, and the direction which this spirit takes, it will not be amiss to lay open somewhat more largely.

First, the people of the colonies are descendants of Englishmen. England, Sir, is a nation which still, I hope, respects, and formerly adored, her freedom. The colonists emigrated from you when this part of your character was most predominant; and they took this bias and direction the moment they parted from your hands. They are therefore not only devoted to liberty, but to liberty according to English ideas and on English principles. Abstract liberty, like other mere abstractions, is not to be found. Liberty inheres in some sensible object; and every nation has formed to itself some favorite point, which by way of eminence becomes the criterion of their happiness. It happened, you know, Sir, that the great contests for freedom in this country were from the earliest times chiefly upon the question of taxing. Most of the contests in the ancient commonwealths turned primarily on the right of election of magistrates, or on the balance among the several orders of the state. The question of money was not with them so immediate. But in England it was otherwise. On this point of taxes the ablest pens and most eloquent tongues have been exercised, the greatest spirits have acted and suffered. In order to give the fullest satisfaction concerning the importance of this point, it was not only necessary for those who in argument defended the excellence of the English Constitution to insist on this privilege of granting money as a dry point of fact, and to prove that the right had been acknowledged in ancient parchments and blind usages to reside in a certain body called an House of Commons: they went much further: they attempted to prove, and they succeeded, that in theory it ought to be so, from the particular nature of a House of Commons, as an immediate

---

Source: Robert A. Smith (ed.), *Edmund Burke on Revolution* (New York: Harper & Row Publishers, 1968), pp. 57–58. Reprinted by permission of Harper & Row.

representative of the people, whether the old records had delivered this oracle or not. They took infinite pains to inculcate, as a fundamental principle, that in all monarchies the people must in effect themselves, mediately or immediately, possess the power of granting their own money, or no shadow of liberty could subsist. The colonies draw from you, as with their lifeblood, these ideas and principles. Their love of liberty, as with you, fixed and attached on this specific point of taxing. Liberty might be safe or might be endangered in twenty other particulars without their being much pleased or alarmed. Here they felt its pulse; and as they found that beat, they thought themselves sick or sound. I do not say whether they were right or wrong in applying your general arguments to their own case. It is not easy, indeed, to make a monopoly of theorems and corollaries. The fact is, that they did thus apply those general arguments; and your mode of governing them, whether through lenity or indolence, through wisdom or mistake, confirmed them in the imagination, that they, as well as you, had an interest in these common principles.

101. TREASONS AND TRAITOROUS CONSPIRACIES

The conflict between Britain and the colonies from Georgia to New Hampshire erupted into open-armed resistance a decade after the Stamp Act. The royal government responded by a decision to put down the rebellion, announced in a proclamation by George III on August 23, 1775. It was directed not only against the insurgents across the ocean but also against their friends in England. "George R." in the text below is *George Rex*, George the King.

George III

Proclamation for Suppressing Rebellion and Sedition, August 23, 1775

GEORGE R.

Whereas many of Our Subjects in divers Parts of Our Colonies and Plantations in North America, misled by dangerous and ill-designing Men, and forgetting the Allegiance which they owe to the Power that has protected and sustained them, after various disorderly Acts committed in Disturbance of the Publick Peace, to the Obstruction of lawful Commerce, and to the Oppression of Our loyal Subjects carrying on the

---

SOURCE: Clarence S. Brigham (ed.), *British Royal Proclamations relating to America, 1603–1783* (New York: Burt Franklin, 1964), pp. 228–29.

same, have at length proceeded to an open and avowed Rebellion, by arraying themselves in hostile Manner to withstand the Execution of the Law, and traitorously preparing, ordering, and levying War against Us; and whereas there is Reason to apprehend that such Rebellion hath been much promoted and encouraged by the traitorous Correspondence, Counsels, and Comfort of divers wicked and desperate Persons within this Realm: To the End therefore that none of Our Subjects may neglect or violate their Duty through Ignorance thereof, or through any Doubt of the Protection which the Law will afford to their Loyalty and Zeal; We have thought fit, by and with the Advice of Our Privy Council, to issue this Our Royal Proclamation, hereby declaring that not only all Our Officers Civil and Military are obliged to exert their utmost Endeavours to suppress such Rebellion, and to bring the Traitors to Justice; but that all Our Subjects of this Realm and the Dominions thereunto belonging are bound by Law to be aiding and assisting in the Suppression of such Rebellion, and to disclose and make known all traitorous Conspiracies and Attempts against Us, Our Crown and Dignity; And We do accordingly strictly charge and command all Our Officers as well Civil as Military, and all other Our obedient and loyal Subjects, to use their utmost Endeavours to withstand and suppress such Rebellion, and to disclose and make known all Treasons and traitorous Conspiracies which they shall know to be against Us, Our Crown and Dignity; and for that Purpose, that they transmit to One of Our Principal Secretaries of State, or other proper Officer, due and full Information of all Persons who shall be found carrying on Correspondence with, or in any Manner or Degree aiding or abetting the Persons now in open Arms and Rebellion against Our Government within any of Our Colonies and Plantations in North America, in order to bring to condign Punishment the Authors, Perpetrators, and Abettors of such traitorous Designs.

Given at Our Court at St. James's the Twenty-third Day of August, One thousand seven hundred and seventy-five, in the Fifteenth Year of Our Reign.

102. AMERICAN INDEPENDENCE

The Declaration of Independence of July 4, 1776, turned the Americans' rebellion into a war against their very status as colonists. Two powerful movements of political habit and ideas flowed together in this act of abjuration. One was the English tradition of parliamentary government; in this the representative assemblies in the colonial provinces played the role of Parliament at Westminster. The other was the Enlightenment, with its theories of popular sovereignty and the natural rights of man. The impact of the former tradition is reflected in the emphasis given by the Declaration to the iniquities of the British monarch and the softer criticism of Parliament; the list of abuses reminded Englishmen of the rights they claimed for themselves. The principles of the Enlightenment are embodied in the eloquent second paragraph, which employs phrases that have made it one of the most memorable brief statements of the democratic idea.

Declaration of Independence, July 4, 1776

In Congress, July 4, 1776

The unanimous Declaration of the thirteen united States of America

When in the Course of human events, it becomes necessary for one people to dissolve the political bands which have connected them with another, and to assume among the Powers of the earth, the separate and equal station to which the Laws of Nature and of Nature's God entitle them, a decent respect to the opinions of mankind requires that they should declare the causes which impel them to the separation.

We hold these truths to be self-evident, that all men are created equal, that they are endowed by their Creator with certain unalienable Rights, that among these are Life, Liberty and the pursuit of Happiness. That to secure these rights, Governments are instituted among Men, deriving their just powers from the consent of the governed, That whenever any Form of Government becomes destructive of these ends, it is the Right of the People to alter or to abolish it, and to institute new Government, laying its foundation on such principles and organizing its powers in such form, as to them shall seem most likely to effect their Safety and Happiness. Prudence, indeed, will dictate that Governments long established should not be changed for light and transient causes; and accordingly all experience hath shown, that mankind are more disposed to suffer, while evils are sufferable, than to right themselves by abolishing the forms to which they are accustomed. But when a long train of abuses and usurpations, pursuing invariably the same Object evinces a design to reduce them under absolute Despotism, it is their right, it is their duty, to throw off such Government, and to provide new Guards for their future security.—Such has been the patient sufferance of these Colonies; and such is now the necessity which constrains them to alter their former Systems of Government. The history of the present King of Great Brit-

---

Source: Ben. Perley Poore (ed.), *The Federal and State Constitutions, Colonial Charters, and Other Organic Laws of the United States,* Part I (Washington, D.C.: Government Printing Office, 1877), pp. 3–5.

ain is a history of repeated injuries and usurpations, all having in direct object the establishment of an absolute Tyranny over these States. To prove this, let Facts be submitted to a candid world.

He has refused his Assent to Laws, the most wholesome and necessary for the public good.

He has forbidden his Governors to pass Laws of immediate and pressing importance, unless suspended in their operation till his Assent should be obtained; and when so suspended, he has utterly neglected to attend to them.

He has refused to pass other Laws for the accommodation of large districts of people, unless those people would relinquish the right of Representation in the Legislature, a right inestimable to them and formidable to tyrants only.

He has called together legislative bodies at places unusual, uncomfortable, and distant from the depository of their Public Records, for the sole purpose of fatiguing them into compliance with his measures.

He has dissolved Representative Houses repeatedly, for opposing with manly firmness his invasions on the rights of the people.

He has refused for a long time, after such dissolutions, to cause others to be elected; whereby the Legislative Powers, incapable of Annihilation, have returned to the People at large for their exercise; the State remaining in the mean time exposed to all the dangers of invasion from without, and convulsions within.

He has endeavoured to prevent the population of these States; for that purpose obstructing the Laws for Naturalization of Foreigners; refusing to pass others to encourage their migration hither, and raising the conditions of new Appropriations of Lands.

He has obstructed the Administration of Justice, by refusing his Assent to Laws for establishing Judiciary Powers.

He has made Judges dependent on his Will alone, for the tenure of their offices, and the amount and payment of their salaries.

He has erected a multitude of New Offices, and sent hither swarms of Officers to harrass our People, and eat out their substance.

He has kept among us, in times of peace, Standing Armies without the Consent of our legislature.

He has affected to render the Military independent of and superior to the Civil Power.

He has combined with others to subject us to a jurisdiction foreign to our constitution, and unacknowledged by our laws; giving his Assent to their Acts of pretended Legislation:

For quartering large bodies of armed troops among us:

For protecting them, by a mock Trial, from Punishment for any Murders which they should commit on the Inhabitants of these States:

For cutting off our Trade with all parts of the world:

For imposing taxes on us without our Consent:

For depriving us in many cases, of the benefits of Trial by Jury:

For transporting us beyond Seas to be tried for pretended offences:

For abolishing the free System of English Laws in a neighbouring Province, establishing therein an Arbitrary government, and enlarging its Boundaries so as to render it at once an example and fit instrument for introducing the same absolute rule into these Colonies:

For taking away our Charters, abolishing our most valuable Laws, and altering fundamentally the Forms of our Governments:

For suspending our own Legislatures, and declaring themselves invested with Power to legislate for us in all cases whatsoever.

He has abdicated Government here, by declaring us out of his Protection and waging War against us.

He has plundered our seas, ravaged our Coasts, burnt our towns, and destroyed the lives of our people.

He is at this time transporting large armies of foreign mercenaries to compleat the works of death, desolation and tyranny, already begun with circumstances of Cruelty & perfidy scarcely paralleled in the most barbarous ages, and totally unworthy the Head of a civilized nation.

He has constrained our fellow Citizens taken Captive on the high Seas to bear Arms against their Country, to become the executioners of their friends and Brethren, or to fall themselves by their Hands.

He has excited domestic insurrections amongst us, and has endeavored to bring on the inhabitants of our frontiers, the merciless Indian Savages, whose known rule of warfare, is an undistinguished destruction of all ages, sexes and conditions.

In every stage of these Oppressions We have Petitioned for Redress in the most humble terms: Our repeated Petitions have been answered only by repeated injury. A Prince, whose character is thus marked by every act which may define a Tyrant, is unfit to be the ruler of a free People.

Nor have We been wanting in attention to our Brittish brethren. We have warned them from time to time of attempts by their legislature to extend an unwarrantable jurisdiction over us. We have reminded them of the circumstances of our emigration and settlement here. We have appealed to their native justice and magnanimity, and we have conjured them by the ties of our common kindred to disavow these usurpations, which, would inevitably interrupt our connections and correspondence. They too have been deaf to the voice of justice and of consanguinity. We must, therefore, acquiesce in the necessity, which denounces our Separation, and hold them, as we hold the rest of mankind, Enemies in War, in Peace Friends.

We, therefore, the Representatives of the united States of America, in

General Congress, Assembled, appealing to the Supreme Judge of the world for the rectitude of our intentions, do, in the Name, and by Authority of the good People of these Colonies, solemnly publish and declare, That these United Colonies are, and of Right ought to be Free and Independent States; that they are Absolved from all Allegiance to the British Crown, and that all political connection between them and the State of Great Britain, is and ought to be totally dissolved; and that as Free and Independent States, they have full Power to levy War, conclude Peace, contract Alliances, establish Commerce, and to do all other Acts and Things which Independent States may of right do. And for the support of this Declaration, with a firm reliance on the Protection of Divine Providence, we mutually pledge to each other our Lives, our Fortunes and our sacred Honor.

103. AN AGRARIAN PARADISE

The American War of Independence was in one sense a rebellion against mercantilism. The author of the Declaration of Independence, Thomas Jefferson (1743-1826), who was perhaps the American thinker most deeply imbued with the ideas of the Enlightenment, went beyond the narrow question of colonial interests versus the advantages of the mother country to the broad issue of the kind of land the new free nation ought to be. His ideal of a rural republic, free of the cankers of industry and urban life, was expressed in his "query" on "manufactures" in his *Notes on the State of Virginia* (1784).

Thomas Jefferson

Notes on the State of Virginia

Query XIX—Manufactures

The present state of manufactures, commerce, interior and exterior trade?

. . . . .

The political æconomists of Europe have established it as a principle that every state should endeavour to manufacture for itself: and this principle, like many others, we transfer to America, without calculating

---

Source: Thomas Jefferson, *Notes on the State of Virginia,* edited by William Peden (Chapel Hill: University of North Carolina Press, 1955), pp. 164–65. Reprinted by permission of the University of North Carolina.

the difference of circumstance which should often produce a difference of result. In Europe the lands are either cultivated, or locked up against the cultivator. Manufacture must therefore be resorted to of necessity not of choice, to support the surplus of their people. But we have an immensity of land courting the industry of the husbandman. Is it best then that all our citizens should be employed in its improvement, or that one half should be called off from that to exercise manufactures and handicraft arts for the other? Those who labour in the earth are the chosen people of God, if ever he had a chosen people, whose breasts he has made his peculiar deposit for substantial and genuine virtue. It is the focus in which he keeps alive that sacred fire, which otherwise might escape from the face of the earth. Corruption of morals in the mass of cultivators is a phenomenon of which no age or nation has furnished an example. It is the mark set on those, who not looking up to heaven, to their own soil and industry, as does the husbandman, for their subsistance, depend for it on the casualties and caprice of customers. Dependance begets subservience and venality, suffocates the germ of virtue, and prepares fit tools for the designs of ambition. This, the natural progress and consequence of the arts, has sometimes perhaps been retarded by accidental circumstances: but, generally speaking, the proportion which the aggregate of the other classes of citizens bears in any state to that of its husbandmen, is the proportion of its unsound to its healthy parts, and is a good-enough barometer whereby to measure its degree of corruption. While we have land to labour then, let us never wish to see our citizens occupied at a work-bench, or twirling a distaff. Carpenters, masons, smiths, are wanting in husbandry: but, for the general operations of manufacture, let our work-shops remain in Europe. It is better to carry provisions and materials to workmen there, than bring them to the provisions and materials, and with them their manners and principles. The loss by the transportation of commodities across the Atlantic will be made up in happiness and permanence of government. The mobs of great cities add just so much to the support of pure government, as sores do to the strength of the human body. It is the manners and spirit of a people which preserve a republic in vigour. A degeneracy in these is a canker which soon eats to the heart of its laws and constitution.

CHAPTER XI

THE BEGINNINGS OF ECONOMIC MODERNIZATION

THE FUNDAMENTALS of modernization of economic life were undertaken in the 18th century. Although transformations in agriculture and business as well as in industry were involved, it is customary to refer to the whole process, or to its central aspect, as the Industrial Revolution. Looked at over the scale of many centuries, the term "revolution" remains apt in indicating a relative rapidity of change, but within the framework of individual lives the economic events of the latter part of the early modern period moved at a slow pace. In any case, the development of industrial processes in which the basic mode of production was by machines in factories was dependent upon simultaneous changes in agriculture and commerce.

During the 18th century, the innovations of Low Countries farmers which broke through the constraints of the old agriculture began to be adopted elsewhere, notably in England. At the same time, foodstuffs from overseas, although at first only such semiluxuries as sugar, began to be available. Thus the possibility that agriculture could require the labors of a smaller share of the population, releasing the majority to work in other sectors of the economy, became evident.

104. PEASANT ENSERFMENT IN RUSSIA

In most of western and some of central Europe during the early modern era, serfdom as a system of binding peasants to the land and to their masters ceased to exist as an effective system in practice, even when legal vestiges remained on the law books. Manorial dues became more of an obligation upon the peasant's land than upon the peasant himself. However, at this same time in eastern European countries such as Prussia, Poland, and Russia, serfdom, which had been relatively light or even nonexistent in the medieval period, was rigidly clamped upon the peasantry. This is illustrated by the provisions of Chapter XI of the Russian Code of Laws of 1649, which concerned the peasantry. The following three articles from the Code illustrate the spirit of the chapter, which contained 34 items.

The Law on the Peasants, 1649

1. Any peasants of the Sovereign and labourers of the crown villages and black volosts who have fled from the Sovereign's crown villages and from the black volosts and live on the land of the Patriarch, metropolitans, archbishops, bishops or the monasteries or the boyars, chamberlains and the men of the Council or the chamber and the sewers, bearers of insignia and the Moscow gentlemen and the clerks and the attendants, town gentlemen and the junior boyars and the foreigners and any lords holding an estate by inheritance or service and [those peasants and labourers] are in the inquisition registers which the officers in the Service Tenure Department submitted to other Departments after the Moscow fire of the past year, 134, [1] those fugitive peasants, or their fathers, who are recorded as the Sovereign's, and those fugitive peasants and labourers of the Sovereign, being sought out, are to be brought to the crown villages of the Sovereign and to the black volosts to their old lots according to the registers of inquisition with wives and children and with all their peasant property without term of years.

2. Also should there be any lords holding an estate by inheritance or service who start to petition the Sovereign about their fugitive peasants and labourers and say that their peasants and labourers who have fled from them live in the crown villages of the Sovereign and in black volosts

---

SOURCE: R. E. F. Smith, *The Enserfment of the Russian Peasantry* (Cambridge, England: Cambridge University Press, 1968), pp. 141–42, 144–45. Reprinted by permission of Cambridge University Press.

[1] The fire of 1626 destroyed many documents in the archives of the Departments in Moscow [note of editor Smith].

or among the artisans in the artisan quarters of towns or among the musketeers, cossacks or among the gunners, or among any other serving men in the towns beyond Moscow or in the Ukraine or on the land of the Patriarch, metropolitans, archbishops and bishops or the monasteries or the boyars, chamberlains and the men of the Council and the chamber and the sewers, bearers of insignia, the Moscow gentlemen and the clerks and the attendants, town gentlemen and the junior boyars and the foreigners and any lords holding an estate by inheritance or service, then those peasants and labourers in accordance with law and the [right of] search are to be handed over according to the inquisition registers which the officers handed in to the Service Tenure Department after the Moscow fire of the past year, 134, if those, their fugitive peasants, are entered under them in those registers, or if after these inquisitions these same peasants or their children were entered in accordance with new grants to anyone in registers of allotment or withdrawal. And fugitive peasants and labourers are to be handed over from flight according to the registers to men of every rank without term of years.

. . . . .

9. But if any peasants and labourers recorded [as living] under anyone in the enumeration registers of the past years, 154 and 155,[2] after those enumerations ran away, or henceforward begin to run away, from those people under whom they were recorded in the registers, those runaway peasants and labourers and their brethren and children and nephews and grandchildren with their wives and children and with all their property, with their grain, standing and threshed, are to be handed over from flight to those people from whom they ran away, according to the enumeration registers, without term of years, and henceforward no one is by any means to accept the peasants of others or to hold them.

105. A SOLDIER AND THE POOR

One of the most eloquent defenses of the poor during the early modern era came from one of its greatest soldiers. Sébastien Le Prestre, Marquis de Vauban (1633-1707), was a military engineer, a master of fortress construction and siegecraft. In recognition of his achievements, Louis XIV made him a marshal of France, a rank until then always limited to field commanders. Vauban was more than a soldier, however. Especially in his later years, he was concerned with economic matters, and in his *Project for a Royal Tithe* (1706) he made a proposal that confounded and angered the government he

[2] 1645/6 and 1646/7.

had served so long. Put one tax—the king's tithe or tenth—in place of the whole snarled system of taxation in France, he urged, and treat the working people of countryside and town, not officeholders and men of idle wealth, as the true human resources of the country. Despite his immense reputation, his book was banned and confiscated.

Sébastien Le Prestre de Vauban

Project for a Royal Tithe

. . . . .

Throughout the investigations which I have been able to do in the several years that I have devoted to them, I have observed very clearly that in the very recent period almost one tenth of the people has been reduced to beggary and is engaged in begging; of the other nine tenths, there are five who are not in a position to give alms to the former because they themselves are reduced to very nearly the same condition; of the four others which remain, three are in difficulties and burdened with debts and lawsuits; and the last tenth, among which I include all military men, ecclesiastical and secular judges, the whole upper nobility, the nobility of distinction, and the military and civilian officeholders, wealthier merchants and rich townsmen living on incomes, does not number a hundred thousand families. I do not think I would be lying if I said that there are not ten thousand families, small or big, which can be said to be in absolutely easy circumstances; and if you were to remove the financiers and their open and concealed allies and adherents, those who are supported by the king's bounty, a few merchants, etc., I am certain that there would not be many left.

. . . . .

Furthermore, it is the little people who enrich the king and his whole kingdom by their labor and their trade. It is they who contribute all the soldiers and sailors for his army and many of the officers, all merchants and the lower judiciary. It is they who perform the work of the various trades and crafts. It is they who do all the trading and manufacturing of this kingdom, who furnish all the farmers, farmhands and vinegrowers, who keep and feed the cattle, who sow and reap the grain, who dress the vines and make the wine. In a few words, it is they who do the heavy work and the vile work in the countryside and the towns.

SOURCE: Eugène Daire (ed.), *Économistes financiers du XVIIIe siècle: Vauban, Project d'une dîme royale* . . . (Paris: Guillaumin, 1843), pp. 34–35, 46–47. Translated by Herbert H. Rowen.

This is what they really are, the part of the people of whom I speak, who have suffered so much and suffer so greatly at the very time that I write. We may hope that the introduction of the Royal Tithe could put all this right in less than fifteen years and restore the kingdom to a full abundance of men and wealth. For when the people will be less oppressed, they will be readier to marry, they will dress and eat better, their children will be more robust and better educated; they will take better care of their affairs. Finally they will work with more strength and courage when they see that the greatest part of what they earn will not be taken from them.

It is obvious that the greatness of kings is measured by the number of their subjects. This is what constitutes their wealth, their happiness, their riches, their strength, their good fortune, and all the esteem which they possess in the world. One could do nothing better, therefore, for their advantage and their glory, than to remind them frequently of this maxim; for, since it is what constitutes their happiness, they cannot give too much attention to the preservation and increase of the people, who should be so dear to them.

I realized long ago that this preface was becoming too long. Yet I cannot decide to bring it to an end until I have stated what I think about the limits which may be placed on the Royal Tithe, which I believe has been sufficiently studied so that I can say what I feel about it.

It has seemed to me, therefore, that we should not go above the Tenth or below the Twentieth [10 and 5 percent]; in the former case, the burden would be too great, and in the latter, not enough revenue would be produced to meet current expenses.

One can work between these two extremes according to what the state needs, and never otherwise, for it is obvious that the more is taken from the people, the more money is drawn out of trade, and that the best employed money in the kingdom is that which remains in the hands of merchants, where it is never useless or idle.

106. THE GROWING AND WEAVING OF WOOL

The principal industry of England, as well as the most important segment of agriculture after the production of grain, was the wool trade and the woolgrowing upon which it rested. These are described in an English state document of 1615 entitled "Reasons to Prove the Convenience of Buying and Selling of Wool," extracts from which appear below.

Classification of Woolgrowers and Clothiers, 1615

The breeders of woolle in all countries are of three sorts.

1. First those that are men of great estate, having both grounds and stocke of their own and are beforehand in welth. Theis [These] cann afford to delay the selling of their woolls and to stay the clothiers leesure for the payment to increase the price. The number of theis is small.

2. Those that doe rent the King's noblemen's and gent[lemen]'s grounds and deale as largely as either their stocke or creditt will afford. Theis are many and breed great store of wooll; most of them doe usually either sell their woolls beforehand, or promise the refusal of them for money which they borrow att the spring of the yeare to buy them sheep to breed the woole, they then having need of money to pay their Lady-day rent and to dubble their stocke upon the grounde as the spring time requireth, and at that tyme the Clothiers disburse their stocke in yarns to lay up in store against hay time and harvest when their spyning fails. Soe that theis farmers and the clothiers have greatest want of money at one time.

3. The generall number of husbandmen in all the woolle countries that have smale livings, whereof every one usually hath some woolle though not much. Theis are many in number in all Countries and have great store of woolle though in smalle parcells. Many of theis also doe borrow money of the wooll merchant to buye sheep to stocke their comons. Their parcells being so small, the tymes of selling soe divers, the distance of place so great between the Clothier and them, it would be their undoing to stay the clothiers leisure for the tyme of their sale or to be subject to him for the price. . . .

Theis woolls are usually converted by fower sorts of people.

1. The riche clothier that buyeth his woolls of the grower in the woolle countries, and makes his whole years provision beforehand, and layes it up in stowre, and in the winter tyme hath it spunne by his owne spinsters and woven by his owne weavers and fulled by his owne tuckers, and all at the lowest rate for wages. Theis clothiers could well spare the woolle buyers that they might likewise have woolle at their owne prizes and the rather because many of them be Brogging clothiers and sell againe very much if not the most of the woolle they buye.

2. The second is the meaner clothier that seldome or never travells into the woolle country to buy his woolle, but borrowes the most parte of it att the markett, and setts many poore on worke, clothes it presently, and

---

Source: George Unwin, *Industrial Organization in the Sixteenth and Seventeenth Centuries* (Oxford; England: Clarendon Press, 1904), pp. 234–36.

sells his cloath in some countries upon the bare thred as in Devonshire and Yorkshire, and others dresse it and sell it in London for ready money, and then comes to the woolle market and payes th' old debte and borrowes more. Of this sort there are great store, that live well and growe riche and sett thousands on woorke; they cannot misse the woolle chapman, for if they doe they must presently put off all their worke folks and become servants to the riche clothier for 4*d.* or 6*d.* a daye which is a poore living.

The third sorte are such clothiers that have not stocke enough to bestowe, some in woolle and some in yarne, and to forbeare some in cloth as the rich clothiers doe, and they buy butt little or no woolle but doe weekely buy their yarn in the marketts, and presently make it into cloth and sell it for ready money and so buy yarn again, which yarn is weekly brought into the markett by a great number of poore people that will not spin to the clothier for smale wages; but have stock enough to sett themselves on woorke and doe weekly buy their woolle in the market by very small parcells according to their use and weekely returne it in yarne, and make good proffit thereof, having the benefit both of their labour and of the merchandise, and live exceeding well. Theis yarnmakers are soe many in number that it is supposed by men of judgement that more than half the cloathes that is made in Wilts, Gloucester and Somersettshire is made by the means of theis yarn makers and poore clothiers that depend weekely upon the woolle chapmen which serves them weekely with woolles either for money or credit.

4. The fourth sorte is of them of the new drapery which are thousands of poore people inhabiting neare the ports and costs from Yarmouth to Plymouth and in many great cities and townes, as London, Norwich, Colchester, Canterbury, South[ton] [Southampton], Exter, and many others. These people by theire great industry and skill doe spend a great parte of the course woolls growing in the kingdom, and that att as high a price or higher than the clothiers doe the finest woolls of this countrye as appeareth by a particular hereunto annexed.

107. THE OLDEN WAY OF MAKING IRON

The following description of the method of producing iron in England before the innovations of the 18th century is taken from Robert Plot, *Natural History of Staffordshire* (1686). It is important because it shows how far machinery had been introduced into the productive process and how dependent the whole process was upon the supply of charcoal at the end of the 17th century. The incipient exhaustion of the forests, which provided the wood that was made into charcoal, provided much of the impetus for finding a way to make iron with fossil coal (the "sea-cole" of this account) in the years that followed.

Robert Plot

Natural History of Staffordshire

An Account of the Method of Producing Iron at the End of the Seventeenth Century

When they have gotten their *Ore* before 'tis fit for the *furnace,* they burn or calcine it upon the open ground, with small charcoal, wood, or sea-cole, to make it break into small pieces, which will be done in 3 days, and this they call *annealing* it, or fiting it for the furnace. In the mean while they also heat their *furnace* for a weeks time with charcoal without blowing it, which they call *seasoning* it, and then they bring the *Ore* to the *furnace* thus prepared, and throw it in with the charcole in baskets *vicissim i.e.*, a basket of *Ore,* and then a basket of coal S.SS. where by two vast pair of *bellows* placed behind the *furnace,* and compress'd alternatly by a large wheel turned by water, the fire is made so intense, that after 3 days time the metall will begin to run, still after increasing, till at length in fourteenights time they can run a *Sow* and *piggs* once in 12 hours, which they do in a bed of sand before the mouth of the *furnace,* wherein they make one larger furrow than the rest, next the *Timp* (where the metall comes forth) which is for the *Sow,* from whence they draw two or three and twenty others (like the *labells* of a *file* in *Heraldry*) for the *piggs,* all which too they make greater or lesser according to the quantity of their Metall: into these when their *Receivers* are full they let it forth, which is made so very fluid by the violence of the fire, that it not only runs to the utmost distance of the *furrows* but stands boiling in them for a considerable time: before it is cold, that is when it begins to blacken at top, and the *red* to goe off, they break the *Sow* and the *pigs* off from one another, and the *sow* into the same length with the pigs, though in the running it is longer and bigger much, which is now done wtith ease; whereas if

---

Source: Thomas Southcliffe Ashton, *Iron and Steel in the Industrial Revolution* (Manchester, England: Manchester University Press, 1951), pp. 233–34. Reprinted by permission of Manchester University Press.

let alone till they are quite cold, they will either not break at all, or not without difficulty. . . .

From the *Furnaces*, they bring their *Sows* and *pigs* of *Iron* when broken asunder, and into lengths, to the *Forges;* which are of two sorts, but commonly (as at *Cunsall*) standing together under the same roof; one whereof they call the *Finery*, the other the *Chafery:* they are both of them *open hearths*, upon which they place great heaps of *coal* [*i.e.*, charcoal], which are blown by bellows like to those of the *Furnaces*, and compressed the same way, but nothing near so large. In these two *forges* they give the *Sow* and *piggs* 5 several *heats*, before they are perfectly wrought into *barrs*. First in the *Finery* they are melted down as thin as lead, where the *Metall* in an hour thickens by degrees into a lump or mass, which they call a *loop*, this they bring to the great *Hammer* raised by the motion of a *waterwheel*, and first beat it into a thick square, which they call a *half bloom*. Then [secondly] they put it into the Finery again for an hour, and then bring it again to the same *Hammer*, where they work it into a *bloom*, which is a square barr in the middle, and two square knobs at the ends, one much less then the other, the smaller being call'd the *Ancony* end, and the greater the *Mocket head*. And this is all they doe at the *Finery*. Then 3 the *Ancony end* is brought to the *Chafery*, where after it has been heated for a quarter of an hour, it is also brought to the *Hammer*, and there beat quite out to a *bar*, first at that end; and after that, the *Mocket head* is brought also 4. to the *chafery*, which being *thick*, requires two *heats*, before it can be wrought under the *Hammer* into bars of such shapes and sizes as they think fittest for *Sale*.

Whereof, those they intend to be cut into *rodds*, are carryed to the *slitting Mills*, where they first break or cut them cold with the force of one of the *Wheels* into short lengths; then they are put into a *furnace* to be heated red hot to a good height, and then brought singly to the *Rollers*, by which they are drawn even, and to a greater length: after this another *Workman* takes them whilst hot and puts them through the *Cutters*, which are of divers sizes, and may be put on and off, according to pleasure: then another lays them straight also whilst hot, and when cold binds them into faggots, and then they are fitting for sale. . . .

Thus I say the *Iron-works* are exercised in their *perfection*, and all their principal *Iron* undergoes all the forementiou'd preparations; not but that for several purposes, as for the *backs* of *Chimneys, Garden-rolls*, and such like; they use a sort of *cast-Iron* which they take out of the *Receivers* of the *Furnaces*, as soon as it is melted, in great *Ladles*, and pour it into *moulds* of fine sand, in like manner as they cast the other softer *Metalls*. Thus the ingenious *Will. Chetwynd* of *Rugeley*, Esq; at *Madeley* furnace, cast. *Iron-Rolls* for gardens, hollow like the *Mills* for *Sugar Canes*, of 5, 6, 7 or 800 weight a piece. . . . For such purposes as these, this serves well enough, but for others it will not, for it is so brittle, that being heated, with one blow of a hammer it will break all to pieces.

108. PHYSIOCRACY AND FREE TRADE

During the later 18th century the doctrines of mercantilism came under attack in France and Great Britain. In each case the criticism reflected the particular characteristics of the nation's economic and political life. In France the critics of mercantilism, who gave their principles the name of "Physiocracy" (the rule of nature), were government administrators and their friends. Their emphasis was upon the needs of agriculture, specifically the need to encourage its modernization so that it could be transformed from a form of production whose chief aim was subsistence to a commercialized system in which it was considered a business primarily concerned with production for the market.

As this meant the abolition of the complex manorial system, whch continued under a much modified form of collaborative tillage combined with a medley of duties and rights, the physiocratic program naturally met with fierce resistance from most farmers. Furthermore, the removal of restrictions on the transport of grain within the country endangered the bread supply, especially in times of shortage. Thus the attempt of Anne Robert Jacques Turgot to act upon this basis during his brief period as finance minister (1774–76) by issuing an edict for free trade in corn led to bread riots. Physiocracy was closely linked to the Enlightenment program of reforms that sought to increase individual freedom through governmental action against privileged groups.

Turgot's friend François Quesnay (1694-1774) advocated free trade in his article on "Grain" or "Corn" (*blé* in French means cereal grains in general, not just wheat) in the *Encyclopedia* of Diderot and D'Alembert, parts of which are given below. A physician by training, Quesnay rose to be the personal doctor of Louis XIV.

François Quesnay

On Grain

X. *The advantages of external trade do not consist in the increase of monetary wealth.* The surplus of wealth procured by a nation's external trade may

---

SOURCE: Ronald L. Meek, *The Economics of Physiocracy: Essays and Translations* (Cambridge, Mass.: Harvard University Press, 1963), pp. 77–81. By permission of Harvard University Press and George Allen & Unwin Ltd., London.

not take the form of a surplus of monetary wealth, because external trade with foreign countries may be conducted on the basis of an exchange for other commodities which are consumed by the nation in question. But what this nation comes into possession of is none the less wealth, which it could by means of thrift convert into monetary wealth for other uses.

Raw produce, moreover, considered as a commodity, is at the same time both monetary wealth and real wealth. A husbandman who sells his corn to a merchant is paid in money. With this money he pays the proprietor, the *taille*, and his servants and workmen, and buys the commodities which he needs. The merchant who sells the corn to a foreign country, and buys another commodity from it, or who trades with it on a barter basis, resells on his return the commodity he has brought back and with the money he receives once again buys corn. Thus corn, considered as a commodity, represents monetary wealth for the sellers and real wealth for the buyers.

Thus saleable produce ought always to be regarded by a state equally as monetary wealth and as real wealth, which subjects may make use of as it suits them.

A nation's wealth is not regulated by the amount of monetary wealth. Monetary wealth can increase or diminish without anyone noticing it, for it is always available in a state, by reason of its quantity or its velocity of circulation, in proportion to the abundance and the value of raw produce. Spain, which owns the treasure of Peru, is always impoverished by its needs. England maintains its opulence by means of its real wealth; the paper which represents money in that country has a value which is assured by trade and by the revenue of the nation's property.

Thus it is not the greater or lesser quantity of monetary wealth which determines the wealth of a state; and the prohibition of the export of money from a kingdom, to the detriment of profitable trade, can only be based on some harmful prejudice or other.

What is necessary for the maintenance of a state is true wealth, i.e. wealth which is always renascent, always sought after and always paid for, in order that it may have the enjoyment of it, procure itself conveniences, and satisfy the needs of life.

XI. *The state of the balance of trade between different nations does not enable us to ascertain the advantages of trade for each nation and the state of its wealth.* For some nations may be richer in men and in landed property than others; and the latter may have a smaller internal trade, a smaller consumption, and a greater external trade than the former.

Moreover, some nations may have a greater re-export trade than others. The trade which returns them the purchase price of the commodities which they resell constitutes a larger item in their balance, but this trade is not as advantageously based as that of other nations which have a smaller trade but which export their own products.

Trade in manufactured commodities is also deceptive because in the value of the product the value of the raw materials is confused with the value of the labour of manufacture, whereas it ought to be distinguished from it.

XII. *It is by the internal and external trade of a nation, and above all by the state of its internal trade, that its wealth may be judged.* For if it consumes a large quantity of its produce at high prices, its wealth will be proportionate to the abundance and price of the produce it consumes, because this produce in fact constitutes wealth in proportion to its abundance and expensiveness; and by reason of the fact that it can be sold, it can be put to any other use in case of special need. It is sufficient if there is a basis of real wealth.

XIII. *No nation which draws the best possible product from its land, its men, and its navigation ought ever to be envious of the trade of its neighbours.* For it could not with evil intent do anything to encroach upon its neighbours' trade without thereby disorganizing and injuring itself, particularly with respect to the mutual trade which it has established with them.

Thus trading nations which are rivals or even enemies ought to pay more attention to maintaining or if possible extending their own trade, than to trying to do direct damage to that of others. They ought even to favour it, because the mutual trade of nations is reciprocally maintained by the wealth of the buyers and the sellers.

XIV. *In mutual trade, the nations which sell the most necessary or most useful commodities have an advantage over those which sell luxury goods.* A nation whose landed property ensures for it a trade in raw produce, and also, as a consequence, an internal trade in manufactured commodities, is independent of other nations. It trades with the latter only for the purpose of maintaining, facilitating, and extending its external trade; and in order to preserve its independence and its advantage in mutual trade it ought as far as possible to obtain from other nations only luxury goods, and to sell to them commodities necessary to satisfy the needs of life.

The other nations will believe that because of the real value of these different commodities this mutual trade is more advantageous to them. But the advantage always lies with the nation which sells the most useful and necessary commodities.

For then its trade is based on the needs of the others; it sells to them only its surplus, and the burden of its purchases is borne only by its opulence. Their interest in selling to it is greater than its need to buy from them; and it is easier for it to cut down on luxuries than it is for the others to economize on necessities.

It should also be noted that states which devote themselves to the manufacture of luxury goods experience serious vicissitudes. For when times are bad, trade in luxury goods slackens, and the workers find themselves without bread and without work.

Given free trade, France could bring forth an abundance of produce of primary necessity, which would be sufficient both for a large consumption and a large external trade, and which could maintain in the kingdom a large trade in manufactured goods.

But the state of her population does not permit her to employ a large number of men in making luxury goods; and it would even be in her interests, for the sake of facilitating external trade in her raw produce, to maintain mutual trade with foreign countries on the basis of the purchase of luxury goods.

Moreover, she ought not to aspire to an all-embracing general trade. She ought to sacrifice certain of the less important branches of trade in favour of other branches which are more profitable to her and which would increase and assure the revenue of the kingdom's landed property.

Nevertheless all trade ought to be free, because it is in the interests of the merchants to devote themselves to those branches of external trade which are the safest and most profitable.

It is enough for the government to watch over the expansion of the revenue of the kingdom's property; not to put any obstacles in the way of industry; and to give the people the opportunity to spend as they choose;

To revive agriculture by means of vigorous trading activity in those provinces where produce has become valueless;

To do away with prohibitions and hindrances which are detrimental to internal trade and mutual external trade;

To abolish or reduce the excessive rights to charge river dues and tolls, which swallow up the revenues of those remote provinces in which produce can only be sold if it is transported over long distances; those to whom these rights belong will be adequately compensated by their share in the general increase in the revenue of the kingdom's property.

It is no less necessary to do away with the privileges which provinces, towns, and townships have contrived to secure for their own private advantage.

It is also important to facilitate everywhere communications and the transport of commodities, by putting roads and river navigation in order.[1]

[1] Country roads and roads communicating with the main highways, the towns, and the markets, are either lacking or in poor condition almost everywhere in the provinces, and this is a serious obstacle to trading operations. Yet it seems that this could be remedied in a few years. The proprietors are too interested in the sale of the produce which is grown on their land to be unwilling to contribute to the expense of repairing these roads. A small

It is also essential that trade in the produce of the provinces should not be subjected to temporary and arbitrary prohibitions and licences, which ruin the countryside under the delusive pretext of assuring abundance for the towns. The towns subsist through the expenditure of the proprietors who live in them; thus, by destroying the revenue of landed property, this practice brings no advantage to the towns and no good to to the state.

The power to control the nation's revenue should not be left to the mercy of subordinate or private bodies.

The export of *corn* by individual provinces should never be restricted on the grounds that their supplies become exhausted before the other provinces are able to replenish them, so that the inhabitants may for several months be subjected to a scarcity of food which is correctly attributed to the exportation.

For when freedom of export is general, the amount of *corn* sent away is hardly noticeable, since the merchants draw on all parts of the kingdom and above all on the provinces where *corn* is at a low price.

Then there are no longer any provinces where produce may become valueless. Agriculture revives everywhere in proportion to sales.

The progress of trade goes hand in hand with that of agriculture; and exportation never takes away more than a surplus which would not come into existence in its absence, and which always maintains abundance and increases the kingdom's revenue.

This increase in revenue expands population and consumption, because expenditure increases and provides gains which attract men.

In this way a kingdom can in a short time progress to a high degree of power and prosperity. Thus by very simple means a sovereign can win victories within his own state which are much more advantageous than those which he could win over his neighbours. Progress is rapid; under Henry IV the impoverished kingdom, burdened with debts, soon became a country of abundance and wealth.

---

tax could therefore be levied on them, assessed at the rate of one sou per livre of the *taille* of their farmers, a tax from which farmers and peasants who had no property would be exempt. The roads to be repaired would be decided upon by the intendants of each district, after consultation with the inhabitants, who would then have the work carried out by entrepreneurs. The most impassable places would be repaired first, and the roads would be successively improved; the farmers and peasants would then be made responsible for their maintenance. Similar arrangements could be made with the provinces in respect of those rivers which could be made navigable. Some provinces have been so fully seized with the utility of such works that they have themselves asked for authority to spend money on them. But the needs of the state have sometimes deprived them of funds earmarked for this purpose; and this lack of success has nipped in the bud arrangements which would have been very conducive to the well-being of the state [note by Quesnay].

109. MERCANTILISM AS ECONOMIC FOLLY

The system of favoring domestic industry and commerce over foreign competitors by means of high tariff walls or outright exclusions came under criticism by economic thinkers whose field of vision encompassed not just the national but the world economy. Of these the most systematic and the most influential was the Scotsman Adam Smith (1723-1790). He taught moral philosophy at the University of Glasgow; traveled to France and Geneva, where he met many of the leading Enlightenment thinkers; and returned home to work on his great study of the economic system of his time, *An Inquiry into the Nature and Causes of the Wealth of Nations,* which was published in 1776. Some of its key ideas had already been put forward by David Hume and others were similar to the analysis of the mercantile system already made by the Physiocrats, but *The Wealth of Nations,* by its careful study of economic practices and principles, became the work on which all modern economic theory was ultimately founded.

Smith argued for the removal of government controls over the economic initiative of individuals except in rare cases of national necessity, such as support of the supply of merchant seamen. He also analyzed industrial production upon the basis of division of labor, although he did not take into account the transformation of industry by machinery that was then beginning, and saw freedom of enterprise as leading to the general good. Some key sections of *The Wealth of Nations* are reproduced here.

Adam Smith

The Wealth of Nations

OF THE DIVISION OF LABOR

The greatest improvement in the productive powers of labour, and the greater part of the skill, dexterity, and judgment with which it is anywhere directed or applied, seem to have been the effect of the division of labour.

SOURCE: Adam Smith, *An Inquiry into the Nature and Causes of the Wealth of Nations,* edited by James E. Thorold Rogers, 2d ed. (Oxford, England: Clarendon Press, 1880), Vol. I, pp. 5–7, 9–11, 25–26, 28–31.

The effects of the division of labour, in the general business of society, will be more easily understood by considering in what manner it operates in some particular manufactures. It is commonly supposed to be carried furthest in some very trifling ones; not perhaps that it really is carried further in them than in others of more importance: but in those trifling manufactures which are destined to supply the small wants of but a small number of people, the whole number of workmen must necessarily be small; and those employed in every different branch of the work can often be collected into the same workhouse, and placed at once under the view of the spectator. In those great manufactures, on the contrary, which are destined to supply the great wants of the great body of the people, every different branch of the work employs so great a number of workmen, that it is impossible to collect them all into the same workhouse. We can seldom see more, at one time, than those employed in one single branch. Though in such manufactures, therefore, the work may really be divided into a much greater number of parts than in those of a more trifling nature, the division is not near so obvious, and has accordingly been much less observed.

To take an example, therefore, from a very trifling manufacture, but one in which the division of labour has been very often taken notice of, the trade of the pin-maker; a workman not educated to this business (which the division of labour has rendered a distinct trade), nor acquainted with the use of the machinery employed in it (to the invention of which the same division of labour has probably given occasion), could scarce, perhaps, with his utmost industry, make one pin in a day, and certainly could not make twenty. But in the way in which this business is now carried on, not only the whole work is a peculiar trade, but it is divided into a number of branches, of which the greater part are likewise peculiar trades. One man draws out the wire, another straights it, a third cuts it, a fourth points it, a fifth grinds it at the top for receiving the head; to make the head requires two or three distinct operations; to put it on is a peculiar business, to whiten the pins is another; it is even a trade by itself to put them into the paper; and the important business of making a pin is, in this manner, divided into about eighteen distinct operations, which in some manufactories are all performed by distinct hands, though in others the same man will sometimes perform two or three of them. I have seen a small manufactory of this kind where ten men only were employed, and where some of them consequently performed two or three distinct operations. But though they were very poor, and therefore but indifferently accommodated with the necessary machinery, they could, when they exerted themselves, make among them about twelve pounds of pins in a day. There are in a pound upwards of four thousand pins of a middling size. Those ten persons, therefore, could make among them upwards of forty-eight thousand pins in a day. Each person, therefore, making a tenth part of forty-eight thousand pins, might be considered as making four thousand eight hundred pins in a day. But if they had all wrought separately and independently, and without any of them having been educated to this peculiar business, they certainly could not each of them have made twenty, perhaps not one pin in a day; that is, certainly, not the two hundred and fortieth, perhaps not the four thousand eight hundredth part of what they are at present capable of performing, in consequence of a proper division and combination of their different operations.

In every other art and manufacture, the effects of the division of labour are similar to what they are in this very trifling one; though in many of them, the labour can neither be so much subdivided, nor reduced to so great a simplicity of operation. The division of labour, however, so far as it it can be introduced, occasions, in every art, a proportionable increase of the productive powers of labour. . . .

. . . . .

This great increase of the quantity of work, which, in consequence of the division of labour, the same number of people are capable of performing, is owing to three different circumstances: first, to the increase of dexterity in every particular workman; secondly, to the saving of the time which is commonly lost in passing from one species of work to another; and lastly, to the invention of a great number of machines which facilitate and abridge labour, and enable one man to do the work of many.

First, the improvement of the dexterity of the workman necessarily increases the quantity of the work he can perform; and the division of labour, by reducing every man's business to some one simple operation, and by making this operation the sole employment of his life, necessarily increases very much the dexterity of the workman. A common smith, who, though accustomed to handle the hammer, has never been used to make nails, if upon some particular occasion he is obliged to attempt it, will scarce, I am assured, be able to make above two or three hundred nails in a day, and those too very bad ones. A smith who has been accustomed to make nails, but whose sole or principal business has not been that of a nailer, can seldom with his utmost diligence make more than eight hundred or a thousand nails in a day. I have seen several boys under twenty years of age who had never exercised any other trade but that of making nails, and who, when they exerted themselves, could make, each of them, upwards of two thousand three hundred nails in a day. The making of a nail, however, is by no means one of the simplest operations. The same person blows the bellows, stirs or mends the fire as there is occasion, heats the iron, and forges every part of the nail: in forging the head too he is obliged to change his tools. The different operations into which the making of a pin, or of a metal button, is subdivided, are all of them much more simple, and the dexterity of the person, of whose life it has been the sole business to perform them, is usually much greater. The rapidity with which some of the operations of those manufactures are performed, exceeds what the human hand could, by those who had never seen them, be supposed capable of acquiring.

Secondly, the advantage which is gained by saving the time commonly lost in passing from one sort of work to another, is much greater than we should at first view be apt to imagine it. It is impossible to pass very quickly from one kind of work to another, that is carried on in a different place, and with quite different tools. A country weaver, who cultivates a small farm, must lose a good deal of time in passing from his loom to the field, and from the field to his loom. When the two trades can be carried on in the same workhouse, the loss of time is no doubt much less. It is even in this case, however, very considerable. A man commonly saunters a little in turning his hand from one sort of employment to another. When he first begins the new work he is seldom very keen and hearty; his mind, as they say, does not go to it, and for some time he rather trifles than applies to good purpose. The habit of sauntering and of indolent careless application, which is naturally, or rather necessarily, acquired by every country workman who is obliged to change his work and his tools every half hour, and to apply his hand in twenty different ways almost every day of his life, renders him almost always slothful and lazy, and incapable of any vigorous application even on the most pressing occasions. Independent, therefore, of his deficiency in point of dexterity, this cause alone must always reduce considerably the quantity of work which he is capable of performing.

Thirdly, and lastly, everybody must be sensible how much labour is facilitated and abridged by the application of proper machinery. It is unnecessary to give any example. I shall only observe, therefore, that the invention of all those machines by which labour is so much facilitated and abridged, seems to have been originally owing to the division of labour. Men are much more likely to discover easier and readier methods of attaining any object, when the whole attention of their minds is directed towards that single object, than when it is dissipated among a great variety of things. But in consequence of the division of labour, the whole of every man's attention comes naturally to be directed towards some one very simple object. It is naturally to be expected, therefore, that some one or other of those who are employed in each particular branch of labour should soon find out easier and readier methods of performing their own particular work, wherever the nature of it admits of such improvement. A great part of the machines made use of in those manufactures in which labour is most subdivided, were originally the inventions of common workmen, who, being each of them employed in some very simple operation, naturally turned their thoughts towards finding out easier and readier methods of performing it. Whoever has been much accustomed to visit such manufactures, must frequently have been shown very pretty machines, which were the inventions of such workmen, in order to facilitate and quicken their own particular part of the work. In the first fire-engines, a boy was constantly employed to open and shut alternately the communication between the boiler and the cylinder, according as the piston either ascended or descended. One of those boys, who loved to play with his companions, observed that, by tying a string from the handle of the valve which opened this communication to another part of the machine, the valve would open and shut without his assistance, and leave him at liberty to divert himself with his play-fellows. One of the greatest improvements that has been made upon this machine, since it was first invented, was in this manner the discovery of a boy who wanted to save his own labour.

. . . . .

Of Restraints upon the Importation from Foreign Countries of Such Goods as Can Be Produced at Home

By restraining, either by high duties, or by absolute prohibitions, the importation of such goods from foreign countries as can be produced at home, the monopoly of the home market is more or less secured to the domestic industry employed in producing them. Thus the prohibition of importing either live cattle or salt provisions from foreign countries secures to the graziers of Great Britain the monopoly of the home market for butcher's-meat. The high duties upon the importation of corn, which in times of moderate plenty amount to a prohibition, give a like advantage to the growers of that commodity. The prohibition of the importation of foreign woollens is equally favourable to the woollen manufactures. The silk manufacture, though altogether employed upon foreign materials, has lately obtained the same advantage. The linen manufacture has not yet obtained it, but is making great strides towards it. Many other sorts of manufacturers have, in the same manner, obtained in Great Britain, either altogether, or very nearly a monopoly against their countrymen. The variety of goods of which the importation into Great Britain is prohibited, either absolutely, or under certain circumstances, greatly exceeds what can easily be suspected by those who are not well acquainted with the laws of the customs.

That this monopoly of the home market frequently gives great encouragement to that particular species of industry which enjoys it, and frequently turns towards that employment a greater share of both the labour and stock of the society than would otherwise have gone to it, cannot be doubted. But whether it tends either to increase the general industry of the society, or to give it the most advantageous direction, is not, perhaps, altogether so evident.

The general industry of the society never can exceed what the capital of the society can employ. As the number of workmen that can be kept in employment by any particular person must bear a certain proportion to his capital, so the number of those that can be continually employed by all the members of a great society, must bear a certain proportion to the whole capital of that society, and never can exceed that proportion. No regulation of commerce can increase the quantity of industry in any society beyond what its capital can maintain. It can only divert a part of it into a direction into which it might not otherwise have gone; and it is by no means certain that this artificial direction is likely to be more advantageous to the society than that into which it would have gone of its own accord.

. . . . .

The produce of industry is what it adds to the subject or materials upon which it is employed. In proportion as the value of this produce is great or small, so will likewise be the profits of the employer. But it is only for the sake of profit that any man employs a capital in the support of industry; and he will always, therefore, endeavour to employ it in the support of that industry of which the produce is likely to be of the greatest value, or to exchange for the greatest quantity either of money or of other goods.

But the annual revenue of every society is always precisely equal to the exchangeable value of the whole annual produce of its industry, or rather is precisely the same thing with that exchangeable value. As every individual, therefore, endeavours as much as he can both to employ his capital in the support of domestic industry, and so to direct that industry that its produce may be of the greatest value, every individual necessarily labours to render the annual revenue of the society as great as he can. He generally, indeed, neither intends to promote the public interest, nor knows how much he is promoting it. By preferring the support of domestic to that of foreign industry, he intends only his own security; and by directing that industry in such a manner as its produce may be of the greatest value, he intends only his own gain, and he is in this, as in many other cases, led by an invisible hand to promote an end which was no part of his intention. Nor is it always the worse for the society that it was no part of it. By pursuing his own interest he frequently promotes that of the society more effectually than when he really intends to promote it. I have never known much good done by those who affected to trade for the public good. It is an affectation, indeed, not very common among merchants, and very few words need be employed in dissuading them from it.

What is the species of domestic industry which his capital can employ, and of which the produce is likely to be of the greatest value, every individual, it is evident, can, in his local situation, judge much better than any statesman or lawgiver can do for him. The statesman, who should attempt to direct private people in what manner they ought to employ their capitals, would not only load himself with a most unnecessary attention, but assume an authority which could safely be trusted, not only to no single person, but to no council or senate whatever, and which would nowhere be so dangerous as in the hands of a man who had folly and presumption enough to fancy himself fit to exercise it.

To give the monopoly of the home market to the produce of domestic industry, in any particular art or manufacture, is in some measure to direct private people in what manner they ought to employ their capitals, and must, in almost all cases, be either a useless or a hurtful regulation. If the produce of domestic can be brought there as cheap as that of foreign industry, the regulation is evidently useless. If it cannot, it must generally be hurtful. It is the maxim of every prudent master of a family, never to attempt to make at home what it will cost him more to make than to buy. The tailor does not attempt to make his own shoes, but buys them of the shoemaker. The shoemaker does not attempt to make his own clothes, but employs a tailor. The farmer attempts to make neither the one nor the other, but employs those different artificers. All of them find it for their interest to employ their whole industry in a way in which they have some advantage over their neighbours, and to purchase with a part of its produce, or, what is the same thing, with the price of a part of it, whatever else they have occasion for.

What is prudence in the conduct of every private family, can scarce be folly in that of a great kingdom. If a foreign country can supply us with a commodity cheaper than we ourselves can make it, better buy it of them with some part of the produce of our own industry, employed in a way in which we have some advantage. The general industry of the country, being always in proportion to the capital which employs it, will not thereby be diminished, no more than that of the above-mentioned artificers, but only left to find out the way in which it can be employed with the greatest advantage. It is certainly not employed to the greatest advantage, when it is thus directed towards an object which it can buy cheaper than it can make. The value of its annual produce is certainly more or less diminished, when it is thus turned away from producing commodities evidently of more value than the commodity which it is directed to produce. According to the supposition, that commodity could be purchased from foreign countries cheaper than it can be made at home. It could, therefore, have been purchased with a part only of the commodities, or, what is the same thing, with a part only of the price of the commodities, which the industry employed by an equal capital would have produced at home, had it been left to follow its natural course. The industry of the country, therefore, is thus turned away from a more to a less advantageous employment, and the exchangeable value of its annual produce, instead of being increased, according to the intention of the lawgiver, must necessarily be diminished by every such regulation.

By means of such regulations, indeed, a particular manufacture may sometimes be acquired sooner than it could have been otherwise, and after a certain time may be made at home as cheap or cheaper than in the foreign country. But though the industry of the society may be thus carried with advantage into a particular channel sooner than it could have been otherwise, it will by no means follow that the sum total, either of its industry or of its revenue, can ever be augmented by any such regulation. The industry of the society can augment only in proportion as its capital augments, and its capital can augment only in proportion to what can be gradually saved out of its revenue. But the immediate effect of every such regulation is to diminish its revenue, and what diminishes its revenue is certainly not very likely to augment its capital faster than it would have augmented of its own accord, had both capital and industry been left to find out their natural employments.

Though for want of such regulations the society should never acquire the proposed manufacture, it would not, upon that account, necessarily be the poorer in any one period of its duration. In every period of its duration its whole capital and industry might still have been employed, though upon different objects, in the manner that was most advantageous at the time. In every period its revenue might have been the greatest which its capital could afford, and both capital and revenue might have been augmented with the greatest possible rapidity.

The natural advantages which one country has over another in producing particular commodities are sometimes so great, that it is acknowledged by all the world to be in vain to struggle with them. By means of glasses, hot-beds, and hot-walls, very good grapes can be raised in Scotland, and very good wine too can be made of them, at about thirty times the expense for which at least equally good can be brought from foreign countries. Would it be a reasonable law to prohibit the importation of all foreign wines, merely to encourage the making of claret and burgundy in Scotland? But if there would be a manifest absurdity in turning towards any employment thirty times more of the capital and industry of the country than would be necessary to purchase from foreign countries an equal quantity of the commodities wanted, there must be an absurdity, though not altogether so glaring, yet exactly of the same kind, in turning towards any such employment a thirtieth or even a three-hundredth part more of either. Whether the advantages which one country has over another be natural or acquired, is in this respect of no consequence. As long as the one country has those advantages and the other wants them, it will always be more advantageous for the latter rather to buy of the former than to make. It is an acquired advantage only which one artificer has over his neighbour who exercises another trade; and yet they both find it more advantageous to buy of one another than to make what does not belong to their particular trades.

110. THE MANY USES OF MAIZE

The central problem in the old agricultural system of Europe had been the dependence upon the cereal grasses—wheat, rye, barley and the like—for bread grain. These crops not only exhausted the fertility of the soil in a few years, necessitating either fertilizing it or letting it lie fallow; they also had a low ratio of crop to seed. One element of the agricultural revolution was concerned with devising ways to break out of the dependence on fallow; another was the introduction into the European diet of a new crop from America, maize, or Indian corn. Its crop/seed ratio was immensely better than that of the cereal grasses, and its productivity per acre was much higher. Maize gradually came into use in Europe, especially during the 18th century, as its advantages were discovered and made known.

A distinguished Swedish botanist, Peter Kalm (1716-1779), who visited the British and French colonies in North America from 1748 to 1751, described these advantages in an extensive article on maize, its cultivation and its uses, in the *Proceedings* of the Swedish Royal Academy of Sciences after his return home. Parts of his article are given below.

Peter Kalm

Description of Maize

From time immemorial, long before the Europeans discovered America, the Americans, not only in North America, but also in all parts

SOURCE: Esther Louise Larsen, "Peter Kalm's Description of Maize, How It Is Planted and Cultivated in North America, together with the Many Uses of This Crop Plant," *Agricultural History*, Vol. IX, No. 1 (January 1935), pp. 101–2, 109–11. Reprinted by permission of *Agricultural History*.

of the West Indies, Peru, Mexico, the Continent, etc., planted maize and used it as their food.

Maize is also called *Turkiskt Hvete* in Swedish. Herbalists refer to the plant as *Zea.* For names used by other botanists one may consult Archiater Linnaeus, *Hort*[*us*] *Ups*[*aliensis*], 281, [and his] *Hort*[*us*] *Cliff*[*ortianus*], 437. The Swedes and Dutch in America call the plant *Mays* and *Magis;* the French, *Blé d'Inde;* the English, *Indian Corn;* the Iroquois, *Ohnasta;* the New England savages, *Ewáchim-neash;* and the savages who formerly occupied New Sweden, but who are now completely and entirely exterminated, *Jaéskung.*

Although maize was not known in the so-called Old World, i.e., Europe, Asia, and Africa, until after Columbus discovered America and the Europeans introduced the plant for cultivation, it may now be said to be cultivated in all parts of the world. Some people wish to maintain that the *Triticum Bactrianum* of Pliny, or perhaps his *Milium indicum,* which were introduced into Italy during the time of Nero and described in *Plinii* [*Secundi*] *Nat* [*uralis*] *Hist* [*oriae*], Book 18, ch. 7, was maize. Other authorities have definitely disproved the idea that the plants described by Pliny are maize, and shown that it cannot be the same, but that it is the African wheat or *Holcus Linnaei.*

. . . . .

Now I will come to the uses of maize, which are so numerous. I doubt if any other species of grain exists which alone may be used for so many purposes both for man and animals.

To begin with, it is one of the most productive plants in the whole world, wherefore it is called by some "the lazy man's crop." I have counted on a single ear 650 clean and healthy kernels, and on each stalk commonly two to three ears. An ear is rarely found which has less than 300 kernels. In addition, this crop has this advantage—the kernels do not spill away as in the case of rye and other grains. On the contrary, great difficulty is apt to be encountered in loosening the kernels. In America this crop is considered a failure if it does not yield two hundred times the corn planted. It is to be noted that a large household seldom plants over 2 bushels, in fact, rarely this much in order to raise food for an entire year, and in addition, some for other purposes.

Let us recall what has previously been discussed: Maize can freeze several times during the spring and still come up from the same root; it stands more heat and drought than any other crop plant; it grows in much poorer soil; it grows rapidly in dry and sandy places; it is not subject to injury by excess moisture as other crops, etc.

If the leaves of maize are removed from the stalk while they are still green, i.e., before they have dried by themselves in the sun, and put together in a covered stack, they will provide food for horses and cows, which is preferable to clover or other good hay. On the other hand, if the leaves dry by themselves out on the stalks, the horses and cattle will not eat them, unless they lack all other food. Warm water poured on maize leaves which are dried green makes a fodder which provides the cows with both food and drink, and increases the amount of milk considerably. During the winter these leaves are cut in pieces, just as we cut straw for provender for horses. Horses prefer this fodder to clover hay. When the maize ears are large, but the kernels on them still soft, it is customary to remove the ears from the stalks on which they are growing in the field. The husks covering the kernels are torn off. The ears are then placed in front of a fire to roast until they become light brown. These ears are considered a delicacy by both Europeans and savages. The savages plague strangers and guests who visit them at that time by offering them roasted ears. If maize had been known to the Israelites, I would say that these ears were the same as the dried ears mentioned in the Bible. But here there is no room for conjecture. Later in the season the savages do not roast the green ears, but cook and eat them, and they actually taste quite good. It is even customary with many to take these green ears where they stand in the field and eat them immediately, raw as they are. I have often done so myself, and to my taste, the kernels are as good as sweet-sugared milk.

While the maize stalks are green, and before the ears are ripe, there is a clear water between the nodes of the stalk, which is as sweet as sugar. Various people have made both syrups and sugar from maize, but this conversion has not been considered profitable. I have seen the Europeans, as well as the American savages, cut off the maize stalks in the field, chew them to pieces between their teeth, and suck out the sweet juice. [John] Lawson, in his *Description* [*i.e.*, *History*] *of Carolina*, p. 75 [(London, 1714)], says that some people crush the stalks and make from them a very palatable drink.

Maize kernels are tightly fastened to the cob (the stalk of the ear). To pick them loose with the fingers would be difficult and rather slow work. The kernels would not come loose by threshing. Therefore, when one needs the maize kernels loose from the ear, either for grinding or for other purposes, one takes a tub or any vessel, puts a long thick hinge or any other piece of iron with an edge directly over the vessel. This piece of iron is bound fast to the vessel at both ends. Against the edge of the iron the side of the ear is placed and thus the kernels are scraped off. They fall down into the tub or vessel. A little technique is required before one can do this easily. Others use a slower method. They loosen the kernels by means of placing the ears in a large wooden mortar and pounding them slowly. Neither the Europeans nor the savages separate the kernels from the ear before they need them for food or other purposes, as they keep better when attached to the cob.

In most of the English colonies the farmers make their bread from maize. In Maryland even the aristocracy and the wealthy eat hardly any other bread. If a stranger comes to them, they place before him both wheat and maize bread, allowing him the freedom to choose whichever he prefers; they themselves prefer the maize bread. But if the bread is made entirely of maize, one does not find it so good. The best is made of rye and maize flour mixed. From wheat and maize flour one also gets fine bread. In America this bread is commonly baked in the form of large loaves. It is a very wholesome bread and always keeps the bowels well regulated. I know that various people, describers of plants as well as travelers, who have written about maize, have said that too much maize for food causes constipation, and even skin eruptions, scurvy, and itch. This I had read and heard discussed, here at home in Sweden, before I left for America. I had also read those who claim that maize had been unjustly criticized. When I reached America and observed people who ate almost nothing but maize and looked as well and happy as those who eat the best and cleanest rye or wheat bread, I often told them what I had read and heard about maize. At the same time I asked them if it did not cause constipation and skin eruptions. They answered all of one accord that no more wholesome food exists and that they had never had these symptoms which are attributed to maize. I then determined to experiment on myself. Maize was a food which I had scarcely seen, much less tasted. I had just come to a strange climate; it should certainly show its effect on me. I ate, then, during the whole first winter I was in America hardly any other bread, only maize alone or maize and rye flour mixed. However, I had no digestive disturbances, at least not more than usual. I found no such effects as those attributed to maize—quite the opposite. I can never wish to be in better health than I was at that time. The boy, Jungstrom, who accompanied me, reacted similarly. Others who have written of North America attribute to maize the same laxative quality which I found and for that reason they recommend that it be mixed with wheat, to counteract the binding constipating effect of the latter. The results attributed to the use of maize are due either to climate or to some other factor, which man has not carefully investigated.

111. THE NEW FARMING LOOKS AT THE OLD

The development of a new kind of agriculture, one capable of feeding expanding populations without the built-in limitation of fertility in the old farming, was an essential link in the industrialization process. One of the most energetic voices for the new farming was that of Arthur Young (1741-1820). While not successful himself as a farmer, Young became the spokesman of the progressive agriculture of his time. He edited the *Annals of Agriculture* from 1784 to 1809 and became secretary of the English Board of Agriculture in 1793. His most famous book, *Travels in France during the Years 1787, 1788 and 1789*, published in 1792, was a detailed description of French agriculture at the end of the Old Regime. He stigmatized particularly the retention of the backward practice of maintaining fallow and open fields.

Arthur Young

Travels in France

Courses of Crops

We cannot but admit that France is in possession of a soil and even of a husbandry that is to be ranked very high amongst the best in Europe. Flanders, part of Artois, the rich plain of Alsace, the banks of the Garonne, and a considerable part of Quercy, are cultivated more like gardens than farms. The rapid succession of crops, the harvest of one being but the signal of sowing immediately for a second, can scarcely be carried to greater perfection, and this in a point perhaps of all others essential to good husbandry, when such crops are so justly distributed as we generally find them in these provinces; cleaning and ameliorating ones being made the preparation for such as foul and exhaust. These are provinces which even an English farmer might visit with advantage. Such praise however cannot be given indiscriminately, for fallows disgrace in some rich districts the finest soils imaginable. A country can hardly be worse cultivated than Picardy, Normandy and the Pays de Beauce, every acre of which provinces would admit the exclusion of fallows, with as much propriety as Flanders itself. In the Pays de Caux, where fallows are very much excluded [*sic*] for want of understanding the right arrangement of crops, their noble soil is full of beggary and weeds.

To detail all the barbarous rotation which ignorance has spread through Bretagne, Maine and Anjou would be tedious The general feature of their management is to pare and burn the fields exhausted, abandoned, and by time recovered, that a succession of crops may bring it

---

Source: Arthur Young, *Travels in France during the Years 1787, 1788, and 1789*, edited by Constantia Maxwell (Cambridge, England: Cambridge University Press, 1929), pp. 288–93. Reprinted by permission of Cambridge University Press.

once more into the same situation. A change of the rotation of crops is the only thing to alter the face of these provinces. . . .

The general arrangement of crops throughout Lorraine and Franche Comté being the common rotation of a third fallow, a third wheat, or rye, and a third barley or oats, has resulted from the great quantity of open land therein subject to common rights. It is however a disgrace to the cultivators, that they too often pursue the same miserable routine in their enclosures. It would be useless to dwell on such husbandry. It is enough to class these provinces among the worst cultivated ones (vines excepted) that are to be found in the kingdom, and considering the extent of the open fields, there is very little probability of their amelioration.

In Sologne, the poverty of the farmers, the waste state of every part of the country, result in no inconsiderable degree from the courses of crops practised; the least and most obvious change of them would give a new face to this desolate province. Where the land is good, they crop without mercy, and where it is bad, they have nothing but fallows and weeds, instead of turnips and sainfoin.

In the two provinces of the Bourbonnais and Nivernais, one feature is found throughout them; 1, fallow; 2, rye; a system to which they must be strangely partial, for it is found in a country of which nine-tenths are enclosed, and at the command of farmers to sow what they please. It is not produce and success that should make them in love with fallows, for the farmers are as poor as their crops. The common produce is four times the seed, and they have often less, and with all this ploughing and fallowing, the soil is in such a state of degradation, that they actually find it exhausted by their management, and to restore it to some degree of fertility they leave it to weeds and broom for 7 or 8 years, in order to recruit the soil, which fallows cannot effect. The world perhaps cannot afford a completer instance of the futility of the practice.

In considering, with respect to the national interests, the proper courses of crops for France, two circumstances should be had in remembrance; it is the quantity of forest necessary in a country that either has not coal, or does not use it; and the vast tracts that are under vines. They should be mentioned to show, that while the quantity of arable land is thus prodigiously lessened, attention to banish fallows, and introduce proper courses of crops, becomes of the highest importance. When we reflect, that from a sixth to a seventh of the kingdom is occupied by wood, and that the space covered by vines is exceedingly great, at the same time that the wastes are in some provinces of enormous extent, it will appear amazing how so numerous a people are fed, with a third or fourth of all their arable land encumbered, not cleaned, by barren fallows. When Louis XIV beggared his people in order to place a grandson of France on the throne of Spain, and to acquire Flanders, Alsace etc., he would have rendered his kingdom infinitely richer, more prosperous and more powerful, had he banished the fallows from half-a-dozen of his provinces, or introduced turnips in some others; there is scarcely a step he could have taken in such an improvement of his agriculture which would not have given him more subjects and more wealth than any of his conquered provinces.

Enclosures

The principal districts of enclosure which I viewed are, all Bretagne, the western part of Normandy, with the northern part of the Seine, most of Anjou and Maine, as far as near Alençon. To the south of the Loire an immense range of country is enclosed; Bas Poitou, Touraine, Sologne, Berry, Limousin, the Bourbonnais, and much of the Nivernais; and from Montcenis in Burgundy to St Ponçin [St Pourçain-sur-Sioule] in Auvergne, all is enclosed. There is some open country in the Angoumois, and the eastern part of Poitou, but more is enclosed. Quercy is partly so; but the whole district of the Pyrenees, from Perpignan to Bayonne, extending to Auch, and almost to Toulouse, is all (wastes excepted) thickly enclosed. Provence, especially about Avignon, is not without enclosures; Dauphiné has more. The whole range of the mountainous district of Auvergne, Velay, Vivarais and Cevenois contains many; Franche Comté and Burgundy, especially the former, have large tracks enclosed; Lorraine has some, and Flanders has them throughout. Add to this most of the vineyards, woods and forests, and meadows of the kingdom, and it will not be thought too large an allowance to suppose one-half of it in this state. In such a calculation it would be absurd to pretend to accuracy; it is a guess, founded on actual observation and innumerable notes taken on the spot. Some of the enclosed provinces are chequered by open fields, and every open province is chequered by tracks that are enclosed.

If the husbandry varied in the enclosed fields from that of the unenclosed ones, there would be nothing surprising in it, but the marvellous folly is, that in nine-tenths of all the enclosures of France, the system of management is precisely the same as in the open fields; that is to say, fallows as regularly prevail, and consequently the cattle and sheep of a farm are nothing in comparison of what they ought to be. Flanders and Alsace, and in general the very rich soils, are well cultivated, but not everywhere, for the noble loams of Bernay to Elbeuf, and those of the Pays de Caux, are disgraced with fallows. Sologne is enclosed, yet it is the most miserable province in France. The Bourbonnais and great part of the Nivernais are enclosed, yet the course pursued is:—1, fallow; 2, rye; and 1, fallow; 2, rye; 3, left to weeds and broom—and all these on soils, as Bretagne, Sologne and the Bourbonnais, highly improvable and capable of the best Norfolk husbandry. With such miserable systems, of what good are enclosures? . . .

To enter largely into the advantages of enclosures, in such a work as this, and at this time of day, would be superfluous; it is sufficient to remark, that without a regular system of enclosures no cattle can be kept, except on the Flemish system of constant confinement in stables, stalls, or yards; and this method, when the lands which are to yield the food are distant from the home stall, is inconvenient and expensive. With open-field farms, much dispersed, it is impossible to follow the Flemish system; not only because the established rotation excludes the proper plants for cattle, but because, if they were raised, they could not be daily carted home, without committing trespasses on other people; therefore, it should always be remembered, that cattle and enclosure are synonymous terms. Without enclosure the half of France cannot possibly support the requisite stock of cattle and sheep; and without such stock, a good and productive husbandry is utterly impracticable.

112. FOOD PRODUCTION AND POPULATION GROWTH

The optimism of agricultural reformers that new methods of cultivation and new crops would expand the produce of the soil to fully meet the needs of man was not shared by a sober-eyed English economist, Thomas Malthus (1766-1834). Malthus introduced into the relationship of tillage and harvest an element which had hitherto been studied separately—the size and growth of populations. He called attention to the tendency of living forms to expand their numbers at an often fantastic geometric rate if not held back by contrary natural forces, such as the limitation of food supplies, disease, predators, and the like. Since even the best of agricultural improvements could hardly hope to increase the supply of food by more than an "arithmetic" rate (mere doubling every so often, instead of compounding), the population would always expand to and beyond the limits of agricultural production, and the natural checks would again begin to operate inexorably.

Malthus, a clergyman by profession, urged the importance of human controls on population growth, not the newly invented contraceptive devices of France but continence, late marriage, and other "moral" means. Malthus's great exposition, *An Essay on the Principle of Population*, published in 1798, contributed not only to the creation of the social science of demography but also to the Darwinian theory of evolution in the next century, by its emphasis upon the struggle for existence. Extracts from the first two chapters are given below.

Thomas Malthus

An Essay on the Principle of Population

In an inquiry concerning the improvement of society, the mode of conducting the subject which naturally presents itself, is,

1. To investigate the causes that have hitherto impeded the progress of mankind towards happiness; and,

2. To examine the probability of the total or partial removal of these causes in future.

To enter fully into this question, and to enumerate all the causes that have hitherto influenced human improvement, would be much beyond the power of an individual. The principal object of the present essay is to examine the effects of one great cause intimately united with the very nature of man; which, though it has been constantly and powerfully operating since the commencement of society, has been little noticed by the writers who have treated this subject. The facts which establish the existence of this cause have, indeed, been repeatedly stated and acknowledged; but its natural and necessary effects have been almost totally overlooked; though probably among these effects may be reckoned a very considerable portion of that vice and misery, and of that unequal distribution of the bounties of nature, which it has been the unceasing object of the enlightened philanthropist in all ages to correct.

The cause to which I allude, is the constant tendency in all animated life to increase beyond the nourishment prepared for it.

It is observed by Dr. Franklin, that there is no bound to the prolific nature of plants or animals, but what is made by their crowding and interfering with each other's means of subsistence. Were the face of the earth, he says, vacant of other plants, it might be gradually sowed and overspread with one kind only, as for instance with fennel: and were it empty of other inhabitants, it might in a few ages be replenished from one nation only, as for instance with Englishmen.

This is incontrovertibly true. Through the animal and vegetable kingdoms Nature has scattered the seeds of life abroad with the most profuse and liberal hand; but has been comparatively sparing in the room and the nourishment necessary to rear them. The germs of existence contained in this earth, if they could freely develop themselves, would fill

---

Source: Thomas R. Malthus, *An Essay on the Principle of Population* (Homewood, Ill.: Richard D. Irwin, 1963), pp. 1–7. Reprinted by permission of Richard D. Irwin, Inc.

millions of worlds in the course of a few thousand years. Necessity, that imperious, all-pervading law of nature, restrains them within the prescribed bounds. The race of plants and the race of animals shrink under this great restrictive law; and man cannot by any efforts of reason escape from it.

In plants and irrational animals, the view of the subject is simple. They are all impelled by a powerful instinct to the increase of their species; and this instinct is interrupted by no doubts about providing for their offspring. Wherever therefore there is liberty, the power of increase is exerted; and the superabundant effects are repressed afterwards by want of room and nourishment.

The effects of this check on man are more complicated. Impelled to the increase of his species by an equally powerful instinct, reason interrupts his career, and asks him whether he may not bring beings into the world, for whom he cannot provide the means of support. If he attend to this natural suggestion, the restriction too frequently produces vice. If he hear it not, the human race will be constantly endeavouring to increase beyond the means of subsistence. But as, by that law of our nature which makes food necessary to the life of man, population can never actually increase beyond the lowest nourishment capable of supporting it, a strong check on population, from the difficulty of acquiring food, must be constantly in operation. This difficulty must fall somewhere, and must necessarily be severely felt in some or other of the various forms of misery, or the fear of misery, by a large portion of mankind. . . .

It may safely be pronounced, therefore, that population, when unchecked, goes on doubling itself every twenty-five years, or increases in a geometrical ratio.

The rate according to which the productions of the earth may be supposed to increase, it will not be so easy to determine. Of this, however, we may be perfectly certain, that the ratio of their increase in a limited territory must be of a totally different nature from the ratio of the increase of population. A thousand millions are just as easily doubled every twenty-five years by the power of population as a thousand. But the food to support the increase from the greater number will by no means be obtained with the same facility. Man is necessarily confined in room. When acre has been added to acre till all the fertile land is occupied, the yearly increase of food must depend upon the melioration of the land already in possession. This is a fund, which, from the nature of all soils, instead of increasing, must be gradually diminishing. But population, could it be supplied with food, would go on with unexhausted vigour; and the increase of one period would furnish the power of a greater increase the next, and this without any limit. . . .

Europe is by no means so fully peopled as it might be. In Europe there is the fairest chance that human industry may receive its best direction. The science of agriculture has been much studied in England and Scotland; and there is still a great portion of uncultivated land in these countries. Let us consider at what rate the produce of this island might be supposed to increase under circumstances the most favourable to improvement.

If it be allowed that by the best possible policy, and great encouragements to agriculture, the average produce of the island could be doubled in the first twenty-five years, it will be allowing, probably, a greater increase than could with reason be expected.

In the next twenty-five years, it is impossible to suppose that the produce could be quadrupled. It would be contrary to all our knowledge of the properties of land. The improvement of the barren parts would be a work of time and labour; and it must be evident to those who have the slightest acquaintance with agricultural subjects, that in proportion as cultivation extended, the additions that could yearly be made to the former average produce must be gradually and regularly diminishing. That we may be the better able to compare the increase of population and food, let us make a supposition, which, without pretending to accuracy, is clearly more favourable to the power of production in the earth, than any experience we have had of its qualities will warrant.

Let us suppose that the yearly additions which might be made to the former average produce, instead of decreasing, which they certainly would do, were to remain the same; and that the produce of this island might be increased every twenty-five years, by a quantity equal to what it at present produces. The most enthusiastic speculator cannot suppose a greater increase than this. In a few centuries it would make every acre of land in the island like a garden.

If this supposition be applied to the whole earth, and if it be allowed that the subsistence for man which the earth affords might be increased every twenty-five years by a quantity equal to what it at present produces, this will be supposing a rate of increase much greater than we can imagine that any possible exertions of mankind could make it.

It may be fairly pronounced, therefore, that, considering the present average state of the earth, the means of subsistence, under circumstances the most favourable to human industry, could not possibly be made to increase faster than in an arithmetical ratio.

The necessary effects of these two different rates of increase, when brought together, will be very striking. Let us call the population of this island eleven millions; and suppose the present produce equal to the easy support of such a number. In the first twenty-five years the population would be twenty-two millions, and the food being also doubled, the means of subsistence would be equal to this increase. In the next twenty-five years, the population would be forty-four millions, and the means of subsistence only equal to the support of thirty-three millions. In the next period the population would be eighty-eight millions, and the means of subsistence just equal to the support of half that number. And, at the conclusion of the first century, the population would be a hundred and seventy-six millions, and the means of subsistence only equal to the support of fifty-five millions, leaving a population of a hundred and twenty-one millions totally unprovided for.

Taking the whole earth, instead of this island, emigration would of course be excluded; and, supposing the present population equal to a thousand millions, the human species would increase as the numbers, 1, 2, 4, 8, 16, 32, 64, 128, 256, and subsistence as 1, 2, 3, 4, 5, 6, 7, 8, 9. In two centuries the population would be to the means of subsistence as 256 to 9; in three centuries as 4096 to 13, and in two thousand years the difference would be almost incalculable.

In this supposition no limits whatever are placed to the produce of the earth. It may increase for ever and be greater than any assignable quantity; yet still the power of population being in every period so much superior, the increase of the human species can only be kept down to the level of the means of subsistence by the constant operation of the strong law of necessity, acting as a check upon the greater power.

Of the general Checks to Population, and the Mode of their Operation

The ultimate check to population appears then to be a want of food, arising necessarily from the different ratios according to which population and food increase. But this ultimate check is never the immediate check, except in cases of actual famine.

The immediate check may be stated to consist in all those customs, and all those diseases, which seem to be generated by a scarcity of the means of subsistence; and all those causes, independent of this scarcity, whether of a moral or physical nature, which tend prematurely to weaken and destroy the human frame.

These checks to population, which are constantly operating with more or less force in every society, and keep down the number to the level of the means of subsistence, may be classed under two general heads—the preventive, and the positive checks.

The preventive check, as far as it is voluntary, is peculiar to man, and arises from that distinctive superiority in his reasoning faculties, which enables him to calculate distant consequences. The checks to the indefinite increase of plants and irrational animals are all either positive, or, if preventive, involuntary. But man cannot look around him, and see the distress which frequently presses upon those who have large families; he cannot contemplate his present possessions or earnings, which he now nearly consumes himself, and calculate the amount of each share, when with very little addition they must be divided, perhaps, among seven or eight, without feeling a doubt whether, if he follow the bent of his inclinations, he may be able to support the offspring which he will probably bring into the world. In a state of equality, if such can exist, this would be the simple question. In the present state of society other considerations occur. Will he not lower his rank in life, and be obliged to give up in great measure his former habits? Does any mode of employment present itself by which he may reasonably hope to maintain a family? Will he not at any rate subject himself to greater difficulties, and more severe labour, than in his single state? Will he not be unable to transmit to his children the same advantages of education and improvement that he had himself possessed? Does he even feel secure that, should he have a large family, his utmost exertions can save them from rags and squalid poverty, and their consequent degradation in the community? And may he not be reduced to the grating necessity of forfeiting his independence, and of being obliged to the sparing hand of Charity for support?

These considerations are calculated to prevent, and certainly do prevent, a great number of persons in all civilised nations from pursuing the dictate of nature in an early attachment to one woman.

If this restraint do not produce vice, it is undoubtedly the least evil that can arise from the principle of population. Considered as a restraint on a strong natural inclination, it must be allowed to produce a certain degree of temporary unhappiness; but evidently slight, compared with the evils which result from any of the other checks to population; and merely of the same nature as many other sacrifices of temporary to permanent gratification, which it is the business of a moral agent continually to make.

113. A NEW SOURCE OF POWER

The crucial step in the transformation of the old economic system into the new, which is generally called the Industrial Revolution, was the invention of an adequate source of power to drive machinery. The steam engine invented by the Scotsman James Watt (1736–1819) meant that the operators of mills and mines were no longer dependent on variable winds or streams as a source of power. The procedure involved in the purchase of a Watt steam engine is illustrated by the letters exchanged between a prospective customer, Samuel Walker & Co., steelmakers, and the firm of (Matthew) Boulton & Watt, manufacturers of the engine.

Correspondence on Ordering a Watt Steam Engine

Samuel Walker to Messrs. Boulton & Watt

ROTHERHAM, May 15th, 1781

GENTN.

We have some works upon a river, wh. in general supplies us well with water; but in dry seasons we are much retarded for want of water. In order to make up this defect in some measure, we are intending to build a fire engine, either in the old or common manner, or under the sanction of your patent. We should therefore be glad to know on what terms we can be permitted to go on under the latter. We have coal of our own geting laid down at the Work at about 2¾d. cwt. and are thinking of a cylinder with 36 or 43 in. diamr., and eight foot stroke, and suppose we may work the engine 3 to 6 months in the year, according as the seasons are wet or dry.—Quere, on what terms we can be permited to go on with either of the above cylinders, as to time, & sum, or what sum in hand you will give us a commission to go on without further interruption.

We hope you will be moderate in your demands, which may be a means of introducing your engines into this country, & without which I imagine you can not expect any thing scarce from this neighbourhood. Your reply *as soon as you can* will oblige Gentn.

Your etc.

N.B. We can have small coal which is got very near to us laid down at our works at about 1½d. cwt.

Messrs. Boulton & Watt to Messrs. Samuel Walker & Co.

BIRMINGHAM, 22 May 1781

SIRS,

We are favoured with yours of 15th instant, requesting to know the general terms on which we conduct our engine business. In answer thereto we beg leave to send you a printed draught of an agreement such as we and the other contracting parties execute, and this we think the clearest way of explaining our terms which are in short as follows—

We contract to make all the necessary plans, sections and drawings for the masons, carpenters, founders, smiths and for all things belonging to the engine. We superintend the execution and erection, and we guarantee

---

SOURCE: M. W. Flinn (ed.), *Readings in Economic and Social History* (New York: St. Martin's Press, 1964), pp. 100–103. Reprinted by permission of St. Martin's Press, Inc., Macmillan & Co., Ltd.; and Macmillan London and Basingstoke.

the good performance of the engine without any profit or advantage arising from any part of the materials, work, or workmen whatsoever, and we grant our licence for using the same during the term of our Act of Parliament for which we ask an annual sum equal to the value one third of the coals saved by the use of our engine when compared with one of the common construction.

As our profits arise from the superiority of our engine, you will perceive the reasonableness of our requiring it to be erected according to our plans and directions, besides, we lay some stress upon the character of our engines and ourselves, as well as upon our profits. We have now nearly erected more than fifty engines, and you may be assured that experience hath taught us to make our species of engines better than could be done without such experience. Although we have the highest opinion of you, as founders, as mechanicks, and as men yet we must beg you will permit us to offer you an opinion and advice in the present case. But first it is necessary to premise that we have already articled to erect 16 large engines this summer, and that as many of them are to be in Cornwall, our Mr. Watt will be under the necessity of residing in the county most of the summer and that it falls to his lot to make the plans, sections and all the drawings. Secondly. Although the proprietors of Ketley Iron Works, near Coalbrookdale condescended to take our advice in employing another founder to cast the whole of the first engine they erected of our construction and bore the cylinder, and thereby they became better judges of the requisite than they otherwise would have been, yet nevertheless we have had much extra trouble in making minute drawings and giving the necessary direction to them for casting and making some of our engines at their own works this summer for which purpose they have erected a boring machine similar to that which Mr. Wilkinson bores our cylinders with at Bersham for it is impossible to bore them so true by the old method as our engines absolutely require to be bored. From your workmen never having cast and never erected one of our engines, from our present engagements being such as cannot allow the time to instruct a new set of people in all that is necessary for the founder, the smith, and the engineer to know from your being at present provided as we suppose with the means of boring sufficiently true, we are induced to advise you to permit us to provide you with such of the castings as relate to the engine and of the beam and as to the pumps etc. We have not the least doubt of your executing them as well as they can be done. In this case we presume it may be possible for us to erect you an engine in the course of this year but otherwise it will not, as we think it our duty to our employers and ourselves to fulfill the engagements we have already entered into, which are now almost more than we can do this year. We beg you will not infer from anything herein said that we are under any engagement with any founders whatsoever or that we have any partiality to one more than to another, further than as we have been at great pains in instructing those we have hitherto employed. We are ready to grant you licences to cast and erect our engines when once you have become masters of the subject and we are persuaded your candour will allow us to judge of that matter. In respect to our claim for profits we again repeat that we ask for no money in hand, that as you say your engine will not work constantly, there can be no calculation grounded upon the dryness of the seasons yet to come, and therefore we propose to put two counters upon the beam, you to keep the key of one, and we of the other and that you shall pay us an agreed sum for every ten thousand strokes the engine actually makes, and if at any time after when you from experience are better qualified to calculate its value than you now are, we shall be willing to agree with you for a specific sum in lieu of an annual claim.

The coal mines in Yorkshire will not pay us for our attention on that business and therefore we have in general declined engine orders where coals are of less value than four or five shillings per ton, particularly as we have hitherto been overloaded with business where coals are at a high price, and as we shall apply our engines to a variety of purposes and manufactories they have never yet been applied to, and for which they are wanted. We have had many public trials made between our engine and the common engine and in some of them ours proved more than four times better and in none so little as three times better and therefore, to save future trouble and expence we have lately determined to rate our engine at three times better than the old one, hence the following calculations will show the value of our claims as we burn but one third of the coal so there will be but one third of the expence in the wear of boilers and there are other savings of which we do not claim any part.

Cylinder 36 inches diameter with an 8 feet stroke in it will work 10 or 12 strokes per minute with an equal beam under the load of 10178 pounds or it will be equal to 81424 pounds one foot high per stroke.
10,000 strokes will consume 33 cwts. of coals when loaded as above and a common engine would consume 99 cwts of coals in raising an equal weight to an equal height.

Hence there is saved 66 cwts of which we claim one third part 22 cwts at 2¾d is equal to 5d or 6d per thousand.

A cylinder 43 inches diar. with an 8 ft. stroke in it will work 10 or 12 strokes per minute with an equal beam under a load of 14522 pounds or it will be equal to 116176 pounds one foot high per stroke, and will require 46½ cwts of coals for every 10,000 strokes. A common engine doing equal work would consume 46½ × 3 = 139½ cwts.
Hence there is saved in 10,000 strokes 93 cwts. of which we claim the

value of one third, viz. 31 cwts at 2¾d is 7s 1d for every 10,000 strokes.

We estimate the quality of your coals to be about equal to the general run of our Staffordshire coals, which we do not consider of so good a quality as the best Newcastle coals by about twenty five per cent in respect to their powers in the evaporation of water.

As we are both now at home and will be so for two or three weeks we should be glad to have your answer as soon as convenient, that if we agree to erect your engine we may know how to forecast our other business.

CHAPTER XII

THE POLITICS OF EUROPE: THE EIGHTEENTH CENTURY

NEW FORCES BEGAN to appear on the European political scene during the 18th century. Although the practice of politics continued to be directed at the aggrandizement of the power, wealth, and prestige of the privileged groups, the Enlightenment brought new emphasis to the debate over the legitimacy of states and the efficacy of their politics.

At the start of the century, monarchy was still the established form of government virtually everywhere in Europe and was little questioned. And while the liberated American colonies of Great Britain had created a new republic across the ocean by the close of the century, in the Dutch Republic, for example, the stadholder was made a virtual monarch.

Movements with well-defined democratic aims were taking shape, however. They brought together the democracy implicit in the political philosophy of the Enlightenment, the interests of the classes that were excluded from participation in political activity in monarchical and aristocratic states, and the experience of rule by representative assemblies in former eras. By the middle of the century the democratic movement began to meet resistance from established governments and turned to the same weapon—force—that baronial rebels had used against centralizing rulers. Until the coming of the French Revolution in 1789, the American Revolution was the crowning success of this movement. Elsewhere, however, as in Geneva and Holland, similar forces were thwarted, although only by foreign intervention.

114. FREEDOM AND THE PRESERVATION OF PRIVILEGE

The Enlightenment did not have a simple, universal political program, as opponents of the French Revolution were to declare decades later. Exactly what its central political tenet—the duty of the state to serve the people—meant in practice depended upon who was using the state, in what circumstances, and to what purpose. This may be seen in the remonstrance addressed by the Parlement of Paris to Louis XVI on March 2, 1776, which attacked a royal edict prepared by the reforming finance minister, Turgot. This edict abolished the *corvée* system of compulsory labor and replaced it with a tax on all classes of society, including the First and Second Estates (the clergy and nobility), which had not been subject to either the *taille*, or general land tax, or the *corvée*. The remonstrance breathes the spirit of goodwill and justice in the abstract but makes clear that it considers the king's duty to be the preservation of the system of privileged status groups *(états)* on which his government in effect depended.

During the reign of Louis XVI, the long struggle between the parlements (law courts) and absolute monarchy rose to a peak of fury. The judges invoked the rights of free subjects against royal despotism in defense of their privileges, while the royal bureaucracy, in seeking to overcome the resistance of the privileged groups to reforms, notably in taxation, had to intensify the right of government to rule and the duty of subjects to obey. Despite the glorious simplicities of the propaganda battle then, and of the historical debate which has reflected it since, the issues at stake were complex. They could be simplified only by a violence that also falsified them.

Remonstrance of the Parlement of Paris to Louis XVI, March 2, 1776

SIRE,

. . . Your parlement realizes that the edict substituting a tax on land of universal, unlimited and perpetual nature, for the *corvées*, under color of the apparent relief which it grants to the people, may have seemed at first glance to be an act of benefaction inspired by the love of mankind.

But at the same time, Sire, your parlement has had no doubt that had Your Majesty reflected further upon it, he would have discovered that this was an operation which would be a burden for the very people that

SOURCE: Jules Flammermont (ed.), *Remonstrances du Parlement de Paris au XVIIIe siécle*, Vol. III (Paris: Imprimerie Nationale, 1898), pp. 277–79, 286–88, 290, 292. Translated by Herbert H. Rowen.

You wish to succor and would be in opposition to the feelings of justice by which you are moved.

Justice, Sire, is the first duty of kings; when it is lacking, the loftiest qualities can result in the most deplorable consequences. It is justice which sets the true worth on deeds of kings and which, when it puts the mark of greatest reverence upon their reigns, consecrates their memory forever.

The first rule of justice is to preserve to each what is his own. It is the fundamental rule of natural law, the law of nations, and of civil government, and it consists not only in maintaining the rights of property but also in protecting those rights which are personal in character and derive from the prerogatives of birth and status.

It follows from this rule of law and equity that any system which would tend, under the appearance of humanity and benefaction, to establish equality of rights and destroy distinctions necessary in a well-ordered monarchy, would soon bring disorder in its train, as the inevitable consequence of absolute equality. It would bring about the overthrow of civil society, which remains harmonious only because of this gradation of powers, authority, preeminence and distinctions which keeps each man in his place and protects all ranks from confusion.

This order depends not only upon the policies of every good government; it has its source in what God has established. The infinite and unalterable wisdom in the plan of the Universe included an unequal distribution of strength and talent, and the inevitable result in the order of society is the inequality of men's status. This is the law of the Universe which holds sway in every state despite the efforts of the human mind, and it maintains in turn the order on which the government itself rests.

How many, therefore, are the dangers of a project which is the product of an unacceptable system of equality, whose first result is to abolish the distinctions between the orders of the state by imposing upon all of them the selfsame yoke of the territorial tax!

. . . . .

We have not done enough, Sire, when we only depict to you in their entirety the illusion of the new system of *corvées*, its drawbacks, and its dangers for the people. We must present broader ideas to you, and we must draw your attention to the attacks which this system would constitute upon the status of persons and the principles on which the Monarchy was founded.

The constitutional organization of the French monarchy provides for its composition by several distinct and separate social orders. Such distinctions of status and persons derives from the way the Nation came into being; it arose with its customs and is the precious chain which binds the Sovereign to his subjects.

"If there were no distinction between the status of persons, disorder and confusion would necessarily result," says one of the most enlightened of our authors.[1] "We cannot live with an equality of status: some must command and others must obey. The sovereign lords command everyone within their states, sending their orders to the magnates, the magnates theirs to men of lesser rank, and they in turn to those of lower rank, and these to the people."

Within the assemblage constituted by these different orders, *every man in your kingdom is subject to you,* and all are obligated to contribute to the needs of the state. But order and general harmony are always to be found in these very contributions. The personal service of the Clergy consists in fulfilling all functions relating to education, the practice of religion, and in contributing to the relief of the unfortunate by the gift of alms. The Nobility devotes its blood to the defense of the state and assists the Sovereign with its counsels. The lowest class of the Nation, who cannot render services of such distinction to the state, meets its obligations by paying taxes, engaging in business, and performing manual labor.

This, Sire, is the ancient rule of the duties and obligations of your subjects.

Although all were equal in their loyalty and their submission, the difference of status among them was never lost, and the nature of their services derived essentially from their status.

"The service of the nobles is also noble; a noble is not required to pay the *taille* nor to perform base compulsory labor, but to serve in war and other deeds of noble character."

These institutions are not such as have been developed by chance, which time can change. It would be necessary to overthrow the entire constitution of France to abolish them. Legislative acts can change what was created by legislation; but what has been rendered fit and proper for a nation by its distinctive spirit, its customs, the general wish of the nation during its formation and the whole course of its government, cannot be changed.

The Monarchy owes its brilliance and its glory to its ancient constitution. It is the Nobility which laid the foundations of that constitution, which erected its structure, and which has supported it since; it is they who carried the Crown into the Royal House and kept it there. Without the Nobility, the kings are without strength and the people without defenders. This is taught to us by the testimony of the sovereigns themselves.

"And because the principal strength of our kingdom consists in the

---

[1] Loyseau, *Des Ordres.* [Charles Loyseau was the most distinguished legal scholar in France in the first half of the 17th century.]

Nobility," said Henry III, "whose diminution would weaken the state, we desire and intend that it should be protected and maintained in its ancient honors, rights, liberties, and customary immunities."

If the Nobility is degraded, if its original birthrights are taken from it, it would soon lose its spirit, its courage, and the elevation of soul which characterizes it. This body, which is unalterable in its worth and its loyalty, cannot permit change or diminution of the honors and distinctions which are due to the birth and the service of its members.

. . . . .

It is in accordance with these principles and examples that your parlement, Sire, pleads with Your Majesty to consider the provisions and consequences of the edict which you have sent to us.

By releasing from compulsory labor the lowest class of the citizens who have been subject to it until now, the edict thrusts this burden upon the two orders of the state which have never been bound to carry it before. All differences among your subjects are lost; the nobleman and the churchman become subject to compulsory labor, or, what amounts to the same thing, they all become subject to the tax which is to replace compulsory labor.

This is not a battle of the rich against the poor, Sire, as some have sought to persuade you. It is a question of status and one of the most important ones, for what is involved is whether all your subjects can and should be treated without distinction, whether no more differences of status, rank, titles and preeminence are to be accepted among them. To subject the nobles to a tax to buy out the *corvée*, in violation of the precept that *no one is subject to compulsory labor who is not subject to the* taille, is to decide that they are subject to compulsory labor. Once this principle is accepted, they could be compelled to perform compulsory labor at once if the *corvée* were reestablished.

. . . . .

These truths and these principles, Sire, will all strike home to Your Majesty's heart. You will easily grasp all the abuse and the peril in this baneful equality which some seek to establish among your subjects; your justice will enlighten your charity and your humanity. You will no longer look upon the edict providing for conversion of the *corvées* into a tax except as an illusion for those of your subjects whom you wish to relieve, and you will realize that a territorial tax of unlimited quantity, by absorbing forever a portion of the revenues, reduces the value of the funds and constitutes a real attack upon the property of citizens of every order.

Finally, after giving consideration to the law and constitution of this state, Your Majesty will no longer remain in doubt that this plan, against which the parlement protests only in the performance of its duty, obviously tends toward the destruction of the original liberties of nobles and churchmen, to the confusion of the orders, and to the overthrow of the principles upon which the Monarchy was founded.

115. PARLIAMENT BEFORE REFORM

The British parliamentary system was generally taken as the model of good government by those who believed in the ultimate mastery of government by those who were ruled. It was not until late in the 18th century that a new breed of reformers subjected this system to attack because, they said, its claim to speak for the people was unwarranted. These "Radicals," who were deeply influenced by the most extreme Enlightenment doctrines, advocated reform of abuses as a method of salvaging Parliament for popular government. Their leader during the sixties and seventies was John Wilkes (1727-1797), who was repeatedly expelled from the House of Commons after he had been elected for Middlesex. This was a county, although it was within the urban limits of London, and it therefore had a broader suffrage than boroughs did. When Wilkes was elected lord mayor of London in 1774, Commons finally seated him. In the House, Wilkes supported the cause of the Americans and continued his defense of the principle of a free press. He also called attention to the anomaly of "rotten boroughs," which sent members to Commons even though such territories had long since ceased to be populous or even inhabited. The following speech was delivered on March 21, 1776.

John Wilkes

Speech in Parliament, March 21, 1776

A motion was made, and the Question was put, "That leave be given to bring in a Bill, for a just and equal Representation of the People of England in Parliament." Mr. Wilkes said,

Mr. Speaker, All wise governments, and well-regulated states, have been careful to mark and correct the various abuses, which a considerable length of time almost necessarily creates. Among these, one of the most striking and important in our country is, the present unfair and inadequate representation of the people of England in Parliament. It is now

---

Source: S. MacCoby (ed.), *The English Radical Tradition, 1763–1914* (New York: New York University Press, 1957), pp. 28–32. Reprinted by permission of A. & C. Black Ltd. Publishers, London.

become so partial and unequal from the lapse of time, that I believe almost every gentleman in the House will agree with me in the necessity of its being taken into our most serious consideration . . . It appears, sir, from the writs remaining in the King's Remembrancer's office in the Exchequer that no less than 22 towns sent members to the Parliament in the 23rd, 25th, and 26th, of Edward I which have long ceased to be represented. The names of some of them are scarcely known to us, such as those of Canebrig and Bamburg in Northumberland, Pershore and Brem in Worcestershire, Jarvall and Tykhull in Yorkshire. What a happy fate, sir, has attended the boroughs of Gatton and Old Sarum, of which, although *ipsae periere ruinae*[1], the names are familiar to us, the clerk regularly calls them over, and four respectable gentlemen represent their departed greatness . . . Great abuses, it must be owned, contrary to the primary ideas of the English constitution, were committed by our former princes, in giving the right of representation to several paltry boroughs, because the places were poor and dependent on them, or on a favourite over-grown peer. The landmarks of the constitution have often been removed. The marked partiality for Cornwall, which single county still sends, within one, as many members as the whole kingdom of Scotland, is striking. It arose from yielding to the crown in tin and lands a larger hereditary revenue than any other English county, as well as from the duchy being in the crown, and giving an amazing command and influence. By such abuses of our princes the constitution was wounded in its most vital part. Henry VIII restored two members, Edward VI twenty, Queen Mary four, Queen Elizabeth twelve, James I sixteen, Charles I eighteen, in all seventy-two. The alterations by creation in the same period were more considerable, for Henry VIII created thirty-three, Edward VI twenty-eight, Queen Mary seventeen, Queen Elizabeth twelve, James I eleven; in all 137 . . . I am satisfied, sir, the sentiments of the people cannot be justly known at this time from the resolutions of a Parliament, composed as the present is, even though no undue influence was practiced after the return of the members to the House, even supposing for a moment the influence of all the baneful arts of corruption to be suspended, which, for a moment, I believe, they have not been under the present profligate administration.

. . . From the majority of electors only in the boroughs, which return members to this House, it has been demonstrated that this number of 254 members elected by no more than 5,723 persons, generally the inhabitants of Cornish, and other very insignificant boroughs . . . Are these the men to give laws to this vast empire, and to tax this wealthy nation? I do not mention all the tedious calculations, because gentlemen may find

[1] Translation of the Latin: "their very remains are lost."

them at length in the works of the incomparable Dr. Price, in Postlethwaite, and in Burgh's Political Disquisitions . . . Lord Chancellor Talbot supposed the majority of this House was elected by 50,000 persons, and he exclaimed against the injustice of that idea. More accurate calculations than his Lordship's, and the unerring rules of political arithmetic, have shown the injustice to be vastly beyond what his Lordship even suspected . . .

The Americans with great reason insist, that the present war is carried on, contrary to the sense of the nation, by a ministerial junto, and an arbitrary faction, equally hostile to the rights of Englishmen and the claims of Americans. The various addresses to the throne from most numerous bodies, praying that the sword may be returned to the scabbard, and all hostilities cease, confirm this assertion . . . Our history furnishes frequent instances of the sense of Parliament running directly counter to the sense of the nation. It was notoriously of late the case in the business of the Middlesex election. I believe the fact to be equally certain in the grand American dispute, at least as to the actual hostilities now carrying on against our brethren and fellow-subjects. The proposition before us will bring the case to an issue, and from a fair and equal representation of the people, America may at length distinguish the real sentiments of freemen and Englishmen.

I do not mean, sir, at this time, to go into a tedious detail of all the various proposals, which have been made for redressing this irregularity in the representation of the people . . . I will at this time, sir, only throw out general ideas, that every free agent in this kingdom should, in my wish, be represented in Parliament; that the metropolis, which contains in itself a ninth part of the people, and the counties of Middlesex, York, and others, which so greatly abound with inhabitants, should receive an increase in their representation; that the mean, and insignificant boroughs, so emphatically stiled *the rotten part of our constitution,* should be lopped off, and the electors in them thrown into the counties; and the rich, populous, trading towns, Birmingham, Manchester, Sheffield, Leeds and others, be permitted to send deputies to the great council of the nation.

The disfranchising of the mean, venal, and dependent boroughs would be laying the axe to the root of corruption and treasury influence, as well as aristocratical tyranny . . . I wish, sir, an English Parliament to speak the free, unbiased sense of the body of the English people, and of every man among us . . . The meanest mechanic, the poorest peasant and day-labourer, has important rights respecting his personal liberty, that of his wife and children, his property, however inconsiderable, his wages, his earnings, the very price and value of each day's hard labour, which are in many trades and manufactures regulated by the power of Parliament . . . Some share therefore in the power of making those laws, which deeply interest them, and to which they are expected to pay obedience should be reserved even to this inferior, but most useful set of men in the community. We ought always to remember this important truth acknowledged by every free state, that all government is instituted for the good of the mass of the people to be governed; that they are the original fountain of power, *and even of revenue,* and in all events the last resource . . .

116. THE JUSTICE OF PETER THE GREAT

If revolution is the attempt to transform society by the use of force, no man was ever more of a revolutionary than Peter I, Tsar of Russia (1672-1725), whom history remembers as Peter the Great. Building on a tradition of rivalry with and imitation of the West that went back several centuries, Peter was the fiercest Westernizer in the whole history of Russia. During his famous long voyage to western Europe in 1697 and 1698, there was a rebellion in Moscow of the Streltsi, the musketeers who garrisoned the capital. They resented the innovations already obvious in the tsar's policy, particularly those military reforms that threatened their own self-satisfied repose. They also spoke for the complaints of the old boyar aristocracy to which they belonged, whom the tsar brutally shoved aside when they would not humbly do his bidding. Peter sped back to Moscow, where, although the uprising had long since been put down, he oversaw the trial and execution of the rebels. The ferocity of the executions shocked foreign observers, like the Austrian legation secretary who recorded his impressions in a Latin diary.

Diary of an Austrian Diplomat at the Court of Peter the Great, 1698

. . . . .

The sentence being thus framed so as to include all the Strelitz so no tardy repentance was attended with impunity for the crime. For before the Czar's Majesty had set out on his travels a mutiny of the same Strelitz had taken place, on the appeasing of which they were pardoned on condition of never daring to attempt such a course again. This condition

Source: *Diary of an Austrian Secretary of Legation at the Court of Czar Peter the Great,* translated from the original Latin by the Count Mac Donnell (London: Bradbury & Evans, 1863), Vol. I, pp. 100–106.

was recorded in a public written instrument, by which they bound themselves, even if no law were in force for treason against Majesty, to every torment that could be thought of, to the most cruel tortures, and to the penalty of death itself, in case by renewed contumacy towards the Sovereign's weal they should admit of anything contrary to their sworn allegiance, and their debt of most humble respect. All confirmed this sanction of the Czar with their own signature, &c.; those who did not know how to write marking with a cross in token of their approval. This was an aggravating fact which closed up the avenue of mercy, and appointed rigorous justice the avenger of treason.

The First Execution—10th October, 1698

To this exhibition of avenging justice the Czar's Majesty invited all the ambassadors of foreign sovereigns, as if it were to assert anew on his return that sovereign prerogative of life and death which the rebels had disputed with him.

The barracks in Bebraschentsko end in a bare field which rises to the summit of a rather steep hill. This was the place appointed for the executions. Here were planted the gibbet stakes, on which the foul heads of these confessedly guilty wretches were to be set, to protract their ignominy beyond death. There the first scene of the tragedy lay exposed. The strangers that had gathered to the spectacle were kept aloof from too close approach; the whole regiment of guards was drawn up in array under arms. A little further off, on a high *tumulus* in the area of the place, there was a multitude of Muscovites, crowded and crushing together in a dense circle. A German Major was then my companion; he concealed his nationality in a Muscovite dress, besides which he relied upon his military rank and the liberty that he might take in consequence of being entitled by reason of his being in the service of the Czar to share in the privileges of the Muscovites. He mingled with the thronging crowd of Muscovites, and when he came back announced that five rebel heads had been cut off in that spot by an axe that was swung by the noblest arm of all Muscovy. The river Jausa flows past the barracks in Bebraschentsko, and divides them in two.

On the opposite side of this stream there were a hundred criminals set upon those little Muscovite carts which the natives call Sbosek, awaiting the hour of the death they had to undergo. There was a cart for every criminal, and a soldier to guard each. No priestly office was to be seen; as if the condemned were unworthy of that pious compassion. But they all bore lighted tapers in their hands, not to die without light and cross. The horrors of impending death were increased by the piteous lamentations of their women, the sobbing on every side, and the shrieks of the dying that run upon the sad array. The mother wept for her son, the daughter deplored a parent's fate, the wife lamenting a husband's lot, bemoaned along with the others, from whom the various ties of blood and kindred drew tears of sad farewell. But when the horses, urged to a sharp pace, drew them off to the place of their doom, the wail of the women rose into louder sobs and moans. As they tried to keep up with them, forms of expression like these bespoke their grief, as others explained them to me: "Why are you torn from me so soon? Why do you desert me? Is a last embrace then denied me? Why am I hindered from bidding him farewell?" With complaints like these they tried to follow their friends when they could not keep up with their rapid course. From a country seat belonging to General Schachin one hundred and thirty more Strelitz were led forth to die. At each side of all the city gates there was a gibbet erected, each of which was loaded with six rebels on that day.

When all were duly brought to the place of execution, and the half dozens were duly distributed at their several gibbets, the Czar's Majesty, dressed in a green Polish cloak, and attended by a numerous suite of Muscovite nobles, came to the gate where, by his Majesty's command, the imperial Lord Envoy had stopped in his own carriage, along with the representatives of Poland and Denmark. Next them was Major-General de Carlowiz, who had conducted his Majesty on his way from Poland, and a great many other foreigners, among whom the Muscovites mingled round about the gate. Then the proclamation of the sentence began, the Czar exhorting all the bystanders to mark well its tenor. As the executioner was unable to dispatch so many criminals, some military officers, by command of the Czar, came under compulsion to aid in this butcher's task. The guilty were neither chained nor fettered; but logs were tied to their legs, which hindered them from walking fast, but still allowed them the use of their feet. They strove of their own accord to ascend the ladder, making the sign of the cross towards the four quarters of the world; they themselves covered their eyes and faces with a piece of linen (which is a national custom); very many putting their necks into the halter sprang headlong of themselves from the gallows, in order to precipitate their end. There were counted two hundred and thirty that expiated their flagitious conduct by halter and gibbet.

The Second Execution—13th October, 1698

Although all those that were accomplices of the rebellion were condemned to death, yet the Czar's Majesty would not dispense with strict investigation. The more so as the unripe years and judgment of many seemed to bespeak mercy, as they were, as one may say, rather victims of error than of deliberate crime. In such case the penalty of death was commuted into some corporal infliction—such as, for instance, the cutting off of their ears and noses, to mark them with ignominy for life—a life to be passed, not as previously, in the heart of the realm, but in various and barbarous places on the frontiers of Muscovy. To such places fifty were transported today, after being castigated in the manner prescribed.

117. SERVITUDE IN TSARIST RUSSIA

The reforms of Peter the Great were directed toward increasing the power of the Russian state against Europe, as well as toward making the nobility—the old boyars and the newly ennobled bureaucrats and officers—obedient and competent servants of the crown. The great tsar did not even conceive of improving the condition of the peasantry, much as he enjoyed mingling with workmen in the shipyards of Holland during his visit to the West. His successors continued his policies with greater or lesser effectiveness, but by the time Catherine II was put on the throne in 1762 by a palace revolution, it had become necessary for the ruler of Russia to hold the loyalty of the nobility by emancipating them from the obligation of service to the crown and at the same time removing the last limitations upon their control of their peasants. The condition of the peasants, whom it is customary to describe as serfs, was hard to distinguish from that of outright slaves, and they are described as such in the letters on Russian conditions written by an English visitor, William Richardson (1743-1814) during 1768 and 1769. His *Anecdotes of the Russian Empire* were published in 1783.

William Richardson

Anecdotes of the Russian Empire

. . . . .

I believe sincerely that no despot, or, if you like the term better, no absolute monarch, ever ruled with more prudence, or studied the welfare of his people with more rectitude of intention, than the present Empress of Russia. Yet it is impossible for a native of Britain, giving an account

---

SOURCE: William Richardson, *Anecdotes of the Russian Empire in a Series of Letters Written, a Few Years Ago, from St. Petersburg* (London: Frank Cass & Co., Ltd., 1968), pp. 193–200.

of this country to an Englishman, not to express such feelings and reflections, as a comparison between the British government, and that of other nations, must naturally suggest.

The peasants in Russia, that is to say, the greatest part of the subjects of this empire, are in a state of abject slavery; and are reckoned the property of the nobles to whom they belong, as much as their dogs and horses. Indeed, the wealth of a great man in Russia is not computed by the extent of land he possesses, or by the quantity of grain he can bring to market, but by the number of his slaves. Those belonging to Prince Sherebatoff, and constituting his fortune, are said to be no less in number than a hundred and twenty-seven thousand.

Every slave pays about a ruble yearly to his owner; and if he be in the way of making money, the tribute he pays is augmented. In general, every Russian nobleman allots to the peasants that belong to him, a certain portion of land to be cultivated by them, the produce of which, except what suffices for their own maintenance, is paid to the proprietor. Sometimes those slaves practise trades, or engage in traffic [commerce]; and all such persons pay a much greater sum yearly to their owners, than is done by the labourer of the ground. In fact, a Russian peasant has no property; every thing he possesses, even the miserable raiment that shelters him from the cold, may be seized by his master as his own.—A carpenter, being known to have made some money, was commanded by the rapacious steward of a rapacious Knaez [prince], to give two hundred rubles to his owner. The man obeyed, and brought the money in copper. "I must have it in silver," said the steward. The slave, denying that he had so much, was instantly scourged till he promised to fulfil the demand. He brought the silver, and the covetous superior retained both the silver and copper.—You will easily conceive, that men in this situation, if they are ever enabled to improve their fortunes, will conceal their wealth, and assume an external appearance of indigence and misery.

The owner has also the power of selling his slave, or of hiring his labour to other persons; and, it happens sometimes, that a Knaez, or Boyard, shall give a slave to a neighbouring Boyard in exchange for a dog or a horse. The owner may also inflict on his slaves whatever punishment he pleases, and for any sort of offence. It is against law, indeed, to put any of them to death; yet it happens, sometimes, that a poor slave dies of the wounds he receives from a passionate and unrelenting superior. I have heard, that not long ago a lady at Moscow, the sister of Marischal S———, was convicted of having put to death upwards of seventy slaves, by scourging, and by inflicting upon them other barbarous punishments. It was a matter of amusement with her to contrive such modes of punishment as were whimsical and unusual. Such enormity, however, notwithstanding her rank, and the great power which the nobility have over their slaves, was not to pass with impunity. She was tried, was found guilty, and condemned to stand in the market-place, with a label on her breast declaring her crime, and to be shut up in a dungeon. But she, who had felt no reluctance in making her fellow-creatures suffer the most inhuman torments, and had even amused herself with the variety of their sufferings, had such a sense of her rank, and such lively feelings of her own disgrace, that pride, shame, and resentment deprived her of her reason. In truth, both the crime and the punishment seem to me strongly marked with the characters of depravity.

As a Russian peasant has no property, can enjoy none of the fruits of his own labour more than is sufficient to preserve his existence, and can transmit nothing to his children but the inheritance of wretched bondage, he thinks of nothing but the present. You are not, of consequence, to expect of them much industry and exertion. Exposed to corporal punishment, and put on the footing of irrational animals, how can they possess that spirit and elevation of sentiment which distinguish the natives of a free state? Treated with so much inhumanity, how can they be humane? I am confident, that most of the defects which appear in their national character, are in consequence of the despotism of the Russian government.

I mentioned that the revenue of a Russian nobleman arises from those lands which are cultivated by his slaves; and sometimes in their being employed in other occupations than tillage. They often come from distant provinces, and are either employed as domestic slaves, mechanics, or as day-labourers, at Moscow, Petersburg, and other cities. In these cases they must have certificates and a written permit, specifying their names, owners, and the time they are allowed to be absent. When they come to any great town, with a view of remaining there, and engaging themselves in any work, the person who employs them must lodge their certificates with the master of the police in the place where they are about to reside. After remaining their allotted time, they must return to their former owners, and must be accountable to them for every thing they have earned.—To these practices the Empress alludes in the following passages, in her instructions to the deputies assembled for making laws: —"It seems too, that the method of exacting their revenues, invented by the lords, diminishes both the inhabitants, and the spirit of agriculture, in Russia. Almost all the villages are heavily taxed. The lords, who seldom or never reside in their villages, lay an impost on every head, of one, two, or even five rubles, without the least regard to the means by which the peasants may be able to raise this money. It is highly necessary that the law should prescribe a rule to the lords, for a more judicious method of raising their revenues; and oblige them to levy such a tax as tends least to separate the peasant from his house and family: this would be the means by which agriculture would become more extensive, and population more increased in the empire. Even now, some husbandmen do not see their houses for fifteen years together, and yet pay the tax annually to their respective lords; which they procure in towns at a vast distance from their families, and wander over the whole empire for that purpose."

Another hardship to which the Russian peasants are exposed, is, that they are obliged to marry whatsoever persons, or at what time their superiors please. Every slave who is a father, pays a certain tax to his owner for each of his children; and the owner is therefore solitious that a new progeny be raised as soon as possible. Marriages of this sort must produce little happiness; neither husband nor wife are very studious of conjugal fidelity: hence the lower classes are as profligate as can possibly be conceived; and, in such circumstances, we cannot expect that they will have much care of their children.

The condition of those peasants who are immediate slaves of the crown, is reckoned less wretched than the condition of those who belong to the nobility; and they are of three kinds: The first are those who, having either secretly, or by the favour of a humane superior, been able to procure as much money as may enable them to purchase their freedom, have also the good luck to live under a superior who is equitable enough to free them for the sum they offer. Such persons, and their children, are ever after immediate slaves of the crown. On the same footing are all priests and their children; though the dependence of the inferior upon the superior clergy, is sometimes as grievous as the most painful bondage. Soldiers also, and their children; and this class includes the whole body of the nobility, are immediate slaves of the crown.

118. EIGHTEENTH-CENTURY WARFARE

The ultimate argument of politics in the early modern period, as always, was power, and power meant employing the instrument of armies (or, for countries on the sea, navies). No ruler was more effective in the use of that instrument than Frederick II, King of Prussia, who employed it in two great wars—the War of the Austrian Succession and the Seven Years' War—to raise his kingdom from a second-rate to a first-rate power. Frederick, who reigned from 1740 to 1786, paid close attention to the development of the art of war and gave a clear description of the character of warfare in the 18th century in several of his works. A distinguished modern military historian, Jay Luvaas, assembled Frederick's writings on war into a book based on material in the king's *History of My Own Times*, his *Anti-Machiavel*, and his *Military Instruction* for his generals. The selection below is from *History of My Own Times.*

Frederick II

History of My Own Times

. . . . .

The Emperor Ferdinand I kept an army of scarcely 30,000 men. Charles VI in the war of 1733 paid 170,000 without oppressing his people. Louis XIII maintained 60,000; Louis XIV 220,000 and even as many as 360,000 during the War of the Spanish Succession. Since this time every prince, even the most petty, has augmented his military forces in imitation. In the war of 1683, Louis XIV raised as many men as he could in order to have a decided superiority over his enemies. He disbanded none after the peace, which forced the Emperor and the German princes to keep as large an army on hand as they could afford. Once established, this custom was perpetuated.

War became increasingly expensive. The provisions for the magazines swallowed up enormous sums, since large numbers of cavalry had to be maintained and assembled in their cantonments before the opening of the campaign and the season for forage.

The infantry of standing armies underwent an almost total change as a result of tacticians' efforts to bring it to perfection. Before the War of the Spanish Succession half of the men in each battalion carried pikes and the other matchlocks, and they fought armed six deep. The pikes were used against cavalry, their muskets kept up a weak fire, and their matches often made them misfire or flash in the pan. These inconveniences brought about a change in weapons: pikes and matchlocks were discarded and replaced by fusils and bayonets, combining the formidable effect of fire and sword. With this increase in firepower the battalions step by step diminished their depth, which gave them a more extensive front. That military mechanic, the Prince of Anhalt, introduced iron ramrods and placed the ranks three deep.

The late king, by his infinite assiduity, introduced a wonderful order and discipline among his troops and a precision hitherto unknown in Europe in their movements and maneuvers. The Prussian battalion became a walking battery: the speed with which the Prussian could reload trebled the firepower and made him the equal of three adversaries. Other nations afterwards imitated the Prussians, but with less success.

SOURCE: Reprinted with permission of The Macmillan Company from *Frederick the Great on the Art of War*, edited by Jay Luvaas, pp. 69–75.

Charles XII had introduced the custom of adding two cannon to each battalion. In Berlin cannon were cast of three, six, twelve, and twenty-four pounds—light enough to be worked by hand and advanced in battle with the battalion to which each belonged. All these new inventions transformed an army into a moving fortress, against which every approach was formidable and murderous.

The French in 1672 invented transportable copper pontoons. This easy way of constructing bridges rendered rivers useless as barriers. To the French also is due the art of attack and defense of fortresses—Vauban especially approached perfection in the art of fortification. . . .

This age has seen the revival of light-armed troops: the Austrian pandours, the French legions, the Prussian free battalion, and the hussars, originally from Hungary but imitated in all other armies, have replaced the Numidian and Parthian cavalry so famous in the Roman wars. Any uniform was unknown to the ancient military; and it is not a century since this practice was generally adopted.

The Composition of Armies

Experience has shown that the national troops of a state are always the most serviceable. . . . I agree with Machiavelli that a state is generally but ill served by mercenary troops, because they can never act with as much fidelity and courage as men who fight for their possessions and families. It is particularly dangerous for a prince to allow the people to languish in a state of inactivity and to grow soft and effeminate at a time when the fatigues of war harden and discipline their neighbors.

It has often been observed that a nation that recently emerged from a Civil War is far superior in valor to its neighbors, for in a Civil War all the people are soldiers. There is more room for merit and less for favor, and every man has more frequent opportunities to discover and improve his military talents.

There are some particular cases, however, that must be excepted from Machiavelli's general rule. If a country does not produce a sufficient number of men for raising a complete army and replacing the losses in war, mercenary troops are absolutely necessary for supplying the needs of the state. In this case, several expedients are found for removing the difficulties and dangers to which a state is exposed by employing mercenaries. The mercenaries are mixed with the native troops so as not to make a separate and independent body. Both are subject to the same discipline in order to make them equally faithful, and particular care is taken that the number of foreign troops does not exceed that of the national ones. . . .

Most European armies consist of national and mercenary troops. Those who inhabit cities or who till the soil are exempted from military service upon paying a certain tax for maintaining the soldiers who defend them. For this reason our armies for the most part are composed of the dregs of society—sluggards, rakes, debauchees, rioters, undutiful sons, and the like, who have as little attachment to their masters or concern about them as do foreigners. How different are these armies from those of the Romans, who conquered the world. Desertions, which are now so frequent in all armies, were unknown among the Romans. Those who fought for their families, their household gods, their fellow-citizens, and everything that was dear to them never betrayed so many interests by their cowardice and desertion. It is the security of the sovereign princes of Europe at present that their troops are so much alike that in this respect they have no advantage over one another. Only the Swedes are citizens, peasants, and soldiers at the same time but, on the other hand, when the Swedes march off to war there are too few inhabitants left at home to till the soil. Therefore their power is by no means formidable. They can execute nothing without ruining themselves in the long run, as well as their enemies.

A King ought not to make war solely with foreign troops. If possible he should depend upon none but his own, and he should export rather than import auxiliaries. Prudence will teach him that he must put himself in a condition of fearing neither his enemies nor his friends. . . . Such powers as have no need of mixed or auxiliary troops ought certainly not to employ them, but as few European princes are in such a situation, I believe that they are in no danger from their auxiliaries as long as these do not outnumber their own troops. . . . As for the Swiss troops in the service of France . . . it is certain the French have owed many victories to their valor and conduct and reaped signal advantages from their service—so much so, in fact, that if the Swiss and Germans employed in the French infantry were to be dismissed, their army would be much less formidable than it is at present.

Our regiments are composed half of our own people and half of foreigners who have been enrolled for money. The latter have no particular attachment to our service and wait only for the first opportunity to desert. The question therefore is to prevent desertion.

The composition of my troops requires infinite attention on the part of those who command them. It is necessary always to make them observe the most exact discipline and to take great care for their welfare. It is also necessary that Prussian soldiers be better fed than nearly any other troops in Europe.

Some of our generals contend that a man is only a man, and that if the loss of one is made good the particular individual involved does not effect the whole. This may apply to other armies but it is not true of ours. If a well-trained soldier deserts and is replaced by another who is equally well-trained, then it is a matter of no consequence. But if a soldier who has been trained in the use of arms for two years in order to give him a certain degree of proficiency should desert and be replaced by a bad subject, or not be replaced at all, eventually the consequences will be injurious.

We have seen that through the negligence of officers in this particular, regiments have lost their reputation and have found themselves diminished by desertion. Such a loss weakens the army at a time when it is essential for it to be at full strength. You will lose your best forces if you do not give this matter the greatest attention, and you will not be in a position to make good your losses. Although Prussia is well populated, it is doubtful whether you will find many men with the stature of my soldiers, and even assuming that you could, does it follow that they could be drilled overnight?

An army is composed for the most part of idle and inactive men. Unless the general keeps a constant eye over them and forces them to perform their duty this machine, which is artificial and cannot be made perfect, soon will disintegrate, and in the final analysis only the concept of a disciplined army will remain.

It is therefore necessary to accustom the troops to work without letup. The experience of those who have not been deficient in this respect offers convincing proof that it is very necessary to keep the soldiers busy and that every day there are abuses to be corrected which pass unobserved by those who make no attempt to discover them.

This constant and painful attention may appear harsh to a general, but its consequences will bear good dividends. What advantage will he not gain with troops so brave, so smart, and so well disciplined? A general who would pass for a foolhardy person would only be acting by established rules with us. He can run any risk and undertake any enterprise that man is capable of executing. Besides, the soldiers will not allow a man to remain amongst them who is capable of any weakness; one would certainly not notice this in the other armies.

I have seen officers and common soldiers dangerously wounded who nevertheless would refuse to abandon their posts or fall to the rear to have their wounds dressed. With troops such as these one could conquer the entire world if the victories were not as fatal to oneself as to the enemies. For you can undertake anything with them provided you do not let them lack provisions. On the march you will outstrip the enemy by speed; if you attack the enemy in a wood you will force him from it; if you make your men climb a mountain you will disperse anyone who offers resistance and then the battle becomes only a massacre. If you send your cavalry into action they will charge through and demolish the enemy at sword's point.

But since it is not enough merely to have good troops, and since a general through ignorance, loses all of his advantages, I will speak [later] of the qualities of a general and give rules which in part I have experimented with at my own expense, and in part the great generals have given me.

119. ENLIGHTENED DESPOTISM AND RELIGION

The endeavor of some rulers to put the ideas of the Enlightenment into practice in their own countries by their own authority was one of the significant political movements of the later 18th century. Perhaps the most stubbornly insistent of these "enlightened despots" was the Emperor Joseph II (1741-1790), who reigned from 1765 in the Empire but only became sole head of the Austrian dominions with the death of his mother, Maria Theresa, in 1780. In a single decade, Joseph attempted a host of reforms, from a partial emancipation of serfs to organization for economic progress. His measures to limit the autonomy of the Catholic Church, while he tightened his own control over it, were effective in Austria but kindled a revolution in the Austrian Netherlands (modern Belgium). Two of the emperor's principal edicts granted toleration to Protestants to practice their religion (A), although continuing some advantages to Catholicism, and abolished several contemplative monastic orders (B), whose mystical asceticism particularly offended Joseph.

A. Joseph II

Toleration Patent, 1781

ORDER *In Spiritualibus* TO ALL IMPERIAL AND ROYAL PROVINCIAL GOVERNMENTS

MY DEAR LIEGES!

Being convinced, on the one hand, that all violence to conscience is harmful, and, on the other, of the great benefit accruing to religion and

SOURCE: C. A. Macartney (ed.), *The Habsburg and Hohenzollern Dynasties in the Seventeenth and Eighteenth Centuries* (New York: Walker & Co., 1970), pp. 155–57.

to the State from a true Christian tolerance, We have found Ourselves moved to grant to the adherents of the Lutheran and Calvinist religions, and also to the non-Uniat Greek religion, everywhere, the appropriate private practice of their faith, regardless of whether it had been previously customary or introduced, or not. The Catholic religion alone shall continue to enjoy the prerogative of the public practice of its faith, but members of the two Protestant religions and the existing non-Uniat Greek shall be permitted the private practice thereof in any place where the number of persons, as defined below, and the resources of the inhabitants make it practicable, and where the said non-Catholics do not already enjoy the right of practicing it publicly. In particular, We allow:

Firstly, non-Catholic subjects, where there are one hundred families, even if they are not all domiciled in the locality of the place of worship or of the pastor, but part of them live as much as some hours' distance away, to build a place of worship and school of their own, and those living further away may attend the nearest place of worship (inside Our Hereditary Dominions) as often as they wish, also the pastors belonging to Our Hereditary Dominions may visit the members of their congregations, and may administer the necessary instruction and spiritual and material comfort to the sick, but may not, under pain of severest punishment, prevent a Catholic priest from being called in, if any sick person wishes it.

In respect to the place of worship, We order expressly that it shall not have any chimes, bells, or towers, unless such already exist, or public entrance from the street signifying a church, but otherwise they are free to build it of whatever material they will and shall be completely free to administer their sacraments and celebrate Divine service, both in the place itself and conveyed to the sick in the Chapels of Ease, and to conduct funerals with their pastor in attendance.

Secondly, they are free to appoint their own schoolmasters, who are maintained by the parish, but shall be subject to the supervision of the Provincial Schools Directorate in respect of methods of instruction and discipline. In particular, We allow:

Thirdly, to the non-Catholic inhabitants of a locality, the choice of their pastors, if they pay for and support the same, but where the authorities provide these services they must enjoy the right of presentation; but We reserve to Ourselves the right of confirmation, in such fashion that where there are Protestant Consistories, the confirmation is given through them, and where there are none, granted through the existing Protestant Consistories in Teschen or Hungary, until conditions call for the establishment in a Province of its own Consistory.

Fourthly: the *jura stolae* remain reserved to the Parish Ordinary, as in Silesia.

Fifthly: the jurisdiction in respect of matters affecting the religion of non-Catholics shall be exercised by the administrative officials of the Province, assisted by one of their own pastors and theologians; this Court shall render judgment in accordance with their religious tenets, but appeal shall lie from this to Our Chancellery.

Sixthly: the issue by non-Catholics of the reversals on marriage, hitherto customary, in respect of the upbringing of the children in the Catholic faith is to cease altogether from now on; where the father is a Catholic, all children, of either sex, are to be brought up without question in the Catholic religion, this being to be regarded as a prerogative of the ruling religion; where, however, the father is Protestant and the mother Catholic, the sex of the child shall decide.

Seventhly: non-Catholics are in future admitted under dispensation to buy houses and real property, to acquire municipal domicile and practice as master craftsmen, to take up academic appointments and posts in the public service, and are not to be required to take the oath in any form contrary to their religious tenets, nor, unless they themselves wish it, to attend processions or functions of the ruling religion. The sole criteria in all choices or appointments to official posts are—as has long been the case in Our army, without the least difficulty and with great benefit—to be the candidate's integrity and competence, and also his Christian and moral way of life; difference of religion is to be disregarded. Dispensations to acquire property, municipal domicile, and master craftsmen's licences are to be issued by the Kreis authorities in towns under manorial jurisdiction; in Royal and *laibgeding* boroughs, by the Provincial Cameral offices, where such exist; failing them, by Our Provinicial Government. They are to be issued without difficulty. Should, however, the authority find any objection to an application suggesting that it ought to be rejected, a reasoned report is to be sent to the Provincial Government, and thence to the Chancellery, for Our decision.

In cases of the *jus incolatus* of the upper classes, the Provincial Government is to give its opinion, and the dispensation is to be granted by Our Bohemian-Austrian Court Chancellery.

Provincial Governments are to communicate this Our decision to all Kreis offices, magistrates, and manorial authorities through printed circulars, of which a larger number than the usual is to be run off. Further, printers and publishers in the Province are permitted to hand these printed circulars to any person asking for them and thus secure adequate dissemination thereof also in other Provinces.

B. Joseph II

Monasteries Patent, 1781

ORDER *In Spiritualibus* (JANUARY 1, 1781)

We have found fit, for good and sufficient reasons, to abolish all Houses of the following Orders in Our Hereditary Lands and to make the following dispositions with respect to their members and property:

1. All Houses, Monasteries, Hospices, or whatever else these spiritual houses of communal life are called, of the male Orders of the Carthusians and Camaldolites and the Eremites or so-called *Waldbrüder*, and the female Orders of the Carmelites, Sisters of St. Clare, Capuchines, and Franciscans are dissolved, and the communal life of the persons in them is to cease.

2. The processes of dissolution shall be as follows: On receipt of this Rescript, the Provincial Government shall send to each House of the said Orders a qualified Commissioner with the necessary instructions and written authority, together with a skilled man from the Cameral accounting office, with the mission of informing the Superiors and all the communities, in the most deferential and kindly fashion, of Our decision, and intimating to them that henceforward no male or female novices or other members of the Order who have not yet taken their vows shall be permitted to do so. The instruction is to be taken down in writing and signed by the Father or Mother Superior and the head of the House, in witness that they have received the order. Next, the Commissioner shall demand the keys of the cashboxes, treasuries, archives, and stores, and shall seal up everything not necessary for daily use in the church and the house so long as the members of the Order remain there, leaving unsealed what is necessary for their day-to-day purposes. An inventory shall then immediately be drawn up, and the valuation put in the hands of a skilled and honest lay official, who shall supply the religious with their daily needs until they disperse.

3. The Superiors, the bursars, and all persons officially concerned with the administration of the real and personal property of the Monastery, Church, or chapel of the communities, whether priests or lay brothers or sisters, or secular persons, are to make a sworn statement to the Commission in the enclosed form. . . . The Commissioner shall further

---

SOURCE: C. A. Macartney (ed.), *The Habsburg and Hohenzollern Dynasties in the Seventeenth and Eighteenth Centuries* (New York: Walker & Co., 1970), pp. 158–60.

warn them to observe their oath, under pain of severe penalty. This is to be recorded in the official minute.

4. The Commissioner's work is not to be hampered by any obstacle, not excluding the Enclosure, which must always be open for the Commissioner. He must carry out his duties with seemliness and dignity, but for precaution's sake, every Diocesan should be asked to order the Cloister to carry out all orders exactly.

5. After the real and personal property has been taken over, an inventory is to be drawn up in duplicate, one copy to go to the Provincial authorities, the other to be sent to Vienna. The administration of the whole property is to be entrusted to the Camera, which has to see that until their discharge and the payment of their pensions the clergy are provided with food and clothing as hereto, but without superfluity or hospitality.

6. All objects in the cells or the Superior's lodgings serving personal use, such as pictures, books, furniture, and utensils, shall be left with their owners; an inventory is to be taken of these objects also, but when their owners leave the House the owners shall be permitted to take these objects with them.

Furthermore, it is to be made known to all, orally or in writing, that: (a) Persons who have not yet taken their vows receive a single gratuity of 150 florins, and must leave the Cloister within four weeks; they may take with them what they brought with them. (b) Religious of either sex may leave Austria and go to religious Houses abroad; in that case they are to be given passports and adequate journey money, but no further pension. (c) Those wishing to transfer to other orders are given, on application, every facility and an annual pension of 150 florins; but if they become Brothers of Charity [*Barmberzige Brüder*] or Piarists, the pension shall be 300 florins, and for women becoming Sisters of Elizabeth, 200 florins, paid out of the Cameral funds. Persons entering the secular priesthood are to receive an annual pension of 300 florins, besides the Princely grant *titulo mensae* until provided with a living. If a Carthusian Abbot [sic] transfers to the secular clergy, he is to receive 800 florins a year until provided with a benefice. (d) The regulation procedure is to be followed in respect of release from religious vows. This applies also, *mutatis mutandis*, to nuns. (e) Monks of Orders whose rules enjoin them to live quietly and peaceably, aloof from all worldly things, may continue to live according to the rule of their Order, but must take up their residence in a House of another Order, to which House the stipend for their maintenance shall then be paid. No one is to remain in the dissolved Houses of the male Orders unless he is too aged and infirm to be received in another House or by relatives. Such cases are to be reported. Professed nuns who do not transfer to anther Order may remain together in a designated convent, but the Provincial authorities and the Ordinary shall prescribe to them a way of living and a spiritual Superior.

7. Circle officers shall order the Eremites or *Waldbrüder*, whether serving as Church sacristans or not, to discard their hermit's dress forever within fourteen days. Where foundations exist, they may continue to serve as sacristans or schoolmasters, but must be registered.

8. The church valuables are listed in the inventory. The report is to state whether the inhabitants of the locality wish for Divine Service to continue to be celebrated in the church. The Commissioners are to make sensible and appropriate dispositions.

120. AN ENLIGHTENED DESPOT ON TYRANNY AND POWER

The Empress Catherine II of Russia, who reigned from 1762 to 1796, "believed" in the Enlightenment, whatever that term might mean to a ruler who could not have applied its principles if she had wanted to, knew it, and made little attempt to do so beyond some codification of the laws. It is interesting, therefore, to read two short pieces from her so-called "memoirs." The first is an attack upon the tyrants who so frequently ruled Russia, the second an even more savage criticism of a plan by noble conspirators under one of her predecessors to make Russia a constitutional monarchy dominated by the nobility.

Catherine II

Memoirs on Tyrants and Autocratic Government

It is not surprising that Russia had many tyrants among her sovereigns. The nation is naturally restless, ungrateful, and filled with informers and men who under the pretext of zeal try to turn everything in their path to their own profit.

One must be acknowledgeable and enlightened to distinguish real zeal from false and good intentions in words from those in deeds. A man who knows little will in such cases be either weak or a tyrant, according to his degree of intelligence. Only education and knowledge of mankind supply the golden mean.

. . . . .

SOURCE: From *The Memoirs of Catherine The Great* edited by Dominique Maroger and translated by Moura Budberg, pp. 290, 294.

If there existed someone extravagant enough to say: you believe that the grandeur of the Russian Empire demands an autocratic ruler, but I set no value on this grandeur, so long as every citizen lives happily—I would reply to this madman: you should know that if your government became a republic, it would lose all its power and the land would become the prey of anyone who cared to seize it. I would like to see whether you would care to become, with your principles, the victim of Tartar hordes and whether your life under their rule would be happy.

Dolgoruki's irresponsible plan, when the Empress Anne came to the throne, would have infallibly dragged the State towards destruction, but luckily the common sense of the majority upset it.[1] The decision of the Council to allow the fleet to disintegrate and not to reconstitute the Army would have been the best way to let jealous neighbours divide Russia among themselves as they pleased. . . .

121. THE DUAL MEANING OF BALANCE OF POWER

The complications of the European system of multiple sovereign states, with its recurrent tension between the possible ascendancy of a single overpowering state and the combined resistance of lesser rivals, led to the emergence of the notion of "balance of power." It was a metaphor used in two ways. One was that of equilibrium, with no state able to outweigh all the others; the other was that of the counterweight, the ability of a given state or group of states to "hold the balance" against the others to its own advantage. Both meanings are discernible in a discussion of British policy in the peace negotiations to end the War of the Spanish Succession that was presented by the English journalist and novelist Daniel Defoe (c. 1659-1731) in his *Review of the State of the British Nation*, a magazine of comment, for May 20, 1712.

Daniel Defoe

Review of the State of the British Nation, May 20, 1712

. . . . .

From hence I say, that you had never so good Terms of Peace offer'd *notwithstanding so many Victories*, as the *Partition* offer'd by the late King:

---

[1] A secret Council composed of eight members of the nobility was to limit the Empress's power with the support of the clergy. The Senate and the aristocracy disbanded it, exiled the members, and then had them tortured to death [translator's note].

Source: Arthur Wellesley Secord (ed.), *Defoe's Review*, Vol. VIII (New York: Columbia University Press, 1938), pp. 726–27.

A Treaty so Calculated for a lasting Peace, so effectually forming a true Ballance of Power, that *Europe* must have remain'd for ever at rest.

But now, one Side are for giving it all to *France*, the other are for giving it all to the Emperor, and neither Side know *by it* what they are doing: When the *Tory* was for a Partition, *No*, the *Whig* was for all or none to the Emperor, *not a Foot to* Philip, *no, not to bury him in:* Now the *Whig* would come in for a Partition, but the *Tory* is for *all to Philip:* Both these mad Extremes I have oppos'd from the beginning, *and hope I shall to the End;* the middle Way between both, is the safe, the just, the most Reasonable; as clipping the Wings of both, that neither the *French* with his *Meridian Sun* may scorch us, nor the Voracious *Roman Eagle* may devour us.

My Aim has been all along at PROTESTANT GREATNESS; I am for making no *Popish* Tyrant a Master of *Europe;* I say NONE, neither *French* nor *German*, they are all alike to me; I think the Protestant Powers of *Britain* and *Holland*, ought NOW to hold the *Ballance of Europe*, and not hold the Candle to *Popery* any longer: I have often said, we ought to have some share of this great Prize, who have ventur'd so much *in the Lottery* of the War: We have Erected a *South-Sea Company*, and we ought to demand a Portion for our Trade, that the Commerce of the World may help to make us amends a little, for all the Treasure Expended, and Blood spilt in this Quarrel.

What have we hitherto fought for, if one *Popish* Power shall still possess this Glorious Prize? If ever *St. Peter's* Trumpet sounds another Cruisado, *as formerly it did against the Waldenses* and *Albigenses*, and the Count *de Thoulouse*, how shall we all be crush'd by that very Power we have Erected? Did not *French* and *German* join together, to Oppress and Root out Christ's Church from the Earth?

But a Partition puts an End to the whole Strife, *France* may have enough to gratifie his Ambition, the Emperor enough to make him a Match for *France; Britain* and *Holland* such a share of Commerce, Wealth, *and especially Naval Strength*, as may make them United, a Superior Power to the other two, and able to maintain the Protestant Interest, let *Popery* and the *Devil* do their worst.

What can any Man say, why WE, *of all the Confederates*, should have no Advantage by the Peace? Why the Protestant Religion, and the Protestant Churches of *Germany*, should weigh nothing in all our Cogitations about Peace? Wretched Politicians! Will ye Erect a *Popish* Tyranny in *Europe* above the Protestant Interest, when you have it in your Hands to Secure the Protestant Religion against them all?

This is what I have always made the Subject of my Schemes, *and these are my Reasons for it;* I have been sufficiently abused for it on the *Whig*

Side, and now the *Tory* Side are against me in it, and still I thank God I see no Reason to alter my Mind; I see no Force in any Arguments against a Partition: Both Sides have push'd on their Party-Interests against it, but still I must say, *as it was ever my Opinion,* no safe Peace can be obtain'd, without some Dismemberings of the *Spanish* Monarchy, so I see no Convincing Reason to alter my Opinion, that I scorn to do it without a Convincing Reason for any Party or Person in the World.

What Ballance of Power can be Establish'd in *Europe,* if the *Spanish* Monarchy be left whole, to Encline in a War *this Way* or *that* in one dead Weight? The Wealth of the *Indies* is so great, that whoever joins with *Spain,* will beat all the World by the meer Force of Money, will Conquer the rest, *au Coup d'Argent:* No Equality which is the great Safety of Nations, can be supposed here; nothing can do it without a PARTITION; let us see the Wise Heads of this Age do it any other Way if they can.

122. THE GOBBLING UP OF POLAND

The balance of power sometimes operated to protect the smaller states against one overweening power, but on other occasions it was practiced by a coalition of powers against a weak state. This happened during the three partitions of Poland in 1772, 1793, and 1795. In the first, Russia and Prussia agreed to take adjacent bands of territory, and Austria, after some hesitation, later joined them in its own annexations. It was followed two decades later by the second and third partitions, which wiped the centuries-old monarchical republic of Poland from the map. How such outright seizures could be justified may be seen in the introductory statements to the treaties of partition, reproduced below.

Partition Treaties of 1772, 1793, and 1795

FIRST PARTITION OF POLAND

TREATY OF THE FIRST PARTITION OF POLAND BETWEEN RUSSIA AND PRUSSIA ST. PETERSBURG, JULY 14/25, 1772.

In the name of the Very Sainted Trinity.

The spirit of faction, turmoils and civil war that has been agitating the Kingdom of Poland for so many years, and the anarchy which every day

SOURCE: Fred L. Israel (ed.), *Major Peace Treaties of Modern History, 1648–1967.* (New York: Chelsea House Publishers, 1967), pp. 351, 415–16, 421. Reprinted with permission of Chelsea House Publishers, a division of Chelsea House Educational Communications, Inc. in association with McGraw-Hill Inc.

gathers there new forces to the point of annihilating all the authority of a regular government, causing justified fears of a forthcoming total decomposition of the State, and of disturbing the interests of all her neighbors, impairing the good harmony existing among them, and kindling a general war, now, due to these disturbances, difficulties resulted between Her Imperial Majesty of all the Russias and the Ottoman Porte; at the same time, the neighboring powers of the Republic have ancient and legitimate claims and rights which they have never been able to maintain and which they risk to lose forever, unless they take measures to assert them and reinstall tranquility and order in the interior of this Republic and secure for her a political existence more in harmony to the interests of her neighbors. . . .

Second Partition of Poland

Agreement Concluded between Her Imperial Majesty of all the Russias and His Majesty, the King of Prussia and subsequently agreed to by His Majesty, the Holy Roman Emperor and Royal Apostolic. St. Petersburg, January 12/23, 1793.

In the Name of the Most Holy and Indivisible Trinity.

The troubles which shake Europe in the wake of the deadly Revolution that has occurred in France present the aspect of an imminent and universal danger in the growth and extension of which they appear liable, if the Powers whose interest it is to maintain order, the only solid foundation for the general safety and peace, do not hasten to make provision by the most rigorous and effective of means. Her Majesty the Empress of all the Russias and His Majesty the King of Prussia, forthwith upon the successful renewal of the treaties of friendship and alliance which have existed between them, have hastened to bring their entire attention to bear upon a matter of such importance, and having communicated with mutual confidence Their ideas and Their thoughts on this matter, They have found all the more cause for concern, for They have seen definite indications that this same spirit of dangerous rebellion and innovation which at present reigns in France is on the verge of breaking out in the Kingdom of Poland, which immediately borders Their respective possessions. This state of affairs has naturally caused Their Imperial and Royal Majesties to realize the necessity for increasing Their precautions and efforts towards protecting Their subjects from the effects of an evil and often contagious example, and at the same time to contrive in such a manner that these efforts might procure both the present and future safety, and compensation for the exorbitant expense which they must inevitably necessitate. . . .

Third Partition of Poland

Treaty of the Third Partition of Poland. St. Petersburg, October 13/24, 1795

In the Name of the Most Holy and Indivisible Trinity.

Her Majesty, the Empress of all the Russias, and His Majesty, the King of Prussia, [desire] to find a more perfect and final accord concerning the stipulations contained in the Declaration issued here at St. Petersburg on December 23, 1794 (January 3, 1795); by the two Imperial Courts and recently transmitted to the Court of Berlin, and [desire] to fix more precisely the limits that are to separate the respective States of three Powers adjoining Poland after the total partition of that state. . . .

CHAPTER XIII

THE FRENCH REVOLUTION

THE DECADE OF THE 1780s in France was marked by economic difficulties that intensified the financial problems of a government already virtually bankrupt but unwilling to let the world—and prospective lenders—know the truth. Last-minute attempts at reform did not bring a solution, and the Estates General, the historic representative assembly of the nation, was convened in May 1789 to inaugurate a decade of political and institutional reorganization in France. The French Revolution took place in the midst of changing governments, foreign and civil war, terror, and sober labors that make it one of the most significant as well as most dramatic events in history.

The monarchy was first constitutionalized and then swept away. Institutions of many centuries' standing were abolished and new ones created almost overnight. Political power ceased to be a matter of right of birth and became the object of political battle, through elections, conspiracies, popular uprisings, and domestic warfare. Groups that had been onlookers in political life became participants who provided leaders for the state, and rival groups began to appear from below, speaking for the poor and the propertyless. But, as the end of the decade came close, no political force had been able to gain the clear allegiance of a majority of the French nation.

The interweaving of war abroad and war within the country became central to the country's fate. As long as foreign war continued, defensive at first and then offensive, France could not reestablish the political calm needed for consolidation of the changes wrought in the first years of the Revolution. But it proved easier to continue war against foreign foes on their territories than to come to terms with them without shaking the confidence of the army on which the revolutionary regime rested.

123. HOW THE BASTILLE FELL: ONE MAN'S STORY

After the fortress of the Bastille was captured by the populace of Paris on July 14, 1789, the participants were asked by the revolutionary city government to present themselves. One of those who did so, at the urging of his relatives, was a clockmaker named J. B. Humbert, who had learned his craft in Switzerland and had witnessed the capture of Geneva by French troops. He came to Paris and took a job with the royal clockmaker. His account of his part in the taking of the Bastille, during which he was the first to reach the tower of the keep, was printed in a pamphlet in which he asked other participants and spectators to confirm his story. His tale vividly recreates the atmosphere of a city in the midst of an insurrection.

J. B. Humbert

Account of July 14, 1789

THE *Journée* OF J. B. HUMBERT

Who was the first to climb on to the towers of the Bastille

My name is J. B. HUMBERT, and I am a native of Langres, working and living in Paris, at Monsieur Belliard's, watchmaker to the King, rue du Hurepoix.

Assuming that I belonged to the district of St-André-des-Arts, I went to that Parish on Monday morning with the rest of the citizens, and patrolled the streets with them all that day and night, armed with swords, the District having no firearms or only a few.

SOURCE: Reprinted by permission of Charles Scribner's Sons from *The Taking of the Bastille: July 14, 1789*, by Jacques Godechot, pp. 280–286. Translated by Jean Stewart.

Overcome with weariness and lack of food and sleep, I left the District at six in the morning. I learned during the course of the morning that arms for the various Districts were being distributed at the Invalides; I promptly went back to inform the Bourgeois of Saint-André, who had gathered together at about half-past twelve. M. Poirier, their Commander, understood the importance of this news, and was preparing to lead some of the citizens thither, but he was unable to set forth, being detained by various people making requests; as these matters seemed to me of very little weight compared to the advantage of procuring arms for the citizens, I seized hold of M. Poirier and took him off, as though by force, together with five or six of the townsfolk. We reached the Invalides at about two o'clock, and we found there a great crowd, which forced us to separate. I do not know what became of the Commander or his company.

I followed the crowd, to get to the cellar where the arms were kept. On the staircase leading to the cellar, seeing a man armed with two muskets, I took one from him, and went up again; but the crowd at the top of the stair was so great that all those who were climbing up were pushed down again, and fell right down into the cellar. Since I was only shaken and not injured by the fall, I picked up a musket which was lying at my feet, and immediately handed it to somebody who had none.

In spite of this horrible tumble, the crowd persisted in going down the stairs, and as nobody could get up again, there was such a crush in the cellar that people were shrieking and gasping for breath.

Many people had fainted; so all those in the cellar who were armed followed the advice someone gave and forced the unarmed crowd to turn and go back, threatening them with the points of their bayonets. The advice succeeded, and as the crowd drew back in terror we took advantage of this moment to form a line and force the people up the stairs.

The crowd went up again, we managed to carry up the people who had fainted, and lay them on a piece of grass near the dome and the moat. After helping and protecting the removal of these people, since my presence seemed superfluous, armed with my gun I searched in vain for my Commander, and then set off for my own District.

As I learned on the way that they were handing out powder at the Hôtel de Ville I hurried thither, and was given about a quarter of a pound, but they gave me no shot, saying that they had none.

As I left the Hôtel de Ville I heard someone say that the Bastille was being besieged. My regret at having no shot prompted an idea which I immediately carried out, namely to buy some small nails, which I got from the grocer's at the *Coin du Roi*, place de la Grève.

There I fixed up and greased my gun.

On leaving the Grocer's, as I was about to load my gun, I was accosted by a Citizen who told me that they were handing out shot at the Hôtel de Ville. So I hurried there, and was given half a dozen pellets of buck-shot.

I immediately set off for the Bastille, loading my gun as I went.

I walked along the embankment as far as the second court of the Arsenal, and there joined a group of people who were preparing to go to the siege.

We found four foot-soldiers of the Watch, armed with guns, and I urged them to come to the siege; as they replied that they had neither powder nor shot, we clubbed together to give each of them enough for two shots. Then they followed us willingly.

As we were passing in front of the Hôtel de la Régie [the Excise Office] they had just broken open two cases of bullets, which were being freely handed out, and I filled one of my coat pockets with them to give to anyone who was short. I still have over three pounds left.

A few paces away I heard a woman calling for help, I promptly went up to her and she told me that *they were setting fire to the saltpetre store.* She added that this was unfair, *because the store had been thrown open and put at the disposal of the citizens as soon as they had asked for it.* I got this woman to take me to the store, and there I found a Barber, *holding a lighted torch in each hand*, with which he was in fact setting fire to the place. I rushed at this Barber and thrust the butt of my gun violently against his stomach, knocking him over. Then, seeing that the barrel of saltpetre had caught fire, I overturned it and succeeded in smothering the flames.

Meanwhile the household staff came to beg me to help them drive out certain ill-intentioned people who had forced their way in and broken into the documents room; I followed them and drove out of the place several individuals who had already smashed some cupboards on the pretext of looking for powder.

Then I left the house, amid general thinks; and having rejoined the soldiers of the Watch to whom I had given powder and shot, I persuaded one of these to stand sentinel in front of the door.

I immediately made my way to the Bastille, passing through the court-yard of the Arsenal; it was about half-past three; the first bridge had been lowered, and the chains cut; but the portcullis barred the way; people were trying to bring in some cannon which had previously been disman-tled; I crossed over by the small bridge and from the further side helped to bring in the two guns.

When they had been set up on their gun-carriages again, everybody with one accord drew up in rows of five or six, and I found myself in the front rank.

In this array we marched to the drawbridge of the fortress; on either side of this I saw two dead soldiers lying; the one on my left was wearing the uniform of the Vintimille regiment; I could not make out that of the soldier lying on my right.

The cannon were then levelled: the bronze gun at the large drawbridge and a small iron one, inlaid with silver, at the small bridge.

This operation forced me to fall out of line; and as we wanted to know whether any offers of peace were forthcoming from the garrison, I undertook to survey the terrace.

While I was occupied with this mission, it was decided to start the attack with musket fire; I hurriedly returned to my post; but my way being blocked by a crowd of people, in spite of the peril I returned by way of the parapet, and resumed my post; I was even forced to step over the body of the soldier from the Vintimille.

We each fired half-a-dozen shots. Then a paper was thrust through an oval gap a few inches across; we ceased fire; one of our number stepped forward and went to the kitchen to fetch a plank so as to collect the paper; this plank was laid on the parapet; many people stood on it to weigh it down: one man started out along it, but just as he was about to take the paper, he was killed by a shot and fell into the moat.

Another man, carrying a flag, immediately dropped his flag and went to fetch the paper, which was then read out loud and clearly, so that everyone could hear.

The contents of this message, which offered capitulation, proving unsatisfactory, we decided to fire the gun; everyone stood aside to let the cannon-ball pass.

Just as we were about to fire, the small drawbridge was lowered; it was promptly filled by a crowd of people, of whom I was about tenth. We found the gate behind the drawbridge closed: after a couple of minutes a Pensioner came to open it, and asked what we wanted: *Give up the Bastille,* I replied, as did everyone else: then he let us in. My first concern was to call for the bridge to be lowered; this was done.

Then I entered the main courtyard (I was about eighth or tenth). The Pensioners were lined up on the right, the Swiss guards on the left; we shouted: *lay down your arms,* which they did, except for one Swiss officer. I went up to him and threatened him with my bayonet, repeating: *lay down your arms.* He appealed to all present: *'Gentlemen, please believe me, I never fired.'*

I immediately said to him: *'How dare you say you never fired, when your lips are still black from biting your cartridge?'* As I said this, I pounced on his sword; another fellow did the same; as the two of us were arguing as to which should have the sword, I happened to glance at a staircase on my left, and I saw three citizens who had gone up five or six steps and were hurrying down again; I immediately left the sword and, armed with my rifle, which I had never abandoned, I rushed over to the staircase to help the citizens, whom I assumed to have been driven back; I rapidly climbed up to the keep, without noticing that nobody was following me; I reached the top of the stairs without meeting anyone either. In the keep I found a Swiss soldier squatting down with his back to me: I aimed my rifle at him, shouting: *lay down your arms;* he turned round in surprise, and laid down his weapons, saying: *'Comrade, don't kill me, I'm for the Tiers État and I will defend you to the last drop of my blood; you know I'm obliged to do my job; but I haven't fired.'*

While he was speaking thus I picked up his rifle, then, poking him in the stomach with my bayonet, I ordered him to hand over his cartridge-case and sling it round my neck, which he did.

Immediately afterwards I went to the cannon that stood just above the drawbridge of the Bastille, in order to push it off its gun-carriage and render it unusable. But as I stood for this purpose with my shoulder under the mouth of the cannon, someone in the vicinity fired at me, and the bullet pierced my coat and waistcoat and wounded me in the neck; I fell down senseless; the Swiss soldier whose life I had spared dragged me on to the staircase, still clutching my gun, so he told me, though I had dropped the one I had taken from the Invalides.

When I recovered from my swoon I found myself sitting on the stairs; the Swiss guard had been shaking me to restore me to consciousness, and he had tried to staunch the blood that was pouring out of my wound with a piece of linen he had cut off my shirt.

Finding myself very weak I decided to go downstairs, asking the Swiss to support me, which he willingly did.

Half way down the stairs we met a number of townsfolk coming up, some in armour and others not; seeing me covered in blood, they assumed that the Swiss must have wounded me, and tried to kill him; I opposed this, and explained the situation. They fortunately took my word for it, and I went my way downstairs, still leaning on him.

When we reached the courtyard together, the Swiss was not allowed to leave, so I was obliged to go out by myself; people made way for me on seeing my blood and my wound.

On the way to the Bastille kitchens I met an army surgeon, who urged me to show him my wound; when he had examined the place, he told me I had a bullet in my neck which he could not extract by himself, and persuaded me to go to a hospital to get it seen to.

On my way there I met somebody who had just been to the Minimes monastery to have a sprained wrist attended to. He immediately took me to the Minimes, where they readily attended to my wound. No bullet was found in it.

As I was seized with a violent thirst they gave me a pewter bowl full of wine and water, which restored my strength. Then I got up joyfully, intending to hurry back to the Bastille.

I immediately got dressed again, I picked up my gun and my cartridge-pouch, but the Minimes who had dressed my wound begged me to change my mind. They assured me that movement would be very bad for my wound, and made me promise to go back home and have some rest, which they thought absolutely indispensable. They offered to take me home, but I refused with thanks.

On my way home I remembered some friends who lived in the rue de la Ferronnerie; I had left them that morning, and they had seemed anxious about the dangers which they foresaw my zeal might lead me into; I went to their house, and four armed Bourgeois escorted me to the rue du Hurepoix. I was greeted with praise wherever I went; but when we reached the Quai des Augustins, we were followed by a crowd of people who mistook me for a malefactor, and twice attempted to put me to death; as I could not explain things to everyone, I was about to be *seized*, when I was recognized by a Bookseller on the Quai, who rescued me from the hands of the crowd and took me into his own home; I was put to bed there and given all thc carc I needed.

I rested until about midnight, when I was woken by repeated cries of *to arms! to arms!* Then I could not resist my longing to be of some further use; I got up, armed myself and went to the guardroom, where I found M. Poirier, the Commanding Officer, under whose orders I remained until the following morning.

124. A RURAL REVOLUTION

What occurred in Paris on July 14, 1789, was a successful insurrection that thwarted counterrevolutionary plans of the Royal Court. What happened less than a month later when the National Assembly met in a dramatic night session on August 4 was immensely more. The event is usually called the abolition of the "feudal system" in France, but not only manorialism (which is what was meant by "feudalism" for the most part) but many other fundamental institutions of the Old Regime were also suppressed. These included such institutions as private ownership of public office ("venality"), tax privileges, local privileges, the system of privileged orders, and various practices of Catholic Church government. This was in fact a social revolution, and in it the driving force was not only the uprising in Paris but even more the widespread rural revolt called the "Great Fear" that had swept France in July. The decree abolishing the feudal system, reprinted below, was decided upon on August 4–5 but actually adopted a week later, on August 11.

rrent Check-Outs summary for Sardar, S
Mon Feb 01 16:05:36 GMT 2016

RCODE: 30114015664983
TLE: The struggle for power in early m
UE DATE: 29 Feb 2016

ARCODE: 30114015830626
ITLE: Worlds made by words : scholarshi
UE DATE: 29 Feb 2016

ARCODE: 30114006531464
ITLE: Culture, society and religion in
DUE DATE: 29 Feb 2016

BARCODE: 3011400[illegible]
TITLE: Early modern Europe : a book of s
DUE DATE: 08 Feb 20[illegible]

Decree of the National Assembly Abolishing the Feudal System, August 11, 1789

ARTICLE I. The National Assembly hereby completely abolishes the feudal system. It decrees that, among the existing rights and dues, both feudal and *censuel*,[1] all those originating in or representing real or personal serfdom *(mainmorte)* or personal servitude, shall be abolished without indemnification. All other dues are declared redeemable, the terms and mode of redemption to be fixed by the National Assembly. Those of the said dues which are not extinguished by this decree shall continue to be collected until indemnification shall take place.

II. The exclusive right to maintain pigeon-houses and dove-cotes is abolished. The pigeons shall be confined during the seasons fixed by the community. During such periods they shall be looked upon as game, and every one shall have the right to kill them upon his own land.

III. The exclusive right to hunt and to maintain unenclosed warrens is likewise abolished, and every land owner shall have the right to kill or to have destroyed on his own land all kinds of game, observing, however, such police regulations as may be established with a view to the safety of the public.

All hunting captainries, including the royal forests, and all hunting rights under whatever denomination, are likewise abolished. Provision shall be made, however, in a manner compatible with the regard due to property and liberty, for maintaining the personal pleasures of the king.

The president of the assembly shall be commissioned to ask of the King the recall of those sent to the galleys or exiled, simply for violations of the hunting regulations, as well as for the release of those at present imprisoned for offences of this kind, and the dismissal of such cases as are now pending.

IV. All manorial courts are hereby suppressed without indemnification. But the magistrates of these courts shall continue to perform their functions until such time as the National Assembly shall provide for the establishment of a new judicial system.

V. Tithes of every description, as well as the dues which have been substituted for them, under whatever denomination they are known or collected (even when compounded for), possessed by secular or regular

---

SOURCE: Department of History, University of Pennsylvania, *Translations and Reprints from the Original Sources of European History* (Philadelphia: University of Pennsylvania Press, n.d.) Vol. I, pp. 2–5. (Footnotes are by the translator-editors.) Reprinted by permission of the University of Pennsylvania Press.

[1] This refers to the *cens*, a perpetual due similar to the payments made by English copyholders.

congregations, by holders of benefices, members of corporations (including the Order of Malta and other religious and military orders,) as well as those devoted to the maintenance of churches, those impropriated to lay persons and those substituted for the *portion congrue,*[2] are abolished, on condition, however, that some other method be devised to provide for the expenses of divine worship, the support of the officiating clergy, for the assistance of the poor, for repairs and rebuilding of churches and parsonages, and for the maintenance of all institutions, seminaries, schools, academies, asylums, and organizations to which the present funds are devoted. Until such provision shall be made and the former possessors shall enter upon the enjoyment of an income on the new system, the National Assembly decrees that the said tithes shall continue to be collected according to law and in the customary manner.

Other tithes, of whatever nature they may be, shall be redeemable in such manner as the Assembly shall determine. Until such regulation shall be issued, the National Assembly decrees that these, too, shall continue to be collected.

VI. All perpetual ground rents, payable either in money or in kind, of whatever nature they may be, whatever their origin and to whomsoever they may be due, as to members of corporations, holders of the domain or appanages or to the Order of Malta, shall be redeemable. *Champarts,*[3] of every kind and under all denominations, shall likewise be redeemable at a rate fixed by the Assembly. No due shall in the future be created which is not redeemable.

VII. The sale of judicial and municipal offices shall be suppressed forthwith. Justice shall be dispensed *gratis.* Nevertheless, the magistrates at present holding such offices shall continue to exercise their functions and to receive their emoluments until the Assembly shall have made provision for indemnifying them.

VIII. The fees of the country priests are abolished, and shall be discontinued so soon as provision shall be made for increasing the minimum salary [*portion congrue*] of the parish priests and the payment to the curates. A regulation shall be drawn up to determine the status of the priests in the towns.

IX. Pecuniary privileges, personal or real, in the payment of taxes are abolished forever. Taxes shall be collected from all the citizens, and from all property, in the same manner and in the same form. Plans shall be considered by which the taxes shall be paid proportionally by all, even for the last six months of the current year.

---

[2] This expression refers to the minimum remuneration fixed for the priests.

[3] The *champart* was the right of the lord to a certain portion of the crops on lands subject to the *cens.*

X. Inasmuch as a national constitution and public liberty are of more advantage to the provinces than the privileges which some of these enjoy, and inasmuch as the surrender of such privileges is essential to the intimate union of all parts of the realm [*empire*], it is decreed that all the peculiar privileges, pecuniary or otherwise, of the provinces, principalities, districts [*pays*], cantons, cities and communes, are once for all abolished and are absorbed into the law common to all Frenchmen.

XI. All citizens, without distinction of birth, are eligible to any office or dignity, whether ecclesiastical, civil or military; and no profession shall imply any derogation.

XII. Hereafter no remittances shall be made for annates or for any other purpose to the court of Rome, the vice-legation at Avignon, or to the nunciature at Lucerne. The clergy of the diocese shall apply to their bishops in regard to the filling of benefices and dispensations, the which shall be granted *gratis* without regard to reservations, expectancies and papal months, all the churches of France enjoying the same freedom.

XIII. The rights of *déport*,[4] of *cotte-morte*,[4] *dépouilles*,[5] *vacat*,[4] *droits censaux*, Peter's pence, and other dues of the same kind, under whatever denomination, established in favor of bishops, archdeacons, archpresbyters, chapters, and regular congregations which formerly exercised priestly functions [*curés primitifs*], are abolished, but appropriate provision shall be made for those benefices of archdeacons and archpresbyters which are not sufficiently endowed.

XIV. Pluralities shall not be permitted hereafter in cases where the revenue from the benefice or benefices held shall exceed the sum of three thousand livres. Nor shall any individual be allowed to enjoy several pensions from benefices, or a pension and a benefice, if the revenue which he already enjoys from such sources exceeds the same sum of three thousand livres.

XV. The National Assembly shall consider, in conjunction with the King, the report which is to be submitted to it relating to pensions, favors and salaries, with a view to suppressing all such as are not deserved and reducing those which shall prove excessive; and the amount shall be fixed which the King may in the future disburse for this purpose.

XVI. The National Assembly decrees that a medal shall be struck in memory of the recent grave and important deliberations for the welfare of France, and that a *Te Deum* shall be chanted in gratitude in all the parishes and the churches of France.

XVII. The National Assembly solemnly proclaims the King, Louis XVI., the *Restorer of French Liberty*.

---

[4] Rights of bishops to the income of benefices during vacancies.

[5] Rights of the convent to the clothes of its deceased members.

XVIII. The National Assembly shall present itself in a body before the King, in order to submit to him the decrees which have just been passed, to tender to him the tokens of its most respectful gratitude and to pray him to permit the *Te Deum* to be chanted in his chapel, and to be present himself at this service.

XIX. The National Assembly shall consider, immediately after the constitution, the drawing up of the laws necessary for the development of the principles which it has laid down in the present decree. The latter shall be transmitted without delay by the deputies to all the provinces, together with the decree of the tenth of this month, in order that it may be printed, published, announced from the parish pulpits, and posted up wherever it shall be deemed necessary.

125. THE COMMONS AND THE NATION

During the months before the Estates General convened, a political debate raged over the rights and privileges of the various orders. The most absolute claim for the exclusive right of the Third Estate (the commoners) to represent the French nation, to the exclusion of the clergy (the first order) and the nobility (the second) came from the pen of a churchman of middling rank, generally known as the Abbé Sieyès although he was a vicar-general for the Bishop of Chartres. (In addition to abbots, the term *abbé* was given to priests without a benefice.) When Emmanuel Joseph Sieyès (1748-1836) took up the cause of the commoners, he published a pamphlet, *What Is the Third Estate?*, which attracted great attention. Key passages are reproduced below. He was elected a deputy to the Third Estate for Paris and played an important role during later phases of the Revolution as a member of the Directory.

Emmanuel Joseph Sieyès

What Is the Third Estate?

. . . . .

What is necessary that a nation should subsist and prosper? Individual effort and public functions.

SOURCE: Department of History, University of Pennsylvania, *Translations and Reprints from the Original Sources of European History* (Philadelphia: University of Pennsylvania Press, n.d.), Vol. VI, pp. 33–35. Reprinted by permission of the University of Pennsylvania Press.

All individual efforts may be included in four classes: 1. Since the earth and the waters furnish crude products for the needs of man, the first class, in logical sequence, will be that of all families which devote themselves to agricultural labor. 2. Between the first sale of products and their consumption or use, a new manipulation, more or less repeated, adds to these products a second value more or less composite. In this manner human industry succeeds in perfecting the gifts of nature, and the crude product increases two-fold, ten-fold, one hundred-fold in value. Such are the efforts of the second class. 3. Between production and consumption, as well as between the various stages of production, a group of intermediary agents establish themselves, useful both to producers and consumers; these are the merchants and brokers: the brokers who, comparing incessantly the demands of time and place, speculate upon the profit of retention and transportation; merchants who are charged with distribution, in the last analysis, either at wholesale or at retail. This species of utility characterizes the third class. 4. Outside of these three classes of productive and useful citizens, who are occupied with real objects of consumption and use, there is also need in society of a series of efforts and pains, whose objects are directly useful or agreeable to the individual. This fourth class embraces all those who stand between the most distinguished and liberal professions and the less esteemed services of domestics.

Such are the efforts which sustain society. Who puts them forth? The Third Estate.

Public functions may be classified equally well, in the present state of affairs, under four recognized heads; the sword, the robe, the church and the administration. It would be superfluous to take them up one by one, for the purpose of showing that everywhere the Third Estate attends to nineteen-twentieths of them, with this distinction; that it is laden with all that which is really painful, with all the burdens which the privileged classes refuse to carry. Do we give the Third Estate credit for this? That this might come about, it would be necessary that the Third Estate should refuse to fill these places, or that it should be less ready to exercise their functions. The facts are well known. Meanwhile they have dared to impose a prohibition upon the order of the Third Estate. They have said to it: "Whatever may be your services, whatever may be your abilities, you shall go thus far; you may not pass beyond!" Certain rare exceptions, properly regarded, are but a mockery, and the terms which are indulged in on such occasions, one insult the more.

If this exclusion is a social crime against the Third Estate; if it is a veritable act of hostility, could it perhaps be said that it is useful to the public weal? Alas! who is ignorant of the effects of monopoly? If it discourages those whom it rejects, is it not well known that it tends to render less able those whom it favors? Is it not understood that every employment from which free competition is removed, becomes dearer and less effective?

In setting aside any function whatsoever to serve as an appanage for a distinct class among citizens, is it not to be observed that it is no longer the man alone who does the work that it is necessary to reward, but all the unemployed members of that same caste, and also the entire families of those who are employed as well as those who are not? Is it not to be remarked that since the government has become the patrimony of a particular class, it has been distended beyond all measure; places have been created, not on account of the necessities of the governed, but in the interests of the governing, etc., etc.? Has not attention been called to the fact that this order of things, which is basely and—I even presume to say—beastly respectable with us, when we find it in reading the History of Ancient Egypt or the accounts of Voyages to the Indies, is despicable, monstrous, destructive of all industry, the enemy of social progress; above all degrading to the human race in general, and particularly intolerable to Europeans, etc., etc.? But I must leave these considerations, which, if they increase the importance of the subject and throw light upon it, perhaps, along with the new light, slacken our progress.

It suffices here to have made it clear that the pretended utility of a privileged order for the public service is nothing more than a chimera; that with it all that which is burdensome in this service is performed by the Third Estate; that without it the superior places would be infinitely better filled; that they naturally ought to be the lot and the recompense of ability and recognized services, and that if privileged persons have come to usurp all the lucrative and honorable posts, it is a hateful injustice to the rank and file of citizens and at the same time a treason to the public weal.

Who then shall dare to say that the Third Estate has not within itself all that is necessary for the formation of a complete nation? It is the strong and robust man who has one arm still shackled. If the privileged order should be abolished, the nation would be nothing less, but something more. Therefore, what is the Third Estate? Everything; but an everything shackled and oppressed. What would it be without the privileged order? Everything, but an everything free and flourishing. Nothing can succeed without it, everything would be infinitely better without the others.

It is not sufficient to show that privileged persons, far from being useful to the nation, cannot but enfeeble and injure it; it is necessary to prove further that the noble order does not enter at all into the social organization; that it may indeed be a burden upon the nation, but that it cannot of itself constitute a nation.

In the first place, it is not possible in the number of all the elementary parts of a nation to find a place for the *caste* of nobles. I know that there are individuals in great number whom infirmities, incapacity, incurable laziness, or the weight of bad habits render strangers to the labors of society. The exception and the abuse are everywhere found beside the rule. But it will be admitted that the less there are of these abuses, the better it will be for the State. The worst possible arrangement of all would be where not alone isolated individuals, but a whole class of citizens should take pride in remaining motionless in the midst of the general movement, and should consume the best part of the product without bearing any part in its production. Such a class is surely estranged to the nation by its indolence.

The noble order is not less estranged from the generality of us by its civil and political prerogatives.

What is a nation? A body of associates, living under a common law, and represented by the same legislature, etc.

Is it not evident that the noble order has privileges and expenditures which it dares to call its rights, but which are apart from the rights of the great body of citizens? It departs there from the common order, from the common law. So its civil rights make of it an isolated people in the midst of the great nation. This is truly *imperium in imperio.*

In regard to its political rights, these also it exercises apart. It has its special representatives, which are not charged with securing the interests of the people. The body of its deputies sit apart; and when it is assembled in the same hall with the deputies of simple citizens, it is none the less true that its representation is essentially distinct and separate: it is a stranger to the nation, in the first place, by its origin, since its commission is not derived from the people; then by its object, which consists of defending not the general, but the particular interest.

The Third Estate embraces then all that which belongs to the nation; and all that which is not the Third Estate, cannot be regarded as being of the nation. What is the Third Estate? It is the whole.

126. THE GOSPEL OF THE REVOLUTION

Some two weeks after the decree abolishing "feudalism," the National Assembly adopted a declaration that reinforced on the level of political principle the actions it had already taken. The "Declaration of the Rights of Man and Citizen" of August 27, 1789, has the same kind of significance as the introductory paragraphs of the American Declaration of Independence—the affirmation of universal goals that justify particular deeds. For all its lofty generalities, the deputies had in mind the specific institutions and practices of the absolute monarchy that they considered to be abuses. The Declaration is therefore both abstract and specific, a battle cry and a bill of rights for a constitution still to be written at the time of its adoption. Nothing in the Declaration looked ahead to the abolition of monarchy, but it was potentially republican in its affirmation of the sovereignty of the nation.

Declaration of the Rights of Man and Citizen, August 27, 1789

. . . . .

The representatives of the French people, organized in National Assembly, considering that ignorance, forgetfulness, or contempt of the rights of man are the sole causes of public misfortunes and of the corruption of governments, have resolved to set forth in a solemn declaration the natural, inalienable, and sacred rights of man, in order that such declaration, continually before all members of the social body, may be a perpetual reminder of their rights and duties; in order that the acts of the legislative power and those of the executive power may constantly be compared with the aim of every political institution and may accordingly be more respected; in order that the demands of the citizens, founded henceforth upon simple and incontestable principles, may always be directed towards the maintenance of the Constitution and the welfare of all.

Accordingly, the National Assembly recognizes and proclaims, in the presence and under the auspices of the Supreme Being, the following rights of man and citizen.

1. Men are born and remain free and equal in rights; social distinctions may be based only upon general usefulness.

2. The aim of every political association is the preservation of the natural and inalienable rights of man; these rights are liberty, property, security, and resistance to oppression.

3. The source of all sovereignty resides essentially in the nation; no group, no individual may exercise authority not emanating expressly therefrom.

4. Liberty consists of the power to do whatever is not injurious to others; thus the enjoyment of the natural rights of every man has for its limits only those that assure other members of society the enjoyment of those same rights; such limits may be determined only by law.

5. The law has the right to forbid only actions which are injurious to

---

SOURCE: Reprinted with permission of The Macmillan Company from *A Documentary Survey of the French Revolution* by John Hall Stewart, pp. 113–15.

society. Whatever is not forbidden by law may not be prevented, and no one may be constrained to do what it does not prescribe.

6. Law is the expression of the general will; all citizens have the right to concur personally, or through their representatives, in its formation; it must be the same for all, whether it protects or punishes. All citizens, being equal before it, are equally admissible to all public offices, positions, and employments, according to their capacity, and without other distinction than that of virtues and talents.

7. No man may be accused, arrested, or detained except in the cases determined by law, and according to the forms prescribed thereby. Whoever solicit, expedite, or execute arbitrary orders, or have them executed, must be punished; but every citizen summoned or apprehended in pursuance of the law must obey immediately; he renders himself culpable by resistance.

8. The law is to establish only penalties that are absolutely and obviously necessary; and no one may be punished except by virtue of a law established and promulgated prior to the offence and legally applied.

9. Since every man is presumed innocent until declared guilty, if arrest be deemed indispensable, all unnecessary severity for securing the person of the accused must be severely repressed by law.

10. No one is to be disquieted because of his opinions, even religious, provided their manifestation does not disturb the public order established by law.

11. Free communication of ideas and opinions is one of the most precious of the rights of man. Consequently, every citizen may speak, write, and print freely, subject to responsibility for the abuse of such liberty in the cases determined by law.

12. The guarantee of the rights of man and citizen necessitates a public force; such a force, therefore, is instituted for the advantage of all and not for the particular benefit of those to whom it is entrusted.

13. For the maintenance of the public force and for the expenses of administration a common tax is indispensable; it must be assessed equally on all citizens in proportion to their means.

14. Citizens have the right to ascertain, by themselves or through their representatives, the necessity of the public tax, to consent to it freely, to supervise its use, and to determine its quota, assessment, payment, and duration.

15. Society has the right to require of every public agent an accounting of his administration.

16. Every society in which the guarantee of rights is not assured or the separation of powers not determined has no constitution at all.

17. Since property is a sacred and inviolable right, no one may be deprived thereof unless a legally established public necessity obviously requires it, and upon condition of a just and previous indemnity.

127. A CALL TO TERROR

The constitutional monarchy fell in September 1792, a victim to three factors—the refusal of Louis XVI to abide by his oath of loyalty to the constitution of 1791, the invasion of France by the armies of Austria and Prussia with the aim of restoring the king's absolute authority, and the consequent political and economic crisis within France. The republican National Convention (so-called because it had the task of writing a new constitution as well as governing), led by the relatively moderate party of the Girondins, proved inept. Generals such as Dumouriez and La Fayette (whom Americans call "Lafayette") turned against the new government and went over to the enemy. The Girondins' adversaries in the Convention, the Jacobins, advocated revolutionary terror to crush the danger to the infant republic. Their program is outlined in a circular sent by the central club of Jacobins in Paris to local branches on April 5, 1793.

Circular from the Paris Jacobins to Local Branches of the Club, April 5, 1793

. . . . .

Friends, we are betrayed! To arms! To arms! The terrible hour is at hand when the defenders of the *Patrie* must vanquish or bury themselves under the bloody ruins of the Republic. Frenchmen, never was your liberty in such great peril! At last our enemies have put the finishing touch to their foul perfidy, and to complete it their accomplice Dumouriez is marching on Paris. The manifest treasons of the generals in coalition with him leave no doubt that this plan of rebellion and this insolent audacity are directed by the criminal faction which has maintained and deified him as it did Lafayette, and which has deceived us, up to the decisive moment, concerning the conduct, conspiracies, defeats, and outrages of this traitor, this impious man who has just effected the arrest of the four commissioners of the Convention and intends to dissolve it. . . .

But, Brothers, not all your dangers are to be found there! . . . You must be convinced of a grievous truth! Your greatest enemies are in your midst, they direct your operations. O Vengeance!!! . . .

SOURCE: Reprinted with permission of The Macmillan Company from *A Documentary Survey of the French Revolution* by John Hall Stewart, pp. 428–30.

Yes, brothers and friends, yes, it is in the Senate that parricidal hands tear at your vitals! Yes, the counter-revolution is in the Government . . . , in the National Convention! It is there, at the center of your security and your hopes, that criminal delegates hold the threads of the web that they have woven with the horde of despots who come to butcher us! . . . It is there that a sacrilegious cabal is directed by the English court . . . and others . . .

But already indignation rouses your courageous patriotism. Let us go, republicans, let us arm! And, without allowing ourselves to be weakened by vain fears concerning our calamities, let our wisdom determine the means of salvation which remain to us; they are as follows:

Let us rise! Yes, let us all rise! Let us arrest all the enemies of our revolution, and all suspected persons. Let us exterminate, without pity, all conspirators, unless we wish to be exterminated ourselves. And to restore to the National Convention, which alone can save us, to restore to it its force and its energy, let the patriotic deputies on mission in the eighty-three departments be dismissed from their posts, let them return as soon as possible; and, following the example of the generous Marseillais, let new apostles of liberty, chosen by you from among your midst, replace these commissioners; let them be sent into the towns and rural districts to facilitate the speediest recruiting, and to kindle patriotism and ferret out traitors.

Let the departments, the districts, the municipalities, and all the popular societies unite and concur in protesting to the Convention, by dispatching thereto a veritable rain of petitions manifesting the formal wish for the immediate recall of all unfaithful members who have betrayed their duty by not wishing the death of the tyrant, and, above all, against those who have led astray so many of their colleagues. Such delegates are traitors, royalists, or fatuous men. The Republic condemns the friends of kings! They are the ones who dismember her, ruin her, and have sworn to annihilate her. Yes, citizens, they are the ones who have formed this criminal and disastrous faction. With them your liberty disappears! And by their prompt expulsion the *Patrie* is saved!!!

Let us all unite equally to demand that the thunder of indictments be loosed against generals who are traitors to the Republic, against prevaricating ministers, against postal administrators, and against all unfaithful agents of the government. Therein lies our most salutary means of defence; but let us repel the traitors and tyrants.

The center of their conspiracy is here: it is in Paris that our perfidious enemies wish to consummate their crime. Paris, the cradle, the bulwark of liberty, is, without doubt, the place where they have sworn to annihilate the holy cause of humanity under the corpses of patriots.

It is against Paris that Dumouriez directs his vengeance, rallying to his party all the Royalists, the Feuillants, the Moderates, and all the craven enemies of our liberty. Therefore, it is at Paris that we must all defend it! And impress this truth firmly on your minds, that Paris, without you, cannot save the Republic. Already the intrepid Marseillais have risen, and it is to forestall their arrival that the nefarious cabal incites the fulfillment of the crimes of Dumouriez the traitor.

Frenchmen! The *Patrie* is threatened with the greatest danger! Dumouriez declares war on the people, and, suddenly become the vanguard of the ferocious enemies of France, a part of his army, seduced by this great criminal, marches on Paris to re-establish the monarchy and dissolve the National Convention.

To arms, Republicans! Fly to Paris; there is the rendezvous of France; Paris must be the headquarters of the Republic.

To arms! To arms! . . . No deliberation, no delay, or liberty is lost! Every means must be utilized to hasten your march. If we are attacked before you arrive, we know how to fight and how to die, and we will surrender Paris only in ashes!!!

Signed, MARAT, *Deputy, President.*
DUBUISSON, *Vice-President.*
JAY, DUQUESNOI, *Deputies.*
COINDRE, DUPEIRET.
CHAMPERTOIS, PRIEUR, *Secretaries.*

128. JACOBIN DICTATORSHIP

The Convention put the Jacobins into power on April 6, 1793, and a new constitution, embodying advanced democratic principles, was adopted on June 22. But the crisis of invasion and civil war continued unabated, the constitution remained in abeyance, and on October 10 a "revolutionary government" with its leadership in the Committee of Public Safety was proclaimed. It was a dictatorship in the sense of the ancient Roman Republic: the Committee was granted full powers, greater than any the most absolute king of France had ever possessed, but they were to be used to save the revolutionary republic and to prepare the way for a return to constitutional rule. The "Reign of Terror" ensued, utilizing brilliant organizational improvisations with relentless force against all enemies, actual or only suspected. The proclamation of October 10, reproduced here, remained in effect even after the fall of Maximilien Robespierre, the Jacobin leader, on July 27 (9th Thermidor), 1794. In October of the following year a new constitution was adopted which established a Directory that governed for five years.

Proclamation of the National Convention, October 10, 1793

Government

1. The provisional government of France is revolutionary until the peace.

2. The provisional Executive Council, the ministers, generals, and constituted bodies are placed under the surveillance of the Committee of Public Safety, which shall render a weekly account thereof to the Convention.

3. Every measure of security is to be taken by the provisional Executive Council, under the authorization of the Committee, which shall render account thereof to the Convention.

4. The revolutionary laws must be executed speedily. The government shall correspond immediately with the districts in measures of public safety.

5. The generals in chief shall be appointed by the National Convention, on the recommendation of the Committee of Public Safety.

6. Since the inertia of the government is the cause of reverses, the periods for execution of decrees and of measures of public safety are fixed. Violation of such periods shall be punished as an attack upon liberty.

Supplies

7. The table of production of grain of every district, made by the Committee of Public Safety, shall be printed and distributed to all members of the Convention, to be put into effect without delay.

8. The necessities of every department shall be estimated by approximation, and shall be guaranteed. The supplies shall be subject to requisition.

9. The table of production of the Republic shall be directed to the representatives of the people, to the Ministers of the Navy and the Interior, and to the administrators of supplies. They shall requisition in the *arrondissements* assigned to them. Paris shall have a special *arrondissement.*

10. Requisitions for the benefit of unproductive departments shall be authorized and regulated by the provisional Executive Council.

11. Paris shall be provisioned on 1 March for one year.

General Security

12. The direction and employment of the revolutionary army shall be regulated immediately so as to repress counter-revolutionaries. The Committee of Public Safety shall present a plan therefor.

13. The Council shall dispatch a garrison into cities where counter-revolutionary movements have arisen. The garrisons shall be paid and maintained by the wealthy people of said cities until the peace.

Finances

14. A court and a jury of accounts shall be created. Such court and jury shall be appointed by the National Convention; they shall be responsible for prosecuting all who have handled public revenues since the Revolution, and with demanding of them an account of their wealth.

The organization of said court is referred to the Committee on Legislation.

129. THE DREAM OF ETERNAL PROGRESS

It has been said that revolution is progress in a state of paroxysm. How ironic it was, then, that the most complete statement of the doctrine of progress evolved by the Enlightenment came at the height of the Reign of Terror, and from a thinker who was its victim. Antoine Nicolas de Caritat (1743-1794) until the Revolution bore the noble title of Marquis de Condorcet, and it was as Condorcet, mathematician, philosopher, and politician, that he is known to history. He was active in the French Revolution until his association with the Girondins led to his persecution by the Jacobins. It was while in hiding that he wrote his *Sketch for a Historical Picture of the Progress of the Human Mind*, and there is a clear reference to his perils in the passages given here. Completed just before his imprisonment and death, probably by suicide, in March 1794, the *Sketch* was published the next year. It anticipates the alliance between democratic liberalism and science (or at least the veneration for science) characteristic of the 19th century, and many of its concepts are still alive in contemporary social thought, in scarcely modified form.

Antoine Nicolas de Caritat, Marquis de Condorcet

Sketch for a Historical Picture of the Progress of the Human Mind

. . . . .

If man can, with almost complete assurance, predict phenomena when he knows their laws, and if, even when he does not, he can still, with great expectation of success, forecast the future on the basis of his experience of the past, why, then, should it be regarded as a fantastic undertaking to sketch, with some pretence to truth, the future destiny of man on the basis of his history? The sole foundation for belief in the natural sciences is this idea, that the general laws directing the phenomena of the universe, known or unknown, are necessary and constant. Why should this principle be any less true for the development of the intellectual and moral faculties of man than for the other operations of nature? Since beliefs founded on past experience of like conditions provide the only rule of conduct for the wisest of men, why should the philosopher be forbidden to base his conjectures on the same foundations, so long as he does not attribute to them a certainty superior to that warranted by the number, the constancy, and the accuracy of his observations?

. . . . .

So we might say that a well directed system of education rectifies natural inequality in ability instead of strengthening it, just as good laws remedy natural inequality in the means of subsistence, and just as in societies where laws have brought about this same equality, liberty, though subject to a regular constitution, will be more widespread, more complete than in the total independence of savage life. Then the social art will have fulfilled its aim, that of assuring and extending to all men enjoyment of the common rights to which they are called by nature.

The real advantages that should result from this progress, of which we can entertain a hope that is almost a certainty, can have no other term than that of the absolute perfection of the human race; since, as the various kinds of equality come to work in its favour by producing ampler sources of supply, more extensive education, more complete liberty, so equality will be more real and will embrace everything which is really of importance for the happiness of human beings.

It is therefore only by examining the progress and the laws of this perfection that we shall be able to understand the extent or the limits of our hopes.

SOURCE: Antoine Nicolas de Condorcet, *Sketch for a Historical Picture of the Progress of the Human Mind*, translated by June Barraclough (New York: Humanities Press, Inc., 1955), pp. 173, 184-85, 199–202. Reprinted by permission of the publisher.

No-one has ever believed that the mind can gain knowledge of all the facts of nature or attain the ultimate means of precision in the measurement, or in the analysis of the facts of nature, the relations between objects and all the possible combinations of ideas. Even the relations between magnitudes, the mere notion of quantity or extension, taken in its fullest comprehension, gives rise to a system so vast that it will never be mastered by the human mind in its entirety, that there will always be a part of it, always indeed the larger part of it that will remain for ever unknown. People have believed that man can never know more than a part of the objects that the nature of his intelligence allows him to understand, and that he must in the end arrive at a point where the number and complexity of the objects that he already knows have absorbed all his strength so that any further progress must be completely impossible.

But since, as the number of known facts increases, the human mind learns how to classify them and to subsume them under more general facts, and, at the same time, the instruments and methods employed in their observation and their exact measurement acquire a new precision; since, as more relations between various objects become known, man is able to reduce them to more general relations, to express them more simply, and to present them in such a way that it is possible to grasp a greater number of them with the same degree of intellectual ability and the same amount of application; since, as the mind learns to understand more complicated combinations of ideas, simpler formulae soon reduce their complexity; so truths that were discovered only by great effort, that could at first only be understood by men capable of profound thought, are soon developed and proved by methods that are not beyond the reach of common intelligence. If the methods which have led to these new combinations of ideas are ever exhausted, if their application to hitherto unsolved questions should demand exertions greater than either the time or the capacity of the learned would permit, some method of a greater generality or simplicity will be found so that genius can continue undisturbed on its path. The strength and the limits of man's intelligence may remain unaltered; and yet the instruments that he uses will increase and improve, the language that fixes and determines his ideas will acquire greater breadth and precision and, unlike mechanics where an increase of force means a decrease of speed, the methods that lead genius to the discovery of truth increase at once the force and the speed of its operations.

. . . . .

Organic perfectibility or deterioration amongst the various strains in the vegetable and animal kingdom can be regarded as one of the general laws of nature. This law also applies to the human race. No-one can doubt that, as preventative medicine improves and food and housing become healthier, as a way of life is established that develops our physical powers by exercise without ruining them by excess, as the two most virulent causes of deterioration, misery and excessive wealth, are eliminated, the average length of human life will be increased and a better health and a stronger physical constitution will be ensured. The improvement of medical practice, which will become more efficacious with the progress of reason and of the social order, will mean the end of infectious and hereditary diseases and illnesses brought on by climate, food, or working conditions. It is reasonable to hope that all other diseases may likewise disappear as their distant causes are discovered. Would it be absurd then to suppose that this perfection of the human species might be capable of indefinite progress; that the day will come when death will be due only to extraordinary accidents or to the decay of the vital forces, and that ultimately the average span between birth and decay will have no assignable value? Certainly man will not become immortal, but will not the interval between the first breath that he draws and the time when in the natural course of events, without disease or accident, he expires, increase indefinitely? . . .

Finally may we not extend such hopes to the intellectual and moral faculties? May not our parents, who transmit to us the benefits or disadvantages of their constitution, and from whom we receive our shape and features, as well as our tendencies to certain physical affections, hand on to us also that part of the physical organization which determines the intellect, the power of the brain, the ardour of the soul or the moral sensibility? Is it not probable that education, in perfecting these qualities, will at the same time influence, modify and perfect the organization itself? Analogy, investigation of the human faculties and the study of certain facts, all seem to give substance to such conjectures which would further push back the boundaries of our hopes.

These are the questions with which we shall conclude this final stage. How consoling for the philosopher who laments the errors, the crimes, the injustices which still pollute the earth and of which he is often the victim is this view of the human race, emancipated from its shackles, released from the empire of fate and from that of the enemies of its progress, advancing with a firm and sure step along the path of truth, virtue and happiness! It is the contemplation of this prospect that rewards him for all his efforts to assist the progress of reason and the defence of liberty. He dares to regard these strivings as part of the eternal chain of human destiny; and in this persuasion he is filled with the true delight of virtue and the pleasure of having done some lasting good which fate can never destroy by a sinister stroke of revenge, by calling back the reign of slavery and prejudice. Such contemplation is for him an asylum, in which the memory of his persecutors cannot pursue him; there he lives in thought with man restored to his natural rights and dignity, forgets man tormented and corrupted by greed, fear or envy; there he lives with his peers in an Elysium created by reason and graced by the purest pleasures known to the love of mankind.

130. A COMMUNIST DREAM

However vehement the revolutionary fervor of the Jacobins, not to speak of the Girondins, their social and economic ideas were built upon whole-hearted acceptance of the principle of private property. Yet a vision of a different kind of society based upon abolition of private property and substitution of one or another pattern of shared production and consumption arose during the immense perturbation of the French Revolution, especially among the poor. It was given political force by Gracchus (born François Noël) Babeuf (1760-1797), a journalist who organized a conspiracy in 1796 to overthrow the Directory with the help of the common soldiers. The insurrection was detected before it gained any strength, and its promotors, including Babeuf, were tried for treason and guillotined. Babeuf presented his ideas in unusually terse form in his speech of defense. The italicized material in the selection below is either direct or indirect quotation from his earlier writings.

Gracchus Babeuf

The Defense of Gracchus Babeuf before the High Court of Vendôme

I wrote:

Man's condition ought not to have deteriorated in passing from a state of nature to a state of social organization. In the beginning the soil belonged to none, its fruits to all. The introduction of private property was a piece of trickery put over on the simple and unsuspecting masses. The laws that buttressed property operated inevitably to create social classes—privileged and oppressed, masters and slaves.

The law of inheritance is a sovereign wrong. It breeds misery even from the second generation. Two sons of a rich man receive equal shares of their father's fortune. One son has but one child, the other, twelve. Of these twelve each receives only a twelfth part of the fortune of his uncle and the twenty-fourth part of the

---

Source: John Anthony Scott (ed. and trans.), *The Defense of Gracchus Babeuf before the High Court of Vendôme* (Amherst: The University of Massachusetts Press, 1967), pp. 52–58. Reprinted by permission of the University of Massachusetts Press.

fortune of his grandfather. This portion is not enough to live on; and so twelve poor men must work for one rich one. Hence we find masters and servants among the grandchildren of a single man.

The law of alienability is no less unjust. This one man, already master over all the other grandchildren in the same line, pays what he will for the work that they must do for him. Their wages are insufficient to maintain life and they are obliged to sell their meager inheritance to their master. They become landless men; and, if they have children of their own, these inherit nothing.

The gulf between rich and poor, rulers and ruled, proceeds from yet another cause, the difference in value and in price that arbitrary opinion attaches to the diverse products of toil and manufacture. Thus a watchmaker's working day has been valued twenty times higher than a ploughman's or laborer's. The wages of the watchmaker enable him to get possession of the inheritance of twenty ploughmen whom he is thus in a position to expropriate, and enhance his own condition.

These three roots of our public woes—heredity, alienability, and the differing values which arbitrary opinion assigns to different types of social product—proceed from the institution of private property. All the evils of society flow from them. They isolate the people from each other; they convert every family into a private commonwealth, pit it against society at large, and dedicate it with an ever growing emphasis to inequality in all its vicious, suicidal forms.

I formulated these observations and came to think of them as self-evident truths. It did not take me very long to draw the following conclusions:

If the earth belongs to none and its fruits to all; if private ownership of public wealth is only the result of certain institutions that violate fundamental human rights; then it follows that this private ownership is a usurpation; and it further follows that all that a man takes of the land and its fruits beyond what is necessary for sustenance is theft from society.

And being drawn from one conclusion to another, believing as I did that no truth must be permitted to remain hidden from the minds of men, I became convinced of the truth of the following ideas, which I caused to be published:

All that a citizen lacks for the satisfaction of his various daily needs, he lacks because he has been deprived of a natural property right by the engrossers of the public domain. All that a citizen enjoys beyond what is necessary for the satisfaction of his daily needs he enjoys as a result of a theft from the other members of society. In this way a more or less numerous group of people is deprived of its rightful share in the public domain.

Inheritance and alienability are institutions destructive of basic human rights.

The plea of superior ability and industry is an empty rationalization to mask the machinations of those who conspire against human equality and happiness. It is ridiculous and unfair to lay claim to a higher wage for the man whose work requires more concentrated thought and more mental effort. Such effort in no way expands the capacity of the stomach. No wage can be defended over and above what is necessary for the satisfaction of a person's needs.

The worth of intelligence is only a matter of opinion, and it still remains to be determined if natural, physical strength is not of equal worth. Clever people have set a high value upon the creations of their minds; if the toilers had also had a hand in the ordering of things, they would doubtless have insisted that brawn is entitled to equal consideration with brain and that physical fatigue is no less real than mental fatigue.

If wages are not equalized, the clever and persevering are given a licence to rob and despoil with impunity those less fortunately endowed with natural gifts. In this way the economic equilibrium of society is upset, for nothing has been more conclusively proven than the maxim: a man only succeeds in becoming rich through the spoliation of others.

All our civic institutions, our social relationships, are nothing else but the expression of legalized barbarism and piracy, in which every man cheats and robs his neighbor. In its festering swamp our swindling society generates vice, crime, and misery of every kind. A handful of well-intentioned people band together and wage war on these evils, but their efforts are futile. They can make no headway because they do not tackle the problem at its roots, but apply palliatives based upon the distorted thinking of a sick society.

It is clear from the foregoing that whatever a man possesses over and above his rightful share of the social product has been stolen. It is therefore right and proper to take this wealth back again from those who have wrongfully appropriated it. Even a man who shows that he can do the work of four, and who consequently demands the wages of four, will still be an enemy of society; he is using criminal means to shake the social order and to obliterate its sacred equality. Common sense tells us, with no small emphasis, that we should curb a man of this type and drive him out as if he had the plague. At the very least he should be allowed to perform no more than one man's work and to lay claim to no more than one man's pay. The human species alone has made insane value distinctions between one of its members and another. As a result, the human species alone has been obliged to experience misery and want. There is no need for men to lack those things which nature has provided for all, though, of course, if want should arise as a result of the unavoidable calamities of wind, storm, flood, or famine, such privation must be borne and shared equally by all.

The creations of the human hand and mind become the property of society, part of the nation's capital, from the very moment that thinkers and workers bring these creations into being. Invention is the fruit of prior investigation and effort. The most recent workers in the field reap their reward as a result of the social labors of their predecessors in a society that nurtures invention and that aids the scientific worker in his task. It is clear that if knowledge is a social product it must be shared by all alike.

It is a truth, which only ignorant or prejudiced people are likely to contest, that if knowledge were made available to all alike, it would serve to make men roughly equal in ability and even in talent. Education is a monstrosity when it is unequally shared, since then it becomes the exclusive patrimony of a section of society; it becomes, in the hands of this section, a set of tools, an ideological armory, with the help of which the privileged make war upon the defenseless masses. In this way the rich succeed, with little difficulty, in stifling and deceiving and robbing the people, thus subjecting them to a shameful servitude.

One thinker[1] *expressed a profound truth when he wrote: "Talk as long as you will of the forms of government; it will all be idle speculation until you destroy the seeds of human greed and acquisitiveness." Society must be made to operate in such a way that it eradicates once and for all the desire of a man to become richer, or wiser, or more powerful than others.*

Putting this more exactly, we must try to to bring our fate under control, *try to make the lot of every member of society independent of accidental circumstances, happy or unhappy. We must try to guarantee to each man and his posterity, however numerous, a sufficiency of the means of existence, and nothing more. We must try and close all possible avenues by which a man may acquire more than his fair share of the fruits of toil and the gifts of nature.*

The only way to do this is to organize a communal regime which will suppress private property, set each to work at the skill or job he understands, require each to deposit the fruits of his labor in kind at the common store, and establish an agency for the distribution of basic necessities. This agency will maintain a complete list of people and of supplies, will distribute the latter with scrupulous fairness, and will deliver them to the home of each worker.

A system such as this has been proven practicable by actual experience, for it is used by our twelve armies with their 1,200,000 men. And what is possible on a small scale can also be done on a large one. A regime of this type alone can ensure the general welfare, or, in other words, the permanent happiness of the people—the true and proper object of organized society.

Such a regime, I continued, *will sweep away iron bars, dungeon walls, and bolted doors, trials and disputations, murders, thefts and crimes of every kind; it will sweep away the judges and the judged, the jails and the gibbets—all the torments of body and agony of soul that the injustice of life engenders; it will sweep away enviousness and gnawing greed, pride and deceit, the very catalogue of sins that Man is heir to; it will remove—and how important is this!—the brooding, omnipresent fear that gnaws always and in each of us concerning our fate tomorrow, next month, next year, and in our old age, concerning the fate of our children and of our children's children.*

[1] Abbé Morelly, an early writer on collectivism whose dates are unknown [editor's comments].

131. THE ENCHANTMENT OF THE REVOLUTION

The French Revolution was admired by all those in other lands for whom it was the hope of putting the ideals of Enlightened Reason into practice. Some remained admirers to the end, but others, like the English Romantic poet William Wordsworth (1770-1850), turned away when revolutionary France became a terrorist dictatorship and a conqueror of nations. Yet Wordsworth was still able, in 1804, to recapture in his poem on the "French Revolution as It Appeared to Enthusiasts at Its Commencement" the quality of the days when it was "bliss . . . in that dawn to be alive."

William Wordsworth

French Revolution

FRENCH REVOLUTION AS IT APPEARED TO ENTHUSIASTS AT ITS COMMENCEMENT

Oh! pleasant exercise of hope and joy!
For mighty were the auxiliars which then stood
Upon our side, we who were strong in love!
Bliss was it in that dawn to be alive,
But to be young was very heaven!—Oh! times,
In which the meagre, stale, forbidding ways
Of custom, law, and statute, took at once
The attraction of a country in romance!
When Reason seemed the most to assert her rights,
When most intent on making of herself
A prime Enchantress—to assist the work
Which then was going forward in her name!
Not favoured spots alone, but the whole earth,
The beauty wore of promise, that which sets
(As at some moment might not be unfelt
Among the bowers of paradise itself)
The budding rose above the rose full blown.
What temper at the prospect did not wake
To happiness unthought of? The inert
Were roused, and lively natures rapt away!
They who had fed their childhood upon dreams,
The playfellows of fancy, who had made

SOURCE: *The Poetical Works of William Wordsworth,* edited by William Knight (Edinburgh, Scotland; William Patterson, 1883), Vol. III, pp. 118–19.

All powers of swiftness, subtilty, and strength
Their ministers,—who in lordly wise had stirred
Among the grandest objects of the sense,
And dealt with whatsoever they found there
As if they had within some lurking right
To wield it;—they, too, who, of gentle mood,
Had watched all gentle motions, and to these
Had fitted their own thoughts, schemers more mild,
And in the region of their peaceful selves;—
Now was it that both found, the meek and lofty
Did both find, helpers to their heart's desire,
And stuff at hand, plastic as they could wish;
Were called upon to exercise their skill,
Not in Utopia, subterranean fields,
Or some secreted island, Heaven knows where!
But in the very world, which is the world
Of all of us,—the place where in the end
We find our happiness, or not at all!

132. THE PRINCIPLE OF COUNTERREVOLUTIONARY INTERVENTION

During the summer of 1791, Emperor Leopold II and King Frederick William II of Prussia responded with double-tongued words to the pressures from the French Royal Court and the *émigrés* (refugee aristocrats) for invasion of France to restore the absolute monarchy. They issued a declaration at Pillnitz, in Saxony, affirming their right to intervene in France; but they hedged their willingness to act by making it conditional upon England's participation, which they did not at all expect. The French revolutionaries, however, read the declaration at its face value, and it therefore contributed to the exacerbation of relations that led to war the next spring. The doctrine of the right of intervention on behalf of an endangered regime, or to establish a new one, was to become part of an unwritten but almost universally practiced "law of nations" for all kinds of governments in the next decades and centuries. It was, of course, a direct violation of the principle of sovereignty of nations that all states proclaimed, at least for themselves.

The Declaration of Pillnitz, August 27, 1791

His Majesty, the Emperor, and his Majesty, the King of Prussia, having given attention to the wishes and representations of *Monsieur* (the brother

---

SOURCE: Department of History, University of Pennsylvania, *Translations and Reprints from the Original Sources of European History* (Philadelphia: University of Pennsylvania Press, n.d.), Vol. I, pp. 34–35. Reprinted by permission of the University of Pennsylvania Press.

of the King of France), and of M. le Comte d'Artois, jointly declare that they regard the present situation of his majesty the King of France, as a matter of common interest to all the sovereigns of Europe. They trust that this interest will not fail to be recognized by the powers, whose aid is solicited, and that in consequence they will not refuse to employ, in conjunction with their said majesties, the most efficient means in proportion to their resources to place the King of France in a position to establish, with the most absolute freedom, the foundations of a monarchical form of government, which shall at once be in harmony with the rights of sovereigns and promote the welfare of the French nation. In that case [*Alors et dans ce cas*] their said majesties the Emperor and the King of Prussia are resolved to act promptly and in common accord with the forces necessary to obtain the desired, common end.

In the meantime they will give such orders to their troops as are necessary in order that these may be in a position to be called into active service.

LEOPOLD. FREDERICK WILLIAM

PILLNITZ, August 27, 1791

133. REVOLUTION IN FRANCE: A REBUTTAL

Edmund Burke, the British statesman who had defended the cause of the Americans in their War of Independence, responded to the Revolution in France in a wholly contrary way. Where he had seen the rebellion in America as a conservative force, Burke considered the French Revolution, even in its earliest and relatively mild stages, as a crime. In his *Reflections on the Revolution in France*, published only a year after the Revolution began, he portrayed it as the result of an attempt to put into practice the political theories of the Enlightenment. He denied the principles of sovereignty of the people and social utilitarianism with an eloquent disquisition on the historical roots of government and society. But he seems to have had no sense of the actual political quarrels in France on the eve of 1789, notably the struggle between an erratically reformist monarchy and a stubbornly standpat aristocracy. Burke's rebuttal was directed to English Radicals, specifically Dr. Richard Price, who defended the French cause. Some important selections from the *Reflections* are given here.

Edmund Burke

Reflections on the Revolution in France

. . . . .

Compute your gains: see what is got by those extravagant and presumptuous speculations which have taught your leaders to despise all their predecessors, and all their contemporaries, and even to despise themselves, until the moment in which they become truly despicable. By following those false lights, France has bought undignified calamities at a higher price than any nation has purchased the most unequivocal blessings! France has bought poverty by crime! France has not sacrificed her virtue to her interest; but she has abandoned her interest, that she might prostitute her virtue. All other nations have begun the fabric of a new government, or the reformation of an old, by establishing originally, or by enforcing with greater exactness some rites or other of religion. All other people have laid the foundations of civil freedom in severer manners, and a system of a more austere and masculine morality. France, when she let loose the reins of regal authority, doubled the licence, of a ferocious dissoluteness in manners, and of an insolent irreligion in opinions and practices; and has extended through all ranks of life, as if she were communicating some privilege, or laying open some secluded benefit, all the unhappy corruptions that usually were the disease of wealth and power. This is one of the new principles of equality in France.

France, by the perfidy of her leaders, has utterly disgraced the tone of lenient council in the cabinets of princes, and disarmed it of its most potent topics. She has sanctified the dark suspicious maxims of tyrannous distrust; and taught kings to tremble at (what will hereafter be called) the delusive plausibilities, of moral politicians. Sovereigns will consider those who advise them to place an unlimited confidence in their people, as subverters of their thrones; as traitors who aim at their destruction, by leading their easy good-nature under specious pretences, to admit combinations of bold and faithless men into a participation of their power. This alone (if there were nothing else) is an irreparable calamity to you and to mankind. Remember that your parliament of Paris told your king, that in calling the states together, he had nothing to fear but the prodigal excess of their zeal in providing for the support of the throne. It is right that these men should hide their heads. It is right that

---

SOURCE: Edmund Burke, *Reflections on the Revolution in France and on the Proceedings in Certain Societies in London Relative to That Event*, edited by William B. Todd (New York: Holt, Rinehart & Winston, 1959), pp. 43–45, 71–73, 103–6, 117.

they should bear their part in the ruin which their counsel has brought on their sovereign and their country. Such sanguine declarations tend to lull authority asleep; to encourage it rashly to engage in perilous adventures of untried policy; to neglect those provisions, preparations, and precautions, which distinguish benevolence from imbecillity; and without which no man can answer for the salutary effect of any abstract plan of government or of freedom. For want of these, they have seen the medicine of the state corrupted into its poison. They have seen the French rebel against a mild and lawful monarch, with more fury, outrage, and insult, than ever any people has been known to rise against the most illegal usurper, or the most sanguinary tyrant. Their resistance was made to concession; their revolt was from protection; their blow was aimed at an hand holding out graces, favours, and immunities.

This was unnatural. The rest is in order. They have found their punishment in their success. Laws overturned; tribunals subverted; industry without vigour; commerce expiring; the revenue unpaid, yet the people impoverished; a church pillaged, and a state not relieved; civil and military anarchy made the constitution of the kingdom; every thing human and divine sacrificed to the idol of public credit, and national bankruptcy the consequence; and to crown all, the paper securities of new, precarious, tottering power, the discredited paper securities of impoverished fraud, and beggared rapine, held out as a currency for the support of an empire, in lieu of the two great recognized species that represent the lasting conventional credit of mankind, which disappeared and hid themselves in the earth from whence they came, when the principle of property, whose creatures and representatives they are, was systematically subverted.

. . . . .

Government is not made in virtue of natural rights, which may and do exist in total independence of it; and exist in much greater clearness, and in a much greater degree of abstract perfection: but their abstract perfection is their practical defect. By having a right to every thing they want every thing. Government is a contrivance of human wisdom to provide for human *wants*. Men have a right that these wants should be provided for by this wisdom. Among these wants is to be reckoned the want, out of civil society, of a sufficient restraint upon their passions. Society requires not only that the passions of individuals should be subjected, but that even in the mass and body as well as in the individuals, the inclinations of men should frequently be thwarted, their will controlled, and their passions brought into subjection. This can only be done *by a power out of themselves;* and not, in the exercise of its function, subject to that will and to those passions which it is its office to bridle and subdue. In this sense the restraints on men, as well as their liberties, are to be reckoned among their rights. But as the liberties and the restrictions vary with times and circumstances, and admit of infinite modifications, they cannot be settled upon any abstract rule; and nothing is so foolish as to discuss them upon that principle.

The moment you abate any thing from the full rights of men, each to govern himself, and suffer any artificial positive limitation upon those rights, from that moment the whole organization of government becomes a consideration of convenience. This it is which makes the constitution of a state, and the due distribution of its powers, a matter of the most delicate and complicated skill. It requires a deep knowledge of human nature and human necessities, and of the things which facilitate or obstruct the various ends which are to be pursued by the mechanism of civil institutions. The state is to have recruits to its strength, and remedies to its distempers. What is the use of discussing a man's abstract right to food or to medicine? The question is upon the method of procuring and administering them. In that deliberation I shall always advise to call in the aid of the farmer and the physician, rather than the professor of metaphysics.

The science of constructing a commonwealth or renovating it, or reforming it, is, like every other experimental science, not to be taught *à priori.* Nor is it a short experience that can instruct us in that practical science; because the real effects of moral causes are not always immediate; but that which in the first instance is prejudicial may be excellent in its remoter operation; and its excellence may arise even from the ill effects it produces in the beginning. The reverse also happens; and very plausible schemes, with very pleasing commencements, have often shameful and lamentable conclusions. In states there are often some obscure and almost latent causes, things whch appear at first view of little moment, on which a very great part of its prosperity or adversity may most essentially depend. The science of government being therefore so practical in itself, and intended for such practical purposes, a matter which requires experience, and even more experience than any person can gain in his whole life, however sagacious and observing he may be, it is with infinite caution that any man ought to venture upon pulling down an edifice which has answered in any tolerable degree for ages the common purposes of society, or on building it up again, without having models and patterns of approved utility before his eyes.

. . . . .

I almost venture to affirm, that not one in a hundred amongst us participates in the "triumph" of the Revolution Society. If the king and queen of France, and their children, were to fall into our hands by the chance of war, in the most acrimonious of all hostilities (I deprecate such an event, I deprecate such hostility) they would be treated with another sort of triumphal entry into London. We formerly have had a king of France in that situation; you have read how he was treated by the victor in the field; and in what manner he was afterwards received in England. Four hundred years have gone over us; but I believe we are not materially changed since that period. Thanks to our sullen resistance to innovation, thanks to the cold sluggishness of our national character, we still bear the stamp of our forefathers. We have not (as I conceive) lost the generosity and dignity of thinking of the fourteenth century; nor as yet have we subtilized ourselves into savages. We are not the converts of Rousseau; we are not the disciples of Voltaire; Helvétius has made no progress amongst us. Atheists are not our preachers; madmen are not our lawgivers. We know that *we* have made no discoveries; and we think that no discoveries are to be made, in morality; nor many in the great principles of government, nor in the ideas of liberty, which were understood long before we were born, altogether as well as they will be after the grave has heaped its mould upon our presumption, and the silent tomb shall have imposed its law on our pert loquacity. In England we have not yet been completely embowelled of our natural entrails; we still feel within us, and we cherish and cultivate, those inbred sentiments which are the faithful guardians, the active monitors of our duty, the true supporters of all liberal and manly morals. We have not been drawn and trussed, in order that we may be filled, like stuffed birds in a museum, with chaff and rags, and paltry, blurred shreds of paper about the rights of man. We preserve the whole of our feelings still native and entire, unsophisticated by pedantry and infidelity. We have real hearts of flesh and blood beating in our bosoms. We fear God; we look up with awe to kings; with affection to parliaments; with duty to magistrates; with reverence to priests; and with respect to nobility.[1] Why? Because when such ideas are brought before our minds, it is *natural* to be so affected; because all other feelings are false and spurious, and tend to corrupt our minds, to vitiate our primary morals, to render us unfit for rational liberty; and by teaching us a servile, licentious, and abandoned insolence, to be our low sport for a few holidays, to make us perfectly fit for, and justly deserving of slavery, through the whole course of our lives.

You see, Sir, that in this enlightened age I am bold enough to confess, that we are generally men of untaught feelings; that instead of casting

---

[1] The English are, I conceive, misrepresented in a Letter published in one of the papers, by a gentleman thought to be a dissenting minister.—When writing to Dr. Price, of the spirit which prevails at Paris, he says, "The spirit of the people in this place has abolished all the proud *distinctions* which the *king* and *nobles* had usurped in their minds; whether they talk of *the king, the noble, or the priest,* their whole language is that of the most *enlightened and liberal amongst the English.*" If this gentleman means to confine the terms *enlightened and liberal* to one set of men in England, it may be true. It is not generally so. [Burke's note]

away all our old prejudices, we cherish them to a very considerable degree, and, to take more shame to ourselves, we cherish them because they are prejudices; and the longer they have lasted, and the more generally they have prevailed, the more we cherish them. We are afraid to put men to live and trade each on his own private stock of reason; because we suspect that this stock in each man is small, and that the individuals would do better to avail themselves of the general bank and capital of nations, and of ages. Many of our men of speculation, instead of exploding general prejudices, employ their sagacity to discover the latent wisdom which prevails in them. If they find what they seek, and they seldom fail, they think it more wise to continue the prejudice, with the reason involved, than to cast away the coat of prejudice, and to leave nothing but the naked reason; because prejudice, with its reason, has a motive to give action to that reason, and an affection which will give it permanence. Prejudice is of ready application in the emergency; it previously engages the mind in a steady course of wisdom and virtue, and does not leave the man hesitating in the moment of decision, sceptical, puzzled, and unresolved. Prejudice renders a man's virtue his habit; and not a series of unconnected acts. Through just prejudice, his duty becomes a part of his nature.

. . . . .

Society is indeed a contract. Subordinate contracts for objects of mere occasional interest may be dissolved at pleasure—but the state ought not to be considered as nothing better than a partnership agreement in a trade of pepper and coffee, callico or tobacco, or some other such low concern, to be taken up for a little temporary interest, and to be dissolved by the fancy of the parties. It is to be looked on with other reverence; because it is not a partnership in things subservient only to the gross animal existence of a temporary and perishable nature. It is a partnership in all science; a partnership in all art; a partnership in every virtue, and in all perfection. As the ends of such a partnership cannot be obtained in many generations, it becomes a partnership not only between those who are living, but between those who are living, those who are dead, and those who are to be born. Each contract of each particular state is but a clause in the great primaeval contract of eternal society, linking the lower with the higher natures, connecting the visible and invisible world, according to a fixed compact sanctioned by the inviolable oath which holds all physical and all moral natures, each in their appointed place.

CHAPTER XIV

NAPOLEON, CONQUEROR AND CONQUERED

WHEN THE REVOLUTIONARY governments were still unable to maintain power or disbar rivals in 1799 except with the aid of an army, it was the army, in the person of General Napoleon Bonaparte, which made itself the ruler of the country. Napoleon, who declared himself emperor of the French in 1804, sought to terminate the revolutionary crisis by consolidating its institutional changes and reconciling the politically influential classes within a monarchy that was both enlightened and tyrannical. But Napoleon was more like Frederick the Great of Prussia than any of his predecessors in France; he was a gifted military commander driven by an obsessive need for domination and glory. With the resources of one of Europe's greatest states at his disposal, he launched a series of campaigns that brought Europe closer to rule by a single man than it had been since the time of Charlemagne.

The Napoleonic Empire, much as it dazzled observers, also aroused deep resistance in Europe. The age-old dynastic monarchies joined forces, however hesitantly, with passionate popular nationalism. England, safe behind the oaken walls of its fleet, was a perpetual foe and a source of strength to whoever would fight the "Corsican tyrant." The failure of the Spanish and Russian campaigns brought Napoleon's end, his first abdication in 1814, and then the final flight in 1815 after Waterloo. The Bourbon monarchy was restored in France, and the victors turned to the task of restoring the old order.

134. THE MIND OF A CONQUEROR AND RULER

The French Revolution gave way in 1799 to a military ruler, General Napoleon Bonaparte. However much he was a creature of his times, he was also to a significant extent the maker of events, and his personal attitudes and characteristics therefore assumed broad historical importance. The following selections from his writings and from conversations with him recorded by others reveal the quality of his mind and the ideas that moved this enlightened and tyrannical despot.

Napoleon Bonaparte

Notes and Conversations

[Manuscript, "Dialogue on Love," before 1793]. . .

Bonaparte: I do not ask you for the definition of love. I was in love once, and I remember it well enough not to require those metaphysical definitions that merely confuse matters. I do more than deny its existence. I believe it to be harmful to society, to individual happiness—in short, I believe that . . . it would be the merciful deed of a protective divinity to rid us of love and to liberate the world from it. . . .

[Conversation, 1817] I have never loved, really loved, except, perhaps, Josephine—a little—and at that, because I was twenty-seven when I met her. I liked Marie Louise a great deal. I rather agree with Gassion, who said that he did not love life enough to give it to other beings.

. . . . .

[Manuscript, early 1790s] But ambition, that immoderate desire to satisfy vanity or intemperance, which, never sated, leads Alexander from Thebes to Persia, from the Granicus to Issus, from Issus to Arbela, from Arbela to India—ambition causes him to conquer and ravage the world and yet fails to appease him. The same ardor still consumes him, and in his delirium he no longer knows what course he should give it. In his agitation he goes astray. . . . Alexander believes himself a god, he thinks himself the son of Jupiter, and he wants to make others believe it. . . .

Ambition, which overthrows governments and private fortunes,

SOURCE: J. Christopher Herold (ed. and trans.), *The Mind of Napoleon* (New York: Columbia University Press, 1955), pp. 10–11, 46, 79, 160, 162–63, 220–23, 243. Reprinted by permission of the Columbia University Press.

which feeds on blood and crimes, ambition . . . is, like all inordinate passions, a violent and unthinking fever that ceases only when life ceases—like a conflagration which, fanned by a pitiless wind, ends only after all has been consumed.

. . . . .

[Conversation, 1800] My policy is to govern men the way the great majority wants to be governed. This, I believe, is the only way in which it is possible to acknowledge the sovereignty of the people. By making myself Catholic I brought the war in the Vendée to an end. By becoming a Moslem I established myself in Egypt. By acting ultramontane I won the minds of the Italians. If I governed a nation of Jews, I should restore the temple of Solomon. Thus I shall talk freedom in the free part of Santo Domingo; I shall confirm slavery in the Ile de France [Mauritius] and even in the slave part of Santo Domingo—with the reservation that I shall soften and limit slavery wherever I maintain it and shall restore order and discipline wherever I maintain freedom.

. . . . .

[Conversation with Talleyrand, late 1813, as related by Talleyrand to Mme de Rémusat] You must know that I am not in the least afraid of committing an act of cowardice if it were useful to me. Look here, at bottom there is nothing either noble or base in this world. My character possesses all those qualities that are capable of strengthening my power and of deceiving those who imagine that they know me. Frankly, I am a coward, indeed I am—essentially a coward. I give you my word of honor that I would not experience the least repugnance toward committing what the world calls a dishonorable action.

[Conversation, April 1815] Don't talk to me of goodness, of abstract justice, of natural law. Necessity is the highest law; public welfare is the highest justice. Unto each day the evil thereof; to each circumstance its own law; each man according to his nature.

[Conversation, 1815] A distinction must be made between the actions of a sovereign, who acts as a collective person, and those of a private individual, who has only his own feelings to consider. Politics allows and even commands the one to do what would be inexcusable in the other.

[Conversation, 1817] Governments keep their promises *only* when they are forced or when it is to their advantage to do so.

. . . . .

[Repeated saying] A true master of politics is able to calculate, down to the smallest fraction, the advantages to which he may put his very faults.

[Conversation, December 1812] They think I am stern, even hard-hearted. So much the better—this makes it unnecessary for me to justify my reputation. My firmness is taken for callousness. I shall not complain, since this notion is responsible for the good order that is prevailing, so that there is nothing that needs to be repressed. . . . Look here, Caulaincourt, I am human. No matter what some people say, I too have entrails, a heart—but the heart of a sovereign. I am not moved by the tears of a duchess, but the sufferings of the people touch me.

[Conversation, 1816] Remember that a man, a true man, never hates. His rages and his bad moods never last beyond the present moment—like electric shocks. A man made for public life and authority never takes account of personalities; he only takes account of things, of their weight and their consequences.

[Conversation, 1816] A stateman's heart must be in his head. . . .

[Conversation, 1800] The question is not whether there is a large group that is hostile to me. The question is whether in each class to the people some chord responds to me. There are many Frenchmen who have ten such chords. Everywhere in Europe, some chord is for me. There are people who respond to my laws, others to my victories—everywhere there is at least one chord. All that needs be done is to touch it.

. . . . .

[Dictation, Saint Helena] A military leader must possess as much character as intellect *(esprit).* Men who have a great deal of intellect and little character are the least suited; they are like a ship whose masts are out of proportion to the ballast; it is preferable to have much character and little intellect. Those men whose intellect is mediocre and whose character is in proportion are likely to succeed in their profession. The base must equal the height. Generals who possessed intellect and character to an equally high degree were Caesar, Hannibal, Turenne, Prince Eugene [of Savoy], and Frederick [the Great]. . . .

[Letter to General Lauriston, 1804] These three things you must always keep in mind: concentration of strength, activity, and a firm resolve to perish gloriously. They are the three principles of the military art which have disposed luck in my favor in all my operations. Death is nothing, but to live defeated and without glory is to die every day. . . .

[Conversation, 1800s] Military science consists in first calculating all the possibilities accurately and then in making an almost mathematically exact allowance for accident. It is on this point that one must make no mistake; a decimal more or less may alter everything. Now, this apportioning of knowledge and accident can take place only in the head of a genius, for without it there can be no creation—and surely the greatest improvisation of the human mind is that which gives existence to the nonexistent. Accident thus always remains a mystery to mediocre minds and becomes reality for superior men. . . .

[Conversation, Saint Helena, 1815] The issue of a battle is the result of a single instant, a single thought. The adversaries come into each other's presence with various combinations; they mingle; they fight for a length of time; the decisive moment appears; a psychological spark makes the decision; and a few reserve troops are enough to carry it out.

. . . . .

[Conversation, 1805] I have a few ideas that aren't ripe yet, but they are far-reaching. There is not enough sameness among the nations of Europe. European society needs a regeneration. There must be a superior power which dominates all the other powers, with enough authority to force them to live in harmony with one another—and France is best placed for that purpose.

[Conversation, 1816] One of my great conceptions was the agglomeration, the concentration, of those geographic-national entities which revolutions and politics have dissolved or broken up. Thus there are in Europe—though scattered—more than thirty million Frenchmen, fifteen million Spaniards, fifteen million Italians, thirty million Germans. I should have liked to make out of each of these peoples one single and uniform national body. . . .

After this summary process of simplification, it would have been possible to pursue the chimera of the *beau idéal* of civilization, for in this new order of things there was an improved chance of creating everywhere uniform codes, principles, opinions, feelings, outlooks, and interests. Then, perhaps, with the help of the universal spread of education, it would have been permissible to dream of applying the American constitution to the great European family.

135. A TURNING AWAY FROM FRANCE AND THE ENLIGHTENMENT

The impact of revolutionary and particularly Napoleonic France on Europe was intellectually stimulating in the extreme, sometimes by way of imitation but more often by way of rejection. An early follower of the Rousseauean variant of Enlightenment thought and feeling, the German philosopher Johann Gottfried Herder (1744-1803) turned against the French Enlightenment itself. Trained as a theologian, he got his living as a church official at Weimar not for his professional services but to support his work as a philosopher and man of letters. Herder developed the notion of peoples as organisms with life, not mere assemblages of individuals. He emphasized the distinctive character of such nations, particularly as it was embodied in language and folk literature. He also contributed to the distinct breakaway in later 18th-century Germany from the rationalism of the Enlightenment towards a Romantic display of feeling, and he was one of the first to look upon the medieval era with favor instead of rationalist disdain. Some of these ideas are expressed in the following passages from his *Travel Diary* (A) and his *Yet Another Philosophy of History* (B).

A. Johann Gottfried Herder

Travel Diary

. . . . .

Languages, no less than governments, depend in this on the spirit of the age: this becomes striking to the point of being obvious, if one makes comparisons. The same spirit of monarchic manners which Montesquieu so strikingly portrays in his own person dominates his language also. Like the French nation, it has little real virtue, little inner strength; it makes as much as it can out of little, as a machine is moved by a small driving wheel. National strength, the idiomatic quality which clings to its native soil, originality—these it does not have in large measure; the concept of honour, however, without which no person, no book and no phrase is complete—features most prominently in it. A certain nobility of thought, a certain freedom of expression, a *politesse* in the manner of using words and in turning phrases—these are the stamp of the French language as of French manners. The chief concern is not with what a writer should teach others, but with what he himself excels in and what he feels he owes it to himself to teach others. Nobody knows this better than Voltaire and Rousseau, however strongly the latter denies it and however immensely they may differ even in this respect. They show it all the same: the first is vain and bold about his own accomplishments, the second proud and arrogant—both seek for nothing so determinedly as for distinctiveness. Only Voltaire thinks he has already distinguished himself, and merely seeks to show off his wit, while Rousseau continues to search for the novel, the unheardof, the paradoxical, often to an intolerable degree. However strongly Rousseau may combat the *philosophes,* he too appears to be less concerned with the validity, the intrinsic quality, the reasonableness and applicability of his ideas, than with their greatness, their extraordinariness, their novelty, their striking effect. Where he can find these qualities he is a sophist and an apologist. Reasons such as these account for the fact that the French have produced so few philosophers, political writers and historians since for these truth is the

---

Source: F. M. Bernard (ed. and trans.), *J. G. Herder on Social and Political Culture* (Cambridge, England: Cambridge University Press, 1969), pp. 107–9. Reprinted by permission of Cambridge University Press.

prime requirement. Voltaire, however, will gladly sacrifice it to a brainwave, Rousseau to a novelty, and Marmontel to a turn of phrase.

Nowhere is gallantry more finely developed than among this nation. It characterizes the French novel and accounts for the coquetry of the French style generally. Underlying it is a concern with polished rather than deep emotions, with the outward manifestation rather than the inner experience of feeling. Mode of expression, capacity for making instant conquests: these are the all-important considerations. The French style is constantly at pains to show that it knows the secret of the art of living, of the art of making conquests. The subtlety of turns of phrase may mean absolutely nothing, yet it cannot fail to demonstrate the writer's command of style . . . It is the same with the compliments of the journalist; no nation can frame them better, more deliberately, more precisely, more richly than the French; but again this is intended more to show that they can thus frame them—that they are educated people, that they are not coarse like the Germans—than to express an upsurge of sincerity and feeling. Gallantry is the language not of emotion and tenderness but of convention and social intercourse; it indicates that one knows the world.

B. Johann Gottfried Herder

Yet Another Philosophy of History

. . . .

The spirit of "Nordic chivalry" has been compared to the heroic age of the Greeks—and, to be sure, points of comparison do exist—but it seems to me that it is really unique in the sequence of the centuries, resembling nothing but itself. Because it comes between the Romans and us—*quanti viri*—some have treated it with derision; others, somewhat adventurously minded, have exalted it above everything, but it seems to me that it is neither more nor less than a "particular state of the world," whose advantages and disadvantages should not be compared with those of preceding ages: it took its point of departure from these ages, but by ceaseless transformation and aspiration became uniquely itself—on a grand scale!

We can read of the dark sides of this period in any book. Every classical litterateur who takes our regimented century for the *ne plus ultra* of mankind finds occasion to reproach whole centuries for barbarism,

---

Source: F. M. Bernard (ed. and trans.), *J. G. Herder on Social and Political Culture* (Cambridge, England: Cambridge University Press, 1969), pp. 191–94. Reprinted by permission of Cambridge University Press.

wretched constitutional law, superstition and stupidity, lack of manners and taste, and to mock their schools, country seats, temples, monasteries, town halls, guilds, cottages and houses. At the same time, he shouts the praises of the light of our century, or, rather, of its frivolity and exuberance, its warmth in theory and coldness in practice, its apparent strength and freedom, and its real mortal weakness and exhaustion under the weight of unbelief, despotism, and luxury. All the books of our Voltaires, Humes, Robertsons and Iselins are, to the delight of their contemporaries, full of beautiful accounts of how the enlightenment and improvement of the world, philosophy and order, emerged from the bleaker epochs of theism and spiritual despotism. All this is both true and untrue. It is true if, like a child, one holds one colour against another, if one wishes to contrive a bright, contrasty little picture—there is, alas, so much light in our century! It is untrue, if one considers the earlier epoch according to its intrinsic nature and aims, its pastimes and mores, and especially as the instrument of the historical process. Often in these apparently coercive institutions and corporations there was something solid, cohesive, noble and majestic, which we certainly do not feel, nor are scarcely able to feel, with our refined ways, disbanded guilds yet shackled states, and with our innate cleverness and all-embracing cosmopolitanism. You mock the servitude of these times, the simple country seats of the nobility, the numerous little social islands and subdivisions and all that depended on them. You praise nothing so much as the breaking of these ties and know of no greater good which ever happened to mankind than when Europe, and with it the world, became free. Became free? What wishful thinking! If only it were true! If only you could realize what these earlier circumstances (in the absence of which human ingenuity would have been stultified) did in fact achieve: Europe was populated and built up; generations and families, master and servant, king and subject, interacted more strongly and closely with one another; what one is wont to call "simple country seats" prevented the luxuriant, unhealthy growth of the cities, those slagheaps of human vitality and energy, whilst the lack of trade and sophistication prevented ostentation and the loss of human simplicity in such things as sex and marriage, thrift and diligence, and family life generally. The mediaeval guilds and baronies engendered pride in the knights and craftsmen, self-confidence, steadfastness and manliness in their spheres of activity, and checked the worst torment of mankind, the enslavement of lands and souls under a yoke which now, apparently, since the earlier social enclaves have been disbanded, everyone accepts readily and wholeheartedly. How could so many warring republics, so many strong and independent cities, spring up later on? Because the vital forces, on whose sad remains we now live, were planted, nourished and nurtured in the rougher climate of an earlier period. Poor, regimented Europe, devourer and sacrificer of your children, if heaven had not ordained that these barbaric times should precede you and had not maintained them for so long, against various kinds of attack and vicissitude, what would you have been with all your erudition and enlightenment?—a desert.

How strange that anyone in the world should find it hard to understand that light does not nourish men, that order and opulence and so-called free thought can be neither the happiness nor the destiny of everyone. Though they may miss their purpose (after all, what, on the human stage has an abiding purpose?), though they may be accompanied by violence and revolutions, by emotions fraught with enthusiasm or fanaticism, capable of becoming brutal or even atrocious, what power and efficacy feelings, tendencies and actions have as tools in the historical process! The heart and not the head is nourished! It is dispositions and instincts of devotion and chivalry, boldness in love and civic vigour, the constitution of the state, legislation, and religion, which have had unifying effects, not sickly thoughts! I am by no means disposed to defend the perpetual migrations and devastations, the feudal wars and attacks, the armies of monks, the pilgrimages, the crusades. I only want to explain them; to show the spirit which breathed through it all, the fermentation of human forces. The whole species underwent a great cure through violent movement, and, if I may speak so boldly, destiny rewound the giant run-down clock, not, to be sure, without a deafening rattle in the wheels, nor without disturbing the weights from their rest.

How differently I see the times in that light! How more prepared I am to forgive, seeing how ceaselessly they themselves struggled against their defects and strove for improvement. How many slanders are obviously false and exaggerated, since the abuses to which they refer were either later invented by the minds of others or, though existing, were then far more innocuous—if not indeed inevitable—than now. Frequently, too, these abuses were accompanied by compensating good qualities, or else they later revealed themselves to us as the tool of a great good in the future which was not recognized as such at the time. Who, reading this history, will not often wonder what has become of the dispositions and virtues of honour and freedom of these times, of their love and gallantry, their courtesy and fidelity? Their depths have been silted up. Their foundations are shifting, silvery sands, where nothing grows. However that may be, in some respects we would willingly take their devotion and superstition, their obscurity and ignorance, their disorder and unpolished manners, in exchange for our light and our unbelief, our enervated coldness and refinement, our philosophical exhaustion and our human misery. As for the rest, mountain and valley certainly have to have a boundary, and the dark, mighty vault could be nothing other than a dark, mighty, *Gothic* vault!

To assume that human destiny is forever marching forward in giant steps; to believe that depravity is a necessary pre-condition for improvement and order; to argue that there must be shadow in order that there be light, that to unravel the knot of events it must first be tied, that, to produce a clear nectar, fermentation must first remove the impurities: this seems to me to be the corollary of our century's pet philosophy. According to this philosophy, so many corners had first to be forcibly rubbed off before the round, smooth, pretty thing that we are could appear. In the Church, so many abominations, errors, absurdities and blasphemies had first to exist, and all the centuries to struggle, clamour and strive for betterment, before our Reformation, or our splendid and enlightened deism, could come about. Evil politics had to run the whole gamut of horror and abomination before our great art of politics, and all that it entails, could emerge like the morning sun out of the night and the fog. What a beautiful portrayal of the natural order and progress in all things we owe to our brilliant philosophers!

Yet I cannot persuade myself that anything in the kingdom of God is *only* a means—everything is both a means and an end simultaneously, now no less than in the centuries of the past . . .

136. A DOCTRINE FOR COUNTERREVOLUTION

The principles of counterrevolution to reestablish the Old Regime were specifically rooted in divine ordinance and a royalist patriotism by the thinker Joseph de Maistre. The Savoy-born De Maistre (1753-1821) was a diplomat in the service of the King of Sardinia, his sovereign, during the Napoleonic period. Unlike Burke, he had never been a reformer: he was the pure conservative from beginning to end. The first of these selections is taken from his *Considerations on France* (A); the second is from the *Study on Sovereignty* (B).

A. Joseph de Maistre

Considerations on France

Of the Pretended Dangers of a Counter-Revolution

Nowadays it is a very common fallacy to insist on the dangers of a counter-revolution in order to buttress the view that we should not return to a monarchy.

A great number of works intended to persuade Frenchmen to be content with the Republic are only developments of this idea. Their authors rest their argument on the evils inseparable from revolutions; then, pointing out that the monarchy cannot be restored in France without a new revolution, they conclude that it is necessary to maintain the Republic. This gross fallacy, whether it arises from fear or from the desire to mislead, deserves to be carefully discussed. . . .

To carry through the French Revolution it was necessary to overthrow religion, insult morality, violate every propriety, and commit every crime; to do this diabolic work, such a number of vicious men had to be used that perhaps never before had so many vices acted in concert to perform any evil whatever. In contrast, to restore order, the king will call together all the virtues; no doubt, he will wish this, but he will also be forced to it in the very nature of things. His most pressing interest will be to unite justice and mercy; worthy men will come of their own accord to take up positions in the posts where they can be of use; and religion, lending its authority to politics, will give it a power which it can draw only from its august sister.

I have no doubt many men will ask to be shown the basis for these splendid hopes; but can it be believed that the political world progresses haphazardly and that it is not organized, directed, and moved by the same wisdom that reveals itself in the physical world? The guilty hands that overthrow a state necessarily inflict the most grievous wounds; for no free agent can run against the plans of the Creator without bringing down, in the sphere of his activity, evils proportionate to the extent of the crime; and this law springs from the kindness rather than from the justice of the Supreme Being.

But when man works to restore order, he associates himself with the author of order; he is favored by *nature*, that is to say, by the combined working of secondary forces, which are the agents of the Divinity. His action has something divine in it; it is both gentle and authoritative; it forces nothing yet nothing resists it; in carrying out its plans, it restores to health; as it acts, so is calmed that disquiet and painful agitation which are the effect and the symptom of disorder; just as men know that a skillful doctor has put back a dislocated joint by the cessation of pain. . . .

B. Joseph de Maistre

Study on Sovereignty

THE NATIONAL SOUL

Human reason left to its own resources is completely incapable *not only of creating but also of conserving any religious or political association,* because it can only give rise to disputes and because, to conduct himself well, man needs beliefs, not problems. His cradle should be surrounded by dogmas; and, when his reason awakes, all his opinions should be given, at least all those relating to his conduct. Nothing is more vital to him than *prejudices.* Let us not take this word in bad part. It does not necessarily signify false ideas, but only, in the strict sense of the word, any opinions adopted without examination. Now, these kinds of opinion are essential to man; they are the real basis of his happiness and the palladium of empires. Without them, there can be neither religion, morality, nor government. There should be a state religion just as there is a state political system; or rather, religion and political dogmas, mingled and merged together, should together form a *general* or *national mind* sufficiently strong to repress the aberrations of the individual reason which is, of its nature, the mortal enemy of any association whatever because it gives birth only to divergent opinions.

All known nations have been happy and powerful to the degree that they have faithfully obeyed this national mind, which is nothing other than the destruction of individual dogmas and the absolute and general rule of national dogmas, that is to say, useful prejudices. Once let everyone rely on his individual reason in religion, and you will see immediately the rise of anarchy of belief or the annihilation of religious sovereignty. Likewise, if each man makes himself the judge of the principles of government you will see immediately the rise of civil anarchy or the annihilation of political sovereignty. Government is a true religion; it has its dogmas, its mysteries, its priests; to submit it to individual discussion is to destroy it; it has life only through the national mind, that is to say, political faith, which is a *creed.* Man's primary need is that his nascent reason should be curbed under a double yoke; it should be frustrated, and it should lose itself in the national mind, so that it changes its individual existence for another communal existence, just as a river which flows into

---

SOURCE: Reprinted with permission of The Macmillan Company from *The Works of Joseph De Maistre,* edited and translated by Jack Lively, pp. 108–9.

…ocean still exists in the mass of water, but without name and distinct …ality.

What is patriotism? It is this national mind of which I am speaking; it is individual *abnegation.* Faith and patriotism are the two great thaumaturges of the world. Both are divine. All their actions are miracles. Do not talk to them of scrutiny, choice, discussion, for they will say that you blaspheme. They know only two words, *submission* and *belief;* with these two levers, they raise the world. Their very errors are sublime. These two infants of Heaven prove their origin to all by creating and conserving; and if they unite, join their forces and together take possession of a nation, they exalt it, make it divine and increase its power a hundredfold. . . .

But can you, insignificant man, light this sacred fire that inflames nations? Can you give a common soul to several million men? Unite them under your laws? Range them closely around a common center? Shape the mind of men yet unborn? Make future generations obey you and create those age-old customs, those conserving *prejudices,* which are the father of the laws and stronger than them? What nonsense! . . .

137. THE CLARION CALL OF NATIONALITY

No one expressed the spirit of resistance to Napoleon, the conqueror of nations, with greater vigor and grandeur than the German philosopher Johann Gottlieb Fichte (1762-1814). As a metaphysician he ranked well below his master, Kant, and he found his true medium in the crisis of the Napoleonic invasions when he called upon the defeated Germans to rally against the tyrant and defend their own nationality. His *Addresses to the German Nation* (1807–8) marked the rise of a powerful nationalism in a Germany which had grown accustomed to far-reaching particularism during the preceding centuries. Typical are the concluding paragraphs of his *Addresses,* reprinted below.

Johann Gottlieb Fichte

Addresses to the German Nation

. . . . .

Your forefathers unite themselves with these addresses, and make a solemn appeal to you. Think that in my voice there are mingled the voices

---

SOURCE: Johann Gottlieb Fichte, *Addresses to the German Nation,* edited by George Armstrong Kelly, translated by R. F. Jones and G. H. Turnbull (New York: Harper & Row, 1968), pp. 225–29. Reprinted by permission of Harper & Row.

of your ancestors of the hoary past, who with their own bodies stemmed the onrush of Roman world dominion, who with their blood won the independence of those mountains, plains, and rivers which under you have fallen prey to the foreigner. They call to you: "Act for us; let the memory of us which you hand on to posterity be just as honorable and without reproach as it was when it came to you, when you took pride in it and in your descent from us. Until now, the resistance we made has been regarded as great and wise and noble; we seemed the consecrated and the inspired in the divine world purpose. If our race dies out with you, our honor will be turned to shame and our wisdom to foolishness. For if, indeed, the German stock is to be swallowed up in Roman civilization, it were better that it had fallen before the Rome of old than before a Rome of today. The former we resisted and conquered; by the latter you have been ground to dust. Seeing that this is so, you shall now not conquer them with temporal weapons; your spirit alone shall rise up against them and stand erect. To you has fallen the greater destiny, to found the empire of the spirit and of reason, and completely to annihilate the rule of brute physical force in the world. If you do this, then you are worthy of your descent from us."

Then, too, there mingle with these voices the spirits of your more recent forefathers, those who fell in the holy war for the freedom of belief and of religion. "Save our honor too," they cry to you. "To us it was not entirely clear what we fought for; besides the lawful resolve not to let ourselves be dictated to by external force in matters of conscience, there was another and a higher spirit driving us, which never fully revealed itself to us. To you it is revealed, this spirit, if you have the power of vision in the spiritual world; it beholds you with eyes clear and sublime. The varied and confused mixture of sensuous and spiritual motives that has hitherto ruled the world shall be displaced, and spirit alone, pure and freed from all sensuous motives, shall take the helm of human affairs. It was in order that this spirit might have freedom to develop and grow to independent existence—it was for this that we poured forth our blood. It is for you to justify and give meaning to our sacrifice, by setting this spirit to fulfill its purpose and to rule the world. If this does not come about as the final goal to which the whole previous development of our nation has been tending, then the battles we fought will turn out to be a vain and fleeting farce, and the freedom of conscience and of spirit that we won is a vain word, if from now onwards spirit and conscience are to be no more."

There comes a solemn appeal to you from your descendants yet unborn. "You boast of your forefathers," they cry to you, "and link yourselves with pride to a noble line. Take care that the chain does not break off with you; see to it that we, too, may boast of you and use you as an unsullied link to connect ourselves with the same illustrious line. Do not force us to be ashamed of our descent from you as from base and slavish barbarians; do not compel us to conceal our origin, or to fabricate a strange one and to take a strange name, lest we be at once and without further examination rejected and trodden underfoot. As the next generation that you produce turns out to be, so will your reputation be in history; honorable, if they bear honorable witness for you, but disgraceful even beyond your due if your descendants may not speak for you, and the conqueror makes your history. Never yet has a conqueror had sufficient inclination or sufficient knowledge to judge the conquered justly. The more he depreciates them, the more just does he himself stand out. Who can know what great deeds, what excellent institutions, what noble customs of many a people in the ancient world have fallen into oblivion because their descendants were forced under the yoke, while the conqueror wrote an account of them that suited his purpose and there was none to contradict him!"

A solemn appeal comes to you even from foreign countries, insofar as they still understand themselves even to the slightest extent, and still have an eye for their true advantage. Yea, in all nations there are still some souls who cannot even yet believe that the great promises of a realm of justice, reason, and truth for the human race are vain and naught but a baseless delusion, and who, therefore, assume that the present age of iron is but a transition to a better state. These souls, and in them the whole of modern humanity, count upon you. A large part of modern humanity is descended from us, and the rest have received from us their religion and all their civilization. The former solemnly appeal to us by the soil of our common fatherland, which was their cradle, too, and which they have left free for us, the latter by the culture they have received from us as the pledge of a loftier bliss—both appeal to us to preserve ourselves for them too and for their sake, just as we have always been, and not to let the whole organism of the new race that has arisen be violently deprived of this member so important to it; so that, when they come to need our counsel, our example, and our cooperation in striving toward the true goal of earthly life, they will not miss us, to their pain.

All ages, all wise and good men who have ever breathed upon this earth, all their thoughts and intuitions of something loftier, mingle with these voices and surround you and lift up imploring hands to you; even, if one may say so, providence and the divine plan in creating a race of men, a plan which exists only to be thought out by men and to be brought by men into the actual world—the divine plan, I say, solemnly appeals to you to save its honor and its existence.[1] Whether those were right who

---

[1] Though the idealist philosopher can deduce the "world plan," man is solely responsible for its translation from thought to actuality. [Fichte's note]

believed that mankind must always grow better, and that thoughts of a true order and worth of man were no idle dreams, but the prophecy and pledge of the real world that is to be—whether they are to be proved right, or those who continue to slumber in an animal and vegetable existence and mock at every flight into higher worlds—to give a final and decisive judgment on this point is your responsibility. The old world with its glory and its greatness, as well as its defects, has fallen by its own unworthiness and by the violence of your fathers. If there is truth in what has been expounded in these addresses, then are you of all modern peoples the one in whom the seed of human perfection most unmistakably lies, and to whom the lead in its development is committed. If you perish in this your essential nature, then there perishes together with you every hope of the whole human race for salvation from the depths of its miseries. Do not console yourselves with an opinion based on thin air and depending on the mere recurrence of cases that have already happened; do not hope that when the old civilization has fallen a new one will arise once more out of a semibarbarous nation on the ruins of the first. In ancient times there was such a people in existence, equipped with every requirement for such a destiny and quite well known to the civilized people, who have left us their description of it; and they themselves, if they had been able to imagine their own downfall, would have been able to discover in this people the means of reconstruction. To us also the whole surface of the globe is quite well known and all the peoples that dwell thereon. But do we know a people akin to the ancestral stock of the modern world, of whom we may have the same expectation? I think that everyone who does not merely base his hopes and beliefs on idle dreaming, but investigates thoroughly and thinks, will be bound to answer this question with a NO. There is, therefore, no way out; if you go under, all humanity goes under with you, without hope of any future restoration.

This it was, gentlemen, which at the end of these addresses I wanted and was bound to impress upon you, who to me are the representatives of the nation, and through you upon the whole nation.

138. THE CONQUEROR ASKS MERCY

The immensity of the Napoleonic wars ended with the stunning brevity of a letter written by Napoleon from the port of Rochefort on July 13, 1815 after he had lost the last battle at Waterloo. It was addressed to the Prince Regent of Great Britain, the country he had never brought to its knees

Napoleon Bonaparte

Letter to the Prince Regent of England, July 13, 1815

Exposed to the factions which distract my country and to the enmity of the greatest Powers of Europe, I have ended my political career, and I come, like Themistocles, to throw myself upon the hospitality of the British people. I put myself under the protection of their laws, which I claim from your Royal Highness, as the most powerful, the most constant, and the most generous of my enemies.

ROCHEFORT, 13 July 1815

139. FRANCE DEFEATED BUT NOT SUPINE

After the first abdication of Napoleon on April 11, 1814, the triumphant allies designed a treaty at Paris setting boundaries for France and then met in Vienna to work out detailed terms of a general peace settlement. The restored Bourbon King of France, Louis XVIII, sent to Vienna one of the most astute diplomats in all Europe, the Prince of Talleyrand. Charles Maurice de Talleyrand-Périgord (1754-1838) had been a church administrator under the Old Regime, a supporter of the Revolution in its early and late phases, and foreign minister under the Directory and Napoleon. The recklessness of Napoleon's policy of conquests dismayed him, however, and he gave up his post. After the emperor's defeat he was a leader in arranging the restoration of Louis XVIII. It was as the king's foreign minister that Talleyrand went to Vienna in September 1814 to take part in the Congress of Vienna. He tells in his *Memoirs* how he played upon the victors to improve the position of France, turning their denunciations of the "usurper" (Napoleon) to the advantage of the "legitimate" monarch and hence of France itself.

Charles Maurice de Talleyrand Périgord

Memoirs of the Congress of Vienna

I arrived at Vienna September 23, 1814. I went down to the "Hôtel Kaunitz," which had been hired for the French legation. On entering, the porter handed me several letters addressed:—"To Prince Talleyrand, *Hôtel Kaunitz.*" The two names thus side by side appeared to me a good omen. The day after my arrival, I presented myself at the houses of the members of the diplomatic corps. They all seemed to me rather surprised at the little advantage they had derived from the capitulation of Paris. They had just traversed countries that had been ravaged by war for many years, in which they had heard, they said, but words of hatred and vengeance against France, for having overwhelmed them with taxes, and treated them with the arrogance of a victor. My new colleagues assured me that they had been reproached everywhere for their weakness in signing the treaty of Paris. I therefore did not find them very enthusiastic over the satisfaction to be derived from generosity, but rather disposed to excite each other about the pretensions they were to advance. . . .

Thus, at the opening of the negotiations, all the cabinets regarded themselves as being, notwithstanding the peace, in an attitude which, if not hostile, was at least very equivocal, with France! They all thought, more or less, that it would have been to their interest that she should have been more enfeebled still. Unable to do anything in that direction, they endeavoured to diminish, at least, her influence. I saw that they all agreed on those various points.

It remained for me to hope that there would be among the powers some divergence of opinion, when they came to distribute the numerous territories that the war had put at their disposal, each one desiring, either to obtain for himself, or to give to the states dependent upon her, a considerable portion of the conquered territories. It was specially desired, at the same time, to exclude from the division those countries which it was feared would prove too independent. . . .

The opening of congress had been fixed for the 1st of October. I had been at Vienna since September 23, but I had been preceded there by several days, by the ministers who, having directed the war, and repented of peace, wished to take up their advantages again at the congress. It was not long before I was informed that they had already formed a committee, and were holding conferences among themselves, of which a protocol had

---

SOURCE: *Memoirs of the Prince de Talleyrand,* translated by Raphaël Ledos de Beaufort (New York: G. P. Putnam's Sons, 1891), Vol. II, pp. 199–204.

been prepared. Their object was to decide alone, what ought to be submitted to the deliberations of the congress, and that too, without the assistance of either France, Spain, or any power of the second order; to these however they would afterwards communicate, in the form of a proposition what would in reality be a resolution, viz., the different articles they should have determined upon. I made no remonstrances. I continued to see them, without speaking of business. I limited myself to communicating to the ministers of the secondary powers, who had a common interest with me, the dissatisfaction I felt. Discovering also, in the past policy of their countries, traces of confidence in France, they very soon looked upon me as their support, and once assured of their assent in all that I was about to do, I officially pressed the opening of the congress. In my first requests I acted as though I had no knowledge of the conferences that had been held. The opening of the congress was fixed for a certain day. That day passed; I entreated that another should be fixed in the near future. I gave it to be understood that it was necessary that I should not remain too long absent from France. A few replies, evasive at first, caused me to repeat my entreaties. I even went so far as to complain a little, but was finally obliged to make use of the personal influence that I had fortunately acquired in the previous negotiations, over the principal personages of the congress. Prince Metternich, and the Count Nesselrode, not wishing to be disobliging to me, both had me invited to a conference which was to have been held at the office of the minister of foreign affairs. Count de Labrador, minister of Spain, with whom I had the honour to support a common cause in the deliberations of the congress, received the same invitation.

I went to the office of the minister of state at the hour indicated, and found there, Lord Castlereagh, Prince von Hardenberg, Herr von Humboldt, and Herr von Gentz, a man of distinguished talents, who fulfilled the functions of secretary. The protocol of the preceding sittings was on the table. I mention all the details of that first sitting, because it decided the position of France at the congress. Prince Metternich opened it by a few sentences on the duty of the congress to give solidity to the peace which had just been restored to Europe. The Prince von Hardenberg added, that in order to consolidate the peace it was indispensable that the engagements that followed perforce from the war should be religiously kept, and that such was the intention of the allied powers.

Placed by the side of Prince von Hardenberg, I was naturally forced to speak after him, and after having said a few words on the good fortune of France in finding herself in relations of confidence and friendship with all the cabinets of Europe, I remarked that the Prince von Hardenberg had let fall an expression that appeared to me to belong to other times, for that they had both of them spoken of the intentions of the *allied powers.*

I declared that *allied powers*, and a *congress* in which powers that were not allied were to be found, were in my eyes very little able to arrange affairs loyally together. I repeated with some astonishment and even warmth, the word *allied powers* . . . "*allied*," I said, "and against whom? It is no longer against Napoleon—he is on the isle of Elba . . . it is no longer against France; for peace has been made . . . it is surely not against the King of France; he is a guarantee of the duration of that peace. Gentlemen, let us speak frankly; if there are still *allied powers*, I am one too many here."—I perceive that I had produced some impression, and especially on Herr von Gentz. I continued: "And nevertheless if I were not here, I should decidedly be missed. Gentlemen, I am perhaps the only one who asks nothing. Great esteem is all I would have for France. She is sufficiently powerful by her resources, her extent of territory, by the number and intelligence of her inhabitants, by the contiguity of her provinces, by the unity of her administration, by the defences with which nature and art have guaranteed her frontiers. I want nothing, I repeat it, out I bring you a great deal. The presence of a minister of Louis XVIII. consecrates here the principle upon which all social order rests. The first need of Europe is to banish for ever the opinion that right can be acquired by conquest alone, and to cause the revival of that sacred principle of legitimacy from which all order and stability spring. To show to-day that France troubles your deliberations, would be to say that true principles are no longer the only ones that guide you, and that you are unwilling to be just; but that idea is far from me, for we all equally feel that a simple and straightforward path is alone worthy of the noble mission we have to fulfil. In the words of the treaty of Paris: '*Toutes les puissances qui ont été engagées de part et d'autre dans la présente guerre, enverront des plénipotentiaires à Vienne, pour régler, dans un congrès général, les arrangements qui doivent compléter les dispositions du traité de Paris.*'[1] When does the general congress open? When do the conferences begin? These are questions posed by all those whose interests bring them here. If, as is already rumoured, some privileged powers would exercise a dictatorial authority over the congress, I must say that, confining myself to the terms of the treaty of Paris, I could not consent to recognize in this assembly any supreme power in questions that the congress is competent to treat, and that I should heed no proposal that proceeded from them."

After a few moments' silence, Count Labrador made, in his proud and piquant language, a declaration almost identical with my own. Embarrassment was depicted on every face. They denied and explained in the

[1] "All the powers who were on either side engaged in the present war, shall send plenipotentiaries to Vienna, there to settle, at a general congress, the arrangements which are t complete the provisions of the treaty of Paris."

same breath all that had taken place before this meeting. I profited by this moment in order to make a few concessions to the pride that I saw thus hurt. I said that in an assembly as numerous as the congress, where one was obliged to occupy oneself with so many different matters, to regulate questions of the first importance, and to decide a host of secondary interests, it was very difficult, nay even impossible, to reach any result by treating of all these subjects in general assemblies, but that some means of distributing and classifying all the business could be found without wounding either the interest or the dignity of any of the powers.

140. THE VISIONARY TSAR

The downfall of Napoleon followed his disastrous defeat in the invasion of Russia in 1812, when he misread the stubborn will to resist of both people and Tsar (or Emperor) Alexander I. Alexander was in some respects like Napoleon himself, an enthroned Romantic; but where the latter's infinite ambition was linked to a cool realism, Alexander was a man of moods and whims, dangerous because he was so unpredictable. A word portrait of the Russian emperor was given by the Austrian statesman Prince Klemens von Metternich (1773-1859). It holds special interest because Metternich himself, having guided the European resistance to Napoleon as Austrian chancellor (foreign minister), was the perfect diplomat of the old school, as cool and guileful as Napoleon at his best.

Klemens von Metternich

Memoirs

ALEXANDER I, EMPEROR OF RUSSIA, A PORTRAIT

To draw a picture of the Emperor Alexander is a most difficult undertaking.

Napoleon expressed his opinion of this prince in a manner the most apt and striking. In one of our conversations, in the year 1810, he asked me whether I knew the Emperor of Russia intimately. I answered that I had had no personal interview with him, except at the time of his residence in Berlin, in 1805. "Well," replied Napoleon, "the course of

---

SOURCE: Prince Richard Metternich (ed.), *Memoirs of Prince Metternich, 1773–1815*, translated by Mrs. Alexander Napier (New York: Charles Scribner's Sons, 1880), Vol. I, pp. 14–19.

events may bring you and this Prince together again; the Emperor Alexander is an attractive person, quite the man to exercise a singular spell over those with whom he comes in contact. If I were given to yielding to mere impressions, I could like him with all my heart. With so many intellectual advantages and dazzling qualities, there is something in him for which I have no name, and which I cannot better express than by saying that there is always something wanting in him. The most singular thing is, that one cannot foresee, in any given case or special affair, what will be wanting, because that which is wanting changes perpetually."

In foreseeing that the course of events would bring me into close contact with the Emperor Alexander, Napoleon had spoken prophetically, without believing, assuredly, that the fulfilment of his prediction was so near as it really was. Three years afterwards, I was in the most intimate relations with the Emperor of Russia. These relations lasted for thirteen years in a constant interchange of real confidence, of more or less expressed coldness, and of personal and open disagreements. Each of these phases has enabled me to see the correctness of Napoleon's judgment.

Relations so lasting and yet so variable have given me an opportunity of forming an exact idea of the character of this monarch.

For my part, I cannot better give the impressions I received than by summing them up in this sentence; that Alexander's character showed a peculiar mixture of masculine virtues and feminine weaknesses.

The Emperor Alexander certainly possessed mind, but his mind, refined and keen as it was, had no depth; he was as easily led astray by an excess of distrust as by an inclination to erroneous theories. His judgment was always influenced by fanciful ideas; he seized upon them as if by sudden inspiration, and with the greatest eagerness; and they soon gained weight enough to rule him, and make the subjection of his will an easy matter to their originators.

Such ideas soon came to be regarded by him as systems; quick as his mind was, even to an extraordinary versatility, these systems did not assimilate, they followed one another in rapid succession. Devoted to the system whose turn it was, he arrived at the exact opposite by intermediate steps, of which he was not aware, and nothing remained of the convictions with which he had been penetrated but the remembrance of the obligations under which they had placed him to different individuals. Hence arose the number of insurmountable embarrassments which were always pressing on the mind and heart of the Emperor; and the frequent favours bestowed on men and things quite opposite to one another; hence the difficulty to most spectators of understanding his attitude, who was not in a position to penetrate into the true causes of such strange appearances.

The Emperor Alexander's life was worn out between devotion to certain systems and disappointment in their results; the feelings prompted by both moods were spontaneous and vigorous and, strange as it may sound, their course showed a certain periodicity, of which I shall afterwards give pertinent examples.

He was a man of his word, entering with facility into the obligations of the ideas for the moment paramount; he knew how to avoid with delicacy those who might lead him in an opposite direction; but since his mind, from taking up systems so easily, was constantly undergoing changes, this very regard for his given word placed his conscience, as well as his whole attitude, in a situation as painful to himself as injurious to the public cause.

Many contemporaries have wrongly ascribed to Alexander the possession of a restless ambition. In his character there was neither sufficient strength for true ambition, nor sufficient weakness for mere vanity. He acted generally from conviction, and if he seemed now and then somewhat full of pretension, this was connected more with the little victories of a man of the world than with his success as the ruler of a great empire.

His youth passed in a time which is unequalled in the annals of Russia. The government of Catherine gave him the example of a brilliant despotism; in that of Paul, he was himself several times nearly a victim to a despotism mean even in its very choice of forms. It suffices to know what Russia was under these two governments, to conceive that a mind like Alexander's would find there neither models for imitation nor men to advise him.

La Harpe was entrusted by Catherine II. with the first education of Alexander. It is, therefore, not surprising that wrong ideas of liberalism and philanthropy long dominated the pupil of such a master; or that such a wonderful mixture as the lessons of a liberal mentor with the practice of the Russian government must lead his judgment and his action in a wrong direction, far, indeed, beyond the limits in which experience could help him.

The method of education followed by La Harpe was far more suited to fill the mind of his pupil with doctrines wrong in themselves, and ridiculous in their application, than to enrich it with positive knowledge. Convinced, no doubt, that the empire which his pupil would one day be called on to govern was not sufficiently advanced in civilisation to bear immediately the practice of these doctrines, he thought of preparing in the future autocrat a mighty lever, to secure the upheaval of other countries which he considered more ripe for the purpose, and especially his own fatherland, Switzerland. The part of a philanthropic monarch appeared to Alexander the one which would secure to him the palm of certain glory—a glory which was easy to gain by a monarch who was removed from the dangers with which other thrones and the old institutions of Central Europe were surrounded.

Simple in his enjoyments, cool in temperament, with many tastes which were, if I may say so, somewhat plebeian, Alexander was too easily guided not to be taken advantage of by such leaders.

A long observation of the moral peculiarities of this monarch and of his political course led me to discover, what I have called above, the periodicity of his thoughts. This periodicity followed a measure of about five years. I do not know how to express this observation more exactly.

The Emperor seized an idea, and followed it out quickly. It grew in his mind for about two years, till it came to be regarded by him as a system. In the course of the third year he remained faithful to the system he had adopted and learned to love, listened with real fervour to its promoters, and was inaccessible to any calculation as to its worth or dangerous consequences. In the fourth year the sight of those consequences began to calm down his fervour; the fifth year showed an unseemly mixture of the old and nearly extinct system with the new idea. This new idea was often diametrically opposite to the one he had just left. To prove this remark, I will give the following historical facts.

My first connection with the Emperor Alexander took place at the time of my embassy to Berlin in 1805. I found him then liberal in the largest sense of the word, and a bitter enemy of Bonaparte, he loaded him—in his double quality of despot and conqueror— with execrations. In the year 1807 a great change came over his mode of thinking. In 1808 his personal feelings even inclined towards the Emperor of the French. The year 1812 brought a new change in his mood: even if Napoleon had not made war on Russia, Alexander's feelings for him would nevertheless have died away. The old ideas of philanthropy and free-thinking had not only regained the power over his mind, but they even took fire from the spirit of the time. In 1814 they had reached their highest point. In 1815 they had already given way to religious mysticism. In the year 1817, this new turn of mind underwent a great change; and in 1818, I found the Emperor a zealous champion of monarchic and conservative principles, a declared enemy of every revolutionary tendency, and already on his way to return to religious mysticism. He followed this direction till 1823. Then the embarrassments arose which his own counsellors had prepared for him by their policy in the affairs in Greece, and he was able everywhere to see the increase of revolutionary principles, whose germs he, in his blindness, had himself scattered in his own empire in past years. All these painful circumstances caused a visible languor in his mind and feelings. A great weariness of life began to show itself in him. His body, apparently so active, suffered under these moral influences. It was during his residence in Verona towards the end of the year 1822, that Alexander confided to the Emperor Francis, his sure presentiment that his life would not be of long duration. The evil made rapid steps, and in 1825, Alexander died of thorough weariness of life.

BOOK MANUFACTURE

Early Modern Europe: A Book of Source Readings was composed in Video-Comp, printed by offset, and bound at Kingsport Press, Inc. The paper is Perkins & Squier's Glatfelter Old Forge. The internal design was by the F. E. Peacock Publishers, Inc. art department, and the cover was designed by Evelyn Hansen. The type is Janson with Baskerville display.